THE PROCESS OF FICTION

Second Edition

Edited by Barbara McKenzie

University of Georgia

THE
PROCESS
OF
FICTION

CONTEMPORARY STORIES AND CRITICISM

Second Edition

HARCOURT BRACE JOVANOVICH, INC.

New York   Chicago   San Francisco   Atlanta

FOR MARY AND ROBERT ANDERSON

COVER PHOTO: *Detail of "Night Window," a relief construction with reflected color by Hadley Anne Smith, University of Georgia. Used by permission of the artist.*

ISBN: 0–15–571986–6

Library of Congress Catalog Card Number: 73–16733

Printed in the United States of America

ACKNOWLEDGMENTS

MARY MCCARTHY

The statement on page 71 is reprinted from "Settling the Colonel's Hash" from *On the Contrary* by Mary McCarthy. Copyright © 1961 by Farrar, Straus & Giroux, Inc. Reprinted by permission of the publisher. "The Cicerone," Copyright, 1948, by Mary McCarthy, is reprinted from her volume *Cast a Cold Eye* by permission of Harcourt Brace Jovanovich, Inc. "The Unspoiled Reaction" is reprinted by permission of Brandt & Brandt. Copyright © 1946 by Mary McCarthy. First published in *The Atlantic Monthly*, March 1946.

PREFACE

The second edition of *The Process of Fiction,* like its predecessor, brings together two stories by each of ten outstanding contemporary American writers, critical essays that interpret the first story of each pair, and a General Introduction to the technical elements of fiction. New to this edition and reflecting recent developments in experimental writing are stories by Joyce Carol Oates, Donald Barthelme, and John Barth.

Like any art form, the short story holds a key to the life of its time, and the life reflected here is America since Hiroshima. But, though the authors share with one another and with the reader a community of time and place, each story is shaped to its author's own measure. Represented are the wit and intelligence of Mary McCarthy, the scrupulously balanced writing of John Updike, the domestic labyrinths of Joyce Carol Oates, the survivors' dance of Roth and Malamud, the newsreel world of Donald Barthelme, the mythic imagination of John Barth, the quiet drama of Eudora Welty and her remarkable gift for extended, tangible images. There is fury barely controlled by style in James Baldwin and a precise matching of style to social texture by Flannery O'Connor. There are, in short, within this shared universe, reverberations of the complexities of both life and fiction and worlds enough for the most eager imagination.

From its inception, the book was planned to be flexible, offering many approaches and leaving the instructor free to make the crucial decisions of emphasis. If the course aims to explore systematically the technical elements of fiction and the short story as a genre, the instructor may approach the stories through the General Introduction. The first and longer part of the Introduction covers point of view, characters, plot, setting, style, and tone; its intention is to explain and document the elements and techniques of the conventional story. The second part deals with experimental fiction and attempts to show the experimentalists' allegiance to traditional fictional practices as well as their radical departures from them. Questions on the first story by each author reflect the six categories of part one of the Introduction. Readers familiar with prominent theories of fiction will recognize the bases for the discussion but will also, it is hoped, find something new. Student readers will find that all the illustrations of general ideas are drawn from literature they know or will soon know—the stories in this collection.

For courses that emphasize literary criticism, the critical essays and the questions on them may be stressed. The essays, seven of which were written especially for this book, employ a variety of critical approaches. Their interpretations are meant to be illustrative, not prescriptive; indeed, they are intended to show that serious literature *is* open to interpretation. The essays should provide merely a beginning for the student's own analysis; and the more discussion and argument they generate, the more successful they will have been. The questions on the essays—arranged under the headings focus, organization, using the evidence, style, and making literary judgments—encourage the student to be a critic of criticism rather than a passive recipient of it. The annotated secondary bibliography for each author directs the student to further critics and criticism. Important to the concept of this book was the *omission* of critical apparatus for the second story of each pair, leaving students to discover the author's method and achievement on their own. Their explorations are both controlled and extended by the presence of two stories by each author. They will, for example, experience a single author speaking with two distinct voices—as does Philip Roth in the renowned story "Eli, the Fanatic" and in "In Trouble" —and they will encounter more nearly consistent voices in "A Gift from the City" and "The Christian Roommates" by John Updike.

Where the student's expository writing—on literature or other subjects —is central to the course, the contemporaneity of the stories and their themes may stimulate the student's efforts. Furthermore, students can apply to their own writing what they learn from studying and analyzing the critical essays. By means of the questions on the essays especially, they can investigate the process by which any essay is made. Suggested writing assignments on specifically literary themes are included at the end of each section, and the questions on the first story of each pair may also be used as the basis for essays.

Finally, the book may be used simply as an anthology of stories, with the critical and editorial apparatus being ignored.

Most instructors will probably combine approaches, finding their own best uses of this book in the process of teaching with it. The idea of process, of course, is basic to the book. For the fiction writer, it incorporates the stages of discovery and the acts of writing and rewriting that produce a completed verbal form. For the reader, process involves learning that the practice of fiction is a craft and that the reader's responsibility is to participate with imagination and intellect. For both writer and reader, process concerns the knowledge that people are constantly being enlarged by their own experience. As the philosopher J. Bronowski said, "The self is not something fixed inside my head. If it exists at all, my self is a process: the unending process by which I turn new experiences into knowledge." It is my hope that through *The Process of Fiction* students, too, will turn new experiences into knowledge.

I wish to express my gratitude to Judith Greissman, editor of the first edition, whose intelligence and spirit are represented throughout this book. In addition, I would like to thank Eben Ludlow and Carolyn Johnson for their editorial assistance on the second edition and Harry Rinehart for his work on the interior and cover designs of both volumes.

Barbara McKenzie

CONTENTS

CONTENTS

xiv

CONTENTS

THE PROCESS OF FICTION

Second Edition

A GENERAL INTRODUCTION

I   THE PROCESS OF FICTION

W H A T   A   S T O R Y   I S

What a Story Is Not

Asked to "define" a short story, Flannery O'Connor (in the Winter 1959 issue of *Esprit*) described the question as "inspired by the devil who tempts textbook publishers" and then acknowledged,

> The best I can do is tell you what a story is not.
>
> 1. It is not a joke.
> 2. It is not an anecdote.
> 3. It is not a lyric rhapsody in prose.
> 4. It is not a case history.
> 5. It is not a reported incident.
>
> It is none of these things because it has an extra dimension and I think this extra dimension comes about when the writer puts us in the middle of some human action and shows it as it is illuminated and outlined by mystery.

By indirection, O'Connor's list of negative characteristics tells us a great deal about what a story is. Implicit in it are these assumptions: that a story illuminates the human action it depicts (in contradistinction to the anecdote and the joke which are intended primarily to entertain and amuse), that it has a plot and characters (unlike the lyric rhapsody), that it is a work of the imagination (separating it from the case history), that it possesses a formal structure (differentiating it from the reported incident).

Each of these assumptions is compatible with a definition offered by Edgar Allan Poe in a review of Nathaniel Hawthorne's *Twice-Told Tales* (1842). In praising Hawthorne for fashioning the events of his stories to accommodate his thoughts, Poe says of the short story:

> In the whole composition there should be no word written, of which the tendency, direct or indirect, is not to the one preestablished design. And by such means, with such care and skill, a picture is at length painted which leaves in the mind of him who contemplates it with a kindred art, a sense of the fullest satisfaction. . . . Truth is often, and in some very great degree, the aim of the tale.

Poe's dictum has led subsequent writers and critics to place a high value on stories that are well made. As he did, they have admired stories in which: "Not only is all done that should be done, but (what perhaps is an end with more difficulty attained) there is nothing done which should not be. Every word *tells,* and there is not a word that does not tell. . . ." The concept of the well-made story does not presuppose a formulaic approach to story telling (although it can lead to that), but it does suggest an adherence to a formalistic structure—one with a beginning, a middle, and an end; with recognizable characters engaged in recognizable actions; with involvement in a world that bears some resemblance to the readers' own; with truth or revelation as its principal aim.

The well-made story has counterparts in the novel, drama, painting, and film. Yet in each of these arts there also exists a parallel tradition that uses and abuses the conventions of the established genre, resulting in works that turn the tenets of the conventional art-form inside out. Though somewhat stronger in these other arts, this unconventional approach is found even in the short story (the most conservative of literary genres), where it results in stories that *appear* to be no more than reported incidents, case histories, lyric rhapsodies, anecdotes, jokes, or some wild and unruly combination of some or all of these "non-stories." In dealing with such stories in this collection, the reader should remember that appearances are often deceiving and that thus it is the reader's job to see through the deceptions and discover the "extra dimension" that unites conventional and experimental works of fiction.

Accordingly, the scope of this introduction is twofold: its first and largest task being to describe the principal elements of fiction and to explain the conventions of the well-made story; its second, to describe the techniques found most frequently in experimental stories. Because the well-made story is more abundant historically, it is predominant in this collection. And because conventional elements and processes underlie experimental stories—even to the point of becoming subject matter in some—the bulk of this introduction will deal with the technical aspects of traditional fiction. Reversing this emphasis would place the innovation before the standard, the exception before the rule.

This introduction will emphasize throughout that the writing of fiction is a craft, a process, a human activity and that awareness of the tools of this craft and the stages of this process permit the reader to comprehend the complex possibilities of contemporary fiction and to judge the success or failure of a story in demonstrating those possibilities. Axiomatic is the assumption that insight into the process of fiction increases one's appreciation of the substance of fiction. Thus, hopefully, as specific examples are drawn from the stories in this collection, the introduction and stories will serve to illuminate each other.

The reader should be forewarned, however, that no amount of technical knowledge will give him an understanding of a story if he is unwilling to commit himself to it—to contemplate it "with a kindred art." Living in a Gutenberg galaxy, we daily confront a mass of printed matter, from which we attempt to extract information. Of necessity, we learn to skim so that we can, for example, tell someone else "what a story is about." But serious literature requires us to read "vertically," to cut through the resistant and lulling surfaces of prose. This in-depth reading demands that the reader willingly involve himself in the human action of a story—an involvement that permits him to experience the "extra dimension" of fiction.

Words as the Base Metal of Fiction

Language is to the writer what paint is to the painter, marble to the sculptor, or musical notes to the composer. Through language, the short-story writer depicts the human action that is his subject matter. If he is skilled, the words he uses and the form in which he casts them achieve

3

a lasting significance. Like paint, marble, or musical notes, language offers its user a set of "conditions"—a certain body of privileges and restrictions.

An obvious limitation that confronts the story writer is the proliferation and banality of words. Indeed, every art involves a substance common to daily, unheightened existence. There is nothing *exclusive* about paint, marble, or musical notes—each may be used by anyone to express anything or nothing. The writer is like other creative artists: he must overcome and even put to his own uses the ordinariness of his material. His refusal to take words for granted causes him to employ language innovatively. As Eudora Welty has said (in "The Reading and Writing of Short Stories"), "The words in the story we are writing now might as well never have been used before. . . . Stories are *new* things, stories make words new; that is one of their illusions and part of their beauty." In turn, this "newness" may move the reader to unaccustomed responses.

Language is not only commonplace; it is also elusive, its flexibility warring against precise formulation and the communication of single, uncontestable meanings. Once again, a consideration of various materials reveals that each in its own way resists the artist's efforts to give hitherto unshaped substances expressive form. Take, for example, the amorphic quality of paint, or the hardness of marble or bronze. For the writer, however, the elusiveness of words is a mixed blessing. On the one hand, because words are connotative he can create prose that is highly textured—rich in imagery, associations, and multiple meanings. On the other hand, the suggestiveness of language allows the reader to bring his own experiences and associations to what he reads. Accordingly, the writer's intended meaning is often misinterpreted by the "public" reader who has his own "private" connotations and responses.

Still another condition affecting the use of language is its symbolic nature. Like the brush strokes on a canvas or the planes in a statue, a word is never the object or emotion itself but a conventional mark or sound that stands for or suggests the referent. Like the completed canvas or sculpture, the story (as a structure) is also symbolic. It is a representation of characters, events, and objects—a grouping of words arranged sequentially so as to stand for a certain pattern of human action. Thus, the story writer is always at a symbolic remove from his referent—human activity. Paradoxically, the writer's success lies in making us feel the immediacy and intensity of his fictional, symbolic world.

A final disadvantage for the writer of fiction is the tendency of language to lend itself to explanation—to *explain* rather than to *present*. Much of our pleasure in reading fiction comes from the intensity of rendered ex-

4

perience in a story—an intensity achieved in part by the writer's ability to *show,* to present us with a situation so that we perceive it immediately and directly rather than to *tell* us about this same set of circumstances.

Undeniably, part of the enjoyment of literature derives from our recognizing the resistances of the medium. Observing that words are commonplace, we delight in their heightened usage. Understanding that words are imprecise, we respond favorably to the aptly chosen word and to the intentional employment of ambiguity; we take pleasure in the imaginative use of the flexibility of language. Recognizing that words lack immediacy, we appreciate a writer's ability to achieve a seemingly tangible reality.

The Story as Narration

If words provide the base metal of fiction, narration is the form into which they are cast. At its most fundamental level, the purpose of narration is to relate an event or succession of events. Thus, narration—whether oral or written, in verse (epic, ballad, or metrical romance) or prose (parable, fable, tale, story, or novel)—involves people or animals (*characters*) who act and are acted upon (*plot*) and who exist in a certain place and at a certain time (*setting*). Furthermore, narration requires a *narrator,* the *events* he relates, and a *listener* or *reader.*

Narration can be classified as either simple or sophisticated. Anecdotes, case histories, reported incidents, and (usually) jokes are simple narratives —the kind of narration engaged in daily and informally by anyone recounting an incident or series of incidents to anyone else. Simple narration is lucid, entertaining, and often informative. Events follow each other in chronological order. Characters are neatly described and categorized. The "moral" is clearly stated. In contrast, the stories in this collection are sophisticated narratives—narratives that rearrange the order of events to suit the purposes of theme; that yield layers of meaning; that utilize devices not needed and therefore not found in simple narration; and that, in the case of the experimental stories, sometimes manage to conceal their narrative origins.

Like all narratives, the story is a temporal art (rather than a spatial art like sculpture) and is cumulative in its effects. The unity and final meaning of a story depend on seeing how its individual sentences relate to the structure as a whole. Yet this kind of understanding is nearly impossible. "Nothing, no power, will keep a book steady and motionless before us, so that we may have time to examine its shape and design," Percy Lubbock acknowledges in *The Craft of Fiction.* "As quickly as we read it, it melts and shifts in the memory; even at the moment when the last page is turned, a great part of the book, its finer detail, is already vague and doubtful." Less cumulative than the novel only in that it is shorter, even the shortest story resists any attempts to "fix" its moving parts.

The brevity of the story accounts for two significant traits—unity and intensity. The restricted scope of the story allows the author to arrange his material to create a single effect, if he wants to, and thus grants the story a structural and thematic unity nearly unattainable in a longer, more diffuse narrative. Because the story is short enough to be read at one sitting, it benefits (as Poe also notes in his review) from the "immense force derivable from totality," achieving an intensity lacking in a work that is read piecemeal. Brevity also accounts for other attributes of the story: it encourages the depiction of a single aspect of experience, which the story seeks to illuminate rather than to resolve; it prohibits the author from covering great periods of time in copious detail; and it makes natural a focus on one or two characters.

In sophisticated narratives and some simple narratives, the narrator as *teller* of the tale and the author as *creator* are separate entities. Only in certain kinds of simple narration do the narrator and teller possess a single identity. For example, if you tell someone about your summer travels— either actual or imaginary—you are both the creator of the "story" you relate and the teller or narrator. If, however, you describe your travels to someone who relates them to a third party, you have, in essence, established a narrator who is separate from yourself. If you have chosen a narrator congenial to your aims and values, your travels can be made to sound exciting. But an unfriendly narrator can represent these same events as dull and pointless meanderings. A narrator to whom you have given an incomplete account will, of course, give the listener only a partial reckoning. Other relationships between you and your narrator induce other interpretations of these same events. Out of these different relationships comes much of the complexity of interpretive fiction.

Various literary critics have pointed to still another presence in narrative—the author's second self or, to use Wayne C. Booth's term, the *implied author*. According to Booth, the implied author is the image of an author derived from reading his works and must not be confused with the historical or "actual" author, that is, the person who wrote the story or novel. Thus the implied author is an illusion, created anew within the mind of each reader by each new book.

Frequently, the implied author and the historical author do not "match," a disparity that leaves the historical author open to unfair charges of insincerity. For example, although the implied author of *Wise Blood* and *The Violent Bear It Away* appears, to some readers, to be morbid, ill-natured, and atheistic, the historical or "actual" Flannery O'Connor was witty, gracious, and devoutly Catholic. But how nearly the historical author equates with his or her literary image is of little importance in the analysis of fiction. Indeed, as Booth makes clear, the only question of sincerity that properly concerns the reader is the relation between the implied author and the work itself.

> A great work establishes the "sincerity" of the implied author, regardless of how grossly the man who created that author may belie in his *other* forms of conduct the values embodied in his work. For all we know, the only sincere moments of his life may have been lived as he wrote his novel.[1]

When a writer draws heavily on events of his own life for the material of his fiction, he seems intent on merging his two identities—on forcing us to consider his actual or historical self. Of the writers in this collection, Mary McCarthy and James Baldwin exemplify this practice most noticeably. If an obvious connection exists between the fictional and actual events, the reader legitimately may investigate the background of the historical author. But his inquiry should be limited to questions that relate to the practice of fiction—what actual events the writer used, how he transformed them, and why he chose to be his own central idea.

Even the presence of seemingly untransformed portions of autobiography should not make the reader forget that the author he "knows" is the implied author. Accordingly, he should be guided in the analysis of fiction by the values of the consciousness that he senses is directing the behavior of the fictional characters and controlling the events of their world. Often —especially in modern fiction, and most noticeably in the work of the experimentalists—the reader identifies less with the characters and narrator of a novel or short story than with the implied author—the intelligence that superintends the fictional events. In part, identification with the implied author stems from the implicit breadth of his perspective, which, by extending beyond the events of the story, is capable of "correcting" the lopsided world so frequently conveyed by the characters and narrators of modern fiction.

---

[1] Wayne C. Booth, *The Rhetoric of Fiction* (Chicago: Univ. of Chicago Press, 1961), p. 75. For additional comments on the function of the implied author, see Chapter 3, in particular pp. 70–76.

Certainly, recognition of the separate existence of the historical author, the implied author, and the narrator is a first step in understanding the art of fiction—in understanding, for example, that a writer *chooses* the kind and placement of his narrator in any given work and may create a narrator who is totally different in character from himself, and that this narrator, in turn, helps to create our sense of the implied author. As well, the separation of the historical and implied authors from the narrator is responsible for a major structural device in all interpretive fiction—point of view.

POINT OF VIEW

The Function of Point of View

In his essay "Technique as Discovery," the critic Mark Schorer observes, "The difference between content, or experience, and achieved content, or art, is technique." According to Schorer, "When we speak of technique . . . we speak of nearly everything. . . . technique is the only means he [the writer] has of discovering, exploring, developing his subject, of conveying its meaning, and, finally, of evaluating it." Since technique gives a story its "form" or shape, and insofar as form *is* meaning, technique embraces more than technical devices or technical proficiency. By controlling the manner in which the story material is communicated to the reader—a process that makes content *achieved* content—technique determines meaning.

The fiction writer's chief structural resource is *point of view*—at its most fundamental level, the physical vantage point occupied by the narrator in a story or novel and the device by which the writer establishes the "authority" for his fiction. For the writer, point of view is the basic means of ordering and unifying his material. Once he has decided upon the position and, further, upon the disposition of his narrator (choices that are often partly unconscious), all other ingredients of the work must relate to his decision. For the reader, point of view, by affecting the shape of the story, determines how the story material reaches him and how he perceives the fictional events.

The narrator of a story stands in one of two basic relationships to the events of the story: *outside* or *inside* the action. The task of the critical reader is to ascertain the effects of each narrative perspective and disposition. In addition, he must concern himself with the matter of "open" and "closed" consciousnesses and their relation to point of view. An *open consciousness* is a character whose inner thoughts are revealed to the reader. Frequently, the author depicts setting or action through the perceptions of such a character. A *closed consciousness* is a character whose inner thoughts are hidden—making the reader view him through such externals as physical action, dialogue, the reaction of others, and personal appearance. Ultimately, the reader must see how point of view, as Mark Schorer contends, serves as *a mode of thematic definition* (as a way of conveying meaning) as well as *a mode of dramatic definition* (as a determiner of structure).

Outside Points of View

By definition, an outside narrator stands outside the action of the story and is, therefore, not a character in it. With one exception (to be noted later), he relates the events of the story through third-person pronouns. Outside narrators differ in their *dis*positions and may be categorized as either *privileged* or *effaced*.[2]

PRIVILEGED NARRATORS

Although not a character in the fictional world inhabited by the characters, a privileged narrator makes his presence felt through the quality of his mind and personality. Everywhere in the story, his figures of speech, the transitions he provides, and the scope of his judgments convey the sense of a narrator whose overall perspective is outside the frame of action, as in this passage from "Lost in the Funhouse":

> Although Peter must have known as well as Ambrose that the latter, because of his position in the car, would be the first to see the electrical towers of the power plant at V_____, the halfway point of their trip, he leaned forward and slightly toward the center of the car and pretended to be looking for them through the flat pinewoods and tuckahoe creeks along the highway. For as long as the boys could remember, "looking for the Towers" had been a feature of the first half of their excursions to Ocean City, "looking for the standpipe" of the second. Though the game

---

[2] In glossaries or handbooks of fiction, you may find the privileged narrator described as "omniscient." Sometimes, the effaced narrator is referred to as the "scenic," "dramatic," or "objective" point of view.

Position and Disposition of Narrator

	OUTSIDE NARRATORS	
	Privileged	*Effaced*
Identity in story	Not a character	Not a character
Voice	Third-person pronouns (he, she, they, etc.); may occasionally use first-person pronouns	Third-person pronouns
Access to characters' consciousnesses	Unlimited access to consciousnesses of all the characters	No access; does not enter consciousnesses of characters; reveals their thoughts and feelings through dialogue and action
Presence	Calls attention to himself as narrator through: 1. descriptions conveyed in his own voice and reflecting his position outside the events of the story; 2. narrative analysis or interpretation of character, incident, and setting; 3. adoption of perspectives different from his own when he reveals the thoughts of certain characters at close range	Conveys almost no sense of his presence, since he generally gives no long descriptions or narrative analysis and does not adopt different perspectives
Reliability	Generally reliable because he frequently stands close to the implied author	Reliable in that he is "neutral"

INSIDE NARRATORS	
Dramatized	*Restricted*
A character	Not a character
First-person pronouns (I, my, mine, etc.)	Third-person pronouns
Access to consciousness of one character—himself	Access to consciousness of one character or to consciousnesses of a "community" of characters through whose perceptions he conveys the story
Dominates story; relates his own experiences or, as witness, someone else's	Speaks in his own voice but submerges his vision into the character(s) whose perspective(s) serves as narrative focus
Frequently unreliable because his self-knowledge and knowledge of others is imperfect	Ranges from reliable to unreliable, depending on the character(s) whose consciousness(es) he reveals and on the presence or absence of "clues" affirming or negating implicit attitudes and values

was childish, their mother preserved the tradition of rewarding the first to see the Towers with a candy-bar or piece of fruit. She insisted now that Magda play the game: the prize, she said, was "something hard to get nowadays." Ambrose decided not to join in; he sat far back in his seat. Magda, like Peter, leaned forward. . . . The simple strategy for being first to espy the Towers, which Ambrose had understood by the age of four, was to sit on the right-hand side of the car. Whoever sat there, however, had also to put up with the worst of the sun, and so Ambrose, without mentioning the matter, chose sometimes the one and sometimes the other. Not impossibly Peter had never caught on to the trick, or thought that his brother hadn't simply because Ambrose on occasion preferred shade to a Baby Ruth or tangerine.

Able to open the consciousness of any character, the privileged narrator can disclose the attitudes and feelings of characters separated in time and place or even antagonistic to each other. As a result, this kind of narrator affords fiction an inclusiveness in which the reader senses the multiplicity of human life.

Because of his position outside the frame of action and because the author has given him considerable knowledge about the fictional world he governs, the privileged narrator is the most flexible of all narrators. Frequently, he interprets information as he relates it to the reader. Thus, the privileged narrator can be described as having freedom of statement— he is at liberty to summarize, interpret, speculate, and judge. In addition, his outside position grants him freedom of movement—he can use his panoramic view to describe and analyze events from a distance, or he can descend momentarily to the level of action within the story and open the consciousnesses of selected characters, revealing action from their isolated vantage points for brief periods of time. Because of his outside position, he is not aligned in sympathy or knowledge with any character or group of characters, unless the author wishes him to be.

Most eighteenth- and nineteenth-century novelists used this point of view. Its obvious advantage (particularly to the novel) is that the author and his narrator are able to cover great stretches of time and space. But the maneuverings, transitional assists, and interpretive comments of the privileged narrator frequently break the illusion of reality engendered by the people and action he is depicting. At such times, the machinery of narration calls attention to itself and to the story as artifice—an effect only occasionally desirable as a narrative technique.

Because this mode of narration lends itself to explanation and summary, stories related by a privileged narrator are sometimes weak in "specification," or memorable scenes—the charge leveled against Thackeray by Henry James. Such a narrator tends to summarize events and to tell us about characters rather than to present us with the action itself or to let characters unfold through dialogue. Accordingly, there is often a second-handedness, an awareness of the story coming from a narrator and not from the characters (as in stories narrated from inside points of view) or directly (as by an effaced narrator).

Of the stories in this collection, only John Barth's "Lost in the Funhouse" uses a privileged narrator—and then chiefly to mock its conventions. In the style of all privileged narrators, the narrator in this story appears not to be a character: the story is told in the third person (Ambrose, the thirteen-year-old protagonist, is referred to as "he"), and the author, through his narrator, colludes with the reader (Ambrose becomes "our hero" and "our protagonist"). The narrator also interrupts the "story" proper to address the reader directly; most typically these interruptions discuss problems of authorship and conventions of nineteenth-century fiction:

> Plush upholstery prickles uncomfortably through gabardine slacks in the July sun. The function of the beginning of a story is to introduce the principal characters, establish their initial relationships, set the scene for the main action, expose the background of the situation if necessary, plant motifs and foreshadowing where appropriate, and initiate the first complication or whatever of the "rising action." Actually, if one imagines a story called "The Funhouse," or "Lost in the Funhouse," the details of the drive to Ocean City don't seem especially relevant. The *beginning* should recount the events between Ambrose's first sight of the funhouse early in the afternoon and his entering it with Magda and Peter in the evening. The *middle* would narrate all relevant events from the time he goes in to the time he loses his way; middles have the double and contradictory function of delaying the climax while at the same time preparing the reader for it and fetching him to it. Then the *ending* would tell what Ambrose does while he's lost, how he finally finds his way out, and what everybody makes of the experience. So far there's been no real dialogue, very little sensory detail, nothing in the way of a theme. And a long time has gone by already without anything happening; it makes a person wonder.

As we read along, however, we begin to see that the privileged narrator reveals only the consciousness of Ambrose and that his omniscience is a guise—a pose struck by Ambrose, a precocious adolescent who is not only the narrator but the protagonist and also the author's younger self. Throughout the story, Ambrose "tries out" various conventions of traditional fiction—literary symbolism, irony of situation, verbal irony, and sensory detail—but the convention of the privileged narrator is the one that allows Barth to distance himself from the consciousness of his protagonist who, in reality, is forever self-aware and forever commenting on his self-awareness. Further, as in all fiction, point of view is here linked to meaning: the subject matter of this story is less an excursion to Ocean City, Maryland, than it is fiction making. The growing pains Ambrose experiences are the physical counterpart of the conflict between traditional and experimental fiction.

EFFACED NARRATORS

The effaced narrator has little in common with the privileged narrator, apart from standing outside the events of the story. He communicates almost no sense of his own presence, has no individuality, has either an extremely limited access or no access to the consciousnesses of the characters (and therefore does not, strictly speaking, adopt their perspective), and offers little description (much less analysis or interpretation) of events and characters. In stories with an effaced narrator, the events seem to unfold automatically and the characters reveal themselves directly, through dialogue and action.

Fiction employing the effaced narrator resembles drama in structure. Usually, the narrator is noticeable at the beginning of the story, when he sets the scene and introduces the characters, and on those subsequent occasions when the narrative embraces a new character or a change in location. As in drama, dialogue supplies exposition, characterizes the speakers, and advances most of the action. Thus, while the privileged narrator tends to explain and to summarize, the natural bent of the effaced narrator is to present and to dramatize action.

The effaced narrator affords objectivity and immediacy; the reader is present at the action, watching the characters move about and listening to them talk. The story-illusion is not disrupted by intrusions that divert attention to the narrator. The chief limitation of this narrator is that he cannot offer overt analyses without violating his "invisibility." At times, however, if the author's intended meaning is to be made clear, the reader needs explicit interpretation of events and characters.

Donald Barthelme's "City Life" is the only story in this collection told from an effaced narrator point of view. Most of the story is conveyed by dialogue and brief descriptions of physical action, as this passage illustrates:

> Ramona's mother and father came to town from Montana. Ramona's thin father stood on the Porter Street sidewalk wearing a business suit and a white cowboy hat. He was watching his car. He watched from the steps of the house for a while, and then watched from the sidewalk a little, and then watched from the steps again. Ramona's mother looked in the suitcases for the present she had brought.
> —Mother! You shouldn't have brought me such an expensive present!
> —Oh, it wasn't all that expensive. We wanted you to have something for the new apartment.
> —An original gravure by René Magritte!
> —Well, it isn't very big. It's just a small one.
> Whenever Ramona received a letter forwarded to her from her Montana home, the letter had been opened and the words "Oops! Opened by mistake!" written on the envelope. But she forgot that in gazing at the handsome new Magritte print, a picture of a tree with a crescent moon cut out of it.
> —It's fantastically beautiful! Where shall we hang it?
> —How about on the wall?

As in "Lost in the Funhouse," point of view is here distinctly related to theme—to the illumination of experience the story affords. In Barthelme's story, the effaced narrator does not intrude to give us answers, to tell us more about the past of Elsa and Ramona, or to explain their lives in "the complicated city." The meaning of the story lies in the apparent randomness of events, in the intricate arabesques of the characters, and in the absence of explanation.

Inside Points of View

Narration from inside the frame of the story uses either a narrator who is a character or participant in the events he relates—a *dramatized narrator*—or a narrator who, although *not* a character or participant in the story per se, nonetheless relates events from a vantage point inside the story's action—a *restricted narrator*.[3]

The dramatized narrator uses the first-person pronoun "I" to tell his

---

[3] In glossaries or handbooks of fiction, the restricted narrator is sometimes referred to as a "limited omniscient" or "selective omniscient" narrator or as a "limited third-person" narrator.

own story or, as a witness, to relate the adventures of someone else. The restricted narrator stations himself by a character or "community" of characters and conveys the action of the story through the impressions and dialogue of that character, or characters, using third-person pronouns. Yet because the character and the restricted narrator are separate, the narrator can, if he wishes, tell us more than the character could possibly know. On the whole, however, his comments do not suggest a perspective outside the events of the story. That is, he neither editorializes on the action and characters nor provides extended narrative summary.

DRAMATIZED NARRATORS

First-person narration is the oldest manner of story-telling, the mode we use in conversation to relate a personal experience. Its most obvious advantage in literature is the immediate authority it conveys: the reader is predisposed to believe what the "I" is going to tell him. In part, this results from the apparent artlessness of the dramatized narrator, an artlessness that prompted Henry James to call this point of view "that accurst autobiographical form which puts a premium on the loose, the improvised, the cheap and the easy."

Unlike the outside points of view, the dramatized narrator allows events to be viewed through a narrow rather than a wide-angle lens. Often, much background is omitted. Also, the narrator cannot give an account of simultaneous happenings or dissociated scenes unless he resorts to far-fetched devices. The only information that can be transmitted is what the "I" can legitimately know. And what the "I" knows best—or *thinks* he knows best—are his own thoughts and feelings. His understanding of other characters' motivations is severely limited. Thus, he stands opposite the privileged narrator, who can put himself into the minds of as many fictional characters as he wishes. Yet by limiting the perspective, this mode of narration provides the writer with a facile means of ordering his material.

In the case of narrators who tell their own story—such as Nat Lime in "Black Is My Favorite Color" and the unnamed narrator of "This Morning, This Evening, So Soon"—the reader may get a sense of a world thrown out of focus because the narrator's ego is omnipresent. Consider, for example, this passage from "Black Is My Favorite Color":

> Although black is still my favorite color you wouldn't know it from my luck except in short quantities even though I do all right in the liquor store business in Harlem, on Eighth Avenue between 110th and 111th.

I speak with respect. A large part of my life I've had dealings with Negro people, most on a business basis but sometimes for friendly reasons with genuine feeling on both sides. I'm drawn to them. At this time of my life I should have one or two good colored friends but the fault isn't necessarily mine.

In stories where the "I" acts as a witness—where he is ostensibly concerned with telling us about someone else—the sense of the "I" lessens and the fictional world becomes less subjective. The particular disadvantage of the "I" as witness is that he cannot logically know everything about the person whose story he is telling. But this partial ignorance can aid the author, as it does in "Sonny's Blues." The meaning of that story comes from the narrator's growing awareness of what kind of man his brother is. Also, as in all stories where the "I" acts as witness, the narrator, while ostensibly telling us about someone else, reveals a great deal about himself.

RESTRICTED NARRATORS

The restricted narrator is not a character in the story and speaks in third-person pronouns. Like the dramatized narrator, he affords a tightly controlled focus that provides a ready structural unity. Yet this mode avoids the constant references to "I" that is one of the disadvantages of the dramatized narrator. Unlike the privileged narrator, who is able to report or interpret action from the vantage of an outside perspective, the restricted narrator is limited to conveying events and information through the perceptions of the character or "community" of characters whose consciousness he has opened. If the narrator frees himself momentarily from the mind of that character, he nonetheless stays by the character's elbow—securely within the frame of the story. But because the restricted narrator is *not* that character, descriptions are in the narrator's own language—regardless of the narrator's protective coloration and the amount of detail filtered through the character's perceptions. Although the narrator is concealed, his rhetoric greatly influences the shape and, therefore, the meaning of the story. Most of the stories in this collection are told from the point of view of the restricted narrator. But, as you will see from your reading, their rhetorical patterns differ sharply. For example, although the following excerpts are both from stories by Philip Roth, the first ("Eli, the Fanatic") differs noticeably in idiom and rhythm from the second ("In Trouble"):

Here, after all, were peace and safety—what civilization had been working toward for centuries. For all his jerkiness, that was all Ted Heller was asking for, peace and safety. It was what his parents had asked for in the Bronx, and his grandparents in Poland, and theirs in Russia or Austria, or wherever else they'd fled to or from. It was what Miriam was asking for.

She had only received the paper back on Monday morning, a B plus for the very first interpretation she had ever written of a poem in college. Only on Monday she had thought it was going to be her last. Before Roy had finally returned to Fort Kean with his big brave decision made, her recurring thought had been to run away. And now she didn't have to; and she didn't have to marry him either.

The principal limitations of this point of view are similar to those of the dramatized narrator. The restricted narrator cannot tell us about events that are not accessible to the character he stands beside. Also, his customary practice of revealing single or similar consciousnesses prevents him from offering a multiplicity of diverse interior views, such as the privileged narrator characteristically provides. Further, since he is always inside the frame of the story, he cannot comment from any wider perspective.

"The Demonstrators" by Eudora Welty, "The Displaced Person" by Flannery O'Connor, and "Accomplished Desires" by Joyce Carol Oates exemplify different uses of the restricted narrator. "The Demonstrators" is told from the vantage point of Dr. Strickland, the principal character. Except for brief excursions outside the consciousness of the doctor ("The *Sentinel,* owned and edited by Horatio Duckett, came out on Tuesdays."), everything that happens in the story comes to us from his perspective; even the "objective" newspaper account of the double murder is read by the doctor as he sits "in his dining room, finishing breakfast." As a result of seeing events only as they impinge on Dr. Strickland's consciousness, we do not see into the minds of Miss Marcia Pope, the child who summons the doctor, Ruby, Dove, Oree, or Lucille: the consciousnesses of these characters are closed to us. This one-sidedness of view serves the theme of the story, which treats the separation of white men from the black community and the inability of medical knowledge to either sustain or make rich the human lives it ostensibly serves.

In "The Displaced Person," the restricted narrator relates the events of the story through more than one consciousness. But the consciousnesses through which the action is reported are so similar that they exist as aspects of a single consciousness (as in the "double" consciousnesses of the young

American couple in "The Cicerone"). Henry James recognized the usefulness of this practice when he stated that "under certain degrees of pressure" and "when it makes for concentration, . . . a represented community of vision between several parties to the action" is permissible. But, he hastened to add, "I understand no breaking-up of the register, no sacrifice of the recording consistency, that doesn't rather scatter and weaken." In "The Displaced Person," the consciousnesses of the Shortleys and Mrs. McIntyre form such a community of vision. Their similar attitudes give the story a cohesiveness that would not have been possible if the narrator had revealed the minds of the Guizacs, the priest, and the Negroes. Once again, point of view is a mode of thematic definition as well as a way of structuring, for only by sensing the seemingly impenetrable community of ignorance represented by the white Southerners in this story do we understand the true meaning of being displaced.

Unlike Mrs. Shortley and Mrs. McIntyre in "The Displaced Person," Dorie and Barbara in "Accomplished Desires" are outwardly dissimilar. Dorie, a student, is young, untalented, organized, devious, and pretty; Barbara, Mark Arber's wife, is forty-three, talented, disorganized, fair-minded, and open. For most of the story, the two women whose consciousnesses serve as its focal point exhibit little in common except their relationship to Mark. In the end, however, this relationship reveals their deeper commonality. In this story, too, point of view reinforces theme. Never seeing any events or either of the two women from Mark's point of view, we experience only the terrible destructiveness inherent in a marriage that grants professional and personal satisfactions to a husband at the expense of his wife, making her his unwitting victim. Were we to have access to Mark's sensibilities, we would probably discover that he, too, is a victim— of stereotyping, of academe, of the "establishment"—but that would be another story.

Inside points of view are well suited to the short story and, in particular, to the modern story. The reasons are chiefly esthetic: the brevity of the form encourages the exploration of particular moments in time and the consciousness of a single person, and the narrator's position inside the frame of the story ensures an immediacy and authority that heighten the illusion of reality. But the predominance of inside views in the contemporary short story has additional bases. Like the writer, the modern reader is particularly aware that his vision is limited, fragmented, immediate, and egocentric. In first-person narration, the reader knows the dramatized narrator's form of seeing and telling from having related his own experiences or from having listened to the experiences of others. Like the restricted narrator, the reader, in real life, is bound within a particular frame of action, similarly restricted to the perspective of a single consciousness or "community" of consciousnesses.

To many writers, the modern world—with its tremendous movements and forces—seems beyond human control and understanding. The fictional point of view that collapses the perspective of a "know-it-all" narrator and fosters the intimacy of a world restricted to the thoughts and feelings of one character or a "community" of characters offers, among its other advantages, a means of dealing with the external world through an ordering of experience based on the interior lives of individual men. Also, as the worth and workability of the external world have come into question, man's inner life has been made more accessible by the findings of Sigmund Freud, Carl Jung, Otto Rank, and the other investigators of man's subconscious. Not surprisingly, modern writers have used these insights as the form and substance of their fiction.

Frequently, the writer who adopts the inside point of view not only relinquishes his ability to transcend the limits of a particular scene but chooses a perspective that is untrustworthy. Many stories told from the inside come from narrators who are incapable of giving a reliable report. Even when such narrators can get the "facts" straight, their analyses and judgments are often unacceptable.

Reliable and Unreliable Narrators

Wayne C. Booth has observed (in *The Rhetoric of Fiction*) that if we discuss point of view to ascertain its relation to "literary effects," whether the narrator is privileged or limited, or referred to as "I" or "he," can be less important than his moral and intellectual qualities. "If he is discovered to be untrustworthy, then the total effect of the work he relays to us is transformed." In Booth's analysis, a *reliable narrator* "speaks for or acts in accordance with the norms of the work." An *unreliable narrator* speaks and acts against these norms.

The norms of any narrative are the explicit and implicit attitudes and values that help shape the theme, or view of life that a literary work suggests. Integrally related, then, to "meaning," the norms of a work derive from and, in turn, aid in establishing the implied author. By speaking or acting in accord with these attitudes and values, the reliable narrator necessarily stands close to the implied author.

In general, inside narrators are less reliable than outside narrators—often standing at considerable distances from the implied author and hampered further by their limited understanding and inside perspectives. In first-person narration, the narrator is, of course, involved physically and emotionally in the action he not only describes but frequently interprets. Consequently, the unreliability of many dramatized narrators is readily apparent. In "Black Is My Favorite Color," for example, Nat Lime's self-knowledge is so limited that his reasoning fails to explain the complexity of his feelings and situation. But even the apparently trustworthy narrator in "This Morning, This Evening, So Soon" is somewhat unreliable. Unable to come to terms with his past, he is unable to interpret the present objectively. As John V. Hagopian makes clear in his essay on that story, the reader must recognize the narrator's biases if he is to avoid thinking that "he is getting the meaning as well as the action from the narrator."

Quite frequently, restricted narrators are as unreliable as first-person narrators. If they offer no explicit commentary to counteract the biases of the character who serves as their focus, they can be as limited and unreliable as that character. But, because the restricted narrator is *not* telling his own story, any "objective" description (found often in opening and closing paragraphs) and all "subjective" description (descriptions that come from the character's point of view) are in the narrator's own language. Thus, he can direct our attention to the limitations of the character and thereby transcend those limitations. In "The Displaced Person," although the narration stays within the flawed consciousnesses of Mrs. Shortley and Mrs. McIntyre, their ignorance and prejudice become apparent through the "clues" it provides, thus making us aware of the values to which the implied author is committed. In "The Cicerone," for example, the narrator generally stays within the complacent and judgmental consciousnesses of the two Americans. But, to the extent that we are made aware of the couple's limitations, the narrator is suggesting an interpretation different from that voiced by the two characters.

Unlike inside narrators, the privileged narrator is usually reliable. His vantage point and "knowledge" allow him to report and interpret accurately and thereby to support the norms of the work. In "Lost in the Funhouse," despite Barth's parodying the convention of the privileged narrator, the many interruptions and comments that appear to come from the outside narrator endorse ideas and values integral to the "second self" created by Barth. For example:

> When you're lost, the smartest thing to do is stay put till you're found, hollering if necessary. But to holler guarantees humiliation as well as rescue; keeping silent permits some saving of face—you can act surprised

at the fuss when your rescuers find you and swear you weren't lost, if they do. What's more you might find your own way yet, *however belatedly.*

In stories told by an effaced narrator, where insight into the characters comes chiefly from what they say and how they act, the narrator is neither reliable nor unreliable—he is neutral. That is, the question of reliability is beside the point because we accept the convention that we see the action *directly* as if through the viewfinder of a camera, without the narrator acting as a middleman. Obviously, however, descriptions (no matter how minimal), transitions, and the juxtaposition of scenes indicate that a story like "City Life" has a narrator as much as stories like "Lost in the Funhouse," and that this narrator (however subtly) influences our interpretations of characters and actions. Because of his detachment, however, the effaced narrator is trustworthy to the extent that neither his presence nor his comments *interfere* with the action from which the reader must extrapolate norms.

At this point, a reader might wonder why a writer should choose an unreliable narrator. There are two principal advantages. The discrepancy between the reader's conception of a character and that character's self-image can be esthetically and thematically effective, as in "Black Is My Favorite Color." Our awareness of Nat Lime's earnest desire to befriend Negroes and our additional awareness of his inability to comprehend the impossibility of his situation—to understand why, although he gives his "heart," his reward will always be a "kick" in the teeth—make particularly effective the separation of black man from white man in our society. Similarly, although the restricted narrator offers no explicit interpretation in "Everything That Rises Must Converge," we recognize (although Julian does not) the conflict between Julian's fantasies about the Godhigh mansion and his conviction that, unlike his mother's attitude, *his* view of Negroes is enlightened and unprejudiced—a conflict that provides the meaning of the story. The unreliable narrator also gives the writer a way of bringing the reader into the action of the story. Rather than handing him neatly packaged "correct" interpretations, the unreliable narrator engages the reader by making him question the validity of the information and judgments he is receiving.

CHARACTERS

In fiction, the view of life a work suggests—its theme—arises from the human action that is its substance. Because ideas are seen in the context of characters involved with each other and their environment, the reader is made to feel the *human* consequences of hitherto impersonal abstractions. In "This Morning, This Evening, So Soon" and "The Displaced Person," for example, prejudice becomes glaringly real, appalling in its effects because our sympathies have been aroused for its victims who, we realize, include not only the Guizacs but Mrs. McIntyre, and not only the Negro singer but his white countrymen. Thus, chiefly through the characters, the norms of a work are emotive as well as rational.

As readers, we may be intrigued by a writer's style, awed by the wisdom of the implied author, or fascinated by the skillful handling of point of view. But the great emotional appeal of fiction lies in its characters— characters whose lives are displayed before us to admire, scorn, envy, or dislike, but always to engender some emotional response.

It is instructive to compare the ways we get to know fictional characters with the ways we get to know people in real life. Whereas the reality of the actual people we encounter is never in question, one of the writer's principal tasks is to make his characters "real" to us. As E. M. Forster notes in *Aspects of the Novel,* a character becomes real when he lives according to the laws of fiction that govern his existence. He is convincing when he appears credible within the achieved content of a story or novel. In both life and fiction, however, we pay attention to a person's behavior, appearance, speech, gestures, and mannerisms. We take stock of his surroundings, especially the objects he has chosen (such as clothes and furniture); we listen to what other people say about him; we see who his friends and enemies are. But, in fiction, these matters come to us from a narrator. That is, we *hear about* the clothes a character wears, his preferences in architecture, the movies he attends, and so forth. Thus, we are always in a position of seeing a character through the eyes of someone else—the narrator—and, ultimately, of judging the character as the implied author has judged him.

Consequently, the most obvious distinction between the two modes of knowing is also the most significant one for the study of fiction: a character is an imaginative creation. He has only those qualities, capacities, thoughts, and responses that his creator gives him. Further, no matter how well we know a person in real life, we are never *inside* that person's mind as we can be in fiction through the adoption of certain narrative perspectives. The supreme law of fiction has to do with the role of the narrator and his ability to open the consciousnesses of selected characters. Also, in real life we understand the people we encounter imperfectly; in fiction we can understand a character as completely as his creator allows. In real life many attributes of a person are objectively, immediately, and randomly evident, while other qualities may never be recognized by the person himself or by observers of him. In fiction the creator determines what qualities the character has, their order and manner of presentation, their relative importance, and even their place within the creator's own value system.

As in real life, where knowledge about other people depends on their proximity and the nature of our relationship to them, so point of view and the choice of narrator control our relationship to the fictional character and his accessibility to us. For example, the creator who uses inside narrators enables us to know a character through his most private thoughts and responses—letting us perceive the world as the character sees it. Dramatized narrators let us into their minds more readily and openly than do our acquaintances in ordinary life; we also become very close to the character whose intelligence serves the restricted narrator as focus. Similarly, the privileged narrator may give us some description and some action from the inside perspective of characters in the story. On the other hand, the effaced narrator limits us to exterior views of the characters.

The *kinds* of characters a writer creates not only alert us to his intentions but also carry much of the story's meaning. One useful critical distinction is between static and dynamic characters. A *static* character is one whose essential nature does not change in the course of the story. A *dynamic* character is one whose experiences impress him so that his attitudes and (usually) his actions change, and he emerges a different person at the conclusion of the work than he was at the beginning.

Most protagonists in novels are dynamic characters, since the length of the novel allows portrayal of character changes over a logical course of time. In the short story, if a writer depicts a character capable of changing because of his experiences, he often brings the character to the point of discovery and ends the story there. Accordingly, we do not see the character acting on his new insights. The implication is that the two Americans in "The Cicerone," Dr. Strickland in "The Demonstrators," Leo Finkle in "The Magic Barrel," and the narrator in "Sonny's Blues" will act differently in the future, but the narrative does not take us into that future.

Frequently, the short-story writer makes his protagonists static characters. Examples are Nat Lime in "Black Is My Favorite Color," Orson Ziegler in "The Christian Roommates," and the woman in "No Place for You, My Love." In both the novel and the short story, minor characters are almost always static.

Thus, the short story lends itself to revealing various facets of a character (including views of him prior to the narrative present) and to showing the forces of change at work upon him, rather than to depicting character development in the sense of significant behavioral changes. If he wishes, the writer may give considerable information about a new character in one or several paragraphs of extended description. Here the cumulative effect of fiction simply plays against the expectations aroused by the "set piece"—as this method of character revelation has been called. If the writer chooses to reveal his character sequentially, he avoids the set piece and uses the cumulative nature of fiction to let actions, speech, thoughts, and feelings depict the character as the story unfolds.

The relationship between how a character becomes known to us and point of view is significant. A privileged narrator often provides a set piece, as in "Lost in the Funhouse," in which the narrator, assuming the guise of omniscience, tells us in the first two paragraphs that Ambrose and his family have come to Ocean City to celebrate Independence Day—a family that consists of his mother and father, his uncle Karl, his brother Peter who is fifteen, and a friend, Magda G———, who is fourteen, "a pretty and exquisite young lady, who live[s] not far from them on B——— Street in the town of D———, Maryland." Since an effaced narrator portrays characters through action and dialogue, his characters are necessarily revealed sequentially. Most often, a restricted narrator reveals characters sequentially. If a set piece is used, the description occurs after the story is well under way, as in "A Gift from the City." A first-person narrator may begin by explaining himself to us, as Nat Lime does in "Black Is My Favorite Color." More commonly, he reveals himself sequentially, as does the narrator in "Sonny's Blues."

Static characters are almost always *flat* as opposed to *round*—an additional way of classifying characters. Dominated by a single quality or idea, *flat* characters are often representative types. Since the proficient writer can create convincing, even memorable, flat characters in a few sentences, this kind of character is well adapted to the short story. In both the novel and story, minor characters are usually flat as well as static.

Typically, *comic* characters are flat, lending themselves to comic portrayal because they exhibit only a single facet or passion and because they are unchanged by experience. We laugh at distortion and incongruity, and we laugh when we see a certain character mechanically repeating the same foolish actions and suffering the same inevitable consequences. Mrs. Shortley in "The Displaced Person" is a comic character not only because of her gross physical appearance (heightened by descriptions that liken her to nonhuman objects, thus shutting off our sympathy to her as a person) but because of the utter stupidity of her prejudice and the invincibility of her ignorance. Nat Lime can be considered a comic character because of the persistence of his clumsy attempts to befriend Negroes and the inevitable rebuttals that he endures as a consequence. In both these stories, the distortion, obsession, or action is not humorous in itself—physical grossness, prejudice, and alienation are not funny. But because these attitudes are exaggerated and revealed through flat characters—fictional personages whom we see as objects—we are able to merge the character and the quality that he represents into one comic entity.

As a result, flat characters serve the writer whose purpose is satiric, for satire exposes man's follies and in so doing makes fun of them. Distortion is one of the satirist's chief weapons. The already distorted flat character and his generic qualities are useful to him. In "The Cicerone," for example, Polly Grabbe is a satirical portrait. Her flower-bulb fortune, her patronage of the arts, her "hunter's look," and her pilgrimages in search of love make her ridiculous. If the author goes one step further and creates a character almost unrecognizable as a human being, the character becomes a caricature—a person so grotesquely or ludicrously exaggerated that he is only a weird puppet; the characterization of Miss Grabbe verges on caricature. When the author wishes to emphasize ideas, he may make his characters flat to keep our interest away from them as people and focused on his ideas.

Despite the brevity of the story as a form, many writers are able to create *round* characters—characters in whom several traits blend and fight for supremacy. "It is only round people," says Forster, "who are fit to perform tragically for any length of time and can move us to any feelings except humour and appropriateness." Eli Peck in "Eli, the Fanatic," Dorie and Barbara in "Accomplished Desires," and Dr. Strickland in "The Demonstrators" are round characters, depicted so as to arouse us to feelings of pity and, perhaps, fear. In a way, the brevity of the short-story form assists in creating the impression of roundness. The author can sustain an intensity and carry the action through at a high pitch; during the time the character exists before us, he does so very clearly.

As with any ingredient in narration, the kinds of characters a writer creates are appropriate if they serve his purpose. When this happens and when a writer creates characters able to stir our curiosity and arouse concern about their destinies, characters in fiction are truly memorable, whether they be static or dynamic, flat or round, major or minor.

P L O T ,   F O R M ,   A N D   T I M E

Plot

Plot is most simply defined as a series of interrelated actions. Because narration is sequential, plot is fundamental to narrative art. And because actors participate in the actions, plot is linked to characterization. In fact, one mark of serious fiction is the degree to which the action arises from and reflects the traits of the characters, thereby involving the reader in the values and judgments brought into play by the characters. Henry James was concerned with this issue when he asked, "What is character but the determination of incident? What is incident but the illustration of character?" In this general and theoretical sense, plot includes not only physical but metaphysical action—that is, the intellectual and emotional responses of the characters.

Plot is generally set in motion by *conflict,* which, in serious fiction, is both external and internal. External conflict concerns the struggles of the protagonist against an objectified antagonist such as his fellow man ("The Displaced Person"), his physical environment ("How I Contemplated the World from the Detroit House of Correction and Began My Life Over Again"), "fate" ("Lost in the Funhouse"), or a combination of all three forces ("Everything That Rises Must Converge"). If the conflict is also internal, as in "Everything That Rises Must Converge," the action of the story takes place at another level—within the mind of the character. Sometimes he finds himself torn between contrasting loyalties and ways of life ("Eli, the Fanatic"). At other times, he wages his battle against two aspects of himself, usually one that is "idealized" and one that is "real" ("The Magic Barrel").

A conventional way of looking at plot is to see the action of a story moving through five basic stages: (1) *exposition* (explanation of essential information, usually about events that have occurred prior to the narrative present); (2) *complication* or rising action (events that follow the initiation of the conflict by the inciting force); (3) *crisis* or climax (the turning point to which the incidents that constitute the complication have been leading; (4) *falling action* (the less intense action that comes about as a result of the turning point); and (5) *resolution* or dénouement (the resolving or unknotting of the situation).

Although it is convenient, this five-stage approach to plot has limited usefulness for analyzing the plot structure of much modern fiction. In general, contemporary authors omit or modify exposition and resolution (or at least any clear-cut "resolving" or "unknotting"). In "Lost in the Funhouse," for example, John Barth discusses the plot of conventional narrative—once in the passage quoted on page 13, and again in a passage complete with trumped-up diagrams illustrating the five basic stages:

> While there is no reason to regard this pattern as an absolute necessity, like many other conventions it became conventional because great numbers of people over many years learned by trial and error that it was effective; one ought not to forsake it, therefore, unless one wishes to forsake as well the effect of drama or has clear cause to feel that deliberate violation of the "normal" pattern can better effect that effect.

The narrator's concern about plot and his lengthy discussions only serve, of course, to remind us of the absence of action in this story. Ambrose is, by the conclusion, out of the actual funhouse; but the tangible funhouse is less important to the story's meaning than the intangible funhouse that serves as principal metaphor. Within the dark and mirrored mazes of that fanciful structure, Ambrose, it seems clear, will wander all the days of his life.

"Sonny's Blues" by James Baldwin, while on the surface a more conventional narrative than "Lost in the Funhouse," is typical of much modern fiction in its "deliberate violation of the 'normal' pattern." With the opening sentence, Baldwin plunges us into present action and establishes the nature of the conflict: "I read about it in the paper, in the subway, on my way to work." Almost immediately we learn that Sonny "had been picked up, the evening before, in a raid on an apartment downtown, for peddling heroin." Gradually, through the first-person narrator, the past is revealed and we are led into the rising action until we reach the turning point: Sonny's request that his brother visit the nightclub. The remainder of the story constitutes the falling action: the narrator meets the musicians and listens to his brother play the piano. As in many modern stories, the conclusion offers little sense of completion. Instead of resolving the action, Baldwin implies a continuance; the blues that Sonny and the group play takes on a special and immense meaning to the narrator:

Freedom lurked around us and I understood, at last, that he could help us to be free if we would listen, that he would never be free until we did. Yet, there was no battle in his face now. I heard what he had gone through, and would continue to go through until he came to rest in earth. He had made it his: that long line, of which we knew only Mama and Daddy. And he was giving it back, as everything must be given back, so that, passing through death, it can live forever.

Many of the stories in this collection have narrative structures similar to that of "Sonny's Blues"—among them "A Gift from the City," "Eli, the Fanatic," "In Trouble," "The Demonstrators," "Accomplished Desires," "The Displaced Person," and "Everything That Rises Must Converge." Like "Sonny's Blues," these stories bring us quickly into the rising action, letting us pick up background information through dialogue, flashbacks, reflection on the part of characters, and occasional statements by the narrator. In each story, the resolution is ambiguous and frequently subdued.

All fiction represents a selection of incidents. Because the short story is brief, the story writer must be especially selective in the action he relates, omitting certain incidents entirely and summarizing others. When he wishes to condense long periods of time, he relays action through narrative statement or summary. If he decides to dwell at length upon a particular incident, he uses dialogue in addition to detailed description of physical action. Whether a writer relies heavily on summary or depicts action "scenically" depends on the point of view he adopts and the chronological time encompassed by the action. Although the narrator in "Lost in the Funhouse" assumes a position that allows him to summarize action, there is little summary because the physical action occurs within a span of a few hours. Conversely, because the theme of "The Christian Roommates" requires us to know what became of Orson Ziegler after graduation, the last few paragraphs, which are written in the style of a biographical résumé, violate the perspective of the restricted narrator. Updike summarizes the major events of Orson's later years in a manner that contrasts with the rich confusion of his freshman year: "After graduation, he married Emily, attended the Yale School of Medicine, and interned in St. Louis. He is now the father of four children." Since the effaced narrator avoids exposition, action in stories told from this point of view comes to us scenically. A dramatized narrator, such as Nat Lime in "Black Is My Favorite Color," is at liberty to summarize action as well as to involve us in the direct presentation of incidents.

As a writer strives to make his characters convincing within the laws of fiction, so must he make plot—an artificial ordering of events—convincing.

Quite obviously, life is more random than that reflected in fiction, events are less causally connected than those in a story. Consequently, the writer must use chance and coincidence with discretion. *Chance*—an occurrence resulting from unknown or unconsidered forces—is always unanticipated, stemming from neither past action nor the disposition of the characters. *Coincidence* is the accidental coming together of two events that have a particular correspondence. In "Everything That Rises Must Converge," chance causes Julian's mother and a Negro woman to "converge" on the same bus. However, it is coincidence that the women are wearing identical hats. Although chance and coincidence both occur in ordinary life, their presence in fiction calls attention to the story as a fabrication by heightening the "unnaturalness" of its plot. Truth is often stranger than fiction, but successful fiction may seldom be stranger than truth.

Because plot is based on selection and arrangement, the writer is able to employ foreshadowing. *Foreshadowing* occurs when the author hints at subsequent developments through narrative comment, dialogue, setting, atmosphere, imagery, and symbols. Thus, foreshadowing is the writer's chief means of evoking *suspense*—a sense of mystification and anticipation. Too much foreshadowing, however, decreases suspense by making the outcome predictable. In "The Unspoiled Reaction," Mary McCarthy uses foreshadowing to make us aware that the seemingly innocuous and pleasant puppet show will end unhappily. Through the perceptions of the mother, we are told of the "generally anxious, false, and flustered air" of the hostess, of the "air of failure" that hangs over "the whole undertaking, infecting the audience itself with the poison of financial sickness," and of the officiousness of a managerial younger lady who insists that the children move to center seats. Whereas a privileged narrator could have informed us about the suppressed hostility of the puppeteer, the inside perspective in this story ensures the maintenance of suspense by keeping us within the consciousness of the mother. In both the novel and short story, point of view is instrumental in determining the nature and degree of the reader's mystification.

Form

In stories containing a recognizable plot—that at least move through the stages of complication, climax, and falling action—we admire the way in which the author has ordered the interrelated sequence of events to produce a certain effect. For example, we admire the "twinning" that illuminates the conflict and parallel lines of "Everything That Rises Must Converge" and the careful building to a crisis in "The Unspoiled Reaction." But some stories—particularly in contemporary fiction—lack any semblance of a traditional plot structure. In such stories we respond to another kind of ordering—to form.

In 1924, Sherwood Anderson complained, "There was a notion that ran through all storytelling in America, that stories must be built about a plot and that absurd Anglo-Saxon notion that they must point a moral, up-lift the people, make better citizens, etc." The notion of plot, said Ander-son, seemed "to poison all story-telling. What was wanted I thought was form, not plot, an altogether more elusive and difficult thing to come at." *Form* refers to the manner in which the ingredients of a story have been ordered so as to give the narrative a distinguishing shape. In this sense, every story has a form: indeed, plot can be one of the means of achieving form. But in "plotless" stories, form alone provides the esthetic cohesiveness that allows an otherwise random collection of incidents and observations to be recognizable as verbal art.

One of the oldest methods of "plotless" narrative ordering is the episodic. Typically, a journey is undertaken, with the presence of the protagonist and the road upon which he travels, rather than the interrelatedness of the incidents, furnishing continuity. This method of telling extends back to all legendary matter in which the protagonist proves his strength in succes-sive combats or sets out in search of a sacred or magical object. "The Cice-rone" and "No Place for You, My Love" involve journeys that are also quests. At the conclusion of each story, the characters return to their place of departure—physically in "No Place for You, My Love," spiritually in "The Cicerone." In neither story has the quest been successful.

Another way of ordering is to structure the story so that the movement is vertical, as opposed to the horizontal development found in most episodic stories and in stories set in motion by a conflict that is at least partly exter-nal. Eudora Welty's "The Demonstrators" is an example of vertical develop-ment. The initial situation is mysterious: the Negro child discloses neither the nature of her request nor the destination. Only as Dr. Strickland is treating the injured woman is the situation clarified. In all such stories, it is as though a darkened room (like that in the house the doctor visits) were illuminated gradually until its contents were finally visible.

Stories that are developed vertically often gain additional cohesiveness through such interior considerations as the psychological correctness of the apparently random thoughts of the protagonist ("The Demonstra-tors"). Or perhaps the form of the story is strengthened through its pat-terns of imagery ("No Place for You, My Love"), or through the effect

31

of its symbolism ("The Cicerone"), or through the unity and intensity of flashbacks employed to round out the present action ("This Morning, This Evening, So Soon"). Frequently a writer combines these ways of achieving form, as in "The Demonstrators," which is unified by imagery, symbolism, and flashbacks as well as by the psychological wholeness of the protagonist's thoughts.

Time

A story that centers around a vertically revealed situation is frequently close to our notions of inner time—interior time zones that have little correspondence to objective time. "Psychological time" is what is being explored in "The Demonstrators" and in "This Morning, This Evening, So Soon." In these stories, present time moves easily into past events, some of which have occurred within the life of the protagonist while others were enacted in a distant moment of history that has a bearing on the present action. The ramifications of seemingly trivial incidents are explored and described in copious detail because of their importance to the protagonist. As the plastic arts have moved away from representation, so modern fiction has moved away from objective chronological continuity. Further, stories that dissolve rather than resolve (such as "The Demonstrators" and "The Magic Barrel") reinforce our notions of irresolution, of continuance—our awareness that the past continually and inescapably influences the present and that in life there are no conclusive endings except death.

SETTING

Setting is the representation in fiction of the place and time that constitute the environment of the action. Incorporating the tangible and spiritual aspects of physical locations and historical eras, setting includes the depiction of objects and institutions peculiar to certain places and periods—Jim's bulletin board and steel desk in "A Gift from the City," the porcelain cup in "The Demonstrators," and the anachronistic office of marriage broker in "The Magic Barrel."

Closely related to characterization, setting enhances the credibility of the characters by providing a visible context for them. It can also influence, sometimes even control, their lives. As with character and plot, the establishment of setting calls for selectivity by the writer. Often, what he chooses *not* to describe is particularly significant, and frequently what *is* included alerts us to what is missing. For example, in "How I Contemplated . . . ," the copious descriptions of external conditions attest to the affluent, faddish, busy lives of the protagonist's parents and suggest the absence of a warm, nurturing, private family life: the protagonist's house is "classic contemporary. Traditional modern. Attached garage, attached Florida room, attached patio, attached pool and cabana . . ."; a host of magazines and newspapers are subscribed to: *Time, Fortune, Life, Business Week,* the *Wall Street Journal, The New York Times,* the *New Yorker,* the *Saturday Review,* and so forth; there are numerous clubs to which the parents belong, among them: the Detroit Athletic Club, the Detroit Golf Club, the Bloomfield Hills Country Club, and the Bloomfield Art Association.

As the writer may depict a rich variety of characters, so may he set his story in any time or any place—actual or imaginary. He may invent a place and time, creating fanciful landscapes sustained only by his imagination and putting the action backward into a remote era or forward into a visionary future, as Lewis Carroll, William Golding, and Ray Bradbury have done. Conversely, he may depict "real" places or settings that closely resemble actual locations, putting the action in the contemporary period, as the writers in this collection have done. Thus, "The Unspoiled Reaction" takes place in New York City; "No Place for You, My Love" takes place in New Orleans and the adjacent bayou country. The action and characters in "Everything That Rises Must Converge" suggest the milieu of a large Southern city—possibly Atlanta.

By setting his story in a "real" location or in one resembling an actual place, the writer releases a host of associations in the reader. For example, the traditional image of Paris is as a romantic, charming, and beautiful city. In "This Morning, This Evening, So Soon" James Baldwin can assume that most readers "know" this Paris and that they will be sympathetic to the narrator's reluctance to leave the French capital. He can also assume that the reader's notions about Paris will make the setting "visible" without copious description. Similarly, he can take it for granted that the reader is aware of the realities of contemporary America and will thus understand why the protagonist has conflicting feelings about his native land. Despite the fact that different readers view a city like Paris or a country like America somewhat differently, owing to their subjective experiences with the actual place, the general effect of specifying a "real" location is the active engagement of the reader's imagination.

By establishing a "real" setting, the writer can manipulate the reader's knowledge in still another way: he can choose to confirm preconceptions about a particular place or to reverse those expectations. "A Gift from the City," for example, confirms preconceptions about the hostility of urban living. "Eli, the Fanatic" corroborates our belief that many fashionable suburbs, like the fictional Woodenton, are still "restricted." In "The Demonstrators," expectations about the dreariness of life in rural Mississippi are reversed in that the humble setting provides the protagonist with an unexpected sense of man's dignity.

Settings can be particularized, as in "Sonny's Blues" (110th Street, Lenox Avenue, Greenwich Village) and "The Cicerone," in which actual places and streets, such as the Sforza Gallery in Milan and the Via San Ignazio in Rome, document the Americans' journey. Or the setting may be unspecified and general, as in "The Indian Uprising." Here the city is wholly an invention of the author (its streets are named after American military leaders, such as Mark Clark, Chester Nimitz, and so on; the pavements are of a soft yellow; the Comanches constitute the invading force). Yet some details conjure images of cities we have known (there are tall, flat buildings, hospitals, cabdrivers, blue and green maps, gardens, a military band). As a result, the unspecified, invented city becomes all cities and gives the story a desirable universality. On the other hand, by specifying actual locations, a writer can give his story a great deal of realism. In "Sonny's Blues," for example, because we know something about Harlem and its effects on human life, we are predisposed to believe in the reality of the characters and incidents.

Settings can be wholly internal as in "The Unspoiled Reaction," which takes place within the confines of a Broadway theater. Or the setting may be predominantly external, as in "No Place for You, My Love," which takes place on a road south of New Orleans. Most often, however, the setting is both external and internal, with the characters moving from the privateness of interior scenes to the openness of streets and public gathering places, as in "The Cicerone," "A Gift from the City," "Sonny's Blues," and "The Demonstrators." In many stories, setting can be considered internal in still another sense. In stories like "The Demonstrators," the mind of the protagonist furnishes the "setting" for much of the action.

In some stories, the specific setting is insignificant to the theme. In "How I Contemplated . . . ," virtually any wealthy suburb of any large

American city would have served the author's purpose: to reveal the protagonist's terrifying spiritual emptiness amid the suburban opulence of automatic sprinklers, paneled walls, and private police in unmarked cars. In other stories, setting is thematically important. In "Everything That Rises Must Converge," the converging of passengers on a public bus in a Southern city *after* the integration of public transportation causes the conflict that provides most of the meaning of the story.

Settings, like characters, can be viewed as flat or round. Thus, although the setting of "In Trouble" is fraught with possible complexities, Philip Roth's description of Liberty Center does not involve us in its idiosyncrasies. It succeeds, simply, in making this town representative of almost any small midwestern town. On the other hand, a writer may suggest the complexity of a particular setting, as James Baldwin does in "This Morning, This Evening, So Soon," in which the objective and most obvious aspects of Paris and New York City are undercut by subjective and intangible qualities that make inevitable the narrator's return to America.

Like every other aspect of fiction, setting is affected by point of view. In stories told by an effaced narrator, description of setting is customarily objective and brief, with the narrator providing only those details necessary to convey a minimal sense of place. In contrast, there is often copious description in stories related by a privileged narrator, who is at liberty to depict setting either through his own perceptions or through those of his characters. John Barth parodies this convention in "Lost in the Funhouse" when, for example, the narrator complains about the lack of "rendered sensory detail" in his story and then lists specific, sensory images that relate to setting, shifting slyly from reiteration of detail to description of present action:

> The faded distorting mirrors beside Fat May; the impossibility of choosing a mount when one had but a single ride on the great carrousel; the *vertigo attendant on his recognition* that Ocean City was worn out, the place of fathers and grandfathers, straw-boatered men and parasoled ladies survived by their amusements. Money spent, the three paused at Peter's insistence beside Fat May to watch the girls get their skirts blown up. The object was to tease Magda.

In general, the restricted narrator depicts setting dramatically and subjectively through the perceptions of the character or community of characters whose consciousness(es) he is revealing. If the narrator provides expository description, it most often occurs at the beginning of the story, as in "Eli, the Fanatic":

35

> Leo Tzuref stepped out from back of a white column to welcome Eli
> Peck. Eli jumped back, surprised; then they shook hands and Tzuref
> gestured him into the sagging old mansion. At the door Eli turned, and
> down the slope of lawn, past the jungle of hedges, beyond the dark, un-
> trampled horse path, he saw the street lights blink on in Woodenton.
> The stores along Coach House Road tossed up a burst of yellow.

As illustrated in this passage, when a restricted narrator is used, there is
necessarily a shift from objectively rendered description to the subjective
perceptions of the character who serves as the narrative focus.

In the case of a dramatized narrator, the setting is always revealed
through his consciousness. Thus, the narrator in "Sonny's Blues" describes
New York City as he experiences it, mixing description and judgments
freely: "We live in a housing project. . . . The beat-looking grass lying
around isn't enough to make their lives green, the hedges will never hold
out the streets, and they know it. The big windows fool no one, they aren't
big enough to make space out of no space."

Setting is related to mood as well as to point of view. *Mood* refers to the
atmosphere that surrounds and helps to define the world in which the
characters move. Thus mood involves the feeling that emanates from certain locales or accrues from particular actions. Although intangible, mood
can be an unshakeable quality that affects our response to a story, as in real
life we are affected by the atmosphere of certain places. In "The Unspoiled
Reaction," the rainy Monday morning, the gloomy and poorly attended
theater, and the "air of failure" establish an atmosphere of impending disaster, with a mood best described as portentous. In "The Magic Barrel," the
insubstantiality of Pinye Salzman's living quarters enhances the note of
fantasy and magic that permeates this story. In "Everything That Rises
Must Converge," the predetermined route of the bus underscores the feeling of inevitability that dominates this story.

Although regional settings in these stories range from Italy to New
Orleans, the rural South to the Midwest, a dominant locus is the city,
particularly New York City, which provides the setting for "The Unspoiled Reaction," "A Gift from the City," "Black Is My Favorite Color,"
"The Magic Barrel," "Sonny's Blues," and "City Life." "This Morning, This
Evening, So Soon" is set in Paris and New York, "How I Contemplated . . ." in Detroit and Bloomfield Hills, and "The Indian Uprising"
and "Everything That Rises Must Converge" in unspecified cities. The
recurrence of the city as a milieu is not surprising, for the increasing
urbanization of America has produced a significant body of literature
concerned with the values and experiences of urban man.

In an essay titled "How I Write," Eudora Welty observed, "Like a good many other writers, I am myself touched off by place. The place where I am and the place I know, and other places that familiarity with and love for my own make strange and lovely and enlightening to look into, are what set me to writing my stories." In addition, she describes place as "one of the most simple and obvious and direct sources of the short story." But, if the "source" is simple, the substance is usually complex. As these stories attest, the physical and spiritual qualities of setting provide a great and intricate reality.

STYLE

Every writer has a prose style that is distinctly his, and every story he writes carries its mark. Most great authors have been great prose stylists, having created styles suitable to their purposes, and having stamped upon language their own originality and vision. Because characters, incidents, and setting—as well as ideas—can be conveyed only through language, *style* is the visible and invisible manifestation of the writer's intentions. Capable of unifying the separate aspects and segments of a narrative, style relates to the way the historical author views life and to his grasp of the story as a whole.

Style can be loosely conceived as applying to everything in a story, for everything in it involves the writer's use of language. But it is possible to define *style* in a narrower sense on the basis of certain technical aspects of language—specifically, the kinds of words a writer uses (*diction*), how words are combined in sentences (*syntax*), the auditory appeals of language (*rhythm* and *sound*), and the nature and uses of spoken language (*dialogue*). Style also embraces those aspects of language that allow the writer to extend the impact and significance of his narrative—*imagery* and *symbolism*.

Because writers create narrators who speak in a manner appropriate to their position and disposition, style—like the other aspects of fiction—is related to point of view. For example, in "Black Is My Favorite Color," Bernard Malamud submerges his voice into that of his first-person narrator and tells his story in a style appropriate to the limited awareness of Nat Lime. In "The Magic Barrel," a story in which a restricted narrator is

37

used, Malamud adapts his writing to the sensitivity and intelligence of the rabbinical student through whose consciousness the tale is revealed. Although there are stylistic links between the two stories (in particular, the Yiddish-American idiom), they illustrate a necessary aspect of prose style—flexibility.

Diction and Syntax

As noted earlier, *diction* refers to the kinds of words a writer uses. Although every writer is bound by the limits and preferences of his personal vocabulary, he is free to employ words from various levels of usage. He may use the informal language of everyday speech, as Philip Roth does in "In Trouble," a more esoteric vocabulary ("The Cicerone"), or language so lyrical as to approach the poetic ("No Place for You, My Love"). He may use predominantly flat, literal words ("City Life") or richly connotative words ("This Morning, This Evening, So Soon"). His language may be heavily Latinate (leaning toward abstraction) or predominantly Anglo-Saxon (which tends toward concrete depiction). But while the writer's choice of words is directly influenced by his particular needs in a story, these needs are directly influenced by the larger social environment within which he lives. If, as John Updike suggests, we live in "an age of nuance, of ambiguous gestures and psychological jockeying," those qualities are bound to find expression in our literature. Updike's own prose style attests to their presence.

Because *how* something is said affects *what* is said, *syntax*—the arrangement of words into sentences—helps determine meaning and tone. *Loose* sentences, in which the most important idea occurs early in the sentence, mirror the spoken language, suggesting artlessness and honesty that contrast with the deliberateness or artifice implied by *periodic* and *balanced* sentences. Consider the effects of these three sentences from "The Unspoiled Reaction":

loose

> But disaffected as it was, *the audience contained the inevitable minority of enthusiastic cooperators* who rejoice in obeying with ostentatious promptness any command whatsoever, who worship all signs, prohibitions, warnings, and who constitute themselves volunteer deputies of any official person they can find in their neighborhood.

periodic

> As the hand still pursued and it seemed as if no power on earth could prevent the approaching indignity, *the puppet cried out.*

balanced

> Sometimes *the children answered,* speaking their own names softly, with reverence; more often, shyness and delight held them tongue-tied, and *the parent supplied the information.*

In each sentence, the main clause(s) or idea(s) is italicized here for illustrative purposes. As these examples show, periodic and balanced sentences depend on withholding information and equating or paralleling ideas in an effort to create suspense or to stress a point. But here even the loose sentence contains three parallel subordinate clauses. Generally, stories like "The Unspoiled Reaction," with many periodic and symmetrical sentences, appear more contrived because the prose is more controlled than in stories like "Accomplished Desires," which contain a preponderance of asymmetrical loose sentences and natural sounding dialogue. In addition, the reader should observe how the structure and arrangement of sentences affect the general pace of a story. For example, short and relatively simple sentences make the pace of "Black Is My Favorite Color" rapid, as opposed to the slower pace of "The Magic Barrel."

Rhythm and Sound

Unlike the regular rhythm of the conventional poetic line, the rhythm of prose is less regular and more expansive. It depends upon individual stress groups and large intonational patterns rather than upon the repetition of identical metrical feet, as in most poetry. In the following sentence from "Sonny's Blues," the diagonal lines indicate the stress groups—groups of words that contain a unit meaning and one or more stressed syllables:

> And Sonny went all the way back,/ he really began/
> with the spare, flat statement/ of the opening
> phrase of the song.

Additional rhythm comes from the story's intonational pattern—the succession of pitches that occur in the speaking of such larger units as clauses and sentences. It is important to notice, however, that "Sonny's Blues" *is* rhythmical (although irregular), and that the strong cadences heighten the emotionality of the subject matter.

Related to rhythm is the *sound* of individual syllables, words, and sentences. Words that contain a predominance of harsh consonants, such as *b, d, g, k, p,* and *t,* are cacophonous. For example, when the narrator of "Sonny's Blues" states, "But now, abruptly, I hated him. I couldn't stand the way he looked at me, partly like a dog, partly like a cunning child," harsh consonants predominate, drowning out the softer consonants (*h, l, m, n, r,* and *w*) and the vowel sounds, and underscoring the speaker's hatred.

Onomatopoeia indicates an attempt to choose words that are directly imitative of sounds. In "This Morning, This Evening, So Soon," the description of New York City contains the words *shuttling, stamping, pressing, chattering,* and *clanging.* These words are onomatopoetic in that they sound like the characteristic noises of Manhattan. The reader should notice also the presence and effect of alliteration and assonance. *Alliteration* refers to the repetition of consonant sounds, particularly in accented syllables and at the beginnings of words; *assonance* refers to the repetition of vowel sounds in neighboring words. Notice how alliteration (the repeated *s* and *p* sounds, for example) and assonance (the repeated long *e* and long and short *i,* for example) heighten the lyricism and meaning of this description from "The Magic Barrel":

> —score another for Salzman, whom he uneasily sensed to be somewhere around, hiding perhaps high in a tree along the street, flashing the lady signals with a pocket mirror; or perhaps a cloven-hoofed Pan, piping nuptial ditties as he danced his invisible way before them strewing wild buds on the walk and purple grapes in their path.

Used effectively, rhythm and sound can underscore the denotative and connotative meanings of words by communicating moods and attitudes that exist beneath the level of conscious verbal exchange. In prose, these devices serve the writer when they emphasize the meaning and enhance the tonal quality; they work against his purpose when they call attention to themselves.

Dialogue

Since dialogue is basic to fiction, the degree and kind of dialogue in a story is an important aspect of prose style. The reader should observe whether the dialogue is appropriate to the social class, psychic state, and region of the speaker; whether it is stilted or natural, witty or dull; and whether it serves to advance the action by revealing thoughts, feelings, and plot details. Dialogue has much to do with the informality and naturalness of Roth's style in "In Trouble" and with the artificial, reportorial quality of Barthelme's style in "The Indian Uprising." Although dialogue in "The Displaced Person" establishes both Mrs. McIntyre and the Shortleys as rural and Southern, the rhythmic and idiomatic patterns in the Shortleys' speech mark them as poor white trash (despite their self-aggrandizement) and indicate their social inferiority to Mrs. McIntyre. Similarly, in "Everything That Rises Must Converge," Julian's mother announces her middle-class origin through her conversation as clearly as the woman "with protruding teeth and long yellow hair" identifies herself as lower class ("I reckon it might could, . . . but I know for a fact my apartment couldn't get no hotter"). In addition to filling in much useful background information about Orson Ziegler and Henry Palamountain in "The Christian Roommates," dialogue quickly and effectively establishes the different temperaments and resultant tension between the roommates.

Imagery

Imagery may be either literal or figurative. *Literal imagery* refers to the verbal representation of sense experience—that is, to words and phrases that identify, describe, or evoke sensory responses. Accordingly, literal imagery extends to the representation of auditory, tactile, gustatory, olfactory, and kinetic sensations as well as visual, often blending several senses in a single image (as does the word *licked* in the passage printed below). By allowing the reader to experience the sensuous qualities of places, events, and characters, literal imagery aids the writer in creating and sustaining the illusion of reality.

While literal imagery seeks to represent the sensation or object as directly as possible, *figurative imagery* is associative and involves saying one thing in terms of another. A figurative image likens an object, place, event, animal, or human being to something else, which may or may not be in the same category. In fiction, the most common types of figurative images are *simile,* which describes or identifies by explicit analogy (for example, "dry as feathers"); *metaphor,* which describes or identifies by implicit analogy (for example, "inlaid mosaic bands"); and *personification,* which describes or identifies by attributing human qualities to animals, inanimate objects, or abstractions (for example, "tires licked"—licking being a human-animal action). As these examples show, figurative imagery is often sensory, in that the thing being compared (the *tenor*) or what it is compared to (the *vehicle*) or both can evoke sensory responses, like the tactile sense appealed to in "dry as feathers."

Concerning "No Place for You, My Love," Eudora Welty observed, "I was writing of exposure, and the shock of the world." Accordingly, she chose a setting in which "secret and shadow are taken away . . . by the merciless light." The following passage from "No Place for You, My Love" shows how a single literal image combines sense impressions, how figurative imagery is also sensory, and how effective imagery transcends mere decoration.

> The road grew [visual-kinetic, also personification in that growth is a human-animal-organic quality] one with the heat [although a noun, heat conveys a tactile sensation] as it was one with the unseen river. Dead snakes stretched across the concrete like markers [simile-visual]—inlaid mosaic bands [metaphor-visual], dry [tactile] as feathers [simile-tactile-visual], which their tires licked [personification-tactile-gustatory-auditory-visual] at intervals that began to seem clocklike [auditory].
>
> No, the heat faced [personification-visual-kinetic] them—it was ahead. They could see it waving [personification-visual-kinetic] at them, shaken [kinetic-visual] in the air above the white [visual] of the road, always at a certain distance ahead, shimmering [kinetic-visual] finely as a cloth [simile-visual], with running [kinetic-visual] edges of green [visual] and gold [visual-tactile], fire [visual-tactile] and azure [visual].

Closely related to figurative imagery are allusions. An *allusion* is a detailed or general reference to persons, places, events, eras, and objects that exist beyond the framework of the story. Mythology, literature, the Bible, history, and geography are the writer's chief sources of allusions. Frequently, images and allusions form image clusters or patterns that either support the overt and implied meanings of the story or run counter to them, thereby inadvertently destroying the unity of the work. In "No Place for You, My Love," the images evoking heat and sunlight form an image pattern that not only supports but conveys the meaning of the story. The many biblical allusions in "Sonny's Blues" form a pattern that supports and extends the theme.

Symbolism

In the short story or novel, a *symbol* is an object, setting, action, or character that suggests a meaning larger than itself. For example, the porcelain cup in "The Demonstrators" is a symbol of the fragile yet sustaining bond that links the small delta town's black community and white community. The doctor recognizes it as having once belonged to his mother, or his wife's mother, or some other white woman of that generation. But drinking from it after attending the dying black girl, he finds that the cup holds "the whole smell of the house in it." A remnant of the past, a reminder of the subservient role of the blacks, the cup still imparts comfort to those who drink from it—black and white alike.

Symbolism provides the writer with ways of suggesting abstract qualities, attitudes, and ideas through specific, concrete depiction of objects and people in the visible world. By utilizing the symbolic potential of the elements of fiction, the writer can imply his theme without making explicit statements, as most essayists would. Like simile and metaphor, a symbol is suggestive. But unlike these figures of speech, the symbol does not openly compare two objects by describing one in terms of the other; rather, the symbol is a single entity with an objective value separate from the additional meanings its presence suggests. To function as an effective symbol, however, the symbolic entity must either typify or recall (by possession of similar qualities or by association real or imagined) the meaning(s) it suggests.

In "Lost in the Funhouse," the narrator points out that the diving could be used as a literary symbol:

> To go off the high board you had to wait in a line along the poolside and up the ladder. Fellows tickled girls and goosed one another and shouted to the ones at the top to hurry up, or razzed them for bellyfloppers. Once on the springboard some took a great while posing or clowning or deciding on a dive or getting up their nerve; others ran right off. Especially among the younger fellows the idea was to strike the funniest pose or do the craziest stunt as you fell, a thing that got harder to do as you kept on and kept on. But whether you hollered *Geronimo!* or *Sieg heil!*, held your nose or "rode a bicycle," pretended to be shot or did a perfect jacknife or changed your mind halfway down and ended up with nothing, it was over in two seconds, after all that wait.

The symbolism embodied by the diving, while unexplained by the narrator, is, of course, comprehensible to the reader: (1) the clownishness of the divers is a microcosm of the larger carnival atmosphere of the amusement park, (2) the innocent and overt acrobatics on the diving board symbolize the covert sexual acrobatics for which, as Ambrose realizes, "the restaurants and dance halls and test-your-strength machines" are "preparation and intermission," and (3) the variety of attitudes toward the diving symbolizes the variety of responses to life itself. The board-walk, too, functions symbolically. On the boardwalk, where Ambrose walks with his family, frivolity and propriety mingle; under the board-walk, where Ambrose ventures alone, are matchbook covers, cigar butts, Coca-Cola caps, cardboard lollipop sticks, "grainy other things," and a man and woman engaged in a sexual embrace. The boardwalk symbolizes the dichotomy between the exterior, visible world of genteel traditions and the interior, mysterious, dark underside of human sexuality.

Symbols can be classified as either created or conventional. A *created symbol* achieves its suggestiveness from the context in which it appears rather than from its inherent qualities. For example, in "Sonny's Blues," the scene in which the narrator gives the drug addict $5.00 has a created symbolic value. Although any charitable act has a variety of meanings—as does any human action—the full symbolic significance of the narrator's gesture is apparent only within the framework of the story itself: his charity to the man, whom he describes as resembling Sonny, symbolizes his acceptance of Sonny.

In "No Place for You, My Love," the shimmering, intense heat is a *conventional symbol:* heat has long been associated with romance and sexual passion. Readers of fiction have been instilled with the belief that the hot climate of the tropics inflames passions more than does the cold, drier climate of northern countries. But, in this Eudora Welty story, our expectations are reversed. The strong undercurrent of sexuality we sense in the relationship between the two characters never rises to the surface. The heat that seems to nurture this muted romance is, in the end, merely oppressive. As is often the case, the conventional symbol assumes an added significance because of its context. In this instance, additional, specialized meanings come about through the contrast between the con-ventional associations for heat and its disparate associations in the story.

Many conventional symbols can be classified as archetypes, a term that has come into literary criticism chiefly through the work of Carl Jung. Jung postulated the existence of a collective unconscious—a storehouse of racial memories carried about by each individual as part of his psychic inheritance, memories that extend even to pre-human experience. These primordial images, or universal symbols, are termed *archetypes*. In literature, archetypes are embodied in particular images, plot patterns, and character types. Because of the recurrent associations of heat with sexuality in the literature and ritual celebrations of widely separated cultures, heat is not only a conventional symbol but an archetype, and thus reflects something fundamental and shared about human experience.

Close familial relationships are the substance of many archetypal patterns. For example, in the Western world, the relationship between Cain and Abel is the archetypal relationship between brothers. The question Cain evasively and defensively asks after slaying Abel—"Am I my brother's keeper?"—signals that, in the world view represented in the Bible, a key element in the relationship between brothers is responsibility. In the development of Western thought, the meaning of the story has sometimes included the responsibility of each human being for all human beings. Any writer who focuses on the relationship between two brothers establishes automatic, and perhaps unwanted, connections with an awesome, archetypal layer of meaning accessible through the reader's awareness of the Cain-Abel story. A simple narrative can thereby take on some of the attributes of a biblical story—its grandeur, its universality, its concern with morality, and so forth. If he wishes, the writer can provide clues to his intention to establish such associations in our mind. In "Sonny's Blues," Baldwin establishes such a verbal clue when the narrator remembers his mother's warning. "You got to hold on to your brother . . . and don't let him fall, no matter what it looks like is happening to him." That she is telling him to "be his brother's keeper," and that Baldwin is calling upon us to recognize the Cain-Abel analogy seems a reasonable conclusion.

Of the writers in this anthology, John Barth is the one who most deliberately uses archetype and myth. Interpreted as myth, Ambrose's situation in "Lost in the Funhouse" dramatizes the archetype of initiation: the rites of passage that will result in manhood. In the funhouse, Ambrose both loses his identity (symbolized by the name-coin) and regains it. The darkened, convoluted passageways and the various obstacles (the tumbling barrel, the revolving discs, and so on) have their more terrifying counterparts in the wanderings of Odysseus. In these and other respects, "Night-Sea Journey" makes parodic use of the journey into darkness that is so integral to myth and the epic hero.

Because the recognition of symbols provides intellectual enjoyment and because symbols add to the meaning of a story, some readers tend to see symbols in whatever they read. But "symbol-hunting" has its dangers. The most obvious of these is the possibility of the reader's manufacturing symbols where none occur in the narrative or assigning personal and irrelevant meanings to symbols that are clearly present. Frequently, in pursuing the symbolic significance of a work, the reader overlooks the fact that a short story is basically empirical—a narrative woven from the materials of human existence. Without characters and the interest and meaning inherent in their actions, symbolic meanings are only ornament. The literary symbol is significant only as it enlarges the concerns of a specific story. Given these cautionary remarks, however, the reader of this volume should be aware of the importance of symbols in literature. Through their use, the short-story writer, like the novelist, achieves a scope and depth that stretch the boundaries of narrative.

"Style in a writer is a policy about life, not a stunt," Herbert Gold has said in *Fiction of the Fifties*. Because style is the author's personal mark and the signal of his involvement, style reveals a good deal about the underlying attitudes and values in a story, at times over-riding such aspects as characters, plot, and setting and even, one suspects, the author's conscious intentions. For example, an "elegant" and highly symbolic style cannot hide the vacuousness of a story centered around a cliché; neither can a deliberately folksy style conceal the dishonesty of a story that, in some way, falsifies a crucial issue. In the largest sense, as Gold has observed, style *is* the writer's "moral stance."

T O N E

Tone is the most general and elusive aspect in the criticism of fiction, a concept, like style, that embraces the story as a whole. In the most widely accepted meaning of the term, *tone* refers to the author's attitude toward his subject—an attitude that reveals itself not only through explicit statement but implicitly, through all the elements of fiction and all the matters of technique discussed so far—point of view, narrators, characters, plot, form, time, setting, and style. Undeniably, how an author views his subject affects how he depicts that subject. Accordingly, every fictional ingredient, every narrative decision—to use the point of view of the boy's mother in "The Unspoiled Reaction," to violate the perspective of the restricted narrator in "The Christian Roommates," to make the narrator of "Sonny's Blues" a high-school mathematics teacher, to obscure identities in "The Indian Uprising," to include discussions of conventional fictional practices in "Lost in the Funhouse"—and *all* similar choices relate to tone.

Our awareness of tone is largely responsible for creating and sustaining our awareness of the implied author. For, as Wayne C. Booth points out in *The Rhetoric of Fiction,* we determine the implied author from explicit and implicit values in the work itself (the implied author *is* the "core of norms and choices" in a narrative), and in turn see him as the guiding spirit within the narrative—giving us our notion of how to interpret the work. Since serious fiction involves values and judgments, becoming aware of tone is instrumental in helping the reader discover where he stands in the world of values represented in the work—that is, in Booth's phrase, "where the author *wants* him to stand."

Irony

A recurrent tone in modern fiction is the ironic. *Irony* always traffics in disparity, whether it is *verbal irony* (a statement that says one thing but means something else), *irony of situation* (a circumstance in which the outcome is unexpected or inappropriate), or *cosmic irony* (a sense that despite the best intentions of man, fate prevents his success). Linked to point of view and to the manipulation of plot, *dramatic irony* occurs only when the reader possesses knowledge that the characters do not have—information that lets him predict the outcome or resolution. Dramatic irony can be easily achieved in stories that use the privileged narrator, whose broad perspective permits him to give the reader more information than the characters possess. The reader is then in a better position than the characters to predict the conclusion. In stories like "The Unspoiled Reaction," however, dramatic irony is noticeably absent. The inside perspective limits the reader to the consciousness of the boy's mother. Accordingly, the reader's ignorance of the puppeteers prevents him from predicting what will happen, thereby negating the possibility of dramatic irony.

Irony of tone is more pervasive than the accumulated effects of the various forms of irony. In the largest sense, *irony of tone* means that the author acknowledges that existence is a mass of contradictions, that there is no absolute truth, and that to commit oneself to a single belief is an untenable simplification. To communicate his vision, such a writer uses the doubleness of irony. Recognizing that things are not what they seem and that expectations are forever being stymied ("The Cicerone" and "The Unspoiled Reaction"), that the man who tries to act beneficently either

47

fails or hurts the person or cause he tries to serve ("A Gift from the City" and "Black Is My Favorite Color"), that opposites are not really opposite ("Everything That Rises Must Converge"), the author adopts an attitude and rhetoric that allow him to display these incongruities. A reader who fails to recognize when an author is being ironic takes everything literally instead of perceiving the doubleness of the vision. The reader should, therefore, be alert to the devices that signal the presence of irony: verbal techniques such as understatement, overstatement, and paradox; the use of situations that are paradoxical or involve the operation of cosmic irony; and discrepancies between the events of the story and the manner in which they are related.

Inevitably, the presence of irony in fiction establishes a tension within the work. In literature, as in life, tension is a force resulting from the interplay of contrary stresses. The Greek philosopher Heraclitus observed, "As with the bow and the lyre, so with the world: it is the tension of opposing forces that makes the structure one." Thus tension, in literature, is a desirable, unifying, esthetically satisfying quality accruing from any number of opposing forces: characters who oppose each other, the conflict basic to plot, the clash between psychological time and chronological time, and the opposition basic to irony.

If the writer uses understatement, overstatement, or paradox, a tension is set up between what is said and what is meant. Irony of situation and cosmic irony create a tension derived from what should happen and what does happen. Dramatic irony establishes a tension between the reader's knowledge and that of the characters—between his awareness of the outcome and the limited, often fragmentary action he perceives as unfolding in front of him.

At its worst, an author can allow "an all-pervasive 'un-earned' irony to substitute for an honest discrimination among his materials," Booth notes. At its best, irony represents a writer's involvement with his subject, dramatizing not only the disparities of existence but the consequences of disparity, as evidenced by Julian's final recognition in "Everything That Rises Must Converge."

Sympathy and Esthetic Distance

A strong emotive appeal of fiction derives from the reader's sympathetic involvement with the characters. In general, *sympathy* depends upon identification. We sympathize with a character when we understand why he behaves as he does and when, by displaying traits that resemble our own or those of acquaintances, he stirs our sense of what it is to be human. Because the writer is able to manipulate our sympathies to accord with his own attitudes and feelings about the characters, sympathy is linked with tone. For by recognizing those characters with whom the writer *wants* us to sympathize, we gain insight into the author's implicit evaluation of his subject.

Sympathy is closely related to point of view and to open and closed consciousnesses. Since we tend to sympathize with the characters whom we know best, the author controls our sympathies by allowing us to see into the minds of certain characters and by excluding us from the consciousnesses of others. For example, by revealing "The Demonstrators" through the consciousness of Dr. Strickland, Eudora Welty makes sure that we align ourselves with him. Had she opened or revealed the consciousnesses of Dr. Strickland's wife, who requested their separation, or of his patients, or of the black community, we would not only be separated from the doctor but forced to view him in a less favorable light. Certainly, any other perspective or any combination of perspectives would dramatize his ineffectuality. Because the entire story comes to us through Dr. Strickland's perceptions, we admire his lonely battle and hope for his good fortune—a hope partly realized by his recognition of the possibility "that there was still allowed to everybody on earth a self—savage, death-defying, private." Booth's discussion of John Marcher in Henry James's story "The Beast in the Jungle" is enlightening: "By seeing the whole thing through the isolated sufferer's vision we are forced to feel it through his heart. And it is our sense of his isolation, of vulnerability in a world where no one can set him straight, that contributes most to this sympathy." The many characters in this collection who would be unsympathetic if we did not see everything from their vantage point (the American couple in "The Cicerone," Eli Peck, Nat Lime, and others) suggest the extensive use of the inside perspective in modern fiction. They also indicate the thematic necessity for closed or unrevealed consciousnesses.

Closely allied to sympathy is the concept of *esthetic distance:* the degree to which the writer succeeds in objectifying an experience or emotion in his story, and the degree to which the reader is separated from the narrative. To be successful, the writer must use the technical devices that allow him to turn experience into "achieved content." For example, James Baldwin tells a great deal about his life in such essays as "The Discovery of What It Means To Be an American," "Fifth Avenue, Uptown," and "Nobody Knows My Name." From his essays we learn that he faced many of the problems, conflicts, and choices experienced by the narrator in "This

Morning, This Evening, So Soon"—the problems of being an artist, black, and American; the choices of living in Paris and returning to America. From the standpoint of the story, a key question is whether Baldwin, as a writer of fiction, was able to give his own experiences and emotions an objective, esthetic form. If there is too little esthetic distance between the author and his story, the effect of the story as an art form is often ruined— the author's subjectivity muddies the tone and distorts the meaning.

The second aspect of esthetic distance (sometimes identified separately as psychic distance) concerns the separation between the reader and the narrative and the degree of involvement that a writer wishes to elicit from the reader. These considerations include the problem of "over-distancing" and "under-distancing"—highly personal relationships that vary among readers according to their experiences, attitudes, and sensitivity to the nature of narrative art. *Over-distancing* occurs when the reader cannot identify with the story. If the work seems improbable, trivial, beyond his intellectual grasp, or totally divergent from his own views, he will stand at too great a distance from it. The story will leave him cold; he will see nothing in it for him. Quite possibly, "City Life" could have this effect on some readers who might find the characters too neurotic, the action too bizarre, and Ramona's reactions too "unreal" to allow identification.

Under-distancing occurs when the reader becomes too emotionally involved in the work—too subjectively enmeshed in the action and characters to respond esthetically. He does not see the narrative as a work of art. In all probability, an older woman reading "Accomplished Desires" may sympathize so completely with Barbara that (like Barbara) she sees Dorie as victor rather than as victim and fails to realize (until it is too late) the woefully similar situations of both women.

Over-distancing and under-distancing relate to tone: if the reader is too removed from the work, he may miss underlying attitudes and fail to comprehend the significance the story or novel might have, and if esthetic distance is too slight, he may lose himself in the work for his own reasons.

Point of view affects both kinds of esthetic distance. Some points of view make it relatively easy to objectify experiences and emotions; in particular, the effaced narrator permits great objectivity. Similarly, the privileged narrator allows a detachment that is harder to achieve in stories told from the inside points of view unless the author dramatizes the consciousnesses of characters bizarrely different from himself and from the norms of the story. Such a work often becomes ironic, as in "Black Is My Favorite Color" and "Everything That Rises Must Converge." Because inside points of view tend to shorten the distance between the reader and the story, this perspective affects psychic distance by forcing the reader and the story together, especially if the subject matter lends itself to this kind of emotional proximity.

The Absence of Laughter

In *The Lonely Voice: A Study of the Short Story,* Frank O'Connor contends that the short story reveals "an intense awareness of human loneliness," that while the novel adheres "to the classical concept of civilized society, of man as an animal who lives in a community, . . . the short story remains by its very nature remote from the community—romantic, individualistic, and intransigent."

Although the stories in this collection occur within a generalized social context, they convey little sense of community—that is, of a group of individuals related to each other by common interests, working for a common good. For example, even though Jim and Liz in "A Gift from the City" are affected by New York City—the crisis is a peculiarly urban one—we see them as an insular family unit, as Midwesterners not yet assimilated into the city and its ways. They take walks in the city, but they talk to no one; in fact, Jim resents Liz looking at strangers. No children play with their child in the city park. Their only conversations are with the babysitter and an apparently vacuous, if not equally removed, couple—outlanders like themselves. At the conclusion, no longer troubled by the intrusive Negro—who is nonetheless an ambiguous representative of the community —they are engulfed by their insularity and their "happiness."

In "The Magic Barrel," another story that takes place in New York City, there is a similar absence of community. Although Leo Finkle, also an "outlander," is a rabbinical student, he does not appear in the company of scholars and fellow students. Instead, he is either in the streets or subways of the city or in his furnished room, aware, for the first time, of being "unloved and loveless." His isolation from the community is made clear not only in his seeking a marriage broker but, at the conclusion, when he meets Stella at a designated street corner.

If the limits of practical criticism can be transcended and different endings projected for these stories—endings appropriate to a "community-oriented" literature—Liz and Jim might come to terms with New York City rather than draw back from it, content that the menace had mysteriously retreated from them. In "The Magic Barrel," another ending might place Stella and Leo among friends and family, or in a community-centered building such as a synagogue or university, rather than depict them against the loneliness and anonymity of a street corner.

In stories that do convey a sense of community, the protagonist frequently stands at odds to it rather than at one within it. In "Eli, the Fanatic," for example, Eli Peck, a lawyer, begins as the townspeople's spokesman: "'Tell this Tzuref where we stand, Eli. This is a modern community, Eli, we have our families, we pay taxes. . . .'" As the story progresses, however, Eli identifies more with Tzuref, the outsider, than with "the Jewish community of Woodenton." By the story's end, Eli has estranged himself so totally from his fellow suburbanites that he has become the stranger to his chosen community, the outsider who must be subdued and resocialized.

In "Sonny's Blues," the narrator depicts his community, the "vivid, killing streets" of Harlem:

> These streets hadn't changed. . . . Houses exactly like the houses of our past yet dominated the landscape, boys exactly like the boys we once had been found themselves smothering in these houses, came down into the streets for light and air and found themselves encircled by disaster. Some escaped the trap, most didn't.

Although the narrator ostensibly has escaped the trap, in truth, his salvation as a man rests on his identifying with his past, his brother, and, by extension, with his community.

In part, the brevity of the short story accounts for the writer's neglect of community. Describing the short-story writer, Frank O'Connor observes, "Because his frame of reference can never be the totality of a human life, he must be forever selecting the point at which he can approach it, and each selection he makes contains the possibility of a new form as well as the possibility of a complete fiasco." The use of inside points of view also contributes to the absence of community, to the "lonely voice" of the short story. The inside perspective underscores the selectivity of the writer's vision by remaining inside the consciousness of a single character and, often, within a single physical space.

In its own way, the absence of community in the short story is partly responsible for another characteristic of the stories in this collection—the absence of laughter. If laughter needs an echo, the absence of community precludes the sounding board that a representation of society provides. This point is well illustrated by a story that is not included here: William

Faulkner's "Spotted Horses." For it is the sense of community that heightens the humorous action of that comic yarn. Through his narrator, Faulkner links past with present, supplying a partial history of Flem Snopes (in this instance, Flem's first appearance as Jody Varner's clerk):

> One morning about ten years ago the boys was just getting settled down on Varner's porch for a little talk and tobacco, when here come Flem out from behind the counter, with his coat off and his hair all parted, like he might have been clerking for Varner for ten years already. Folks all knowed him; it was a big family of them about five miles down the bottom. That year, at least.

Further, the characters in the story *act* as members of a community. They are knowledgeable about each other's present activities and concerned for each other's welfare, even for someone as doltish as Henry Armstid. In the sense that the community as a whole is duped by Flem, the jokes—the "deals" that he pulls—are always at the expense of the community at large. As a group, the "boys" on Varner's porch can laugh at their own collective naiveté and stupidity in being, forever, the hapless victims of Flem's schemes. The comic action is played against this recognition and thereby heightened. A recognizable social milieu affords an enclosure for an isolated action that gives the action something to bounce against. By being greater than the characters and events of the story, such a frame of reference offers a necessary sense of resonance.

This does not mean that the stories in this collection are entirely without comedy. As noted in the discussion of characters, there are comic characters, such as Mr. and Mrs. Shortley in "The Displaced Person." Further, there are comic incidents, as in the interplay between Mr. and Mrs. Shortley (in particular, the account of Chauncy Shortley's courting). And there is also much verbal comedy, as in Mrs. Shortley's distorted concept of Europeans. But there is little overt laughter in these stories, which is due not only to the relative absence of physical humor of the kind present in "Spotted Horses" but also to the writers' apparent disinclination to provoke overt laughter.

The absence of laughter or laughter-producing situations in these stories is not surprising, for laughter implies superiority: we laugh *at* something—at incongruity, distortion, or repetition. In the main, however, not only do we find ourselves sympathetic to most of the characters in these stories but we also sense that the authors themselves view their characters sympathetically, having created them out of respect and concern. For it is through his fictional personages that the author represents the profundity and baffling complexity of modern experience. Even when there are moments of comedy, as in "The Displaced Person," there is always the larger vein of concern—of awareness of the moral ambiguities of contemporary society, or of impending disaster, rendering the comedy subordinate to the tragic implications of the cumulative action.

The content of contemporary experience, too, militates against laughter. The fragmentary nature of existence means that readers do not bring to fiction a shared body of experiences and values that would provide an implicit sounding board. Also, the post-Hiroshima world—the world reflected and refracted in these stories—is not a pervasively joyous place. Buchenwald, Hiroshima, the Berlin Wall, Dallas-Memphis-Los Angeles, Watergate, stand as natural symbols of the post-World War II world. What they suggest is horrifying and, because they share a fundamental irrationality, absurd.

Yet the reader must not confuse the absence of laughter in these stories with nihilism. Even the bleakest story, "The Indian Uprising," posits a reasonably happy ending; although a captive of the Comanches, the narrator is being held by their Clemency Committee. In most of the stories, there is a sense that on the individual and familial level, life will go on. These stories do not represent a death of the human spirit but a questioning of it—a dramatization of where man has been. Although the inexperienced reader may initially seize upon despair as their dominant tone, he will discover that the tones are rich and complex, signifying in a variety of ways not negation but an affirmation of life.

Being able to see beyond subject matter to attitude involves establishing the proper esthetic distance—one that permits enough identification so that the stories have a meaning, yet one that prevents an emotional involvement so subjective that the stories cannot be viewed as art but only as accounts of catastrophe, of breakdowns on a private and public scale, comparable to those reported daily in newspapers and newcasts. That is, the reader must understand that these stories are a representation of life—verbal structures that involve a heightening and a patterning, that permit esthetic pleasure and offer an interpretation of the action they present. As should be evident by now, the serious author is conveying attitudes about life through narrative. This is the province of tone. The most inclusive element of fiction—the one that unifies a work and communicates impressions and attitudes that we are asked to absorb—tone brings the reader closest to grasping the story as a whole.

II THE PROCESS OF FICTION AS FICTION

In the *Poetics,* Aristotle describes tragedy as being "an imitation, not of men as such, but of action and life, of happiness and misery"; and, for centuries, imitation, or mimesis, has been as basic to the novel and short story as it has been to drama. Indeed, the contention that a novelist should *show* events or characters in action rather than *tell* us about them stems from a belief in art as mimesis. Mimetic art attempts to hide the hand of the artist behind his creation and, at the same time, to make the creation disappear as the "life" it represents takes over in our consciousnesses. The conventions of traditional fiction, as represented by the well-made story or novel, aid the writer in achieving this goal: by minimizing the fiction as literary construct they help the writer convince us that we are experiencing "reality."

But some modern writers of fiction want us not only to see their hands at work but to continuously acknowledge their creations as literary fabrications. One way in which they prompt this acknowledgment is by having their works call attention to the fiction-making process itself—either by making the protagonist a very self-conscious writer or by using the elements and process of fiction as subject matter. In *Bech: A Book,* John Updike does both: his hero is a writer who comments frequently on the episodes in which he appears. "I wonder if it *is* me, enough me, purely me," the fictional Bech complains to Updike:

> My childhood seems out of Alex Portnoy and my ancestral past out of I. B. Singer. I get a whiff of Malamud in your city breezes, and am I paranoid to feel my "block" an ignoble version of the more or less noble renunciations of H. Roth, D. Fuchs, and J. Salinger? Withal, something Waspish, theological, scared, and insulatingly ironical that derives, my wild surmise is, from you.

Characters in conventional fiction are seldom writers and almost never call attention to themselves as invented personages; indeed, the author's intention ordinarily is to convince us of the reality of his characters—not to remind us that he created them. By reversing these conventional principles in *Bech: A Book,* Updike undercuts its fiction as mimesis. Among the experimental stories in this collection, "Lost in the Funhouse" by John Barth and "How I Contemplated . . ." by Joyce Carol Oates contain similar assaults on illusion.

To appreciate stories and novels that use the process of fiction as fiction, a reader must know enough about conventional fiction to perceive the experimentalist's elaborate use of it as subject matter. Almost all the techniques of conventional fiction appear—however hidden and distorted—in the fiction of the experimentalists. Thus, in this section the elements of the well-made story will be discussed again—but, this time, only as they relate to experimental writing; as before, examples will be drawn from the stories in this collection. Nothing in the discussion is meant to suggest that experimental stories are *better than* or *inferior to* stories that can be classified as "well-made." Experimental stories are only *different from* fiction that places more emphasis on mimesis—and not always radically different, as a full reading of this introduction should indicate.

W O R D S   A S   T H E   B A S E   M E T A L   O F   F I C T I O N

Never more true.

When asked about the subject of his painting, the contemporary nonrepresentational artist often explains that painting itself is the subject of his painting. In the same way, the experimental writer often maintains that words are the subject of his stories, novels, or plays. In many experimental plays—such as Harold Pinter's *Old Times,* for example—the action of the drama lies only in words; the play itself is not an imitation of action as in conventional drama. Similarly, in stories like "The Indian Uprising," words are what the story is about; the surface of the prose demands attention in the same way that the surface of an abstract painting demands scrutiny—and appreciation. In the manner of nonrepresentational painters, who are free to make their statements entirely by the arrangement of paint on canvas, Donald Barthelme and other experimental writers use words as self-contained entities that, when arranged in a certain order, create a new form that is its own meaning. Though his words are still symbolic constructs, the experimentalist minimizes their symbolic value and, most typically, uses them to appeal to the reader's imagination rather than to summon up physical realities.

Thus, the words of experimental fiction call attention to themselves; we are forced to *see* them. And when we do we often see that familiar words have been used in unfamiliar ways. Aware that in many exchanges words mean little or nothing ("Let me make one thing perfectly clear," "I enjoyed meeting you," "That was a delicious dinner"), the experimentalists refresh the language by making us pay attention to words we might otherwise dismiss. For instance, many of their words are placed in awkward and disruptive contexts that undercut their usual symbolic meanings, as in this excerpt from "The Indian Uprising":

"The only form of discourse of which I approve," Miss R. said in her dry, tense voice, "is the litany. I believe our masters and teachers as well as plain citizens should confine themselves to what can safely be said. Thus when I hear the words *pewter, snake, toad, Fad #6 sherry, serviette, fenestration, crown, blue* coming from the mouth of some public official, or some raw youth, I am not disappointed. Vertical organization is also possible," Miss R. said, "as in

> pewter
> snake
> tea
> Fad #6 sherry
> serviette
> fenestration
> crown
> blue.

I run to liquids and colors," she said, "but you, you may run to something else, my virgin, my darling, my thistle, my poppet, my own."

Because of its emphasis on "reading the lines themselves," experimental fiction has been described as a return to a more verbal kind of writing. John Barth expresses this concept in *Chimera* when the writer-hero of "Dunyazadiad" acknowledges: "It's in words that the magic is—Abracadabra, Open Sesame, and the rest—but the magic words in one story aren't magical in the next. . . ."

POINT OF VIEW

Much havoc here.

Consistency of point of view is basic to fiction in which mimesis is accorded a high value. Violations of the established point of view call attention to themselves and therefore disrupt the illusion that we are experiencing reality. Indeed, in realistic fiction we admire an author's ability to conceal himself in his narrator and the narrator's "ability" to conceal himself in the character (by adopting the character's perspective, idiom, and so on). These disappearances aid our suspension of disbelief by allowing us to overlook the story as fabrication. Therefore, if a writer wants us to be consciously aware of his fiction as a made object, he is likely to deny the convention and fashion a narrator who is both noticeable and inconsistent. In portions of "Lost in the Funhouse," John Barth appears to have created a privileged narrator:

> Count a generation as thirty years: in approximately the year when Lord Baltimore was granted charter to the province of Maryland by Charles I, five hundred twelve women—English, Welsh, Bavarian, Swiss—of every class and character, received into themselves the penises the intromittent organs of five hundred men, ditto, in every circumstance and posture, to conceive the five hundred twelve ancestors of the two hundred fifty-six ancestors of the et cetera et cetera et cetera et cetera et cetera et cetera et cetera et cetera of the author, of the narrator, of this story, *Lost in the Funhouse.*

Eventually, however, the clues of the passage become clearer, and we realize that Ambrose is a dramatized narrator telling his own story in the third person and, in the process, using and discussing the conventions of traditional fiction—including that of the privileged narrator.

The narrator of Barthelme's "The Indian Uprising" is also a dramatized narrator but, unlike Ambrose, discloses only the vaguest autobiographical information. Events come to us from the narrator's perspective, but the inadequacy of the personal information we have about him makes that perspective ambiguous. The characters we meet in the story are friends, or at least acquaintances, of the narrator, but their specific relationship to him is often unclear. In the collection's essay on the story, the narrator is described as being "little more than the voice that records actions, statements, and allusions. More completely here than in other fiction, the narrator is words." The same can be said of the long-distance swimmer-narrator of "Night-Sea Journey"—another dramatized narrator, another inside perspective. But whose? In an author's note, Barth tells us, tongue in cheek, that the narrator is not

> as many reviewers took him to be, a fish. If he were, their complaint that his eschatological and other speculations are trite would be entirely justified; given his actual nature, they are merely correct, and perhaps illumine certain speculations of Lord Raglan, Carl Jung, and Joseph Campbell.

If not a fish, then who or what is this narrator who describes himself as "tale bearer of a generation"? Who belongs to this voice that speculates, complains, aggrandizes his condition, and then downgrades it? The identity of the improbable, misanthropic narrator lies in the story for the reader to discover. And when he does, he will also find that the author has been there all along—inside his creation, so to speak. Narrators in experimental fiction, such as Barth's, are diverse, sometimes elusive, sometimes outrageous, and often inconsistent. Further, even when he adopts an established point of view, like that of the dramatized narrator, the experimentalist typically ignores its conventional strengths: the enhancement of mimesis ("Lost in the Funhouse" and "How I Contemplated . . ." are antimimetic) and the engagement of the reader's sympathy for the narrator (the narrator of "The Indian Uprising" is, at best, viewed neutrally).

CHARACTERS

Flat, round, major, minor, static, dynamic, sympathetic, unsympathetic, all too human, inhuman, half-human.

Not concerned with fiction as an imitation of life, the experimentalist is under no pressure to create characters that are recognizable human types —or even human in the sense of having human form. One way of demonstrating the reality of fiction is through the reader's identification with the characters—at least with the protagonist who is usually, in the terminology used previously, round. When we identify with a character, we are considering the fictional personage enough like ourselves to see ourselves mirrored, however obliquely, in him. The character is "real" because we are real. The dramatized narrator of "How I Contemplated . . ." becomes a round character as the reader puts the bits and pieces of her personal history together. And when this happens, the relationship between the reader and the character changes: the reader no longer sees the character as object but views her as subject in much the same manner as he views himself. In this instance, the reader probably experiences pity for the girl as he recognizes her inability to reconcile her experiences, as a woman, with Simon and her customary behavior, as a daughter, with her parents. "How I Contemplated . . ." is different, however, from much experimental fiction in that its plot and characters, when reconstructed sequentially, run a course between journalism (newspaper account of runaway teenager from wealthy suburb) and soap opera (also the tale of a runaway but with more emphasis on drugs, sex, and the girl's ventures into shoplifting). The form of the story is new, but its substance comes straight out of melodrama.

Freedom from verisimilitude opens up the possibility of inventing characters no sane reader would identify with or consider "real": hence, the characters in "Night-Sea Journey" and "The Indian Uprising." Some experimental characters, however, edge closer to being the kind of flesh-and-blood personages found in conventional fiction. At least Elsa, Ramona, and Charles ("City Life") have names; Ramona has parents who come from Montana to visit her in New York City; Ramona is jealous of Elsa, and so forth. But these Barthelme figures are still as flat as paper dolls, and their involvements in fashionable movements and relationships never really engage the reader's sympathies. Yet the characters, while overly affected, are nonetheless curiously affecting. Their meaning, we sense, lies not in how well they conform to our images of ourselves or other people we know but in how well they and their stereotypical relationships comment on the patterns of many contemporary lives.

Offering advice to aspiring writers, Somerset Maugham observed that if the writer "takes care" of his characters, the rest of the story or novel will "take care" of itself. In this spirit, writers of conventional fiction usually attempt from the outset to make the protagonist "real." No such goal burdens the writers of experimental fiction. However, their relative liberty has a concomitant restriction: by giving up sympathetic, round characters with whom the reader can identify, the experimentalists relinquish pathos, a dependable ingredient for a successful story. Much of learning what experimental fiction is about concerns discovering what the author has chosen as substitutes for such proven ingredients.

PLOT

Nonexistent.

"Night-Sea Journey" has no plot; neither does "Lost in the Funhouse," "How I Contemplated . . . ," "The Indian Uprising," or "City Life." Although these stories depict events that share an ideational relationship, none of them attempts to construct a tightly woven narrative that develops its plot through the five customary stages: exposition, rising action, turning point, falling action, and resolution. "Night-Sea Journey," as the title implies, takes the form of a journey, but the journey is less important in this story than the philosophizing. The story is really an extended interior monologue: its substance is the questions the dramatized narrator asks and the quirky, humorous "personality" that unfolds. In "Lost in the Funhouse," as noted earlier, the conventions of traditional plotting though often mentioned are severely absent from the structure of the story itself.

In a similar vein, "How I Contemplated . . ." is presented as a series of notes outlined by the protagonist-narrator for an essay she is to write for an English class. However, though ostensibly well ordered, her thoughts are random—past and present are mixed within one paragraph:

> The girl lies sleepless, wondering. Why here, why not there? Why Bloomfield Hills and not jail? Why jail and not her pink room? Why downtown Detroit and not Sioux Drive? What is the difference? Is Simon all the difference? The girl's head is a parade of wonders. She is nearly sixteen, her breath is marvelous with wonders, not long ago she was coloring with crayons and now she is smearing the landscape with paints that won't come off and won't come off her fingers either. She says to the matron *I am not talking about anything,* not because everyone has warned her not to talk but because, because she will not talk; because she won't say anything about Simon, who is her secret. And she says to the matron, *I won't go home,* up until that night in the lavatory when everything was changed. . . . "No, I won't go home I want to stay here," she says, listening to her own words with amazement.

Casting the story in the form of an annotated outline precludes the use of foreshadowing or suspense. It also rules out the use of coincidence and chance as formalistic narrative stratagems.

In "City Life," the action becomes a paradigm of modern life in a city of apartments furnished with "paper things from a Japanese store"—and with equally impermanent relationships. Two girls, roommates, move to the city and attend law school:

> —You are the only two girls ever to be admitted to our Law School, the Dean observed. Mostly, we have men. A few foreigners. Now I am going to tell you three things to keep an eye on: 1) Don't try to go too far too fast. 2) Wear plain clothes. And 3) Keep your notes clean. And if I hear the words "Yoo hoo" echoing across the quadrangle, you will be sent down instantly. We don't use those words in this school.
>
> —I like what I already know, Ramona said under her breath.
>
> Savoring their matriculation, the two girls wandered out to sample the joys of Pascin Street. They were closer together at this time than they had ever been. Of course, they didn't want to get too close together. They were afraid to get too close together.
>
> Elsa met Jacques. He was deeply involved in the struggle.

Elsa and Jacques have an affair; Elsa becomes pregnant and Elsa and Jacques marry; Ramona begins seeing several men, becomes pregnant, and has an illegitimate child; she brings the child with her to law school and becomes the center of controversy, and so on. The inability to assign a father to Ramona's child is humorous proof of the ambiguity of cause and effect relationships in this story. Yet the sketchily presented action does contain the story's meaning: that "cities are erotic, in a depressing way"—Moonbelly earns a gold record for his best-selling song, "Cities Are Centers of Copulation." The plot is like a schematic for a carefully and intricately engineered stereophonic set: the circuitry works, but the city is a system that "cannot withstand close scrutiny."

By not involving us in action that purports to be a representation of life, by not arousing our curiosity about what happens next or about the fate of the characters, by not appealing to our sense of mystification, the experimental writer relinquishes elements of conventional fiction that appeal to most readers. For mystery, the experimentalist substitutes predictability; for surprise, inevitability; for action, metaphysical speculation; for idiosyncratic happenings, stereotypical behavior; for causality, a series of events (or, quite simply, outrageous, unexplained behavior); and in place of linear development he offers a mosaic.

SETTING

*Varied: A suburban department store. A house of correction. A fun-
house. A city besieged by Comanches. A metropolis. A law school. An
interior sea.*

Since the characters in experimental fiction are not obliged to be believable, the settings in which they are placed need not enhance their
credibility. And most often they do not. "Lost in the Funhouse," however,
does make full use of its setting on both literal and metaphysical levels. In
"How I Contemplated . . . ," setting is also important to the story's literal meaning; yet in the Detroit described by the narrator the

> temperature is always 32°. Fast-falling temperatures. Slow-rising tempera-
> tures. Wind from the north-northeast four to forty miles an hour, small-
> craft warnings, partly cloudy today and Wednesday changing to partly
> sunny through Thursday . . . small warnings of frost, soot warnings,
> traffic warnings, hazardous lake conditions for small craft and swimmers,
> restless Negro gangs, restless cloud formations, restless temperatures ach-
> ing to fall out the very bottom of the thermometer or shoot up over the
> top and boil everything over in red mercury.

> Detroit's temperature is 32°. Fast-falling temperatures. Slow-rising tem-
> peratures. Wind from the north-northeast four to forty miles an
> hour. . . .

A similar description is given of Bloomfield Hills, the suburban community in which the narrator lives. But no matter how carefully the realistic
details are compiled, no matter how many names and how much chrome
and glass are mentioned, there is nonetheless something unbalanced in
the description: as with Detroit, the image of Bloomfield Hills is stretched
and twisted by the protagonist's imagination.

The metropolis of "City Life" is not intended to convince through the
representation of copious, physical detail. Barthelme suggests; the reader
supplies the recognition. The author is after *city-ness,* not a realistic depiction of one particular city; the same purpose is served by the invented
city in "The Indian Uprising." In Barth's "Night-Sea Journey," the setting
is a mysterious, strangely dark, interior sea in whose troubled waters swim-

mers are beset by whirlpool, poisoned cataract, and sea convulsion. Only toward the end does the sea sweeten and calm, and the protagonist hear a "song, or summons from the near upstream."

In experimental writing, as in all fiction, the setting should match the characters and action: it is a good match if the setting provides an appropriate milieu; the match is a better one if the setting initiates some of the action. There exists no official map for the cities of Barthelme's fiction; nor is there a Coast Guard chart for Barth's internal sea. But then, in both instances, no guide is needed.

STYLE

Diverse. Lyrical, flat, Latinate, evocative, clichéd, pedantic, self-conscious, serious, humorous, resonant, outrageous, parodic, banal, arcane, convoluted, simplistic, rich in specification, vague, cluttered, lean, mythic, all of the above, none of the above.

In "Lost in the Funhouse," John Barth affects a style that alternates between a mock seriousness full of specific, realistic detail and a fragile and evocative lyricism. But "Night-Sea Journey," his other story in this collection, often reads like a philosophical discourse:

> Swimming itself I find at best not actively unpleasant, more often tiresome, not infrequently a torment. Arguments from function and design don't impress me; granted that we can and do swim, that in a manner of speaking our long tails and streamlined heads are "meant for" swimming; it by no means follows—for me, at least—that we *should* swim, or otherwise endeavor to "fulfill our destiny." Which is to say, Someone Else's destiny, since ours, so far as I can see, is merely to perish, one way or another, soon or late. The heartless zeal of our (departed) leaders, like the blind ambition and good cheer of my own youth, appalls me now; for the death of my comrades I am inconsolable. If the night-sea journey has justification, it is not for us swimmers ever to discover it.

In "How I Contemplated . . . ," Joyce Carol Oates adopts the vocabulary of her heroine; the style is matter-of-fact; the word choice is simple; sentences are left incomplete; the narrator refers to herself in both the first and third persons. Here, as in all fiction, style is important to an understanding of meaning, for in the banality of the protagonist's language—in its fragmentation, its rationalizing, and its abrupt shifts in time and place—as well as in the infrequent poetic outcries, is revealed the divided self of the narrator.

Though the language Barthelme employs in "The Indian Uprising" is usually specific, the words seem to relate to one another only tangentially:

"What is the situation?" I asked.
"The situation is liquid," he said. "We hold the south quarter and they hold the north quarter. The rest is silence."

This story and the collection's other experimental fiction also abound in unexplained brand names, jargon from commerce and politics, intellectual commonplaces, and the itemization of ordinary household objects, as illustrated by the following excerpts from "The Indian Uprising," "Lost in the Funhouse," and "How I Contemplated . . .":

a tin frying pan; two-litre bottles of red wine; three-quarter-litre bottles of Black & White; aquavit; cognac; vodka; gin; Fad #6 sherry; a hollow-core door in birch veneer on black wrought-iron legs; a blanket, red-orange with faint blue stripes; a red pillow and a blue pillow

a black 1936 Lasalle sedan; Lucky Strikes; Baby Ruths; an El Producto cigar box; candied apples-on-a-stick; syrup-coated popcorn; Noxzema

Kleenex; hairpins; safety pins; a broken pencil; a blue ballpoint pen; "a purse-size compact of Cover Girl Make-Up, Ivory Rose . . . Her lipstick is Broken Heart"

When the context allows, experimental fiction offers much specification but no explication; thus, this passage from "City Life":

Elsa and Ramona watched the Motorola television set in their pajamas.
—What else is on? Elsa asked.
Ramona looked in the newspaper.
—On 7 there's "Johnny Allegro" with George Raft and Nina Foch. On 9 "Johnny Angel" with George Raft and Claire Trevor. On 11 there's "Johnny Apollo" with Tyrone Power and Dorothy Lamour. On 13 is "Johnny Concho" with Frank Sinatra and Phyllis Kirk. On 2 is "Johnny Dark" with Tony Curtis and Piper Laurie. On 4 is "Johnny Eager" with Robert Taylor and Lana Turner. On 5 is "Johnny O'Clock" with Dick

Powell and Evelyn Keyes. On 31 is "Johnny Trouble" with Stuart Whitman and Ethel Barrymore.
—What's this one we're watching?
—What time is it?
—Eleven-thirty-five.
—"Johnny Guitar" with Joan Crawford and Sterling Hayden.

Most readers will not need an explanation of the particular contemporary situation depicted in Barthelme's passage: the plethora of choice that, as evidenced by indistinguishable television listings, reveals itself as no choice at all.

There are, however, dangers in itemizing without explanation, for the banality may overwhelm and lead us nowhere. In the novella *Snow White,* Barthelme defends the manufacturing of plastic buffalo humps:

They are "trash," and what in fact could be more useless or trashlike? It's that we want to be on the leading edge of this trash phenomenon, the everted sphere of the future, and that's why we pay particular attention, too, to those aspects of language that may seem as a model of the trash phenomenon.

Experimental writers like Barthelme respond to the unprecedented pervasiveness of the mass culture by syphoning off its energies and gestures; in doing so, they hope to make the popular culture reveal something about itself. This, however, is a very difficult task. Popular culture is a hard act for the fiction writer to follow, particularly when both reader and author are engulfed in it: familiarity tends to breed imperceptiveness; nearness blinds. And moreover, the products of the popular culture are often easier to swallow than the bittersweet fruits of fiction.

Also characteristic of much experimental fiction are frequent and cataclysmic shifts in mood. In "How I Contemplated . . . ," the narrator, sitting in her pink room and listening to the maid vacuum in the adjacent bedroom, remembers Simon, her lover:

Each day he needs a certain amount of money. He devours it. It wasn't love he uncoiled in me with his hollowed-out eyes and his courteous smile, that remnant of a prosperous past, but a dark terror that needed to press itself flat against him, or against another man . . . but he was the first, he came over to me and took my arm, a claim. We struggled on the stairs and I said, *Let me loose, you're hurting my neck, my face,* it was such a surprise that my skin hurt where he rubbed it, and afterward we

66

lay face to face and he breathed everything into me. In the end he turned me in.

In "The Indian Uprising," a description of the torture of a captured Comanche is followed by a declaration of love and drunkenness. The constructing of a table takes place at the same time as the filming of a pornographic movie. Language, too, contradicts, as when Miss R. addresses the narrator: "I despise you, my boy, *mon cher,* my heart." Similar shifts occur in Barthelme's "City Life":

> A large wedding scene
> Charles measures the church
> Elsa and Jacques bombarded with flowers
> Fathers and mothers riding on the city railway
> The minister raises his hands
> Evacuation of the sacristy: bomb threat
> Black limousines with ribbons tied to their aerials
> Several men on balconies who appear to be signalling, or applauding
> Traffic lights
> Pieces of blue cake
> Champagne.

These dislocations, with their accompanying shifts in mood, parallel what is for most Americans an everyday occurrence: the evening news as presented on television. There, war, assassinations, natural disasters, plane crashes, sporting accidents, stock market quotations, and glimpses of life's lighter moments are offered in a far more intensive staccato.

Because it tends to be more verbal than conventional writing, experimental fiction is replete with wordplays: double-entendres, allusions, puns, archaisms, and echoes and paraphrases of earlier literature. "Night-Sea Journey" contains scores of verbal tricks and turns: puns like *joie de nager* and *tale-bearer;* sly and twisted paraphrases of contemporary poetry ("I have seen the best swimmers of my generation go under"); Biblical echoes ("Except ye drown, ye shall not reach the Shore of Light"); and allusions to Victorian prose and poetry (the swimmers' sodden cry of onward and upward, the narrator's reflection, "Ours not to stop and think; ours but to swim and sink"). Similarly in "City Life," the Dean of the Law School tells Ramona and Elsa to keep their notes clean; Elsa and Jacques have a large wedding—Charles measures the church; and Ramona has a lover named Vercingetorix who is leader of the firemen. As these examples show, the prose is self-conscious; but calling attention to the way in which it is written is not a defect if the story is meant to be viewed as a created object. In *Snow White,* Barthelme describes the men who live with Snow White as reading

> books that have a lot of *dreck* in them, matter which presents itself as not wholly relevant (or indeed, at all relevant) but which, carefully attended to, can supply a kind of "sense" of what is going on. This "sense" is not to be obtained by reading between the lines (for there is nothing there in those white spaces) but by reading the lines themselves.

As noted earlier, because words constitute the meaning of much experimental writing, we are supposed to read the lines for themselves, finding the sense in them. A great deal of the fiction is therefore, deliberately unsymbolic because symbols suggest meanings larger than themselves. But because the experimentalists draw from the practices of conventional fiction, the white spaces on the page are seldom truly empty, especially when the writer engages in wordplay. For then a word may become more than itself: to the degree that it takes on double and triple meanings, it will expand into the adjacent white spaces. But the dislocations, the tricks, the posturings, the jolting syntax, and the shifts in mood all force us to pay attention to the words, and that can be a good beginning.

TONE: THE ABSENCE OF LAUGHTER

Not true.

There is laughter in works of experimental fiction, but the source of the laughter is primarily wordplay and only secondarily action. Thus, the response is generally a smile. If there is overt laughter, it is usually the author's. Indeed, in much experimental fiction, like "Lost in the Funhouse" or "Night-Sea Journey," the reader senses the writer standing off to one side, laughing at his own jokes. If there is a community in such fiction, it exists directly between the reader and the writer. One critic contends that Barth's mind is more interesting than any of Barth's books—it is "perceived through the books, of course, but it could be perceived as being let down."

Sometimes the laugh is based on an inside joke, as in "Lost in the Funhouse." A reader unaware of Barth's parody of conventional fiction would miss half the fun: he would simply be lost. The conception as well as the execution of "Night-Sea Journey" is humorous only when you have discovered the identity of the narrator, for then the philosophical speculations, given the source, assume an added humorous poignancy. The questions are serious, but the context is not, and the comedy reveals itself in the discrepancy. Similarly in "City Life," there is humor in the law professor's remarks, in the matter of the virgin birth, in the law student's defense of Ramona, in Moonbelly's popular songs. Even "The Indian Uprising" has elements of humor—in the scenes with the schoolteacher, in the use of hollow-core doors as love tokens, in the ingredients of the barricades. Among the experimental fiction collection here, only "How I Contemplated . . ." appears absolutely humorless. In it, hostility, brutality, emptiness, the desperate need to be loved, and society's insulating proprieties are unrelieved by any trace of the comic.

On the whole, however, experimental stories evince a playfulness noticeably absent in fiction in which the characters and events are closer to "real life" counterparts. Generally, the experimentalist takes pleasure in word games, in verbal jests, in artifices, in imagizing absurdity and then triumphing over it through the form his story takes. He delights in mockery and parody, in bringing to the reader amusement as well as instruction, in discovering older fictional genres like the fable and the fairy tale, in thumbing his nose at conventions and cramming his story with trash only to emerge impishly clean at its conclusion if the fiction has been a success, in *not* being afraid to be lost in the funhouse.

FORM

Fitting.

As should be evident, experimental fiction is not formless, although, on the surface, its structuring may appear random. Time shifts occur without transitions but with great precision. Events in stories like "City Life" appear arbitrary; however, upon closer examination, they show an inevitability that their unexplained presentation at first concealed. Without plot to lend narrative causality, the form of these stories comes from other elements: from diction, imagery, syntax, irony, and tone; from an intuitive "felt" patterning; from a sensibility that shapes the whole; from the story's calling attention to itself. The materials of literary construction are not concealed in stories like "Lost in the Funhouse" and "How I Contemplated . . . ." In structures such as these, the beams, braces, and uprights are exposed. Sometimes the plumbing, too, is visible; occasionally you can even hear it.

The reader who needs the verisimilitude of stories that depict overt action (however minimal) and characters that are more or less recognizable (and perhaps even likable) will probably not enjoy reading experimental stories—and he will not be alone. The writer-hero of "Dunyazadiad" complains that the only readers of "artful fiction" in America today are "critics, other writers, and unwilling students who, left to themselves, [prefer] music and pictures to words." This is a small following, but it is not destined to remain so if you enlarge your definition of the story to include "artful fiction"—allowing the genre to be "a vehicle for the many voices of the intellect and verbal innovation" rather than solely "a story-telling machine," and recognizing that even if the current interest in experimentation wanes,

> linear sequential omniscient narrative will never be the same again. Or to put it another way it has become possible again, because it has a much richer context of alternatives, because it is no longer low-grade entertainment or a "classic" but has resumed serious negotiations with philosophy, politics, and that re-opened debate on how we see.[5]

Like all arts, fiction would become moribund if its elements settled rigidly into place. We do not expect this stasis in film, for example, where the flourishing avant-garde is usually cited as proof of the genre's vitality. The same flexibility must be accorded the story. For, if the truth be known, the house of fiction is always being renewed and enlarged, even if the changes are not evident at first glance. And it is thus both large and intricate; its possibilities seemingly endless. This introduction will have succeeded if it has revealed some of the building materials and some of the compartments; the exploration of the remaining ones and the familiarity that comes from firsthand experience are left for you, the reader, to enjoy.

‡ For an enlightening discussion of publishing and contemporary fiction, see Charles Newman, "The Uses and Abuses of Death: A Little Rumble Through the Remnants of Literary Culture," *TriQuarterly*, 26 (Winter 1973), 3–41.

Every short story, at least for me, is a little act of discovery. A cluster of details presents itself to my scrutiny, like a mystery that I will understand in the course of writing or sometimes not fully until afterward, when, if I have been honest and listened to these details carefully, I will find that they are connected and that there is a coherent pattern. This pattern is in experience itself; you do not impose it from the outside and if you try to, you will find that the story is taking the wrong tack, dribbling away from you into artificiality or inconsequence. A story that you do not learn something from while you are writing it, that does not illuminate something for you, is dead, finished before you started it.

FROM *Settling the Colonel's Hash*

MARY McCARTHY

Mary McCarthy was born in Seattle in 1912. Orphaned at six, she was brought up by guardians and grandparents. *Memories of a Catholic Girlhood* (1957), a collection of autobiographical essays, vividly recounts her troubled childhood years.

After graduating from Vassar—birthplace of *The Group* (1963)—McCarthy settled in New York City, where she reviewed books for *The New Republic* and *The Nation*. In 1937 she became the drama editor of *Partisan Review*, which was then a Marxist, anti-Stalinist publication; her theatre column appeared in that magazine for many years. It was the distinguished critic Edmund Wilson, to whom she was then married, who encouraged McCarthy to write fiction. "Cruel and Barbarous Treatment," her first published story, was printed in *The Southern Review* (Spring 1939) and is collected with later stories in *The Company She Keeps* (1942). In addition to writing, McCarthy has taught at Bard and Sarah Lawrence colleges.

McCarthy's nonfiction writing has included literary and dramatic criticism, essays describing and evaluating contemporary cultural and political movements (for example, her Vietnam reports), and books on Venice and Florence. In fact, many critics consider her most at home in the critical essay. She acknowledges, "Whatever way I write was really, I suppose, formed critically. That is, I learned to write reviews and criticism and then write novels so that however I wrote, it was formed that way." The two stories reprinted here exhibit many characteristics of informal essays: they are personal (revealing attitudes of their author), full of analytically descriptive statement, witty (with heavy doses of bookish humor), and curiously inconclusive, as if they were only attempts at explaining the particularities of an event, person, or place.

THE CICERONE

When they first met him, in the *wagons-lits,* he was not so nervous. Tall, straw-colored, standing smoking in the corridor, he looked like an English cigarette. Indeed, there was something about him so altogether parched and faded that he seemed to bear the same relation to a man that a Gold Flake bears to a normal cigarette. English, surely, said the young American lady. The young American man was not convinced. If English, then a bounder, he said, adjusting his glasses to peer at the stranger with such impassioned curiosity that his eyes in their light-brown frames seemed to rush dangerously forward, like strange green headlights on an old-fashioned car. As yet, he felt no unusual interest in the stranger who had just emerged from a compartment; this curiosity was his ordinary state of being.

It was so hard, the young lady complained, to tell a bounder in a foreign country; one was never sure; those dreadful striped suits that English gentlemen wear . . . and the Duke of Windsor talking in a cockney accent.

Here on the Continent, continued the young man, it was even more confusing, with the upper classes trying to dress like English gentlemen and striking the inevitable false notes; the dukes all looked like floorwalkers, but every man who looked like a floorwalker was unfortunately not a duke. Their conversation continued in an agreeable rattle-rattle. Its inspiration, the Bounder, was already half-dismissed. It was not quite clear to either of them whether they were trying to get into European society or whether this was simply a joke that they had between them. The young man had lunched with a viscountess in Paris and had admired her house and her houseboat, which was docked in the Seine. They had poked their heads into a great many courtyards in the Faubourg St. Germain, including the very grandiose one, bristling with guards who instantly ejected them, that belonged to the Soviet Embassy. On the whole, architecture, they felt, provided the most solid answer to their social curiosity: the bedroom of Marie Antoinette at the Petit Trianon had informed them that the French royal family were dwarfs, a secret already hinted at in Mme Pompadour's bedroom at the Frick museum in New York; in Milan, they would meet the Sforzas through the agency of their Castello; at Stra, on the Brenta, they would get to know the Pisani. They had read Proust, and the decline of the great names in modern times was accepted by them as a fact; the political speeches of the living Count Sforza suggested the table-talk of Mme Verdurin, gracing with her bourgeois platitudes the board of an ancient house. Nevertheless, the sight of a rococo ceiling, a great swaying crystal chandelier, glimpsed at night through an open second-story window, would come to them like an invitation which is known to exist but which has been incomprehensibly lost in the mails; a vague sadness descended, yet they did not feel like outsiders.

Victors in a world war of unparalleled ferocity, heirs of imperialism and the philosophy of the enlightenment, they walked proudly on the dilapidated streets of Europe. They had not approved of the war and were pacifist and bohemian in their sympathies, but the exchange had made them feel rich, and they could not help showing it. The exchange had turned them into a prince and a princess, and, considering the small bills, the weekly financial anxieties that attended them at home, this was quite an accomplishment. There was no door, therefore, that, they believed, would not open to them should they present themselves fresh and crisp as two one-dollar bills. These beliefs, these dreams, were, so far, no more to them than a story children tell each other. The young man, in fact, had found his small role as war-profiteer so distasteful and also so frightening that he had refused for a whole week to go to his money-changer and had cashed his checks at the regular rate at the bank. For the most part, their practical, moral life was lived, guidebook in hand, on the narrow streets and in the cafés of the Left Bank—they got few messages at their hotel.

Yet occasionally when they went in their best clothes to a fashionable bar, she wearing the flowers he had bought her (ten cents in American money), they hoped in silent unison during the first cocktail for the Dr.-Livingstone-I-presume that would discover them in this dark continent. And now on the train that was carrying them into Italy, the European illusion quickened once more within them. They eyed every stranger with that suspension of disbelief which, to invert Wordsworth, makes its object poetical. The man at the next table had talked all through lunch to two low types with his mouth full, but the young man remained steady in his conviction that the chewer was a certain English baronet traveling to his villa in Florence, and he had nearly persuaded the young lady to go up and ask him his name. He particularly valued the young lady today because, coming from the West, she entered readily into conversation with people she did not know. It was a handicap, of course, that there were two of them ("My dear," said the young lady, "a couple looks so complete"), but they were not inclined to separate—the best jockey in a horse race scorns to take a lighter weight. Unfortunately, their car, except for the Bounder at the other end, offered very little scope to his imaginative talent or her loquacity.

But, as they were saying, Continental standards were mysteriously different; at the frontier at Domodossola a crowd gathered on the rainy platform in front of their car. Clearly there was some object of attraction here, and, dismissing the idea that it was herself, the young lady moved to the window. Next to her, a short, heavy, ugly man with steel-rimmed spectacles was passing some money to a person on the platform, who immediately hurried away. Other men came up and spoke in undertones through the window to the man beside her. In all of this there was something that struck the young lady as strange—so much quiet and so much motion, which seemed the more purposeful, the more businesslike without its natural accompaniment of sound. Her clear, school-teacher-on-holiday voice intruded resolutely on this quarantine. *"Qu'est-ce que se passe?"* she demanded. *"Rien,"* said her neighbor abruptly, glancing at her and away with a single, swiveling movement of the spectacled eyes. *"C'est des amis qui rencontrent des amis."* Rebuffed, she turned back to the young man. "Black market," she said. "They are changing money." He nodded, but seeing her thoughts travel capably to the dollar bills pinned to her underslip, he touched her with a cautioning hand. The dead, noncommittal face beside her, the briefcase, the noiseless, nondescript young men on the platform, the single laugh that had rung out in the Bounder's end of the car when the young lady had put her question, all bade him beware: this black market was not for tourists. The man who had hurried away came back with a dirty roll of bills which he thrust through the window. *"Ite, missa est,"* remarked the young lady sardonically, but the man beside her gave no sign of having heard; he continued to gaze immovably at the thin young men before him, as though the transaction had not yet been digested.

At this moment, suddenly, a hubbub of singing, of agitated voices shouting slogans was heard. A kind of frenzy of noise, which had an unruly, an unmistakably seditious character, moved toward the train from somewhere outside the shed. The train gave a loud puff. "A revolution!" thought the young lady, clasping the young man's hand with a pang of terror and excitement; he, like everyone else in the car, had jumped to his feet. A strange procession came into sight, bright and bedraggled in the rain—an old woman in a white dress and flowered hat waving a large red flag, two or three followers with a homemade-looking bouquet, and finally a gray-bearded old man dressed in an ancient frock coat, carrying an open old-fashioned black umbrella and leaping nimbly into the air. Each of the old man's hops was fully two yards high; his thin legs in the black trousers were jack-knifed neatly under him; the umbrella maintained a perfect perpendicular; only his beard flew forward and his coat-tails back; at the summit of each hop, he shouted joyously, *"Togliatti!"* The demonstration was coming toward the car, where alarm had given way to amazement; Steel Glasses alone was undisturbed by the appearance of these relics of political idealism; his eyes rested on them without expression. Just as they gained the protection of the shed, the train, unfortunately, began to move. The followers, lacking the old man's gymnastic precision, were haphazard with the bouquet; it missed the window, which had been opened for the lira-changing, and fell back into the silent crowd. The train picked up speed.

In the compartment, the young man was rolling on the seat with laughter; he was always the victim of his emotions, which—even the pleasurable ones—seemed to overrun him like the troops of some marauding army. Thus happiness, with him, had a look of intensest suffering, and the young lady clucked sympathetically as he gasped out, *"The Possessed, The Possessed."* To the newcomer in the compartment, however, the young man's condition appeared strange. "What is the matter with him?" the young man, deep in the depths of his joy, heard an odd, accented little voice asking; then the young lady's voice was explaining, "Dostoevski . . . a small political center . . . a provincial Russian town." "But no," said the other voice, "it is Togliatti, the leader of *Italian* Communists who is in the next compartment. He is coming from the Peace Conference where he talks to Molotov." The words, *Communist, Molotov, Peace Conference,* bored the young man so much that he came to his senses instantly, sat up, wiped his glasses, and perceived that it was the Bounder who was in the compartment, and to whom the young lady was now re-explaining that her friend was laughing because the scene on the platform had reminded him of something in a book. "But no," protested the Bounder, who was still convinced that the young lady had not understood *him.* He appeared to come to some sort of decision and ran out into the corridor, returning with a Milanese newspaper folded to show an item in which the words, *Togliatti, Parigi, Pace,* and *Molotov* all indubitably figured. The young lady, weary of explanation, allowed a bright smile as of final comprehension to pass over her features and handed the paper to the young man, who could not read Italian either; in such acts of submission their conversations with Europeans always ended. They had got used to it, but they sometimes felt that they had stepped at Le Havre into some vast cathedral where a series of intrusive custodians stood between them and the frescoes relating with tireless patience the story of the Nativity. Europeans, indeed, seemed to them often a race of custodians, didactic automatons who answered, like fortune-telling machines, questions to which one already knew the answer or questions which no one would conceivably ask.

True to this character, the Bounder, now, had plainly taken a shine to the young lady, who was permitting him to tell her facts about the Italian political situation which she had previously read in a newspaper. That her position on Togliatti was identical with his own, he assumed as axiomatic, and her dissident murmurs of correction he treated as a kind of linguistic static. Her seat on the *wagons-lits* spoke louder to him than words; she could never persuade him that she hated Togliatti from the *left,* any more than she could convince a guide in Paris of her indifference to Puvis de Chavannes. Her attention he took for assent, and only the young man troubled him, as he had troubled many guides in many palaces and museums by lingering behind in some room he fancied; an occasional half-smothered burst of laughter indicated to the two talkers that he was still in the Dostoevski attic. But the glances of tender understanding that the young lady kept rather pointedly turning toward her friend were an explanation in pantomime; his alarms stilled, the visitor neatly drew up his trousers and sat down.

They judged him to be a man about forty-two years old. In America he might have passed for younger; he had kept his hair, light-brown and slightly oiled, with a ripple at the brow and a half-ripple at the back; his figure, moreover, was slim—it had not taken on that architectural form, those transepts, bows, and barrel-vaulting, that with Americans demonstrate (how quickly often!) that the man is no longer a boy but an Institution. Like the young lady's hairdresser, like the gay little grocer on Third Avenue, he had retained in middle age something for which there is no English word, something *trés mignon*, something *gentil*, something *joli garçon*. It lay in a quickness and lightness of movement, in slim ankles, small feet, thin, agile wrists, in a certain demure swoop of lowering eyelids, in the play of lashes, and the butterfly flutter of the airy white handkerchief protruding from the breast pocket. It lay also in a politeness so eager as to seem freshly learned and in a childlike vanity, a covert sense of performance, in which one could trace the swing of the censer and the half-military, half-theatrical swish of the altar-boy's skirts.

But if this sprightliness of demeanor and of dress gave the visitor an appearance of youthfulness, it also gave him, by its very exaggeration, a morbid appearance of age. Those quick, small smiles, those turns of the eye, and expressive raisings of the eyebrow had left a thousand tiny wrinkles on his dust-colored face; his slimness too had something cadaverous in it—chicken-breasted he appeared in his tan silk gabardine suit. And, oddly enough, this look of premature senility was not masculine but feminine. Though no more barbered and perfumed than the next Italian man, he evoked the black mass of the dressing-table and the hand-mirror; he reminded them of that horror so often met in Paris, city of beauty, the well-preserved woman in her fifties. At the same time, he was unquestionably a man; he was already talking of conquests. It was simply, perhaps, that the preservation of youth had been his main occupation; age was the specter he had dealt with too closely; like those middle-aged women he had become its intimate through long animosity.

Yet just as they had decided that he was a man somehow without a profession (they had come to think in unison and needed the spoken word only for a check), he steered himself out of a small whirlpool of ruffled political feelings and announced that he was in the silk business. He was returning from London, and had spent a week in Paris, where he had been short of francs and had suffered a serious embarrassment when taking a lady out to lunch. The lady, it appeared, was the wife of the Egyptian delegate to the Peace Conference, whom he had met—also—on the *wagons-lits*. There was a great deal more of this, all either very simple or very complicated, they were unable to say which, for they could not make out whether he was telling the same story twice, or, whether, as in a folk tale, the second story repeated the pattern of the first but had a variant ending. His English was very odd; it had a speed and a precision of enunciation that combined with a vagueness of grammar so as to make the two Americans feel that they were listening to a foreign language, a few words of which they could recognize. In the same way, his anecdotes had a wealth and circumstantiality of detail and an overall absence of form, or at least so the young lady, who was the only one who was listening, reported later to the young man. The young man, who was tone-deaf, found the visitor's conversation reminiscent of many concerts he had been taken to, where he could only distinguish the opening bars of any given work; for him, Mr. Sciarappa's stories were all in their beginnings, and he would interrupt quite often with a reply square in the middle, just as, quite often, he used to break in with wild applause when the pianist paused between the first and second movements of a sonata.

But at the mention of the silk business, the young man's eyes had once more burned a terrifying green. With his afflamed imagination, he was at the same time extremely practical. Hostile to Marxist theory, he was marxist in personal matters, having no interest in people's opinions, or even, perhaps, in their emotions (the superstructure), but passionately, madly curious as to what people did and how they made their money (the base). He did not intend that Mr. Sciarappa (he had presented his card) should linger forever in Paris adding up the lunch bill of the Egyptian delegate's wife. Having lain *couchant* for the ten minutes that human politeness required, he sprang into the conversation with a question: did the *signor* have an interest in the silk mills at Como? And now the visitor betrayed the first signs of nervousness. The question had suggested knowledge that was at least second-hand. The answer remained obscure. Mr. Sciarappa did not precisely own a factory, nor was he precisely in the exporting business. The two friends, who were not lacking in common humanity, precipitately turned the subject to the beauty of Italian silks, the superiority of Italian tailoring to French or even English tailoring, the chic of Italian men. The moment passed, and a little later, under the pretense of needing her help as a translator, Mr. Sciarappa showed the young lady a cablegram dated London which seemed to be a provisional order for a certain quantity of something, but the garbled character of the English suggested that the cable had been composed—in London—by Mr. Sciarappa himself. Nevertheless, the Americans accepted the cablegram as a proof of their visitor's *bona fides,* though actually it proved no more than that he was in business, that is, that he existed in the Italy of the post-war world.

The troubled moment, in fact, had its importance for them only in

79

retrospect. A seismographic recording of conditions in the compartment would have shown only the faintest tremor. The desire to believe the best of people is a prerequisite for intercourse with strangers; suspicion is reserved for friends. The young lady in particular, being gregarious, took the kindest view of everyone; she was under the impression that she was the only person in the world who told lies. The young man today fell in with her gullibility, with her "normal" interpretations of life, because he saw that they were heading for friendship with Mr. Sciarappa and felt as yet no positive objections to the idea. They were alone in Italy; a guide would be useful. Moreover, Mr. Sciarappa had announced that he was going on to Rome, where he lived with his parents, at midnight. Already he had invited them to join him for a drink in Milan in the famous Galleria; the worst they could expect was a dinner à trois. Therefore, he acted, temporarily, on the young lady's persuasion that their visitor was an ordinary member of the upper middle classes in vaguely comfortable circumstances, in other words, that he was an abstraction; in the same way, certain other abstract beliefs of hers concerning true love and happiness had conveyed him, somewhat more critical and cautious, into this compartment with her on a romantic journey into Italy.

But, just as it had come as a surprise to him that love should go on from step to step, that it should move from city to country and cross an ocean and part of a continent, so in Milan it was with a vague astonishment that he beheld Mr. Sciarappa remove his baggage from the taxi in front of their hotel and hurry inside ahead of him to inquire for a room. For the next three days, the trio could be seen any evening promenading, arm in arm, down the long arcade of the Galleria, past the crowded little tables with the pink, and the peach, and the lime, and the orange colored tablecloths, walking with the air of distinguished inseparables, the two tall men and the tallish young lady with a large black hat. Or at noon they could be found there, perspiring and not so distinguished, sipping Americanos, Mr. Sciarappa's favorite drink, at the café with the orange tablecloths, which Mr. Sciarappa considered the cheapest. At night, they appeared at Giannino's or Crispi's (not so expensive as Biffi's but better food, said Mr. Sciarappa), restaurants where Mr. Sciarappa made himself at home, sending back the wine which the Americans had ordered and getting in its place some thinner and sourer vintage of which he had special knowledge. The one solid trait the two friends could discover in Mr. Sciarappa's character was a rooted abhorrence of the advertised first-rate, of best hotels, top restaurants, principal shopping streets, famous vineyards; and, since for the first time in many years they saw themselves in a position to command these advantages, they found this trait of Mr. Sciarappa's rather a cross. In American money, the difference between the best and the mediocre was trifling; indeed even in Italian money, it was often nonexistent. They tried to convince Mr. Sciarappa of this, but their computations he took as an insult to himself and his defeated country. His lip would curl into a small, angry sneer that looked as if it had come out of a permanent-wave machine. "Ah, you Americans," he would say, "your streets are paved with dollars."

The two friends, after the first night, spent on bad beds in an airless room hung with soiled lace curtains, moved with a certain thump into the best hotel next door. They would not have stayed in any case, for the young man had a horror of the sordid, and the best hotel proved, when you counted breakfast, to be cheaper than its second-rate neighbor. Nevertheless, in the circumstances, the move had a significant tone—they hoped to fray, if not to sever, their connection with Mr. Sciarappa, and perhaps also, to tell the truth, to insult him a little. The best hotel, half-requisitioned by the Allied armies, smiled on them with brass and silver insignia, freshly washed summer khaki and blond, straight, water-combed American hair; when Mr. Sciarappa came for cocktails in the same gabardine suit, he looked somehow like a man in prison clothes or the inmate of a mental institution. The young lady, who was the specialist in sentiments, felt toward him sorrow, shame, triumph.

They could not make out what he wanted of them.

Whatever business had, on the train, been hurrying him on to Rome had presumably lost its urgency. He never mentioned it again; indeed, the three spoke very little together, and it was this that gave them that linked and wedded look. During the day he disappeared, except for the luncheon apéritif. He went to Como, to Genoa, and, once, in the Galleria, they saw him with an unshaven, white-haired, morose-looking man whom he introduced as his brother-in-law. In restaurants, he was forever jumping up from the table with a gay little wave of the hand to greet a party that was in the act of vanishing into the dark outdoors. Though he was a man who twitched with sociability, whose conversation was a veritable memo pad of given names, connections, ties, appointments, he seemed to be unknown to the very waiters whom he directed in the insolent style of an old customer. The brother-in-law, who plainly disliked him, and they themselves, whom he hated, were his only friends.

The most remarkable symptom of this hatred, which ate into the conversation leaving acid holes of boredom, which kept him glancing at other tables as though in hope of succor or release, was a tone of unshakable, impolite disbelief. "Ah, I am not such a fool," his pretty face would almost angrily indicate if they told him that they had spent their morning in the castle-fort of the Sforzas, where beneath the ramparts bombed by the Liberators, a troupe of Italian players with spotlights lent by the American army was preparing to do an American pacifist play. Every statement volunteered by the two friends broke on the edge of Mr. Sciarappa's contempt like the very thinnest alibi; parks and the public buildings they described to him became as transparent as falsehoods—anyone of any experience knew there were no such places in Milan. When they praised the wicked-looking Filippo Lippi Madonna they had seen in the Sforza Gallery, Mr. Sciarappa and his disaffected brother-in-law, who was supposed to speak no English, exchanged, for the first time, a fraternal, sidewise look: a masterpiece, indeed, their incredulous eyebrows ejaculated—they had heard that story before.

That Mr. Sciarappa should question their professions of enthusiasm was perhaps natural. His own acquaintance with Italy's artistic treasures seemed distant; they had had the reputation with him of being much admired by English and American tourists; the English and American airforces, however, had quoted them, as he saw, at a somewhat lower rate. Moreover, it was as if the devaluation of the currency had, for Mr. Sciarappa's consistent thought, implicated everything Italian; cathedrals, pictures, women had dropped with the lira. He could not imagine that anyone could take these things at their Baedeker valuation, any more than he could imagine that anyone in his right mind would change dollars into lira at the official rate. The two friends soon learned that to praise any Italian product, were it only a bicycle or a child in the street, was an insult to Mr. Sciarappa's intelligence. They would be silent—and eventually were—but the most egregious insult, the story that they had come to Italy as tourists, they could not wipe away.

He felt himself to be the victim of an imposture, that was plain. But did he believe that they were rich pretending to be poor, or poor pretending to be rich? They could not tell. On the whole, it seemed as if Mr. Sciarappa's suspicions, like everything else about him, had a certain flickering quality; the light in him went on and off, as he touched one theory or another, cruising in his shaft like an elevator. And, as the young man said, you could not blame Mr. Sciarappa for wondering: was it in the character of a rich man or a poor that they stayed in the best hotel, which was slightly less expensive than an American auto-camp?

The obscurity of their financial position justified Mr. Sciarappa's anger. Nevertheless, though sympathetic, they grew tired of spending their evenings with a stranger who was continually out of sorts because he could not make up his mind whether they were worth swindling. "We did not come to Italy to see Mr. Sciarappa," they would say to each other every night as they rode up in the elevator, and would promise themselves to evade this time, without fail, the meeting he had fixed for the next day. Yet as noon came on the following morning, they would find that they were approaching the Galleria. He is waiting, they would say to each other, and without discussion they would hurry on toward the café with the orange tablecloths, where they were late but never quite late enough to miss Mr. Sciarappa.

He was never glad to see them. He rose to acknowledge them with a kind of bravura laziness of his tall "English" figure, one shoulder lifted in a shrug of ennui or resignation. He kissed the young lady's hand and said to the young man perfunctorily, and sometimes with a positive yawn, "Hello, sit down, my dear." One of his odd little tricks was to pretend that they were not together. The young man's frequent absences of mind he treated literally, when it suited him, as if they were absences of body, and once he carried this so far as to run his fingers up and down the young lady's bare arm as the three of them rode in a taxi, inquiring as he did so, in the most civil tone imaginable, whether she found her friend satisfactory. His conversation was directed principally to the young lady, but for all that he had no real interest in her. It was the young man whom he watched, often in the mirror of her face, which never left her friend as he talked wildly, excitedly, extravagantly, with long wrists flung outward in intensity of gesture: did Mr. Sciarappa see beauty and strangeness in him or the eccentricity of money? Or was he merely trying to determine which it was that she saw?

It was irresistible that they should try to coax Mr. Sciarappa (or Scampi, as they had begun to call him, after fried crayfish-tails, his favorite dish) out into the open. The name of a certain lady, middlingly but authentically rich, who was expecting to see them in Venice, began to figure allusively, alluringly, in their conversation. These pointers that they directed toward Polly Herkimer Grabbe had at first a merely educational purpose. National pride forbade that they should allow Scampi to take them for rich Americans when a really good example of the genre existed only a day's journey away. But their first references to the flower-bulb heiress, to her many husbands, her collection of garden statuary, her career as an impresario of modern architecture, failed, seemingly, to impress Scampi; he raised his eyes briefly from the plate of Saltimbocca (Jump-in-your-mouth) that he was eating, and then returned to his meal. The language difficulties made it sometimes impossible to tell whether Mr. Sciarappa really heard what they said. They had remarked once, for example, in conversational desperation, that they had come to Italy to retrace the footsteps of Lord Byron: they were on their way from Lausanne, where he had composed "The Prisoner of Chillon" in a bedroom of the Hotel Angleterre, to Venice to visit his house on the Grand Canal. "Ah well, my dear," said Mr. Sciarappa, "if he is an English lord, you do not have to worry; his house will not be requisitioned, and you will have the use of his gondolier." There had been no way the young man could find of preventing the young lady from supplying the poet's dates, and now, it seemed, Scampi was under the impression that everyone they knew in Venice was dead. It required the largest brush-strokes to bring Miss Grabbe to life for him. By the third night, when the young man had finished a wholly invented account of Miss Grabbe's going through the customs with a collection of obscene fountain statuary, Mr. Sciarappa showed interest and inquired how old Miss Grabbe was. The next evening, at cocktails, he had an auto-pullman ticket to Venice.

He was leaving the next morning at seven. The two Americans, remembering that the flower-bulb heiress was, after all, their friend, felt appalled and slightly frightened at what they had done. They thought of dropping some note of warning into the letter of introduction which of course they would have to write. But then they reflected that if Miss Grabbe was richer than they, she was also proportionately shrewder: glass bricks only could Mr. Sciarappa sell her for that submarine architectural salon she spoke of opening in the depths of the Grand Canal. Miss Grabbe's intelligence was flighty (she had once forgotten to include the furnace in a winter house that so hugged the idea of warmth that the bathtubs were done in buff), but her estimates were sharp; no contractor or husband had ever padded a bill on her; she always put on her glasses to add up a dinner check. Men, it was true, had injured her, and movements had left her flat, but these misadventures she had cheerfully added to her capital. An indefatigable Narcissa, she adapted herself spryly to comedy when she perceived that the world was smiling; she was always the second to laugh at a pratfall of her spirit. Mr. Sciarappa, at worst, could only be another banana-peel on the vaudeville stage of her history. It was possible, of course, that he might bore her, thought the two friends, reasoning from experience; this alone she would not forgive them, yet Miss Grabbe's judgments of men were often strikingly lenient—she had been unattached when they left her in Paris.

Besides, Mr. Sciarappa was looking quite presentable this evening, even though he had not yet changed his suit. Bright, eager, intensely polite, useful, informative, he seemed once more the figure they had seen in the train corridor; some innocent, cavalier hope that had died in those long

Milan evenings had revived in him, as the expectation of parting made the two friends recede from him a little and become strangers once more. The letter of introduction wrote itself out, somehow, more affectionately than the friends had planned it. "Enclosed," it said, "please find Mr. Sciarappa, who has been most helpful to us in Milan."

Signorina Grabbe was waiting alone with a gondola in the orange-lampshade glow of a Canaletto sunset when their autobus drew up, two days later, at the station. Against the Venetian panorama of white domes and pink towers, Mr. Sciarappa was so pronouncedly absent that it seemed an indelicacy to inquire after him. The two friends, whom solitude and a consciousness of indiscretion had worked up to a pitch of anxiety and melodramatic conjecture, now felt slightly provoked that Miss Grabbe had not, in this short interval, been married or murdered for her money. At the very least, they had expected to be scolded for sending her that curious envoy, but Mr. Sciarappa's arrival seemed barely to have disturbed Miss Grabbe, who had been busy, so she said, with an inner experience. "Your friend turned up," she remarked at last, in the tone of one who acknowledges a package. "What on earth did you find to talk to him about?" The young man groaned. Miss Grabbe had put her rich, plump, practiced finger on the flaw in Mr. Sciarappa as prosaically as if he had been a piece of yardgoods —was there nothing more to be said of him? "We found him rather odd," the young man murmured in half-apology. "Oh, my dear," said Miss Grabbe, raising her dyed black eyebrows, "all the men you meet on the *wagons-lits* are like that. You must go to the little *campos* and the *trattorias* to meet the real Italians."

And as Miss Grabbe went on to talk, in the dipping, swaying gondola, of the intense, insular experience she had found, blazing as the native *grappa*, in the small, hot squares, the working-class restaurants and dirty churches of Venice, Mr. Sciarappa seemed indeed a poor thing to have offered her, a gimcrack souvenir such as one might have bought in a railway station. The young man blushed angrily as he felt his own trip and that of the young lady shrink to fit inside Mr. Sciarappa's nipped-in gabardine suit. He was only saved from despair by a memory of Miss Grabbe, as he had last seen her in Paris, alone, with her hunter's look, and three saucers under her vermouth glass, at a table in a Left Bank café—"Isn't it divine?" she had called out to him; "don't you love it, don't you hate New York?"

Compared to Miss Grabbe, he perceived, he himself and the young lady would always appear to skim the surface of travel. They were tourists; Miss Grabbe was an explorer. Looking at the two ladies as they sat facing him

in the gondola, he saw that their costumes perfectly expressed this difference: the young lady's large black hat, long gloves, high-heeled shoes, and
nylon stockings were a declaration of nationality and a stubborn assertion
of the pleasure-principle (what a nuisance that hat had been as it scraped
against his neck on the autobus, on the train, in the Metro in Paris); Miss
Grabbe's snood and sandals, her bright glass-bead jewelry, her angora
sweater, and shoulder-strap leather handbag, all Italian as the *merceria*, she
wore in the manner of a uniform that announced her mobility in action and
her support of the native products. Moreover, her brown face had a
weather-beaten look, as though it had been exposed to the glare of many
merciless suns; and her eyes blazed out of the sun-tan powder around them
with the bright blue stare of a scout; only her pretty, tanned legs suggested
a life less hardy—they might have been going to the beach. Like Mr.
Sciarappa (for all his little graces), Miss Grabbe seemed to have been
parched and baked by exposure, hardened and chapped by the winds of rebuff and failure. In contrast, the young lady, with her pallor and her smile,
looked faintly unreal, like a photograph of a girl whose engagement has just
been announced. And the young man felt himself joined to her in this shel-
tered and changeless beatitude; at the same time, in the company of Miss
Grabbe as in that of Mr. Sciarappa, he was aware of a slight discomfort, a
sense of fatuity, like the brief, antagonized embarrassment he noticed in
himself whenever, in answer to the inevitable question, he replied, with a
touch of storminess, that he was traveling in Europe for pleasure.

That he and the young lady were happy became, in this context, a
crime, or, at best, a breach of taste, like the conspicuous idleness of the rich.
They could hardly, he remarked to himself, be expected to give up their
mutual delight because others were not so fortunate; they had already settled this question with regard to steak and *cotolette*. Yet, catching Miss
Grabbe's eye measuring his happiness in the gondola, he felt inclined to
withdraw his feelings to some more private place, just as certain sensitive
patrons of restaurants preferred nowadays to feast indoors, secure from the
appraisal of the poor. His state, as he well knew, was of peculiar interest to
Miss Grabbe: for twenty years, Polly Grabbe had made herself famous by
coming to Europe, semi-annually, in pursuit of love. These sorties of hers
had the regularity and the directness of buyers' trips that are signalized by
a paid notice in the Paris *Herald*, announcing to the dressmaking trade
that Miss Blank of Franklin Simon is staying at the Crillon. Under the eye
of that transatlantic experience, the young man felt a little discomfited, as if
he had been modeling a housedress before a cosmopolite audience. He had
no wish to judge Miss Grabbe, yet he felt installed in a judgment by the

dream of perpetual monogamy into which the young lady had invited him. In an effort to extricate himself, he inquired of Miss Grabbe very civilly, as one traveler to another, how she found the Venetian men, but the heiress only stared at him coldly and asked what he took her for.

Miss Grabbe was aware of her legend; it half-pleased her, and yet she resented it, for, at bottom, she was naively unconscious of the plain purport of her acts. She imagined that she came abroad out of a cultural impatience with America; in her own eyes, she was always a rebel against a commercial civilization. She hoped to be remembered for her architectural experiments, her patronage of the arts, her championship of personal freedom, and flattered herself that in Europe this side of her was taken seriously. Men in America, she complained, thought only about business, and the European practice of making a business of love seemed to her, in contrast, the mark of an advanced civilization. Sexual intercourse, someone had taught her, was a quick transaction with the beautiful, and she proceeded to make love, whenever she traveled, as ingenuously as she trotted into a cathedral: men were a Continental commodity of which one naturally took advantage, along with the wine and the olives, the bitter coffee and the crusty bread. Miss Grabbe, despite her boldness, was not an original woman, and her boldness, in fact, consisted in taking everything literally. She made love in Europe because it was the thing to do, because European lovers were superior to American lovers ("My dear," she told the young lady, "there's all the difference in the *world*—it's like comparing the very best California claret to the simplest little *vin du pays*"), because she believed it was good for her, especially in hot climates, and because one was said to learn languages a great deal more readily in bed. The rapid turnover of her lovers did not particularly disconcert her; she took a quantitative view and sought for a *wealth* of sensations. She liked to startle and to shock, yet positively did not understand why people considered her immoral. A prehensile approach, she inferred, was laudable where values were in question—what was the beautiful *for,* if not to be seized and savored?

For Polly Grabbe, as for the big luxury liners and the small school teachers with their yearly piety of Europe, the war had been an enforced hiatus. Though she had wished for the defeat of Hitler and been generous with money to his victims, in her heart she had waited for it to be over with a purely personal impatience. She was among the first to return when travel was once again permitted, an odd, bedizened, little figure, alighting gallantly from the plane, making a spot of color among the American businessmen, her vulturine co-passengers, who were descending on Europe to "look after" their investments. Conditions in Paris shocked these men, deep in their business sense, and Miss Grabbe was dismayed also; her own investment had been swept away. She could not take up where she had left off: people were dead or dispersed or in prison; her past stood about her in fragments, a shattered face looming up here and there like a house-wall in a bombed city; normalcy was far away. But Miss Grabbe did not lack courage. She had learned how to say good-bye and to look ahead for the next thing. Paris, she quickly decided, was beautiful but done for, a shell from which the life had retreated out into the suburbs where a few old friends still persisted, a shell now inhabited by an alien existentialist gossip, and an alien troupe of young men who cadged drinks from her in languid boredom and made love only to each other. Her trip to Italy, therefore, had the character of a farewell and a new beginning, and the hotel suite, into which she now showed the two friends, resembled a branch office which had been opened but was not yet in full operation.

The wide *letto matrimoniale* in the bedroom, the washstand, and the bidet with the towel over it, the dressing-table on which were arranged, very neatly and charmingly, Miss Grabbe's toilet waters and perfumes, her powders and lucite brush and comb, her lipsticks, orange sticks, and tweezers, all had an air unmistakably functional, to which the books and magazines, the cigarettes and pretty colored postcards set out, invitingly, in the sitting room contributed their share, so that it was not so surprising as it might have been to see, when the balcony doors were opened, the figure of Mr. Sciarappa lounging on the terrace, like a waiting client, with a copy of *Life*.

This conception of his position, however, seemed not to have struck Mr. Sciarappa. He was there, it seemed, simply for the practical joke of it, for their shrieks, for Miss Grabbe's discomfiture. He laughed at them with candid merriment, saying, "*Caro,* I give you a surprise." The two friends had not seen him so lively since one night in Milan when a tired fat woman, running for a tramcar, had failed to catch it. He showed no inclination at all to step into the role that stood there, ready for him to try on. He had come, he said, as a courier, proposing to take them to dinner, to the Piazza San Marco, to Harry's Bar, where the smart English officers went and the international set with their electric-blue suits, blonde mistresses, heavy jaws, and decorations from Balkan kings. With all these little offices and services, his mind was completely occupied. His original mission, Miss Grabbe, had plainly dropped into some *oubliette* of his faculties, and the two friends, observing him, could nearly have sworn that his sole purpose in coming to Venice had been to prepare a place for them, like Jesus for his disciples in Heaven.

Dinner, however, soon restored him to his normal state of disaffection. Once the four were seated upstairs, in the yellow lamplight at Quadri's, he was his old self, bored, petulant, abstracted. He jumped up from his chair with almost indecent agility to speak to a bearded gentleman in a respectable suit of clothes, and came back finally to announce that this was Prince Rucellai, an illustrious Florentine nobleman who practiced the trade of antique-dealer. In the manner of all Mr. Sciarappa's native acquaintances, the prince at once quitted the restaurant, but Mr. Sciarappa's attention went with him out into the square, abandoning the Americans summarily for the evening. It was as if he suffered from some curious form of amnesia that made him mislay his purpose halfway on the road to accomplishment. He was in Venice and could not remember why, and he stayed on hoping, somehow, for a refreshment of his memory. Now and then, during the following days, the Americans would find him looking at them with a curious concentration, as though their appearance might recall to him his motive in seeking their society. From Miss Grabbe, on the contrary, whose emeralds should have furnished him his clue, he persistently averted his eyes.

The little bohemian heiress, in fact, was the center of his inattention, an inattention principled and profound. From the very first night, apparently, she had associated herself in his mind with culture, and hence, merely by talking about them, she had fallen into the class of objects—cathedrals, works of art, museums, palaces maintained by the state—which, by being free to all, were valuable, in his opinion, to none. And by the same trick by which he substituted an empty space for the cathedral in the Piazza San Marco, he "vanished" Miss Grabbe from the table at dinner. The possibility of her buying a palazzo, which she spoke of continually, he simply declined to credit. His business interest, it would seem, was far too deep to be aroused by it, and no commission could be large enough to make him expand his idea of money to accommodate within it the living heresy of Miss Grabbe. All over Venice, volunteer real-estate agents were at work for her, the concierge at the Grand Hotel, the lift-boy, a gondolier, two Communist painters in a studio across the Canal. Mr. Sciarappa only smiled impatiently whenever this project was mentioned, and once he nudged the young lady and significantly tapped his head.

Miss Grabbe, for her part, was unaware of his feelings. The first evening on the balcony, she had expressed herself strongly against him. Pointing dramatically to the blue lagoon, the towers, the domes, the clouds, the Palladian front of San Giorgio, all as pink and white, as airy, watery, clear, and neat as the bottles and puffs on her own dressing-table, she had taken the young man's arm and invited him to choose. "My dear, why do you see him? He is not our sort," she had said. "Life is too short. He will spoil Venice for you if you let him." The young man had simply stared. Mr. Sciarappa was a nuisance, but he felt no inclination to trade him for the Venetian "experience." The bargain was too sharp for his nature. If Mr. Sciarappa obstructed the European view he also replaced it. The mystery of Europe lay in him as solidly as in the stones of Venice, and it was somewhat less worn by previous inquisitive travelers. Night after night, he and the young lady would sit up examining Mr. Sciarappa with the refined passion of connoisseurs. It was true that sometimes at the dinner-hour they would try to give him the slip, yet they felt a certain relief whenever he rose from behind a potted plant in the hotel lobby to claim, once again, their company. He had become a problem for them in both senses of the word: the impossibility of talking *with* him was compensated for by the possibilities of talking about him, and the detachment of their attitude was, they felt, atoned for by their neighborliness in the physical sphere. How much, in fact, they had come to feel that they owed Mr. Sciarappa their company, they did not recognize until the afternoon, extraordinary to them, when he was not on hand to collect the debt.

The day of the fiesta he silently disappeared. Like everyone else in Venice he had been planning on the occasion. Colored lanterns had been attacked to the gondolas, floats were being decked, and rumors, gay as paper flowers, promised a night of license, masking, and folly. A party of English tourists was expected; Miss Grabbe was trying on eighteenth-century court costumes with the Communists across the Canal. Apparently, Mr. Sciarappa had set this as the date of his own liberation, for at the apéritif hour he was not to be seen, either at the hotel or, as he had stipulated, in the Piazza. The two friends connected his disappearance with the arrival of the English tourists, for at the first mention of their existence, his mind had ducked underground, into the tunnel where his real life was conducted. They had known him long enough to see him as a city of Catacombs, and to interpret his lapses of attention as signs of the keenest interest; his silences were the camouflaged entrances to the Plutonian realm of his thoughts. Nevertheless, they felt slightly shocked and abandoned. Like many intellectual people, they were alarmed by the confirmation of theories—was the world as small as the mind? They telephoned their hotel twice, but their friend had left no messages for them, and, disturbed, they allowed Miss Grabbe to go off with her maskers while they watched on the cold jetty the little gondolas chasing up and down the Canal in pursuit of the great floating orchestra which everybody had seen in the afternoon but which now, like Mr. Sciarappa, had unaccountably disappeared.

Some time later, they perceived Mr. Sciarappa alone in a gondola that was rapidly making for the pier. They would not have recognized him had he not called out effusively, "Ah, my friends, I am looking for you all over Venice tonight."

The full force of this lie was lost on them, for they were less astonished to find Scampi in a falsehood than to find him in a new suit. In dark blue and white stripes, he stepped out of the gondola; gold links gleamed at his wrists; his face was soft from the barbershop, and a strong fragrance of Chanel caused passers-by to turn to stare at them. The bluish-white glare from the dome of San Giorgio, lit up for the occasion, fell on him, accentuating the moment. The heavier material had added a certain substantiality to him; like the men in Harry's Bar, he looked sybaritic, prosperous, and vain. But this transfiguration was, it became clear, merely the afterglow of some hope that had already set for him. Wherever he had been, he had failed to accomplish his object, if indeed he had had an object beyond the vague adventure of a carnival night. He was more nervous than ever, and he invited them to join him on the Canal in the manner of a man who is weighing the security of companionship against the advantages of the lone hand. The two friends declined, and he put off once more in the gondola, saying, "Well, my dears, you are right; it is just a tourist fiesta." The two retired to their window to wonder whether the English tourists, and not themselves or Miss Grabbe, had not been, after all, the real Venetian attraction. The *Inglesi's* arrival might well have been anticipated in a newspaper, particularly since they had the reputation of being rich collectors of furniture. Mr. Sciarappa's restless behavior, irrational in a pursuer who has already come up with his prey, was appropriate enough to the boredom and anxiety of waiting. Indeed, sometimes, watching him drum on the table, they had said to themselves that he behaved toward them like a passenger who is detained between trains in a provincial railroad station and vainly tries to interest himself in the billboard and the ticket collector.

Miss Grabbe had taken very little part in all this mental excitement. So far as the two friends could see, he had no erotic interest for her. She was as adamant to his virility as he to the evidence of her money—it would have disturbed all her preconceptions to discover sex in a business suit. She received his disappearance calmly, saying, "I thought you wanted to get rid of him—he has probably found bigger fish." In general, after her first protest, she had grown accustomed to Mr. Sciarappa, in the manner of the rich.

For her he did not assume prominence through the frequency of his attendance, but on the contrary he receded into the surroundings in the fashion of a piece of furniture that is "lived with." She opened and closed him like a guidebook whenever she needed the name of a hotel or a hairdresser or had forgotten the Italian for what she wanted to say to the waiter. Having money, she had little real curiosity; she was not a dependent of the world. It did not occur to her to inquire why he had come, nor did she ask when he would leave. She too spoke of him as "Scampi," but tolerantly, without resentment, as nice women call a dog a rascal. She was not, despite appearances, a woman of strong convictions; she accepted any current situation as normative and was not anxious for change. Her money had made her insular; she was used to a mercenary circle and had no idea that outside it lovers showed affection, friends repaid kindness, and husbands did not ask an allowance or bring their mistresses home to bed. So now she accepted Mr. Sciarappa's dubious presence without particular question; it struck her as far less unnatural than the daily affection she witnessed between the young man and the young lady. She domesticated all the queerness of his being with them in Venice. "My dear," she remonstrated with the young man, "he simply wants to sell us something," dissipating Sciarappa as succinctly as if he had been a Fuller Brush man at the door. It irritated them slightly that she would not see the problem of Sciarappa, and they did not guess that now, when they had given up expecting it, she would grapple with their problem more matter-of-factly than they. While the two friends slept, through the night of the fiesta she and Mr. Sciarappa made love; when he departed, in dressing-gown and slippers, she thanked him "for a very pleasant evening."

Mr. Sciarappa, however, did not stay to cement the relationship. He left Venice precipitately, as though retreating ahead of Miss Grabbe's revelations. He was gone the next afternoon, without spoken adieus, leaving behind him a list of the second-best restaurants in Florence for the young lady, with an asterisk marking the ones where he was personally known to the headwaiter. "Unhappily," his note ran, "one cannot be on a holiday forever." On a final zigzag of policy he had careened away from them into the inexplicable. Now that he had declared himself in action, his motives seemed the more obscure. What, in fact, had he been up to? It was impossible to find out from Miss Grabbe, for to her mind sex went without explanations; it seemed to her perfectly ordinary that two strangers who were indifferent to each other should spend the night locked in the privacies of love.

Sitting up in bed, surrounded by hot-water bottles (for she had caught cold in her stomach), she received the two friends at tea-time and related her experiences of the night, using confession matter-of-factly, as a species of feminine hygiene, to disinfect her spirit of any lingering touch of the man. Scampi, she said, accepting the nickname from the young man as a kind of garment for the Italian gentleman, who seemed to stand there before them, shivering and slightly chicken-breasted in the nude, Scampi, she said, was very nice, but not in any way remarkable, the usual Italian man. He had taken her back from the fiesta, where the orchestra had never been found and she had grown tired of the painters, who looked ridiculous in costume when no one else was dressed. He had pinched her bottom on the Riva and undressed her on the balcony; they had tussled and gone to bed. Upon the cold stage of Miss Grabbe's bald narrative, he capered in and out like a grotesque, now naked, chasing her naked onto the balcony, now gorgeous in a silk dressing-gown and slippers tiptoeing down the corridor of the hotel, now correct in light tan pajamas dutifully, domestically, turning out the light. For a moment, they saw him all shrunken and wizened ("My dear, he is much older than you think," said Miss Grabbe confidentially), and another glimpse revealed him in an aspect still more intimate and terrible, tossing the scapular he wore about his neck, and which hung down and interfered with his love-making, back again and again, lightly, flippantly, recklessly, over his thin shoulder.

"Stop," cried the young lady, seizing the young man's hands and pressing them in an agony of repentance in her own bosom. "Does it shock you?" inquired Miss Grabbe, lifting her black eyebrows. "Darling, you *gave* me Sciarappa."

"No, no," begged the young lady, for it seemed to her that this was not at all what they had wanted, this mortal exposé, but that, on the contrary, they had had in mind something more sociological, more humane—biographical details, Mr. Sciarappa's relation with his parents, his social position, his business, his connection with the Fascist state. But of all this, of course, Miss Grabbe could tell them nothing. The poor Italian, hunted down, defenseless, surprised in bed by a party of intruders, had yielded nothing but his manhood. His motives, his status, his true public and social self, everything that the young lady now called "the really interesting part about him," he had carried off with him to Rome intact. He was gone and had left them with his skin, withered, dry, unexpectedly old. Through Miss Grabbe, they had come as close to him bodily as the laws of nature permit, and there at the core there was nothing—they had known him better in the Galleria in Milan. As for the affective side of him, the emotions and sentiments, here too he had eluded them. Miss Grabbe's net had been too coarse to catch whatever small feelings had escaped him during the encounter.

A sense of desolation descended on the room, the usual price of confidences. It was a relief when one of the Communist painters came in with some lira, which Miss Grabbe put in her douche-bag. The two friends exchanged a glance of illumination. Had this repository for his country's debased currency proved too casual for Mr. Sciarappa's sense of honor? Was this the cause of his flight? If so, was it the lira or his manhood that was insulted? Or were the two, in the end, indistinguishable?

The two friends could never be sure, and when they left Venice shortly afterwards they were still debating whether some tactlessness of Miss Grabbe's had set Scampi at last in motion or whether his own action, by committing him for an hour or so, had terrified him into instant removal. He was a theoretician of practice so pure, they said to each other on the bus, that any action must appear to him as folly because of the risks to his shrewdness that it involved, a man so worldly that he saw the world as a lie too transparent to fool Rino Sciarappa, who was clever and knew the ropes. As they passed through the bony Apennines, the landscape itself seemed to wear a face baked and disabused as Mr. Sciarappa's own, and thus to give their theories a geological and national cast. The terraced fields lay scorched, like Mr. Sciarappa's wrinkles, on the gaunt umber-colored hillsides; like his vernal hopes, plants sprang up only to die here, and the land had the mark of wisdom—it too had seen life. After these reflections, it was a little anticlimactic to meet, half an hour after their arrival in Florence, the face of Italian history, whose destination had been announced as Rome. "He is following us, but he is ahead," said the young man, abandoning historical explanations forever. Only one conclusion seemed possible—he must be a spy.

In Florence, at any rate, he appeared to be acquainted; he introduced them to a number of American girls who worked in United States offices and to one or two young men who wore American uniforms. All of these people, as he had once promised them in Venice, called him by his first name; yet when the dinner-hour drew near the whole party vanished as agilely as Mr. Sciarappa, and the two friends found themselves once more going to his favorite restaurant, drinking his favorite wine, and being snubbed first by the waiter and then by their impatient guide. If he was a spy, however, his superiors must at last have given him a new assignment, for the next day he left Florence, not without giving the young lady his restaurant key to Rome.

In Rome, curiosity led them, at long last, and with some reluctance, to investigate his address, which he had written out in the young lady's address book long ago, on the train, outside Domodossola, when their acquaintance had promised to be of somewhat shorter duration. As their steps turned into the dusty Via San Ignazio, they felt their hearts quicken. The European enigma and its architectural solution lay just before them, around a bend in the street, and they still, in spite of everything, should not have been surprised to find a renaissance palace, a coat of arms, and a liveried manservant just inside the door. But the house was plain and shabby; it was impossible to conceive of Mr. Sciarappa's gabardines proceeding deftly through the entrance. Looking at this yellow house, at the unshaven tenant in his undershirt regarding them from the third-story window, and the mattress and the geranium in the fourth, the two friends felt a return of that mortification and unseemly embarrassment they had experienced in Miss Grabbe's bedroom. This house too was an obscenity, like the shrunken skin and the scapular, but it also was a shell which Rino Sciarappa did not truly inhabit. By common consent, they turned silently away from it, with a certain distaste which, oddly enough, was not directed at Mr. Sciarappa or his residence, but, momentarily, at each other. The relation between pursuer and pursued had been confounded, by a dialectic too subtle for their eyes.

THE ARID PLAIN
OF "THE CICERONE"

Barbara McKenzie

"English, surely," the young American lady says, eying the "tall, straw-colored" stranger who stood smoking in the corridor of the *wagon-lit*. Unconvinced, her companion concedes, "If English, then a bounder." Their conversation continues "in an agreeable rattle-rattle" as they discuss the problems of detecting "a bounder in a foreign country." Thus Mary McCarthy begins her story about two young Americans (unnamed and unmarried) traveling together in Europe shortly after the end of World War II. For the most part, she writes from an inside point of view, using as her narrative focus the double consciousness of the American couple. Yet, in reality, this double consciousness is single. Different in their characteristic external responses, the young Americans are basically alike, having come "to think in unison" and needing "the spoken word only for a check."

Intrigued by Europe, they are also puzzled and challenged by its mystery. Although they are tourists and are ostensibly traveling in Italy for pleasure, the couple is determined to penetrate the "Continental standards" that they sense as "mysteriously different" and even, although they question their own seriousness, "to get into European society." Architecture, they believe, provides "the most solid answer to their social curiosity." Thus they seek to understand the Sforzas "through the agency of their Castello" and "to know the Pisani" by visiting Stra, on the Brenta. Putting great stock in appearances, they find their penchant for categorizing thwarted by upper-class Europeans who, trying "to dress like English gentlemen," strike "the inevitable false notes."

But "The Cicerone" is less about the adventures of two Americans in search of Europe than it is about American attitudes toward the Continent. To dramatize this wider purpose, Miss McCarthy uses Rino Sciarappa, the cicerone, and introduces a third American, Polly Grabbe. Basic to the symbolic structure of the story is the assumption that Sciarappa is the personification of post-war Europe. "The mystery of Europe lay in him as solidly as in the stones of Venice, and it was somewhat less worn by previous in-

quisitive travelers." To the American couple, the Italian is "a city of Catacombs" whose "real life" is conducted in the "tunnel" of his mind. The
cicerone's appearance underscores his identification with Europe—in particular, post-war Italy. His slenderness is cadaverous and his quick and light
movements, effete. He reminds the young lady and young man "of that
horror so often met in Paris, city of beauty, the well-preserved woman in
her fifties." Even "the terraced fields" are "like Mr. Sciarappa's wrinkles."
Moreover, the land bears "the mark of wisdom—it too had seen life." The
different ways in which the young American couple and Miss Grabbe relate to Sciarappa clarify different but similar American attitudes toward
Europe. Conversely, the disbelieving and contemptuous Italian expresses a
conventional attitude of Europe toward America: "'Ah, you Americans,'"
he remarks, "'your streets are paved with dollars.'"

Like Rino Sciarappa, the young American couple behaves in a manner
that, similar to "the young lady's large black hat, long gloves, high-heeled
shoes, and nylon stockings," acts as "a declaration of nationality." The
young man who walks "proudly on the dilapidated streets of Europe" is un-
abashedly curious. Little interested in people's opinions or in their emotions, he is "passionately, madly curious as to what people did and how they
made their money." Uneasy in "his small role as war-profiteer," he nonetheless avoids the black market in favor of cashing "his checks at the regular
rate at the bank" for only a single week. The young lady shares the in-
quisitiveness of her companion. An active verbalizer, she is adept at label-
ing sentiments, at dissecting shades of feeling, of making subtle distinctions. She is both aggressive and gullible. Being gregarious, she "took the
kindest view of everyone" and believed that "she was the only person in the
world who told lies."

The relationship that develops between Rino Sciarappa and the two
Americans is as deserved as it is bizarre. Since the narrator does not enter
the Italian's mind, the Italian is an enigma not only to the young man and
young lady but to the reader as well. Stymied by the cicerone's uncertain
grasp of English syntax, the Americans seek to ascertain his place in the
social hierarchy and thereby to "understand" Europe not through what he
says but through more tangible, external means. But neither his appearance nor his professed occupation allows them to turn him into a demon-
strable abstraction. Equally unknowable are his reasons for staying with
them in the role of cicerone.

The term "cicerone" derives from the name of the Roman orator Cicero
and refers to his learning or eloquence. It was first applied to learned Italian antiquarians whose function was to provide visitors with information

about the antiquities of a place. Subsequently, the meaning was widened to include ordinary professional guides. But in neither the original nor the later sense is Sciarappa a cicerone, and herein lies the central irony of the story at its literal and satirical levels. Not valuing the art treasures of Italy and, in fact, not valuing post-war Italy, he cannot credit tourism as a legitimate motive for the Americans' being in Italy any more than he can credit as honest their enthusiastic response to Italy's art objects and buildings: "it was as if the devaluation of the currency had, for Mr. Sciarappa's consistent thought, implicated everything Italian; cathedrals, pictures, women had dropped with the lira." Further, since cathedrals, works of art, museums, and palaces maintained by the state were free to all, Sciarappa considers them as valuable to none. Equally peculiar—for a guide—is the "one solid trait" that the two Americans discover in his character, his "rooted abhorrence of the advertised first-rate, of best hotels, top restaurants, principal shopping streets, famous vineyards." In an interplay of internal emotions and external forces, Miss McCarthy balances Sciarappa against the Americans. Neither the Italian nor the Americans can assign each other to a social class. The young man and young lady sense that Sciarappa believes himself to be the victim of an imposture. "But did he believe that they were rich pretending to be poor, or poor pretending to be rich? They could not tell." Their partial understanding of the Italian's hostility does not preclude their lessening sympathy toward him and their increasing impatience at devoting evenings to a "stranger who was continually out of sorts because he could not make up his mind whether they were worth swindling." Later, in Venice, they find themselves in the same kind of situation: "He had become a problem for them in both senses of the word: the impossibility of talking *with* him was compensated for by the possibilities of talking about him, and the detachment of their attitude was, they felt, atoned for by their neighborliness in the physical sphere."

This kind of balancing, this interplay between abhorrence and attraction, supply and demand, is apparent in other short stories by Miss McCarthy. In "The Genial Host," for example, Margaret Sargent realizes that she exists in a strange symbiotic relationship with Pflaumen the host. His price for providing dinner parties where she meets eligible young men is that she inform him of resulting emotional liaisons. In "The Friend of the Family," the husband and wife discover the usefulness of the unobtrusive and dull Francis Cleary. His company is not sprightly but neither is it demanding or upsetting, and thus they find themselves cultivating this mutually satisfactory friend, even to the point of wooing him in order to maintain the delicate balance of their own social relationship. Further evidence can be found in "The Weeds," where the wife, after trying to break away from her husband and start a new life in New York City, returns to her husband, defeated by the inevitable changes that five years have wrought in herself, her friends, and the social patterns she had known as a single woman. Modifying her demands, she goes back to her insensitive and dogmatic husband because she needs the structured situation he offers her.

In a similar way, the Americans find themselves drawn to the distrustful and uncommunicative cicerone, despite the absence of a common meeting ground. In fact, they need him precisely because he is different from them, for they sense the mystery of Europe in his enigmatic disaffection. If they can understand Sciarappa, they reason, they can understand Europe. Consequently they try to coax the Italian "out into the open." Their bait is Polly Grabbe, a "middling but authentically rich" American whom they are to meet in Venice. Well known for her semi-annual pilgrimages to Europe in search of love and for her collection of garden statuary, the flower-bulb heiress provides a means for them to trap Sciarappa into revealing himself. If he wishes money, Polly Grabbe has enough to precipitate him into some decisive action. If he seeks a mistress, Miss Grabbe is accessible.

But the relationship that develops between Sciarappa and the American heiress fails to reveal the inner nature of the Italian. Shrewd and flighty, relentless in her search for experience and lenient in her judgments of men, Miss Grabbe fails to provoke the cicerone into disclosing his motivation. Throughout, Polly Grabbe refuses to see anything transcendent about the man and interprets his behavior on the basis of her own limitations. Instead of seeing "the problem of Sciarappa," she warns the Americans that he will spoil Venice for them. Commenting on Sciarappa's disappearance on the day of the fiesta, she says, " 'I thought you wanted to get rid of him—he has probably found bigger fish.' " At another time, she tells the young man, " 'My dear, he simply wants to sell us something.' "

It is inevitable, therefore, that she should relate to Sciarappa in her own way—as a convenient directory of people and places and, finally, as a lover. Her graphic confession after a night of lovemaking (" 'he is much older than you think' ") dramatizes the polarities between her and the young Americans. The young lady begs her to stop because she knows that "this mortal exposé" is not what they had wanted; "on the contrary, they had had in mind something more sociological, more humane—biographical details, Mr. Sciarappa's relation with his parents, his social position, his business, his connection with the Fascist state." The revelation of Miss Grabbe yields only an image of Sciarappa "hunted down, defenseless, surprised in bed by a party of intruders." The motives, status, and true public self of the Italian—" 'the really interesting part about him' "—continue to elude them.

As they travel to Florence, they note that the "landscape itself seemed to wear a face baked and disabused as Mr. Sciarappa's own." Geography and man merge when they unexpectedly encounter the cicerone in Florence. Baffled, the young man admits, " 'He is following us, but he is ahead.' " In Rome, where their persistent curiosity causes them to "investigate" the address of the Italian, they do so with quickened expectation. "The European enigma and its architectural solution lay just before them, around a bend in the street." Their discovery that his house is "plain and shabby" makes them feel as mortified and embarrassed as when they had listened to Polly Grabbe's confession. "This house too was an obscenity, like the shrunken skin and the scapular, but it was also a shell which Rino Sciarappa did not truly inhabit." Their shame causes them to turn away, aware that "the relation between pursuer and pursued had been confounded, by a dialectic too subtle for their eyes."

What has happened is that their net—architecture—is, like Miss Grabbe's, "too coarse to catch" the mystery of the Italian. The distaste the American couple feels for each other is really an objectifying of what each finds repugnant in himself. In their alikeness, each is subdued by the grossness he sees reflected in the other person. Thus the story folds back on itself, and the two Americans are again standing at a distance from the secrets of Europe, reduced, at least momentarily, from their hopeful curiosity on the *wagons-lits* or their naive, optimistic belief that someone would "discover them in this dark continent."

The dialectic that confounds the relation between pursuer and pursued has to do with the interchangeability of the two entities. Ostensibly Sciarappa is the pursuer. The American couple and Miss Grabbe see him as wanting something from them. What the young lady and young man discover is that they are also pursuers in a pursuit externalized by their image of the cicerone "hunted down" in Miss Grabbe's bed, by their finding him waiting for them in Florence, and by their "investigation" of his residence in Rome. The dialectic resulting from this exchange of roles is indeed too subtle for their eyes to detect. Externals such as houses and clothes are forever incapable of explaining an entity as elusive as Rino Sciarappa, who had, quite literally, "careened away from them into the inexplicable."

The conclusion of "The Cicerone" makes the formal design of the story apparent. It began with the two young Americans, opened to include Rino

Sciarappa (as the first sentence suggested), and then widened to encompass the flower-bulb heiress. After this relative fullness, the story closed in on itself again, finally returning to the isolated consciousness of the American couple. Such formal balancing of plot and characters parallels and enhances the delicate balance of the social relationships that form the story's content.

In commenting on her technique as a writer, Mary McCarthy has said, "With characters, I do try at least to be as exact as possible about the essence of a person, to find the key that works the person both in real life and in the fiction." Yet, despite scrupulous delineation of dress (Miss Grabbe's and the young lady's "costumes"), history (Miss Grabbe's past), mannerisms (the young man's unleashed hilarity), subtleties of feeling (the young lady is a "specialist in sentiments"), the reader remains at considerable psychic distance from the characters. This "gulf" is inevitable in the case of Polly Grabbe and the cicerone—characters whose consciousnesses are closed to us. But we are removed even from those characters whose perceptions serve as narrative focus—the young couple. This separation is widened by Miss McCarthy's failure to name her central characters: They are anonymous Americans of cultivated sensibility.

As a fiction writer, however, Miss McCarthy most often bases her characters on persons whom she has known. The facts of her life frequently supply the "facts" of her fiction. Many knowledgeable readers have noted the similarities between Mary McCarthy and the young lady, Miss McCarthy's third husband and the young man, and a famous real-life American heiress and Polly Grabbe. It is as though by drawing them from real-life models Miss McCarthy *assumes* their "life-likeness" in fiction. In truth, however, the characters in "The Cicerone" are little more than two-dimensional puppets maneuvered into place by the author. A consequence of their "flatness," of the *manner* in which they are made "real," is their distance from us. In turn, this distance compounds our lack of sympathy toward them.

Ironically, the "person" we are closest to in "The Cicerone" is the implied author—that is, the image of Mary McCarthy we construct from reading the story. In the first paragraph, it is Miss McCarthy (not the young man or young woman) who compares Sciarappa to "an English cigarette," finding that the Italian bears "the same relation to a man that a Gold Flake bears to a normal cigarette." In this same paragraph, it is Miss McCarthy, again speaking directly through her narrator, who likens the young man's eyes to "strange green headlights on an old-fashioned car."

Throughout the story, various similes, metaphors, allusions, and turns of phrase come not from the characters but, unfiltered, from the narrator who, serving as the author's agent, displays her brilliant command of language.

Yet Miss McCarthy's unwillingness or inability to create round, sympathetic characters is basic to her method and purpose as a writer. Fundamental to her intention is the depiction of characters that are representative types as well as singular entities. Her ability to see and describe generically is partly responsible for her ability to write satirically. In "The Cicerone," the Americans and Sciarappa are satirical portraits of representative types. Concomitantly, satire allows Miss McCarthy to accomplish her larger social purpose in this story.

For through Sciarappa and the Americans she is embodying national attributes and attitudes. Parasitic, unyielding, and nervous, Rino Sciarappa *is* Europe. Remember Polly Grabbe's confession, " 'My dear, he is much older than you think.' " He is also faded and secretive. To the Americans, he is "the face of Italian history." Even his purposelessness, his lack of occupation, identifies him with a Europe recovering from a devastating war. Polly Grabbe and her flower-bulb fortune represent more than American materialism, vulgarity, and artistic pretension. Quite literally, Polly Grabbe "grabs" at Europe through the agency of the cicerone. Accepting Sciarappa as a lover, she causes him to strip himself physically in a gesture that parallels her requisitioning of Europe's art treasures. The young American couple wants to strip Europe spiritually and intellectually, but, in their persistence, they are as gross as Miss Grabbe. The tone-deaf young man and the gullible young lady differ in kind but not degree from the heiress in their quest to understand the social hierarchy and heritage of Europe and to lay bare its spiritual essence. That they fail with Sciarappa is symptomatic of their larger failure.

The life depicted in "The Cicerone" is bleak and hopeless. In many ways, the war-torn, humbled, unyielding Europe Miss McCarthy describes has echoes of T. S. Eliot's "The Waste Land," which also imagizes a parched and barren land. Like Eliot's personages, the young Americans are dry and sterile people who intellectualize their experience as they attempt, unsuccessfully, to intellectualize Europe and its mystery. In the manner of the inhabitants of "The Waste Land," they have lost touch with the past and cannot participate in its rituals, as their inability to share in the bacchanalian experience of the fiesta suggests. Paralleling Eliot's poem, the failure in sexual relationships in "The Cicerone" suggests the malaise of the wider society. Having recognized the disadvantages of traveling together—

"('My dear,' said the young lady, 'a couple looks so complete')"—the young Americans accept their "handicap" like "the best jockey" in a horse race who "scorns to take a lighter weight." Although Rino Sciarappa gives himself to Polly Grabbe in a night of adequate though not extraordinary lovemaking, he rejuvenates neither himself nor his partner. Instead, he leaves Venice the next morning, offering as a reminder of himself a list of second-best restaurants and hotels. That Polly Grabbe stores the devalued currency of Italy in her douche-bag is a fitting and final symbol for all that is incongruous and debased in the arid plain of "The Cicerone."

QUESTIONS

The Cicerone

POINT OF VIEW 1. That the story is being told by a restricted narrator who focuses on the consciousnesses of the American couple is apparent in such statements as "But, just as it had come as a surprise to him that love should go on from step to step, that it should move from city to country and cross an ocean and part of a continent, so in Milan it was with a vague astonishment that he beheld Mr. Sciarappa remove his baggage from the taxi in front of their hotel and hurry inside ahead of him to inquire for a room." As mentioned in the essay, however, the narrator frequently makes objective statements that come from the "author" and not from the characters. For example, "The desire to believe the best of people is a prerequisite for intercourse with strangers; suspicion is reserved for friends." Cite at least three other places in the story where the narrator inserts similar epigrams. What attitudes does the implied author communicate through such statements? In particular, how is your response to the young man and young woman shaped by these statements?

CHARACTERS 2. If it is possible to contend that the Americans seek to understand Europe by understanding Sciarappa, is it also possible to say that Sciarappa seeks to understand his own country through understanding the Americans? Why do you suppose the Italian chose to stay with the Americans as long as he did? 3. At one point in the story, the narrator refers to Polly Grabbe as "a really good example of the genre" of a "middlingly but authentically rich" American. Thus the American heiress can be considered an exhibition of Mary McCarthy's skill as a satirist and her stance as a short-story writer. Discuss this statement, taking into account the brief "inside" view of Miss Grabbe and the lavish similes and metaphors that occur in the "set-piece" descriptions.

PLOT 4. Although the narrative structure of "The Cicerone" consists of a series of episodes (in the manner of all narratives that embody a journey), the story is nonetheless unified. Discuss the various ways in which McCarthy has created a coherent story. 5. Foreshadowing occurs throughout the narrative. Even the first sentence, "When they first met him, in the *wagons-lits*, he was not so nervous," hints that, in later meetings, the Italian will become increasingly nervous. Find at least three other examples of foreshadowing. Does foreshadowing serve any esthetic function? 6. The rather lengthy description of the events that occur at Domodossola is neither padding nor a digression. What insights into the young man and young lady are revealed through this episode? How does this episode contribute to your understanding of the story as a whole?

SETTING 7. Mary McCarthy describes Venice more graphically than she does Milan, Florence, or Rome. Examine how she depicts Venice so that this particular Italian city becomes vivid to the reader. In particular, examine her use of sense imagery and allusions.

STYLE 8. Throughout the story, there are many references to money. For example, "There was no door, therefore, that, they believed, would not open to them should they present themselves fresh and crisp as two one-dollar bills." Find as many other literal and figurative references to money as you can. How do these references affect the meaning of the story? 9. Does Sciarappa's professed occupation have any symbolic significance?

TONE 10. What is ironic about the title? 11. The story makes very little use of direct dialogue. Accordingly, we seldom perceive the characters directly as they speak to each other in their own voices. Most often, our sense of the characters comes from indirect discourse and extended description. In the main, we feel and perceive as Mary McCarthy feels and perceives. How does this distance and the resulting decrease in our sympathy for the characters shape the theme of the story?

The Arid Plain of "The Cicerone"

FOCUS 1. In what ways (if any) do the first and second paragraphs prepare you for a statement of the essay's thesis in paragraph three? 2. As mentioned in the General Introduction, technique (in the sense Mark Schorer uses that term) provides an important means of discovery—a means of revealing the "meaning" of a short story. Find at least three instances where the essayist uses fictional technique to discover meaning.

ORGANIZATION   3. After the introductory material and the discussion of the events of the story (pp. 96-100), the essay reaches what could be a logical conclusion. But instead of stopping, it takes a new turn. Is this new turn related to the essay's focus? Or is it unrelated, causing the essay to be disunified? Explain.   4. In one sense, the discussion (pp. 98-99) of stories by Mary McCarthy other than "The Cicerone" is an interruption, for it breaks into the explanation of the plot and characters of "The Cicerone." Is there any justification for this interruption? What does it contribute to the essay as a whole?

USING THE EVIDENCE   5. The essay contends that "the Americans and Sciarappa are satirical portraits of representative types." Can you find evidence in the story to support this contention? Is there any justification for the essayist not developing this observation in the essay?   6. How does the essay support the contention that the "double consciousness" of the young man and young lady is, in reality, "single"? From your reading of the story, can you find additional evidence to support or contradict this interpretation?   7. In response to the Americans' finding Sciarappa's house "a shell" that he "did not truly inhabit," the essay states that "Externals such as houses and clothes are forever incapable of explaining an entity as elusive as Rino Sciarappa." Is it possible to argue that the young Americans are *unwilling* to accept what the house says about Sciarappa and that what the house and other externals represent might, indeed, be close to the mark? Has the essay ignored any evidence from the story that would support this contention? How would such an interpretation alter the essay's analysis of the young man and the young lady?

STYLE   8. Discuss the appropriateness (or inappropriateness) of the allusions to "The Waste Land" in the concluding paragraphs of the essay.

MAKING LITERARY JUDGMENTS   9. In saying that "The Cicerone" is "less about the adventures of two Americans in search of Europe than it is about American attitudes toward the Continent," the essay indicates that the story is concerned more with ideas than with characters. Do you agree that the story is idea-centered?   10. The essay describes the characters in "The Cicerone" as two-dimensional figures despite the wealth of knowledge we possess about their appearance and feelings. Yet the essay finds this "flatness" suitable to McCarthy's purposes. Discuss the validity of this observation.

THE UNSPOILED
REACTION

In the theater lobby everyone at first mistook her for another patron (a grandmother, perhaps), though the fact that she wore an unstylish close-fitting hat, antique earrings, and no coat and had a generally anxious, false, and flustered air should have announced her status: she was a hostess, or, rather, one of those *entrepreneuses* masquerading as hostesses who are inevitably associated with benefits, club luncheons, lectures, alumnae teas, with all gatherings whose intention is not primarily pleasure.

Here, in the theater, on a rainy Monday morning, she was an anomaly, for in New York, in the Times Square neighborhood, relations between management and customer are, by common consent, austerely professional. Consequently her intervention at the door came as a perceptible shock to each parent and child; it demanded a slight adjustment of focus. "Haven't we seen you before?" She addressed the child, and the face that turned up to her in each case showed bewilderment and pleasure. Only a moment before, the child had been an anonymous consumer bent on mass gratification; this magic question turned him back into his human self, and the child, unless he were totally hardened, blushed.

"What is your name?" the lady continued, and now even the parent was drawn in and smiled tenderly, sharing for an instant with this unknown but plainly intuitive person the holy miracle of his child's identity. Sometimes the children answered, speaking their own names softly, with reverence; more often, shyness and delight held them tongue-tied, and the parent supplied the information. "It's for Sunny," the lady added, in a sort of whispered nudge at the parent, who came to himself with a start. The explanation, if it told him nothing else (who or what was Sunny, anyway?), told him unmistakably that he had been a fool just now—he ought to have suspected the utilitarian motive. Angry and disillusioned, he passed into the poorly lit auditorium, the remnants of the smile, the fond, fatuous smile, still tugging at the corners of his mouth.

But at once the sight of so many empty places (hardly twenty persons were seated in a cluster down in front) brought a sentiment of pity for the woman outside. Clearly, these puppeteers were in a bad way; not even the rain, not even Monday, not even the too high price of admission, could explain or palliate the smallness of the house. An air of failure hung over the whole undertaking, infecting the audience itself with the poison of financial sickness, so that even the most healthy, the most fortunate parents and children, sitting there in little groups in the bad light, with the dismal smell of damp wool and dead cigarettes all about them, had the look of derelicts huddled together.

So strong indeed was the sense of misery that the more sensitive parents felt an impulse to remove their children from this house of death and were only prevented by the practical difficulties (how to explain?) and by the habit of chivalry toward the poor and ill-favored. If the rat does *not* leave the sinking ship, his only recourse is to identify himself with its fortunes; so the parents, having committed themselves to this unhappy enterprise, immediately experienced the symptoms of solidarity. They began to tell themselves that the attendance could have been worse (after all, it *was* Monday and it *was* raining), to clock off each new arrival with a feeling of personal triumph, and finally to lean forward in their seats and will people into the theater as passengers in a decrepit car lean forward to will the car up a long grade. *converts*

These exercises in kinesthetic magic, in which, from their clenched fists and closed eyes, one would say nearly the whole audience was engaging, were cut short by another woman, younger and more openly managerial than the first, a progressive school teacher in genus if not in actuality, one accustomed to giving orders in the form of requests. "Will you please take an outside seat?" she said, leaning over and tapping surprised parents on the shoulder.

Some mothers and fathers did as they were bid at once, almost apologetically. Others were slow and showed even a certain disposition to stand on their rights. Still others (the most well-fed and polished) pretended not to hear. "This does not apply to me," their deaf backs declared.

When it became plain that she was not going to be obeyed without further explanation (for her little air of authority had stirred up latent antagonism in an audience which had disposed itself to pity but not to be ruled by her), she walked down an empty row and took hold of the back of a seat, in the manner of an informal lecturer. "We like to have the children together in the middle," she announced with that excess of patience that suggests that patience is really out of place. "These puppet plays are intended for *children*. We want to reach the children as a group. We want them to be free of adult influences. We want an unspoiled reaction."

This fetched even the most stubborn, for it hinted to every adult in the audience that he was the snake in this paradise of innocence, that there was something intrinsically disgusting in the condition of being grown-up. There was a great shuffling of coats, hats, and handbags. Mothers dropped packages on the floor, a little girl cried, but at length the resettlement was accomplished, and the sheep were separated from the goats.

Whenever a new party came in, the earlier arrivals would, out of a kind of concerted malice, allow the parent to get herself well lodged in the center block of seats before breaking it to her that she was out of place. Indeed, the greater part of the audience was disinclined to make the revelation at all; its original feelings of mistrust had returned; it saw something ugly in this arbitrary manipulation of the natural order of seating, this planned spontaneity. Though it looked forward to the confounding of the newcomer, it would not take the side of the management; in an attitude of passive hooliganism it waited for the dark.

But disaffected as it was, the audience contained the inevitable minority of enthusiastic coöperators who rejoice in obeying with ostentatious promptness any command whatsoever, who worship all signs, prohibitions, warnings, and who constitute themselves volunteer deputies of any official person they can find in their neighborhood. These coöperators nudged, tapped, poked, signaled, relayed admonitory whispers along rows of children, until every misplaced adult became conscious of the impropriety of his position and retreated, in confusion, to the perimeter of the house. By the time the curtain went up, the adults formed three sides of a box which contained the children but left the cover open to receive the influences of the stage.

Almost at once the object of the first lady's question became apparent. Laboriously, the curtains of the miniature stage parted and an unusually small puppet, dressed as a boy, was revealed, bowing and dancing in a veritable tantrum of welcome. This was Sunny. "Hello, boys and girls," he began in the shrieky voice that is considered *de rigueur* for puppets and marionettes. "Welcome to our theater." "Hello, Sunny," replied a self-assured child, patently the son of one of the coöperators. He had been here before, and he did what was expected of him. "Hello, John, how are you today?" the puppet screamed in answer, and now he passed from child to child, speaking to each by name.

The children, for the most part, looked at each other in wonder and astonishment. They were at a loss to account for the puppet's knowing them; they did not relate cause and effect and doubtless had already forgotten the question and answer in the lobby. After the first consternation, the voices that answered the gesticulating creature grew louder and firmer. The children were participating. Each one was anxious to show himself more at home than his neighbor, and soon they were treating the puppet with positive familiarity, which he encouraged, greeting every bold remark from the audience with peals of shrill artificial laughter. Before the actual play began he had drawn all but the very youngest and shyest into an atmosphere of audacity.

Along the sides of the human box, the parents were breathing easier. Gladly they divested themselves of their original doubts. It was enough that the children were entering into the spirit of the thing. That reciprocity between player and audience, lost to us since the medieval mysteries, and mourned by every theoretician of the drama, was here recovered, and what did it matter if the production was a mockery, a cartoon of the art of drama? What did it matter that the children's innocence had been taken advantage of, that the puppet who seemed to know them knew only their names? And as for the seating arrangements, perhaps in the modern world all spontaneity had to be planned; as with crop control and sex, the "unspoiled reaction" did not come of itself; it was the end-product of a series of maneuvers.

The curtains closed on Sunny, with the children yelling, "Good-bye." The main attraction, "Little Red Riding Hood," was about to begin, when a party of late-comers made its way down the aisle. There were eight or ten children and a dispirited-looking young teacher. They took places in the very first row and were a little slow getting seated. The children kept changing places, and the teacher was either ineffectual or a principled anti-disciplinarian, for she made no real effort to interpose her authority.

The curtains on the stage above them moved, as if with impatience, and a human hand and then a face, grotesquely enlarged to eyes adjusted to the scale of puppets, appeared and then quickly withdrew. This apparition was terrifying to everyone but those for whom it was intended, the school of children in front, who had as yet no standard of comparison and continued their bickering unperturbed. The face had come and gone so abruptly that nobody could be sure whether it belonged to a man or a woman; it left the audience with a mere sense of some disembodied anger—a deity was displeased. Could this be Sunny? the parents wondered.

At length, the party in the front row composed itself. Little Red Riding Hood and her basket were revealed as the curtains lurched back. To the left of the puppet stage, a little box opened, and there was Sunny, ready with a prologue, adjuring the children to watch out for Little Red Riding Hood as if she were their own little sister. The box closed, the action began, and the children took Sunny at his word. From the house a series of warnings and prophecies of disaster followed the little red puppet out its door. "Look out," the children called. "Don't obey your Mummy." "Eat the basket yourself."

In all these admonitions none were louder than the party in the front row. These children, indeed, appeared to be the ideal audience for Sunny and his troupe; they were the unspoiled reaction in test-tube purity. While other boys and girls hung back, murmured their comments, or simply parroted the cries of the bolder children, the ones down in front were inventive and various in their advice—so much so that it seemed hardly possible that the play could go on without the actors' taking cognizance of what these untrammeled children were saying, and one almost expected Little Red Riding Hood to sail off from her lines into pure improvisation, and a kind of *commedia dell' arte* to ensue. But the puppets kept rigidly to the text, oblivious of interruptions and suggestions, and the usual situation was reversed—it was not the audience which was unresponsive but the players.

By the middle of the second scene, when the wolf had made his appearance, the whole theater was in a condition of wild excitement. Some children were taking the side of the wolf, urging him to make a good dinner, and some, traditionalists even in unrestraint, remained loyal to the grandmother. The contest on the stage was transported into the pit.

*

At the end of the second scene, Sunny came out once more, and now the boldness of the children perfectly matched the provocations of the puppet. Saucy answer met impudent question. Sunny was beside himself; from time to time, a witticism from the house would capsize him altogether and he would lie panting on the stage, gasping out the last exhausted notes of the hee-hee-hee. Liberty and equality reached such a pitch of frenzy that it seemed the most natural thing in the world that a boy from the front row should climb up onto the stage to speak directly to Sunny.

The audience watched him go without the slightest sense of a breach of decorum. The puppet, however, drew back into his box at the approach of the child. Slowly, his cloth body began to wriggle and twist in an uncanny pantomine of distaste and fear. The child put out his hand to touch the puppet, and now the doll was indubitably alive. A shudder ran through it; it shrank back against the curtains and doubled itself up, as though to leave no intimate surface exposed to the violator's touch.

As the hand still pursued and it seemed as if no power on earth could prevent the approaching indignity, the puppet cried out. But its voice had changed; the falsetto shriek had become a human scream. "Sunny doesn't like that," called an agonized woman's voice from behind the curtain. The note of hysteria struck home to the boy, separating him from his intention. He leaped back, stumbled toward the stairs, slipped on them, and fell into the orchestra pit. Two of the fathers rushed forward. The teacher joined them, peering anxiously over the brink. The child was retrieved, unhurt, and firmly put back into his seat. In the commotion, Sunny had disappeared.

Fortunately, the children hardly missed him. For the moment, they were more interested in the mechanics of the little boy's fall than in its cause. "What is an orchestra pit?" they called out to the mothers who had tried to explain, and some got out of their seats, proposing to investigate. "Afterwards, afterwards," the mothers' voices ordered. "The show is going to begin again."

But was it? The parents, glancing at each other, wondered. Had they not witnessed, just now, one of those ruptures which are instantly and irrevocably permanent, since they reveal an aversion so profound that no beginning, i.e., no cause can be assigned to it, and hence no end, no solution can be predicted? Like guests sitting around a dinner table which the hostess has just quitted to pack her trunk in a fury, the parents fidgeted, waiting for a sign which would tell them that it was not really necessary to go home to meet again the emptiness of their own devices, yet knowing perfectly well that the only thing to do was to go and go at once, before anything else happened. But inertia, the great minimizer, provided them with the usual excuses. They told themselves that they were letting their imaginations run away with them, that nothing of any consequence had happened—an incompetent teacher had let her charge misbehave.

And as the minutes passed and the curtains did not move, the sentiment of the audience turned sharply against the teacher. "Damn fool of a woman," murmured the father of a boy to the pretty mother of a girl. "I certainly wouldn't send a child to *her* school," replied the mother, brightening up. As if aware of the whispers of criticism, the teacher stiffened in her seat and stared blindly forward, feigning unconsciousness.

In the middle of the house, the children were also turning the experience over, clumsily trying to fix the blame, but they were not so adroit, so practiced as their parents, and small frowns of dissatisfaction wrinkled their brows. "Was that little boy naughty?" called a little girl's voice, at last. "Yes," answered her mother, without a moment's hesitation. "Oh," said the little girl, but her look remained troubled.

"And *now*, boys and girls—" It was Sunny, cordial as ever, and the third scene was about to start. There was no doubt that the puppet was himself again; he bowed, he clapped his hands, he danced, he screeched, in his old dionysiac style. Bygones were bygones, all was forgiven, childhood was off on another spree.

Yet the children at first were wary and glanced toward their parents, seeking instruction, for they no longer knew what was expected of them. The parents nodded encouragement, and as the children still hesitated, the adults screwed their own faces into grimaces of pleasure, till everywhere the children looked, on the sides of the audience or, above them, on the stage, there was a large, energetic smile bidding them enjoy themselves. The more docile children began to laugh, rather mechanically; others joined in, and in a few moments the crisis was past and the mood of abandon tentatively re-established. The play proceeded, and before long the children were barking and howling like wolves, the timid little girl was whimpering with terror, and the parents were quietly rejoicing in the fact that another morning had been got through without serious damage to the children or emotional cost to themselves.

The last scruple died as Little Red Riding Hood was rescued and the play came safely to an end. The curtains closed, but the children were not quite disposed to go. They remained clapping and shouting in their seats, while their parents gathered up hats and coats.

At this moment, when all danger seemed past and former fears groundless and even morbid, the same little boy in the front row jumped up and asked his teacher a question. "Yes," she said, in a voice that penetrated the whole auditorium, "I think it will be all right for you to go backstage now."

Something in the teacher's tone arrested everyone; even those parents who had succeeded in getting their children halfway up the aisle now paused to watch as the party in the front row made a little procession up the stairs. The drama was not quite over; a reconciliation must follow between the puppet and the child; the child must handle the puppet, but ceremoniously, backstage, and with the puppet's permission.

Indulgently, the audience waited. The little procession reached the stage. Other children, emboldened, were starting down the aisle after it, when the curtains parted. There, her white hair disheveled, her well-bred features working with rage, stood the woman everyone had met in the lobby and who was now instantly identifiable as the apparition of anger, the face between the curtains. "Get out, get out of here, get out." She barred the way of the approaching group. "You dreadful, horrible children."

The voice, screaming, was familiar too; it was, of course, Sunny's. "You horrible, horrible children," she repeated, her *r*'s trilling out in a kind of reflex of gentility. The children turned and ran, and she pursued them to the stairs, a trembling figure of terrible malevolence, in whom could be discerned, as in a triple exposure, traces of the gracious hostess and the frolicsome puppet.

From behind the curtains came someone to seize her. A man from the box office ran down the aisle to pacify the teacher, who, now seeing herself on firm ground, was repeating over and over again, "That is no way to talk to a child." The audience did not wait to see the outcome. In shame and silence, it fled out into the rain, pursued by the sound of weeping which intermingled with the word *child*, as pronounced by the teacher in a tone of peculiar piety and reverence, her voice genuflecting to it as though to the Host.

SUGGESTIONS FOR WRITING

The Stories

1. The setting establishes and controls much of the action of "The Cicerone." Write an essay in which you discuss the significance of setting in this story.

2. The essay contends that the life depicted in "The Cicerone" is "bleak and hopeless." Yet this story is not without humor. Discuss the kinds of humor (verbal humor, humor growing out of character and incident) and the function of humor in "The Cicerone."

3. Examine the relationship between point of view, foreshadowing, and suspense in "The Unspoiled Reaction."

4. As in "The Cicerone," the narrator in "The Unspoiled Reaction" superimposes "her" own voice upon that of the character whose perceptions serve as narrative focus. Consider the following description: "But disaffected as it was, the audience contained the inevitable minority of enthusiastic coöperators who rejoice in obeying with ostentatious promptness any command whatsoever, who worship all signs, prohibitions, warnings, and who constitute themselves volunteer deputies of any official person they can find in their neighborhood." Write an essay in which you show how the narrator (through the similes, metaphors, analogies, and allusions embodied in direct statement) shapes your response to the story.

5. Stated broadly, the theme of "The Unspoiled Reaction" accrues from the conflict of *innocence* versus *knowledge*. More specifically, the puppeteers (hypocritical, motivated by self-interest) *use* the gullibility of the children to perpetrate what is, in actuality, a hoax. Yet, the parents are almost as guilty as the puppeteers, for, during most of the action of the story, they are allies of the puppeteers. Furthermore, the children do much to bring about their own destruction—the end of their innocence. Write an essay in which you discuss the thematic implications of such an interpretation.

Other Works by Mary McCarthy

1. Mary McCarthy has been acclaimed for her depiction of mid-twentieth-century liberals. Discuss her dramatization of the paradoxes of liberalism in *The Oasis* and *The Groves of Academe*.

2. Accepting the definition of a novel of manners as that which deals with the social customs, manners, conventions, and habits of a definite social class at a particular time and place, discuss *A Charmed Life* as a contemporary novel of manners.

3. *The Group* has been described by McCarthy as "a kind of mock-chronicle novel. . . . about the idea of progress. . . . seen in the female sphere, the feminine sphere." With this description in mind, analyze the success and failure of satire in this novel.

4. Examine the role and concept of nature in *Birds of America*.

5. McCarthy has been praised for her ability to create memorable minor characters. Discuss the *minor* characters in *A Charmed Life, The Group,* and *Birds of America.*

6. Both *The Group* and *Birds of America* concern change. Explore the theme of *change* in these two novels.

B I B L I O G R A P H Y

Primary

The Company She Keeps. New York: Harcourt, Brace & World, 1942. (Originally published by Simon and Schuster.) Short stories.

The Oasis. New York: Random House, 1949. A novella.

Cast a Cold Eye. New York: Harcourt, Brace & World, 1950. Short stories and autobiographical essays.

The Groves of Academe. New York: Harcourt, Brace & World, 1952. A novel.

A Charmed Life. New York: Harcourt, Brace & World, 1955. A novel.

Sights and Spectacles: 1937–1956. New York: Farrar, Straus & Giroux, 1956. Theatre criticism.

Venice Observed. New York: Reynal, 1956. Art, history, travel.

Memories of a Catholic Girlhood. New York: Harcourt, Brace & World, 1957. Autobiographical essays.

The Stones of Florence. New York: Harcourt, Brace & World, 1959. Art, history, travel.

On the Contrary: Articles of Belief, 1946–1961. New York: Farrar, Straus & Giroux, 1961. Essays.

Mary McCarthy's Theatre Chronicles, 1937–1962. New York: Farrar, Straus & Giroux, 1963. Theatre criticism.

The Group. New York: Harcourt, Brace & World, 1963. A novel.

Vietnam. New York: Harcourt, Brace & World, 1967. A report.

Hanoi. New York: Harcourt, Brace & World, 1968. Essays and letters.

Writing on the Wall and Other Literary Essays. New York: Harcourt Brace Jovanovich, 1970. Literary criticism.

Birds of America. New York: Harcourt Brace Jovanovich, 1971. A novel.

Medina. New York: Harcourt Brace Jovanovich, 1972. A report.

Secondary

Aldridge, John W. "Mary McCarthy: Princess Among the Trolls" in *A Time to Murder and Create: The Contemporary Novel in Crisis.* New York: David McKay, 1966. A highly contentious analysis of McCarthy's writing and her literary reputation.

Auchincloss, Louis. *Pioneers & Caretakers: A Study of 9 American Women Novelists.* Minneapolis: Univ. of Minnesota Press, 1965. Devotes the final chapter to a broad view of the fiction of Mary McCarthy.

Brower, Brock. "Mary McCarthyism." *Esquire,* 58 (July 1962), 62–67, 113. An amusing and informative biographical sketch.

Goldman, Sherli Evens. *Mary McCarthy: A Bibliography.* New York: Harcourt, Brace & World, 1968.

Grumbach, Doris. *The Company She Kept: A Revealing Portrait of Mary McCarthy.* New York: Coward-McCann, 1967. A full-length critical biography based on the author's conviction that "the fiction of Mary McCarthy is autobiographical to an extraordinary degree, in the widest sense of autobiography."

Hardwick, Elizabeth. "Mary McCarthy" in *A View of My Own: Essays in Literature and Society.* New York: Farrar, Straus & Giroux, 1963. An excellent brief appraisal of McCarthy as a writer and as a person.

McKenzie, Barbara. *Mary McCarthy.* New York: Twayne, 1966. A full-length critical study of McCarthy's collected writing.

Niebuhr, Elisabeth. "The Art of Fiction XXVII." *The Paris Review,* 27 (Winter–Spring 1962), 58–94. Reprinted in *Writers at Work, Second Series.* New York: Viking Press, 1963. An interview with Mary McCarthy that affords helpful insights into her writing.

Pritchett, V. S. "Ironical Aviary." *New York Review of Books,* 16 (June 3, 1971), 13–15. A review of *Birds of America* that finds the novel "a topical allegory about intellectual pollution."

Rahv, Philip. "The Editor Interviews Mary McCarthy." *Modern Occasions,* 1 (Fall 1970), 14–25. A discussion of literature and politics.

Schlueter, Paul. "The Dissections of Mary McCarthy" in *Contemporary American Novelists,* ed. by Harry T. Moore. Carbondale, Ill.: Southern Illinois Univ. Press, 1964. A brief examination of McCarthy's fictional techniques.

Stock, Irvin. *Mary McCarthy.* Minneapolis: Univ. of Minnesota Press, 1968 (No. 72 of the University of Minnesota Pamphlets on American Writers). An overview of McCarthy's writing that posits that her "contempt" and "cutting satire" accrue "not from an intellectual's superciliousness but from an intellectual's hunger for the ordinary decencies and delights of life."

Few writers since Joyce would risk [as Salinger does] such a wealth of words upon events that are purely internal and deeds that are purely talk. We live in a world, however, where the decisive deed may invite the holocaust, and Salinger's conviction that our inner lives greatly matter peculiarly qualifies him to sing of an America where, for most of us, there seems little to do but to feel. Introversion, perhaps, has been forced upon history; an age of nuance, of ambiguous gestures and psychological jockeying on a national and private scale, is upon us, and Salinger's intense attention to gesture and intonation helps make him, among his contemporaries, a uniquely pertinent literary artist. As Hemingway sought the words for things in motion, Salinger seeks the words for things transmuted into human subjectivity. His fiction, in its rather grim bravado, its humor, its privacy, its wry but persistent hopefulness, matches the shape and tint of present American life. It pays the price, however, of becoming dangerously convoluted and static.

FROM a review of J. D. Salinger's novel *Franny and Zooey*

JOHN UPDIKE

John Updike was born in Shillington, a small town in Pennsylvania, in 1932. His father taught at the local high school. After graduating from Harvard *summa cum laude* in English Literature, Updike spent a year in England on a Knox fellowship at the Ruskin School of Drawing and Fine Art at Oxford. He then joined the staff of the *New Yorker* as a reporter for the "Talk of the Town" column and also contributed parodies, humorous essays, light verse, and short stories to the magazine. *The Carpentered Hen* (1958) contains many of his early *New Yorker* poems. Updike resigned his staff position in 1957 to devote himself to writing serious fiction but has continued to publish many short stories, essays, and poems in the *New Yorker*. *Assorted Prose* (1965) contains the best of his nonfiction pieces. Updike lives in Ipswich, Massachusetts, with his wife and four children.

Updike's fiction has won such honors as a 1960 National Institute of Arts and Letters Award, for *The Poorhouse Fair*, and the 1964 National Book Award in Fiction, for *The Centaur*. Some of his critics, lavish in their praise for his technical virtuosity, condemn him for an apparent triviality of subject matter. Yet, in almost everything Updike has written, there is an important and integral plane of metaphysical as well as physical action. In the two stories that follow, Updike's facility with syntax and narrative structure should not obscure the reader's vision of the philosophical issues bulwarking each story.

A GIFT
FROM THE CITY

Like most happy people, they came from well inland. Amid this city's mysteries, they had grown very close. When the phone on his desk rang, he knew it was she. "Jim? Say. Something awful has happened."

"What?" His voice had contracted and sounded smaller. He pictured his wife and small daughter attacked by teen-agers, derelicts, coal men, beneath the slender sparse trees of Tenth Street; oh if only love were not immaterial! If only there were such a thing as enchantment, and he could draw, with a stick, a circle of safety around them that would hold, though they were on Tenth near Fifth and he forty blocks north.

"I guess it shouldn't be awful but it's so upsetting. Martha and I were in the apartment, we had just come back from the park, and I was making tea for her tea party—"

"Nnn. And?"

"And the doorbell rang. And I didn't know who could be calling, but

I pressed the buzzer and went to the stairs, and there was this young Negro. It seemed strange, but then he looked awfully frightened and really smaller than I am. So I stood at the banister and he stood on the middle of the stairs, and he told me this story about how he had brought his family up from North Carolina in somebody else's truck and they had found a landlord who was giving them a room but they had no furniture or food. I couldn't understand half of what he said." Her voice broke here.

"Poor Liz. It's all right, he didn't expect you to."

"He kept saying something about his wife, and I *couldn't* understand it."

"You're O.K. now, aren't you?"

"Yes I'm O.K., let me finish."

"You're crying."

"Well it was awfully strange."

"What did he *do?*"

"He didn't *do* anything. He was very nice. He just wanted to know if there were any odd jobs I could let him do. He'd been all up and down Tenth Street just ringing doorbells, and nobody was home."

"We don't have any odd jobs."

"That's what I said. But I gave him ten dollars and said I was sorry but this was all I had in the house. It's all I did have."

"Good. That was just the right thing."

"Was it all right?"

"Sure. You say the poor devil came up in a truck?" James was relieved: the shadow of the coal man had passed; the enchantment had worked. It had seemed for a moment, from her voice, that the young Negro was right there in the apartment, squeezing Martha on the sofa.

"The point is, though," Liz said, "now we don't have any money for the weekend, and Janice is coming tomorrow night so we can go to the movies, and then the Bridges on Sunday. You know how she eats. Did you go to the bank?"

"Dammit, no. I forgot."

"Well, *dar*ling."

"I keep thinking we have lots of money." It was true; they did. "Never mind, maybe they'll cash a check here."

"You think? He was really awfully pathetic, and I couldn't tell if he was a crook or not."

"Well, even if he was he must have needed the money; crooks need money too."

"You think they *will* cash a check?"

"Sure. They love me."

"The really awful thing I haven't told you. When I gave him the ten dollars he said he wanted to thank you—he seemed awfully interested in you—and I said, Well, fine, but on Saturdays we were in and out all day, so he said he'd come in the evening. He really wants to thank you."

"He does."

"I told him we were going to the movies and he said he'd come around before we went."

"Isn't he rather aggressive? Why didn't he let *you* thank me for him?"

"Darley, I didn't know *what* to say."

"Then it's not the Bridges we need the money for; it's him."

"No, I don't think so. You made me forget the crucial part: He said he has gotten a job that starts Monday, so it's just this weekend he needs furniture."

"Why doesn't he sleep on the floor?" James could imagine himself, in needful circumstances, doing that. In the Army he had done worse.

"He has his *family*, Jim. Did you want me not to give him anything— to run inside and lock the door? It would have been easy to do, you know."

"No, no, you were a wonderful Christian. I'm proud of you. Anyway, if he comes before the movie he can't very well stay all night."

This pleasant logic seemed firm enough to conclude on, yet when she had hung up and her voice was gone, the affair seemed ominous again. It was as if, with the click of the receiver, she had sunk beneath an ocean. His own perch, twenty-two stories above Park Avenue, swayed slightly, with the roll of too many cigarettes. He ground his present one into a turquoise ashtray, and looked about him, but his beige office at Dudevant & Smith (Industrial and Package Design) offered an inappropriate kind of comfort. His youth's high hopes—he had thought he was going to be a painter—had been distilled into a few practical solids: a steel desk, a sponge chair, a drawing board the size of a dining table, infinitely adjustable lighting fixtures, abundant draftsman's equipment, and a bulletin board so fresh it gave off a scent of cork. Oversized white tacks fixed on the cork several flattering memos from Dudevant, a snapshot, a studio portrait of Liz, and a four-color ad for the Raydo shaver, a shaver that James had designed, though an asterisk next to the object dropped the eye to the right-hand corner, to Dudevant's name, in elegantly modest sans-serif. This was all right; it was in the bargain. James's anonymity had been honestly purchased. Indeed, it seemed they couldn't give him enough; there was always some bonus or adjustment or employee benefit or Christmas present appearing on his desk, in one of those long blue envelopes that spelled "money" to his mind as surely as green engravings.

His recent fortunes had been so good, James had for months felt that

paranoid about city

some harsh blow was due. Cautious, he gave Providence few opportunities to instruct him. Its last chance, except for trips in the car, had been childbirth, and Liz had managed that with a poised animal ease, one Thursday at dawn. As the months passed harmlessly, James's suspicion increased that the city itself, with its steep Babylonian surfaces, its black noon shadows, its godless millions, was poised to strike. He placated the circumambient menace the only way he knew—by giving to beggars. He distributed between one and two dollars a day to Salvation Army singers, degraded violinists, husky blind men standing in the center of the pavement with their beautiful German shepherds, men on crutches offering yellow pencils, mumbling drunks anxious to shake his hand and show him the gash beneath their hats, men noncommittally displaying their metal legs in subway tunnels. Ambulatory ones, given the pick of a large crowd, would approach him; to their vision, though he dressed and looked like anyone else, he must wear, with Byzantine distinctness, the aureole of the soft touch.

Saturday was tense. James awoke feeling the exact shape of his stomach, a disagreeable tuber. The night before, he had tried to draw from Liz more information about her young Negro. "How was he dressed?"

"Not badly."

"Not badly!"

"A kind of sport coat with a red wool shirt open at the neck, I think."

"Well why is he all dolled up if he has no money? He dresses better than I do."

"It didn't seem *terribly* strange. You know he *would* have *one* good outfit."

"And he brought his wife and *seven* children up here in the cab of a truck?"

"I said seven? I just have the feeling it's seven."

"Sure. Seven dwarfs, seven lively arts, seven levels of Purgatory . . ."

"It couldn't have been in the cab, though. It must have been in the truck part. He said they had no furniture or anything except what they wore."

"Just the rags on their backs. Son of a bitch."

"This is so unlike you, darling. You're always sending checks to Father Flanagan."

"He only asks me once a year and at least he doesn't come crawling up the stairs after my wife."

James was indignant. The whole tribe of charity seekers, to whom he had been so good, had betrayed him. On Saturday morning, down on

Eighth Street buying a book, he deliberately veered away, off the curb and into the gutter, to avoid a bum hopefully eying his lapels. At lunch the food lacked taste. The interval between the plate and his face exasperated him; he ate too fast, greedily. In the afternoon, all the way to the park, he maintained a repellent frown. When Liz seemed to dawdle, he took over the pushing of the carriage himself. A young colored man in Levis descended the steps of a brick four-story and peered up and down the street uncertainly. James's heart tripped. "There he is."

"Where?"

"Right ahead, looking at you."

"Aren't you scary? That's not him. Mine was really short."

At the park his daughter played in the damp sand by herself. No one seemed to love her; the other children romped at selfish games. The slatted shadow of the fence lengthened as the sun drew closer to the tops of the N.Y.U. buildings. Beneath this orange dying ball a yelping white played tennis with a tall Negro on an asphalt court, beneath the variously papered wall of a torn-down building. Martha tottered from the sandbox to the seesaw to the swings, in her element and fearless. Strange, the fruit of his seed was a native New Yorker; she had been born in a hospital on Twenty-ninth Street. He rescued her at the entry to the swing section, lifted her into one, and pushed her from the front. Her face dwindled and loomed, dwindled and loomed; she laughed, but none of the other parents or children gave a sign of hearing her. The metal of the swing was icy; this was September. A chill, end-of-summer breeze weighed restlessly on the backs of his hands.

When they returned to the apartment, after four, safe, and the Negro was not there, and Liz set about making tea as on any other day, his fears were confounded, and he irrationally ceased expecting anything bad to happen. Of course they gave the baby her bath and ate their dinner in peace; by pure will he was keeping the hateful doorbell smothered. And when it did ring, it was only Janice their baby-sitter, coming up the stairs with her grandmotherly slowness.

He warned her, "There's a slight chance a young Negro will be coming here to find us," and told her, more or less, the story.

"Well don't worry, I won't let him in," Janice said in the tone of one passing on a particularly frightening piece of gossip. "I'll tell him you're not here and I don't know when you'll be back." She was a good-hearted, unfortunate girl, with dusty tangerine hair. Her mother in Rhode Island was being filtered through a series of hopeless operations. Most of her weekends were spent up there, helping her mother die. The salary Janice earned as a stenographer at NBC was consumed by train fares and long-distance phone calls; she never accepted her fee at the end of a night's sitting without saying, with a soft one-sided smile wherein ages of Irish wit were listlessly deposited, "I hate to take it, but I need the money."

"Well, no, don't be rude or anything. Tell him—and I don't think he'll come, but just in case—we'll be here Sunday."

"The Bridges, too," Liz pointed out.

"Yeah, well, I don't think he'll show. If he's as new here as you said he was, he probably can't find the place again."

"You know," Janice said to Liz, "you really can't be so softhearted. I admire you for it, and I feel as sorry for these people as you do, but in this town, believe me, you don't dare trust anybody, literally *any*body. A girl at work beside me knows a man who's as healthy as you or me, but he goes around on crutches and makes a hundred and twenty dollars a week. Why, that's more than any of us who work honestly make."

James smiled tightly, insulted twice; he made more than that a week, and he did not like to hear he was being defrauded by pitiable souls on the street who he could see were genuinely deformed or feeble-minded or alcoholic.

After a pause, Liz gently asked the girl, "How is your mother?"

Janice's face brightened and was not quite so overpowered by the orange hair. "Oh, on the phone last night she sounded real high and mighty. The P. T.A. has given her some job with a drive for funds, something she could do with pencil and paper, without getting up. I've told you how active she had been. She was all for getting out of bed. She said she can feel, you know, that it's out of her body now. But when I talked to the doctor last Sunday, he said we mustn't hope too much. But he seemed very proud of the operation."

"Well, good luck," James said, jingling the change in his pocket.

Janice shook her finger. "You have a good time. He isn't going to get in if I'm here, *that* you can depend on," she assured them, misunderstanding, or perhaps understanding more than necessary.

The picture was excellent, but just at the point where John Wayne, after tracking the Comanches from the snowbound forests of Montana to the blazing dunes of Border Country, was becoming reconciled to the idea of his niece cohabiting with a brave, James vividly remembered the bum who had wobbled toward him on Eighth Street—the twisted eye, the coat too small to button, the pulpy mouth with pathetic effort trying to frame the first words. The image made him squirm in his seat and pull away from Liz's hand. They decided not to stay for the second feature. Liz said her eyes smarted from the Vistavision. They were reluctant to go home so early; Janice counted on them to last out the double feature. But the service at the luncheonette was swift; the sodas—weak things, scarcely frothy at all, just tan liquid in a paper cone—were quickly drained; and the main streets of the Village, thronged with gangsters and hermaphrodites, seemed to James a poor place to stroll with his wife. Liz caught the attention of every thug and teen-ager they passed. "Stop it," he said. "You'll get me knifed."

"Darling. There's no law against people's eyes."

"There should be. They think you're a whore out with her pimp. What makes you stare at everybody?"

"Faces are *interesting*. Why are you so uninterested in people?"

"Because every other day you call up the office and I have to come rescue you from some damn bugaboo you've enticed up the stairs. No wonder Dudevant is getting set to fire me."

"Let's go home if you want to rave."

"We can't. Janice needs the money, the bloodsucker."

"It's nearly ten. She charges a dollar an hour, after all."

As they advanced down Tenth from Fifth he saw a slight blob by their gate which simply squinting did not erase. He did not expect ever to see Liz's Negro, who had had his chance at dinner. Yet when it was clear that a man *was* standing there, wearing a hat, James hastened forward, glad at last to have the enemy life-size and under scrutiny. They seemed to know each other well; James called "Hi!" and grasped the quickly offered hand, the palm waxy and cool, like a synthetic fabric.

"I just wanted . . . *thank* . . . such a fine gentleman," the Negro said, in a voice incredibly thin-spun, the thread of it always breaking.

"Have you been waiting long?" Liz asked.

"No, well . . . the lady upstairs, she said you'd be back. When the man in the taxi let me go from the station . . . came on back to thank such wonderful people."

"I'm awfully sorry," James told him. "I thought you knew we were going off to the movies." His own voice sounded huge—a magnificent instrument. He must not be too elaborately courteous; Liz was terribly alive to him in regard to vanity or condescension. She was unfair; his natural, heartfelt impulse at this moment was toward elaborate courtesy.

"You were at the police station?" Liz asked. Their previous encounter seemed to have attuned her to the man's speech.

". . . how I do appreciate." He was still speaking to James, ignoring Liz completely. This assumption that he, as head of the family, superseded all its other elements, and that in finding him the Negro had struck the fountainhead of his good fortune, made James panicky. He had been raised to believe in democratic marriages. Further, the little Negro seemed to need specifically maternal attention. He trembled softly under his coat, and it was not that cold; the night was warmer than the late afternoon had been.

The Negro's clothes, in the dimness of outdoors, did not look as shabby as James would have liked. As for his being young, James could distinguish no marks of either youth or age.

"Well, come on inside," he said.

"Aaaah . . . ?"

"Please," Liz said.

They entered the little overheated vestibule, and immediately the buzzer rasped at the lock, signalling that Janice had been watching from the window. She ran to the banister and shouted down in a whisper, "Did he get in? Has he told you about the taxi-driver?"

James, leading the group, attained the top of the stairs. "How was Martha?" he asked, rather plainly putting first things first.

"An absolute angel. How was the movie?"

"Quite good, really. It really was."

"I was honestly afraid he'd kill him."

They shuffled each other into the room. "I gather you two have met, then," James said to Janice and the Negro. The girl bared her teeth in a kindly smile that made her look five years older, and the Negro, who had his hat already in his hands and was therefore unable to tip it, bent the brim slightly and swiftly averted his head, confronting a striped canvas Liz had done, titled *Swans and Shadows*.

At this juncture, with these two showing these sinister signs of rapport, Liz deserted him, easing into the bedroom. She was bothered by fears that Martha would stop breathing among the blankets. "Before the doorbell rang, even," Janice talked on, "I could hear the shouting on the street—Oh, it was something. He said terrible things. And then the bell rang, and I answered it, like you had said to, and *he* said—" She indicated the Negro, who was still standing, in a quiet plaid sport coat.

"Sit down," James told him.

"—and *he* said that the taxi-driver wanted money. *I* said, 'I don't have any. I don't have a red cent, honestly.' You know when I come over I never think to bring my purse." James recalled she could never make change. There was usually an amount she was left owing them, "toward next time."

"I *tol* him," the Negro said, "there were these fine people, in this house here. The lady in there, she told me you'd be *here*."

James asked, "Where did you take a taxi *from?*"

The Negro sought refuge in contemplation of his hat, pendent from one quivering hand. "Please, Mister . . . the lady, she knows about it." He looked toward the bedroom door.

Janice rescued him, speaking briskly: "He told me the driver wanted two thirty, and I said, 'I don't have a cent.' Then I came in here and hunted, you know, to see if you left any around—sometimes there's some tens under the silver bowl."

"Oh, yes," James said.

"Then I went to the window to signal—I'm scared to death of going downstairs and locking myself out—and down on the street there was this crowd, from across the street at Alex's, and it looked like when he went back to tell the driver, the driver grabbed him; there was a lot of shouting, and some woman kept saying 'Cop.' "

Liz reëntered the room.

"He grab me here," the Negro humbly explained. He touched with his little free hand the open collar of his red wool shirt.

"So I guess then they went to the police station," Janice concluded lamely, disappointed to discover that her information was incomplete.

Liz, assuming that the police-station part of the story had been told when she was out of the room, took this to be the end, and asked, "Who wants some coffee?"

"No thanks, Betty," Janice said. "It keeps me awake."

"It keeps everybody awake," James said. "That's what it's supposed to do."

"Oh, no, Ma'am," the Negro said. "I couldn't do that." Uneasily shifting his face toward James, though he kept his eyes on the lamp burning above Janice's head, he went on, "I tolem at the station how there were these people. I had your address, cause the lady wrote it down on a little slip."

"Uh-huh." James assumed there was more to come. Why wasn't he still at the police station? Who paid the driver? The pause stretched. James felt increasingly remote; it scarcely seemed his room, with so strange a guest in it. He tilted his chair back, and the Negro sharpened as if through the wrong end of a telescope. There was a resemblance between the Negro's head and the Raydo shaver. The inventive thing about that design—the stroke of mind, in Dudevant's phrase—had been forthrightly paring away the space saved by the manufacturer's improved, smaller motor. Instead of a symmetrical case, then, in form like a tapered sugar sack, a squat, asymmetrical shape was created, which fitted, pleasingly weighty, in the user's hand like a religious stone full of mana. Likewise, a part of the Negro's skull had been eliminated. His eyes were higher in his head than drawing masters teach, and had been set shallowly on the edges where the planes of the face turned sideways. With a smothered start James realized that Janice, and Liz leaning in the doorway of the kitchen, and the Negro too, were expecting him to speak—the man of the situation, the benefactor. "Well, now, what *is* your trouble?" he asked brutally.

The coffee water sang, and Liz, after wrinkling her expressive high forehead at him, turned to the stove.

The Negro feebly rubbed the slant of his skull. "Aaaah? . . . appreciate the kindness of you and the lady . . . generous to a poor soul like me nobody wanted to help."

James prompted. "You and your wife and—how many children?"

"Seven, Mister. The oldest boy ten."

"—*have* found a place to live. Where?"

"Yessir, the man say he give us this room, but he say he can't put no beds in it, but I found this other man willing to give us on loan, you know, until I go to my job. . . . But the wife and children, they don't have no bed to rest their heads. Nothing to eat. My children are tired."

James put a cigarette in the center of his mouth and said as it bobbled, "You say you *have* a job?"

"Oh yes Mister, I went to this place where they're building the new road to the tunnel, you know, and *he* tol *me* as soon as I get in one day's work, he can give me that money, toward my pay. He ast if I could do the work and I said, 'Yes, sir, any kind of work you give I can do.' He said the pay was two dollar seventy cents for every hour you work."

"Two seventy? For heaven's sake. Twenty dollars a day just laboring?"

"Yes, pushing the wheelbarrow . . . he said two seventy. I said, 'I can do any kind of work you give. I'm a hard worker.'"

To James he looked extremely frail, but the happy idea of there existing a broad-shouldered foreman willing to make him a working citizen washed all doubts away. He smiled and insisted, "So it's really just this weekend you need to get over."

"Thas right. Starting Monday I'll be making two seventy every hour. The wife, she's as happy as anybody could be."

The wife seemed to have altered underfoot, but James let it pass; the end was in sight. He braced himself to enter the realm of money. Here Janice, the fool, who should have left the minute they came home, interrupted with, "Have you tried any agencies, like the Salvation Army?"

"Oh, yes, Miss. All. They don't care much for fellas like me. They say they'll give us money to get *back,* but as for staying—they won't do a damn thing. Boy, you come up here in a truck, you're on your own. Nobody help me except these people."

The man he probably was with his friends and family was starting to show. James was sleepy. The hard chair hurt; the Negro had the comfortable chair. He resented the man's becoming at ease. But there was no halting it; the women were at work now.

"Isn't that awful," Janice said. "You wonder why they have these agencies."

"You say you need help, your wife ain't got a place to put her head, they give you money to go *back.*"

Liz entered with two cups of coffee. Hers, James noticed, was just half full; he was to bear the larger burden of insomnia. The cup was too hot to hold. He set it on the rug, feeling soft-skinned and effeminate in the eyes of this hard worker worth twenty dollars a day.

"Why did you decide to leave North Carolina?" Liz asked.

"Missis, a man like me, there's no chance there for him. I worked in the cotton and they give me thirty-five cents an hour."

"Thirty-five cents?" James said. "That's illegal, isn't it?"

The Negro smiled sardonically, his first facial expression of the evening. "Down there you don't tell them what's legal." To Liz he added, "The wife, Ma'am, she's the bravest woman. When I say, 'Let's go,' she said, 'Thas right, let's give oursels a chance.' So this man promise he'd take us up in the cab of the truck he had . . ."

"With all seven children?" James asked.

The Negro looked at him without the usual wavering. "We don't have anybody to leave them behind."

"And you have no friends or relatives here?" Liz asked.

"No, we don't have no friends, and until you were so kind to me it didn't look like we'd find any either."

Friends! In indignation James rose and, on his feet, had to go through the long-planned action of placing two ten-dollar bills on the table next to the Negro. The Negro ignored them, bowing his head. James made his speech. "Now, I don't know how much furniture costs—my wife gave me the impression that you were going to make the necessary payment with the ten. But here is twenty. It's all we can spare. This should carry you over until Monday, when you say you can get part of your salary for working on the Lincoln tunnel. I think it was very courageous of you to bring your family up here, and we want to wish you lots of luck. I'm sure you and your wife will make out." Flushing with shame, he resumed his post in the hard chair.

Janice bit her lip to cure a smile and looked toward Liz, who said nothing.

The Negro said, "Aeeh . . . Mister . . . can't find words to press, such fine *people*." And, while the three of them sat there, trapped and stunned, he tried to make himself cry. He pinched the bridge of his nose and shook his head and squeezed soft high animal sounds from his throat, but when he looked up, the grainy whites of his eyes were dry. Uncoordinated with this failure, his lips writhed in grief. He kept brushing his temple as if something were humming there. "Gee," he said. "The wife . . . she tol me, you got to go back and thank that man. . . ."

The Negro's sense of exit seemed as defective as his other theatrical skills. He just sat there, shaking his head and touching his nose. The bills on the table remained ignored—taboo, perhaps, until a sufficiently exhausting ritual of gratitude was performed. James, to whom rudeness came hard, teetered in his chair, avoiding all eyes; at the root of the Negro's demonstration there was either the plight he described or a plight that had made him lie. In either case, the man must be borne. Yet James found him all but unbearable; the thought of his life as he described it, swinging, blithe moron, from one tenuous vine of charity to the next—the truck driver, the landlord, Liz, the furniture man, the foreman, now James—was sickening, giddying. James said courteously, "Maybe you'd better be getting back to her."

"Iiih," the Negro sighed, on an irrelevant high note, as if he produced the sound with a pitch pipe.

James dreaded that Liz would start offering blankets and food if the Negro delayed further—as he did, whimpering and passing the hatbrim through his hands like an endless rope. While Liz was in the kitchen filling a paper bag for him, the Negro found breath to tell James that he wanted to bring his wife and all his family to see him and his missis, tomorrow, so they could all express gratitude. "Maybe there's some work . . . washing the floors, anything, she's so happy, until we can pay back. Twenty, gee." His hand fled to his eyes.

"No, don't you worry about us. That thirty dollars"—the record must be kept straight—"you can think of as a gift from the city."

"Oh I wouldn't have it no other way. You let my wife do all your work tomorrow."

"You and she get settled. Forget us."

Liz appeared with an awkward paper bag. There were to be no blankets, he deduced; his wife's stance seemed edged with defiance.

Talkative as always when a guest was leaving, James asked, "Now, do you know how to get back? For heaven's sake don't take a taxi. Take a bus and then the subway. Where is your place?"

"Aaaah . . . right near where that Lexington Avenue is."

"Where on Lexington? What cross street?"

"Beg pardon, Mister? I'm sorry, I don't make sense I'm so thrilled."

"What cross street? How far *up* on Lexington?"

"The, ah, hundred twenty-nine."

As James, with an outlander's simple pride in "knowing" New York, gave detailed instructions about where to board the Fourteenth Street bus, where to find the subway kiosk after so many stops, and how to put the token in the turnstile, the words seemed to bounce back, as if they were finding identical information already lodged in the Negro's brain. He concluded, "Just try to resist the temptation to jump in a taxicab. That would have cost us two thirty if we'd been home. Now here, I'll even give you bus fare and a token." Dredging a handful of silver from his coat pocket, he placed a nickel and a dime and a token in the svelte little palm and, since the hand did not move, put two more dimes in it, then thought, *Oh hell,* and poured all the coins in—over a dollar's worth.

"Now I'm penniless," he told the colored man.

"Thank eh, you too Missis, so much, and you Miss."

They wished him luck. He shook hands all around, hoisted the bag with difficulty into his arms, and walked murmuring through the door James held open for him.

"Four blocks up, to Fourteenth Street," James called after him, adding in a normal voice, "I know damn well he'll take a taxi."

"It's awfully good-hearted of you," Janice said, "but about giving all that money, I-don't-know."

"Ah, well," said James, doing a small dance step, "money is dross."

Liz said, "I *was* surprised, darley, that you gave him *two* bills."

"You *were?* These are times of inflation. You can't buy seven air-conditioned Beautyrest mattresses for ten dollars. He's shown a great gift for spending; he ran through your ten like a little jack rabbit. We never did find out where it went to."

Janice, Irishly earnest, still grappled with the moral issue. She spoke more to Liz than to him. "I don't doubt he needs the money—Oh, you should have heard the things that cabby said, or maybe you shouldn't. But then who doesn't need money? You and I need money, too."

"Which reminds me," James said. He looked at the electric clock in the kitchen: 11:20. "We came home, didn't we, around ten? Seven-thirty to ten—two and a half. Two and a half dollars. You can't change a ten, can you?"

The girl's face fell. "Honestly, I never remember to bring my purse. But you could owe me to next time. . . ."

"I hate to do that. You need the money." He couldn't believe the girl would take a surplus of $7.50 from him.

"That-I-do," Janice admitted cheerfully, gathering up her coat and a limp black book stamped simply with a cross. *Her mother,* James thought, and felt the prayers rising about them.

"Wait," Liz said. "I think in my purse. I lied to him when I said I had nothing in the house but the ten." They found the purse and were indeed able to piece together, out of paper and silver, the fee.

Spited, Janice said, "For your sakes, I sure hope he doesn't bother you again. This little island has more different kinds of crooks on it than you or I could imagine existed. Some of them could out-act old Larry Olivier himself."

"I really don't see how he can do this laboring job," Liz said, with a tactful appearance of agreeing. "Why, just that little bag I gave him almost knocked him over." When Janice was gone, she asked, "Do you think she expected us to pay her for the hour and a half she stayed to watch the Negro?"

"Heaven knows. I feel vile."

"Where?"

"Everywhere. I feel like a vile person."

"Why? You were fine. You were awfully, awfully good."

From her hasty kiss on his cheek he gathered that, surprisingly, she meant it.

Sunday, husk among days, was full of fear. Even in gay times James felt on this day like a nameless statue on an empty plaza. Now he dared not go out, either to church or to the newsstand. Last night's episode had the color of a public disgrace. The Negro was everywhere. James holed up in his inadequate cave. The walls seemed transparent, the floors sounding boards. The Negro's threat to return had smashed the windows and broken the burglar locks. Never on a morning had he wished so intensely to be back in Ontauk, Minnesota, his birthplace. The town had over seven thousand residents now, and a city manager instead of a mayor, and since the war the creek that ran through its center and drained its few mills had been robbed of its Indian name and called the Douglas Mac-Arthur River; but the cars still parked higgledy-piggledy on the crooked, shaded streets, and he would still have a place, his father's son.

Liz and James lived four doors down from an Episcopal church. There was not an inch of air between the masonry of any of the buildings. When the church bells rang, their apartment quivered sonorously. Enveloped in this huge dead hum, he fought the picture of seven fuzz-haired children squeezed into the cab of a truck, roadside lights flickering in their faces, the dark of the Carolina fields slipping away, great whoring cities bristling and then falling back, too, and then the children dozing, except for the oldest, a boy of ten, who remained awake to stare unblinking at the bent-necked blue lights of the Jersey Turnpike, the jet carpet carrying them to the sorcerer's palace, where Harlem was choked with Cadillacs and white men on subways yielded their seats to colored ladies. James hated the Negro chiefly because he was tactless. Janice's mother, the sores of street beggars—this was misery, too, but misery that knew its limits, that kept an orbit and observed manners. But in his perfect ignorance the Negro was like one of those babies born with its heart in front of its ribs. He gave no protection. You touched him and you killed him. Now that he had found this Northern man—the promised man—so free with money, he would be back today, and again tomorrow, with an even greater gift of mumbled debts. Why not? Thirty was nothing to James. He could give away a flat three thousand, and then thirty every week—more than thirty, fifty—and he and Liz would still be richer than the Negro. Between him and the Negro the ground was unimpeded, and only a sin could be placed there as barrier.

By afternoon the focus of James's discomfort had shifted from the possibility that the Negro had told the truth to the possibility that he had not. Reliving his behavior in this light was agonizing. He shuddered above the depths of fatuity the Negro must have seen in his clumsy kindness. If the story had been a fraud, the impatience of James's charity was its one saving grace. The bits of abruptness, the gibes about the taxi shone in memory like jewels among refuse. The more he thought, the more he raged, aloud and privately. And the angrier he grew at the Negro, the less he wanted to see him, the more he dreaded him, an opponent invincibly armed with the weapon of having seen him as a fool. And those seven clambering children, and the wife bullying Liz.

He only wanted to hide his head in the haven of the Bridges' scheduled visit. They saw him as others saw him and knew his value. He would bask in their lucid external view.

Then mercifully it *was* dark, and his friends had come.

Rudy Bridges was also from Ontauk, Minnesota. He had been two classes ahead of James in the high school, a scholastic wonder, the more so because his father was a no-account who died of tuberculosis the year Rudy graduated. In the nine years since, Rudy's buttercup hair had thinned severely, but the spherical head and the chubby lips of the prig had remained constant. *His* great hopes had been boiled down to instructing three sections of Barnard girls in American history. His wife came from Maryland. Augustina was a pale and handsome woman with an uncompromising, uptilted nose that displayed its nostrils. She wore her abundant chestnut hair strictly parted in the middle—a madonna for the Piston Age. They had no children, and with elaborate managing, just enough money. James loved them as guests. In their own home, Rudy talked too much about his special field, domestic fiscal policy between Grant and Wilson, a desert of dullness where the lowliest scholar could be king. And Augustina, careful of the budget, went hungry and thirsty and inhibited everyone. Away from home she drank and ate beautifully.

James tiptoed into the bedroom with their heavy coats. Martha was cased in her crib like a piece of apparatus manufacturing sleep. He heard Liz talking and, returning, asked, "Is she telling you about how we're running the Underground Railway?"

"Why, no, James," Augustina said slowly.

"I was telling them the accident Martha had in the park," Liz said.

"Yeah, the poor kid just ran right into the swings," he said, no doubt duplicating the story.

"Now, James," Rudy said, "what is this mad tale about the Underground Rail*road?*" Years of teaching had perfected his speech habit of pronouncing everything, clichés and all, with artificial distinctness. Throughout James's recital of the Negro story he kept saying "Ah yes," and when it was over and, like Janice the night before, James seemed to have reached an insufficient conclusion, Rudy felt compelled to clarify: "So the chances are these seven children are going to show up in the middle of supper."

"Oh dear," Augustina said with mock alarm. "Do you have enough food?"

Rudy, beside her on the sofa, attacked the tale pedantically. "Now. You say he was well dressed?"

"Sort of. But after all it was Saturday night." James didn't get the smile he expected.

"Did you look at his shoes?"

"Not much."

"Would you say his accent was Southern or neutral?"

"Well, your wife's the only Southerner I know. His speech was so peculiar and high, I couldn't tell. Certainly he didn't talk like you. Or me."

"And at one point he used the word 'thrilled.'"

"Yeah, that got me, too. But look: there were odd things, but when a man is in such a dither anyway—"

Augustina broke in, addressing Liz. "Did James *really* just hand him thirty dollars?"

"Thirty-one and a token," James corrected.

Rudy laughed excessively—he had no sense of humor, so when he laughed it was too hard—and lifted his golden glass in toast. Augustina, to back him up, gripped hers, which was already empty. "James," Rudy said, "you're the soul of charity."

It was flattering, of course, but it wasn't the way he thought they should take it. The point really wasn't the thirty dollars at all; hard as it was to explain without seeming to ridicule Rudy's salary, thirty dollars was nothing.

"It doesn't seem to *me*," he said, "that he would have such an unlikely story, with so many authentic overtones, unless it were true. He didn't look at all like a Harlem Negro—his head was uncanny—and he seemed to know about North Carolina and the relief agencies—"

"Nonsense, James. There are a hundred—a thousand—ways of obtaining such information. For instance: he quoted thirty-five cents an hour as his old wage. Well, *you* could research that. *Is* thirty-five cents an hour standard pay in the cotton belt? To be frank, it sounds low to me."

"That was the thing," Liz said, "that made me begin to wonder."

James turned on her, surprised and stung. "Damn it, the trouble with people like you who are passed from one happy breadwinner to the next without missing a damn meal is that you refuse to admit that outside your own bubble anybody can be suffering. Of *course* people starve. Of *course* children die. Of *course* a man will pay a quarter an hour if nobody makes him pay more. Jesus."

"However," Rudy went on, "mere dollar-and-cents quotations mean very little; the relative value, purchasewise, of, for instance, ten cents, 'a thin dime'—"

James's harangue had agitated Augustina; her nostrils darted this way and that, and when she heard her husband's voice drone, she turned those marvelous staring apertures directly on him. Not insensitive, he slowly climbed out of his brain, sensed the heat in the room, and, the worst thing possible, fell silent.

The silence went on. Liz was blushing. James held his tongue, by way of apology to her. Rudy's brittle gears shifted, his mouth flipped open, and he considerately said, "No, joke about it as we will, a problem in sheer currency can very seriously affect real people. To take an example, in the states of the Confederacy in the decade after the surrender of Appomattox—that is, from the year eighteen sixty-five to the year eighteen seventy-*four* . . ."

On Monday James's office was waiting for him. The white-headed tacks made his personal constellation on the cork. The wastebasket had been emptied. A blue envelope lay on the steel desk. Otherwise, not so much as a pen nib had been disturbed; the drawing he had been working on when Liz called still lay by the telephone, its random placement preserved like the handiwork of a superbly precious being.

He did his work all day with great precision, answering letters, making order. His office encouraged the illusion that each passage of life was on a separate sheet, and could be dropped into the wastebasket, and destroyed by someone else in the night. One job he gave his mind was to keep the phone from ringing. Whether the Negro came or not, with his tattered children or not, from ten to five let the problem belong to Liz. It was of her making. There should be, in a man's life, hours when he has never married, and his wife walks in magic circles she herself draws. It was little enough to ask; he had sold his life, his chances, for her sake. The phone did not ring, except once: Dudevant, effusive.

As he made his way home, through indifferent crowds, the conviction grew that she had wanted to call and had been balked by the cold pressure he had applied at the other end of the line. He would find her clubbed, and his daughter cut in two. He wondered if he would be able to give a good enough description of the Negro to the police. He saw himself in the station stammering, blushing, despised by the policemen; had it been their wives, they would have been there, knotting their fists, baring their teeth. Through this daydream ran the cowardly hope that the killer would not still be there, lingering stupidly, so that James would have to struggle with him, and be himself injured.

Liz waited until he was in the apartment and his coat was off before she communicated her news. Her tone was apprehensive. "He came again, when Martha was having her nap. I went to the stairs—I was terribly busy cleaning up. He said the man who promised to sell him the furniture wouldn't give him the beds if he didn't give him ten dollars more, and I asked him why he wasn't at his job, and he said something about Wednesday, I don't know. I told him we had given him all we could, and I didn't have a dollar—which was true; you went off with all the money and we have nothing for supper. Anyway, he seemed to have expected it, and was really very nice. So I guess he was a crook."

"Thank God," he said, and they never saw the Negro again, and their happiness returned.

CHARITY
IN "A GIFT FROM THE CITY"

John M. Warner

Although it dramatizes an encounter between a young white couple from Minnesota and a Negro from North Carolina, "A Gift from the City" is neither a civil rights tract nor, except tangentially, an exploration of race relations. Rather, the story is an ironic fable that deals with the true nature of charity. It centers in the fall of the white couple from a state of innocence into a kind of "knowing" that enables them to live in the hostile environment of the large city.

In this story the city is seen as depersonalized and dehumanizing. The first sentences suggest that the city exists as a force that accelerates a modern tendency toward impersonality: "Like most happy people, they came from well inland. Amid this city's mysteries, they had grown very close." Updike suggests that this couple's happiness is something that they achieve in spite of the city and also something that they must guard from the city. Later in the story James reflects,

> Never on a morning had he wished so intensely to be back in Ontauk, Minnesota, his birthplace. The town had over seven thousand residents now, and a city manager instead of a mayor, and since the war the creek that ran through its center and drained its few mills had been robbed of its Indian name and called the Douglas MacArthur River; but the cars still parked higgledy-piggledy on the crooked, shaded streets, and he would still have a place, his father's son.

Even Ontauk is not impervious to changes for the worse: The creek has been "robbed" of its Indian name for that of a war hero. Nevertheless, this inland city seems more hospitable to happiness and a sense of belonging than the vast impersonality of New York.

At the park, James notices that "his daughter played in the damp sand by herself. No one seemed to love her; the other children romped at selfish games." And as he pushes Martha in the swing, "she laughed, but none of the other parents or children gave a sign of hearing her." Such impersonality is, however, typical of what James later calls the "Piston Age." Indeed, as James and Liz walk after the movie, the main streets of Greenwich Village seem "thronged with gangsters and hermaphrodites," and James himself berates Liz for showing what could be a dangerous interest in people's faces. The couple find in the Village nothing of the sense of community that characterizes Ontauk. In fact, "Village" becomes a grimly ironic name for a place where neighborly values cannot exist.

The modern city not only alienates and isolates, making man homeless as well as friendless, it also destroys man's dreams and reduces his spiritual hopes to materialistic achievements. James finds that

> his youth's high hopes—he had thought he was going to be a painter—
> had been distilled into a few practical solids: a steel desk, a sponge chair,
> a drawing board the size of a dining table, infinitely adjustable lighting
> fixtures, abundant draftsman's equipment, and a bulletin board so fresh
> it gave off a scent of cork.

The Raydo shaver he has designed and the long blue bonus envelopes from the satisfied Mr. Dudevant become for James the physical symbols of the material world for which he has sold out his higher spiritual quest.

Still, what differentiates James and Liz from the Dudevants and the Janices of the city is their effort to resist its dehumanizing aspect. Almost through a physical act of willing James creates a safe and "magic" world for his family. At the opening of the story, having heard for the first time of the Negro, James wishes that there were "such a thing as enchantment, and he could draw, with a stick, a circle of safety around them that would hold, though they were on Tenth near Fifth and he forty blocks north." And later, he reflects, "the enchantment had worked." The enchantment consists simply in the young couple's effort to maintain a fragile but nevertheless real state of humanism and love within the dehumanized and loveless world of the large city.

How do they attempt this? Whether consciously or not, they try to adhere to a central Christian tenet: Charity. When Liz first tells James that she has given the Negro ten dollars, he replies, without irony, "you were a wonderful Christian. I'm proud of you." Later, Rudy Bridges tells James that he is "the soul of charity." The longer they live in the city, the more James feels it necessary to avoid giving Providence "opportunities to instruct him": "James's suspicion increased that the city itself, with its steep Babylonian surfaces, its black noon shadows, its godless millions, was poised to strike. He placated the circumambient menace the only way he knew—by giving to beggars." In a godless city, James tries in the only way he knows how to remain Christian, hoping to find in religious action protection for his family.

The action of the story serves, however, to demonstrate Updike's sense of the inadequacy of James and Liz's conception of charity and their necessary and inevitable "fall" into the corruption of the modern, materialistic Babylon. The "enchanted" state the couple achieve always seems tenuous, and James always fears its collapse. Fear and anxiety are a permanent part of his response to his environment for this reason. The first telephone call from Liz causes him to fear for her safety. After she hangs up, "the affair seemed ominous again." Their apartment appears a "safe" refuge on Saturday before the Negro has appeared, but "Sunday, husk among days, was full of fear." James's "charity" has developed out of this fear. Rather than genuinely concerning himself with the objects of his charity, James has simply used his kindnesses to them as a way of forestalling disaster, of placating the "circumambient menace." By his good deeds James sought to prolong the "enchantment" of his happiness.

The reason the encounter with the Negro becomes so important in this story is that he represents a different kind of charitable case from those James has encountered before.

> James hated the Negro chiefly because he was tactless. Janice's mother, the sores of street beggars—this was misery, too, but misery that knew its limits, that kept an orbit and observed manners. But in his perfect ignorance the Negro was like one of those babies born with its heart in front of its ribs. He gave no protection. You touched him and you killed him.

The Negro serves as a catalyst for bringing out two major points about charity—points that James and Liz finally cannot face. First, as the quotation illustrates, the Negro insistently focuses the attention of the charitable act on the object of charity itself. He does not simply accept his money graciously and disappear, thus allowing James his self-satisfied sense of having done a good deed. Rather, the Negro obtrudes himself relentlessly on James, and thus forces the white man to see not himself giving money but the condition of the person to whom he is giving it. This shift in perspective is uncomfortable because it makes the charitable act seem more inadequate in the true Christian sense. As James reflects, "Thirty was nothing. . . . He could give away a flat three thousand, and then thirty every week—more than thirty, fifty—and he and Liz would still be richer than the Negro." True charity concerns itself with the object not with the act, but such concern can be uncomfortable in a materialistic society that places a high value on the possession of goods and property. The encounter with the Negro makes James aware for the first time of the uncomfortable recognitions that a "true Christian" must make.

Secondly, the Negro raises the question of the validity of the charitable act. Is his case real or is it simply a fake designed to exploit gullible people? Throughout the story James has resisted the idea that his charity might be misplaced. When Janice tells her story of the healthy man who makes a hundred and twenty dollars a week by posing as a beggar, James "smiled tightly . . . he did not like to hear he was being defrauded by pitiable souls on the street who he could see were genuinely deformed or feeble-minded or alcoholic." But by Sunday afternoon, James begins considering the Negro's case as possibly malicious. "Reliving his behavior in this light was agonizing. He shuddered above the depths of fatuity the Negro must have seen in his clumsy kindness. If the story had been a fraud, the impatience of James's charity was its one saving grace."

No true charity can be without concern for the authenticity of its object; a mere gullible giving cannot be mistaken for a Christian impulse, for it lacks that proper self-respect without which there can be no true concern for others. On the other hand, an obsessive interest in the authenticity of the charitable demand made upon one can also be destructive. One has to have a proper concern for the validity of the charitable impulse, but to allow this concern to degenerate into a morbid fear of being "taken" is a perversion of one's humanity. As Updike sees it, one of the great threats of city life (and, ironically, one of its gifts) is the growing dehumanization of personal relationships as people become less and less willing to accept the sometimes ambiguous implications of their charitable acts.

Such is the threat that James and Liz are not able to resist. Their being from the West, their "inlandness," has been their protection before, for they still try to abide by the more charitable view of human relations that developed out of the sense of community in Ontauk. But as James finds his "youth's high hopes" of being an artist ending in designing Raydo razors, so the couple find their charitable impulse being corrupted into a final selfishness by the moral ambiguities the Negro presents.

This "fall" from grace is prefigured throughout the story by the growing tendency of the couple (particularly James) to react to people not as humans but as objects. The complexities and ambiguities in having to react to human beings in human situations can, obviously, best be removed by considering them abstractly. Thus, on Saturday, while he is waiting for the Negro to appear, James becomes angry, thinking that the "whole *tribe* of charity seekers, to whom he had been so good, had betrayed him." James's growing materialism is revealed when Janice's comment that the pseudocripple makes "more than any of us who work honestly" insults him because "he made more than that a week." His initiation into the nuances of charitable action causes him more and more to treat people as objects, rather than as humans. Thus, the Village street is crowded with "gangsters and hermaphrodites"; Janice becomes the "bloodsucker"; the Negro becomes "some damn bugaboo" or "the enemy." Even the baby Martha "was cased in her crib like a piece of apparatus manufacturing sleep."

During the interview between James and the Negro, the young white man's feelings are varied and complex. On the one hand, he would like to respond to the Negro humanly. For this reason, the fact that another person (the foreman) apparently has put trust in the Negro is curiously comforting to James: "To James he looked extremely frail, but the happy idea of there existing a broad-shouldered foreman willing to make him a working citizen washed all doubts away." For James, the foreman's belief in the Negro authenticates him as a human being, as someone on whom James's charity can properly be bestowed. Rather ominous, however, is James's recognition in the same scene that there was "a resemblance between the Negro's head and the Raydo shaver." It would be convenient if all the complexities the Negro raises could be reduced to problems of design like that of the Raydo razor which "fitted, pleasingly weighty, in the user's hand like a religious stone full of mana."

These foreshadowings of the corruption of the young couple's humanness reach their fruition in the last section of the story. There James spends the day at the office, working "with great precision . . . making order." Life has not revealed itself as very tidy or neat, but "his office encouraged the illusion that each passage of life was on a separate sheet, and could be dropped into the wastebasket, and destroyed by someone else in the night." Another sign of James's demoralization is that he gives the problem of the Negro to Liz, feeling that it "was little enough to ask; he had sold his life, his chances, for her sake." Finally, as the sign of his total degeneration, walking home, he daydreams, not about building enchanted castles for his family, but about their having been cruelly murdered by the outraged Negro. "Through this daydream ran the cowardly hope that the killer would not still be there, lingering stupidly, so that James would have to struggle with him, and be himself injured." Fortunately, James is spared this ordeal, for Liz informs him that the Negro indeed returned, seeking more money, but left quietly (and, as it turns out, permanently) on finding that no more charity would be forthcoming. They rejoice that the Negro turned out to be a crook, thereby relieving them of the strain of Christian charity. Updike ironically concludes, "their happiness returned."

The Bible exhorts that man must "live in" the world but not "be of" it. That is, man must recognize his existence in a social context and his actions must inevitably conform in part to that context. But man must beware of letting his values become totally dependent upon that context. Updike clearly delineates the fall of an average young couple intent upon maintaining their humanness but incapable finally of accepting the complexities and ambiguities of charitable action. After their test, their initiation experience, their "happiness" returns, but we must regard it as a debased happiness. It perhaps represents a withdrawal from the world of enchantment, but its foundation rests on an impersonal, dehumanized, selfish society: It is the logical and ultimate "gift from the city."

QUESTIONS

A Gift from the City

POINT OF VIEW 1. Angry at the possibility of his being duped by the Negro, James looks forward to the Bridges' visit. "They saw him as others saw him and knew his value. He would bask in their lucid external view." Ironically, however, because Updike has chosen to reveal the story through the perceptions of James, the reader views James from the inside. Assuming, therefore, that we share James's self-image because we share his vantage point, would he (as he thinks) appear strong and invulnerable if viewed from the outside—that is, through the eyes of the Bridges, Janice, or the Negro? Discuss. 2. Although the Negro is a pivotal character, Updike has chosen *not* to reveal the workings of his mind. In what way is the "problem" of charity heightened by treating the Negro as a closed consciousness? 3. On occasion, the narrator abandons the subjective perceptions of James to insert passages that reflect an apparently objective point of view. After examining the content of three such passages, explain what they have in common and why Updike chose to "leave" James's consciousness to give the reader this information.

CHARACTERS 4. Analyze the relation between James and the baby-sitter. Why does Janice try "to cure a smile" when James gives the Negro $20.00 and makes "his speech"? Is Janice another object of James's charity? In what way does she intensify the conflict? How does she represent the city? 5. Examine the relationship of James and Liz. Is Liz always truthful? Is there evidence that James blames Liz for his not being a painter? Explain. 6. How are Rudy Bridges and James similar?

PLOT 7. In one sense, the visit of Rudy and Augustina Bridges seems gratuitous—needlessly delaying the resolution. What justifications can you find for including this episode in the story? 8. Some critics have objected to Updike's evasiveness as a writer, charging him with setting up a problem and then employing some happenstance that allows him to resolve the story without bringing his protagonist into any meaningful confrontation with that problem. Does "A Gift from the City" have this flaw? Explain.

SETTING 9. Does Updike succeed in conveying both the tangible and intangible aspects of his Manhattan setting? If so, what details does he select to convey the complex reality of New York City?

STYLE 10. As well as utilizing many images that suggest dehumanization, Updike builds a cluster of images around the concept of fear—an all-embracing concept that obscures the variety of activities (work, recreation, family life) and the relationships that figure in the story. Find as many images of fear as you can. How do they help to imply the theme of the story?

TONE 11. How does the religious imagery used in the story help to shape the theme? 12. In the first line of the story, Updike describes James and Liz as being "happy." Yet there is little evidence of their "happiness," even prior to the appearance of the Negro. Is the description of their condition as "happy" evidence of an ironical tone? Cite other evidence in support of the contention that irony is the dominant tone in this story. 13. Perhaps nowhere in the story is Updike's irony less subtle and his judgments less ambiguous than in the paragraph introducing the Bridges:

> Rudy Bridges was also from Ontauk, Minnesota. He had been two classes ahead of James in the high school, a scholastic wonder, the more so because his father was a no-account who died of tuberculosis the year Rudy graduated. In the nine years since, Rudy's buttercup hair had thinned severely, but the spherical head and the chubby lips of the prig had remained constant. *His* great hopes had been boiled down to instructing three sections of Barnard girls in American history. His wife came from Maryland. Augustina was a pale and handsome woman with an uncompromising, uptilted nose that displayed its nostrils. She wore her abundant chestnut hair strictly parted in the middle—a madonna for the Piston Age. They had no children, and with elaborate managing, just enough money. James loved them as guests. In their own home, Rudy talked too much about his special

field, domestic fiscal policy between Grant and Wilson, a desert of dullness where the lowliest scholar could be king. And Augustina, careful of the budget, went hungry and thirsty and inhibited everyone. Away from home she drank and ate beautifully.

The tone—the underlying attitude—is clear: Updike thoroughly dislikes the Bridges. To see how crucial tone is to characterization, rewrite the paragraph, taking as your tone an attitude of sympathy, affection, and admiration for the Bridges. Try to stick to the facts Updike offers, embroidering on them as little as possible. Achieve most of your desired effect through the *language* in which you present the facts.

Charity in "A Gift from the City"

FOCUS 1. The essay describes the story as centering in the fall of James and Liz from "a state of innocence into a kind of 'knowing.'" Does the essay relate this "knowledge" to the theme of charity? If so, how?

ORGANIZATION 2. The first sentence states that the story "is neither a civil rights tract nor, except tangentially, an exploration of race relations." Why do you suppose the essayist felt it necessary or desirable to make that statement? In what way *is* this story a tangential exploration of race relations? 3. In what way does the essayist's emphasis on the city serve to unify the essay? 4. Is there any parallel between the plot of the story and the organization of evidence and explanation in the essay? If so, what is it?

USING THE EVIDENCE 5. Why does the essayist describe the dehumanization of personal relationships as, "ironically," one of the city's gifts? 6. The essay contends that James and Liz are different from "the Dudevants and the Janices" because they attempt to resist the city's dehumanizing aspect. Is there any evidence in the essay to prove that Dudevant and Janice are, indeed, dehumanized? 7. How does the essayist support his contention that James's "charity" has developed out of his "fear"?

STYLE 8. Comment on the manner in which the essayist has used quotations from the story in his analysis.

MAKING LITERARY JUDGMENTS 9. The essay terms the story an ironic fable. What literary qualities in the story support this judgment? 10. By treating the story as an ironic fable, does the essay slight the story as a piece of realistic fiction? Discuss. 11. After stating that the last three words of the story are ironical, the essay treats the irony as evaluative— as qualifying overt meaning and surface action. Do you agree with this judgment? Explain.

THE CHRISTIAN
ROOMMATES

Orson Ziegler came straight to Harvard from the small South Dakota town where his father was the doctor. Orson, at eighteen, was half an inch under six feet tall, with a weight of 164 and an I.Q. of 152. His eczematous cheeks and vaguely irritated squint—as if his face had been for too long transected by the sight of a level horizon—masked a definite self-confidence. As the doctor's son, he had always mattered in the town. In his high school he had been class president, valedictorian, and captain of the football and baseball teams. (The captain of the basketball team had been Lester Spotted Elk, a full-blooded Chippewa with dirty fingernails and brilliant teeth, a smoker, a drinker, a discipline problem, and the only boy Orson ever had met who was better than he at anything that mattered.) Orson was the first native of his town to go to Harvard, and would probably be the last, at least until his son was of age. His future was firm in his mind: the pre-med course here, medical school either at Harvard, Penn, or Yale, and then back to South Dakota, where he had his wife already selected and claimed and primed to wait. Two nights before he left for Harvard, he had taken her virginity. She had cried, and he had felt foolish, having, somehow, failed. It had been his virginity, too. Orson was sane, sane enough to know that he had lots to learn, and to be, within limits, willing. Harvard processes thousands of such boys and restores them to the world with little apparent damage. Presumably because he was from west of the Mississippi and a Protestant Christian (Methodist), the authorities had given him as a freshman roommate a self-converted Episcopalian from Oregon.

When Orson arrived at Harvard on the morning of Registration Day, bleary and stiff from the series of airplane rides that had begun fourteen hours before, his roommate was already installed. "H. Palamountain" was floridly inscribed in the upper of the two name slots on the door of Room 14. The bed by the window had been slept in, and the desk by the window was neatly loaded with books. Standing sleepless inside the door, inertly clinging to his two heavy suitcases, Orson was conscious of another presence in the room without being able to locate it; optically and mentally, he focused with a slight slowness.

The roommate was sitting on the floor, barefoot, before a small spinning wheel. He jumped up nimbly. Orson's first impression was of the wiry quickness that almost magically brought close to his face the thick-lipped, pop-eyed face of the other boy. He was a head shorter than Orson, and wore, above his bare feet, pegged sky-blue slacks, a lumberjack shirt whose throat was dashingly stuffed with a silk foulard, and a white cap such as Orson had seen before only in photographs of Pandit Nehru. Dropping a suitcase, Orson offered his hand. Instead of taking it, the roommate touched his palms together, bowed his head, and murmured something Orson didn't catch. Then he gracefully swept off the white cap, revealing a narrow crest of curly blond hair that stood up like a rooster's comb. "I am Henry Palamountain." His voice, clear and colorless in the way of West Coast voices, suggested a radio announcer. His handshake was metallically firm and seemed to have a pinch of malice in it. Like Orson, he wore glasses. The thick lenses emphasized the hyperthyroid bulge of his eyes and their fishy, searching expression.

"Orson Ziegler," Orson said.

"I know."

Orson felt a need to add something adequately solemn, standing as they were on the verge of a kind of marriage. "Well, Henry"—he lamely lowered the other suitcase to the floor—"I guess we'll be seeing a lot of each other."

"You may call me Hub," the roommate said. "Most people do. However, call me Henry if you insist. I don't wish to diminish your dreadful freedom. You may not wish to call me anything at all. Already I've made three hopeless enemies in the dormitory."

Every sentence in this smoothly enunciated speech bothered Orson, beginning with the first. He himself had never been given a nickname; it was the one honor his classmates had withheld from him. In his adolescence he had coined nicknames for himself—Orrie, Ziggy—and tried to insinuate them into popular usage, without success. And what was meant by "dreadful freedom"? It sounded sarcastic. And why might he not wish to call him anything at all? And how had the roommate had the time to make enemies? Orson asked irritably, "How long have you *been* here?"

"Eight days." Henry concluded every statement with a strange little pucker of his lips, a kind of satisfied silent click, as if to say, "And what do you think of *that?*"

Orson felt that he had been sized up as someone easy to startle. But he slid helplessly into the straight-man role that, like the second-best bed, had been reserved for him. "That *long?*"

"Yes. I was totally alone until the day before yesterday. You see, I hitch-hiked."

"From *Oregon?*"

"Yes. And I wished to allow time enough for any contingency. In case I was robbed, I had sewed a fifty-dollar bill inside my shirt. As it turned out, I made smooth connections all the way. I had painted a large cardboard sign saying 'Harvard.' You should try it sometime. One meets some very interesting Harvard graduates."

"Didn't your parents worry?"

"Of course. My parents are divorced. My father was furious. He wanted me to fly. I told him to give the plane fare to the Indian Relief Fund. He never gives a penny to charity. And, of course, I'm old. I'm twenty."

"You've been in the Army?"

Henry lifted his hands and staggered back as if from a blow. He put the back of his hand to his brow, whimpered "Never," shuddered, straightened up smartly, and saluted. "In fact, the Portland draft board is after me right now." With a preening tug of his two agile hands—which did look, Orson realized, old: bony and veined and red-tipped, like a woman's—he broadened his foulard. "They refuse to recognize any conscientious objectors except Quakers and Mennonites. My bishop agrees with them. They offered me an out if I'd say I was willing to work in a hospital, but I explained that this released a man for combat duty and if it came to that I'd just as soon carry a gun. I'm an excellent shot. I mind killing only on principle."

The Korean War had begun that summer, and Orson, who had been nagged by a suspicion that his duty was to enlist, bristled at such blithe pacifism. He squinted and asked, "What *have* you been doing for two years, then?"

"Working in a plywood mill. As a gluer. The actual gluing is done by machines, but they become swamped in their own glue now and then. It's a kind of excessive introspection—you've read *Hamlet?*"

"Just *Macbeth* and *The Merchant of Venice.*"

"Yes. Anyway. They have to be cleaned with solvent. One wears long rubber gloves up to one's elbows. It's very soothing work. The inside of a gluer is an excellent place for revolving Greek quotations in your head. I memorized nearly the whole of the *Phaedo* that way." He gestured toward his desk, and Orson saw that many of the books were green Loeb editions of Plato and Aristotle, in Greek. Their spines were worn; they looked read and reread. For the first time, the thought of being at Harvard frightened him. Orson had been standing between his suitcases and now he moved to unpack. "Have you left me a bureau?"

"Of course. The better one." Henry jumped on the bed that had not been slept in and bounced up and down as if it were a trampoline. "And I've given you the bed with the better mattress," he said, still bouncing, "and the desk that doesn't have the glare from the window."

"Thanks," Orson said.

Henry was quick to notice his tone. "Would you rather have my bed? My desk?" He jumped from the bed and dashed to his desk and scooped a stack of books from it.

Orson had to touch him to stop him, and was startled by the tense muscularity of the arm he touched. "Don't be silly," he said. "They're exactly alike."

Henry replaced his books. "I don't want any bitterness," he said, "or immature squabbling. As the older man, it's my responsibility to yield. Here. I'll give you the shirt off my back." And he began to peel off his lumberjack shirt, leaving the foulard dramatically knotted around his naked throat. He wore no undershirt.

Having won from Orson a facial expression that Orson himself could not see, Henry smiled and rebuttoned the shirt. "Do you mind my name being in the upper slot on the door? I'll remove it. I apologize. I did it without realizing how sensitive you would be."

Perhaps it was all a kind of humor. Orson tried to make a joke. He pointed and asked, "Do I get a spinning wheel, too?"

"Oh, *that.*" Henry hopped backward on one bare foot and became rather shy. "That's an experiment. I ordered it from Calcutta. I spin for a half hour a day, after Yoga."

"You do Yoga, too?"

"Just some of the elementary positions. My ankles can't take more than five minutes of the Lotus yet."

"And you say you have a bishop."

The roommate glanced up with a glint of fresh interest. "Say. You listen, don't you? Yes. I consider myself an Anglican Christian Platonist strongly influenced by Gandhi." He touched his palms before his chest, bowed, straightened, and giggled. "My bishop hates me," he said. "The one in Oregon, who wants me to be a soldier. I've introduced myself to the bishop here and I don't think he likes me, either. For that matter, I've antagonized my adviser. I told him I had no intention of fulfilling the science requirement."

"For God's sake, why *not?*"

"You don't really want to know."

Orson felt this rebuff as a small test of strength. "Not really," he agreed.

"I consider science a demonic illusion of human *hubris.* Its phantasmal nature is proved by its constant revision. I asked him, 'Why should I waste an entire fourth of my study time, time that could be spent with Plato, mastering a mass of hypotheses that will be obsolete by the time I graduate?' "

"My Lord, Henry," Orson exclaimed, indignantly defending the millions of lives saved by medical science, "you can't be serious!"

"Please. Hub. I may be difficult for you, and I think it would help if you were to call me by my name. Now let's talk about you. Your father is a doctor, you received all A's in high school—I received rather mediocre grades myself—and you've come to Harvard because you believe it affords a cosmopolitan Eastern environment that will be valuable to you after spending your entire life in a small provincial town."

"Who the hell told you all this?" The recital of his application statement made Orson blush. He already felt much older than the boy who had written it.

"University Hall," Henry said. "I went over and asked to see your folder. They didn't want to let me at first, but I explained that if they were going to give me a roommate, after I had specifically requested to live alone, I had a right to information about you, so I could minimize possible friction."

"And they *let* you?"

"Of course. People without convictions have no powers of resistance." His mouth made its little satisfied click, and Orson was goaded to ask, "Why did *you* come to Harvard?"

"Two reasons." He ticked them off on two fingers. "Raphael Demos and Werner Jaeger."

Orson did not know these names, but he suspected that "Friends of yours?" was a stupid question, once it was out of his mouth.

But Henry nodded. "I've introduced myself to Demos. A charming old scholar, with a beautiful young wife."

"You mean you just went to his house and pushed yourself *in?*" Orson heard his own voice grow shrill; his voice, rather high and unstable, was one of the things about himself that he liked least.

Henry blinked, and looked unexpectedly vulnerable, so slender and bravely dressed, his ugly, yellowish, flat-nailed feet naked on the floor, which was uncarpeted and painted black. "That isn't how I would describe it. I went as a pilgrim. He seemed pleased to talk to me." He spoke carefully, and his mouth abstained from clicking.

That he could hurt his roommate's feelings—that this jaunty apparition had feelings—disconcerted Orson more deeply than any of the surprises he had been deliberately offered. As quickly as he had popped up, Henry dropped to the floor, as if through a trapdoor in the plane of conversation. He resumed spinning. The method apparently called for one thread to be wound around the big toe of a foot and to be kept taut by a kind of absent-minded pedal motion. While engaged in this, he seemed hermetically sealed inside one of the gluing machines that had incubated his garbled philosophy. Unpacking, Orson was slowed and snagged by a complicated mood of discomfort. He tried to remember how his mother had arranged his bureau drawers at home—socks and underwear in one, shirts and handkerchiefs in another. Home seemed infinitely far from him, and he was dizzily conscious of a great depth of space beneath his feet, as if the blackness of the floor were the color of an abyss. The spinning wheel steadily chuckled. Orson's buzz of unease circled and settled on his roommate, who, it was clear, had thought earnestly about profound matters, matters that Orson, busy as he had been with the practical business of being a good student, had hardly considered. It was also clear that Henry had thought unintelligently. This unintelligence ("I received rather mediocre grades myself") was more of a menace than a comfort. Bent above the bureau drawers, Orson felt cramped in his mind, able neither to stand erect in wholehearted contempt nor to lie down in honest admiration. His mood was complicated by the repugnance his roommate's physical presence aroused in him. An almost morbidly clean boy, Orson was haunted by glue, and a tacky ambience resisted every motion of his unpacking.

The silence between the roommates continued until a great bell rang ponderously. The sound was near and yet far, like a heartbeat within the bosom of time, and it seemed to bring with it into the room the muffling foliation of the trees in the Yard, which to Orson's prairie-honed eyes had looked tropically tall and lush; the walls of the room vibrated with leaf shadows, and many minute presences—dust motes, traffic sounds, or angels of whom several could dance on the head of a pin—thronged the air and made it difficult to breathe. The stairways of the dormitory rumbled. Boys dressed in jackets and neckties crowded the doorway and entered the room, laughing and calling "Hub. Hey, Hub."

"Get up off the floor, dad."

"Jesus, Hub, put your shoes on."

"Pee-yew."

"And take off that seductive sarong around your neck."

"Consider the lilies, Hub. They toil not, neither do they spin, and yet I say unto you that Solomon in all his glory was not arrayed like one of these."

"Amen, brothers!"

"Fitch, you should be a preacher."

They were all strangers to Orson. Hub stood and smoothly performed introductions.

In a few days, Orson had sorted them out. That jostling conglomerate, so apparently secure and homogeneous, broke down, under habitual exposure, into double individuals: roommates. There were Silverstein and Koshland, Dawson and Kern, Young and Carter, Petersen and Fitch.

Silverstein and Koshland, who lived in the room overhead, were Jews from New York City. All Orson knew about non-biblical Jews was that they were a sad race, full of music, shrewdness, and woe. But Silverstein and Koshland were always clowning, always wisecracking. They played bridge and poker and chess and Go and went to the movies in Boston and drank coffee in the luncheonettes around the Square. They came from the "gifted" high schools of the Bronx and Brooklyn respectively, and treated Cambridge as if it were another borough. Most of what the freshman year sought to teach them they seemed to know already. As winter approached, Koshland went out for basketball, and he and his teammates made the floor above bounce to the thump and rattle of scrimmages with a tennis ball and a wastebasket. One afternoon, a section of ceiling collapsed on Orson's bed.

Next door, in Room 12, Dawson and Kern wanted to be writers. Dawson was from Ohio and Kern from Pennsylvania. Dawson had a sulky, slouching bearing, a certain puppyish facial eagerness, and a terrible temper. He was a disciple of Anderson and Hemingway and himself wrote as austerely as a newspaper. He had been raised as an atheist, and no one in the dormitory incited his temper more often than Hub. Orson, feeling that he and Dawson came from opposite edges of that great psychological realm called the Midwest, liked him. He felt less at ease with Kern, who seemed Eastern and subtly vicious. A farm boy driven by an unnatural sophistication, riddled with nervous ailments ranging from conjunctivitis to hemorrhoids, Kern smoked and talked incessantly. He and Dawson maintained between them a battery of running jokes. At night Orson could hear them on the other side of the wall keeping each other awake with improvised parodies and musical comedies based on their teachers, their courses, or their fellow-freshmen. One midnight, Orson distinctly heard Dawson sing, "My name is Orson Ziegler, I come from South Dakota." There was a pause, then Kern sang back, "I tend to be a niggler, and masturbate by quota."

Across the hall, in 15, lived Young and Carter, Negroes. Carter was from Detroit and very black, very clipped in speech, very well dressed, and apt to collapse, at the jab of a rightly angled joke, into a spastic giggling fit that left his cheeks gleaming with tears; Kern was expert at breaking Carter up. Young was a lean, malt-pale colored boy from North Carolina, here on a national scholarship, out of his depth, homesick, and cold. Kern called him Br'er Possum. He slept all day and at night sat on his bed playing the mouthpiece of a trumpet to himself. At first, he had played the full horn in the afternoon, flooding the dormitory and its green envelope of trees with golden, tremulous versions of languorous tunes like "Sentimental Journey" and "The Tennessee Waltz." It had been nice. But Young's sombre sense of tact—a slavish drive toward self-effacement that the shock of Harvard had awakened in him—soon cancelled these harmless performances. He took to hiding from the sun, and at night the furtive spitting sound from across the hall seemed to Orson, as he struggled into sleep, music drowning in shame. Carter always referred to his roommate as "Jonathan," mouthing the syllables fastidiously, as if he were pronouncing the name of a remote being he had just learned about, like Rochefoucauld or Demosthenes.

Cattycorner up the hall, in unlucky 13, Petersen and Fitch kept a strange household. Both were tall, narrow-shouldered, and broad-bottomed; physiques aside, it was hard to see what they had in common, or why Harvard had put them together. Fitch, with dark staring eyes and the flat full cranium of Frankenstein's monster, was a child prodigy from Maine, choked with philosophy, wild with ideas, and pregnant with the seeds of the nervous breakdown he was to have, eventually, in April. Petersen was an amiable Swede with a transparent skin that revealed blue veins in his nose. For several summers he had worked as a reporter for the Duluth *Herald.* He had all the newsman's tricks: the side-of-the-mouth quip, the nip of whiskey, the hat on the back of the head, the habit of throwing still-burning cigarettes onto the floor. He did not seem quite to know why he was at Harvard, and in fact did not return at the end of the freshman year. But, while these two drifted toward their respective failures, they made a strangely well-suited couple. Each was strong where the other was helpless. Fitch was so uncoördinated and unorganized he could not even type; he would lie on his bed in pajamas, writhing and grimacing, and dictate a tangled humanities paper, twice the requested length and mostly about books that had not been assigned, while Petersen, typing with a hectic two-finger system, would obligingly turn this chaotic monologue into "copy." His patience verged on the maternal. When Fitch appeared for a meal wearing a coat and tie, the joke ran in the dormitory that Petersen had dressed him. In return, Fitch gave Petersen ideas out of the superabundance painfully cramming his big flat head. Petersen had absolutely no ideas; he could neither compare, contrast, nor criticize St. Augustine and Marcus Aurelius. Perhaps having seen, so young, so many corpses and fires and policemen and prostitutes had prematurely blighted his mind. At any rate, mothering Fitch gave him something practical to do, and Orson envied them.

He envied all the roommates, whatever the bond between them— geography, race, ambition, physical size—for between himself and Hub Palamountain he could see no link except forced cohabitation. Not that living with Hub was superficially unpleasant. Hub was tidy, industrious, and ostentatiously considerate. He rose at seven, prayed, did Yoga, spun, and was off to breakfast, often not to be seen again until the end of the day. He went to sleep, generally, at eleven sharp. If there was noise in the room, he would insert rubber plugs in his ears, put a black mask over his eyes, and go to sleep anyway. During the day, he kept a rigorous round of appointments: he audited two courses in addition to taking four, he wrestled three times a week for his physical-training requirement, he wangled tea invitations from Demos and Jaeger and the Bishop of Massachusetts, he attended free evening lectures and readings, he associated himself with Phillips Brooks House and spent two afternoons a week supervising slum boys in a Roxbury redevelopment house. In addition, he had begun to take piano lessons in Brookline. Many days, Orson saw him only at meals in the Union, where the dormitory neighbors, in those first fall months when their acquaintance was crisp and young and differing interests had not yet scattered them, tended to regroup around a long table. In these months there was often a debate about the subject posed under their eyes: Hub's vegetarianism. There he would sit, his tray heaped high with a steaming double helping of squash and lima beans, while Fitch would try to locate the exact point at which vegetarianism became inconsistent. "You eat eggs," he said.

"Yes," Hub said.

"You realize that every egg, from the chicken's point of reference, is a newborn baby?"

"But in fact it is not unless it has been fertilized by a rooster."

"But suppose," Fitch pursued, "as sometimes happens—which I happen to know, from working in my uncle's henhouse in Maine—an egg that *should* be sterile has in fact been fertilized and contains an embryo?"

"If I see it, I naturally don't eat that particular egg," Hub said, his lips making that satisfied concluding snap.

Fitch pounced triumphantly, spilling a fork to the floor with a lurch of his hand. "But *why?* The hen feels the same pain on being parted from an egg whether sterile or fertile. The embryo is unconscious—a vegetable. As a vegetarian, you should eat it with special relish." He tipped back in his chair so hard he had to grab the table edge to keep from toppling over.

"It seems to me," Dawson said, frowning darkly—these discussions, clogging some twist of his ego, often spilled him into a vile temper—"that psychoanalysis of hens is hardly relevant."

"On the contrary," Kern said lightly, clearing his throat and narrowing his pink, infected eyes, "it seems to me that there, in the tiny, dim mind of the hen—the minimal mind, as it were—is where the tragedy of the universe achieves a pinpoint focus. Picture the emotional life of a hen. What does she know of companionship? A flock of pecking, harsh-voiced gossips. Of shelter? A few dung-bespattered slats. Of food? Some flecks of mash and grit insolently tossed on the ground. Of love? The casual assault of a polygamous cock—cock in the Biblical sense. Then, into this heartless world, there suddenly arrives, as if by magic, an egg. An egg of her own. An egg, it must seem to her, that she and God have made. How she must cherish it, its beautiful baldness, its gentle lustre, its firm yet somehow fragile, softly swaying weight."

Carter had broken up. He bent above his tray, his eyes tight shut, his dark face contorted joyfully. "Puhleese," he gasped at last. "You're making my stomach hurt."

"Ah, Carter," Kern said loftily, "if that were only the worst of it. For then, one day, while the innocent hen sits cradling this strange, faceless, oval child, its little weight swaying softly in her wings"—he glanced hopefully at Carter, but the colored boy bit his lower lip and withstood the jab—"an enormous man, smelling of beer and manure, comes and tears the egg from her grasp. And why? Because *he*"—Kern pointed, arm fully extended, across the table, so that his index finger, orange with nicotine, almost touched Hub's nose—"*he,* Saint Henry Palamountain, wants more eggs to eat. 'More eggs!' he cries voraciously, so that brutal steers and faithless pigs can continue to menace the children of American mothers!"

Dawson slammed his silver down, got up from the table, and slouched out of the dining room. Kern blushed. In the silence, Petersen put a folded slice of roast beef in his mouth and said, chewing, "Jesus, Hub, if somebody else kills the animals you might as well eat 'em. They don't give a damn any more."

"You understand nothing," Hub said simply.

"Hey, Hub," Silverstein called down from the far end of the table. "What's the word on milk? Don't calves drink milk? Maybe you're taking milk out of some calf's mouth."

Orson felt impelled to speak. *"No,"* he said, and his voice seemed to have burst, its pitch was so unsteady and excited. "As anybody except somebody from New York would know, milch cows have weaned their calves. What I wonder about, Hub, is your shoes. You wear leather shoes."

"I do." The gaiety left Hub's defense of himself. His lips became prim.

"Leather is the skin of a steer."

"But the animal has already been slaughtered."

"You sound like Petersen. Your purchase of leather goods—what about your wallet and belt, for that matter?—encourages the slaughter. You're as much of a murderer as the rest of us. More of one—because you think about it."

Hub folded his hands carefully in front of him, propping them, almost in prayer, on the table edge. His voice became like that of a radio announcer, but an announcer rapidly, softly describing the home stretch of a race. "My belt, I believe, is a form of plastic. My wallet was given to me by my mother years ago, before I became a vegetarian. Please remember that I ate meat for eighteen years and I still have an appetite for it. If there were any other concentrated source of protein, I would not eat eggs. Some vegetarians do not. On the other hand, some vegetarians eat fish and take liver extract. I would not do this. Shoes are a problem. There is a firm in Chicago that makes non-leather shoes for extreme vegetarians, but they're very expensive and not comfortable. I once ordered a pair. They killed my feet. Leather, you see, 'breathes' in a way no synthetic substitute does. My feet are tender; I have compromised. I apologize. For that matter, when I play the piano I encourage the slaughter of elephants, and in brushing my teeth, which I must do faithfully because a vegetable diet is so heavy in carbohydrates, I use a brush of pig bristles. I am covered with blood, and pray daily for forgiveness." He took up his fork and resumed eating the mound of squash.

Orson was amazed; he had been impelled to speak by a kind of sympathy, and Hub had answered as if he alone were an enemy. He tried to defend himself. "There are perfectly wearable shoes," he said, "made out of canvas, with crêpe-rubber soles."

"I'll look into them," Hub said. "They sound a little sporty to me."

Laughter swept the table and ended the subject. After lunch Orson walked to the library with the beginnings of indigestion; a backwash of emotion was upsetting his stomach. There was a growing confusion inside him he could not resolve. He resented being associated with Hub, and yet felt attacked when Hub was attacked. It seemed to him that Hub deserved credit for putting his beliefs into practice, and that people like Fitch and Kern, in mocking, merely belittled themselves. Yet Hub smiled at their criticism, took it as a game, and fought back in earnest only at Orson, forcing him into a false position. Why? Was it because in being also a Christian he alone qualified for serious rebuke? But Carter went to church, wearing a blue pin-striped suit with a monogrammed handkerchief peaked in the breast pocket, every Sunday; Petersen was a nominal Presbyterian; Orson had once seen Kern sneaking out of Mem Chapel; and even Koshland observed his holidays, by cutting classes and skipping lunch. Why, therefore, Orson asked himself, should Hub pick on him? And why should he care? He had no real respect for Hub. Hub's handwriting was childishly large and careful and his first set of hour exams, even in the course on Plato and Aristotle, had yielded a batch of C's. Orson resented being condescended to by an intellectual inferior. The knowledge that at the table he had come off second best galled him like an unfair grade. His situation with Hub became in his head a diagram in which all his intentions curved off at right angles and his strengths inversely tapered into nothing. Behind the diagram hung the tuck of complacence in Hub's lips, the fishy impudence of his eyes, and the keenly irksome shape and tint of his hands and feet. These images—Hub disembodied—Orson carried with him into the library, back and forth to classes, and along the congested streets around the Square; now and then the glaze of an eye or the flat yellowish nail of a big toe welled up distinctly through the pages of a book and, greatly magnified, slid with Orson into the unconsciousness of sleep. Nevertheless, he surprised himself, sitting one February afternoon in Room 12 with Dawson and Kern, by blurting, "I hate him." He considered what he had said, liked the taste of it, and repeated, "I hate the bastard. I've never hated anybody before in my life." His voice cracked and his eyes warmed with abortive tears.

They had all returned from Christmas vacation to plunge into the weird limbo of reading period and the novel ordeal of midyear exams. This was a dormitory, by and large, of public-school graduates, who feel the strain of Harvard most in their freshman year. The private-school boys, launched by little Harvards like Exeter and Groton, tend to glide through this year and to run aground later on strange reefs, foundering in alcohol, or sinking into dandified apathy. But the institution demands of each man, before it releases him, a wrenching sacrifice of ballast. At Christmas, Orson's mother thought he looked haggard, and set about fattening him up. On the other hand, he was struck by how much his father had aged and shrunk. Orson spent his first days home listening to the mindless music on the radio, hours of it, and driving through farmland on narrow straight roads already banked bright with plowed snow. The South Dakota sky had never looked so open, so clean; he had never realized before that the high dry sun that made even sub-zero days feel warm at noon was a local phenomenon. He made love to his girl again, and again she cried. He said to her he blamed himself, for ineptitude; but in his heart he blamed her. She was not helping him. Back in Cambridge, it was raining, raining in January, and the entryway of the Coop was full of gray footprints and wet bicycles and Radcliffe girls in slickers and sneakers. Hub had stayed here, alone in their room, and had celebrated Christmas with a fast.

In the monotonous, almost hallucinatory month of rereading, outlining, and memorizing, Orson perceived how little he knew, how stupid he was, how unnatural all learning is, and how futile. Harvard rewarded him with three A's and a B. Hub pulled out two B's and two C's. Kern, Dawson, and Silverstein did well; Petersen, Koshland, and Carter got mediocre grades; Fitch flunked one subject, and Young flunked three. The pale Negro slunk in and out of the dorm as if he were diseased and marked for destruction; he became, while still among them, a rumor. The suppressed whistling of the trumpet mouthpiece was no longer heard. Silverstein and Koshland and the basketball crowd adopted Carter and took him to movies in Boston three or four times a week.

After exams, in the heart of the Cambridge winter, there is a grateful pause. New courses are selected, and even the full-year courses, heading into their second half, sometimes put on, like a new hat, a fresh professor. The days quietly lengthen; there is a snowstorm or two; the swimming and squash teams lend the sports pages of the *Crimson* an unaccustomed note of victory. A kind of foreshadow of spring falls bluely on the snow. The elms are seen to be shaped like fountains. The discs of snow pressed by boots into the sidewalk by Albiani's seem large precious coins; the brick buildings, the arched gates, the archaic lecterns, and the barny mansions along Brattle Street dawn upon the freshman as a heritage he temporarily possesses. The thumb-worn spines of his now familiar textbooks seem proof of a certain knowingness, and the strap of the green book bag tugs at his wrist like a living falcon. The letters from home dwindle in importance. The hours open up. There is more time. Experiments are made. Courtships begin. Conversations go on and on; and an almost rapacious desire for mutual discovery possesses acquaintances. It was in this atmosphere, then, that Orson made his confession.

Dawson turned his head away as if the words had menaced him personally. Kern blinked, lit a cigarette, and asked, "What don't you like about him?"

"Well"—Orson shifted his weight uncomfortably in the black but graceful, shapely but hard Harvard chair—"it's little things. Whenever he gets a notice from the Portland draft board, he tears it up without opening it and scatters it out the window."

"And you're afraid that this incriminates you as an accessory and they'll put you in jail?"

"No—I don't know. It seems exaggerated. He exaggerates everything. You should see how he prays."

"How do you know how he prays?"

"He shows me. Every morning, he gets down on his knees and *throws* himself across the bed, his face in the blanket, his arms way out." He showed them.

"God," Dawson said. "That's marvellous. It's medieval. It's more than medieval. It's Counter-Reformation."

"I mean," Orson said, grimacing in realization of how deeply he had betrayed Hub, "I pray, too, but I don't make a show of myself."

A frown clotted Dawson's expression, and passed.

"He's a saint," Kern said.

"He's *not*," Orson said. "He's not intelligent. I'm taking Chem 1 with him, and he's worse than a child with the math. And those Greek books he keeps on his desk, they look worn because he bought them second-hand."

"Saints don't have to be intelligent," Kern said. "What saints have to have is energy. Hub has it."

"Look how he wrestles," Dawson said.

"I doubt if he wrestles very *well*," Orson said. "He didn't make the freshman team. I'm sure if we heard him play the piano, it'd be awful."

"You seem to miss the point," Kern said, eyes closed, "of what Hub's all about."

"I know goddam well what he thinks he's all about," Orson said, "but it's fake. It doesn't go. All this vegetarianism and love of the starving Indian—he's really a terribly cold bastard. I think he's about the coldest person I've ever met in my life."

"I don't think Orson thinks that, do you?" Kern asked Dawson.

"No," Dawson said, and his puppyish smile cleared his cloudy face. "That's not what Orson the Parson thinks."

Kern squirmed. "Is it Orson the Parson, or Orson the Person?"

"I think Hub is the nub," Dawson said.

"Or the rub," Kern added, and both burst into grinding laughter. Orson felt he was being sacrificed to the precarious peace the two roommates kept between themselves, and left, superficially insulted but secretly flattered to have been given, at last, a nickname of sorts: Orson the Parson.

Several nights later they went to hear Carl Sandburg read in New Lecture Hall—the four adjacent roommates, plus Fitch. To avoid sitting next to Hub, who aggressively led them into a row of seats, Orson delayed, and so sat the farthest away from the girl Hub sat directly behind. Orson noticed her immediately; she had a lavish mane of coppery red hair which hung down loose over the back of her seat. The color of it, and the abundance, reminded him, all at once, of horses, earth, sun, wheat, and home. From Orson's angle she was nearly in profile; her face was small, with a tilted shadowy cheekbone and a pale prominent ear. Toward the pallor of her profile he felt an orgasmic surge; she seemed suspended in the crowd and was floating, a crest of whiteness, toward him. She turned away. Hub had leaned forward and was saying something into her other ear. Fitch overheard it, and gleefully relayed it to Dawson, who whispered to Kern and Orson; *"Hub said to the girl, 'You have beautiful hair.'"*

Several times during the reading, Hub leaned forward to add something more into her ear, each time springing spurts of choked laughter from Fitch, Dawson, and Kern. Meanwhile, Sandburg, his white bangs as straight and shiny as a doll's wig of artificial fibre, incanted above the lectern and quaintly strummed a guitar. Afterward, Hub walked with the girl into the outdoors. From a distance Orson saw her white face turn and crumple into a laugh. Hub returned to his friends with the complacent nick in the corner of his mouth deepened, in the darkness, to a gash.

It was not the next day, or the next week, but within the month that Hub brought back to the room a heap of red hair. Orson found it lying like a disastrous corpse on a newspaper spread on his bed. "Hub, what the hell is this?"

Hub was on the floor playing with his spinning wheel. "Hair."

"*Human* hair?"

"Of course."

"Whose?"

"A girl's."

"What happened?" The question sounded strange; Orson meant to ask, "What girl's?"

Hub answered as if he had asked that question. "It's a girl I met at the Sandburg reading; you don't know her."

"This is *her* hair?"

"Yes. I asked her for it. She said she was planning to cut it all off this spring anyway."

Orson stood stunned above the bed, gripped by an urge to bury his face and hands in the hair. "You've been *seeing* her?" This effeminate stridence in his voice: he despised it and only Hub brought it out.

"A little. My schedule doesn't allow for much social life, but my adviser has recommended that I relax now and then."

"You take her to movies?"

"Once in a while. She pays her admission, of course."

"Of *course*."

Hub took him up on his tone. "Please remember I'm here on my savings alone. I have refused all financial assistance from my father."

"Hub"—the very syllable seemed an expression of pain—"what are you going to do with her hair?"

"Spin it into a rope."

"A *rope*?"

"Yes. It'll be very difficult; her hair is terribly fine."

"And what will you do with the rope?"

"Make a knot of it."

"A *knot*?"

"I think that's the term. I'll coil it and secure it so it can't come undone and give it to her. So she'll always have her hair the way it was when she was nineteen."

"How the hell did you talk this poor girl into it?"

"I didn't talk her into it. I merely offered, and she thought it was a lovely idea. Really, Orson, I don't see why this should offend your bourgeois scruples. Women cut their hair all the time."

"She must think you're insane. She was humoring you."

"As you like. It was a perfectly rational suggestion, and my sanity has never been raised as an issue between us."

"Well, *I* think you're insane. Hub, you're a *nut.*"

Orson left the room and slammed the door, and didn't return until eleven, when Hub was asleep in his eye mask. The heap of hair had been transferred to the floor beside the spinning wheel, and already some strands were entangled with the machine. In time a rope was produced, a braided cord as thick as a woman's little finger, about a foot long, weightless and waxen. The earthy, horsy fire in the hair's color had been quenched in the process. Hub carefully coiled it and with black thread and long pins secured and stiffened the spiral into a disc the size of a small saucer. This he presented to the girl one Friday night. The presentation appeared to satisfy him, for, as far as Orson knew, Hub had no further dates with her. Once in a while Orson passed her in the Yard, and without her hair she scarcely seemed female, her small pale face fringed in curt tufts, her ears looking enormous. He wanted to speak to her; some obscure force of pity, or hope of rescue, impelled him to greet this wan androgyne, but the opening word stuck in his throat. She did not look as if she pitied herself, or knew what had been done to her.

Something magical protected Hub; things deflected from him. The doubt Orson had cast upon his sanity bounced back onto himself. As spring slowly broke, he lost the ability to sleep. Figures and facts churned sluggishly in an insomnious mire. His courses became four parallel puzzles. In mathematics, the crucial transposition upon which the solution pivoted consistently eluded him, vanishing into the chinks between the numbers. The quantities in chemistry became impishly unstable; the unbalanced scales clicked down sharply and the system of interlocked elements that fanned from the lab to the far stars collapsed. In the history survey course, they had reached the Enlightenment, and Orson found himself disturbingly impressed by Voltaire's indictment of God, though the lecturer handled it calmly, as one more dead item of intellectual history, neither true nor false. And in German, which Orson had taken to satisfy his language requirement, the words piled on remorselessly, and the existence of languages other than English, the existence of so many, each so vast, intricate, and opaque, seemed to prove cosmic dementia. He felt his mind, which was always more steady than quick, grow slower and slower. His chair threatened to adhere to him, and he would leap up in panic. Sleepless, stuffed with information he could neither forget nor manipulate, he became prey to obsessive delusions; he became convinced that his girl in South Dakota had taken up with another boy and was making love to him happily, Orson having shouldered the awkwardness and blame of taking her virginity. In the very loops that Emily's ballpoint pen described in her bland letters to him he read the pleased rotundity, the inner fatness of a well-loved woman. He even knew the man. It was Spotted Elk, the black-nailed Chippewa, whose impassive nimbleness had so often mocked Orson on the basketball court, whose terrible ease and speed of reaction had seemed so unjust, and whose defense—he recalled now—Emily had often undertaken. His wife had become a whore, a squaw; the scraggly mute reservation children his father had doctored in the charity clinic became, amid the sliding transparencies of Orson's mind, his own children. In his dreams—or in those limp elisions of imagery which in the absence of sleep passed for dreams—he seemed to be rooming with Spotted Elk, and his roommate, who sometimes wore a mask, invariably had won, by underhanded means, the affection and admiration that were rightfully his. There was a conspiracy. Whenever Orson heard Kern and Dawson laughing on the other side of the wall, he knew it was about him, and about his most secret habits. This ultimate privacy was outrageously invaded; in bed, half-relaxed, he would suddenly see himself bodily involved with Hub's lips, Hub's legs, with Hub's veined, vaguely womanish hands. At first he resisted these visions, tried to erase them; it was like trying to erase ripples on water. He learned to submit to them, to let the attack—for it was an attack, with teeth and sharp acrobatic movements—wash over him, leaving him limp enough to sleep. These dives became the only route to sleep. In the morning he would awake and see Hub sprawled flamboyantly across his bed in prayer, or sitting hunched at his spinning wheel, or, gaudily dressed, tiptoeing to the door and with ostentatious care closing it softly behind him; and he would hate him—hate his appearance, his form, his manner, his pretensions with an avidity of detail he had never known in love. The tiny details of his roommate's physical existence—the wrinkles flickering beside his mouth, the slightly withered look about his hands, the complacently polished creases of his leather shoes—seemed a poisonous food Orson could not stop eating. His eczema worsened alarmingly.

By April, Orson was on the verge of going to the student clinic, which had a department called Mental Health. But at this point Fitch relieved him by having, it seemed, his nervous breakdown for him. For weeks, Fitch had been taking several showers a day. Toward the end he stopped going to classes and was almost constantly naked, except for a towel tucked around his waist. He was trying to complete a humanities paper that was already a month overdue and twenty pages too long. He left the dormitory only to eat and to take more books from the library. One night around nine, Petersen was called to the phone on the second-floor landing. The Watertown police had picked Fitch up as he was struggling through the underbrush on the banks of the Charles four miles away. He claimed he was walking to the West, where he had been told there was enough space to contain God, and proceeded to talk with wild animation to the police chief about the differences and affinities between Kierkegaard and Nietzsche. Hub, ever alert for an opportunity to intrude in the guise of doing good, went to the hall proctor—a spindly and murmurous graduate student of astronomy engaged, under Harlow Shapley, in an endless galaxy count—and volunteered himself as an expert on the case, and even conferred with the infirmary psychologist. Hub's interpretation was that Fitch had been punished for *hubris*. The psychologist felt the problem was fundamentally Oedipal. Fitch was sent back to Maine. Hub suggested to Orson that now Petersen would need a roommate next year. "I think you and he would hit it off splendidly. You're both materialists."

"I'm *not* a materialist."

Hub lifted his dreadful hands in half-blessing. "Have it your way. I'm determined to minimize friction."

"Dammit, Hub, all the friction between us comes from *you.*"

"How? What do I do? Tell me, and I'll change. I'll give you the shirt off my back." He began to unbutton, and stopped, seeing that the laugh wasn't going to come.

Orson felt weak and empty, and in spite of himself he cringed inwardly, with a helpless affection for his unreal, unreachable friend. "I don't know, Hub," he admitted. "I don't know what it is you're doing to me."

A paste of silence dried in the air between them.

Orson with an effort unstuck himself. "I think you're right, we shouldn't room together next year."

Hub seemed a bit bewildered, but nodded, saying, "I told them in the beginning that I ought to live alone." And his hurt eyes bulging behind their lenses settled into an invulnerable Byzantine stare.

One afternoon in middle May, Orson was sitting stumped at his desk, trying to study. He had taken two exams and had two to go. They stood between him and release like two towering walls of muddy paper. His position seemed extremely precarious: he was unable to retreat and able to advance only along a very thin thread, a high wire of sanity on which he balanced above an abyss of statistics and formulae, his brain a firmament of winking cells. A push would kill him. There was then a hurried pounding up the stairs, and Hub pushed into the room carrying cradled in his arm a metal object the color of a gun and the size of a cat. It had a red tongue. Hub slammed the door behind him, snapped the lock, and dumped the object on Orson's bed. It was the head of a parking meter, sheared from its post. A keen quick pain cut through Orson's groin. "For God's sake," he cried in his contemptible high voice, "what's *that?*"

"It's a parking meter."

"I *know,* I can *see* that. Where the hell did you *get* it?"

"I won't talk to you until you stop being hysterical," Hub said, and crossed to his desk, where Orson had put his mail. He took the top letter, a special delivery from the Portland draft board, and tore it in half. This time, the pain went through Orson's chest. He put his head in his arms on the desk and whirled and groped in the black-red darkness there. His body was frightening him; his nerves listened for a third psychosomatic slash.

There was a rap on the door; from the force of the knock, it could only be the police. Hub nimbly dashed to the bed and hid the meter under Orson's pillow. Then he pranced to the door and opened it.

It was Dawson and Kern. "What's up?" Dawson asked, frowning as if the disturbance had been created to annoy him.

"It sounded like Ziegler was being tortured," Kern said.

Orson pointed at Hub and explained, "He's castrated a parking meter!"

"I did not," Hub said. "A car went out of control on Mass. Avenue and hit a parked car, which knocked a meter down. A crowd gathered. The head of the meter was lying in the gutter, so I picked it up and carried it away. I was afraid someone might be tempted to steal it."

"Nobody tried to stop you?" Kern asked.

"Of course not. They were all gathered around the driver of the car."

"Was he hurt?"

"I doubt it. I didn't look."

"You didn't *look!*" Orson cried. "You're a great Samaritan."

"I am not prey," Hub said, "to morbid curiosity."

"Where were the police?" Kern asked.

"They hadn't arrived yet."

Dawson asked, "Well why didn't you wait till a cop arrived and give the meter to him?"

"Why should I give it to an agent of the State? It's no more his than mine."

"But it *is,*" Orson said.

"It was a plain act of Providence that placed it in my hands," Hub said, the corners of his lips dented securely. "I haven't decided yet which charity should receive the money it contains."

Dawson asked, "But isn't that stealing?"

"No more stealing than the State is stealing in making people pay money for space in which to park their own cars."

"Huh," Orson said, getting to his feet. "You give it back or we'll both go to jail." He saw himself ruined, the scarcely commenced career of his life destroyed.

Hub turned serenely. "I'm not afraid. Going to jail under a totalitarian regime is a mark of honor. If you had a conscience, you'd understand."

Petersen and Carter and Silverstein came into the room. Some boys from the lower floors followed them. The story was hilariously retold. The meter was produced from under the pillow and passed around and shaken to demonstrate the weight of pennies it contained. Hub always carried, as a vestige of the lumberjack country he came from, an intricate all-purpose pocket knife. He began to pry open the little money door. Orson came up behind him and got him around the neck with one arm. Hub's body stiffened. He passed the head of the meter and the open knife to Carter, and then Orson experienced sensations of being lifted, of flying, and of lying on the floor, looking up at Hub's face, which was upside down in his vision. He scrambled to his feet and went for him again, rigid with anger and yet, in his heart, happily relaxed; Hub's body was tough and quick and satisfying to grip, though, being a wrestler, he somehow deflected Orson's hands and again lifted and dropped him to the black floor. This time, Orson felt a blow as his coccyx hit the wood; yet even through the pain he perceived, gazing into the heart of this marriage, that Hub was being as gentle with him as he could be. And that he could try in earnest to kill Hub and be in no danger of succeeding was also a comfort. He renewed the attack and again enjoyed the tense defensive skill that made Hub's body a kind of warp in space through which his own body, after an ecstatic instant of contention, was converted to the supine position. He got to his feet and would have gone for Hub the fourth time, but his fellow-freshmen grabbed his arms and held him. He shook them off and without a word returned to his desk and concentrated down into his book, turning the page. The type looked extremely distinct, though it was trembling too hard to be deciphered.

The head of the parking meter stayed in the room for one night. The next day, Hub allowed himself to be persuaded (by the others; Orson had stopped speaking to him) to take it to the Cambridge police headquarters in Central Square. Dawson and Kern tied a ribbon around it, and attached a note: "Please take good care of my baby." None of them, however, had the nerve to go with Hub to the headquarters, though when he came back he said the chief was delighted to get the meter, and had thanked him, and had agreed to donate the pennies to the local orphans' home. In another week, the last exams were over. The freshmen all went home. When they returned in the fall, they were different: sophomores. Petersen and Young did not come back at all. Fitch returned, made up the lost credits, and eventually graduated *magna cum* in History and Lit. He now teaches in a Quaker prep school. Silverstein is a bio-chemist, Koshland a lawyer. Dawson writes conservative editorials in Cleveland, Kern is in advertising in New York. Carter, as if obliged to join Young in oblivion, disappeared between his junior and senior years. The dormitory neighbors tended to lose sight of each other, though Hub, who had had his case shifted to the Massachusetts jurisdiction, was now and then pictured in the *Crimson*, and once gave an evening lecture, "Why I Am an Episcopalian Pacifist." As the litigation progressed, the Bishop of Massachusetts rather grudgingly vouched for him, and by the time of his final hearing the Korean War was over, and the judge who heard the case ruled that Hub's convictions were sincere, as witnessed by his willingness to go to jail. Hub was rather disappointed at the verdict, since he had prepared a three-year reading list to occupy him in his cell and was intending to memorize all four Gospels in the original Greek. After graduation, he went to Union Theological Seminary, spent several years as the assistant rector of an urban parish in Baltimore, and learned to play the piano well enough to be the background music in a Charles Street cocktail lounge. He insisted on wearing his clerical collar, and as a consequence gave the bar a small celebrity. After a year of overriding people of less strong convictions, he was allowed to go to South Africa, where he worked and preached among the Bantus until the government requested that he leave the country. From there he went to Nigeria, and when last heard from—on a Christmas card, with French salutations and Negro Magi, which arrived, soiled and wrinkled, in South Dakota in February—Hub was in Madagascar, as a "combination missionary, political agitator, and soccer coach." The description struck Orson as probably facetious, and Hub's childish and confident handwriting, with every letter formed individually, afflicted him with some of the old exasperation. Having vowed to answer the card, he mislaid it, uncharacteristically.

Orson didn't speak to Hub for two days after the parking-meter incident. By then, it seemed rather silly, and they finished out the year sitting side by side at their desks as amiably as two cramped passengers who have endured a long bus trip together. When they parted, they shook hands, and Hub would have walked Orson to the subway kiosk except that he had an appointment in the opposite direction. Orson received two A's and two B's on his final exams; for the remaining three years at Harvard, he roomed uneventfully with two other colorless pre-med students, named Wallace and Neuhauser. After graduation, he married Emily, attended the Yale School of Medicine, and interned in St. Louis. He is now the father of four children and, since the death of his own father, the only doctor in the town. His life has gone much the way he planned it, and he is much the kind of man he intended to be when he was eighteen. He delivers babies, assists the dying, attends the necessary meetings, plays golf, and does good. He is honorable and irritable. If not as much loved as his father, he is perhaps even more respected. In one particular only—a kind of scar he carries without pain and without any clear memory of the amputation—does the man he is differ from the man he assumed he would become. He never prays.

SUGGESTIONS   FOR   WRITING

The Stories

1. Examine the many references to money in "A Gift from the City." Is money and its uses symptomatic of what is wrong with contemporary urban living? Write an essay in which you discuss the function of money in this story.

2. The essay describes James and Liz as undergoing an "initiation experience" that brings them from a state of innocence to a state of "knowing." Write an essay in which you show that "The Christian Roommates" is structured around a similar "fall" into knowledge.

3. While "A Gift from the City" concerns itself with public charity, "The Christian Roommates" deals with private charity. Compare and contrast these two treatments of charity, showing the relation between theme and characterization in each story.

4. Discuss the function of irony in "The Christian Roommates."

5. Several years after their graduation from Harvard, Orson received a Christmas card from Hub. "The description struck Orson as probably facetious, and Hub's childish and confident handwriting, with every letter formed individually, afflicted him with some of the old exas-

peration." Describe the nature of Orson's "exasperation," and why, even as a grown man, Hub annoys him.

Other Works by John Updike

1. In *Desperate Faith*, Howard Harper points out the relationship of some of the stories to the novels, that is, that "Ace in the Hole" is the prototype of *Rabbit, Run*, and "Flight" and "Pigeon Feathers" echo *The Centaur*. Write an essay describing the relationship (in terms of characters, plot, setting, and theme) between one or more Updike stories and a novel—*Rabbit, Run, The Centaur, Of the Farm,* or *Couples*.

2. Examine *The Poorhouse Fair* as a utopian novel. Be sure to discuss its implicit criticism of contemporary society.

3. Updike has said that he conceived *The Centaur* as a "contrasting companion" to *Rabbit, Run*. Write an essay in which you compare and contrast the two novels.

4. Discuss the function of myth in *The Centaur*.

5. Many reviewers find little to praise in *Couples*. Putting himself in this number, William Gass writes, "It's hard to see how anyone could take this diagrammatic melodrama seriously, least of all its author, even though he often seems to." And Charles T. Samuels says of Updike: "Committing himself to banal characters, his dialogue seldom rises above their level. . . . As for the plot—when Updike gets around to it, he concocts an improbable mixture of Boccaccio and Victorian melodrama." Yet, as Updike explains it, *Couples* is an attempt at heightened verisimilitude that approaches fantasy. Write an essay in which you evaluate this novel and come to your own opinion about its literary merit.

6. Compare one or more elements of *Rabbit, Run* (such as characters, setting, plot, theme, imagery) with a similar element (or elements) of *Rabbit Redux*.

7. Explore the structural and thematic ramifications of the novelist-as-protagonist in *Bech: A Book*.

JOHN UPDIKE

BIBLIOGRAPHY

Primary

The Carpentered Hen. New York: Harper & Row, 1958. Poems.
The Poorhouse Fair. New York: Alfred A. Knopf, 1959. A novel.
The Same Door. New York: Alfred A. Knopf, 1959. Short stories.
Rabbit, Run. New York: Alfred A. Knopf, 1960. A novel.
Pigeon Feathers. New York: Alfred A. Knopf, 1962. Short stories.
The Centaur. New York: Alfred A. Knopf, 1963. A novel.
Telephone Poles and Other Poems. New York: Alfred A. Knopf, 1963. Poems.
Assorted Prose. New York: Alfred A. Knopf, 1965. Essays.
Of the Farm. New York: Alfred A. Knopf, 1965. A novel.
The Music School. New York: Alfred A. Knopf, 1966. Short stories.
Couples. New York: Alfred A. Knopf, 1968. A novel.
Midpoint and Other Poems. New York: Alfred A Knopf, 1969. Poems.
Bech: A Book. New York: Alfred A. Knopf, 1970. A novel.
Rabbit Redux. New York: Alfred A. Knopf, 1971. A novel.
Museums and Women and Other Stories. New York: Alfred A. Knopf, 1972. Short stories.

Secondary

Aldridge, John W. "The Private Vice of John Updike" in *A Time to Murder and Create: The Contemporary Novel in Crisis.* New York: David McKay, 1966. Contends that Updike possesses neither "an interesting mind" nor "remarkable gifts."
Burchard, Rachael C. *John Updike: Yea Sayings.* Carbondale, Ill.: Southern Illinois Univ. Press, 1971. Emphasizes Updike as religious searcher rather than as writer.
Finkelstein, Sidney. *Existentialism and Alienation in American Literature.* New York: International Publishers, 1965. Discusses the relationship between alienation and technique in *Rabbit, Run* and *The Centaur.*
Galloway, David D. *The Absurd Hero in American Fiction.* Austin: Univ. of Texas Press, 1966. Devotes a chapter ("The Absurd Man

as Saint") to a discussion of the protagonists in *The Poorhouse Fair, Rabbit, Run,* and *The Centaur.*

Gass, William H. "Cock-A-Doodle-Doo" in *Fiction and the Figures of Life.* New York: Alfred A. Knopf, 1970. An appropriately witty review of *Couples.*

Hamilton, Alice, and Kenneth Hamilton. *John Updike: A Critical Essay.* Grand Rapids, Mich.: William B. Eerdmans Publishing Co., 1967. A thematic study emphasizing Updike's relation to Christianity.

Hamilton, Alice, and Kenneth Hamilton. *The Elements of John Updike.* Grand Rapids, Mich.: William B. Eerdmans Publishing Co., 1970. An expanded version of *John Updike: A Critical Essay* that concentrates almost totally on the patterns of meaning in Updike's fiction.

Harper, Howard M., Jr. *Desperate Faith: A Study of Bellow, Salinger, Mailer, and Updike.* Chapel Hill: Univ. of North Carolina Press, 1967. Explores the increasing depth and integrity of Updike's fiction.

Hicks, Granville. "Generations of the Fifties: Malamud, Gold, and Updike" in *The Creative Present,* ed. by Nona Balakian and Charles Simmons. Garden City, N.Y.: Doubleday, 1963. Links Updike with Malamud and Gold in their shared preoccupation with "the theme of redemption."

Mizener, Arthur. "The American Hero as High-school Boy: Peter Caldwell" in *The Sense of Life in the Modern Novel.* Boston: Houghton Mifflin, 1963. Examines the "discontinuity of substance and style" in *The Centaur.*

Samuels, Charles Thomas. "The Art of Fiction XLII: John Updike." *Paris Review,* 45 (Winter 1968), 84–117. Informative interview that provides insight into Updike's fictional theories.

Samuels, Charles Thomas. *John Updike.* Minneapolis: Univ. of Minnesota Press, 1969 (No. 79 of the University of Minnesota Pamphlets on American Writers). An examination of the major subjects and themes.

Tanner, Tony. "A Compromised Environment" in *City of Words: American Fiction from 1950–1970.* London: Jonathan Cape Ltd., 1971. Discusses Updike's fiction; posits that "Updike shares that vision of entropy so common among contemporary American writers."

Taylor, Larry E. *Pastoral and Anti-Pastoral Patterns in John Updike's Fiction.* Carbondale, Ill.: Southern Illinois Univ. Press, 1971. Introduction provides brief history of the pastoral; remaining chapters show tension in Updike's fiction between pastoralism and anti-pastoralism and between an enthusiasm for nature and a criticism of it.

Ward, J. A. "John Updike's Fiction." *Critique,* 5 (Spring–Summer 1962), 27–40. An examination of technique and meaning in *The Same Door, The Poorhouse Fair, Rabbit, Run,* and *Pigeon Feathers.*

The American writer in the middle of the 20th century has his hands full in trying to understand, and then describe, and then make credible much of the American reality. It stupefies, it sickens, it infuriates, and finally it is even a kind of embarrassment to one's own meager imagination. The actuality is continually outdoing our talents, and the culture tosses up figures almost daily that are the envy of any novelist.

. . .

It is the tug of reality, its mystery and magnetism, that leads one into the writing of fiction—what then when one is not mystified, but stupefied? not drawn but repelled?

. . .

That our communal predicament is a distressing one, is a fact that weighs upon the writer no less, and perhaps even more, than his neighbor—for to the writer the community is, properly, both his subject and his audience. And it may be that when the predicament produces in the writer not only feelings of disgust, rage, and melancholy, but impotence, too, he is apt to lose heart and finally, like his neighbor, turn to other matters, or to other worlds; or to the self, which may, in a variety of ways, become his subject, or even the impulse for his technique.

FROM *Writing American Fiction*

PHILIP ROTH

Philip Roth was born in Newark, New Jersey, in 1933. He graduated from Bucknell University and received a master's degree from the University of Chicago, where he taught English literature from 1956 to 1958. Since then he has been a visiting lecturer at several universities—including Princeton, the State University of New York at Stony Brook, and the University of Pennsylvania. Roth's literary honors include a National Institute of Arts and Letters grant and a Guggenheim fellowship. In 1970, he was elected a member of the National Institute of Arts and Letters.

Goodbye, Columbus (1959), Roth's first book, brought him not only widespread critical acclaim but the 1960 National Book Award for fiction. Composed of a novella and five short stories, this work is set, for the most part, in the region Roth knew best as a boy—the environs of New York City. In *Letting Go* (1962) and *When She Was Good* (1967), Roth uses his later knowledge of the people and institutions of the Midwest. These novels, however, are marred by contrivance and by long lapses into prosaicness. In contrast, some of his more recent works—*Portnoy's Complaint* (1969), *The Breast* (1972), *The Great American Novel* (1973)—are extraordinary displays of energy, imagination, and literary resourcefulness.

Roth's adroitness at capturing the idioms and rhythms of American speech is evident in all his fiction, whether he is writing of suburban Jews, as in "Eli, the Fanatic," or Midwestern Anglo-Saxon Protestants, as in "In Trouble."

ELI, THE FANATIC

Leo Tzuref stepped out from back of a white column to welcome Eli Peck. Eli jumped back, surprised; then they shook hands and Tzuref gestured him into the sagging old mansion. At the door Eli turned, and down the slope of lawn, past the jungle of hedges, beyond the dark, untrampled horse path, he saw the street lights blink on in Woodenton. The stores along Coach House Road tossed up a burst of yellow—it came to Eli as a secret signal from his townsmen: "Tell this Tzuref where we stand, Eli. This is a modern community, Eli, we have our families, we pay taxes . . ." Eli, burdened by the message, gave Tzuref a dumb, weary stare.

"You must work a full day," Tzuref said, steering the attorney and his briefcase into the chilly hall.

Eli's heels made a racket on the cracked marble floor, and he spoke above it. "It's the commuting that's killing," he said, and entered the dim room Tzuref waved open for him. "Three hours a day . . . I came right from the train." He dwindled down into a harp-backed chair. He expected it would be deeper than it was and consequently jarred himself on the sharp bones of his seat. It woke him, this shiver of the behind, to his business. Tzuref, a bald shaggy-browed man who looked as if he'd once been very fat, sat back of an empty desk, halfway hidden, as though he were settled on the floor. Everything around him was empty. There were no books in the bookshelves, no rugs on the floor, no draperies in the big casement windows. As Eli began to speak Tzuref got up and swung a window back on one noisy hinge. "May and it's like August," he said, and with his back to Eli, he revealed the black circle on the back of his head. The crown of his head was missing! He returned through the dimness—the lamps had no bulbs—and Eli realized all he'd seen was a skullcap. Tzuref struck a match and lit a candle, just as the half-dying shouts of children at play rolled in through the open window. It was as though Tzuref had opened it so Eli could hear them.

"Aah, now," he said. "I received your letter."

Eli poised, waiting for Tzuref to swish open a drawer and remove the letter from his file. Instead the old man leaned forward onto his stomach, worked his hand into his pants pocket, and withdrew what appeared to be a week-old handkerchief. He uncrumpled it; he unfolded it; he ironed it on the desk with the side of his hand. "So," he said.

Eli pointed to the grimy sheet which he'd gone over word-by-word with his partners, Lewis and McDonnell. "I expected an answer," Eli said. "It's a week."

"It was so important, Mr. Peck, I knew you would come."

Some children ran under the open window and their mysterious babble —not mysterious to Tzuref, who smiled—entered the room like a third person. Their noise caught up against Eli's flesh and he was unable to restrain a shudder. He wished he had gone home, showered and eaten dinner, before calling on Tzuref. He was not feeling as professional as usual—the place was too dim, it was too late. But down in Woodenton they would be waiting, his clients and neighbors. He spoke for the Jews of Woodenton, not just himself and his wife.

"You understood?" Eli said.

"It's not hard."

"It's a matter of zoning . . ." and when Tzuref did not answer, but only drummed his fingers on his lips, Eli said, "We didn't make the laws . . ."

"You respect them."

"They protect us . . . the community."

"The law is the law," Tzuref said.

"Exactly!" Eli had the urge to rise and walk about the room.

"And then of course"—Tzuref made a pair of scales in the air with his hands—"The law is not the law. When is the law that is the law not the law?" He jiggled the scales. "And vice versa."

"Simply," Eli said sharply. "You can't have a boarding school in a residential area." He would not allow Tzuref to cloud the issue with issues. "We thought it better to tell you before any action is undertaken."

"But a house in a residential area?"

"Yes. That's what residential means." The DP's English was perhaps not as good as it seemed at first. Tzuref spoke slowly, but till then Eli had mistaken it for craft—or even wisdom. "Residence means home," he added.

"So this is my residence."

"But the children?"

"It is their residence."

"*Seventeen* children?"

"Eighteen," Tzuref said.

"But you *teach* them here."

"The Talmud. That's illegal?"

"That makes it school."

Tzuref hung the scales again, tipping slowly the balance.

"Look, Mr. Tzuref, in America we call such a place a boarding school."

"Where they teach the Talmud?"

"Where they teach period. You are the headmaster, they are the students."

Tzuref placed his scales on the desk. "Mr. Peck," he said, "I don't believe it . . ." but he did not seem to be referring to anything Eli had said.

"Mr. Tzuref, that is the law. I came to ask what you intend to do."

"What I *must* do?"

"I hope they are the same."

"They are." Tzuref brought his stomach into the desk. "We stay." He smiled. "We are tired. The headmaster is tired. The students are tired."

Eli rose and lifted his briefcase. It felt so heavy packed with the grievances, vengeances, and schemes of his clients. There were days when he carried it like a feather—in Tzuref's office it weighed a ton.

"Goodbye, Mr. Tzuref."

"Sholom," Tzuref said.

Eli opened the door to the office and walked carefully down the dark tomb of a corridor to the door. He stepped out on the porch and, leaning against a pillar, looked down across the lawn to the children at play. Their voices whooped and rose and dropped as they chased each other round the old house. The dusk made the children's game look like a tribal dance. Eli straightened up, started off the porch, and suddenly the dance was ended. A long piercing scream trailed after. It was the first time in his life anyone had run at the sight of him. Keeping his eyes on the lights of Woodenton, he headed down the path.

And then, seated on a bench beneath a tree, Eli saw him. At first it seemed only a deep hollow of blackness—then the figure emerged. Eli recognized him from the description. There he was, wearing the hat, that hat which was the very cause of Eli's mission, the source of Woodenton's upset. The town's lights flashed their message once again: "Get the one with the hat. What a nerve, what a nerve . . ."

Eli started towards the man. Perhaps he was less stubborn than Tzuref, more reasonable. After all, it was the law. But when he was close enough to call out, he didn't. He was stopped by the sight of the black coat that fell down below the man's knees, and the hands which held each other in his lap. By the round-topped, wide-brimmed Talmudic hat, pushed onto the back of his head. And by the beard, which hid his neck and was so soft and thin it fluttered away and back again with each heavy breath he took. He was asleep, his sidelocks curled loose on his cheeks. His face was no older than Eli's.

Eli hurried towards the lights.

The note on the kitchen table unsettled him. Scribblings on bits of paper had made history this past week. This one, however, was unsigned. "Sweetie," it said, "I went to sleep. I had a sort of Oedipal experience with the baby today. Call Ted Heller."

She had left him a cold soggy dinner in the refrigerator. He hated cold soggy dinners, but would take one gladly in place of Miriam's presence. He was ruffled, and she never helped that, not with her infernal analytic powers. He loved her when life was proceeding smoothly—and that was when she loved him. But sometimes Eli found being a lawyer surrounded him like quicksand—he couldn't get his breath. Too often he wished he were pleading for the other side; though if he were on the other side, then he'd wish he were on the side he was. The trouble was that sometimes the law didn't seem to be the answer, *law* didn't seem to have anything to do with what was aggravating everybody. And that, of course, made him feel foolish and unnecessary . . . Though that was not the situation here—the townsmen had a case. But not *exactly,* and if Miriam were awake to see Eli's upset, she would set about explaining his distress to him, understanding him, forgiving him, so as to get things back to Normal, for Normal was where they loved one another. The difficulty with Miriam's efforts was they only upset him more; not only did they explain little to him about himself or his predicament, but they convinced him of *her* weakness. Neither Eli nor Miriam, it turned out, was terribly strong. Twice before he'd faced this fact, and on both occasions had found solace in what his neighbors forgivingly referred to as "a nervous breakdown."

Eli ate his dinner with his briefcase beside him. Halfway through, he gave in to himself, removed Tzuref's notes, and put them on the table, beside Miriam's. From time to time he flipped through the notes, which had been carried into town by the one in the black hat. The first note, the incendiary:

To whom it may concern:

Please give this gentleman the following: Boys shoes with rubber heels and soles.

> 5 prs size 6c
> 3 prs size 5c
> 3 prs size 5b
> 2 prs size 4a
> 3 prs size 4c
> 1 pr size 7b
> 1 pr size 7c

Total 18 prs. boys shoes. This gentleman has a check already signed. Please fill in correct amount.

> L. Tzuref
> Director, Yeshivah of
> Woodenton, N.Y.
> (5/8/48)

"Eli, a regular greenhorn," Ted Heller had said. "He didn't say a word. Just handed me the note and stood there, like in the Bronx the old guys who used to come around selling Hebrew trinkets."

"A Yeshivah!" Artie Berg had said. "Eli, in Woodenton, a Yeshivah! If I want to live in Brownsville, Eli, I'll live in Brownsville."

"Eli," Harry Shaw speaking now, "the old Puddington place. Old man

179

Puddington'll roll over in his grave. Eli, when I left the city, Eli, I didn't plan the city should come to me."

Note number two:

Dear Grocer:

Please give this gentleman ten pounds of sugar. Charge it to our account, Yeshivah of Woodenton, NY—which we will now open with you and expect a bill each month. The gentleman will be in to see you once or twice a week.

L. Tzuref, Director
(5/10/48)

P.S. Do you carry kosher meat?

"He walked right by my window, the greenie," Ted had said, "and he nodded, Eli. He's my *friend* now."

"Eli," Artie Berg had said, "he handed the damn thing to a *clerk* at Stop N' Shop—and in that hat yet!"

"Eli," Harry Shaw again, "it's not funny. Someday, Eli, it's going to be a hundred little kids with little *yamalkahs* chanting their Hebrew lessons on Coach House Road, and then it's not going to strike you funny."

"Eli, what goes on up there—my kids hear strange sounds."

"Eli, this is a modern community."

"Eli, we pay taxes."

"Eli."

"Eli!"

"*Eli!*"

At first it was only another townsman crying in his ear; but when he turned he saw Miriam, standing in the doorway, behind her belly.

"Eli, sweetheart, how was it?"

"He said no."

"Did you see the other one?" she asked.

"Sleeping, under a tree."

"Did you let him know how people feel?"

"He was sleeping."

"Why didn't you wake him up? Eli, this isn't an everyday thing."

"He was tired!"

"Don't shout, please," Miriam said.

" 'Don't shout. I'm pregnant. The baby is heavy.' " Eli found he was getting angry at nothing she'd said yet; it was what she was going to say.

"He's a very heavy baby the doctor says," Miriam told him.

"Then sit *down* and make my dinner." Now he found himself angry about her not being present at the dinner which he'd just been relieved that she wasn't present at. It was as though he had a raw nerve for a tail, that he kept stepping on. At last Miriam herself stepped on it.

"Eli, you're upset. I understand."

"You *don't* understand."

She left the room. From the stairs she called, "I do, sweetheart."

It was a trap! He would grow angry knowing she would be "understanding." She would in turn grow more understanding seeing his anger. He would in turn grow angrier . . . The phone rang.

"Hello," Eli said.

"Eli, Ted. So?"

"So nothing."

"Who is Tzuref? He's an American guy?"

"No. A DP. German."

"And the kids?"

"DP's too. He teaches them."

"What? What subjects?" Ted asked.

"I don't know."

"And the guy with the hat, you saw the guy with the hat?"

"Yes. He was sleeping."

"Eli, he sleeps with the *hat*?"

"He sleeps with the hat."

"Goddam fanatics," Ted said. "This is the twentieth century, Eli. Now it's the guy with the hat. Pretty soon all the little Yeshivah boys'll be spilling down into town."

"Next thing they'll be after our daughters."

"Michele and Debbie wouldn't look at them."

"Then," Eli mumbled, "you've got nothing to worry about, Teddie," and he hung up.

In a moment the phone rang. "Eli? We got cut off. We've got nothing to worry about? You worked it out?"

"I have to see him again tomorrow. We can work something out."

"That's fine, Eli. I'll call Artie and Harry."

Eli hung up.

"I thought you said *nothing* worked out." It was Miriam.

"I did."

"Then why did you tell Ted *something* worked out?"

"It did."

"Eli, maybe you should get a little more therapy."

"That's enough of that, Miriam."

"You can't function as a lawyer by being neurotic. That's no answer."

"You're ingenious, Miriam."

She turned, frowning, and took her heavy baby to bed.

The phone rang.

"Eli, Artie. Ted called. You worked it out? No trouble?"

"Yes."

"When are they going?"

"Leave it to me, will you, Artie? I'm tired. I'm going to sleep."

In bed Eli kissed his wife's belly and laid his head upon it to think. He laid it lightly, for she was that day entering the second week of her ninth month. Still, when she slept, it was a good place to rest, to rise and fall with her breathing and figure things out. "If that guy would take off that crazy hat. I know it, what eats them. If he'd take off that crazy hat everything would be all right."

"What?" Miriam said.

"I'm talking to the baby."

Miriam pushed herself up in bed. "Eli, please, baby, shouldn't you maybe stop in to see Dr. Eckman, just for a little conversation?"

"I'm fine."

"Oh, sweetie!" she said, and put her head back on the pillow.

"You know what your mother brought to this marriage—a sling chair and a goddam New School enthusiasm for Sigmund Freud."

Miriam feigned sleep, he could tell by the breathing.

"I'm telling the kid the truth, aren't I, Miriam? A sling chair, three months to go on a *New Yorker* subscription, and *An Introduction to Psychoanalysis*. Isn't that right?"

"Eli, must you be aggressive?"

"That's all you worry about, is your insides. You stand in front of the mirror all day and look at yourself being pregnant."

"Pregnant mothers have a relationship with the fetus that fathers can't understand."

"Relationship my ass. What is my liver doing now? What is my small intestine doing now? Is my island of Langerhans on the blink?"

"Don't be jealous of a little fetus, Eli."

"I'm jealous of your island of Langerhans!"

"Eli, I can't argue with you when I know it's not me you're really angry with. Don't you see, sweetie, you're angry with yourself."

"You and Eckman."

"Maybe he could help, Eli."

"Maybe he could help you. You're practically lovers as it is."

"You're being hostile again," Miriam said.

"What do you care—it's only *me* I'm being hostile towards."

"Eli, we're going to have a beautiful baby, and I'm going to have a perfectly simple delivery, and you're going to make a fine father, and there's absolutely no reason to be obsessed with whatever is on your mind. All we have to worry about—" she smiled at him "—is a name."

Eli got out of bed and slid into his slippers. "We'll name the kid Eckman if it's a boy and Eckman if it's a girl."

"Eckman Peck sounds terrible."

"He'll have to live with it," Eli said, and he went down to his study where the latch on his briefcase glinted in the moonlight that came through the window.

He removed the Tzuref notes and read through them all again. It unnerved him to think of all the flashy reasons his wife could come up with for his reading and rereading the notes. "Eli, why are you so *preoccupied* with Tzuref?" "Eli, stop getting *involved*. Why do you think you're getting *involved*, Eli?" Sooner or later, everybody's wife finds their weak spot. His goddam luck he had to be neurotic! Why couldn't he have been born with a short leg.

He removed the cover from his typewriter, hating Miriam for the edge she had. All the time he wrote the letter, he could hear what she would be saying about his not being *able* to let the matter drop. Well, her trouble was that she wasn't *able* to face the matter. But he could hear her answer already: clearly, he was guilty of "a reaction formation." Still, all the fancy phrases didn't fool Eli: all she wanted really was for Eli to send Tzuref and family on their way, so that the community's temper would quiet, and the calm circumstances of their domestic happiness return. All she wanted were order and love in her private world. Was she so wrong? Let the world bat its brains out—in Woodenton there should be peace. He wrote the letter anyway:

Dear Mr. Tzuref:

Our meeting this evening seems to me inconclusive. I don't think there's any reason for us not to be able to come up with some sort of compromise that will satisfy the Jewish community of Woodenton and the Yeshivah and yourself. It seems to me that what most disturbs my neighbors are the visits to town by the gentleman in the black hat, suit, etc. Woodenton is a progressive suburban community whose members, both Jewish and

Gentile, are anxious that their families live in comfort and beauty and serenity. This is, after all, the twentieth century, and we do not think it too much to ask that the members of our community dress in a manner appropriate to the time and place.

Woodenton, as you may not know, has long been the home of well-to-do Protestants. It is only since the war that Jews have been able to buy property here, and for Jews and Gentiles to live beside each other in amity. For this adjustment to be made, both Jews and Gentiles alike have had to give up some of their more extreme practices in order not to threaten or offend the other. Certainly such amity is to be desired. Perhaps if such conditions had existed in prewar Europe, the persecution of the Jewish people, of which you and those 18 children have been victims, could not have been carried out with such success—in fact, might not have been carried out at all.

Therefore, Mr. Tzuref, will you accept the following conditions? If you can, we will see fit not to carry out legal action against the Yeshivah for failure to comply with township Zoning ordinances No. 18 and No. 23. The conditions are simply:

1. The religious, educational, and social activities of the Yeshivah of Woodenton will be confined to the Yeshivah grounds.

2. Yeshivah personnel are welcomed in the streets and stores of Woodenton provided they are attired in clothing usually associated with American life in the 20th century.

If these conditions are met, we see no reason why the Yeshivah of Woodenton cannot live peacefully and satisfactorily with the Jews of Woodenton—as the Jews of Woodenton have come to live with the Gentiles of Woodenton. I would appreciate an immediate reply.

> Sincerely,
> ELI PECK, Attorney

Two days later Eli received his immediate reply:

Mr. Peck:
    The suit the gentleman wears is all he's got.

> Sincerely,
> LEO TZUREF, Headmaster

Once again, as Eli swung around the dark trees and onto the lawn, the children fled. He reached out with his briefcase as if to stop them, but they were gone so fast all he saw moving was a flock of skullcaps.

"Come, come . . ." a voice called from the porch. Tzuref appeared from behind a pillar. Did he *live* behind those pillars? Was he just watching the children at play? Either way, when Eli appeared, Tzuref was ready, with no forewarning.

"Hello," Eli said.

"Sholom."

"I didn't mean to frighten them."

"They're scared, so they run."

"I didn't do anything."

Tzuref shrugged. The little movement seemed to Eli strong as an accusation. What he didn't get at home, he got here.

Inside the house they took their seats. Though it was lighter than a few evenings before, a bulb or two would have helped. Eli had to hold his briefcase towards the window for the last gleamings. He removed Tzuref's letter from a manila folder. Tzuref removed Eli's letter from his pants pocket. Eli removed the carbon of his own letter from another manila folder. Tzuref removed Eli's first letter from his back pocket. Eli removed the carbon from his briefcase. Tzuref raised his palms. ". . . It's all I've got . . ."

Those upraised palms, the mocking tone—another accusation. It was a crime to keep carbons! Everybody had an edge on him—Eli could do no right.

"I offered a compromise, Mr. Tzuref. You refused."

"Refused, Mr. Peck? What is, is."

"The man could get a new suit."

"That's all he's got."

"So you told me," Eli said.

"So I told you, so you know."

"It's not an insurmountable obstacle, Mr. Tzuref. We have stores."

"For that too?"

"On Route 12, a Robert Hall—"

"To take away the one thing a man's got?"

"Not take away, *replace*."

"But I tell you he has nothing. *Nothing*. You have that word in English? *Nicht? Gornisht?*"

"Yes, Mr. Tzuref, we have the word."

"A mother and a father?" Tzuref said. "No. A wife? No. A baby? A little ten-month-old baby? No! A village full of friends? A synagogue where you knew the feel of every seat under your pants? Where with your eyes closed you could smell the cloth of the Torah?" Tzuref pushed out of his chair, stirring a breeze that swept Eli's letter to the floor. At the window he leaned out, and looked, beyond Woodenton. When he turned he was shaking a finger at Eli. "And a medical experiment they performed on him yet! That leaves nothing, Mr. Peck. Absolutely nothing!"

"I misunderstood."

"No news reached Woodenton?"

"About the suit, Mr. Tzuref. I thought he couldn't afford another."

"He can't."

They were right where they'd begun. "Mr. Tzuref!" Eli demanded. *"Here?"* He smacked his hand to his billfold.

"Exactly!" Tzuref said, smacking his own breast.

"Then we'll buy him one!" Eli crossed to the window and taking Tzuref by the shoulders, pronounced each word slowly. "We-will-pay-for-it. All right?"

"Pay? What, diamonds!"

Eli raised a hand to his inside pocket, then let it drop. Oh stupid! Tzuref, father to eighteen, had smacked not what lay under his coat, but deeper, under the ribs.

"Oh . . ." Eli said. He moved away along the wall. "The suit is all he's got then."

"You got my letter," Tzuref said.

Eli stayed back in the shadow, and Tzuref turned to his chair. He swished Eli's letter from the floor, and held it up. "You say too much . . . all this reasoning . . . all these conditions . . ."

"What can I do?"

"You have the word 'suffer' in English?"

"We have the word suffer. We have the word law too."

"Stop with the law! You have the word suffer. Then try it. It's a little thing."

"They won't," Eli said.

"But you, Mr. Peck, how about you?"

"I am them, they are me, Mr. Tzuref."

"Aach! You are us, we are you!"

Eli shook and shook his head. In the dark he suddenly felt that Tzuref might put him under a spell. "Mr. Tzuref, a little light?"

Tzuref lit what tallow was left in the holders. Eli was afraid to ask if they couldn't afford electricity. Maybe candles were all they had left.

"Mr. Peck, who made the law, may I ask you that?"

"The people."

"No."

"Yes."

"Before the people."

"No one. Before the people there was no law." Eli didn't care for the conversation, but with only candlelight, he was being lulled into it.

"Wrong," Tzuref said.

"We make the law, Mr. Tzuref. It is our community. These are my neighbors. I am their attorney. They pay me. Without law there is chaos."

"What you call law, I call shame. The heart, Mr. Peck, the heart is law! God!" he announced.

"Look, Mr. Tzuref, I didn't come here to talk metaphysics. People use the law, it's a flexible thing. They protect what they value, their property, their well-being, their happiness—"

"Happiness? They hide their shame. And you, Mr. Peck, you are shameless?"

"We do it," Eli said, wearily, "for our children. This is the twentieth century . . ."

"For the goyim maybe. For me the Fifty-eighth." He pointed at Eli. "That is too old for shame."

Eli felt squashed. Everybody in the world had evil reasons for his actions. Everybody! With reasons so cheap, who buys bulbs. "Enough wisdom, Mr. Tzuref. Please. I'm exhausted."

"Who isn't?" Tzuref said.

He picked Eli's papers from his desk and reached up with them. "What do you intend for us to do?"

"What you must," Eli said. "I made the offer."

"So he must give up his suit?"

"Tzuref, Tzuref, leave me be with that suit! I'm not the only lawyer in the world. I'll drop the case, and you'll get somebody who won't talk compromise. Then you'll have no home, no children, nothing. Only a lousy black suit! Sacrifice what you want. I know what I would do."

To that Tzuref made no answer, but only handed Eli his letters.

"It's not me, Mr. Tzuref, it's them."

"They are you."

"No," Eli intoned, "I am me. They are them. You are you."

"You talk about leaves and branches. I'm dealing with under the dirt."

"Mr. Tzuref, you're driving me crazy with Talmudic wisdom. This is that, that is the other thing. Give me a straight answer."

"Only for straight questions."

"Oh, God!"

Eli returned to his chair and plunged his belongings into his case. "Then, that's all," he said angrily.

Tzuref gave him the shrug.

"Remember, Tzuref, you called this down on yourself."

"I did?"

Eli refused to be his victim again. Double-talk proved nothing.

"Goodbye," he said.

But as he opened the door leading to the hall, he heard Tzuref.

"And your wife, how is she?"

"Fine, just fine." Eli kept going.

"And the baby is due when, any day?"

Eli turned. "That's right."

"Well," Tzuref said, rising. "Good luck."

"You know?"

Tzuref pointed out the window—then, with his hands, he drew upon himself a beard, a hat, a long, long coat. When his fingers formed the hem they touched the floor. "He shops two, three times a week, he gets to know them."

"He *talks* to them?"

"He sees them."

"And he can tell which is my wife?"

"They shop at the same stores. He says she is beautiful. She has a kind face. A woman capable of love . . . though who can be sure."

"*He* talks about *us*, to *you*?" demanded Eli.

"You talk about us, to her?"

"Goodbye, Mr. Tzuref."

Tzuref said, "Sholom. And good luck—I know what it is to have children. Sholom," Tzuref whispered, and with the whisper the candles went out. But the instant before, the flames leaped into Tzuref's eyes, and Eli saw it was not luck Tzuref wished him at all.

Outside the door, Eli waited. Down the lawn the children were holding hands and whirling around in a circle. At first he did not move. But he could not hide in the shadows all night. Slowly he began to slip along the front of the house. Under his hands he felt where bricks were out. He moved in the shadows until he reached the side. And then, clutching his briefcase to his chest, he broke across the darkest spots of the lawn. He aimed for a distant glade of woods, and when he reached it he did not stop, but ran through until he was so dizzied that the trees seemed to be running beside him, fleeing not towards Woodenton but away. His lungs were nearly ripping their seams as he burst into the yellow glow of the Gulf station at the edge of town.

*

"Eli, I had pains today. Where were you?"

"I went to Tzuref."

"Why didn't you call? I was worried."

He tossed his hat past the sofa and onto the floor. "Where are my winter suits?"

"In the hall closet. Eli, it's May."

"I need a strong suit." He left the room, Miriam behind him.

"Eli, talk to me. Sit down. Have dinner. Eli, what are you doing? You're going to get moth balls all over the carpet."

He peered out from the hall closet. Then he peered in again—there was a zipping noise, and suddenly he swept a greenish tweed suit before his wife's eyes.

"Eli, I love you in that suit. But not now. Have something to eat. I made dinner tonight—I'll warm it."

"You've got a box big enough for this suit?"

"I got a Bonwit's box, the other day. Eli, *why?*"

"Miriam, you see me doing something, let me do it."

"You haven't eaten."

"I'm *doing* something." He started up the stairs to the bedroom.

"Eli, would you please tell me what it is you want, and why?"

He turned and looked down at her. "Suppose this time you give me the reasons *before* I tell you what I'm doing. It'll probably work out the same anyway."

"Eli, I want to help."

"It doesn't concern you."

"But I want to help *you,*" Miriam said.

"Just be quiet, then."

"But you're upset," she said, and she followed him up the stairs, heavily, breathing for two.

"Eli, what now?"

"A shirt." He yanked open all the drawers of their new teak dresser. He extracted a shirt.

"Eli, batiste? With a tweed suit?" she inquired.

He was at the closet now, on his knees. "Where are my cordovans?"

"Eli, why are you doing this so compulsively? You look like you *have* to do something."

"Oh, Miriam, you're supersubtle."

"Eli, stop this and talk to me. Stop it or I'll call Dr. Eckman."

Eli was kicking off the shoes he was wearing. "Where's the Bonwit box?"

"Eli, do you want me to have the baby right *here!*"

Eli walked over and sat down on the bed. He was draped not only with his own clothing, but also with the greenish tweed suit, the batiste shirt, and under each arm a shoe. He raised his arms and let the shoes drop onto the bed. Then he undid his necktie with one hand and his teeth and added that to the booty.

"Underwear," he said. "He'll need underwear."

"Who!"

He was slipping out of his socks.

Miriam kneeled down and helped him ease his left foot out of the sock. She sat with it on the floor. "Eli, just lie back. Please."

"Plaza 9-3103."

"What?"

"Eckman's number," he said. "It'll save you the trouble."

"Eli—"

"You've got that goddam tender 'You need help' look in your eyes, Miriam, don't tell me you don't."

"I don't."

"I'm not flipping," Eli said.

"I know, Eli."

"Last time I sat in the bottom of the closet and chewed on my bedroom slippers. That's what I did."

"I know."

"And I'm not doing that. This is not a nervous breakdown, Miriam, let's get that straight."

"Okay," Miriam said. She kissed the foot she held. Then, softly, she asked, "What *are* you doing?"

"Getting clothes for the guy in the hat. Don't tell me why, Miriam. Just let me do it."

"That's all?" she asked.

"That's all."

"You're not leaving?"

"No."

"Sometimes I think it gets too much for you, and you'll just leave."

"What gets too much?"

"I don't *know*, Eli. Something gets too much. Whenever everything's peaceful for a long time, and things are nice and pleasant, and we're expecting to be even happier. Like now. It's as if you don't think we *deserve* to be happy."

"Damn it, Miriam! I'm giving this guy a new suit, is that all right?

From now on he comes into Woodenton like everybody else, is that all right with you?"

"And Tzuref moves?"

"I don't even know if he'll take the suit, Miriam! What do you have to bring up moving!"

"Eli, I didn't bring up moving. Everybody did. That's what everybody wants. Why make everybody un*happy*. It's even a law, Eli."

"Don't tell me what's the law."

"All right, sweetie. I'll get the box."

"*I'll* get the box. Where is it?"

"In the basement."

When he came up from the basement, he found all the clothes neatly folded and squared away on the sofa: shirt, tie, shoes, socks, underwear, belt, and an old gray flannel suit. His wife sat on the end of the sofa, looking like an anchored balloon.

"Where's the green suit?" he said.

"Eli, it's your loveliest suit. It's my favorite suit. Whenever I think of you, Eli, it's in that suit."

"Get it out."

"Eli, it's a Brooks Brothers suit. You say yourself how much you love it."

"Get it out."

"But the gray flannel's more practical. For shopping."

"Get it out."

"You go overboard, Eli. That's your trouble. You won't do anything in moderation. That's how people destroy themselves."

"I do *everything* in moderation. That's my trouble. The suit's in the closet again?"

She nodded, and began to fill up with tears. "Why does it have to be *your* suit? Who are you even to decide to give a suit? What about the others?" She was crying openly, and holding her belly. "Eli, I'm going to have a baby. Do we need all *this?*" and she swept the clothes off the sofa to the floor.

At the closet Eli removed the green suit. "It's a J. Press," he said, looking at the lining.

"I hope to hell he's happy with it!" Miriam said, sobbing.

A half hour later the box was packed. The cord he'd found in the kitchen cabinet couldn't keep the outfit from popping through. The trouble was there was too much: the gray suit *and* the green suit, an oxford shirt as well as the batiste. But let him have two suits! Let him have three, four, if only this damn silliness would stop! And a hat—of course! God, he'd almost forgotten the hat. He took the stairs two at a time and in Miriam's closet yanked a hatbox from the top shelf. Scattering hat and tissue paper to the floor, he returned downstairs, where he packed away the hat he'd worn that day. Then he looked at his wife, who lay outstretched on the floor before the fireplace. For the third time in as many minutes she was saying, "Eli, this is the real thing."

"Where?"

"Right under the baby's head, like somebody's squeezing oranges."

Now that he'd stopped to listen he was stupefied. He said, "But you have two more weeks . . ." Somehow he'd really been expecting it was to go on not just another two weeks, but another nine months. This led him to suspect, suddenly, that his wife was feigning pain so as to get his mind off delivering the suit. And just as suddenly he resented himself for having such a thought. God, what had he become! He'd been an unending bastard towards her since this Tzuref business had come up— just when her pregnancy must have been most burdensome. He'd allowed her no access to him, but still, he was sure, for good reasons: she might tempt him out of his confusion with her easy answers. He could be tempted all right, it was why he fought so hard. But now a sweep of love came over him at the thought of her contracting womb, and his child. And yet he would not indicate it to her. Under such splendid marital conditions, who knows but she might extract some promise from him about his concern with the school on the hill.

Having packed his second bag of the evening, Eli sped his wife to Woodenton Memorial. There she proceeded not to have her baby, but to lie hour after hour through the night having at first oranges, then bowling balls, then basketballs, squeezed back of her pelvis. Eli sat in the waiting room, under the shattering African glare of a dozen rows of fluorescent bulbs, composing a letter to Tzuref.

Dear Mr. Tzuref:

The clothes in this box are for the gentleman in the hat. In a life of sacrifice what is one more? But in a life of no sacrifices even one is impossible. Do you see what I'm saying, Mr. Tzuref? I am not a Nazi who would drive eighteen children, who are probably frightened at the sight of a firefly, into homelessness. But if you want a home here, you must accept what we have to offer. The world is the world, Mr. Tzuref. As you would say, what is, is. All we say to this man is change your clothes. Enclosed are two suits and two shirts, and everything else he'll need, including a new hat. When he needs new clothes let me know.

We await his appearance in Woodenton, as we await friendly relations with the Yeshivah of Woodenton.

He signed his name and slid the note under a bursting flap and into the box. Then he went to the phone at the end of the room and dialed Ted Heller's number.

"Hello."

"Shirley, it's Eli."

"Eli, we've been calling all night. The lights are on in your place, but nobody answers. We thought it was burglars."

"Miriam's having the baby."

"At home?" Shirley said. "Oh, Eli, what a fun-idea!"

"Shirley, let me speak to Ted."

After the ear-shattering clatter of the phone whacking the floor, Eli heard footsteps, breathing, throat-clearing, then Ted. "A boy or a girl?"

"Nothing yet."

"You've given Shirley the bug, Eli. Now she's going to have *our* next one at home."

"Good."

"That's a terrific way to bring the family together, Eli."

"Look, Ted, I've settled with Tzuref."

"When are they going?"

"They're not exactly going, Teddie. I settled it—you won't even know they're there."

"A guy dressed like 1000 B.C. and I won't know it? What are you thinking about, pal?"

"He's changing his clothes."

"Yeah, to what? Another funeral suit?"

"Tzuref promised me, Ted. Next time he comes to town, he comes dressed like you and me."

"What! Somebody's kidding somebody, Eli."

Eli's voice shot up. "If he says he'll do it, he'll do it!"

"And, Eli," Ted asked, "he said it?"

"He said it." It cost him a sudden headache, this invention.

"And suppose he doesn't change, Eli. Just suppose. I mean that *might* happen, Eli. This might just be some kind of stall or something."

"No," Eli assured him.

The other end was quiet a moment. "Look, Eli," Ted said, finally, "he changes. Okay? All right? But they're still up there, aren't they? *That* doesn't change."

"The point is you won't know it."

Patiently Ted said, "Is this what we asked of you, Eli? When we put our faith and trust in you, is that what we were asking? We weren't concerned that this guy should become a Beau Brummel, Eli, believe me. We just don't think this is the community for them. And, Eli, we isn't me. The Jewish members of the community appointed me, Artie, and Harry to see what could be done. And we appointed you. And what's happened?"

Eli heard himself say, "What happened, happened."

"Eli, you're talking in crossword puzzles."

"My wife's having a baby," Eli explained, defensively.

"I realize that, Eli. But this is a matter of zoning, isn't it? Isn't that what we discovered? You don't abide by the ordinance, you go. I mean I can't raise mountain goats, say, in my backyard—"

"This isn't so simple, Ted. People are involved—"

"People? Eli, we've been through this and through this. We're not just dealing with people—these are religious fanatics is what they are. Dressing like that. What I'd really like to find out is what goes on up there. I'm getting more and more skeptical, Eli, and I'm not afraid to admit it. It smells like a lot of hocus-pocus abracadabra stuff to me. Guys like Harry, you know, they think and they think and they're afraid to admit what they're thinking. I'll tell you. Look, I don't even know about this Sunday school business. Sundays I drive my oldest kid all the way to Scarsdale to learn Bible stories . . . and you know what she comes up with? This Abraham in the Bible was going to kill his own *kid* for a sacrifice. She gets nightmares from it, for God's sake! You call that religion? Today a guy like that they'd lock him up. This is an age of science, Eli. I size people's feet with an X-ray machine, for God's sake. They've disproved all that stuff, Eli, and I refuse to sit by and watch it happening on my own front lawn."

"Nothing's happening on your front lawn, Teddie. You're exaggerating, nobody's sacrificing their kid."

"You're damn right, Eli—I'm not sacrificing mine. You'll see when you have your own what it's like. All the place is, is a hideaway for people who can't face life. It's a matter of *needs*. They have all these superstitions, and why do you think? Because they can't face the world, because they can't take their place in society. That's no environment to bring kids up in, Eli."

"Look, Ted, see it from another angle. We can convert them," Eli said, with a half a heart.

"What, make a bunch of Catholics out of them? Look, Eli—pal, there's a good healthy relationship in this town because it's modern Jews and Protestants. That's the point, isn't it, Eli? Let's not kid each other, I'm not Harry. The way things are now are fine—like human beings. There's going to be no pogroms in Woodenton. Right? 'Cause there's no fanatics, no crazy people—" Eli winced, and closed his eyes a second—"just people who respect each other, and leave each other be. Common sense is the ruling thing, Eli. I'm for common sense. Moderation."

"Exactly, exactly, Ted. I agree, but common sense, maybe, says make this guy change his clothes. Then maybe—"

"Common sense says that? Common sense says to me they go and find a nice place somewhere else, Eli. New York is the biggest city in the world, it's only 30 miles away—why don't they go there?"

"Ted, give them a chance. Introduce them to common sense."

"Eli, you're dealing with *fanatics*. Do they display common sense? Talking a dead language, that makes sense? Making a big thing out of suffering, so you're going oy-oy-oy all your life, that's common sense? Look, Eli, we've been through all this. I don't know if you know—but there's talk that *Life* magazine is sending a guy out to the Yeshivah for a story. With pictures."

"Look, Teddie, you're letting your imagination get inflamed. I don't think *Life's* interested."

"But I'm interested, Eli. And we thought you were supposed to be."

"I am," Eli said, "I am. Let him just change the clothes, Ted. Let's see what happens."

"They live in the medieval ages, Eli—it's some superstition, some *rule*."

"Let's just *see*," Eli pleaded.

"Eli, every day—"

"One more day," Eli said. "If he doesn't change in one more day . . ."

"What?"

"Then I get an injunction first thing Monday. That's that."

"Look, Eli—it's not up to me. Let me call Harry—"

"You're the spokesman, Teddie. I'm all wrapped up here with Miriam having a baby. Just give me the day—them the day."

"All right, Eli. I want to be fair. But tomorrow, that's all. Tomorrow's the judgment day, Eli, I'm telling you."

"I hear trumpets," Eli said, and hung up. He was shaking inside—Teddie's voice seemed to have separated his bones at the joints. He was still in the phone booth when the nurse came to tell him that Mrs. Peck would positively not be delivered of a child until the morning. He was to go home and get some rest, he looked like *he* was having the baby. The nurse winked and left.

But Eli did not go home. He carried the Bonwit box out into the street with him and put it in the car. The night was soft and starry, and he began to drive the streets of Woodenton. Square cool windows, apricot-colored, were all one could see beyond the long lawns that fronted the homes of the townsmen. The stars polished the permanent baggage carriers atop the station wagons in the driveways. He drove slowly, up, down, around. Only his tires could be heard taking the gentle curves in the road.

What peace. What incredible peace. Have children ever been so safe in their beds? Parents—Eli wondered—so full in their stomachs? Water so warm in its boilers? Never. Never in Rome, never in Greece. Never even did walled cities have it so good! No wonder then they would keep things just as they were. Here, after all, were peace and safety—what civilization had been working toward for centuries. For all his jerkiness, that was all Ted Heller was asking for, peace and safety. It was what his parents had asked for in the Bronx, and his grandparents in Poland, and theirs in Russia or Austria, or wherever else they'd fled to or from. It was what Miriam was asking for. And now they had it—the world was at last a place for families, even Jewish families. After all these centuries, maybe there just had to be this communal toughness—or numbness—to protect such a blessing. Maybe that was the trouble with the Jews all along— too soft. Sure, to live takes guts . . . Eli was thinking as he drove on beyond the train station, and parked his car at the darkened Gulf station. He stepped out, carrying the box.

At the top of the hill one window trembled with light. What *was* Tzuref doing up there in that office? Killing babies—probably not. But studying a language no one understood? Practicing customs with origins long forgotten? Suffering sufferings already suffered once too often? Teddie was right—why keep it up! However, if a man chose to be stubborn, then he couldn't expect to survive. The world is give-and-take. What sense to sit and brood over a suit. Eli would give him one last chance.

He stopped at the top. No one was around. He walked slowly up the lawn, setting each foot into the grass, listening to the shh shhh shhhh his shoes made as they bent the wetness into the sod. He looked around. Here there was nothing. Nothing! An old decaying house—and a suit.

On the porch he slid behind a pillar. He felt someone was watching him. But only the stars gleamed down. And at his feet, off and away, Woodenton glowed up. He set his package on the step of the great front door. Inside the cover of the box he felt to see if his letter was still there.

When he touched it, he pushed it deeper into the green suit, which his fingers still remembered from winter. He should have included some light bulbs. Then he slid back by the pillar again, and this time there was something on the lawn. It was the second sight he had of him. He was facing Woodenton and barely moving across the open space towards the trees. His right fist was beating his chest. And then Eli heard a sound rising with each knock on the chest. What a moan! It could raise hair, stop hearts, water eyes. And it did all three to Eli, plus more. Some feeling crept into him for whose deepness he could find no word. It was strange. He listened—it did not hurt to hear this moan. But he wondered if it hurt to make it. And so, with only stars to hear, he tried. And it did hurt. Not the bumble-bee of noise that turned at the back of his throat and winged out his nostrils. What hurt buzzed down. It stung and stung inside him, and in turn the moan sharpened. It became a scream, louder, a song, a crazy song that whined through the pillars and blew out to the grass, until the strange hatted creature on the lawn turned and threw his arms wide, and looked in the night like a scarecrow.

Eli ran, and when he reached the car the pain was only a bloody scratch across his neck where a branch had whipped back as he fled the greenie's arms.

The following day his son was born. But not till one in the afternoon, and by then a great deal had happened.

First, at nine-thirty the phone rang. Eli leaped from the sofa—where he'd dropped the night before—and picked it screaming from the cradle. He could practically smell the hospital as he shouted into the phone, "Hello, yes!"

"Eli, it's Ted. Eli, he *did* it. He just walked by the store. I was opening the door, Eli, and I turned around and I swear I thought it was you. But it was him. He still walks like he did, but the clothes, Eli, the clothes."

"Who?"

"The greenie. He has on man's regular clothes. And the suit, it's a beauty."

The suit barreled back into Eli's consciousness, pushing all else aside. "What color suit?"

"Green. He's just strolling in the green suit like it's a holiday. Eli . . . is it a Jewish holiday?"

"Where is he now?"

"He's walking straight up Coach House Road, in this damn tweed job. Eli, it worked. You were right."

"We'll see."

"What next?"

"We'll see."

He took off the underwear in which he'd slept and went into the kitchen where he turned the light under the coffee. When it began to perk he held his head over the pot so it would steam loose the knot back of his eyes. It still hadn't when the phone rang.

"Eli, Ted again. Eli, the guy's walking up and down every street in town. Really, he's on a tour or something. Artie called me, Herb called me. Now Shirley calls that he just walked by our house. Eli, go out on the porch you'll see."

Eli went to the window and peered out. He couldn't see past the bend in the road, and there was no one in sight.

"Eli?" He heard Ted from where he dangled over the telephone table. He dropped the phone into the hook, as a few last words floated up to him—"Eliyousawhim . . . ?" He threw on the pants and shirt he'd worn the night before and walked barefoot on to his front lawn. And sure enough, his apparition appeared around the bend: in a brown hat a little too far down on his head, a green suit too far back on the shoulders, an unbuttoned-down button-down shirt, a tie knotted so as to leave a two-inch tail, trousers that cascaded onto his shoes—he was shorter than that black hat had made him seem. And moving the clothes was that walk that was not a walk, the tiny-stepped shlumpy gait. He came round the bend, and for all his strangeness—it clung to his whiskers, signaled itself in his locomotion—he looked as if he belonged. Eccentric, maybe, but he belonged. He made no moan, nor did he invite Eli with wide-flung arms. But he did stop when he saw him. He stopped and put a hand to his hat. When he felt for its top, his hand went up too high. Then it found the level and fiddled with the brim. The fingers fiddled, fumbled, and when they'd finally made their greeting, they traveled down the fellow's face and in an instant seemed to have touched each one of his features. They dabbed the eyes, ran the length of the nose, swept over the hairy lip, until they found their home in the hair that hid a little of his collar. To Eli the fingers said, *I have a face, I have a face at least.* Then his hand came through the beard and when it stopped at his chest it was like a pointer—and the eyes asked a question as tides of water shifted over them. *The face is all right, I can keep it?* Such a look was in those eyes that Eli was still seeing them when he turned his head away. They were the hearts of his jonquils, that only last week had appeared—they were the leaves on his birch, the bulbs in his coach lamp, the droppings on his lawn: those eyes were the eyes in his head. They were his, he had made them. He turned and went into his house and when he peeked out the side of the window, between shade and molding, the green suit was gone.

The phone.

"Eli, Shirley."

"I saw him, Shirley," and he hung up.

He sat frozen for a long time. The sun moved around the windows. The coffee steam smelled up the house. The phone began to ring, stopped, began again. The mailman came, the cleaner, the bakery man, the gardener, the ice cream man, the League of Women Voters lady. A Negro woman spreading some strange gospel calling for the revision of the Food and Drug Act knocked at the front, rapped the windows, and finally scraped a half-dozen pamphlets under the back door. But Eli only sat, without underwear, in last night's suit. He answered no one.

Given his condition, it was strange that the trip and crash at the back door reached his inner ear. But in an instant he seemed to melt down into the crevices of the chair, then to splash up and out to where the clatter had been. At the door he waited. It was silent, but for a fluttering of damp little leaves on the trees. When he finally opened the door, there was no one there. He'd expected to see green, green, green, big as the doorway, topped by his hat, waiting for him with those eyes. But there was no one out there, except for the Bonwit's box which lay bulging at his feet. No string tied it and the top rode high on the bottom.

The coward! He couldn't do it! He couldn't!

The very glee of that idea pumped fuel to his legs. He tore out across his back lawn, past his new spray of forsythia, to catch a glimpse of the bearded one fleeing naked through yards, over hedges and fences, to the safety of his hermitage. In the distance a pile of pink and white stones— which Harriet Knudson had painted the previous day—tricked him. "Run," he shouted to the rocks, "Run, you . . ." but he caught his error before anyone else did, and though he peered and craned there was no hint anywhere of a man about his own size, with white, white, terribly white skin (how white must be the skin of his body!) in cowardly retreat. He came slowly, curiously, back to the door. And while the trees shimmered in the light wind, he removed the top from the box. The shock at first was the shock of having daylight turned off all at once. Inside the box was an eclipse. But black soon sorted from black, and shortly there was the glassy black of lining, the coarse black of trousers, the dead black of fraying threads, and in the center the mountain of black: the hat. He picked the box from the doorstep and carried it inside. For the first time in his life he *smelled* the color of blackness: a little stale, a little sour, a little old, but nothing that could overwhelm you. Still, he held the package at arm's length and deposited it on the dining room table.

Twenty rooms on a hill and they store their old clothes with me! What am I supposed to do with them? Give them to charity? That's where they came from. He picked up the hat by the edges and looked inside. The crown was smooth as an egg, the brim practically threadbare. There is nothing else to do with a hat in one's hands but put it on, so Eli dropped the thing on his head. He opened the door to the hall closet and looked at himself in the full-length mirror. The hat gave him bags under the eyes. Or perhaps he had not slept well. He pushed the brim lower till a shadow touched his lips. Now the bags under his eyes had inflated to become his face. Before the mirror he unbuttoned his shirt, unzipped his trousers, and then, shedding his clothes, he studied what he was. What a silly disappointment to see yourself naked in a hat. Especially in that hat. He sighed, but could not rid himself of the great weakness that suddenly set on his muscles and joints, beneath the terrible weight of the stranger's strange hat.

He returned to the dining room table and emptied the box of its contents: jacket, trousers, and vest (it smelled deeper than blackness). And under it all, sticking between the shoes that looked chopped and bitten, came the first gleam of white. A little fringed serape, a gray piece of semi-underwear, was crumpled at the bottom, its thready border twisted into itself. Eli removed it and let it hang free. What is it? For warmth? To wear beneath underwear in the event of a chest cold? He held it to his nose but it did not smell from Vick's or mustard plaster. It was something special, some Jewish thing. Special food, special language, special prayers, why not special BVD's? So fearful was he that he would be tempted back into wearing his traditional clothes—reasoned Eli—that he had carried and buried in Woodenton everything, including the special underwear. For that was how Eli now understood the box of clothes. The greenie was saying, Here, I give up. I refuse even to be tempted. We surrender. And that was how Eli continued to understand it until he found he'd slipped the white fringy surrender flag over his hat and felt it clinging to his chest. And now, looking at himself in the mirror, he was momentarily uncertain as to who was tempting who into what. Why *did* the greenie leave his clothes? Was it even the greenie? Then who was it? And why? But, Eli, for Christ's sake, in an age of science things don't happen like that. Even the goddam pigs take drugs . . .

Regardless of who was the source of the temptation, what was its end, not to mention its beginning, Eli, some moments later, stood draped in black, with a little white underneath, before the full-length mirror. He had to pull down on the trousers so they would not show the hollow of his ankle. The greenie, didn't he wear socks? Or had he forgotten them? The mystery was solved when Eli mustered enough courage to investigate the trouser pockets. He had expected some damp awful thing to happen to his fingers should he slip them down and out of sight—but when at last he jammed bravely down he came up with a khaki army sock in each hand. As he slipped them over his toes, he invented a genesis: a G.I.'s present in 1945. Plus everything else lost between 1938 and 1945, he had also lost his socks. Not that he had lost the socks, but that he'd had to stoop to accepting these, made Eli almost cry. To calm himself he walked out the back door and stood looking at his lawn.

On the Knudson back lawn, Harriet Knudson was giving her stones a second coat of pink. She looked up just as Eli stepped out. Eli shot back in again and pressed himself against the back door. When he peeked between the curtain all he saw were paint bucket, brush, and rocks scattered on the Knudsons' pink-spattered grass. The phone rang. Who was it— Harriet Knudson? Eli, there's a Jew at your door. *That's me.* Nonsense, Eli, I saw him with my own eyes. *That's me, I saw you too, painting your rocks pink.* Eli, you're having a nervous breakdown again. Jimmy, Eli's having a nervous breakdown again. Eli, this is Jimmy, hear you're having a little breakdown, anything I can do, boy? Eli, this is Ted, Shirley says you need help. Eli, this is Artie, you need help. Eli, Harry, you need help you need help . . . The phone rattled its last and died.

"God helps them who help themselves," intoned Eli, and once again he stepped out the door. This time he walked to the center of his lawn and in full sight of the trees, the grass, the birds, and the sun, revealed that it was he, Eli, in the costume. But nature had nothing to say to him, and so stealthily he made his way to the hedge separating his property from the field beyond and he cut his way through, losing his hat twice in the underbrush. Then, clamping the hat to his head, he began to run, the threaded tassels jumping across his heart. He ran through the weeds and wild flowers, until on the old road that skirted the town he slowed up. He was walking when he approached the Gulf station from the back. He supported himself on a huge tireless truck rim, and among tubes, rusted engines, dozens of topless oil cans, he rested. With a kind of brainless cunning, he readied himself for the last mile of his journey.

"How are you, Pop?" It was the garage attendant, rubbing his greasy hands on his overalls, and hunting among the cans.

Eli's stomach lurched and he pulled the big black coat round his neck.
"Nice day," the attendant said and started around to the front.

"Sholom," Eli whispered and zoomed off towards the hill.

The sun was directly overhead when Eli reached the top. He had come
by way of the woods, where it was cooler, but still he was perspiring beneath his new suit. The hat had no sweatband and the cloth clutched his
head. The children were playing. The children were always playing, as
if it was that alone that Tzuref had to teach them. In their shorts, they
revealed such thin legs that beneath one could see the joints swiveling as
they ran. Eli waited for them to disappear around a corner before he came
into the open. But something would not let him wait—his green suit. It
was on the porch, wrapped around the bearded fellow, who was painting
the base of a pillar. His arm went up and down, up and down, and the
pillar glowed like white fire. The very sight of him popped Eli out of the
woods onto the lawn. He did not turn back, though his insides did. He
walked up the lawn, but the children played on; tipping the black hat, he
mumbled, "Shhh . . . shhhh," and they hardly seemed to notice.

At last he smelled paint.

He waited for the man to turn to him. He only painted. Eli felt suddenly that if he could pull the black hat down over his eyes, over his
chest and belly and legs, if he could shut out all light, then a moment
later he would be home in bed. But the hat wouldn't go past his forehead.
He couldn't kid himself—he was there. No one he could think of had
forced him to do this.

The greenie's arm flailed up and down on the pillar. Eli breathed
loudly, cleared his throat, but the greenie wouldn't make life easier for
him. At last, Eli had to say "Hello."

The arm swished up and down; it stopped—two fingers went out after
a brush hair stuck to the pillar.

"Good day," Eli said.

The hair came away; the swishing resumed.

"Sholom," Eli whispered and the fellow turned.

The recognition took some time. He looked at what Eli wore. Up
close, Eli looked at what he wore. And then Eli had the strange notion
that he was two people. Or that he was one person wearing two suits.
The greenie looked to be suffering from a similar confusion. They stared
long at one another. Eli's heart shivered, and his brain was momentarily
in such a mixed-up condition that his hands went out to button down the
collar of his shirt that somebody else was wearing. What a mess! The
greenie flung his arms over his face.

"What's the matter . . ." Eli said. The fellow had picked up his bucket and brush and was running away. Eli ran after him.

"I wasn't going to hit . . ." Eli called. "Stop . . ." Eli caught up and grabbed his sleeve. Once again, the greenie's hands flew up to his face. This time, in the violence, white paint spattered both of them.

"I only want to . . ." But in that outfit Eli didn't really know what he wanted. "To talk . . ." he said finally. "For you to look at me. Please, just *look* at me . . ."

The hands stayed put, as paint rolled off the brush onto the cuff of Eli's green suit.

"Please . . . please," Eli said, but he did not know what to do. "Say something, speak *English*," he pleaded.

The fellow pulled back against the wall, back, back, as though some arm would finally reach out and yank him to safety. He refused to uncover his face.

"Look," Eli said, pointing to himself. "It's your suit. I'll take care of it."

No answer—only a little shaking under the hands, which led Eli to speak as gently as he knew how.

"We'll . . . we'll moth-proof it. There's a button missing"—Eli pointed —"I'll have it fixed. I'll have a zipper put in . . . Please, please—just look at me . . ." He was talking to himself, and yet how could he stop? Nothing he said made any sense—that alone made his heart swell. Yet somehow babbling on, he might babble something that would make things easier between them. "Look . . ." He reached inside his shirt to pull the frills of underwear into the light. "I'm wearing the special underwear, even . . . Please," he said, "*please, please, please*" he sang, as if it were some sacred word. "Oh, *please* . . ."

Nothing twitched under the tweed suit—and if the eyes watered, or twinkled, or hated, he couldn't tell. It was driving him crazy. He had dressed like a fool, and for what? For this? He reached up and yanked the hands away.

"There!" he said—and in that first instant all he saw of the greenie's face were two white droplets stuck to each cheek.

"Tell me—" Eli clutched his hands down to his sides—"Tell me, what can I do for you, I'll do it . . ."

Stiffly, the greenie stood there, sporting his two white tears.

"Whatever I can do . . . Look, look, what I've done *already*." He grabbed his black hat and shook it in the man's face.

And in exchange, the greenie gave him an answer. He raised one hand to his chest, and then jammed it, finger first, towards the horizon. And with what a pained look! As though the air were full of razors! Eli followed the finger and saw beyond the knuckle, out past the nail, Woodenton.

"What do you want?" Eli said. "I'll bring it!"

Suddenly the greenie made a run for it. But then he stopped, wheeled, and jabbed that finger at the air again. It pointed the same way. Then he was gone.

And then, all alone, Eli had the revelation. He did not question his understanding, the substance or the source. But with a strange, dreamy elation, he started away.

On Coach House Road, they were double-parked. The Mayor's wife pushed a grocery cart full of dog food from Stop N' Shop to her station wagon. The President of the Lions Club, a napkin around his neck, was jamming pennies into the meter in front of the Bit-in-Teeth Restaurant. Ted Heller caught the sun as it glazed off the new Byzantine mosaic entrance to his shoe shop. In pinkened jeans, Mrs. Jimmy Knudson was leaving Halloway's Hardware, a paint bucket in each hand. Roger's Beauty Shoppe had its doors open—women's heads in silver bullets far as the eye could see. Over by the barbershop the pole spun, and Artie Berg's youngest sat on a red horse, having his hair cut; his mother flipped through *Look*, smiling: the greenie had changed his clothes.

And into this street, which seemed paved with chromium, came Eli Peck. It was not enough, he knew, to walk up one side of the street. That was not enough. Instead he walked ten paces up one side, then on an angle, crossed to the other side, where he walked ten more paces, and crossed back. Horns blew, traffic jerked, as Eli made his way up Coach House Road. He spun a moan high up in his nose as he walked. Outside no one could hear him, but he felt it vibrate the cartilage at the bridge of his nose.

Things slowed around him. The sun stopped rippling on spokes and hubcaps. It glowed steadily as everyone put on brakes to look at the man in black. They always paused and gaped, whenever he entered the town. Then in a minute, or two, or three, a light would change, a baby squawk, and the flow continue. Now, though lights changed, no one moved.

"He shaved his beard," Eric the barber said.

"Who?" asked Linda Berg.

"The . . . the guy in the suit. From the place there."

Linda looked out the window.

"It's Uncle Eli," little Kevin Berg said, spitting hair.

"Oh God," Linda said, "Eli's having a nervous breakdown."

"A nervous breakdown!" Ted Heller said, but not immediately. Immediately he had said "Hoooly . . ."

Shortly, everybody in Coach House Road was aware that Eli Peck, the nervous young attorney with the pretty wife, was having a breakdown. Everybody except Eli Peck. He knew what he did was not insane, though he felt every inch of its strangeness. He felt those black clothes as if they were the skin of his skin—the give and pull as they got used to where he bulged and buckled. And he felt eyes, every eye on Coach House Road. He saw headlights screech to within an inch of him, and stop. He saw mouths: first the bottom jaw slides forward, then the tongue hits the teeth, the lips explode, a little thunder in the throat, and they've said it: Eli Peck Eli Peck Eli Peck Eli Peck. He began to walk slowly, shifting his weight down and forward with each syllable: E–li–Peck–E–li–Peck–E–li–Peck. Heavily he trod, and as his neighbors uttered each syllable of his name, he felt each syllable shaking all his bones. He knew who he was down to his marrow—they were telling him. Eli Peck. He wanted them to say it a thousand times, a million times, he would walk forever in that black suit, as adults whispered of his strangeness and children made "Shame . . . shame" with their fingers.

"It's going to be all right, pal . . ." Ted Heller was motioning to Eli from his doorway. "C'mon, pal, it's going to be all right . . ."

Eli saw him, past the brim of his hat. Ted did not move from his doorway, but leaned forward and spoke with his hand over his mouth. Behind him, three customers peered through the doorway. "Eli, it's Ted, remember Ted . . ."

Eli crossed the street and found he was heading directly towards Harriet Knudson. He lifted his neck so she could see his whole face.

He saw her forehead melt down to her lashes. "Good morning, Mr. Peck."

"Sholom," Eli said, and crossed the street where he saw the President of the Lions.

"Twice before . . ." he heard someone say, and then he crossed again, mounted the curb, and was before the bakery, where a delivery man charged past with a tray of powdered cakes twirling above him. "Pardon me, Father," he said, and scooted into his truck. But he could not move it. Eli Peck had stopped traffic.

He passed the Rivoli Theater, Beekman Cleaners, Harris' Westinghouse, The Unitarian Church, and soon he was passing only trees. At Ireland Road he turned right and started through Woodenton's winding streets. Baby carriages stopped whizzing and creaked—"Isn't that . . ."

Gardeners held their clipping. Children stepped from the sidewalk and tried the curb. And Eli greeted no one, but raised his face to all. He wished passionately that he had white tears to show them . . . And not till he reached his own front lawn, saw his house, his shutters, his new jonquils, did he remember his wife. And the child that must have been born to him. And it was then and there he had the awful moment. He could go inside and put on his clothes and go to his wife in the hospital. It was not irrevocable, even the walk wasn't. In Woodenton memories are long but fury short. Apathy works like forgiveness. Besides, when you've flipped, you've flipped—it's Mother Nature.

What gave Eli the awful moment was that he turned away. He knew exactly what he could do but he chose not to. To go inside would be to go halfway. There was more . . . So he turned and walked towards the hospital and all the time he quaked an eighth of an inch beneath his skin to think that perhaps he'd chosen the crazy way. To think that he'd *chosen* to be crazy! But if you chose to be crazy, then you weren't crazy. It's when you didn't choose. No, he wasn't flipping. He had a child to see.

"Name?"

"Peck."

"Fourth floor." He was given a little blue card.

In the elevator everybody stared. Eli watched his black shoes rise four floors.

"Four."

He tipped his hat, but knew he couldn't take it off.

"Peck," he said. He showed the card.

"Congratulations," the nurse said. ". . . the grandfather?"

"The father. Which room?"

She led him to 412. "A joke on the Mrs?" she said, but he slipped in the door without her.

"Miriam?"

"Yes?"

"Eli."

She rolled her white face towards her husband. "Oh Eli . . . Oh, Eli."

He raised his arms. "What could I do?"

"You have a son. They called all morning."

"I came to see him."

"Like *that*!" she whispered harshly. "Eli, you can't go around like that."

"I have a son. I want to see him."

"Eli, why are you doing this to me!" Red seeped back into her lips. "*He's* not your fault," she explained. "Oh, Eli, sweetheart, why do you feel guilty about everything? Eli, change your clothes. I forgive you."

"Stop forgiving me. Stop understanding me."

"But I love you."

"That's something else."

"But, sweetie, you *don't* have to dress like that. You didn't do anything. You don't have to feel guilty because . . . because everything's all right. Eli, can't you see that?"

"Miriam, enough reasons. Where's my son?"

"Oh, please, Eli, don't flip now. I need you now. Is that why you're flipping—because I need you?"

"In your selfish way, Miriam, you're very generous. I want my son."

"Don't flip now. I'm afraid, now that he's out." She was beginning to whimper. "I don't know if I love him, now that he's out. When I look in the mirror, Eli, he won't be there . . . Eli, Eli, you look like you're going to your own funeral. Please, can't you leave well enough *alone*? Can't we just have a family?"

"No."

In the corridor he asked the nurse to lead him to his son. The nurse walked on one side of him, Ted Heller on the other.

"Eli, do you want some help? I thought you might want some help."

"No."

Ted whispered something to the nurse; then to Eli he whispered, "Should you be walking around like this?"

"Yes."

In his ear Ted said, "You'll . . . you'll frighten the kid . . ."

"There," the nurse said. She pointed to a bassinet in the second row and looked, puzzled, to Ted. "Do I go in?" Eli said.

"No," the nurse said. "She'll roll him over." She rapped on the enclosure full of babies. "Peck," she mouthed to the nurse on the inside.

Ted tapped Eli's arm. "You're not thinking of doing something you'll be sorry for . . . are you, Eli? Eli—I mean you know you're still Eli, don't you?"

In the enclosure, Eli saw a bassinet had been wheeled before the square window.

"Oh, Christ. . . ." Ted said. "You don't have this Bible stuff on the brain—" And suddenly he said, "You wait, pal." He started down the corridor, his heels tapping rapidly.

Eli felt relieved—he leaned forward. In the basket was what he'd come to see. Well, now that he was here, what did he think he was going to say to it? I'm your father, Eli, the Flipper? I am wearing a black hat, suit, and fancy underwear, all borrowed from a friend? How could he admit to this reddened ball—*his* reddened ball—the worst of all: that Eckman would shortly convince him he wanted to take off the whole business. He couldn't admit it! He wouldn't do it!

Past his hat brim, from the corner of his eye, he saw Ted had stopped in a doorway at the end of the corridor. Two interns stood there smoking, listening to Ted. Eli ignored it.

No, even Eckman wouldn't make him take it off! No! He'd wear it, if he chose to. He'd make the kid wear it! Sure! Cut it down when the time came. A smelly hand-me-down, whether the kid liked it or not!

Only Teddie's heels clacked; the interns wore rubber soles—for they were there, beside him, unexpectedly. Their white suits smelled, but not like Eli's.

"Eli," Ted said, softly, "visiting time's up, pal."

"How are you feeling, Mr. Peck? First child upsets everyone. . . ."

He'd just pay no attention; nevertheless, he began to perspire, thickly, and his hat crown clutched his hair.

"Excuse me—Mr. Peck. . . ." It was a new rich bass voice. "Excuse me, rabbi, but you're wanted . . . in the temple." A hand took his elbow, firmly; then another hand, the other elbow. Where they grabbed, his tendons went taut.

"Okay, rabbi. Okay okay okay okay okay okay. . . ." He listened; it was a very soothing word, that okay. "Okay okay everything's going to be okay." His feet seemed to have left the ground some, as he glided away from the window, the bassinet, the babies. "Okay easy does it everything's all right all right—"

But he rose, suddenly, as though up out of a dream, and flailing his arms, screamed: *"I'm the father!"*

But the window disappeared. In a moment they tore off his jacket—it gave so easily, in one yank. Then a needle slid under his skin. The drug calmed his soul, but did not touch it down where the blackness had reached.

ELI AGONISTES:
PHILIP ROTH'S KNIGHT OF FAITH

James R. Hollis

> *Does the age really need a ridiculous exhibition by a reli-*
> *gious enthusiast in order to get something to laugh at, or does*
> *it not need rather that such an enthusiastic figure should*
> *remind it of that which has been forgotten?* [1]

Søren Kierkegaard

Philip Roth's parabolic "Eli, the Fanatic" is ostensibly concerned with the problem of being a Jew in a secure but secularized promised land. By affirming their tradition Eli and his friends risk alienating their neighbors; by displaying their differences they threaten the myths of tolerance and fraternity that lull their neighbors into self-righteous sleep. Though the technique and atmosphere of the story are highly reminiscent of such Jewish writers as Isaac B. Singer and Bernard Malamud, the issue Roth raises is not necessarily a "Jewish" issue, although the reason Roth seems to treat the dilemma of Eli and his friends so sensitively may be because of his own Jewish heritage. Eli's perplexities are part of a larger existential crisis that seems universal in its application. His task is the old Socratic directive to know himself, to discover who he is, where he has come from, and what he must do to affirm his identity. Insofar as he undertakes this imperative Eli becomes more than an assimilated suburban Jew. He becomes what the nineteenth-century thinker Søren Kierkegaard called the Knight of Faith, the solitary individual who must sojourn in regions of private terror before he may uncover the name and norm of his identity.

Eli is of the Prufrock legion: weary, without joy, unsure of himself, and given to "nervous breakdowns." He is an apparently successful lawyer with a last name sufficiently ambiguous to ease his assimilation into the

---

[1] Søren Kierkegaard, *Fear and Trembling*, tr. by Walter Lowrie (Princeton, N.J.: Princeton Univ. Press, 1941), p. 157.

gentile culture. But Eli is a man with a charge. He is selected to represent the modern, suburban Jews on a mission to the DP's, whose presence serves to remind them of their troubled heritage.

The "progressive" Jews of Woodenton thought they had escaped the past, that they had fled forever from the ghettos of Nuremburg, Warsaw, and Brownsville. But the past has come to haunt them in the guise of the Yeshivah. They are embarrassed by the garb, ancient rituals, and cabbalistic mutterings of the intruders. The response of Eli's wife, Miriam, is typical.

> All she wanted really was for Eli to send Tzuref and family on their way, so that the community's temper would quiet, and the calm circumstances of their domestic happiness return. All she wanted were order and love in her private world. Was she so wrong? Let the world bat its brains out—in Woodenton there should be peace.

It is because the newcomers threaten that peace, because the demands of their Talmudic law challenge their presumed liberation from the ghetto that the "progressive" Jews of Woodenton turn to civil law to extricate themselves from their embarrassing dilemma. In his confrontation with Leo Tzuref, the teacher of the ancient law of Moses, Eli, the practitioner and representative of the secular law, confronts his opposite. The irony of their juxtaposition is underlined by Roth in the letter that Eli sends to Tzuref. In the letter two demands are made: that the residents of the school confine their activities to its grounds and that they wear a certain attire when venturing into the city. Thus the displaced persons once again find those who demand their confinement to a ghetto. This time, however, they are enjoined to hide their Star of David and keep the world ignorant of their uniqueness.

As an envoy, however, Eli is a failure. His rational arguments, prepared as though they were briefs before some imposing tribunal, are undercut by Tzuref's replies, which are so concise, so simple as to be enigmatic. "The suit the gentleman wears is all he's got," he tells Eli. In suggesting that the man visit the local Robert Hall clothier, Eli fails to understand that the act of wearing the clothes of a despised creed is the only affirmation remaining to a man whose life has been stricken by the instruments of terror. Since Eli is neither willing nor ready to make a like affirmation of his identity, he retreats into his legal arguments. Fearing the moral ambiguities that have suddenly opened before him, he reflexively declares,

> Without law there is chaos.
> What you call law, I call shame. The heart, Mr. Peck, the heart is law! God!

The teacher advances, and Eli fails to understand, the truth of Pascal's conclusion that "the heart has reasons that reason knows not."

Until he is capable of discovering the reasons of the heart, Eli must content himself with the reasons of the intellect. His peers reason that they have a good thing going, that there will be "no pogroms in Woodenton." For the *Heilsgeschichte*, the redemptive history of a people's suffering, they would substitute the togetherness of the Jaycees. Even at home Eli finds himself in the presence of alien but thoroughly rational deities. Miriam worships Dr. Eckman, high priest of the Freudian cult. In supplanting Jerusalem with Vienna, the dispensation of Yahweh with that of Freud, Miriam unsuccessfully attempts to find a new comfort, a new peace that passes understanding. Thus Eli and his friends fanatically avoid fanaticism on behalf of common sense and rational moderation. Until Eli recognizes that he must be a fanatic in any case, he will not know himself or the god he must affirm.

Hardly the stuff of heroes, hardly a paladin to defend the ark of the covenant, Eli nevertheless undergoes an ordeal of the self and emerges triumphant. His medical history is ample testimony to his sensitivity, and it is precisely because he is sensitive that Eli is capable of being deeply touched and of responding to voices that cry to him from his heritage. Strange things happen to him when he visits the Yeshivah. Once, crossing the porch, he emerges from behind a pillar to see children playing. In the half-light they seem to be participating in a tribal dance or ritual evocation. On two occasions Tzuref materializes before his eyes by stepping from behind the pillar. Eli wonders if Tzuref in fact lives behind the pillar. In these strange encounters the young attorney wanders down the haunted corridors of his Hebraic experience. In the half-light he probes the depth of his unconscious and finds there a sacred circle of dancing children, his children, his people. The pillar itself seems symbolic of the monolithic, masculine Yahweh from whose shadows Tzuref, the bearer of the word, steps into the light. It is in these primal explorations of the unconscious that Eli, whose name is the Hebrew word for "the exalted one," begins to confront his true identity.

Eli had misguidedly given his suit to the "greenie" and found to his consternation that the gift had been returned in the form of the hated black garb. It is painful for Eli to recognize that clothes are symbolic vestments, outward metaphors for the inner man. By donning his clothes, Eli assumes the burdens of the "greenie" and accepts the terrible cost that is exacted from the man of spiritual integrity. When he puts on the clothing, Eli finds that his protective phantasies and comforting fictions wither away. He looks older, more tired, and yet the face he discerns in the mirror is really his face. He knows now who has hidden beneath his skin all those years.

Armed with this new knowledge, Eli returns to the Yeshivah to find the "greenie" painting the pillar on the porch. The pillar glows like white fire, and like the burning bush, beckons the wandering child of Israel. The "greenie" turns to confront Eli and they recognize themselves not as opposites but *"semblables, frères."* But the ordeal of Eli is not ended. He is not to be permitted to absent himself from the world and live apart. The "greenie's" arm points to Woodenton, the arena wherein Eli must make his affirmation. He is not to be permitted a self-indulgent religion, for the child of Israel is most often recognized, like Odysseus of Ithaca, Coriolanus of Rome, Jesus of Nazareth, by the wounds he has suffered for his people. As he walks through the town, Eli's wounds are obvious to those who look on. Yet Eli measures his tread with his name, "Eli Peck, Eli Peck . . . ." He knows who he is for the first time. In the Hebraic tradition the act of naming symbolizes the act of creation. Coincidental with his own rebirth is the birth of Eli's son, the affirmation of a tradition and the continuity of past and present. Eli now understands, in Eliot's formulation, "not only the pastness of the past, but of its presence."

Those who have not understood the nature of Eli's quest conclude that his behavior is a manifestation of his dementia. They try to numb his pain, forgetting that suffering is often a necessary result of profound commitment. What they do not recognize is "that he'd *chosen* to be crazy." It is in this moment of existential crisis that Eli chooses to suffer, to affirm the absurd, to learn who he is whatever it may cost. The radical character of his commitment will puzzle his peers and perhaps frighten them. They will want to agree that he is mad. In *Fear and Trembling* Kierkegaard describes the knowledge of such a madman who

> knows that it is beautiful to be born as the individual who has the universal as his home, his friendly abiding-place, which at once welcomes him with open arms when he would tarry in it. But he knows also that higher than this there winds a solitary path, narrow and steep; he knows that it is terrible to be born outside the universal, to walk without meeting a single traveler. He knows very well where he is and how he is related to men. Humanly speaking, he is crazy and cannot make himself intelligible to anyone.[2]

The sanity of Eli's peers is a stratagem to protect their proprieties. They

[2] *Ibid.,* p. 115.

live at the expedient level where there are always pragmatic goods and necessary evils. But Eli has gone beyond expedience to the point of existential significance, to what Kierkegaard, in speaking of Eli's spiritual ancestor Abraham, describes as the moment of "either / or."

> Either the individual as the individual is able to stand in an absolute relation to the absolute (and then the ethical is not the highest) / or Abraham is lost—he is neither a tragic hero, nor an aesthetic hero.[3]

In pushing himself to the point of either / or, Eli finds the courage to respond to the absolutes of the spirit and reject the entreaties of expediency. He is a strange man still, but a Knight of the Faith need not answer to less "exalted" proprieties.

How is it possible, then, for us to conclude that Eli Peck triumphs? Is he not "mad"? Is he not in disgrace? The course of Eli's behavior reveals a pattern that students of myth have called the "hero-quest." This quest is three-fold: The hero leaves his home, journeys through a series of crises in the world, and, if he is not destroyed in the process, returns home. But he is, upon returning to the point of origin, not the same man who first ventured forth. His consciousness is tempered by experience, *his* experience. Now his homeland is *his* homeland, chosen by him, and not merely the place where he was born.

Eli Peck is not overtly the hero type, and yet one may see in his effort to come to terms with his ancestral "homeland" a spiritual quest of heroic dimensions. Eli, as the other "progressives" of Woodenton, is tempted to deny his kinship with the community of DP's and to shun its demands upon him. But he courageously takes upon himself the consequences of his choice to identify with the DP's and, paradoxically, recovers his home amid a community of homeless. To the "progressives" who would rather be secure by not being different, such an act is madness. Is Eli mad, then? Of course. But as Wordsworth wisely concluded when asked his opinion of Blake, "There are some who say this man is mad, but I prefer the madness of this man to the sanity of others."

[3] *Ibid.*, p. 175.

QUESTIONS

Eli, the Fanatic

POINT OF VIEW 1. Discuss the relationship between the "greenie" and Eli. In particular, explain how Roth uses the "greenie," whose consciousness remains closed to the reader, as a means of unlocking and displaying the feelings and thoughts of Eli. ("Greenie," incidentally, is short for "greenhorn," a disparaging term that was sometimes applied to new immigrants.)

CHARACTERS 2. In "Eli, the Fanatic," the past penetrates the narrative present. From the information Roth supplies, describe the past of Eli, Tzuref, and the "greenie," and explain the significance of their individual histories on the present action of the story. 3. Assuming that Roth had the biblical Eli (cf. I Samuel 4:11-18) in mind when he created the fictional Eli, what does that identification contribute to the characterization and to your understanding of the story? 4. Explain Miriam's and Ted's positions in regard to the Yeshivah. In what ways does Ted serve as a foil to Eli?

PLOT 5. In this story, there is an *anagnorisis*, or recognition scene, that is similar to those in classical tragedy. Locate this scene. Then examine its structure.

SETTING 6. What details has Roth chosen in order to convey the tangible and intangible qualities of Woodenton? 7. How does the setting precipitate and intensify the external and internal conflict in this story?

STYLE 8. Eli's name means "the exalted one." What might be the implications of the Yeshivah director's name? of Eli's wife's name? 9. Using at least three passages of extended dialogue in the story, show how the dialogue grows naturally out of the speaker, helps to characterize him, and advances the action. Examine the use of idioms in the dialogue. Finally, discuss how Roth captures the rhythm of various kinds of conversation—note, especially, when the character is trying to explain himself or a principle to someone else, when he is engaged in heated argument, and when he tries to shield himself. 10. Find at least three symbols in the story. How do they contribute to its meaning?

TONE 11. Examine the relationship between sympathy and point of view in this story. Take into account Eli's isolation and extreme responses, the "reasonableness" of other characters, and the use of the restricted narrator. 12. Throughout the story, there is a rich vein of humor— growing out of incident, character, and language. Find examples of these three kinds of comedy. Discuss the effect of humor on the meaning of the story.

Eli Agonistes: Philip Roth's Knight of Faith

FOCUS 1. How does the epigraph from Kierkegaard indicate the focus of the essay? 2. Many modern critics base their approach to literature on existentialism—a philosophy that asserts that every man defines himself (asserts his identity) through his choices. To the existentialist "existence precedes essence." Through action, an individual creates his own reality, replete with its own system of meaning. At various points in the essay, the essayist makes clear that his approach is that of the existentialist critic. Find as many examples of this bias as you can.

ORGANIZATION 3. Every paragraph in the essay either focuses on Eli or includes mention of him. Using this observation as a guide, examine the organization of the essay.

USING THE EVIDENCE 4. How does the essay support the contention that the juxtaposition of Eli Peck and Leo Tzuref is ironical? 5. What evidence supports construing the pillar as "symbolic of the monolithic, masculine Yahweh"?

STYLE 6. The prose style in the essay is rather allusive and baroque. For example, "He is not to be permitted a self-indulgent religion, for the child of Israel is most often recognized, like Odysseus of Ithaca, Coriolanus of Rome, Jesus of Nazareth, by the wounds he has suffered for his people." Examine how the style reinforces the subject matter.

MAKING LITERARY JUDGMENTS 7. The essay describes "Eli, the Fanatic" as parabolic. Explain the meaning of the term. In what ways is the story parabolic? Is this a valid judgment? 8. In discussing the conclusion of the story the essayist implies that he favors Eli's madness to the sanity of the Woodenton "progressives." If you adopt a critical perspective other than existentialism, can you support a less optimistic interpretation of the ending—one that sees Eli's nervous breakdown as a sign of an apparently complete and perhaps irreversible personality disorder?

IN TROUBLE

That morning when the alarm rang at six thirty, she went off to the bathroom to stick a finger down her throat before the other girls started coming in to brush their teeth. This made her feel herself again, provided she skipped breakfast afterward, and avoided the corridor back of the dining hall, and forced soda crackers down her throat from time to time during the morning. Then she could get through the day's classes pretending that she was the same girl in the same body, and in the same way too—alone.

But what about last night? What about Roy saying he was willing to do his duty by her? The fainting spells had ended two weeks back, and the nausea she could starve to death every morning, but now that Roy's body seemed to be inhabited by some new person—by a man, a responsible, upright, decent man, what she had been pleading with that coward to be for weeks!—the truth came in upon her as it never had before. *A new person was inhabiting hers as well.*

She was stunned. Her predicament was real. It was no plot she had invented to bring them all to their senses. It was no scheme to force them to treat her like flesh and blood, like a human being, like a girl! And it was not going to disappear either, just because somebody besides herself was at long last taking it seriously. It was real! Something was happening which she was helpless to stop! Something was growing inside her body, and without her permission!

And I don't want to marry him! He only said yes because he's afraid— of his family, of me, of everything! He's a weak, frightened, hopeless, childish idiot who if he lives to be a hundred will never be a proper husband or a proper father or even half of a whole human being!

The sun wasn't even above the trees as she ran across Pendleton Park to downtown Fort Kean.

She had to wait an hour in the station for the first bus to the north. Her books were in her lap; she had some idea that she could study on the way up and be back for her two thirty, but then she had not yet a clear idea of why she was suddenly rushing home to Liberty Center, or what would happen there. On the bench in the empty station she tried to calm herself by reading the English assignment she had planned to do in her free hour before lunch; and during lunch, which she didn't eat anyway. "Here you will have a chance to examine, and then practice, several skills used in writing effective sentences. The skills presented are those—"

She didn't want to marry him! He was the last person in the world she would ever want to marry!

She began gagging only a little way beyond Fort Kean. When he heard her, the driver pulled to the side of the road. She dropped out the back door and threw her soiled handkerchief into a puddle. Aboard again, she sat in the rear corner praying that she would not be ill, or faint, or begin to sob. She must not think of food; she must not even think of the crackers she had forgotten in her flight from the dorm; she must not think of what she was going to say, or to whom.

What *was* she going to say?

"Here you will have a chance to examine, and then practice, several skills used in writing effective sentences. The skills presented are those used by writers of the models in the Description Section—" Years ago there was a farm girl at L. C. High who took so large a dose of castor oil to try to make the baby come out that she blew a hole in her stomach. She contracted a terrible case of peritonitis, and lost the baby, but afterward, because she had come so close to dying, everyone forgave her, and kids who hadn't even noticed her before—"Here you will have a chance to examine, and then practice, several skills used in writing—" Curt Bonham, the basketball star . . . He had been a year ahead of her. In March of his last term he and a friend had tried to walk home across the river one night while the ice was breaking up, and Curt had drowned. His whole class voted unanimously to dedicate the yearbook to him, and his graduation photograph appeared all by itself on the opening page of "The Liberty Bell." And beneath the black-bordered picture was written:

Smart lad, to slip betimes away
From fields where glory does not stay . . .
ELLIOT CURTIS BONHAM
1930-1947

"What is it?" her mother asked when she came through the front door. "Lucy, what are you doing here? What's the matter?"

"I got here by bus, Mother. That's how people get from Fort Kean to Liberty Center. Bus."

"But what is it? Lucy, you're so pale."

"Is anyone else home?" she asked. "Where is everyone?"

"Daddy Will took Grandma over to the market in Winnisaw."

"And he went to work? Your husband?"

"Lucy, what is it? Why aren't you in school?"

"I'm getting married Christmas Day," she said, moving into the parlor. Sadly her mother spoke. "We heard. We know."

"How did you hear?"

"Lucy, weren't you going to tell us?"

"We only decided last night. How did you hear, Mother?"

"Roy's father spoke to Daddy."

"Daddy Will?"

"To your father."

"Oh? And what came of that, may I ask?"

"Well, he took your side. Well, that's what came of it. Lucy, I'm answering your question. He took your side, and without a moment's hesitation. Despite our not having been properly told by our own daughter the day of her own wedding—"

"What did he say, Mother? Exactly."

"He told Mr. Bassart he couldn't speak for Roy, of course— He told Mr. Bassart we feel you are mature enough to know your own mind—"

"Well, maybe I'm not!"

"Lucy, you can't think everything he does is wrong just because he does it: He *believes* in you."

"Tell him not to then!"

"Dear—"

"I'm going to have a baby, Mother. So please tell him not to!"

"Lucy—you are?"

"Yes! Of course I am! Why else would I marry that idiot! I hate him, Mother! I can't stand his guts!"

She ran off to the kitchen just in time to be sick in the sink.

She was put to bed in her room. "Here you will have a chance—" The book slid off the bed onto the floor. What was there to do now but wait?

The mail fell through the slot in the hallway and onto the welcome mat. The vacuum cleaner started up. The car pulled into the driveway. She heard her grandmother's voice down on the front porch. She slept.

Her mother brought her tea and toast. "I told Grandma it was the grippe," she whispered to her daughter. "Is that all right?"

Would her grandmother believe that she had come home because of the grippe? Where was Daddy Will? What had she told *him?*

"He didn't even come inside, Lucy. He'll be back this afternoon."

"Does he know I'm home?"

"Not yet."

Home. But why not? For years they had complained that she acted contemptuous of everything they said or did; for years they complained that she refused to let them give her a single word of advice; she lived among them like a stranger, like an enemy even, unfriendly, uncommunicative, nearly unapproachable. Well, could they say she was behaving like their enemy today? She had come home. So what were they going to do?

She drank some of the tea. She sank back into the pillow her mother had fluffed up for her and drew one finger lightly round and round her lips. Lemon. It smelled so nice. Forget everything else. Just wait. Time will pass. Eventually something will have to be done.

She fell asleep with her face on her fingers.

Her grandmother came up the stairs carrying a wet mustard plaster. The patient let her nightgown be unbuttoned. "That'll loosen it up," said Grandma Berta, pressing it down. "The two important things, rest and heat. Plenty of heat. Much as you can possibly stand," and she piled two blankets more onto the patient.

Lucy closed her eyes. Why hadn't she done this at the start instead of suffering all these weeks while Roy Bassart made up his mind whether or not to do his duty and be a man? Why hadn't she just gotten into bed and left it all to them? Wasn't that what they were always wanting to be, her family?

She was awakened by the piano. Her mother's students had begun to arrive for their lessons. She thought, *"But I don't have the grippe."* But then she drove the thought, and the panic that accompanied it, right from her mind.

It must have begun snowing while she was asleep. She pulled a blanket off the bed, wrapped it around her, and at the window put her mouth on the cold glass and watched the cars sliding down the street. The window began to grow warm where her mouth was pressed against it. Breathing in and out, she could make the circle of steam on the glass expand and contract. What would happen when her grandmother found out what really was wrong with her? And her grandfather, when he got home? And her father!

She had forgotten to tell her mother not to tell him. Maybe she wouldn't anyway. But then would anything happen?

She scuffed with her slippers across the old worn rug and got back into her bed. She thought to pick her English book up from the floor and work a little on those sentences; instead she got way down under the blankets, and with her faintly lemony fingers under her nose, slept for the sixth or seventh time.

Beyond the window it was dark, though from where she sat propped up in bed the snow could be seen floating through the light of the street-lamp across the street. Her father knocked on her door and asked if he could come in.

"It's not locked," was her response.

"Well," he said, stepping into the room, "so this is how the rich spend their days. Not bad."

She could tell that his words had been prepared. She did not look up from the blanket, but began to smooth it out with her hand. "I have the grippe."

"Smells to me," he said, "like you've been eating hot dogs."

She did not smile or speak.

"I tell you what it smells like. Smells like Comiskey Park, down in Chicago."

"Mustard plaster," she finally said.

"Well," he said, giving the door a push so that it closed, "that's one of your grandmother's real pleasures in life. That's one," he said, lowering his voice, "and the other is—no, I think that about covers it."

She only shrugged, as though she had no opinions on people's habits one way or the other. Was he clowning because he knew, or because he didn't know? She saw from the corner of her eye that the pale hairs on the back of his hands were wet; he had washed up before coming into her room.

The smell of dinner cooking below caused her to begin to feel ill.

"Mind if I sit at the foot here?" he said.

"If you want to."

She mustn't be sick, not again. She mustn't arouse in him a single suspicion. Oh, she did not want him to know, ever!

"Let's see," he was saying. "Do I want to or don't I want to? I want to."

She yawned; he sat.

"Well," he said, "nice and cozy up here."

She stared straight ahead into the snowy evening.

"Winter's coming in with a rush this time," he said.

He was so close to her, how could she not? She glanced quickly over at him. "I suppose." She turned back to the window instantly and was able to collect herself in that way. She could not remember the last time she had looked directly into his eyes.

"Did I ever tell you," he said, "about the time I sprained my ankle when I was working at McConnell's? It swelled way up, and I came home, and your grandmother just lit up all over. Hot compresses, she said. So I sat down in the kitchen and rolled up my trouser leg. You should have seen her boiling up the water on the stove. Somehow it reminded me of all those cannibals over in Africa. She can't see how it can be good for you, unless it hurts or smells bad."

Suppose she just blurted out the truth to him?

"A lot of people like that," he said. "So," and gave her foot a squeeze where it stuck up at the end of the bed, "how's school going, Goosie?"

"All right."

"I hear you're learning French. *Parlez-vous?*"

"French is one of my subjects, yes."

"And let's see—what else? You and me haven't had a good conversation in a long time now, have we?"

She did not answer.

"Oh, and how's Roy doing?"

Instantly she said, "Fine."

Her father took his hand off her foot at last. "Well," he said, "we heard, you know, about the wedding."

"Where's Daddy Will?"

"I'm talking to you right now, Lucy. What do you want him for while I'm talking to you?"

"I didn't say I wanted him. I only asked where he was."

"Out," her father said. "Your grandfather is out!"

"Isn't he even going to have dinner?"

"He went out!" He rose from the bed. "I don't ask where he goes, or when he eats. How do I know where he is? He's out!" And he left the room.

In a matter of seconds, her mother appeared.

"What happened now?"

"I asked where Daddy Will is, that's all," Lucy answered. "What's wrong with that?"

"But is Daddy Will your father or is your father your father?"

"*But you told him,*" she burst out.

"Lucy," said her mother, shutting the door, "lower your voice."

"But you did. You told him! And I didn't say you should!"

"Lucy, you came home; dear, you said—"

"I don't want him to know! It's not his business!"

"Now you must stop, unless you want others to know too."

"But I don't care who knows! I'm not ashamed! And don't start crying, Mother!"

"Then let him talk to you, *please*. He wants to."

"Oh, does he?"

"Lucy, you have to listen to him. You have to give him a chance."

She turned and hid her face in the pillow. "I didn't want him to *know*, Mother."

Her mother sat on the bed and put her hand on the girl's hair.

"And," said Lucy, moving back, "what was he going to say, anyway? Why didn't he just say it out, if he had anything to say?"

"Because," her mother pleaded, "you didn't give him the chance."

"Well, I'm giving *you* a chance, Mother."

There was a silence.

"Tell me!"

"Lucy—dear, what would you think—what would you say—what would you think, I mean—of going for a visit—"

"Oh, no."

"*Please* let me finish. Of going to visit your father's cousin Vera. In Florida."

"And is that his idea of what to do with me?"

"Lucy, till this is over. For a little while."

"Nine months is no little while, Mother—"

"But it would be warm there, and pleasant—"

"Oh," she said, beginning to cry into the pillow, "very pleasant. Why doesn't he ship me off to a home for wayward girls; wouldn't that be even easier?"

"Don't say that. He doesn't want to send you anywhere, you know that."

"He wishes I'd never been born, Mother. He thinks I'm why everything is so wrong with *him*."

"That's not *so*."

"Then," she said sobbing, "he'd have one less responsibility to feel guilty about. If he even felt guilty to begin with."

"But he does, terribly."

"Well, he should!" she said. "He is!"

Some twenty minutes after her mother had run from the room, her grandfather knocked. Daddy Will was wearing his lumber jacket and held his cap in his hands. The brim was dark where the snow had dampened it.

"Hey, I hear somebody's been asking for me."

"Hullo."

"You sound like death-warmed-over, my friend. You ought to be outside and feel the wind. Then you'd really appreciate being sick in bed."

She did not answer.

"Stomach settle down?" he asked.

"Yes."

He pulled a chair over to the side of the bed. "How's about another mustard plaster? Berta called me at the Erwins, and on the way home I stopped and bought a whole fresh packet. So just say when."

She turned and looked at the wall.

"What is it, Lucy? Maybe you want Dr. Eglund. That's what I told Myra—"

He pulled the chair right up close. "Lucy, I never saw anything like the change in your father this time," he said softly. "Not a drop—not a single solitary drop, Lucy. He is taking this whole decision of yours right in his stride. You set a date, and it was just fine with him. Fine with all of us, Lucy—whatever you think is going to make you and Roy happy."

"I want my mother."

"Don't you feel good again? Maybe the doctor—"

"I want my mother! My mother, and not him!"

She was still looking at the wall when her door opened.

"Myra," her father said, "sit over there. Sit, I said."

"Yes."

"All right, Lucy. Turn over." He was standing by the side of the bed. "Roll over, I said."

"Lucy," her mother begged, "look at us, please."

"I don't have to see that his shoes are shined and his jaw is set and what a new man he is. I don't have to see his necktie, or him either!"

"Lucy—"

"Myra, be quiet. If she wants to act like a two-year-old at a time like this, let her."

She whispered, "Look who's talking about two-year-olds."

"Listen, young lady. Your back talk doesn't faze me one way or the other. There have always been smart-aleck teen-agers, and there always will be, especially this generation. You just listen to me, that's all, and if you're too ashamed to look me in the eye—"

"Ashamed!" she cried, but she did not move.

"Are you or are you not going to visit Cousin Vera?"

"I don't even *know* Cousin Vera."

"That isn't what I'm asking."

"I can't go off alone to someone I don't even know—and what? Make up filthy lies for the neighbors—?"

"But they wouldn't be lies," said her mother.

"What would they be, Mother. The truth?"

"They would be *stories*," her father said. "That you have a husband overseas—in the Army."

"Oh, you know all about stories, I'm sure; but I tell the truth!"

"Then," he said, "just what do you intend to do about getting into trouble with somebody you say you can't even stand?"

She turned violently from the wall as though she intended to hurl herself at him. "Don't you take such a tone with me! Don't you dare!"

"I am not taking any tone!"

"Because I am not ashamed—not in front of you I'm not!"

"Now watch it, you, just watch it. Because I can still give you a licking, smart as you think you are."

"Oh," she said bitterly, "can you?"

"Yes!"

"Go ahead then."

"Oh, wonderful," he said, and walked to the window, where he stood as though looking outside. "Just wonderful."

"Lucy," said her mother, "if you don't want to go to Cousin Vera's, then what do you want to do? Just tell us."

"You're the parents. You were always *dying* to be the parents."

"Now look," said her father, turning to face her once again. "First, Myra, you sit down. And stay down. And you," he said, waving a finger at his daughter, "you give me your attention, do you hear? Now there is a crisis here, you understand that? There is a crisis here involving my daughter, and I am going to deal with it, and it's going to be dealt with."

"Fine," said Lucy. "Deal."

"Then be *still*," her mother pleaded, "and let him talk." But when she made a move to the bed her husband looked at her and she retreated.

"Now either I'm going to do it," he said, speaking between his teeth to his wife, "or I'm not. Now which is it?"

She lowered her eyes.

"Unless, of course, you want to call your daddy in," he said.

"I'm sorry."

"Now," said her father, "if you wanted to marry that Roy Bassart— such as we understood you did, Lucy—that would be one thing. But this is something else entirely. Who he is I see pretty clear now, and the less said about him the better. I understand the whole picture, so there is just no need for raising voices. He was older, back from the service, and just thought to himself he could come back here last year and take advantage of a young seventeen-year-old high school girl. And that's what he did. But he is his father's business, Lucy, and we will have to leave it to his high and mighty father, the big schoolteacher, to teach something into that boy's hide. Oh, his father thinks he is very superior and all in his ways, but I guess he is going to have another guess coming now. But my concern is with you, Lucy, and what is uppermost to you. Do you understand that? My concern is your going to college, which has always been your dream, right? Now, the question is this, do you still want your dream, or don't you?"

She did not favor him with a reply.

"OK," he said, "I am going to go ahead on my assumption that you do, just as you always did. Now, next—to give you your dream I am going to do anything I can— Are you listening to me? Anything that is going to give it to you, do you follow me? Because what that so-called ex-G.I. has done to you, which I would like to put my hands around his throat for, well, that is not going to just take away your dream, lock, stock, and barrel . . . Now, anything," he went on, "even something that isn't usual and ordinary, and that might to some folks seem very—out of the question." He came close to the bed so that he could speak without being heard outside the room. "Now, do you know what *anything* means, before I go to the next step?"

"Giving up whiskey?"

"I want you to go to college, it means! I have given up whiskey, for your information!"

"Really?" she asked. "Again?"

"Lucy, since Thanksgiving," her mother began.

"Myra, you be still."

"I was only telling her—"

"But *I* will tell her," he said. "*I* will do the telling!"

"Yes," his wife said softly.

"Now," he said, turning back to Lucy, "drink is neither here nor there. Drink is not the issue."

"Oh, no?"

"No! A baby is!"

And that made her look away.

"An illegitimate baby is," he said again. "And if you don't *want* that illegitimate baby," his voice had fallen almost to a whisper now, "then maybe we will have to arrange that you don't have it. If Cousin Vera's is still something you are going to consider out of the question."

"It absolutely is! I will not spend nine months lying! I will not get big and pregnant and lie!"

"Shhh!"

"Well, I won't," she muttered.

"OK." He wiped his mouth with his hand. "Then let's do this in order. And without voice-raising, as there are other people who live in this house."

"We're the other people who live here."

"Be still!" he said. "Everybody knows that without your back talk!"

"Then just what are you proposing to me? Say it!"

Her mother rushed to the bed at last. "Lucy," she said, taking hold of her hand, "Lucy, it's only to help *you*—"

And then her father took hold of the other hand, and it was as though some current were about to pass through the three of them. She closed her eyes, waited—and her father spoke. And she let him. And she saw the future. She saw herself seated between her two parents as her father drove them across the bridge to Winnisaw. It would be early morning. The doctor would only just have finished with his breakfast. He would come to the door to greet them, and her father would shake his hand. In his office the doctor would seat himself behind a big dark desk, and she would sit in a chair, and her parents would be together on a sofa, while the doctor explained to them exactly what he was going to do. He would have all his medical degrees right up on the wall, in frames. When she went off with him into the little white operating room, her mother and father would smile at her from the sofa. And they would wait there until it was time to bundle her up and take her home.

When her father had finished, she said, "But it must cost a fortune."

"The object isn't the money, honey," he said.

"The object is you," said her mother.

How nice that sounded. Like a poem. She was just beginning to study poetry, too. Her last English composition had been an interpretation of "Ozymandias." She had only received the paper back on Monday morning, a B plus for the very first interpretation she had ever written of a poem in college. Only on Monday she had thought it was going to be her last. Before Roy had finally returned to Fort Kean with his big brave decision made, her recurring thought had been to run away. And now she didn't have to; and she didn't have to marry him either. Now she could concentrate on one thing and one thing only, on school, on French, history, poetry . . .

> The object isn't money,
> The object is you.

"But where," she asked softly, "will you get it all?"

"Let me worry about that," her father said. "OK?"

"Will you work?"

"Wow," he said to Myra. "She sure don't pull her punches, your daughter here." The red that had risen into his cheeks remained, even as he tried to maintain a soft joking tone. "Come on, Goosie, what do you say? Give me a break, huh? Where do you think I've been all day today, anyway? Taking a stroll on the boulevard? Playing a tennis game? What do you think I've been doing all my life since I was eighteen years old, and part-time before that? Work, Lucy, just plain old work, day in and day out."

"Not at one job," she said.

"Well, so I moved around—that's true—"

She was going to cry; they were talking!

"Look," he said, "why don't you think of it this way. You have a daddy who is a jack of all trades. You should be proud. Come on, Goosie-pie, how about a smile like I used to get back in prehistoric times?"

She felt her mother squeeze her hand.

"Look," he said, "why do you think people always hire Duane Nelson no matter what? Because he sits around twiddling his thumbs, or because he knows every kind of machine there is, inside out? Now which? That's not a hard question, is it, for a smart college girl?"

Afterward she would read in bed. She would have her assignments mailed up to her while she recuperated in her bed. Yes, a college girl. And without Roy. He wasn't so bad, he just wasn't for her, that was all. He would just disappear, and she could begin to make friends at school, friends to bring home with her when she came to visit on the weekend. For things would have changed.

Could that be? At long last those terrible days of hatred and solitude, over? To think—she could begin again to talk to her family, to tell them about all the things she was studying, to show them her papers. Stuck into her English book right there on the floor was the essay she had written on "Ozymandias." B plus, and across the front the professor had written, "Excellent paragraph development; good understanding of meaning; good use of quotation; but please don't stuff your sentences so." And maybe she *had* overdone the main topic sentence somewhat, but her intention had been to state at the outset all those ideas that she would later take up in the body of the essay. "Even a great king," her paper began, "such as Ozymandias apparently had been, could not predict or control what the future, or Fate, held in store for him and his kingdom; that, I think, is the message that Percy Bysshe Shelley, the poet, means for us to come away with from his romantic poem 'Ozymandias,' which not only reveals the theme of the vanity of human wishes—even a king's— but deals also with the concept of the immensity of 'boundless and bare' life and the inevitability of the 'colossal wreck' of everything, as compared to the 'sneer of cold command,' which is all many mere mortals have at their command, unfortunately."

"But is he clean?" she asked.

"A hundred percent," her father said. "Spotless, Lucy. Like a hospital."

"And how old is he?" she asked.

"Oh," her father said, "middle-aged, I'd say."

A moment passed. Then: "That's the catch, isn't it?"

"What kind of catch?"

"He's too old."

"Now what do you mean 'too old'? If anything, he's real experienced."

"But is this all he does?"

"Lucy, he's a regular doctor who does this as a special favor, that's all."

"But he charges, you said."

"Well, sure, he charges."

"Then it's not a special favor. He does it for money."

"Well, everybody has got bills to meet. Everybody has got to be paid for what they do."

But she saw herself dead. The doctor would be no good, and she would die.

"How do you know about him?"

"Because," and here he stood and hitched up his trousers. "Through a friend," he finally said.

"Who?"

"Lucy, I'm afraid maybe that's got to be a secret."

"But where did you hear about him?" Where *would* he hear about such a doctor? "At Earl's famous Dugout of Buddies? At a *saloon?*"

"Lucy, that's not necessary," said her mother.

Her father walked to the window again. He cleared a pane with the palm of his hand. "Well," he said, "it's stopped snowing. It's stopped snowing, if anybody cares."

"All I meant—" Lucy began.

"Is what?" He had turned back to her.

"Is—do you know anybody who he's ever done it to, that's all?"

"Yes, I happen to, for your information!"

"And they're alive?"

"For your information, yes!"

"Well, it's my life. I have a right to know."

"Why don't you just trust me! I'm not going to kill you!"

"Oh, Duane," her mother said, "she *does!*"

"Don't speak for me, Mother!"

"Hear that?" he cried to his wife.

"Well, he might just be some quack drinking friend, who says he's a doctor or something. Well, how do I know, Mother? Maybe it's even Earl himself in his red suspenders!"

"Yeah, that's who it is," her father shouted. "Earl Duval! Sure! What's the matter with you? You think I don't mean it when I say I want you to finish college?"

"Dear, he does. You're his daughter."

"That doesn't mean he knows whether a doctor is good or not, Mother. Suppose I die!"

"But I just told you," he cried, shaking a fist at her, "you won't!"

"But how do you know?"

"Because she didn't, did she!"

"Who?"

No one had to speak for her to understand.

"Oh, no." She dropped slowly back against the headboard.

Her mother covered her face with her hands.

"When?" said Lucy.

"But she's alive, isn't she?" He was pulling at his shirt with his hands. "Answer the point I'm making! I am speaking! She did not die! She did not get hurt in any way at all!"

"Mother," she said, turning to her, "when?"

But her mother only shook her head. Lucy got up out of the bed. "Mother, when did he make you do that?"

"He didn't make me."

"Oh, Mother," she said, standing before her. "You're my *mother*."

"Lucy, you were a little girl. It was in the Depression times. It was long ago. Oh, it's all forgotten. Daddy Will, Grandma, they don't know," she whispered, "don't have to—"

"But the Depression was over when I was three, when I was four."

"What?" her father cried. "Are you kidding?" To his wife he said, "Is she kidding?"

"Lucy," her mother said, "we did it for you."

"Oh, yes," she said, moving backward onto her bed, "for me, everything was for me."

"Lucy, we couldn't have another baby. Not when we were so far behind and trying so to fight back—"

"But if only he did his job! If he only stopped being a coward!"

"Look," he said, coming angrily at her, "you don't even know when the Depression was, or what it was, either—so *watch what you say!*"

"I do too know!"

"The whole country was behind the eight ball, not just me! If you want to call names, you call the whole United States of America names!"

"Oh, sure, the whole *world*."

"Don't you know history?" he cried. "Don't you know anything?" he demanded.

"I know what you made her do, you!"

"But," her mother cried, "I *wanted* to."

"Did you hear that?" he shouted. "Did you hear what your mother just said to you?"

"But you're the man!"

"I am also a human being!"

"That's no excuse!"

"Oh, what am I arguing with you for? You don't know *a* from *z* as far as life is concerned, and you never will! You wouldn't know a man's job if I did it!"

Silence.

"Hear, Mother? Hear your husband?" said Lucy. "Did you hear what he just said, right out in the open?"

"Hear what I *mean*," he cried.

"But what you *said*—"

"I don't care! Stop trapping me! I came in here to solve a crisis, but how can I do it when nobody lets me even begin? Or end! You'd rather trap me—throw me in jail like you did already! That's what you'd rather do! You'd rather humiliate me in this whole town, and make me looked down on as the town joke!"

"Town *drunk!*"

"Drunk?" he said. "Town drunk? You ought to see the town drunk. You think I'm the town drunk? Well, you ought to just see a town drunk, and then think what you're saying twice before you say it. You don't know what a town drunk is. You don't know what anything is! You—you just want me behind bars—that's your big wish in life, and always has been!"

"It's not."

"It is."

"But that's *over*," cried Myra.

"Sure it's over," said her father. "Sure, people just forget how a daughter threw her own father in jail. Called up the police at the age of fifteen because her own father had one lousy beer too many! Sure, people don't talk about that behind your back. People don't like to tell stories on a person, oh, no. People are always giving other people a chance to change and get their strength back. Sure, that's what this little scene is all about too. You bet it is. Oh, she's got me fixed, boy—and that's the way it's going to be. That's how brilliant she is, your so-called college girl scholarship daughter. Well, go ahead, so-called daughter who knows all the answers, solve your own life. Because I'm not good enough for a person like you, and never have been. What am I anyway? The town drunk to you."

He pulled open the door and went loudly down the stairs. They could hear him in the parlor, bellowing at Daddy Will. "Go ahead, Mr. Carroll. You're the only one can solve things around here. Go ahead, it's Daddy Will everyone wants around here anyway. I'm just extra anyway. I'm just along for the ride, we all know that."

"Shouting won't help anything, Duane—"

"Right, right you are, Berta. Nothing will help anything around here."

"Willard," said Berta, "tell this person—"

"What's the trouble, Duane? What's the fuss?"

"Oh, nothing you can't fix, Willard. Because you're the big daddy, and me, I'm just along for the ride."

"Willard, where is he going? Dinner is all ready."

"Duane, where are you going?"

"I don't know. Maybe I'll go down and see old Tom Whipper."

"Who's he?"

"The town drunk, Willard! That's who the town drunk is, damn it— Tom Whipper!"

The door slammed, and then the house was silent except for the whispering that began downstairs.

Lucy lay without moving on the bed.

Her mother was crying.

"Mother, why, *why* did you let him make you do that?"

"I did what I had to," said her mother mournfully.

"You didn't! You let him trample on your dignity, Mother! You were his doormat! His slave!"

"Lucy, I did what was necessary," she said, sobbing.

"That's not always right, though! You have to do what's *right!*"

"It was." She spoke as in a trance. "It was. It was."

"It wasn't! Not for you! He degrades you, Mother, and you let him! Always! All our lives!"

"Oh, Lucy, whatever we say, our suggestions, you refuse."

"I refuse—I refuse to live your life again, Mother, that's what I refuse!" And so she was married to Roy Bassart on Christmas Day.

SUGGESTIONS FOR WRITING

The Stories

1. Explore the language of dialogue in "In Trouble." You may find question 9 on p. 214 a useful point of departure and you may include in your essay a comparison of the dialogue in "In Trouble" with that in "Eli, the Fanatic."

2. Examine the patterns of imagery in "Eli, the Fanatic," showing how imagery contributes to the meaning of this story.

3. Compare and contrast Miriam in "Eli, the Fanatic" with Liz in "A Gift from the City."

4. Although we never "meet" Roy Bassart (Roy does not participate in the present action of the story), he is nonetheless real as a character in the fictional world of "In Trouble." Write a character sketch of Roy, showing how Roth makes Roy "visible" to the reader.

5. Although we learn that Lucy does not love Roy, write an essay in which you show why Lucy's decision to marry Roy is inevitable.

6. Through action and dialogue as well as through her unspoken thoughts, Lucy reveals herself as a highly neurotic young woman— at times appearing superior, defensive, independent, childish, scared, and hostile. Write a character sketch of Lucy, taking into account these contradictory aspects of her behavior, and also discussing the complex relationship that exists between Lucy and her father.

Other Works by Philip Roth

1. Consult such works as Frederic I. Carpenter's *American Literature and the Dream* (1955) and R. W. B. Lewis's *The American Adam* (1955). Then write an essay in which you interpret *Goodbye, Columbus* as a mid-twentieth century embodiment of the American Dream.

2. Stanley Edgar Hyman criticizes the "architectural weakness" of *Letting Go*, saying that it never "becomes a novel, with a unified dramatic action, but falls apart into two narratives which have only a pat complementarity." Either defend or attack this criticism.

3. Compare and contrast *Main Street* by Sinclair Lewis with *When She Was Good*.

4. *Our Gang* can be considered a fictionalized treatment of "Politics and the English Language" by George Orwell. Read this essay and show the parallels between it and Roth's political satire.

5. Compare and contrast Alex Portnoy (*Portnoy's Complaint*) and David Alan Kepesh (*The Breast*) in terms of their sexuality.

6. Compare *The Breast* with Kafka's "The Metamorphosis" and Gogol's "The Nose."

7. *The Great American Novel,* Bernard Malamud's *The Natural,* Robert Coover's *The Universal Baseball Association,* and Mark Harris's *The Southpaw* are all baseball novels. Compare and contrast Roth's novel with one of these others. Also, try to explain why baseball can be treated as myth.

BIBLIOGRAPHY

Primary

Goodbye, Columbus and Five Short Stories. Boston: Houghton Mifflin, 1959. A novella and short stories.

"Writing American Fiction." *Commentary,* 31 (March 1961), 223–33. Literary criticism. In the September 1961, issue of *Commentary,* pp. 250–52, Roth replies to letters that attack aspects of his article.

Letting Go. New York: Random House, 1962. A novel.

When She Was Good. New York: Random House, 1967. A novel.

Portnoy's Complaint. New York: Random House, 1969. A novel.

Our Gang. New York: Random House, 1971. Political satire.

The Breast. New York: Holt, Rinehart and Winston, 1972. A novella.

The Great American Novel. New York: Holt, Rinehart and Winston, 1973. A novel.

Secondary

Fiedler, Leslie A. *Waiting for the End.* New York: Stein and Day, 1964. Considers Roth in relation to other American-Jewish writers who are creating "America's last Jews."

Hyman, Stanley Edgar. "A Novelist of Great Promise" in *On Contemporary Literature,* ed. by Richard Kostelanetz. New York: Avon Books, 1964. Reprinted from *The New Leader* of June 11, 1962. A review of *Letting Go.*

Kazin, Alfred. "Tough-minded Mr. Roth" in *Contemporaries.* Boston: Little, Brown, 1962. A review of *Goodbye, Columbus.*

Larner, J. "Conversion of the Jews." *Partisan Review,* 27 (Fall 1960), 760–68. A review of *Goodbye, Columbus.*

Lelchuk, Alan. "On the Breast: An Interview." *New York Review of Books,* 19 (October 19, 1972), 26–28. An interview with Philip Roth.

Malin, Irving. *Jews and Americans.* Carbondale, Ill.: Southern Illinois Univ. Press, 1965. An analysis of the writing of Karl Shapiro, Delmore Schwartz, Isaac Rosenfeld, Leslie Fiedler, Saul Bellow, Bernard Malamud, and Philip Roth.

Meeter, Glenn. *Philip Roth and Bernard Malamud: A Critical Essay.*

Grand Rapids, Mich.: William B. Eerdmans Publishing Co., 1968. Views Roth and Malamud as Jewish romantics whose "effort and in good part their achievement is to keep a religious spirit alive in a secular world."

Peden, William. *The American Short Story*. Boston: Houghton Mifflin, 1964. Contains some brief comments on *Goodbye, Columbus*.

Podhoretz, Norman. "The Gloom of Philip Roth" in *Doings and Undoings*. New York: Farrar, Straus & Giroux, 1964. Contrasts Roth's pessimism in *Making Do* with the optimism of Bellow, Gold, and Styron.

Raban, Jonathan. "The New Philip Roth." *Novel: A Forum on Fiction*, 2 (Winter 1969), 153–63. A review that praises Roth for his concern with the texture of language, his irony, his superb gift for elaborate parody, his capacity to create by suggestion a dominant social and literary ideology, and the social density he achieves with such apparent ease.

Sheed, Wilfrid. "Pity the Poor Wasps." *New York Times Book Review*, June 11, 1967, pp. 5, 50. A review of *When She Was Good*.

The fine story writers seem to be in a sense obstructionists. As if they hold back their own best interests. It's a strange illusion. For if we look to the source of the deepest pleasure we receive from a writer, how surprising it seems that this very source is the quondam obstruction. The fact is, in seeking our source of pleasure we have entered another world again. We are speaking of beauty.

And beauty is not a blatant or promiscuous or obvious quality; indeed at her finest she is somehow associated with obstruction—with reticence of a number of kinds. The beauty of "The Bear" seems tied up intimately with the reluctance to confine the story to its proper time sequence and space measurements; Faulkner makes fantastic difficulty about time and place both, and the result is beauty. Time after time Lawrence refuses to get his story told, to let his characters talk in any natural way; the story is held up forever, and through so delaying and through such refusal on the author's part, we enter the magical world of pure sense, of evocation—the shortest cut known through the woods.

. . .

Where does beauty come from in the short story? Beauty comes from form, from development of idea, from after-effect. It often comes from carefulness, lack of confusion, elimination of waste—and yes, those are the rules. But that can be on occasion a cold kind of beauty, when there are warm kinds. And beware of tidiness. Sometimes spontaneity is the most sparkling kind of beauty.

FROM *The Reading and Writing of Short Stories*

EUDORA WELTY

Eudora Welty's home is Jackson, Mississippi, where she was born in 1909. Her early ambition was to be a painter. She attended Mississippi State College for Women, the University of Wisconsin (graduating in 1929), and Columbia University School of Business, where she studied advertising. Returning to Jackson, she began writing seriously while working at a variety of jobs, including free-lance reporting for local newspapers. As a Work Projects Administration publicity agent, she traveled throughout her native state, interviewing and photographing its people and writing accounts of what she saw and heard.

In 1936, a New York City gallery held a one-man exhibition of her photographic studies of Mississippi Negroes. That same year, *Manuscript* published her first story, "Death of a Traveling Salesman." Soon her stories began to appear in such periodicals as *Southern Review, Prairie Schooner, Atlantic Monthly,* and *New Yorker.* Her first collection of stories, *A Curtain of Green* (1941), for which Katherine Anne Porter wrote the preface, established her as an important young writer. Her subsequent writing has attracted widespread critical praise, and she has received many honors. These include two Guggenheim Fellowships and a 1972 National Institute of Arts and Letters Award in fiction, for *The Optimist's Daughter.*

In Welty's fiction there is a persistent concern not only with the sights and sounds of an objectified "place" but with the intangible, inner life of her protagonist. The two stories in this collection reveal this double and reciprocal concern.

THE DEMONSTRATORS

Near eleven o'clock that Saturday night, the doctor stopped again by his office. He had recently got into playing a weekly bridge game at the club, but tonight it had been interrupted for the third time, and he'd just come from attending to Miss Marcia Pope. Now bedridden, scorning all medication and in particular tranquilizers, she had a seizure every morning before breakfast and often on Saturday night for some reason, but had retained her memory; she could amuse herself by giving out great wads of Shakespeare and *"Arma virumque cano,"* or the like. The more forcefully Miss Marcia Pope declaimed, the more innocent grew her old face—the lines went right out.

"She'll sleep naturally now, I think," he'd told the companion, still in her rocker.

Mrs. Warrum did well, perhaps hadn't hit yet on an excuse to quit that suited her. She failed to be alarmed by Miss Marcia Pope, either in convulsions or in recitation. From where she lived, she'd never gone to school to this lady, who had taught three generations of Holden, Mississippi, its Latin, civics, and English, and who had carried, for forty years, a leather satchel bigger than the doctor's bag.

As he'd snapped his bag shut tonight, Miss Marcia had opened her eyes and spoken distinctly: "Richard Strickland? I have it on my report that Irene Roberts is not where she belongs. Now which of you wants the whipping?"

"It's all right, Miss Marcia. She's still my wife," he'd said, but could not be sure the answer got by her.

In the office, he picked up the city newspaper he subscribed to—seeing as he did so the picture on the front of a young man burning his draft card before a camera—and locked up, ready to face home. As he came down the stairway onto the street, his sleeve was plucked.

It was a Negro child. "We got to hurry," she said.

His bag was still in the car. She climbed into the back and stood there behind his ear as he drove down the hill. He met the marshal's car as both bounced over the railroad track—no passenger rode with the marshal that he could see—and the doctor asked the child, "Who got hurt? Whose house?" But she could only tell him how to get there, an alley at a time, till they got around the cottonseed mill.

Down here, the street lights were out tonight. The last electric light of any kind appeared to be the one burning in the vast shrouded cavern of the gin. His car lights threw into relief the dead goldenrod that stood along the road and made it look heavier than the bridge across the creek.

As soon as the child leaned on his shoulder and he had stopped the car, he heard men's voices; but at first his eyes could make out little but an assembly of white forms spaced in the air near a low roof—chickens roosting in a tree. Then he saw the reds of cigarettes. A dooryard was as packed with a standing crowd as if it were funeral time. They were all men. Still more people seemed to be moving from the nearby churchyard and joining onto the crowd in front of the house.

The men parted before them as he went following the child up broken steps and across a porch. A kerosene lamp was being held for him in the doorway. He stepped into a roomful of women. The child kept going, went to the foot of an iron bed and stopped. The lamp came up closer behind him and he followed a path of newspapers laid down on the floor from the doorway to the bed.

A dark quilt was pulled up to the throat of a girl alive on the bed. A pillow raised her at the shoulders. The dome of her forehead looked thick as a battering ram, because of the rolling of her eyes.

Dr. Strickland turned back the quilt. The young, very black-skinned

woman lay in a white dress with her shoes on. A maid? Then he saw that
of course the white was not the starched material of a uniform but shiny,
clinging stuff, and there was a banner of some kind crossing it in a crumpled red line from the shoulder. He unfastened the knot at the waist and
got the banner out of the way. The skintight satin had been undone at
the neck already; as he parted it farther, the girl kicked at the foot of the
bed. He exposed the breast and then, before her hand had pounced on his,
the wound below the breast. There was a small puncture with little evidence of external bleeding. He had seen splashes of blood on the dress,
now almost dry.

"Go boil me some water. Too much excitement to send for the doctor
a little earlier?"

The girl clawed at his hand with her sticky nails.

"Have you touched her?" he asked.

"See there? And she don't want you trying it either," said a voice in
the room.

A necklace like sharp and pearly teeth was fastened around her throat.
It was when he took that off that the little girl who had been sent for him
cried out. "I bid that!" she said, but without coming nearer. He found no
other wounds.

"Does it hurt you to breathe?" He spoke almost absently as he addressed
the girl.

The nipples of her breast cast shadows that looked like figs; she would
not take a deep breath when he used the stethoscope. Sweat in the airless
room, in the bed, rose and seemed to weaken and unstick the newspapered
walls like steam from a kettle already boiling; it glazed his own white hand,
his tapping fingers. It was the stench of sensation. The women's faces
coming nearer were streaked in the hot lamplight. Somewhere close to the
side of his head something glittered; hung over the knob of the bedpost,
where a boy would have tossed his cap, was a tambourine. He let the
stethoscope fall, and heard women's sighs travel around the room, domestic
sounds like a broom being flirted about, women getting ready for company.

"Stand back," he said. "You got a fire on in here?" Warm as it was,
crowded as it was in here, he looked behind him and saw the gas heater
burning, half the radiants burning blue. The girl, with lips turned down,
lay pulling away while he took her pulse.

The child who had been sent for him and then had been sent to heat
the water brought the kettle in from the kitchen too soon and had to be
sent back to make it boil. When it was ready and in the pan, the lamp was
held closer; it was beside his elbow as if to singe his arm.

"Stand back," he said. Again and again the girl's hand had to be forced away from her breast. The wound quickened spasmodically as if it responded to light.

"Ice pick?"

"You right this time," said voices in the room.

"Who did this to her?"

The room went quiet; he only heard the men in the yard laughing together. "How long ago?" He looked at the path of newspapers spread on the floor. "Where? Where did it happen? How did she get here?"

He had an odd feeling that somewhere in the room somebody was sending out beckoning smiles in his direction. He lifted, half turned his head. The elevated coal that glowed at regular intervals was the pipe of an old woman in a boiled white apron standing near the door.

He persisted. "Has she coughed up anything yet?"

"Don't you know her?" they cried, as if he never was going to hit on the right question.

He let go the girl's arm, and her hand started its way back again to her wound. Sending one glowing look at him, she covered it again. As if she had spoken, he recognized her.

"Why, it's Ruby," he said.

Ruby Gaddy *was* the maid. Five days a week she cleaned up on the second floor of the bank building where he kept his office and consulting rooms.

He said to her, "Ruby, this is Dr. Strickland. What have you been up to?"

"Nothin'!" everybody cried for her.

The girl's eyes stopped rolling and rested themselves on the expressionless face of the little girl, who again stood at the foot of the bed watching from this restful distance. Look equalled look: sisters.

"Am I supposed to just know?" The doctor looked all around him. An infant was sitting up on the splintery floor near his feet, he now saw, on a clean newspaper, a spoon stuck pipelike in its mouth. From out in the yard at that moment came a regular guffaw, not much different from the one that followed the telling of a dirty story or a race story by one of the clowns in the Elks' Club. He frowned at the baby; and the baby, a boy, looked back over his upside down spoon and gave it a long audible suck.

"She married? Where's her husband? That where the trouble was?"

Now, while the women in the room, too, broke out in sounds of amusement, the doctor stumbled where he stood. "What the devil's running in here? Rats?"

242

"You wrong there."

Guinea pigs were running underfoot, not only in this room but on the other side of the wall, in the kitchen where the water had finally got boiled. Somebody's head turned toward the leaf end of a stalk of celery wilting on top of the Bible on the table.

"Catch those things!" he exclaimed.

The baby laughed; the rest copied the baby.

"They lightning. Get away from you so fast!" said a voice.

"Them guinea pigs ain't been caught since they was born. Let you try."

"Know why? 'Cause they's Dove's. Dove left 'em here when he move out, just to be in the way."

The doctor felt the weight recede from Ruby's fingers, and saw it flatten her arm where it lay on the bed. Her eyes had closed. A little boy with a sanctimonious face had taken the bit of celery and knelt down on the floor; there was scrambling about and increasing laughter until Dr. Strickland made himself heard in the room.

"All right. I heard you. Is Dove who did it? Go on. Say."

He heard somebody spit on the stove. Then:

"It's Dove."

"Dove."

"Dove."

"Dove."

"You got it right that time."

While the name went around, passed from one mouth to the other, the doctor drew a deep breath. But the sigh that filled the room was the girl's own, luxuriously uncontained.

"Dove Collins? I believe you. I've had to sew him up enough times on Sunday morning, you all know that," said the doctor. "I know Ruby, I know Dove, and if the lights would come back on I can tell you the names of the rest of you and you know it." While he was speaking, his eyes fell on Oree, a figure of the Holden square for twenty years, whom he had inherited—sitting here in the room in her express wagon, the flowered skirt spread down from her lap and tucked in over the stumps of her knees.

While he was preparing the hypodermic, he was aware that more watchers, a row of them dressed in white with red banners like Ruby's, were coming in to fill up the corners. The lamp was lifted—higher than the dipping shadows of their heads, a valentine tacked on the wall radiated color—and then, as he leaned over the bed, the lamp was brought down closer and closer to the girl, like something that would devour her.

"Now I can't see what I'm doing," the doctor said sharply, and as the light jumped and swung behind him he thought he recognized the anger as a mother's.

"Look to me like the fight's starting to go out of Ruby mighty early," said a voice.

Still her eyes stayed closed. He gave the shot.

"Where'd he get to—Dove? Is the marshal out looking for him?" he asked.

The sister moved along the bed and put the baby down on it close to Ruby's face.

"Remove him," said the doctor.

"She don't even study him," said the sister. "Poke her," she told the baby.

"Take him out of here," ordered Dr. Strickland.

The baby opened one of his mother's eyes with his fingers. When she shut it on him he cried, as if he knew it to be deliberate of her.

"Get that baby out of here and all the kids, I tell you," Dr. Strickland said into the room. "This ain't going to be pretty."

"Carry him next door, Twosie," said a voice.

"I ain't. You all promised me if I leave long enough to get the doctor I could stand right here until." The child's voice was loud.

"O.K. Then you got to hold Roger."

The baby made a final reach for his mother's face, putting out a hand with its untrimmed nails, gray as the claw of a squirrel. The woman who had held the lamp set that down and grabbed the baby out of the bed herself. His legs began churning even before she struck him a blow on the side of the head.

"You trying to raise him an idiot?" the doctor flung out.

"I ain't going to raise him," the mother said toward the girl on the bed.

The deliberation had gone out of her face. She was drifting into unconsciousness. Setting her hand to one side, the doctor inspected the puncture once more. It was clean as the eye of a needle. While he stood there watching her, he lifted her hand and washed it—the wrist, horny palm, blood-caked fingers one by one.

But as he again found her pulse, he saw her eyes opening. As long as he counted he was aware of those eyes as if they loomed larger than the watch face. They were filled with the unresponsing gaze of ownership. She knew what she had. Memory did not make the further effort to close the lids when he replaced her hand, or when he took her shoes off and set them on the floor, or when he stepped away from the bed and again the full lamplight struck her face.

The twelve-year-old stared on, over the buttress of the baby she held to her chest.

"Can you ever hush that baby?"

A satisfied voice said, "He going to keep-a-noise till he learn better."

"Well, I'd like a little peace and consideration to be shown!" the doctor said. "Try to remember there's somebody in here with you that's going to be pumping mighty hard to breathe." He raised a finger and pointed it at the old woman in the boiled apron whose pipe had continued to glow with regularity by the door. "You stay. You sit here and watch Ruby," he called. "The rest of you clear out of here."

He closed his bag and straightened up. The woman stuck the lamp hot into his own face.

"Remember Lucille? I'm Lucille. I was washing for your mother when you was born. Let me see you do something," she said with fury. "You ain't even tied her up! You sure ain't your daddy!"

"Why, she's bleeding inside," he retorted. "What do you think *she's* doing?"

They hushed. For a minute all he heard was the guinea pigs racing. He looked back at the girl; her eyes were fixed with possession. "I gave her a shot. She'll just go to sleep. If she doesn't, call me and I'll come back and give her another one. One of you kindly bring me a drink of water," the doctor continued in the same tone.

With a crash, hushed off like cymbals struck by mistake, something was moved on the kitchen side of the wall. The little boy who had held the celery to catch the guinea pigs came in carrying a teacup. He passed through the room and out onto the porch, where he could be heard splashing fresh water from a pump. He came back inside and at arm's length held the cup out to the doctor.

Dr. Strickland drank with a thirst they all could and did follow. The cup, though it held the whole smell of this house in it, was of thin china, was an old one.

Then he stepped across the gaze of the girl on the bed as he would have had to step over a crack yawning in the floor.

"Fixing to leave?" asked the old woman in the boiled white apron, who still stood up by the door, the pipe gone from her lips. He then remembered her. In the days when he travelled East to medical school, she used to be the sole factotum at the Holden depot when the passenger train came through sometime between two and three in the morning. It was always late. Circling the pewlike benches of the waiting rooms, she carried around coffee which she poured boiling hot into paper cups out of a white-enamelled pot that looked as long as her arm. She wore then, in addition to the apron, a white and flaring head covering—something between a chef's cap and a sunbonnet. As the train at last steamed in, she called the stations. She didn't use a loudspeaker but just the power of her lungs. In all the natural volume of her baritone voice she thundered them out to the scattered and few who had waited under lights too poor to read by—first in the colored waiting room, then in the white waiting room, to echo both times from the vault of the roof: ". . . Meridian. Birmingham. Chattanooga. Bristol. Lynchburg. Washington. Baltimore. Philadelphia. And New York." Seizing all the bags, two by two, in her own hands, walking slowly in front of the passengers, she saw to it that they left.

He said to her, "I'm going, but you're not. You're keeping a watch on Ruby. Don't let her slide down in the bed. Call me if you need me." As a boy, had he never even wondered what her name was—this tyrant? He didn't know it now. He put the cup into her reaching hand. "Aren't you ready to leave?" he asked Oree, the legless woman. She still lived by the tracks where the train had cut off her legs.

"I ain't in no hurry," she replied and as he passed her she called her usual "Take it easy, Doc."

When he stepped outside onto the porch, he saw that there was moonlight everywhere. Uninterrupted by any lights from Holden, it filled the whole country lying out there in the haze of the long rainless fall. He himself stood on the edge of Holden. Just one house and one church farther, the Delta began, and the cotton fields ran into the scattered paleness of a dimmed-out Milky Way.

Nobody called him back, yet he turned his head and got a sideways glimpse all at once of a row of dresses hung up across the front of the house, starched until they could have stood alone (as his mother complained), and in an instant had recognized his mother's gardening dress, his sister Annie's golf dress, his wife's favorite duster that she liked to wear to the breakfast table, and more dresses, less substantial. Elevated across the front of the porch, they were hung again between him and the road. With sleeves spread wide, trying to scratch his forehead with the tails of their skirts, they were flying around this house in the moonlight.

The moment of vertigo passed, as a small black man came up the steps and across the porch wearing heeltaps on his shoes.

"Sister Gaddy entered yet into the gates of joy?"

"No, Preacher, you're in time," said the doctor.

As soon as he left the house, he heard it become as noisy as the yard had been, and the men in the yard went quiet to let him through. From the road, he saw the moon itself. It was above the tree with the chickens in it, it might have been one of the chickens flown loose. He scraped children off the hood of his car, pulled another from position at the wheel, and climbed inside. He turned the car around in the churchyard. There was a flickering light inside the church. Flat-roofed as a warehouse, it had its shades pulled down like a bedroom. This was the church where the sounds of music and dancing came from habitually on many another night besides Sunday, clearly to be heard on top of the hill.

He drove back along the road, across the creek, its banks glittering now with the narrow bottles, the size of harmonicas, in which paregoric was persistently sold under the name of Mother's Helper. The telephone wires along the road were hung with shreds of cotton, the sides of the road were strewn with them too, as if the doctor were out on a paper chase.

He passed the throbbing mill, working on its own generator. No lights ever shone through the windowless and now moonlit sheet iron, but the smell came out freely and spread over the town at large—a cooking smell, like a dish ordered by a man with an endless appetite. Pipes hung with streamers of lint fed into the moonlit gin, and wagons and trucks heaped up round as the gypsy caravans or circus wagons of his father's, or even his grandfather's, stories, stood this way and that, waiting in the yard outside.

Far down the railroad track, beyond the unlighted town, rose the pillow-shaped glow of a grass fire. It was gaseous, unveined, unblotted by smoke, a cloud with the November flush of the sedge grass by day, sparkless and nerveless, not to be confused with a burning church, but like anesthetic made visible.

Then a long beam of electric light came solid as a board from behind him to move forward along the long loading platform, to some bales of cotton standing on it, some of them tumbled one against the others as if pushed by the light; then it ran up the wall of the dark station so you could read the name, "Holden." The hooter sounded. This was a grade crossing with a bad record, and it seemed to the doctor that he had never started over it in his life that something was not bearing down. He stopped the car, and as the train in its heat began to pass in front of him he saw it to be a doubleheader, a loaded freight this time. It was going right on through Holden.

He cut off his motor. One of the sleepers rocked and complained with every set of wheels that rolled over it. Presently the regular, slow creaking reminded the doctor of an old-fashioned porch swing holding lovers in the dark.

He had been carried a cup tonight that might have been his own

247

mother's china or his wife's mother's—the rim not a perfect round, a thin, porcelain cup his lips and his fingers had recognized. In that house of murder, comfort had been brought to him at his request. After drinking from it he had all but reeled into a flock of dresses stretched wide-sleeved across the porch of that house like a child's drawing of angels.

Faintly rocked by the passing train, he sat bent at the wheel of the car, and the feeling of well-being persisted. It increased, until he had come to the point of tears.

The doctor was the son of a doctor, practicing in his father's office; all the older patients, like Miss Marcia Pope—and like Lucille and Oree— spoke of his father, and some confused the young doctor with the old; but not they. The watch he carried was the gold one that had belonged to his father. Richard had grown up in Holden, married "the prettiest girl in the Delta." Except for his years at the university and then at medical school and during his internship, he had lived here at home and had carried on the practice—the only practice in town. Now his father and his mother both were dead, his sister had married and moved away, a year ago his child had died. Then, back in the summer, he and his wife had separated, by her wish.

Sylvia had been their only child. Until her death from pneumonia last Christmas, at the age of thirteen, she had never sat up or spoken. He had loved her and mourned her all her life; she had been injured at birth. But Irene had done more; she had dedicated her life to Sylvia, sparing herself nothing, tending her, lifting her, feeding her, everything. What do you do after giving all your devotion to something that cannot be helped, and that has been taken away? You give all your devotion to something else that cannot be helped. But you shun all the terrible reminders, and turn not to a human being but to an idea.

Last June, there had come along a student, one of the civil-rights workers, calling at his office with a letter of introduction. For the sake of an old friend, the doctor had taken him home to dinner. (He had been reminded of him once tonight, already, by a photograph in the city paper.) He remembered that the young man had already finished talking about his work. They had just laughed around the table after Irene had quoted the classic question the governor-before-this-one had asked, after a prison break: "If you can't trust a trusty, who can you trust?" Then the doctor had remarked, "Speaking of who can you trust, what's this I read in your own paper, Philip? It said some of your outfit over in the next county were forced at gunpoint to go into the fields at hundred-degree temperature and pick cotton. Well, that didn't happen—there isn't any cotton in June."

"I asked myself the same question you do. But I told myself, 'Well, they won't know the difference where the paper is read,'" said the young man.

"It's lying, though."

"We are dramatizing your hostility," the young bearded man had corrected him. "It's a way of reaching people. Don't forget—what they *might* have done to us is even worse."

"Still—you're not justified in putting a false front on things, in my opinion," Dr. Strickland had said. "Even for a good cause."

"*You* won't tell Herman Fairbrothers what's the matter with him," said his wife, and she jumped up from the table.

Later, as a result of this entertainment, he supposed, broken glass had been spread the length and breadth of his driveway. He hadn't seen in time what it wouldn't have occurred to him to look for, and Irene, standing in the door, had suddenly broken into laughter . . .

He had eventually agreed that she have her wish and withdraw herself for as long as she liked. She was back now where she came from, where, he'd heard, they were all giving parties for her. He had offered to be the one to leave. "Leave Holden without its Dr. Strickland? You wouldn't to save your soul, would you?" she had replied. But as yet it was not divorce.

He thought he had been patient, but patience had made him tired. He was so increasingly tired, so sick and even bored with the bitterness, intractability that divided everybody and everything.

And suddenly, tonight, things had seemed just the way they used to seem. He had felt as though someone had stopped him on the street and offered to carry his load for a while—had insisted on it—some old, trusted, half-forgotten family friend that he had lost sight of since youth. Was it the sensation, now returning, that there was still allowed to everybody on earth a *self*—savage, death-defying, private? The pounding of his heart was like the assault of hope, throwing itself against him without a stop, merciless.

It seemed a long time that he had sat there, but the cars were still going by. Here came the caboose. He had counted them without knowing it—seventy-two cars. The grass fire at the edge of town came back in sight.

The doctor's feeling gradually ebbed away, like nausea put down. He started up the car and drove across the track and on up the hill.

Candles, some of them in dining-room candelabra, burned clear across the upstairs windows in the Fairbrothers' house. His own house, next door, was of course dark, and while he was wondering where Irene kept candles for emergencies he had driven on past his driveway for the second time that night. But the last place he wanted to go now was back to the club. He'd only tried it anyway to please his sister Annie. Now that he'd got by Miss Marcia Pope's dark window, he smelled her sweet-olive tree, solid as the bank building.

Here stood the bank, with its doorway onto the stairs to Drs. Strickland & Strickland, their names in black and gilt on three windows. He passed it. The haze and the moonlight were one over the square, over the row of storefronts opposite with the line of poles thin as matchsticks rising to prop the one long strip of tin over the sidewalk, the drygoods store with its ornamental top that looked like opened paper fans held up by acrobats. He slowly started around the square. Behind its iron railings, the courthouse-and-jail stood barely emerging from its black cave of trees and only the slicked iron steps of the stile caught the moon. He drove on, past the shut-down movie house with all the light bulbs unscrewed from the sign that spelled out in empty sockets "BROADWAY." In front of the new post office the flagpole looked feathery, like the track of a jet that is already gone from the sky. From in front of the fire station, the fire chief's old Buick had gone home.

What was there, who was there, to keep him from going home? The doctor drove on slowly around. From the center of the deserted pavement, where cars and wagons stood parked helter-skelter by day, rose the water tank, pale as a balloon that might be only tethered here. A clanking came out of it, for the water supply too had been a source of trouble this sum-mer—a hollow, irregular knocking now and then from inside, but the doctor no longer heard it. In turning his car, he saw a man lying prone and colorless in the arena of moonlight.

The lights of the car fastened on him and his clothes turned golden yellow. The man looked as if he had been sleeping all day in a bed of flowers and rolled in their pollen and were sleeping there still, with his face buried. He was covered his length in cottonseed meal.

Dr. Strickland stopped the car short and got out. His footsteps made the only sound in town. The man raised up on his hands and looked at him like a seal. Blood laced his head like a net through which he had broken. His wide tongue hung down out of his mouth. But the doctor knew the face.

"So you're alive, Dove, you're still alive?"

Slowly, hardly moving his tongue, Dove said: "Hide me." Then he hemorrhaged through the mouth.

Through the other half of the night, the doctor's calls came to him over the telephone—all chronic cases. Eva Duckett Fairbrothers telephoned at daylight.

"Feels low in his mind? Of course he feels low in his mind," he had finally shouted at her. "If I had what Herman has, I'd go down in the back yard and shoot myself!"

The *Sentinel*, owned and edited by Horatio Duckett, came out on Tuesdays. The next week's back-page headline read, "TWO DEAD, ONE ICE PICK. FREAK EPISODE AT NEGRO CHURCH." The subhead read, "No Racial Content Espied."

The doctor sat at the table in his dining room, finishing breakfast as he looked it over.

An employee of the Fairbrothers Cotton Seed Oil Mill and a Holden maid, both Negroes, were stabbed with a sharp instrument judged to be an ice pick in a crowded churchyard here Saturday night. Both later expired. The incident was not believed by Mayor Herman Fairbrothers to carry racial significance.

"It warrants no stir," the Mayor declared.

The mishap boosted Holden's weekend death toll to 3. Billy Lee Warrum Jr. died Sunday before reaching a hospital in Jackson where he was rushed after being thrown from his new motorcycle while on his way there. He was the oldest son of Mrs. Billy Lee Warrum, Rt. 1. Reputedly en route to see his fiance he was pronounced dead on arrival. Multiple injuries was listed as the cause, the motorcycle having speeded into an interstate truck loaded to capacity with holiday turkeys. (See eyewitness account, page 1.)

As Holden marshal Curtis "Cowboy" Stubblefield reconstructed the earlier mishap, Ruby Gaddy, 21, was stabbed in full view of the departing congregation of the Holy Gospel Tabernacle as she attempted to leave the church when services were concluded at approximately 9:30 P.M. Saturday.

Witnesses said Dave Collins, 25, appeared outside the church as early as 9:15 P.M. having come directly from his shift at the mill where he had been employed since 1959. On being invited to come in and be seated he joked and said he preferred to wait outdoors as he was only wearing work clothes until the Gaddy woman, said to be his common-law wife, came outside the frame structure.

In the ensuing struggle at the conclusion of the services, the woman, who was a member of the choir, is believed to have received fatal ice-pick injuries to a vital organ, then to have wrested the weapon from her assailant and paid him back in kind. The Gaddy woman then walked to her mother's house but later collapsed.

Members of the congregation said they chased Collins 13 or 14 yds. in the direction of Snake Creek on the South side of the church then he fell to the ground and rolled approximately ten feet down the bank, rolling over six or seven times. Those present believed him to have succumbed since it was said the pick while in the woman's hand had been seen to drive in and pierce either his ear or his eye, either of which is in close approximation to the brain. However, Collins later managed to crawl unseen from the creek and to make his way undetected up Railroad Avenue and to the Main St. door of an office occupied by Richard Strickland, M.D., above the Citizens Bank & Trust.

Witnesses were divided on which of the Negroes struck the first blow. Percy McAtee, pastor of the church, would not take sides but declared on being questioned by Marshal Stubblefield he was satisfied no outside agitators were involved and no arrests were made.

Collins was discovered on his own doorstep by Dr. Strickland who had been spending the evening at the Country Club. Collins is reported by Dr. Strickland to have expired shortly following his discovery, alleging his death to chest wounds.

"He offered no statement," Dr. Strickland said in response to a query.

Interviewed at home where he is recuperating from an ailment, Mayor Fairbrothers stated that he had not heard of there being trouble of any description at the Mill. "We are not trying to ruin our good reputation by inviting any, either," he said. "If the weatherman stays on our side we expect to attain capacity production in the latter part of next month," he stated. Saturday had been pay day as usual.

When Collins' body was searched by officers the pockets were empty however.

An ice pick, reportedly the property of the Holy Gospel Tabernacle, was later found by Deacon Gaddy, 8, brother of Ruby Gaddy, covered with blood and carried it to Marshal Stubblefield. Stubblefield said it had been found in the grounds of the new $100,000.00 Negro school. It is believed to have served as the instrument in the twin slayings, the victims thus virtually succeeding in killing each other.

"Well, I'm surprised didn't more of them get hurt," said Rev. Alonzo Duckett, pastor of the Holden First Baptist Church. "And yet they expect to be seated in our churches." County Sheriff Vince Lasseter, reached fishing at Lake Bourne, said: "That's one they can't pin the blame on us for. That's how they treat their own kind. Please take note our conscience is clear."

Members of the Negro congregation said they could not account for Collins having left Snake Creek at the unspecified time. "We stood there a while and flipped some bottle caps down at him and threw his cap down after him right over his face and didn't get a stir out of him," stated an official of the congregation. "The way he acted, we figured he was dead. We would not have gone off and left him if we had known he was able to subsequently crawl up the hill." They stated Collins was not in the habit of worshipping at Holy Gospel Tabernacle.

The Gaddy woman died later this morning, also from chest wounds. No cause was cited for the fracas.

The cook had refilled his cup without his noticing. The doctor dropped the paper and carried his coffee out onto the little porch; it was still his morning habit.

The porch was at the back of the house, screened on three sides. Sylvia's daybed used to stand here; it put her in the garden. No other houses were in sight; the gin could not be heard or even the traffic whining on the highway up off the bypass.

The roses were done for, the perennials too. But the surrounding crape-myrtle tree, the redbud, the dogwood, the Chinese tallow tree, and the pomegranate bush were bright as toys. The ailing pear tree had shed its leaves ahead of the rest. Past a falling wall of Michaelmas daisies that had not been tied up, a pair of flickers were rifling the grass, the cock in one part of the garden, the hen in another, picking at the devastation right through the bright leaves that appeared to have been left lying there just for them, probing and feeding. They stayed year round, he supposed, but it was only in the fall of the year that he ever noticed them. He was pretty sure that Sylvia had known the birds were there. Her eyes would follow birds when they flew across the garden. As he watched, the cock spread one wing, showy as a zebra's hide, and with a turn of his head showed his red seal.

Dr. Strickland swallowed the coffee and picked up his bag. It was all going to be just about as hard as seeing Herman and Eva Fairbrothers through. He thought that in all Holden, as of now, only Miss Marcia Pope was still quite able to take care of herself—or such was her own opinion.

DEMONSTRATORS
IN A STRICKEN LAND

Ruth M. Vande Kieft

In Eudora Welty's view of fiction, *place* provides the writer's "endowment" and means of focusing his vision, and *mystery* is celebrated through his vision. Place, she says, provides the "touchstone"; it "shows up, before anything else does, truth and mistakes. In a way place is your honor as it is your wisdom, and would make you responsible to it for what you put down for the truth." [1]

The "home" truth presented in "The Demonstrators" is that of Holden, Mississippi, the small town in a stricken land, held up so steadily before our eyes that only a refusal to look closely allows the moral and esthetic irresponsibility of easy approval or rejection. The enveloping action, the "issues" suggested, are those of the sixties: The title announces that as loudly as any signboard held high by any demonstrator. But just as the human beings who hold the signboards are complex, paradoxical, mysterious, so is the story under the title, so is the specific and universal reality behind the story, so is truth itself.

Close to the center of this historic, tightly knit Southern town is Dr. Strickland, whose activity and compassionate nature place him in the best tradition of his humane profession. He is of the middle generation, carrying on his father's vocation, aware of the demands and interests of both the older and younger generations. He acts quickly and practically, but he also feels, reflects, sorts out. We follow him through a night that does not seem, despite the "freak episode" headlined by the *Sentinel,* all that unusual. It finds him, in a way, simply powerless. For all his skills and good intentions, what has he been able to do for Ruby and Dove, old Miss Pope, the legless Oree, the incurably sick Fairbrothers and his worried wife, the speed-crazed Billy Lee, even his "loved and mourned" daughter and bereaved wife? Violence, disease, and death are his familiar antagonists: They reign as ominously as the dark night; they are as much a felt presence as the racial antagonism, the war, the personal and

---

[1] "How I Write," *Virginia Quarterly*, No. 31 (Spring 1955), pp. 240-51.

social hostilities that make up the troubled, restless, murderous life of the modern world. At best, Dr. Strickland's is a holding action.

But the night is not unrelievedly dark. A light flickers in the church, candles burn from the Fairbrothers' window, cigarette ashes glow, a lighted kerosene lamp shows a hanging valentine radiating color. The same lamp bears down on a dying girl "like something that would devour her," a long beam from a train pushes over cotton bales, car lights pick out dead goldenrod and a dying man rolled in golden cottonseed meal, and a high moon hangs over everything. These lights tell as much of pain and trouble as of love, but together they penetrate darkness and illuminate mysteries.

Dr. Strickland's night journey begins with a call on Miss Marcia Pope, a pillar of the community, who reigned as teacher for more than forty years. Though she is stricken by some strange disease of old age, her authority is undiminished. She still maintains a teacher-schoolboy relationship with the doctor, now calling him on the carpet to give an accounting of his grown-up marital difficulties. She rejects the universal modern palliative, the tranquillizer, and she will go on teaching her "civics" (civilized codes in a democratic land), and declaiming her Shakespeare and Virgil, to the end of her days. She is the first of the demonstrators, old style. Her ornery independence prefigures that of most of the demonstrators in this deeply and subtly interdependent community where a trio of deaths diminishes no one, and everyone.

Back in his office Dr. Strickland picks up his newspaper: A young man is making *his* declaration of independence, burning his draft card publicly to show his revolt against the state and the authorities who make war. He is another demonstrator, new style.

Then a Negro child summons the doctor on a nameless but urgent mission over the tracks. He drives into the dark (the street lights have gone out), reaches his destination, walks through a strangely quiet group of men, and enters a room where a wounded Negro girl lies on an iron bed. For a time the whole atmosphere is like that of a dream—shadowy, vaguely threatening, crowded with vivid and kaleidoscopic impressions, in which the dreamer tries to identify objects, persons, motives, relationships, in order to achieve a solid basis for action. Yet the doctor works efficiently by trained instinct: He knows how to treat his patient, command and reprimand the onlookers, order the highly charged information coming in to him through all five senses and the sixth (intuition). But not without initial mistakes and one total lapse of recognition: the identity of the patient herself.

The witnesses and helpers are neither cooperative nor friendly. They are secret and suspicious, somewhat hostile; the interchange is all question and enigmatic choral answer. They are oddly protective of the girl and her assailant, as though the doctor were an intruder. Reluctantly and bunglingly they carry out his orders. And the patient too is uncooperative about her wound, too private to expose, just below her breast—a heart wound; her bleeding is all internal. She rebels against his searching the wound; she touches it compulsively with sticky, bloodstained fingers.

Finally the doctor identifies the girl as Ruby Gaddy, the maid who cleans his office. Ruby wears a kind of white dress unfamiliar to him, a dress of "skintight satin" with "a banner of some kind crossing it in a crumpled red line from the shoulder." We later learn that Ruby has been at church—her banner seems to be some part of a choir gown, for others are wearing the same "uniform." Ruby lives in a social world whose activities are largely unknown to Dr. Strickland's white, middle-class world. Furthermore, within her social world she has her own private life, and out of it comes her trouble now.

Other identifications follow rapidly. The small girl who fetched the doctor is Ruby's sister Twosie. Guinea pigs running about were left by Dove, Ruby's man, "just to be in the way." It is an ice pick wound, inflicted by Dove. The doctor knows Dove Collins: "I've had to sew him up enough times on Sunday morning, you all know that." Given more light, the doctor would know everybody: Oree, an "inherited" care, is among the first. Then there is Ruby's brother, her baby, her mother, and a pipe-smoking matriarch who may be the grandmother.

Everyone in this hot, overcrowded room is making a private claim to rights and privileges belonging to the self alone by reason of position or authority. Twosie lays claim to Ruby's necklace and demands her right to stay in the room. Ruby is absorbed with dying: Every gesture and expression shows how she demands the dignity and privacy of her final human act. To the doctor her eyes seem filled with "the unresponding gaze of ownership." She rejects her baby, who demands her attention; he cries loudly in protest when she ignores him. Ruby's mother rejects both the baby and her daughter: "I ain't going to raise him," she says. She identifies herself as Lucille, who did the washing for the doctor's mother. Attached to the older generation and their ways, she furiously denies Dr. Strickland's medical competence: "Let me see you do something. . . . You ain't even tied her up! You sure ain't your daddy!" The doctor's retort brings a hush, and when he asks for a drink, it is brought to him in an old china cup.

Seeking out one person in the room with clear authority to watch over Ruby, he fastens on the old pipe-smoking woman in the boiled white apron. Suddenly he recognizes her as a local "tyrant," who had single-handedly run the railroad station at night: dispensed coffee, "thundered" out instructions in her baritone voice, seen to it that baggage and passengers got on the train. She might have been called the Miss Pope of the railroad station: They had both been benevolent despots. Now the doctor, having come to his professional maturity, gives *her* the orders. But he depends on her to carry them out (which she may or may not choose to do: Oree, for one, "ain't in no hurry" to leave and it is impossible to catch the guinea pigs or silence the children).

His call over, the doctor steps out into the night, now flooded with moonlight. Driving back into town and waiting for a long freight train to pass, he has time for reflection. So much of the past has sprung out of memory; so many new impressions are waiting to be sorted out and stored among dear, costly things suffered and loved. And now it is chiefly of relatedness that the doctor becomes aware as the long train of linked cars goes by; "the regular, slow creaking" reminds him of "an old-fashioned porch swing holding lovers in the dark." So also he holds in his mind all Holden's "lovers in the dark," living and dead; lovers aware of themselves and each other, but ignorant, seeing only by the moon's dim but magical illumination, by the light of imagination and love:

> He had been carried a cup tonight that might have been his own mother's china or his wife's mother's—the rim not a perfect round, a thin, porcelain cup his lips and his fingers had recognized. In that house of murder, comfort had been brought to him at his request. After drinking from it he had all but reeled into a flock of dresses stretched wide-sleeved across the porch of that house like a child's drawing of angels.

He had recognized the dresses as those of his mother, sister, and wife. They were stiffly starched, like the spines of independent people who can also "stand alone"; flying about they could even "scratch his forehead"— irritate or wound the mind or feelings. For a moment the clothes seem to be disembodied, nobody's property. They make a vision of peace and blessedness, of his whole family linked with this Negro family, of white man linked with black, older generation with younger. All wear the same clothes, drink from a fragile, common cup with an imperfect rim, share the same human joys and griefs; they are linked by society, tradition, common responsibility and service, personal and impersonal forms of love. But they are also separate, and therein lies the tragedy of human life.

With the résumé of Dr. Strickland's past life and experiences, our vision shifts to the causes and symptoms of this tragic separateness and hostility between persons and races. "It's all right. . . . She's still my wife," Dr. Strickland had defended himself at Miss Pope's inquisition. But it is *not* all right and he knows it. He and his wife are separated, by her wish. The loss of their only child, more intensely loved and served because she was afflicted, has caused his wife to turn her devotion to "an idea." Exactly what, if anything, she has done for the civil-rights cause is not clear, since she is "back now where she came from." But civil rights had provided at least the occasion for her going, if not the reason, as it had provided the occasion for a discussion with a young civil-rights worker entertained in answer to a friend's introduction. Dr. Strickland had challenged the young man's publicity measures—misrepresenting the facts in order to "dramatize" Southern hostility. The doctor does not believe that ends justify means, even for a "good cause"; but his wife counters by accusing him of employing the same strategy on the Mayor, Herman Fairbrothers, by not telling him the nature of his disease. When the doctor suffers retaliation from extremists who strew his driveway with broken glass for entertaining the Northern intruder, his wife laughs. We do not learn why: perhaps because of the irony involved (the doctor is not really a "civil-rights worker"), perhaps because of his unsuspecting innocence, perhaps because she resents his impotence—his learning and skills could not save their daughter Sylvia. And of course, being with him reminds her of Sylvia. In any event, she leaves him, as Dove had left Ruby.

Thinking about everything, the doctor is deeply tired, "so sick and even bored with the bitterness, intractability that divided everybody and everything." Yet he has not forgotten his vision—it had seemed as if "some old, trusted, half-forgotten family friend that he had lost sight of since youth" had assumed his burden. "Was it the sensation, now returning, that there was still allowed to everybody on earth a *self*—savage, death-defying, private?" Hope affects him like an "assault"—what else to a heart resigned to a burden of hopelessness? But too futile and costly a feeling to nourish, it ebbs away, "like nausea put down."

Yet when the doctor drives back through town and sees Dove lying in the moonlight, transfigured by cottonseed meal into a golden form, he is the abstract self of Dr. Strickland's imaginings become visible: "savage, death-defying, private." Dove is the last and best of the demonstrators: A strong, violent man, he fights for his very life. "Blood laced his head like a net through which he had broken." His final plea, to the only man in town who might save him, seems less for protection from the law than for privacy: "Hide me." Then his life blood spills through his mouth.

The impersonal newspaper report supplies many details, but as is usual with newspapers, it tells very little. We do learn some of the circumstances of the slaying, and we learn also of the accidental death of Billy Lee Warrum on a motorcycle en route to see his fiancée. Billy is representative of the restlessness of a generation that has turned to speed and machines as a demonstration of power, power that hurdles him into an early and pointless death.

Reading on and between the lines, as though over Dr. Strickland's shoulder, we learn a great deal more. We learn with what apparent self-satisfaction public leaders of the white community wash their hands of the double murder, suffering, perhaps, some qualms of conscience at the accusations of Northern civil-rights workers like the bearded youth. NOT RESPONSIBLE is the sign demonstrated by the statements of Mayor Fairbrothers, "fair" as a brother and, ironically, a dying man who hopes for fair weather, physically and socially, to encourage industry and enhance the town's reputation; Rev. Alonzo Duckett, who "ducks" his Christian responsibility of loving concern for the Negro community because he expects only the worst from them; and County Sheriff Vince Lasseter, who shows his moral lassitude by fishing and enjoying his clear conscience. Still, these are newspaper statements: Public accusations call forth public rebuttals; blame calls for defense and evasion of responsibility.

"No cause was cited for the fracas," the newspaper reports. But none is needed. It is built into the natures of strong, death-defying people who hate as passionately as they love: It is with pity and fear that we witness in our imaginations this awesome consummation of love and death as the two lovers with sure instinct plunge the weapon alternately into heart and brain, and then walk or run away: Left for dead, they refuse to die. Equally heroic, they are savage, dignified, and above all, *private*. "He offered no statement" is Dr. Strickland's laconic understatement to the press about Dove's last moments, for whatever he has learned on that night of tragedy, he will keep to himself.

The story closes with a brief, poignant elegy, which, like all elegies, ends with hope. It is autumn; the garden, untended by the doctor's wife, is declining, though still bright with color. Sitting on the porch, finishing his morning coffee, Dr. Strickland thinks of his daughter, who used to lie there on her daybed, enjoying the flowers and watching the birds. Then he sees a pair of flickers, the cock in one part of the garden, the hen in another. The birds are separate now—probably in the spring they were together. As he watches, he sees the cock spread a wing, "showy as a zebra's hide." Then the cock turns his head and shows his red seal—

nature's token and stamp of love. The birds are linked with the lovers. Ruby—a gem, deep red. Red for hearts. Ruby had posted her valentine on the wall over her bed. She had also worn a red banner over her breast. Red for violence, for blood. And Dove. The newspaper got that wrong, calling him Dave. Dove, man of violence—no more Saturday night scrapes for him. Dove for peace.

Dr. Strickland picks up his bag, reassuming the burden of his own human care and responsibility. He knows it is not going to be easy. There is no one in all Holden who does not need help, unless it is Miss Marcia Pope, "still quite able to take care of herself—or such was her opinion."

There is one final demonstrator implicit in this story: the author herself. In an article titled "Must the Novelist Crusade?" Eudora Welty defends the writer's independence and privacy, his refusal to take sides on current problems *in his fiction*. He cannot crusade through fiction, she maintains, even if "morality as shown through human relationships is the whole heart of fiction." Crusades spring from crisis, and unless the fiction, like Ibsen's plays or *The Grapes of Wrath* or *A Passage to India,* contains more than the crisis, it will not last. Crusaders must simplify, generalize, work in public, convince by argument. Writers of fiction work with the particular, the complex human personality, the mysteries of the heart, the confusions of an actuality in which "people are not Right and Wrong, Good and Bad, Black and White personified." Crusaders must work by clear daylight, while novelists must also work with the dark, the insoluble, "because surely it was the dark that first troubled us." While crusades are effected in public, "fiction has, and must keep, a private address. For life is *lived* in a private place; where it means anything is inside the mind and heart." While the external incidents with which fiction deals change rapidly, the "instruments of perceiving"—the way the artist sees—stay the same. What is perceived, despite all the changes, is that

> there is a relationship in progress between ourselves and other people; this was the case when the world seemed stable, too. There are relationships of the blood, of the passions and the affections, of thought and spirit and deed. There is the relationship between the races. How can one kind of relationship be set apart from the others? Like the great root system of an old and long-established growing plant, they are all tangled up together; to separate them you would have to cleave the plant itself from top to bottom.

"The Demonstrators" is a delicately balanced portrait of one such intricate root system, part of a long-established growing plant, Holden, Mississippi. The town is now stricken by hostility and suspicion, and threatened by an old internal blight. It has lost a couple of vital young branches, and is about to lose other, older ones. But since the root system reaches deep into the earth, it seems quite possible that Holden will hold.

QUESTIONS

The Demonstrators

POINT OF VIEW 1. Does the narrator enter any consciousness other than that of Dr. Strickland? Taking the theme into consideration, what are the advantages in having a doctor serve as the center of consciousness in this story?

CHARACTERS 2. In what ways is Dr. Strickland different from other members of the white community—for example, Mayor Herman Fairbrothers, Reverend Alonzo Duckett, and Curtis "Cowboy" Stubblefield? 3. In what ways are Miss Marcia Pope and Ruby Gaddy similar? How does their similarity add to the thematic fullness of the story? 4. What does the attitude of the Negroes toward Ruby's dying reveal about their attitudes toward life? 5. How is the doctor's attitude toward Ruby's death similar to and yet different from that of the Negroes? What does this reveal about the doctor's attitude toward life? toward the black community? 6. Is the doctor a developing or static character? Is he a "demonstrator"? If so, how?

PLOT 7. In the opening paragraph, we are told that Miss Pope's companion is Mrs. Warrum. In the newspaper account, we learn that a young motorcyclist, Billy Lee Warrum Jr., was killed. Is this coincidence justified esthetically? thematically? 8. When the doctor is driving the Negro child to their yet unstated destination, he notices that there are no passengers in the marshal's car. How does this detail foreshadow the events that follow? 9. Analyze the devices that build and maintain suspense. 10. Does the action of this story develop along vertical or horizontal lines? If vertical, what serves as the axis for this development? Where would you locate the climax of the story, and why?

SETTING 11. What mood or atmosphere envelops the scene that takes place at Ruby Gaddy's death-bed? 12. Examine the ways in which Ruby's mother's house is revealed—thus taking on an increasing "reality" or presence. 13. Examine the doctor's perception of the natural world.

In what ways does nature contrast with or augment his vision of the world—and, by extension, the theme of the story?

STYLE   14. What differences do you notice between the narrative method and style of the newspaper account and that of the rest of the story—by implication, the difference between journalism and fiction? What marks of the provincial reporter do you detect in the newspaper article?   15. In addition to visual imagery, "The Demonstrators" contains many tactile, auditory, and olefactory images. Cite several examples of these various kinds of images.   16. As the story progresses, it becomes apparent that not only the color red but light and dark have symbolic value. Relate the symbolic significance of light and dark to the theme.

TONE   17. The stories of Eudora Welty are rarely without comic elements. Trace some of these comic elements in "The Demonstrators," distinguishing whether the humor arises from character, incidents, or word choice. What is the esthetic and thematic effect of the presence of humor?   18. Much of the action in "The Demonstrators" is violent— being concerned with a fatal struggle between Ruby and Dove and with the circumstances of their dying. Yet the attitude of the implied author qualifies this violence. In one sense, the tone stands at odds with the subject matter. Explain.

Demonstrators in a Stricken Land

FOCUS   1. In what way does the title of the essay suggest the writer's thesis?   2. The first sentence of the second paragraph of the essay announces the critical approach that will be used in the remainder of it. What is this approach? Why is it well suited to interpretation of this particular story?

ORGANIZATION   3. In the essay, Dr. Strickland is described as a person who "feels, reflects, sorts out." In what way does the organization of the essay parallel the doctor's characteristic responses?   4. Do you agree that demonstrators and demonstrations unify the essay as they unify the story itself? Explain.

USING THE EVIDENCE   5. Upon what evidence does the essayist base her claim that Miss Marcia Pope is "the first of the demonstrators, old style"?   6. According to the essay, what do the starched clothes on the clothesline and the porcelain cup symbolize? What evidence is used to support this interpretation?   7. According to the essayist, what does the color red symbolize in the story? What evidence does the essayist use to support this interpretation? 8. From the story itself, it is clear that Dove is less than admirable: He has deserted his common-law wife, leaving her to bring up what is probably his child; he is a brawler, for we learn that the doctor has had to "sew him up" frequently on Sunday mornings; and, of course, he is a murderer. In describing Dove as "the last and best of the demonstrators," is the essayist ignoring the evidence of Dove's irresponsibility and violent nature? Or does this evidence support her contention? Explain. 9. Why does the essayist state that the story concludes with "a brief, poignant elegy, which, like all elegies, ends with hope"? Does such a statement ignore the implication of the last sentence of the story—in particular the clause, "or such was her own opinion"? 10. From the evidence cited in the essay, in what way do the answers embedded in Eudora Welty's article "Must the Novelist Crusade?" provide illumination for "The Demonstrators"?

STYLE 11. Examine the concluding paragraph of the essay. In what ways is the controlling metaphor linked to the quoted material that precedes it? Why is this metaphor appropriate to the essay as a whole? 12. In what ways is the style of the essay similar to the style of the story?

MAKING LITERARY JUDGMENTS 13. In the passage quoted at the beginning of this section, Eudora Welty speaks of the best story writers as being "in a sense obstructionists." The essay refers to the story and the practice of fiction as necessarily complex and even mysterious. Thus, it seems that some amount of obfuscation is a valuable quality—in that it provides the writer with a way of handling complexity. Do you find that complexity is, indeed, a desirable intrinsic quality in this story? Discuss.

NO PLACE FOR YOU,
MY LOVE

They were strangers to each other, both fairly well strangers to the place, now seated side by side at luncheon—a party combined in a free-and-easy way when the friends he and she were with recognized each other across Galatoire's. The time was a Sunday in summer—those hours of afternoon that seem Time Out in New Orleans.

The moment he saw her little blunt, fair face, he thought that here was a woman who was having an affair. It was one of those odd meetings when such an impact is felt that it has to be translated at once into some sort of speculation.

With a married man, most likely, he supposed, slipping quickly into a groove—he was long married—and feeling more conventional, then, in his curiosity as she sat there, leaning her cheek on her hand, looking no further before her than the flowers on the table, and wearing that hat.

He did not like her hat, any more than he liked tropical flowers. It was the wrong hat for her, thought this Eastern businessman who had no interest whatever in women's clothes and no eye for them; he thought the unaccustomed thing crossly.

It must stick out all over me, she thought, so people think they can love me or hate me just by looking at me. How did it leave us—the old, safe, slow way people used to know of learning how one another feels, and the privilege that went with it of shying away if it seemed best? People in love like me, I suppose, give away the short cuts to everybody's secrets.

Something, though, he decided, had been settled about her predicament —for the time being, anyway; the parties to it were all still alive, no doubt. Nevertheless, her predicament was the only one he felt so sure of here, like the only recognizable shadow in that restaurant, where mirrors and fans were busy agitating the light, as the very local talk drawled across and agitated the peace. The shadow lay between her fingers, between her little square hand and her cheek, like something always best carried about the person. Then suddenly, as she took her hand down, the secret fact was still there—it lighted her. It was a bold and full light, shot up under the brim of that hat, as close to them all as the flowers in the center of the table.

Did he dream of making her disloyal to that hopelessness that he saw very well she'd be cultivating down here? He knew very well that he did not. What they amounted to was two Northerners keeping each other company. She glanced up at the big gold clock on the wall and smiled. He didn't smile back. She had that naïve face that he associated, for no good reason, with the Middle West—because it said "Show me," perhaps. It was a serious, now-watch-out-everybody face, which orphaned her entirely in the company of these Southerners. He guessed her age, as he could not guess theirs: thirty-two. He himself was further along.

Of all human moods, deliberate imperviousness may be the most quickly communicated—it may be the most successful, most fatal signal of all. And two people can indulge in imperviousness as well as in anything else. "You're not very hungry either," he said.

The blades of fan shadows came down over their two heads, as he saw inadvertently in the mirror, with himself smiling at her now like a villain. His remark sounded dominant and rude enough for everybody present to listen back a moment; it even sounded like an answer to a question she might have just asked him. The other women glanced at him. The Southern look—Southern mask—of life-is-a-dream irony, which could turn to pure challenge at the drop of a hat, he could wish well away. He liked naïveté better.

"I find the heat down here depressing," she said, with the heart of Ohio in her voice.

"Well—I'm in somewhat of a temper about it, too," he said.

They looked with grateful dignity at each other.

"I have a car here, just down the street," he said to her as the luncheon party was rising to leave, all the others wanting to get back to their houses and sleep. "If it's all right with— Have you ever driven down south of here?"

Out on Bourbon Street, in the bath of July, she asked at his shoulder, "South of New Orleans? I didn't know there was any south to *here*. Does it just go on and on?" She laughed, and adjusted the exasperating hat to her head in a different way. It was more than frivolous, it was conspicuous, with some sort of glitter or flitter tied in a band around the straw and hanging down.

"That's what I'm going to show you."

"Oh—you've been there?"

"No!"

His voice rang out over the uneven, narrow sidewalk and dropped back from the walls. The flaked-off, colored houses were spotted like the hides of beasts faded and shy, and were hot as a wall of growth that seemed to breathe flower-like down onto them as they walked to the car parked there.

"It's just that it couldn't be any worse—we'll see."

"All right, then," she said. "We will."

So, their actions reduced to amiability, they settled into the car—a faded-red Ford convertible with a rather threadbare canvas top, which had been standing in the sun for all those lunch hours.

"It's rented," he explained. "I asked to have the top put down, and was told I'd lost my mind."

"It's out of this world. *Degrading* heat," she said and added, "Doesn't matter."

The stranger in New Orleans always sets out to leave it as though following the clue in a maze. They were threading through the narrow and one-way streets, past the pale-violet bloom of tired squares, the brown steeples and statues, the balcony with the live and probably famous black monkey dipping along the railing as over a ballroom floor, past the grill-work and the lattice-work to all the iron swans painted flesh color on the front steps of bungalows outlying.

Driving, he spread his new map and put his finger down on it. At the intersection marked Arabi, where their road led out of the tangle and he took it, a small Negro seated beneath a black umbrella astride a box chalked "Shou Shine" lifted his pink-and-black hand and waved them languidly good-by. She didn't miss it, and waved back.

Below New Orleans there was a raging of insects from both sides of the concrete highway, not quite together, like the playing of separated marching bands. The river and the levee were still on her side, waste and jungle and some occasional settlements on his—poor houses. Families bigger than housefuls thronged the yards. His nodding, driving head would veer from side to side, looking and almost lowering. As time passed and the distance from New Orleans grew, girls ever darker and younger were disposing themselves over the porches and the porch steps, with jet-black hair pulled high, and ragged palm-leaf fans rising and falling like rafts of butterflies. The children running forth were nearly always naked ones.

She watched the road. Crayfish constantly crossed in front of the wheels, looking grim and bonneted, in a great hurry.

"How the Old Woman Got Home," she murmured to herself.

He pointed, as it flew by, at a saucepan full of cut zinnias which stood waiting on the open lid of a mailbox at the roadside, with a little note tied onto the handle.

They rode mostly in silence. The sun bore down. They met fishermen and other men bent on some local pursuits, some in sulphur-colored pants, walking and riding; met wagons, trucks, boats in trucks, autos, boats on top of autos—all coming to meet them, as though something of high moment were doing back where the car came from, and he and she were determined to miss it. There was nearly always a man lying with his shoes off in the bed of any truck otherwise empty—with the raw, red look of a man sleeping in the daytime, being jolted about as he slept. Then there was a sort of dead man's land, where nobody came. He loosened his collar and tie. By rushing through the heat at high speed, they brought themselves the effect of fans turned onto their cheeks. Clearing alternated with jungle and canebrake like something tried, tried again. Little shell roads led off on both sides; now and then a road of planks led into the yellow-green.

"Like a dance floor in there." She pointed.

He informed her, "In there's your oil, I think."

There were thousands, millions of mosquitoes and gnats—a universe of them, and on the increase.

A family of eight or nine people on foot strung along the road in the same direction the car was going, beating themselves with the wild palmettos. Heels, shoulders, knees, breasts, back of the heads, elbows, hands, were touched in turn—like some game, each playing it with himself.

He struck himself on the forehead, and increased their speed. (His wife would not be at her most charitable if he came bringing malaria home to the family.)

More and more crayfish and other shell creatures littered their path, scuttling or dragging. These little samples, little jokes of creation, persisted and sometimes perished, the more of them the deeper down the road went. Terrapins and turtles came up steadily over the horizons of the ditches.

Back there in the margins were worse—crawling hides you could not penetrate with bullets or quite believe, grins that had come down from the primeval mud.

"Wake up." Her Northern nudge was very timely on his arm. They had veered toward the side of the road. Still driving fast, he spread his map.

Like a misplaced sunrise, the light of the river flowed up; they were mounting the levee on a little shell road.

"Shall we cross here?" he asked politely.

He might have been keeping track over years and miles of how long they could keep that tiny ferry waiting. Now skidding down the levee's flank, they were the last-minute car, the last possible car that could squeeze on. Under the sparse shade of one willow tree, the small, amateurish-looking boat slapped the water, as, expertly, he wedged on board.

"Tell him we put him on hub cap!" shouted one of the numerous olive-skinned, dark-eyed young boys standing dressed up in bright shirts at the railing, hugging each other with delight that that last straw was on board. Another boy drew his affectionate initials in the dust of the door on her side.

She opened the door and stepped out, and, after only a moment's standing at bay, started up a little iron stairway. She appeared above the car, on the tiny bridge beneath the captain's window and the whistle.

From there, while the boat still delayed in what seemed a trance—as if it were too full to attempt the start—she could see the panlike deck below, separated by its rusty rim from the tilting, polished water.

The passengers walking and jostling about there appeared oddly amateurish, too—amateur travelers. They were having such a good time. They all knew each other. Beer was being passed around in cans, bets were being loudly settled and new bets made, about local and special subjects on which they all doted. One red-haired man in a burst of wildness even tried to give away his truckload of shrimp to a man on the other side of the boat—nearly all the trucks were full of shrimp—causing taunts and then protests of "They good! They good!" from the giver. The young boys leaned on each other thinking of what next, rolling their eyes absently.

A radio pricked the air behind her. Looking like a great tomcat just above her head, the captain was digesting the news of a fine stolen automobile.

At last a tremendous explosion burst—the whistle. Everything shuddered in outline from the sound, everybody said something—everybody else.

They started with no perceptible motion, but her hat blew off. It went spiraling to the deck below, where he, thank heaven, sprang out of the car and picked it up. Everybody looked frankly up at her now, holding her hands to her head.

The little willow tree receded as its shade was taken away. The heat was like something falling on her head. She held the hot rail before her. It was like riding a stove. Her shoulders dropping, her hair flying, her skirt buffeted by the sudden strong wind, she stood there, thinking they all must see that with her entire self all she did was wait. Her set hands, with the bag that hung from her wrist and rocked back and forth—all three seemed objects bleaching there, belonging to no one; she could not feel a thing in the skin of her face; perhaps she was crying, and not knowing it. She could look down and see him just below her, his black shadow, her hat, and his black hair. His hair in the wind looked unreasonably long and rippling. Little did he know that from here it had a red undergleam like an animal's. When she looked up and outward, a vortex of light drove through and over the brown waves like a star in the water.

He did after all bring the retrieved hat up the stairs to her. She took it back—useless—and held it to her skirt. What they were saying below was more polite than their searchlight faces.

"Where you think he come from, that man?"

"I bet he come from Lafitte."

"Lafitte? What you bet, eh?"—all crouched in the shade of trucks, squatting and laughing.

Now his shadow fell partly across her; the boat had jolted into some other strand of current. Her shaded arm and shaded hand felt pulled out from the blaze of light and water, and she hoped humbly for more shade for her head. It had seemed so natural to climb up and stand in the sun.

The boys had a surprise—an alligator on board. One of them pulled it by a chain around the deck, between the cars and trucks, like a toy—a hide that could walk. He thought, Well they had to catch one sometime. It's Sunday afternoon. So they have him on board now, riding him across the Mississippi River. . . . The playfulness of it beset everybody on the ferry. The hoarseness of the boat whistle, commenting briefly, seemed part of the general appreciation.

"Who want to rassle him? Who want to, eh?" two boys cried, looking up. A boy with shrimp-colored arms capered from side to side, pretending to have been bitten.

What was there so hilarious about jaws that could bite? And what danger was there once in this repulsiveness—so that the last worldly evidence of some old heroic horror of the dragon had to be paraded in capture before the eyes of country clowns?

He noticed that she looked at the alligator without flinching at all. Her distance was set—the number of feet and inches between herself and it mattered to her.

Perhaps her measuring coolness was to him what his bodily shade was to her, while they stood pat up there riding the river, which felt like the sea and looked like the earth under them—full of the red-brown earth, charged with it. Ahead of the boat it was like an exposed vein of ore. The river seemed to swell in the vast middle with the curve of the earth. The sun rolled under them. As if in memory of the size of things, uprooted trees were drawn across their path, sawing at the air and tumbling one over the other.

When they reached the other side, they felt that they had been racing around an arena in their chariot, among lions. The whistle took and shook the stairs as they went down. The young boys, looking taller, had taken out colored combs and were combing their wet hair back in solemn pompadour above their radiant foreheads. They had been bathing in the river themselves not long before.

The cars and trucks, then the foot passengers and the alligator, waddling like a child to school, all disembarked and wound up the weed-sprung levee.

Both respectable and merciful, their hides, she thought, forcing herself to dwell on the alligator as she looked back. Deliver us all from the naked in heart. (As she had been told.)

When they regained their paved road, he heard her give a little sigh and saw her turn her straw-colored head to look back once more. Now that she rode with her hat in her lap, her earrings were conspicuous too. A little metal ball set with small pale stones danced beside each square, faintly downy cheek.

Had she felt a wish for someone else to be riding with them? He thought it was more likely that she would wish for her husband if she had one (his wife's voice) than for the lover in whom he believed. Whatever people liked to think, situations (if not scenes) were usually three-way —there was somebody else always. The one who didn't—couldn't— understand the two made the formidable third.

He glanced down at the map flapping on the seat between them, up at his wristwatch, out at the road. Out there was the incredible brightness of four o'clock.

On this side of the river, the road ran beneath the brow of the levee and followed it. Here was a heat that ran deeper and brighter and more intense than all the rest—its nerve. The road grew one with the heat as it was one with the unseen river. Dead snakes stretched across the concrete like markers—inlaid mosaic bands, dry as feathers, which their tires licked at intervals that began to seem clocklike.

No, the heat faced them—it was ahead. They could see it waving at them, shaken in the air above the white of the road, always at a certain distance ahead, shimmering finely as a cloth, with running edges of green and gold, fire and azure.

"It's never anything like this in Syracuse," he said.

"Or in Toledo, either," she replied with dry lips.

They were driving through greater waste down here, through fewer and even more insignificant towns. There was water under everything. Even where a screen of jungle had been left to stand, splashes could be heard from under the trees. In the vast open, sometimes boats moved inch by inch through what appeared endless meadows of rubbery flowers.

Her eyes overcome with brightness and size, she felt a panic rise, as sudden as nausea. Just how far below questions and answers, concealment and revelation, they were running now—that was still a new question, with a power of its own, waiting. How dear—how costly—could this ride be?

"It looks to me like your road can't go much further," she remarked cheerfully. "Just over there, it's all water."

"Time out," he said, and with that he turned the car into a sudden road of white shells that rushed at them narrowly out of the left.

They bolted over a cattle guard, where some rayed and crested purple flowers burst out of the vines in the ditch, and rolled onto a long, narrow, green, mowed clearing: a churchyard. A paved track ran between two short rows of raised tombs, all neatly white-washed and now brilliant as faces against the vast flushed sky.

The track was the width of the car with a few inches to spare. He passed between the tombs slowly but in the manner of a feat. Names took their places on the walls slowly at a level with the eye, names as near as the eyes of a person stopping in conversation, and as far away in origin, and in all their music and dead longing, as Spain. At intervals were set packed bouquets of zinnias, oleanders, and some kind of purple flowers, all quite fresh, in fruit jars, like nice welcomes on bureaus.

They moved on into an open plot beyond, of violent-green grass, spread before the green-and-white frame church with worked flower beds around it, flowerless poinsettias growing up to the windowsills. Beyond was a house, and left on the doorstep of the house a fresh-caught catfish the size of a baby—a fish wearing whiskers and bleeding. On a clothesline in the yard, a priest's black gown on a hanger hung airing, swaying at man's height, in a vague, trainlike, lady-like sweep along an evening breath that might otherwise have seemed imaginary from the unseen, felt river.

With the motor cut off, with the raging of the insects about them, they sat looking out at the green and white and black and red and pink as they leaned against the sides of the car.

"What is your wife like?" she asked. His right hand came up and spread—iron, wooden, manicured. She lifted her eyes to his face. He looked at her like that hand.

Then he lit a cigarette, and the portrait, and the right-hand testimonial it made, were blown away. She smiled, herself as unaffected as by some stage performance; and he was annoyed in the cemetery. They did not risk going on to her husband—if she had one.

Under the supporting posts of the priest's house, where a boat was, solid ground ended and palmettos and water hyacinths could not wait to begin; suddenly the rays of the sun, from behind the car, reached that lowness and struck the flowers. The priest came out onto the porch in his underwear, stared at the car a moment as if he wondered what time it was, then collected his robe off the line and his fish off the doorstep and returned inside. Vespers was next, for him.

After backing out between the tombs he drove on still south, in the sunset. They caught up with an old man walking in a sprightly way in their direction, all by himself, wearing a clean bright shirt printed with a pair of palm trees fanning green over his chest. It might better be a big colored woman's shirt, but she didn't have it. He flagged the car with gestures like hoops.

"You're coming to the end of the road," the old man told them. He pointed ahead, tipped his hat to the lady, and pointed again. "End of the road." They didn't understand that he meant, "Take me."

They drove on. "If we do go any further, it'll have to be by water—is that it?" he asked her, hesitating at this odd point.

"You know better than I do," she replied politely.

The road had for some time ceased to be paved; it was made of shells. It was leading into a small, sparse settlement like the others a few miles back, but with even more of the camp about it. On the lip of the clearing, directly before a green willow blaze with the sunset gone behind it, the row of houses and shacks faced out on broad, colored, moving water that stretched to reach the horizon and looked like an arm of the sea. The houses on their shaggy posts, patchily built, some with plank runways instead of steps, were flimsy and alike, and not much bigger than the boats tied up at the landing.

"Venice," she heard him announce, and he dropped the crackling map in her lap.

They coasted down the brief remainder. The end of the road—she could not remember ever seeing a road simply end—was a spoon shape, with a tree stump in the bowl to turn around by.

Around it, he stopped the car, and they stepped out, feeling put down in the midst of a sudden vast pause or subduement that was like a yawn. They made their way on foot toward the water, where at an idle-looking landing men in twos and threes stood with their backs to them.

The nearness of darkness, the still uncut trees, bright water partly under a sheet of flowers, shacks, silence, dark shapes of boats tied up, then the first sounds of people just on the other side of thin walls—all this reached them. Mounds of shells like day-old snow, pink-tinted, lay around a central shack with a beer sign on it. An old man up on the porch there sat holding an open newspaper, with a fat white goose sitting opposite him on the floor. Below, in the now shadowless and sunless open, another old man, with a colored pencil bright under his hat brim, was late mending a sail.

When she looked clear around, thinking they had a fire burning somewhere now, out of the heat had risen the full moon. Just beyond the trees, enormous, tangerine-colored, it was going solidly up. Other lights just striking into view, looking farther distant, showed moss shapes hanging, or slipped and broke matchlike on the water that so encroached upon the rim of ground they were standing on.

There was a touch at her arm—his, accidental.

"We're at the jumping-off place," he said.

She laughed, having thought his hand was a bat, while her eyes rushed downward toward a great pale drift of water hyacinths—still partly open, flushed and yet moonlit, level with her feet—through which paths of water for the boats had been hacked. She drew her hands up to her face under the brim of her hat; her own cheeks felt like the hyacinths to her, all her skin still full of too much light and sky, exposed. The harsh vesper bell was ringing.

"I believe there must be something wrong with me, that I came on this excursion to begin with," she said, as if he had already said this and she were merely in hopeful, willing, maddening agreement with him.

He took hold of her arm, and said, "Oh, come on—I see we can get something to drink here, at least."

But there was a beating, muffled sound from over the darkening water. One more boat was coming in, making its way through the tenacious, tough, dark flower traps, by the shaken light of what first appeared to be torches. He and she waited for the boat, as if on each other's patience. As if borne in on a mist of twilight or a breath, a horde of mosquitoes and gnats came singing and striking at them first. The boat bumped, men laughed. Somebody was offering somebody else some shrimp.

Then he might have cocked his dark city head down at her; she did not look up at him, only turned when he did. Now the shell mounds, like the shacks and trees, were solid purple. Lights had appeared in the not-quite-true window squares. A narrow neon sign, the lone sign, had come out in bright blush on the beer shack's roof: "Baba's Place." A light was on on the porch.

The barnlike interior was brightly lit and unpainted, looking not quite finished, with a partition dividing this room from what lay behind. One of the four cardplayers at a table in the middle of the floor was the newspaper reader; the paper was in his pants pocket. Midway along the partition was a bar, in the form of a pass-through to the other room, with a varnished, second-hand fretwork overhang. They crossed the floor and sat, alone there, on wooden stools. An eruption of humorous signs, newspaper cut-outs and cartoons, razor-blade cards, and personal messages of significance to the owner or his friends decorated the overhang, framing where Baba should have been but wasn't.

Through there came a smell of garlic and cloves and red pepper, a blast of hot cloud escaped from a cauldron they could see now on a stove at the back of the other room. A massive back, presumably female, with a twist of gray hair on top, stood with a ladle akimbo. A young man joined her and with his fingers stole something out of the pot and ate it. At Baba's they were boiling shrimp.

When he got ready to wait on them, Baba strolled out to the counter, young, black-headed, and in very good humor.

"Coldest beer you've got. And food— What will you have?"

"Nothing for me, thank you," she said. "I'm not sure I could eat, after all."

"Well, I could," he said, shoving his jaw out. Baba smiled. "I want a good solid ham sandwich."

"I could have asked him for some water," she said, after he had gone.

While they sat waiting, it seemed very quiet. The bubbling of the shrimp, the distant laughing of Baba, and the slap of cards, like the beating of moths on the screens, seemed to come in fits and starts. The steady breathing they heard came from a big rough dog asleep in the corner. But it was bright. Electric lights were strung riotously over the room from a kind of spider web of old wires in the rafters. One of the written messages tacked before them read, "Joe! At the boyy!!" It looked very yellow, older than Baba's Place. Outside, the world was pure dark.

Two little boys, almost alike, almost the same size, and just cleaned up, dived into the room with a double bang of the screen door, and circled around the card game. They ran their hands into the men's pockets.

"Nickel for some pop!"

"Nickel for some pop!"

"Go 'way and let me play, you!"

They circled around and shrieked at the dog, ran under the lid of the counter and raced through the kitchen and back, and hung over the stools at the bar. One child had a live lizard on his shirt, clinging like a breast pin—like lapis lazuli.

Bringing in a strong odor of geranium talcum, some men had come in now—all in bright shirts. They drew near the counter, or stood and watched the game.

When Baba came out bringing the beer and sandwich, "Could I have some water?" she greeted him.

Baba laughed at everybody. She decided the woman back there must be Baba's mother.

Beside her, he was drinking his beer and eating his sandwich—ham, cheese, tomato, pickle, and mustard. Before he finished, one of the men who had come in beckoned from across the room. It was the old man in the palm-tree shirt.

She lifted her head to watch him leave her, and was looked at, from all over the room. As a minute passed, no cards were laid down. In a far-off way, like accepting the light from Arcturus, she accepted it that she was more beautiful or perhaps more fragile than the women they saw every day of their lives. It was just this thought coming into a woman's face, and at this hour, that seemed familiar to them.

Baba was smiling. He had set an opened, frosted brown bottle before her on the counter, and a thick sandwich, and stood looking at her. Baba made her eat some supper, for what she was.

"What the old fellow wanted," said he when he came back at last, "was to have a friend of his apologize. Seems church is just out. Seems the friend made a remark coming in just now. His pals told him there was a lady present."

"I see you bought him a beer," she said.

"Well, the old man looked like he wanted *something*."

All at once the juke box interrupted from back in the corner, with the same old song as anywhere. The half-dozen slot machines along the wall were suddenly all run to like Maypoles, and thrown into action—taken over by further battalions of little boys.

There were three little boys to each slot machine. The local custom appeared to be that one pulled the lever for the friend he was holding up to put the nickel in, while the third covered the pictures with the flat of his hand as they fell into place, so as to surprise them all if anything happened.

The dog lay sleeping on in front of the raging juke box, his ribs working fast as a concertina's. At the side of the room a man with a cap on his white thatch was trying his best to open a side screen door, but it was stuck fast. It was he who had come in with the remark considered ribald; now he was trying to get out the other way. Moths as thick as ingots were trying to get in. The card players broke into shouts of derision, then joy, then tired derision among themselves; they might have been here all afternoon—they were the only ones not cleaned up and shaved. The original pair of little boys ran in once more, with the hyphenated bang. They got nickels this time, then were brushed away from the table like mosquitoes, and they rushed under the counter and on to the cauldron behind, clinging to Baba's mother there. The evening was at the threshold.

They were quite unnoticed now. He was eating another sandwich, and she, having finished part of hers, was fanning her face with her hat. Baba had lifted the flap of the counter and come out into the room. Behind his head there was a sign lettered in orange crayon: "Shrimp Dance Sun. PM." That was tonight, still to be.

And suddenly she made a move to slide down from her stool, maybe wishing to walk out into that nowhere down the front steps to be cool a moment. But he had hold of her hand. He got down from his stool, and, patiently, reversing her hand in his own—just as she had had the look of being about to give up, faint—began moving her, leading her. They were dancing.

"I get to thinking this is what we get—what you and I deserve," she whispered, looking past his shoulder into the room. "And all the time, it's real. It's a real place—away off down here . . ."

They danced gratefully, formally, to some song carried on in what must be the local patois, while no one paid any attention as long as they were together, and the children poured the family nickels steadily into the slot machines, walloping the handles down with regular crashes and troubling nobody with winning.

She said rapidly, as they began moving together too well, "One of those clippings was an account of a shooting right here. I guess they're proud of it. And that awful knife Baba was carrying . . . I wonder what he called me," she whispered in his ear.

"Who?"

"The one who apologized to you."

If they had ever been going to overstep themselves, it would be now as he held her closer and turned her, when she became aware that he could not help but see the bruise at her temple. It would not be six inches from his eyes. She felt it come out like an evil star. (Let it pay him back, then, for the hand he had stuck in her face when she'd tried once to be sympathetic, when she'd asked about his wife.) They danced on still as the record changed, after standing wordless and motionless, linked together in the middle of the room, for the moment between.

Then, they were like a matched team—like professional, Spanish dancers wearing masks—while the slow piece was playing.

Surely even those immune from the world, for the time being, need the touch of one another, or all is lost. Their arms encircling each other, their bodies circling the odorous, just-nailed-down floor, they were, at last, imperviousness in motion. They had found it, and had almost missed it: they had had to dance. They were what their separate hearts desired that day, for themselves and each other.

They were so good together that once she looked up and half smiled. "For whose benefit did we have to show off?"

Like people in love, they had a superstition about themselves almost as soon as they came out on the floor, and dared not think the words "happy" or "unhappy," which might strike them, one or the other, like lightning.

In the thickening heat they danced on while Baba himself sang with the mosquito-voiced singer in the chorus of *"Moi pas l'aimez ça,"* enumerating the *ça's* with a hot shrimp between his fingers. He was counting over the platters the old woman now set out on the counter, each heaped with shrimp in their shells boiled to iridescence, like mounds of honeysuckle flowers.

The goose wandered in from the back room under the lid of the counter and hitched itself around the floor among the table legs and people's legs, never seeing that it was neatly avoided by two dancers—who nevertheless vaguely thought of this goose as learned, having earlier heard an old man read to it. The children called it Mimi, and lured it away. The old thatched man was again drunkenly trying to get out by the stuck side door; now he gave it a kick, but was prevailed on to remain. The sleeping dog shuddered and snored.

It was left up to the dancers to provide nickels for the juke box; Baba kept a drawerful for every use. They had grown fond of all the selections by now. This was the music you heard out of the distance at night—out of the roadside taverns you fled past, around the late corners in cities half asleep, drifting up from the carnival over the hill, with one odd little strain always managing to repeat itself. This seemed a homey place.

Bathed in sweat, and feeling the false coolness that brings, they stood finally on the porch in the lapping night air for a moment before leaving. The first arrivals of the girls were coming up the steps under the porch light—all flowered fronts, their black pompadours giving out breathlike feelers from sheer abundance. Where they'd resprinkled it since church, the talcum shone like mica on their downy arms. Smelling solidly of geranium, they filed across the porch with short steps and fingers joined, just timed to turn their smiles loose inside the room. He held the door open for them.

"Ready to go?" he asked her.

Going back, the ride was wordless, quiet except for the motor and the insects driving themselves against the car. The windshield was soon blinded. The headlights pulled in two other spinning storms, cones of flying things that, it seemed, might ignite at the last minute. He stopped the car and got out to clean the windshield thoroughly with his brisk, angry motions of driving. Dust lay thick and cratered on the roadside scrub. Under the now ash-white moon, the world traveled through very faint stars—very many slow stars, very high, very low.

It was a strange land, amphibious—and whether water-covered or grown with jungle or robbed entirely of water and trees, as now, it had the same loneliness. He regarded the great sweep—like steppes, like moors, like deserts (all of which were imaginary to him); but more than it was like any likeness, it was South. The vast, thin, wide-thrown, pale, unfocused star-sky, with its veils of lightning adrift, hung over this land as it hung over the open sea. Standing out in the night alone, he was struck as powerfully with recognition of the extremity of this place as if all other bearings had vanished—as if snow had suddenly started to fall.

He climbed back inside and drove. When he moved to slap furiously at his shirtsleeves, she shivered in the hot, licking night wind that their speed was making. Once the car lights picked out two people—a Negro couple, sitting on two facing chairs in the yard outside their lonely cabin —half undressed, each battling for self against the hot night, with long white rags in endless, scarflike motions.

In peopleless open places there were lakes of dust, smudge fires burning at their hearts. Cows stood in untended rings around them, motionless in the heat, in the night—their horns standing up sharp against that glow.

At length, he stopped the car again, and this time he put his arm under her shoulder and kissed her—not knowing ever whether gently or harshly. It was the loss of that distinction that told him this was now. Then their faces touched unkissing, unmoving, dark, for a length of time. The heat came inside the car and wrapped them still, and the mosquitoes had begun to coat their arms and even their eyelids.

Later, crossing a large open distance, he saw at the same time two fires. He had the feeling that they had been riding for a long time across a face —great, wide, and upturned. In its eyes and open mouth were those fires they had had glimpses of, where the cattle had drawn together: a face, a head, far down here in the South—south of South, below it. A whole giant body sprawled downward then, on and on, always, constant as a constellation or an angel. Flaming and perhaps falling, he thought.

She appeared to be sound asleep, lying back flat as a child, with her hat in her lap. He drove on with her profile beside his, behind his, for he bent forward to drive faster. The earrings she wore twinkled with their rushing motion in an almost regular beat. They might have spoken like tongues. He looked straight before him and drove on, at a speed that, for the rented, overheated, not at all new Ford car, was demoniac.

It seemed often now that a barnlike shape flashed by, roof and all outlined in lonely neon—a movie house at a cross roads. The long white flat road itself, since they had followed it to the end and turned around to come back, seemed able, this far up, to pull them home.

*

A thing is incredible, if ever, only after it is told—returned to the world it came out of. For their different reasons, he thought, neither of them would tell this (unless something was dragged out of them): that, strangers, they had ridden down into a strange land together and were getting safely back—by a slight margin, perhaps, but margin enough. Over the levee wall now, like an aurora borealis, the sky of New Orleans, across the river, was flickering gently. This time they crossed by bridge, high above everything, merging into a long light-stream of cars turned cityward.

For a time afterward he was lost in the streets, turning almost at random with the noisy traffic until he found his bearings. When he stopped the car at the next sign and leaned forward frowning to make it out, she sat up straight on her side. It was Arabi. He turned the car right around.

"We're all right now," he muttered, allowing himself a cigarette.

Something that must have been with them all along suddenly, then, was not. In a moment, tall as panic, it rose, cried like a human, and dropped back.

"I never got my water," she said.

She gave him the name of her hotel, he drove her there, and he said good night on the sidewalk. They shook hands.

"Forgive . . ." For, just in time, he saw she expected it of him.

And that was just what she did, forgive him. Indeed, had she waked in time from a deep sleep, she would have told him her story. She disappeared through the revolving door, with a gesture of smoothing her hair, and he thought a figure in the lobby strolled to meet her. He got back in the car and sat there.

He was not leaving for Syracuse until early in the morning. At length, he recalled the reason; his wife had recommended that he stay where he was this extra day so that she could entertain some old, unmarried college friends without him underfoot.

As he started up the car, he recognized in the smell of exhausted, body-warm air in the streets, in which the flow of drink was an inextricable part, the signal that the New Orleans evening was just beginning. In Dickie Grogan's, as he passed, the well-known Josefina at her organ was charging up and down with *"Clair de Lune."* As he drove the little Ford safely to its garage, he remembered for the first time in years when he was young and brash, a student in New York, and the shriek and horror and unholy smother of the subway had its original meaning for him as the lilt and expectation of love.

SUGGESTIONS FOR WRITING

The Stories

1. In Eudora Welty's story "The Bride of the Innisfallen," the protagonist observes that loneliness is not being physically alone. Rather, "Love with the joy being drawn out of it like anything else that aches —that was loneliness." Write an essay in which you apply this observation to Dr. Strickland and to the theme of "The Demonstrators."

2. Show how the setting in "No Place for You, My Love" affects the characters, action, and theme.

3. Discuss the nature and function of imagery in "No Place for You, My Love."

4. Examine those elements in "No Place for You, My Love" that obstruct your understanding of the story. Then write an essay in which you determine the reasons for your difficulties and the function of each "mystery" that remains unresolved after your close examination of the story.

5. Using the insights Welty affords in "How I Write" (listed in the bibliography that follows), discuss the relationship between point of view, character, and theme in "No Place for You, My Love."

6. In one sense, the plot in "No Place for You, My Love" consists of a journey. At the literal level, the man and woman journey south and west of New Orleans, into the bayou country; on the symbolic level, their journey resembles a descent into hell and a return (as in *The Aeneid* or in Dante's *Inferno*). Write an essay in which you discuss both aspects of the journey described in this story.

Other Works by Eudora Welty

1. Eudora Welty has acknowledged (in "Place in Fiction") that the family provides "a known set of standards to struggle within or against." Examine the function of the family in *Delta Wedding*, showing how the life of each member of the Fairchild family unit is influenced by its membership in that family. Examine, too, the relationship of the family to the surrounding community.

2. Discuss the nature and function of myth in *The Golden Apples*.

3. In "How I Write," Welty states, "Relationship *is* a pervading and changing mystery; it is not words that make it so in life, but words have to make it so in a story. Brutal or lovely, the mystery waits for people wherever they go, whatever extreme they run to." Write an essay in which you show how Welty seeks to embody the "pervading and changing mystery" of relationships in selected stories from one of her short-story collections.

4. In *One Time, One Place,* Eudora Welty describes the camera as "an eye, though—not quite mine, but a quicker and an unblinking one—and it couldn't see pain where it looked, or give any, though neither could it catch effervescence, color, transcience, kindness, or what was not there." Welty's fiction incorporates the camera eye and effervescence, transcience, and "what was not there" as well. Explore what the camera sees and what the story-teller reveals in *Losing Battles.*

5. Both *Delta Wedding* and *Losing Battles* concern the expanded family and its accompanying social ceremonies (weddings, funerals, birthdays, and so on). Compare and contrast these two novels.

6. Describing *Losing Battles,* Louis Rubin says, "Everything is out on the surface, but the art *is* the surface, and every inch of the surface must be inspected." Examine how the surface of *The Optimist's Daughter* contains the meaning of that novel.

BIBLIOGRAPHY

Primary

A Curtain of Green and Other Stories. New York: Doubleday, 1941. Short stories.

The Robber Bridegroom. New York: Doubleday, 1942. A novella.

The Wide Net and Other Stories. New York: Harcourt, Brace & World, 1943. Short stories.

Delta Wedding. New York: Harcourt, Brace & World, 1946. A novel.

The Golden Apples. New York: Harcourt, Brace & World, 1949. Short stories.

Short Stories. New York: Harcourt, Brace & World, 1950. Literary criticism. An abridged version appears in *Atlantic Monthly,* 183 (February and March 1949), 54–58, 46–49, as "The Reading and Writing of Short Stories."

The Ponder Heart. New York: Harcourt, Brace & World, 1954. A novella.

The Bride of the Innisfallen. New York: Harcourt, Brace & World, 1955. Short stories.

"How I Write." *Virginia Quarterly*, 31 (Spring 1955), 240–51. Literary criticism.

"Place in Fiction." *South Atlantic Quarterly*, 55 (January 1956), 57–72. Literary criticism.

"Must the Novelist Crusade?" *Atlantic Monthly*, 216 (October 1965), 104–08. Literary criticism.

Losing Battles. New York: Random House, 1970. A novel.

One Time, One Place: Mississippi in the Depression. New York: Random House, 1971. Photographs with introductory essay.

The Optimist's Daughter. New York: Random House, 1972. A novel.

Secondary

Bryant, Joseph Allen, Jr. *Eudora Welty*. Minneapolis: Univ. of Minnesota Press, 1968 (No. 66 of the University of Minnesota Pamphlets on American Writers). A summary full of predictable observations about Welty's fiction.

Daniel, Robert W. "The World of Eudora Welty," *Hopkins Review*, 6 (Winter 1953), 49–58. Reprinted in *Southern Renascence*, ed. by Louis D. Rubin, Jr. and Robert D. Jacobs. Baltimore: Johns Hopkins Press, 1953. A general analysis of the stories in *A Curtain of Green*, *The Wide Net*, and *The Golden Apples*—with particular emphasis on "June Recital."

Glenn, Eunice. "Fantasy in the Fiction of Eudora Welty" in *A Southern Vanguard*, ed. by Allen Tate. New York: Prentice-Hall, 1947. Reprinted in *Critiques and Essays on Modern Fiction, 1920–1951*, ed. by John W. Aldridge. New York: Ronald Press, 1952. Discusses the role of fantasy in heightening the conflict between the real and the imagined in *A Curtain of Green* and *The Wide Net*.

Gossett, Louise Y. "Violence as Revelation" in *Violence in Recent Southern Fiction*. Durham N.C.: Duke Univ. Press, 1965. Contends that violence in the fiction of Eudora Welty is used to "reveal to characters hitherto unaware of their condition the fact of their aloneness."

Hicks, Granville. "Eudora Welty." *College English*, 14 (November 1952), 69–76. Printed also in *The English Journal*, 41 (November 1952), 461–68. An explication of Welty's various approaches to "the mystery of personality" and a defense of her regionalism.

Jones, Alun R. "The World of Love: The Fiction of Eudora Welty" in *The Creative Present*, ed. by Nona Balakian and Charles Simmons.

New York: Doubleday, 1963. An analysis of the scope and variety of Eudora Welty's fiction—from *A Curtain of Green* to *The Ponder Heart*.

Oates, Joyce Carol. "Eudora's Web." *Atlantic Monthly*, 225 (April 1970), 118–22. A review of *Losing Battles*.

Porter, Katherine Anne. Introduction to *A Curtain of Green*, 1941. Reprinted as Introduction to Modern Library edition of *Selected Stories of Eudora Welty*. New York: Random House, 1954. Also in *The Days Before* by Katherine Anne Porter. New York: Harcourt, Brace & World, 1952. Includes both a short biographical sketch of Eudora Welty and some critical remarks about the stories in *A Curtain of Green*.

Rubin, Louis D., Jr. "Everything Brought Out in the Open: Eudora Welty's *Losing Battles*." *The Hollins Critic*, 7 (June 1970), 1–12. An appreciative, long essay.

Shenandoah, 20 (Spring 1969). An issue devoted to Eudora Welty. Includes "A Note on Jane Austen," an essay by Eudora Welty; and essays about her by such writers as Robert Heilman, Walker Percy, Reynolds Price, Allen Tate, Robert Penn Warren, and Joyce Carol Oates.

Vande Kieft, Ruth M. *Eudora Welty*. New York: Twayne, 1962. A well-documented and insightful full-length study of the fiction of Eudora Welty.

Warren, Robert Penn. "Love and Separateness in Miss Welty," *Kenyon Review*, 6 (Spring 1944), 246–59. Reprinted in Warren's *Selected Essays*. New York: Random House, 1958. A discussion of the pervasiveness of isolation in *A Curtain of Green* and *The Wide Net*.

As a writer I want uncertainty. It's part of life. I want something the reader is uncertain about. It is this uncertainty that produces drama. Keep the reader surprised. That is enormously important to me. A good writer is an imaginative writer.

. . .

My work, all of it, is an idea of dedication to the human. That's basic to every book. If you don't respect man, you cannot respect my work. I'm in defense of the human. If you want to say that, that's it.

My place in literature? It's a phenomenon of time, depending on the quality of my work as I continue to write.

FROM an interview with Haskel Frankel

BERNARD MALAMUD

Bernard Malamud was born in Brooklyn, New York, in 1914. His mother died young and his father worked long hours in his shop, so Malamud was permitted to roam at will throughout the neighborhood. Regarding his childhood, he has said, "There was adventure and a sense that one was a boy. One got to know people all over the neighborhood. This is important." The significance of his profound acquaintance with his neighborhood is apparent in his fiction.

Malamud received a bachelor's degree from the City College of New York and a master's degree in English literature from Columbia. He taught at Oregon State University from 1949 to 1961 and since 1961 has been on the faculty of Bennington College. He is married and the father of two children.

Malamud spent a year in Rome—a setting that appears in several stories—and has also traveled in England and Italy (1963) and in the Soviet Union, France, and Spain (1965). His many awards and honors include a *Partisan Review* fellowship, a Rockefeller grant, a Ford fellowship, and two National Book Awards in fiction—for *The Magic Barrel* (1958) and *The Fixer* (1966).

Opposed to the "mindlessness" and nihilism of much contemporary fiction, Malamud has dedicated himself to portraying man's ability to affirm life amidst such odds as poverty, sickness, prejudice, and persecution. The two stories in this collection attest to Malamud's belief in the richness and potentiality of the human spirit.

BLACK IS
MY FAVORITE COLOR

Charity Sweetness sits in the toilet eating her two hardboiled eggs while I'm having my ham sandwich and coffee in the kitchen.
That's how it goes only don't get the idea of ghettoes. If there's a ghetto
I'm the one that's in it. She's my cleaning woman from Father Divine and
comes in once a week to my small three-room apartment on my day off from
the liquor store. "Peace," she says to me, "Father reached on down and took
me right up in Heaven." She's a small person with a flat body, frizzy hair,
and a quiet face that the light shines out of, and Mama had such eyes before she died. The first time Charity Sweetness came in to clean, a little
more than a year and a half, I made the mistake to ask her to sit down at
the kitchen table with me and eat her lunch. I was still feeling not so hot
after Ornita left but I'm the kind of a man—Nat Lime, forty-four, a bachelor with a daily growing bald spot on the back of my head, and I could
lose frankly fifteen pounds—who enjoys company so long as he has it. So
she cooked up her two hardboiled eggs and sat down and took a small bite

out of one of them. But after a minute she stopped chewing and she got up and carried the eggs in a cup in the bathroom, and since then she eats there. I said to her more than once, "Okay, Charity Sweetness, so have it your way, eat the eggs in the kitchen by yourself and I'll eat when you're done," but she smiles absentminded, and eats in the toilet. It's my fate with colored people.

Although black is still my favorite color you wouldn't know it from my luck except in short quantities even though I do all right in the liquor store business in Harlem, on Eighth Avenue between 110th and 111th. I speak with respect. A large part of my life I've had dealings with Negro people, most on a business basis but sometimes for friendly reasons with genuine feeling on both sides. I'm drawn to them. At this time of my life I should have one or two good colored friends but the fault isn't necessarily mine. If they knew what was in my heart towards them, but how can you tell that to anybody nowadays? I've tried more than once but the language of the heart either is a dead language or else nobody understands it the way you speak it. Very few. What I'm saying is, personally for me there's only one human color and that's the color of blood. I like a black person if not because he's black, then because I'm white. It comes to the same thing. If I wasn't white my first choice would be black. I'm satisfied to be white because I have no other choice. Anyway, I got an eye for color. I appreciate. Who wants everybody to be the same? Maybe it's like some kind of a talent. Nat Lime might be a liquor dealer in Harlem, but once in the jungle in New Guinea in the Second War, I got the idea when I shot at a running Jap and missed him, that I had some kind of a talent, though maybe it's the kind where you have a marvelous idea now and then but in the end what do they come to? After all, it's a strange world.

Where Charity Sweetness eats her eggs makes me think about Buster Wilson when we were both boys in the Williamsburg section of Brooklyn. There was this long block of run-down dirty frame houses in the middle of a not-so-hot white neighborhood full of pushcarts. The Negro houses looked to me like they had been born and died there, dead not long after the beginning of the world. I lived on the next street. My father was a cutter with arthritis in both hands, big red knuckles and swollen fingers so he didn't cut, and my mother was the one who went to work. She sold paper bags from a second-hand pushcart in Ellery Street. We didn't starve but nobody ate chicken unless we were sick or the chicken was. This was my first acquaintance with a lot of black people and I used to poke around on their poor block. I think I thought, brother, if there can be like this, what can't there be? I mean I caught an early idea what life was about. Anyway I met

Buster Wilson there. He used to play marbles by himself. I sat on the curb across the street, watching him shoot one marble lefty and the other one righty. The hand that won picked up the marbles. It wasn't so much of a game but he didn't ask me to come over. My idea was to be friendly, only he never encouraged, he discouraged. Why did I pick him out for a friend? Maybe because I had no others then, we were new in the neighborhood, from Manhattan. Also I liked his type. Buster did everything alone. He was a skinny kid and his brothers' clothes hung on him like worn-out potato sacks. He was a beanpole boy, about twelve, and I was then ten. His arms and legs were burnt out matchsticks. He always wore a brown wool sweater, one arm half unraveled, the other went down to the wrist. His long and narrow head had a white part cut straight in the short woolly hair, maybe with a ruler there, by his father, a barber but too drunk to stay a barber. In those days though I had little myself I was old enough to know who was better off, and the whole block of colored houses made me feel bad in the daylight. But I went there as much as I could because the street was full of life. In the night it looked different, it's hard to tell a cripple in the dark. Sometimes I was afraid to walk by the houses when they were dark and quiet. I was afraid there were people looking at me that I couldn't see. I liked it better when they had parties at night and everybody had a good time. The musicians played their banjos and saxophones and the houses shook with the music and laughing. The young girls, with their pretty dresses and ribbons in their hair, caught me in my throat when I saw them through the windows.

But with the parties came drinking and fights. Sundays were bad days after the Saturday night parties. I remember once that Buster's father, also long and loose, always wearing a dirty gray Homburg hat, chased another black man in the street with a half-inch chisel. The other one, maybe five feet high, lost his shoe and when they wrestled on the ground he was already bleeding through his suit, a thick red blood smearing the sidewalk. I was frightened by the blood and wanted to pour it back in the man who was bleeding from the chisel. On another time Buster's father was playing in a crap game with two big bouncy red dice, in the back of an alley between two middle houses. Then about six men started fist-fighting there, and they ran out of the alley and hit each other in the street. The neighbors, including children, came out and watched, everybody afraid but nobody moving to do anything. I saw the same thing near my store in Harlem, years later, a big crowd watching two men in the street, their breaths hanging in the air on a winter night, murdering each other with switch knives, but nobody moved to call a cop. I didn't either. Anyway, I was just a young kid but I still remember how the cops drove up in a police paddy wagon and broke up the fight by hitting everybody they could hit with big nightsticks. This was in the days before LaGuardia. Most of the fighters were knocked out cold, only one or two got away. Buster's father started to run back in his house but a cop ran after him and cracked him on his Homburg hat with a club, right on the front porch. Then the Negro men were lifted up by the cops, one at the arms and the other at the feet, and they heaved them in the paddy wagon. Buster's father hit the back of the wagon and fell, with his nose spouting very red blood, on top of three other men. I personally couldn't stand it, I was scared of the human race so I ran home, but I remember Buster watching without any expression in his eyes. I stole an extra fifteen cents from my mother's pocketbook and I ran back and asked Buster if he wanted to go to the movies. I would pay. He said yes. This was the first time he talked to me.

So we went more than once to the movies. But we never got to be friends. Maybe because it was a one-way proposition—from me to him. Which includes my invitations to go with me, my (poor mother's) movie money, Hershey chocolate bars, watermelon slices, even my best Nick Carter and Merriwell books that I spent hours picking up in the junk shops, and that he never gave me back. Once he let me go in his house to get a match so we could smoke some butts we found, but it smelled so heavy, so impossible, I died till I got out of there. What I saw in the way of furniture I won't mention—the best was falling apart in pieces. Maybe we went to the movies all together five or six matinees that spring and in the summertime, but when the shows were over he usually walked home by himself.

"Why don't you wait for me, Buster?" I said. "We're both going in the same direction."

But he was walking ahead and didn't hear me. Anyway he didn't answer.

One day when I wasn't expecting it he hit me in the teeth. I felt like crying but not because of the pain. I spit blood and said, "What did you hit me for? What did I do to you?"

"Because you a Jew bastard. Take your Jew movies and your Jew candy and shove them up your Jew ass."

And he ran away.

I thought to myself how was I to know he didn't like the movies. When I was a man I thought, you can't force it.

Years later, in the prime of my life, I met Mrs. Ornita Harris. She was standing by herself under an open umbrella at the bus stop, crosstown

110th, and I picked up her green glove that she had dropped on the wet sidewalk. It was in the end of November. Before I could ask her was it hers, she grabbed the glove out of my hand, closed her umbrella, and stepped in the bus. I got on right after her.

I was annoyed so I said, "If you'll pardon me, Miss, there's no law that you have to say thanks, but at least don't make a criminal out of me."

"Well, I'm sorry," she said, "but I don't like white men trying to do me favors."

I tipped my hat and that was that. In ten minutes I got off the bus but she was already gone.

Who expected to see her again but I did. She came into my store about a week later for a bottle of scotch.

"I would offer you a discount," I told her, "but I know you don't like a certain kind of a favor and I'm not looking for a slap in the face."

Then she recognized me and got a little embarrassed.

"I'm sorry I misunderstood you that day."

"So mistakes happen."

The result was she took the discount. I gave her a dollar off.

She used to come in about every two weeks for a fifth of Haig and Haig. Sometimes I waited on her, sometimes my helpers, Jimmy or Mason, also colored, but I said to give the discount. They both looked at me but I had nothing to be ashamed. In the spring when she came in we used to talk once in a while. She was a slim woman, dark but not the most dark, about thirty years I would say, also well built, with a combination nice legs and a good-size bosom that I like. Her face was pretty, with big eyes and high cheek bones, but lips a little thick and nose a little broad. Sometimes she didn't feel like talking, she paid for the bottle, less discount, and walked out. Her eyes were tired and she didn't look to me like a happy woman.

I found out her husband was once a window cleaner on the big buildings, but one day his safety belt broke and he fell fifteen stories. After the funeral she got a job as a manicurist in a Times Square barber shop. I told her I was a bachelor and lived with my mother in a small three-room apartment on West Eighty-third near Broadway. My mother had cancer, and Ornita said she was very sorry.

One night in July we went out together. How that happened I'm still not so sure. I guess I asked her and she didn't say no. Where do you go out with a Negro woman? We went to the Village. We had a good dinner and walked in Washington Square Park. It was a hot night. Nobody was surprised when they saw us, nobody looked at us like we were against the law. If they looked maybe they saw my new lightweight suit that I bought yesterday and my shiny bald spot when we walked under a lamp, also how pretty she was for a man of my type. We went in a movie on West Eighth Street. I didn't want to go in but she said she had heard about the picture. We went in like strangers and we came out like strangers. I wondered what was in her mind and I thought to myself, whatever is in there it's not a certain white man that I know. All night long we went together like we were chained. After the movie she wouldn't let me take her back to Harlem. When I put her in a taxi she asked me, "Why did we bother?"

For the steak, I wanted to say. Instead I said, "You're worth the bother."

"Thanks anyway."

Kiddo, I thought to myself after the taxi left, you just found out what's what, now the best thing is forget her.

It's easy to say. In August we went out the second time. That was the night she wore a purple dress and I thought to myself, my God, what colors. Who paints that picture paints a masterpiece. Everybody looked at us but I had pleasure. That night when she took off her dress it was in a furnished room I had the sense to rent a few days before. With my sick mother, I couldn't ask her to come to my apartment, and she didn't want me to go home with her where she lived with her brother's family on West 115th near Lenox Avenue. Under her purple dress she wore a black slip, and when she took that off she had white underwear. When she took off the white underwear she was black again. But I know where the next white was, if you want to call it white. And that was the night I think I fell in love with her, the first time in my life though I have liked one or two nice girls I used to go with when I was a boy. It was a serious proposition. I'm the kind of a man when I think of love I'm thinking of marriage. I guess that's why I am a bachelor.

That same week I had a holdup in my place, two big men—both black—with revolvers. One got excited when I rang open the cash register so he could take the money and he hit me over the ear with his gun. I stayed in the hospital a couple of weeks. Otherwise I was insured. Ornita came to see me. She sat on a chair without talking much. Finally I saw she was uncomfortable so I suggested she ought to go home.

"I'm sorry it happened," she said.

"Don't talk like it's your fault."

When I got out of the hospital my mother was dead. She was a wonderful person. My father died when I was thirteen and all by herself she kept the family alive and together. I sat shive for a week and remembered how she sold paper bags on her pushcart. I remembered her life and what she tried to teach me. Nathan, she said, if you ever forget you are a Jew a goy will remind you. Mama, I said, rest in peace on this subject. But if I do something you don't like, remember, on earth it's harder than where you are. Then when my week of mourning was finished, one night I said, "Ornita, let's get married. We're both honest people and if you love me like I love you it won't be such a bad time. If you don't like New York I'll sell out here and we'll move someplace else. Maybe to San Francisco where nobody knows us. I was there for a week in the Second War and I saw white and colored living together."

"Nat," she answered me, "I like you but I'd be afraid. My husband woulda killed me."

"Your husband is dead."

"Not in my memory."

"In that case I'll wait."

"Do you know what it'd be like—I mean the life we could expect?"

"Ornita," I said, "I'm the kind of a man, if he picks his own way of life he's satisfied."

"What about children? Were you looking forward to half-Jewish polka dots?"

"I was looking forward to children."

"I can't," she said.

Can't is can't. I saw she was afraid and the best thing was not to push. Sometimes when we met she was so nervous that whatever we did she couldn't enjoy it. At the same time I still thought I had a chance. We were together more and more. I got rid of my furnished room and she came to my apartment—I gave away Mama's bed and bought a new one. She stayed with me all day on Sundays. When she wasn't so nervous she was affectionate, and if I know what love is, I had it. We went out a couple of times a week, the same way—usually I met her in Times Square and sent her home in a taxi, but I talked more about marriage and she talked less against it. One night she told me she was still trying to convince herself but she was almost convinced. I took an inventory of my liquor stock so I could put the store up for sale.

Ornita knew what I was doing. One day she quit her job, the next day she took it back. She also went away a week to visit her sister in Philadelphia for a little rest. She came back tired but said maybe. Maybe is maybe so I'll wait. The way she said it it was closer to yes. That was the winter two years ago. When she was in Philadelphia I called up a friend of mine from the Army, now CPA, and told him I would appreciate an invitation for an evening. He knew why. His wife said yes right away. When Ornita came back we went there. The wife made a fine dinner. It wasn't a bad time and they told us to come again. Ornita had a few drinks. She looked relaxed, wonderful. Later, because of a twenty-four hour taxi strike I had to take her home on the subway. When we got to the 116th Street station she told me to stay on the train, and she would walk the couple of blocks to her house. I didn't like a woman walking alone on the streets at that time of the night. She said she never had any trouble but I insisted nothing doing. I said I would walk to her stoop with her and when she went upstairs I would go back to the subway.

On the way there, on 115th in the middle of the block before Lenox, we were stopped by three men—maybe they were boys. One had a black hat with a half-inch brim, one a green cloth hat, and the third wore a black leather cap. The green hat was wearing a short coat and the other two had long ones. It was under a street light but the leather cap snapped a six-inch switchblade open in the light.

"What you doin' with this white son of a bitch?" he said to Ornita.

"I'm minding my own business," she answered him, "and I wish you would too."

"Boys," I said, "we're all brothers. I'm a reliable merchant in the neighborhood. This young lady is my dear friend. We don't want any trouble. Please let us pass."

"You talk like a Jew landlord," said the green hat. "Fifty a week for a single room."

"No charge fo' the rats," said the half-inch brim.

"Believe me, I'm no landlord. My store is 'Nathan's Liquors' between Hundred Tenth and Eleventh. I also have two colored clerks, Mason and Jimmy, and they will tell you I pay good wages as well as I give discounts to certain customers."

"Shut your mouth, Jewboy," said the leather cap, and he moved the knife back and forth in front of my coat button. "No more black pussy for you."

"Speak with respect about this lady, please."

I got slapped on my mouth.

"That ain't no lady," said the long face in the half-inch brim, "that's black pussy. She deserve to have evvy bit of her hair shave off. How you like to have evvy bit of your hair shave off, black pussy?"

"Please leave me and this gentleman alone or I'm gonna scream long and loud. That's my house three doors down."

They slapped her. I never heard such a scream. Like her husband was falling fifteen stories.

I hit the one that slapped her and the next I knew I was lying in the gutter with a pain in my head. I thought, goodbye, Nat, they'll stab me for sure, but all they did was take my wallet and run in three different directions.

Ornita walked back with me to the subway and she wouldn't let me go home with her again.

"Just get home safely."

She looked terrible. Her face was gray and I still remembered her scream. It was a terrible winter night, very cold February, and it took me an hour and ten minutes to get home. I felt bad for leaving her but what could I do?

We had a date downtown the next night but she didn't show up, the first time.

In the morning I called her in her place of business.

"For God's sake, Ornita, if we got married and moved away we wouldn't have that kind of trouble that we had. We wouldn't come in that neighborhood any more."

"Yes, we would. I have family there and don't want to move anyplace else. The truth of it is I can't marry you, Nat. I got troubles enough of my own."

"I coulda sworn you love me."

"Maybe I do but I can't marry you."

"For God's sake, why?"

"I got enough trouble of my own."

I went that night in a cab to her brother's house to see her. He was a quiet man with a thin mustache. "She gone," he said, "left for a long visit to some close relatives in the South. She said to tell you she appreciate your intentions but didn't think it will work out."

"Thank you kindly," I said.

Don't ask me how I got home.

Once on Eighth Avenue, a couple of blocks from my store, I saw a blind man with a white cane tapping on the sidewalk. I figured we were going in the same direction so I took his arm.

"I can tell you're white," he said.

A heavy colored woman with a full shopping bag rushed after us.

"Never mind," she said, "I know where he live."

She pushed me with her shoulder and I hurt my leg on the fire hydrant.

That's how it is. I give my heart and they kick me in my teeth.

"Charity Sweetness—you hear me?—come out of that goddamn toilet!"

A COMPLEX
BLACK-AND-WHITE MATTER

Merrill Maguire Skaggs

Bernard Malamud's "Black Is My Favorite Color" is, on the surface, a sketch about the frustrations of a white man who tries to befriend Negroes. For the protagonist of this tale of woe, Malamud chose a character type out of the Yiddish literary tradition—the schlemiel. Irving Howe defines the schlemiel as "the kind of person who just cannot do anything right. He means well; his heart may be warm; he is even capable . . . of feeling great love for his fellow men. But constantly he acts out the Yiddish proverb: . . . [he] lands on his back and bruises his nose." Malamud's Nathan Lime is a schlemiel; as he himself says, "I got the idea . . . that I had some kind of a talent, though maybe it's the kind where you have a marvelous idea now and then but in the end what do they come to?" Transcending the stereotyped outlines of the pratfall-prone schlemiel, however, Nat Lime becomes the agent through which Malamud dramatizes ambivalent racial attitudes, charity's inadequacy as a basis for friendship, and the seemingly insoluble problem of human isolation.

As in all good stories, the method by which this tale is told reflects the writer's attitude toward his subject matter; indeed, the special way Nat Lime reviews his personal history provides an important clue to what Malamud is attempting. Telling a story in the first person normally makes it appear more believable. The first-person narrator implicitly says, "Although this series of events may appear improbable, I saw or experienced them, and I assure you they occurred." But in this story, Malamud makes use of a narrator who is not entirely reliable, whose words must be inspected quite closely if the reader is to deduce "the truth" hiding behind his statements. Such a technique has many variations,[1] for the narrator may mislead either inadvertently or deliberately, through malice, defensiveness, or simply through his own inadequate understanding of events. If he is

[1] Compare, for example, Edgar Allan Poe's "The Cask of Amontillado," Eudora Welty's "Why I Live at the P. O.," Ring Lardner's "You Know Me Al," or Muriel Spark's "You Should Have Seen the Mess."

discussing himself, he may speak with less than total accuracy either because he does not wish the reader to discover his personal weaknesses, or because he does not understand himself as well as an objective reader-observer might. Using an unreliable narrator is hazardous, since the author must trust fate to provide him with readers perceptive enough to recognize the unreliability. But such a narrator provides exceptionally good opportunities for a special kind of ironic effect. The reader who is aware of the narrator's unreliability has a doubleness of vision: Simultaneously, he sees things as an interested party would and as they really are. Thus any story told by an unreliable narrator implicitly comments on human fallibility and on the incompleteness of human understanding.

Of course, a reader may ask how he can know for sure whether to believe exactly what the narrator says, or whether to question what he is told. Since the author has total control over the story, the reader may assume that any series of statements, incidents, or opinions, all of which serve to make him question the narrator's judgment or to undermine trust in the narrator's character, are deliberately meant to create suspicions about the total reliability of what the narrator says.

In "Black Is My Favorite Color," Nat Lime appears in every way sincere, earnest, and full of good intentions. We never have reason to suspect that he is deliberately hedging—telling only part of the facts he remembers. Indeed, the unfavorable light Nat casts on himself by much of what he says convinces us that he is not holding back unflattering information. He seems to be pouring out his heart, as he would say, and with innocent trust baring his past for our inspection. We realize that he is an unreliable narrator, however, when we see that Malamud deliberately undermines our confidence in Nat's sensitivity and forces us to assume that we will see deeper into Nat's problems than Nat can. That is, while we accept the facts Nat gives us (having no other facts available), we question Nat's interpretations of those facts. Malamud forces us to assume the existence of a "truth" deeper than Nat can articulate for us.

The most obvious way in which Malamud undermines confidence in Nat's understanding is by having him speak in clichés: "black is my favorite color"; "I was feeling not so hot"; "who wants everybody to be the same"; "it's a strange world"; and "nobody ate chicken unless we were sick or the chicken was," the last a standard vaudeville joke. Nat is also prone to self-contradiction. When he notes that the only human color is the color of blood, and then immediately adds, "I like a black person, if not because he's black, then because I'm white," he contradicts himself without realizing it; for he immediately begins discussing humans in terms of two colors, neither of which is the color of blood. Similarly, when Nat says first that Buster's street "was full of life," then remarks, "In the night it looked different [and better], it's hard to tell a cripple in the dark," he contradicts himself by first associating the street with liveliness, then comparing it to a cripple. Having just expressed his preference for the street at night, Nat admits that the dark, quiet houses frightened him, then adds that what he actually remembers fondly are the Saturday night parties. But the parties immediately remind him of fights and bloodshed. Thus Nat's description of the colored block goes through five or six steps, each of which contradicts the preceding one.

Nat's holding contradictory attitudes simultaneously constitutes an important (and certainly a familiarly human) facet of his personality. But his contradictory reactions extend beyond the Negro race and the Negro neighborhood to individual Negroes as well. In his descriptions of Ornita and Charity Sweetness, for example, Nat uses words or phrases that to him clearly have negative associations—such as "flat body, frizzy hair," or "lips a little thick and nose a little broad"—and then combines such negative evaluations with high praise, as in "a quiet face that the light shines out of," or "a combination nice legs and a good-size bosom that I like." In such ambivalent responses to others, Nat is certainly not unlike most people. It is necessary to remember that he maintains such contradictions, however, because Malamud calls attention to them so frequently. Clearly they have some bearing on why Negroes react to Nat as they do.

In addition to these revelations of Nat's rather unanalytic mind, Malamud also has Nat speak in the ungrammatical, Yiddish-influenced idioms of New York—such as "I got an eye for color. I appreciate"; "The first time Charity Sweetness came in to clean, a little more than a year and a half, I made the mistake to ask her"—and in rambling, run-on sentences—as in "That's how it goes only don't get the idea of ghettoes"; "If they knew what was in my heart towards them, but how can you tell that to anybody nowadays?" The literary effect of any non-standard idiom or dialect, even if it is only mildly aberrant, is always to make the reader, however fondly he views the speaker, consider himself more educated or socially aware than that speaker.

Nat also arouses our skepticism about his emotional maturity, as when he refers so quickly to his Mama, then identifies himself as a forty-four-year-old bachelor. But he most dramatically illustrates his inadequate emotional grasp of a situation after he repeats Buster Wilson's taunt, "Take your Jew movies and your Jew candy and shove them up your Jew ass," and then explains, "how was I to know he didn't like the movies." Though none of these—the clichés, the contradictions, the ungrammatical idioms, the rambling sentences, the obtuseness—might be considered significant if taken alone, their cumulative effect is to suggest that Nat is far too limited to be a trustworthy authority, even on the basic significance of his own experiences. Indeed, the esthetic effect of Malamud's narrative technique beautifully illustrates one part of Nat's story—his bad luck at communicating with others. And the bad luck extends even to his communication with the reader: The reader, as do the Negroes, begins eventually to assume that there is more to Nat's behavior than Nat, if he were aware enough to make a choice, would probably like him to think. For Nat's repeated failures to communicate appear, by the end of the story, to be the direct results of his inability to analyze motives, and therefore to understand others' responses to him.

In explaining why he repeatedly attempts to befriend colored people despite their rejection of him, Nat asserts simply, "I'm drawn to them." Nat himself appears content with this opaque explanation, but his narrative points to less mysterious reasons for the attraction he feels. In his childhood, he searched out Buster Wilson, he tells us, because he had no other friends in the neighborhood, because he liked Buster's type, and because of his genuine desire to ameliorate the humiliation he had seen Buster experience. He also explains why he feels he can help Buster: "In those days though I had little myself I was old enough to know who was better off, and the whole block of colored houses made me feel bad in the daylight." Nat alludes to a final reason when he mentions the pleasure of wandering down Buster's street during the Saturday night parties, when "the musicians played their banjoes and saxophones and the houses shook with the music and laughing." Here then are the elements that elicited Nat's first ill-rewarded attempt to make contact with a Negro: Nat's own friendlessness, Nat's identification with Buster because "Buster did everything alone," Nat's recognition that Buster needs friends as badly as he, Nat's association of a kind of happiness with Negroes, and Nat's confidence that even in his poverty he can furnish Buster with something Buster needs.

These same factors appear to operate at other stages of Nat's life. In his maturity, Nat is apparently still lonely. The only other whites mentioned in the story are his parents, one or two girls he once dated in high school, and an army buddy whose wife invites Ornita and him for dinner. Nat also seems to assume that he is personally unattractive. He describes himself as "forty-four, a bachelor with a daily growing bald spot on the back of my head, and I could lose frankly fifteen pounds," and he is pleased when people notice him walking with Ornita. He hopes they observe "how pretty she was for a man of my type." Implicitly, then, Nat tells us that he counts on few personal assets to offer others with whom he would normally become intimate.

This feeling of personal inadequacy apparently leads Nat to search for friends among those who he assumes (in this case, mistakenly) will have to accept him, being even less fortunate than he. To assure his acceptance, he relies on generosity and good manners, both of which he always tries to exhibit. He approaches Buster with movie money after witnessing the brutal treatment Buster's father receives from the New York police. His acquaintance with Ornita begins with a chivalrous gesture, and his last beating on the Harlem streets occurs when he insists on a gentleman's duty to see his lady safely home. Although his initial attraction to a Negro may have sprung from his viewing Buster as a loner and outsider like himself, Nat nevertheless tries always to express his affection as bounteously as he can. Why then do his efforts always fail, and why can he identify failure as his "fate with colored people"? The answer provides a key to the racial attitudes dramatized in the story.

Nat dooms himself continually to be rejected despite his overtures of friendship when he overlooks one fact: A patronizing attitude is inherent in his kind of generosity, which is actually a kind of charity. Indeed, it is partly the recognition that someone might need the patronage of so destitute a waif as himself that first drives Nat to try befriending Buster Wilson. And when Buster, and later Ornita, accepts the favors Nat offers, each stands to lose self-respect by becoming an object of charity. Both seem to recognize this fact. Buster refuses to walk home from the movies with Nat, apparently as a public denial that he has agreed to be Nat's guest. The first thing Ornita says to Nat is "I don't like white men trying to do me favors." Nat actually puts his finger on the explanation for Buster's (and Charity's and Ornita's) behavior when he says, "It was a one-way proposition—from me to him." The point is not that Nat deceives himself about the intensity of his feeling for Negroes—there is no reason to doubt his love—but that he never searches beyond the emotion to understand that it originates in a need to be charitable, and therefore to be morally, socially, or economically superior.

Thus Nat always offends in two ways the Negroes he tries to make friends with. First, he insists on doing all the giving. It never occurs to him to take. The one time he enters Buster Wilson's house to get a match, for example, he "died till [he] got out of there." Even when he "takes" Ornita sexually, he immediately decides that he loves her, so that the sexual relationship itself becomes another situation in which he gives more than he receives. Second, and more important, is that in order to keep his own identity firmly established, Nat always thinks of the object of his friendship first as a black, and only later as an individual. Throughout the story, he reveals his bias—though it is admittedly a prejudice *toward* and not *against* —by identifying every Negro he encounters by race. He speaks of his "dealings with Negro people," for example, as if such dealings were different from dealings with people in general. Significantly, he says, "I like a black person if not because he's black, then because I'm white." Nat's descriptions of Ornita emphasize her Negroid lips and nose along with her "better" features, and her racial identity dominates his plans for their first date. "Where do you go out with a Negro woman?" he asks before they meet. As he wonders what is in her mind after they emerge from the movie, he thinks to himself, "whatever is in there it's not a certain white man that I know." Though his love for Ornita is undoubtedly genuine, Nat is unable to escape thinking automatically in racial terms, even during his proposal of marriage: "We'll move someplace else. Maybe to San Francisco. . . . I was there for a week in the Second War and I saw white and colored living together." Indeed, in his encounter with the three Harlem punks, it is Nat's attempt to relate to them *in terms of race* that enrages them: He first lists Negro employees and customers whom he treats well, and then refers to his clerks by their first names, thus indulging in a familiar means of white condescension—the failure to address Negroes by the respectful title of *Mister*. And at the end of the story, he is still categorizing Negroes as a group, thus denying individual differences, when he says, "I give my heart and they kick me in my teeth." From first to last, Nat thinks of his Negro acquaintances always as *they*, never as *we*.

Negroes avoid friendship with Nat, not because they fail to read him correctly, but rather because they sense exactly what is in his heart. They therefore reject a friendship based on their racial rather than individual identities. Further, they avoid a relationship that stems from a love so charitable that the loving member does all the giving, and they must do all the receiving. Such a relationship actually prohibits genuine equality, for all the nobility remains on one side. It is the desire to strip Nat of his sense of personal nobility, after all, that inspires the most anti-Semitic attacks he experiences, both in Williamsburg and in Harlem. Nat's efforts get him nowhere because he makes those efforts in terms of charity. In the past, we understand, he has tried a gentle charity; but with symbolic appropriateness, he ends the story by profanely ordering Charity to "come out of that goddamn toilet!"

At its most complex level, however, "Black Is My Favorite Color" treats a subject more universal than the relationship between New York's Jews and Negroes, the ingratitude with which charitable acts are sometimes met, or the unconscious prejudices that direct human behavior. It rises above such concerns to confront the more fundamental problem of human isolation, of man's separation from his fellows. The story opens with a very concrete image of separation, for Charity Sweetness has chosen to shut herself in the bathroom, where her privacy is presumably inviolable. To eat in Nat Lime's kitchen would be to risk the chance of having to deal with him on a friendly or human basis—that is, as anything other than an employer. Though Nat is eager to be friendly (for he fails to see that his friendship would make working for him seem undesirably complex to a woman who is already satisfied with the community surrounding Father Divine), his efforts have resulted only in widening the gulf between him and his servant. Now Charity Sweetness will not eat in his kitchen at all, whether he is there or not. His being deliberately excluded from her company makes Nat think of ghettoes, in which some people are forcefully separated from others, but he aptly informs the reader, "If there's a ghetto I'm the one that's in it." Certainly it is Nat who is distressed by his inability to climb racial barriers, not Charity. Charity's deliberate decision to eat separately also reminds Nat of Buster Wilson from Williamsburg, who preferred playing marbles left hand against right hand to playing with Nat Lime, and preferred hunger and boredom to Nat's candy and movies. Buster's name evokes in turn the memory of young Nat, once again isolated and alone, who wandered down the Negro block on Saturday nights, wistfully looking through windows (another image of separation) at the musicians, laughing party guests, and pretty girls. The pretty girls whose appearance once caught at Nat's throat remained as inaccessible to him as he felt Ornita was on their first trip to the movies, when they "went in like strangers and . . . came out like strangers." Since this story follows the structural pattern of most Malamud tales, Nat's brief period of hope that he can attain a cherished goal—that his marriage to Ornita will end his separation—dissolves into the futility he feels when Ornita breaks their engagement, leaving him more isolated than ever.

Because Nat Lime is drawn so expertly in Malamud's story, his unsuccessful attempts to communicate with others begin to resemble a general human predicament. By the end of the story Nat's many references to blackness come metaphorically to stand for any chasm separating men from one another. Thus blackness finally acts as a metaphor for the many forces—of which race is only one—that prevent two individuals from loving what is in each other's heart. Our suspicion that Nat Lime's human isolation is no more intense than that of most other men makes the story seem even sadder. For if the humanly fallible, short-sighted, but well-meaning Nathan Lime cannot break out of his ghetto, then what hope indeed is there for those of us with less eager compassion?

QUESTIONS

Black Is My Favorite Color

POINT OF VIEW   1. Frequently, the first-person narrator provides an important source of humor in otherwise serious stories. Find as many instances of comedy as you can in "Black Is My Favorite Color." Then discuss the relation between point of view and humor in this story.   2. As discussed in the General Introduction (pp. 20–22), the unreliable narrator inevitably causes the reader to participate in the story by forcing the reader to assess the "facts" for himself. Analyze your reaction as a reader to "Black Is My Favorite Color." Did you find that you were actively engaged in the story by attempting to "interpret" Nat? Discuss.

CHARACTERS   3. Several times, Nat mentions that, as a boy, he was afraid of the Negroes he encountered and of the Negro neighborhood. Analyze the relationship between Nat's friendliness toward Negroes and his fear.   4. Discuss the element of anti-Semitism in Nat's encounters with Negroes.   5. Charity Sweetness is both an enigmatic and emblematic character. Explain her relation to the theme of the story.

PLOT   6. Nat Lime's mother tells her son that if he forgets that he is a Jew, a goy will remind him. Does a Christian (or Christians) in fact serve as a reminder? If so, who and where?   7. Examine Malamud's rhetorical devices for moving from present to past action. Why is understanding Nat's past so important to the meaning of this story?   8. One critic comments that Malamud's stories follow a consistent form: First, a situation is defined; second, numerous obstacles are presented that prevent the situation from being resolved happily; third, hope is allowed to flare briefly; and fourth, all hope is quelled as a result of an irreversible and disastrous resolution. Is this a satisfactory description of the plot of "Black Is My Favorite Color"? Explain.

SETTING 9. Malamud has set the story in Brooklyn and Harlem, locations that most readers know something about. He has endowed the setting with additional "reality" through careful description of physical details. Show how Nat's boyhood neighborhood is made "real"—even tangible—to us.

STYLE 10. In an interview (*Harper's*, March 1967), Ralph Ellison observed that Jewish writers in America "had to discover that the Jewish American idiom would lend a whole new dimension to the American language." Comment on Malamud's use of this idiom in his creation of character and situation in "Black Is My Favorite Color."

TONE 11. Irony provides a means not only of indicating the complexity of a situation but of evaluating the subject matter. Show how irony influences and shapes your understanding of the meaning of this story. 12. It is possible to argue that the implied author that we sense beyond Nat Lime is generous, deeply committed to his characters, compassionate, and yet aware of the terrible dilemma in which they find themselves. What aspects of the story lend credibility to such a statement? Discuss.

A Complex Black-and-White Matter

FOCUS 1. In the introductory paragraph, the essayist makes very clear not only what the focus of the essay is, but also what it is not. Explain, using evidence from the essay to support your observation.

ORGANIZATION 2. Show how the essay moves from specific considerations (matters of technique, extended discussion of Nat as a person, and so forth) to general, even universal ones.

USING THE EVIDENCE 3. What evidence from the story is cited to support the contention that "Nat Lime appears in every way sincere, earnest, and full of good intentions"? 4. What evidence is cited to support the observation that Malamud wishes us to view Nat as an unreliable narrator? 5. The essay states that Nat's "holding contradictory attitudes simultaneously" is partly responsible for Negroes reacting to Nat as they do. What evidence is cited as illustration of Nat's contradictory attitudes? 6. Cite some of the evidence given to support the statement that "Nat always thinks of the object of his friendship first as a black, and only later as an individual." 7. What evidence from the story is used to support the claim that Nat's "charity" toward Negroes "prohibits genuine equality, for all the nobility remains on one side"?

STYLE   8. What rhetorical considerations led the essayist to supply a rather long definition of schlemiel in the first paragraph?   9. In the second and third paragraphs, the essayist supplies another, even longer definition of a term: that of the unreliable narrator. What is the rhetorical effect of discussing this aspect of narrative technique at this point in the essay?

MAKING LITERARY JUDGMENTS   10. Explain the critical assumptions that permit the essayist to make the following statement: "Because Nat Lime is drawn so expertly in Malamud's story, his unsuccessful attempts to communicate with others begin to resemble a general human predicament."   11. What critical assumptions are behind the statement, "As in all good stories, the method by which this tale is told reflects the writer's attitude toward his subject matter"?   12. Concerning Nat's Yiddish-American dialect, the essayist states, "The literary effect of any non-standard idiom or dialect, even if it is only mildly aberrant, is always to make the reader, however fondly he views the speaker, consider himself more educated or socially aware than that speaker." Do you agree with this statement in regard to "Black Is My Favorite Color"? to other literary works? Explain.

THE MAGIC BARREL

Not long ago there lived in uptown New York, in a small, almost meager room, though crowded with books, Leo Finkle, a rabbinical student in the Yeshivah University. Finkle, after six years of study, was to be ordained in June and had been advised by an acquaintance that he might find it easier to win himself a congregation if he were married. Since he had no present prospects of marriage, after two tormented days of turning it over in his mind, he called in Pinye Salzman, a marriage broker whose two-line advertisement he had read in the *Forward*.

The matchmaker appeared one night out of the dark fourth-floor hallway of the graystone rooming house where Finkle lived, grasping a black, strapped portfolio that had been worn thin with use. Salzman, who had been long in the business, was of slight but dignified build, wearing an old hat, and an overcoat too short and tight for him. He smelled frankly of fish, which he loved to eat, and although he was missing a few teeth, his presence was not displeasing, because of an amiable manner curiously contrasted with mournful eyes. His voice, his lips, his wisp of beard, his bony fingers were animated, but give him a moment of repose and his mild blue eyes revealed a depth of sadness, a characteristic that put Leo a little at ease although the situation, for him, was inherently tense.

He at once informed Salzman why he had asked him to come, explaining that his home was in Cleveland, and that but for his parents, who had married comparatively late in life, he was alone in the world. He had for six years devoted himself almost entirely to his studies, as a result of which, understandably, he had found himself without time for a social life and the company of young women. Therefore he thought it the better part of trial and error—of embarrassing fumbling—to call in an experienced person to advise him on these matters. He remarked in passing that the function of the marriage broker was ancient and honorable, highly approved in the Jewish community, because it made practical the necessary without hindering joy. Moreover, his own parents had been brought together by a matchmaker. They had made, if not a financially profitable marriage—since neither had possessed any worldly goods to speak of—at least a successful one in the sense of their everlasting devotion to each other. Salzman listened in embarrassed surprise, sensing a sort of apology. Later, however, he experienced a glow of pride in his work, an emotion that had left him years ago, and he heartily approved of Finkle.

The two went to their business. Leo had led Salzman to the only clear place in the room, a table near a window that overlooked the lamp-lit city. He seated himself at the matchmaker's side but facing him, attempting by an act of will to suppress the unpleasant tickle in his throat. Salzman eagerly unstrapped his portfolio and removed a loose rubber band from a thin packet of much-handled cards. As he flipped through them, a gesture and sound that physically hurt Leo, the student pretended not to see and gazed steadfastly out the window. Although it was still February, winter was on its last legs, signs of which he had for the first time in years begun to notice. He now observed the round white moon, moving high in the sky through a cloud menagerie, and watched with half-open mouth as it penetrated a huge hen, and dropped out of her like an egg laying itself. Salzman, though pretending through eyeglasses he had just slipped on to be engaged in scanning the writing on the cards, stole occasional glances at the young man's distinguished face, noting with pleasure the long, severe scholar's nose, brown eyes heavy with learning, sensitive yet ascetic lips, and a certain, almost hollow quality of the dark cheeks. He gazed around at shelves upon shelves of books and let out a soft, contented sigh.

When Leo's eyes fell upon the cards, he counted six spread out in Salzman's hand.

"So few?" he asked in disappointment.

"You wouldn't believe me how much cards I got in my office," Salzman replied. "The drawers are already filled to the top, so I keep them now in a barrel, but is every girl good for a new rabbi?"

Leo blushed at this, regretting all he had revealed of himself in a curriculum vitae he had sent to Salzman. He had thought it best to acquaint him with his strict standards and specifications, but in having done so, felt he had told the marriage broker more than was absolutely necessary.

He hesitantly inquired, "Do you keep photographs of your clients on file?"

"First comes family, amount of dowry, also what kind promises," Salzman replied, unbuttoning his tight coat and settling himself in the chair. "After comes pictures, rabbi."

"Call me Mr. Finkle. I'm not yet a rabbi."

Salzman said he would, but instead called him doctor, which he changed to rabbi when Leo was not listening too attentively.

Salzman adjusted his horn-rimmed spectacles, gently cleared his throat and read in an eager voice the contents of the top card:

"Sophie P. Twenty four year. Widow one year. No children. Educated high school and two years college. Father promises eight thousand dollars. Has wonderful wholesale business. Also real estate. On the mother's side comes teachers, also one actor. Well known on Second Avenue."

Leo gazed up in surprise. "Did you say a widow?"

"A widow don't mean spoiled, rabbi. She lived with her husband maybe four months. He was a sick boy she made a mistake to marry him."

"Marrying a widow has never entered my mind."

"This is because you have no experience. A widow, especially if she is young and healthy like this girl, is a wonderful person to marry. She will be thankful to you the rest of her life. Believe me, if I was looking now for a bride, I would marry a widow."

Leo reflected, then shook his head.

Salzman hunched his shoulders in an almost imperceptible gesture of disappointment. He placed the card down on the wooden table and began to read another:

"Lily H. High school teacher. Regular. Not a substitute. Has savings and new Dodge car. Lived in Paris one year. Father is successful dentist thirty-five years. Interested in professional man. Well Americanized family. Wonderful opportunity.

"I knew her personally," said Salzman. "I wish you could see this girl. She is a doll. Also very intelligent. All day you could talk to her about books and theyater and what not. She also knows current events."

"I don't believe you mentioned her age?"

"Her age?" Salzman said, raising his brows. "Her age is thirty-two years."

Leo said after a while, "I'm afraid that seems a little too old."

Salzman let out a laugh. "So how old are you, rabbi?"

"Twenty-seven."

"So what is the difference, tell me, between twenty-seven and thirty-two? My own wife is seven years older than me. So what did I suffer?—Nothing. If Rothschild's a daughter wants to marry you, would you say on account her age, no?"

"Yes," Leo said dryly.

Salzman shook off the no in the yes. "Five years don't mean a thing. I give you my word that when you will live with her for one week you will forget her age. What does it mean five years—that she lived more and knows more than somebody who is younger? On this girl, God bless her, years are not wasted. Each one that it comes makes better the bargain."

"What subject does she teach in high school?"

"Languages. If you heard the way she speaks French, you will think it is music. I am in the business twenty-five years, and I recommend her with my whole heart. Believe me, I know what I'm talking, rabbi."

"What's on the next card?" Leo said abruptly.

Salzman reluctantly turned up the third card:

"Ruth K. Nineteen years. Honor student. Father offers thirteen thousand cash to the right bridegroom. He is a medical doctor. Stomach specialist with marvelous practice. Brother in law owns own garment business. Particular people."

Salzman looked as if he had read his trump card.

"Did you say nineteen?" Leo asked with interest.

"On the dot."

"Is she attractive?" He blushed. "Pretty?"

Salzman kissed his finger tips. "A little doll. On this I give you my word. Let me call the father tonight and you will see what means pretty."

But Leo was troubled. "You're sure she's that young?"

"This I am positive. The father will show you the birth certificate."

"Are you positive there isn't something wrong with her?" Leo insisted.

"Who says there is wrong?"

"I don't understand why an American girl her age should go to a marriage broker."

A smile spread over Salzman's face.

"So for the same reason you went, she comes."

Leo flushed. "I am pressed for time."

Salzman, realizing he had been tactless, quickly explained. "The father came, not her. He wants she should have the best, so he looks around himself. When we will locate the right boy he will introduce him and encourage. This makes a better marriage than if a young girl without experience takes for herself. I don't have to tell you this."

"But don't you think this young girl believes in love?" Leo spoke uneasily.

Salzman was about to gaffaw but caught himself and said soberly, "Love comes with the right person, not before."

Leo parted dry lips but did not speak. Noticing that Salzman had snatched a glance at the next card, he cleverly asked, "How is her health?"

"Perfect," Salzman said, breathing with difficulty. "Of course, she is a little lame on her right foot from an auto accident that it happened to her when she was twelve years, but nobody notices on account she is so brilliant and also beautiful."

Leo got up heavily and went to the window. He felt curiously bitter and upbraided himself for having called in the marriage broker. Finally, he shook his head.

"Why not?" Salzman persisted, the pitch of his voice rising.

"Because I detest stomach specialists."

"So what do you care what is his business? After you marry her do you need him? Who says he must come every Friday night in your house?"

Ashamed of the way the talk was going, Leo dismissed Salzman, who went home with heavy, melancholy eyes.

Though he had felt only relief at the marriage broker's departure, Leo was in low spirits the next day. He explained it as arising from Salzman's failure to produce a suitable bride for him. He did not care for his type of clientele. But when Leo found himself hesitating whether to seek out another matchmaker, one more polished than Pinye, he wondered if it could be—his protestations to the contrary, and although he honored his father and mother—that he did not, in essence, care for the matchmaking institution? This thought he quickly put out of mind yet found himself still upset. All day he ran around in the woods—missed an important appointment, forgot to give out his laundry, walked out of a Broadway cafeteria without paying and had to run back with the ticket in his hand; had even not recognized his landlady in the street when she passed with a friend and courteously called out, "A good evening to you, Doctor Finkle." By nightfall, however, he had regained sufficient calm to sink his nose into a book and there found peace from his thoughts.

Almost at once there came a knock on the door. Before Leo could say enter, Salzman, commercial cupid, was standing in the room. His face was gray and meager, his expression hungry, and he looked as if he would expire on his feet. Yet the marriage broker managed, by some trick of the muscles, to display a broad smile.

"So good evening. I am invited?"

Leo nodded, disturbed to see him again, yet unwilling to ask the man to leave.

Beaming still, Salzman laid his portfolio on the table. "Rabbi, I got for you tonight good news."

"I've asked you not to call me rabbi. I'm still a student."

"Your worries are finished. I have for you a first-class bride."

"Leave me in peace concerning this subject." Leo pretended lack of interest.

"The world will dance at your wedding."

"Please, Mr. Salzman, no more."

"But first must come back my strength," Salzman said weakly. He fumbled with the portfolio straps and took out of the leather case an oily paper bag, from which he extracted a hard, seeded roll and a small, smoked white fish. With a quick motion of his hand he stripped the fish out of its skin and began ravenously to chew. "All day in a rush," he muttered.

Leo watched him eat.

"A sliced tomato you have maybe?" Salzman hesitantly inquired.

"No."

The marriage broker shut his eyes and ate. When he had finished he carefully cleaned up the crumbs and rolled up the remains of the fish, in the paper bag. His spectacled eyes roamed the room until he discovered, amid some piles of books, a one-burner gas stove. Lifting his hat he humbly asked, "A glass tea you got, rabbi?"

Conscience-stricken, Leo rose and brewed the tea. He served it with a chunk of lemon and two cubes of lump sugar, delighting Salzman.

After he had drunk his tea, Salzman's strength and good spirits were restored.

"So tell me, rabbi," he said amiably, "you considered some more the three clients I mentioned yesterday?"

"There was no need to consider."

"Why not?"

"None of them suits me."

"What then suits you?"

Leo let it pass because he could give only a confused answer.

Without waiting for a reply, Salzman asked, "You remember this girl I talked to you—the high school teacher?"

"Age thirty-two?"

But, surprisingly, Salzman's face lit in a smile. "Age twenty-nine."

Leo shot him a look. "Reduced from thirty-two?"

"A mistake," Salzman avowed. "I talked today with the dentist. He took me to his safety deposit box and showed me the birth certificate. She was twenty-nine years last August. They made her a party in the mountains where she went for her vacation. When her father spoke to me the first time I forgot to write the age and I told you thirty-two, but now I remember this was a different client, a widow."

"The same one you told me about? I thought she was twenty-four?"

"A different. Am I responsible that the world is filled with widows?"

"No, but I'm not interested in them, nor for that matter, in school teachers."

Salzman pulled his clasped hands to his breast. Looking at the ceiling he devoutly exclaimed, "Yiddishe kinder, what can I say to somebody that he is not interested in high school teachers? So what then you are interested?"

Leo flushed but controlled himself.

"In what else will you be interested," Salzman went on, "if you not interested in this fine girl that she speaks four languages and has personally in the bank ten thousand dollars? Also her father guarantees further twelve thousand. Also she has a new car, wonderful clothes, talks on all subjects, and she will give you a first-class home and children. How near do we come in our life to paradise?"

"If she's so wonderful, why wasn't she married ten years ago?"

"Why?" said Salzman with a heavy laugh. "—Why? Because she is *partikiler*. This is why. She wants the *best*."

Leo was silent, amused at how he had entangled himself. But Salzman had aroused his interest in Lily H., and he began seriously to consider calling on her. When the marriage broker observed how intently Leo's mind was at work on the facts he had supplied, he felt certain they would soon come to an agreement.

Late Saturday afternoon, conscious of Salzman, Leo Finkle walked with Lily Hirschorn along Riverside Drive. He walked briskly and erectly, wearing with distinction the black fedora he had that morning taken with trepidation out of the dusty hat box on his closet shelf, and the heavy black Saturday coat he had thoroughly whisked clean. Leo also owned a walking stick, a present from a distant relative, but quickly put temptation aside and did not use it. Lily, petite and not unpretty, had on something signifying the approach of spring. She was au courant, animatedly, with all sorts of subjects, and he weighed her words and found her surprisingly sound—score another for Salzman, whom he uneasily sensed to be somewhere around, hiding perhaps high in a tree along the street, flashing the lady signals with a pocket mirror; or perhaps a cloven-hoofed Pan, piping nuptial ditties as he danced his invisible way before them, strewing wild buds on the walk and purple grapes in their path, symbolizing fruit of a union, though there was of course still none.

Lily startled Leo by remarking, "I was thinking of Mr. Salzman, a curious figure, wouldn't you say?"

Not certain what to answer, he nodded.

She bravely went on, blushing, "I for one am grateful for his introducing us. Aren't you?"

He courteously replied, "I am."

"I mean," she said with a little laugh—and it was all in good taste, or at least gave the effect of being not in bad—"do you mind that we came together so?"

He was not displeased with her honesty, recognizing that she meant to set the relationship aright, and understanding that it took a certain amount of experience in life, and courage, to want to do it quite that way. One had to have some sort of past to make that kind of beginning.

He said that he did not mind. Salzman's function was traditional and honorable—valuable for what it might achieve, which, he pointed out, was frequently nothing.

Lily agreed with a sigh. They walked on for a while and she said after a long silence, again with a nervous laugh, "Would you mind if I asked you something a little bit personal? Frankly, I find the subject fascinating." Although Leo shrugged, she went on half embarrassedly, "How was it that you came to your calling? I mean was it a sudden passionate inspiration?"

Leo, after a time, slowly replied, "I was always interested in the Law."

"You saw revealed in it the presence of the Highest?"

He nodded and changed the subject. "I understand that you spent a little time in Paris, Miss Hirschorn?"

"Oh, did Mr. Salzman tell you, Rabbi Finkle?" Leo winced but she went on, "It was ages ago and almost forgotten. I remember I had to return for my sister's wedding."

And Lily would not be put off. "When," she asked in a trembly voice, "did you become enamored of God?"

He stared at her. Then it came to him that she was talking not about Leo Finkle, but of a total stranger, some mystical figure, perhaps even passionate prophet that Salzman had dreamed up for her—no relation to the living or dead. Leo trembled with rage and weakness. The trickster had obviously sold her a bill of goods, just as he had him, who'd expected to become acquainted with a young lady of twenty-nine, only to behold, the moment he laid eyes upon her strained and anxious face, a woman past thirty-five and aging rapidly. Only his self control had kept him this long in her presence.

"I am not," he said gravely, "a talented religious person," and in seeking words to go on, found himself possessed by shame and fear. "I think," he said in a strained manner, "that I came to God not because I loved Him, but because I did not."

This confession he spoke harshly because its unexpectedness shook him.

Lily wilted. Leo saw a profusion of loaves of bread go flying like ducks high over his head, not unlike the winged loaves by which he had counted himself to sleep last night. Mercifully, then, it snowed, which he would not put past Salzman's machinations.

He was infuriated with the marriage broker and swore he would throw him out of the room the minute he reappeared. But Salzman did not come that night, and when Leo's anger had subsided, an unaccountable despair grew in its place. At first he thought this was caused by his disappointment in Lily, but before long it became evident that he had involved himself with Salzman without a true knowledge of his own intent. He gradually realized—with an emptiness that seized him with six hands—that he had called in the broker to find him a bride because he was incapable of doing it himself. This terrifying insight he had derived as a result of his meeting and conversation with Lily Hirschorn. Her probing questions had somehow irritated him into revealing—to himself more than her—the true nature of his relationship to God, and from that it had come upon him, with shocking force, that apart from his parents, he had never loved anyone. Or perhaps it went the other way, that he did not love God so well as he might, because he had not loved man. It seemed to Leo that his whole life stood starkly revealed and he saw himself for the first time as he truly was—unloved and loveless. This bitter but somehow not fully unexpected revelation brought him to a point of panic, controlled only by extraordinary effort. He covered his face with his hands and cried.

The week that followed was the worst of his life. He did not eat and lost weight. His beard darkened and grew ragged. He stopped attending seminars and almost never opened a book. He seriously considered leaving the Yeshivah, although he was deeply troubled at the thought of the loss of all his years of study—saw them like pages torn from a book, strewn over the city—and at the devastating effect of this decision upon his parents. But he had lived without knowledge of himself, and never in the Five Books and all the Commentaries—mea culpa—had the truth been revealed to him. He did not know where to turn, and in all this desolating loneliness there was no *to whom,* although he often thought of Lily but not once could bring himself to go downstairs and make the call. He became touchy and irritable, especially with his landlady, who asked him all manner of personal questions; on the other hand, sensing his own disagreeableness, he waylaid her on the stairs and apologized abjectly, until mortified, she ran from him. Out of this, however, he drew the consolation that he was a Jew and that a Jew suffered. But gradually, as the long and terrible week drew to a close, he regained his composure and some idea of purpose in life: to go on as planned. Although he was imperfect, the ideal was not. As for his quest of a bride, the thought of continuing afflicted him with anxiety and heartburn, yet perhaps with this new knowledge of himself he would be more successful than in the past. Perhaps love would now come to him and a bride to that love. And for this sanctified seeking who needed a Salzman?

The marriage broker, a skeleton with haunted eyes, returned that very night. He looked, withal, the picture of frustrated expectancy—as if he had steadfastly waited the week at Miss Lily Hirschorn's side for a telephone call that never came.

Casually coughing, Salzman came immediately to the point: "So how did you like her?"

Leo's anger rose and he could not refrain from chiding the matchmaker: "Why did you lie to me, Salzman?"

Salzman's pale face went dead white, the world had snowed on him.

"Did you not state that she was twenty-nine?" Leo insisted.

"I give you my word—"

"She was thirty-five, if a day. *At least* thirty-five."

"Of this don't be too sure. Her father told me—"

"Never mind. The worst of it was that you lied to her."

"How did I lie to her, tell me?"

"You told her things about me that weren't true. You made me out to be more, consequently less than I am. She had in mind a totally different person, a sort of semi-mystical Wonder Rabbi."

"All I said, you was a religious man."

"I can imagine."

Salzman sighed. "This is my weakness that I have," he confessed. "My wife says to me I shouldn't be a salesman, but when I have two fine people that they would be wonderful to be married, I am so happy that I talk too much." He smiled wanly. "This is why Salzman is a poor man."

Leo's anger left him. "Well, Salzman, I'm afraid that's all."

The marriage broker fastened hungry eyes on him.

"You don't want any more a bride?"

"I do," said Leo, "but I have decided to seek her in a different way. I am no longer interested in an arranged marriage. To be frank, I now admit the necessity of premarital love. That is, I want to be in love with the one I marry."

"Love?" said Salzman, astounded. After a moment he remarked, "For us, our love is our life, not for the ladies. In the ghetto they—"

"I know, I know," said Leo. "I've thought of it often. Love, I have said to myself, should be a by-product of living and worship rather than its own end. Yet for myself I find it necessary to establish the level of my need and fulfill it."

Salzman shrugged but answered, "Listen, rabbi, if you want love, this I can find for you also. I have such beautiful clients that you will love them the minute your eyes will see them."

Leo smiled unhappily. "I'm afraid you don't understand."

But Salzman hastily unstrapped his portfolio and withdrew a manila packet from it.

"Pictures," he said, quickly laying the envelope on the table.

Leo called after him to take the pictures away, but as if on the wings of the wind, Salzman had disappeared.

March came. Leo had returned to his regular routine. Although he felt not quite himself yet—lacked energy—he was making plans for a more active social life. Of course it would cost something, but he was an expert in cutting corners; and when there were no corners left he would make circles rounder. All the while Salzman's pictures had lain on the table, gathering dust. Occasionally as Leo sat studying, or enjoying a cup of tea, his eyes fell on the manila envelope, but he never opened it.

The days went by and no social life to speak of developed with a member of the opposite sex—it was difficult, given the circumstances of his situation. One morning Leo toiled up the stairs to his room and stared out the window at the city. Although the day was bright his view of it was dark. For some time he watched the people in the street below hurrying along and then turned with a heavy heart to his little room. On the table was the packet. With a sudden relentless gesture he tore it open. For a half-hour he stood by the table in a state of excitement, examining the photographs of the ladies Salzman had included. Finally, with a deep sigh he put them down. There were six, of varying degrees of attractiveness, but look at them long enough and they all became Lily Hirschorn: all past their prime, all starved behind bright smiles, not a true personality in the lot. Life, despite their frantic yoohooings, had passed them by; they were pictures in a brief-case that stank of fish. After a while, however, as Leo attempted to return the photographs into the envelope, he found in it another, a snapshot of the type taken by a machine for a quarter. He gazed at it a moment and let out a cry.

Her face deeply moved him. Why, he could at first not say. It gave him the impression of youth—spring flowers, yet age—a sense of having been used to the bone, wasted; this came from the eyes, which were hauntingly familiar, yet absolutely strange. He had a vivid impression that he had met her before, but try as he might he could not place her although he could al-most recall her name, as if he had read it in her own handwriting. No, this couldn't be; he would have remembered her. It was not, he affirmed, that she had an extraordinary beauty—no, though her face was attractive enough; it was that *something* about her moved him. Feature for feature, even some of the ladies of the photographs could do better; but she leaped forth to his heart—had *lived*, or wanted to—more than just wanted, per-haps regretted how she had lived—had somehow deeply suffered: it could be seen in the depths of those reluctant eyes, and from the way the light enclosed and shone from her, and within her, opening realms of possibil-ity: this was her own. Her he desired. His head ached and eyes narrowed with the intensity of his gazing, then as if an obscure fog had blown up in the mind, he experienced fear of her and was aware that he had received an impression, somehow, of evil. He shuddered, saying softly, it is thus with us all. Leo brewed some tea in a small pot and sat sipping it without sugar, to calm himself. But before he had finished drinking, again with excitement he examined the face and found it good: good for Leo Finkle. Only such a one could understand him and help him seek whatever he was seeking. She might, perhaps, love him. How she had happened to be among the discards in Salzman's barrel he could never guess, but he knew he must urgently go find her.

Leo rushed downstairs, grabbed up the Bronx telephone book, and searched for Salzman's home address. He was not listed, nor was his office. Neither was he in the Manhattan book. But Leo remembered having written down the address on a slip of paper after he had read Salzman's advertisement in the "personals" column of the *Forward*. He ran up to his room and tore through his papers, without luck. It was exasperating. Just when he needed the matchmaker he was nowhere to be found. Fortunately Leo remembered to look in his wallet. There on a card he found his name written and a Bronx address. No phone number was listed, the reason—Leo now recalled—he had originally communicated with Salzman by letter. He got on his coat, put a hat on over his skull cap and hurried to the subway station. All the way to the far end of the Bronx he sat on the edge of his seat. He was more than once tempted to take out the picture and see if the girl's face was as he remembered it, but he refrained, allowing the snapshot to remain in his inside coat pocket, content to have her so close. When the train pulled into the station he was waiting at the door and bolted out. He quickly located the street Salzman had advertised.

The building he sought was less than a block from the subway, but it was not an office building, nor even a loft, nor a store in which one could rent office space. It was a very old tenement house. Leo found Salzman's name in pencil on a soiled tag under the bell and climbed three dark flights to his apartment. When he knocked, the door was opened by a thin, asthmatic, gray-haired woman, in felt slippers.

"Yes?" she said, expecting nothing. She listened without listening. He could have sworn he had seen her, too, before but knew it was an illusion.

"Salzman—does he live here? Pinye Salzman," he said, "the matchmaker?"

She stared at him a long minute. "Of course."

He felt embarrassed. "Is he in?"

"No." Her mouth, though left open, offered nothing more.

"The matter is urgent. Can you tell me where his office is?"

"In the air." She pointed upward.

"You mean he has no office?" Leo asked.

"In his socks."

He peered into the apartment. It was sunless and dingy, one large room divided by a half-open curtain, beyond which he could see a sagging metal bed. The near side of the room was crowded with rickety chairs, old bureaus, a three-legged table, racks of cooking utensils, and all the apparatus of a kitchen. But there was no sign of Salzman or his magic barrel, probably also a figment of the imagination. An odor of frying fish made Leo weak to the knees.

"Where is he?" he insisted. "I've got to see your husband."

At length she answered, "So who knows where he is? Every time he thinks a new thought he runs to a different place. Go home, he will find you."

"Tell him Leo Finkle."

She gave no sign she had heard.

He walked downstairs, depressed.

But Salzman, breathless, stood waiting at his door.

Leo was astounded and overjoyed. "How did you get here before me?"

"I rushed."

"Come inside."

They entered. Leo fixed tea, and a sardine sandwich for Salzman. As they were drinking he reached behind him for the packet of pictures and handed them to the marriage broker.

Salzman put down his glass and said expectantly, "You found somebody you like?"

"Not among these."

The marriage broker turned away.

"Here is the one I want." Leo held forth the snapshot.

Salzman slipped on his glasses and took the picture into his trembling hand. He turned ghastly and let out a groan.

"What's the matter?" cried Leo.

"Excuse me. Was an accident this picture. She isn't for you."

Salzman frantically shoved the manila packet into his portfolio. He thrust the snapshot into his pocket and fled down the stairs.

Leo, after momentary paralysis, gave chase and cornered the marriage broker in the vestibule. The landlady made hysterical outcries but neither of them listened.

"Give me back the picture, Salzman."

"No." The pain in his eyes was terrible.

"Tell me who she is then."

"This I can't tell you. Excuse me."

He made to depart, but Leo, forgetting himself, seized the matchmaker by his tight coat and shook him frenziedly.

"Please," sighed Salzman. *"Please."*

Leo ashamedly let him go. "Tell me who she is," he begged. "It's very important for me to know."

"She is not for you. She is a wild one—wild, without shame. This is not a bride for a rabbi."

"What do you mean wild?"

"Like an animal. Like a dog. For her to be poor was a sin. This is why to me she is dead now."

"In God's name, what do you mean?"

"Her I can't introduce to you," Salzman cried.

"Why are you so excited?"

"Why, he asks," Salzman said, bursting into tears. "This is my baby, my Stella, she should burn in hell."

Leo hurried up to bed and hid under the covers. Under the covers he thought his life through. Although he soon fell asleep he could not sleep her out of his mind. He woke, beating his breast. Though he prayed to be rid of her, his prayers went unanswered. Through days of torment he endlessly struggled not to love her; fearing success, he escaped it. He then concluded to convert her to goodness, himself to God. The idea alternately nauseated and exalted him.

He perhaps did not know that he had come to a final decision until he encountered Salzman in a Broadway cafeteria. He was sitting alone at a rear table, sucking the bony remains of a fish. The marriage broker appeared haggard, and transparent to the point of vanishing.

Salzman looked up at first without recognizing him. Leo had grown a pointed beard and his eyes were weighted with wisdom.

"Salzman," he said, "love has at last come to my heart."

"Who can love from a picture?" mocked the marriage broker.

"It is not impossible."

"If you can love her, then you can love anybody. Let me show you some new clients that they just sent me their photographs. One is a little doll."

"Just her I want," Leo murmured.

"Don't be a fool, doctor. Don't bother with her."

"Put me in touch with her, Salzman," Leo said humbly. "Perhaps I can be of service."

Salzman had stopped eating and Leo understood with emotion that it was now arranged.

Leaving the cafeteria, he was, however, afflicted by a tormenting suspicion that Salzman had planned it all to happen this way.

Leo was informed by letter that she would meet him on a certain corner, and she was there one spring night, waiting under a street lamp. He appeared, carrying a small bouquet of violets and rosebuds. Stella stood by the lamp post, smoking. She wore white with red shoes, which fitted his expectations, although in a troubled moment he had imagined the dress red, and only the shoes white. She waited uneasily and shyly. From afar he saw that her eyes—clearly her father's—were filled with desperate innocence. He pictured, in her, his own redemption. Violins and lit candles revolved in the sky. Leo ran forward with flowers outthrust.

Around the corner, Salzman, leaning against a wall, chanted prayers for the dead.

SUGGESTIONS FOR WRITING

The Stories

1. Compare and contrast the nature and implications of charity in "Black Is My Favorite Color" and "A Gift from the City."

2. An archetypal pattern behind much of Malamud's fiction is the quest. Typically, his protagonists journey (physically and spiritually) in search of experience, love, or a new life. Write an essay in which you describe the nature of the protagonist's quest in "The Magic Barrel."

3. Salzman supplies much of the humor in "The Magic Barrel." As in "Black Is My Favorite Color," Yiddish speech rhythms are largely accountable for what is humorous in the story. Further, as Alfred Kazin has observed, "Malamud has caught as one the guttural toughness of big-city speech and the classic bitterness of Jewish dialogue." Write an essay in which you analyze these two seemingly contradictory facets of Yiddish-American dialogue in "The Magic Barrel."

4. When Leo goes to meet Stella at the conclusion of the story, he sees "that her eyes—clearly her father's—were filled with desperate innocence. He pictured, in her, his own redemption." In either the Old Testament or Russian literature (such works as *Crime and Punishment* or *The Brothers Karamazov*), find a literary antecedent for the union of saint and sinner that results in mutual regeneration. Then write an essay in which you compare and contrast this theme as represented in "The Magic Barrel" and in the source you have chosen.

5. Concerning the concluding scene, one critic has noted, "All the complex meaning is fixed, flashed back upon the story itself in a kind of Joycean epiphany that runs counter to the neatly packaged endings of the naturalistic tale." Write an essay in which you support this critical judgment.

6. Many critics have pointed out parallels between the fiction of Malamud and the work of the painter Marc Chagall. Examine some Chagall

drawings and lithographs. Then, from your reading of "The Magic Barrel," write an essay in which you discuss correspondences (such as "the affecting blend of bitter comedy and wistful nostalgia" and elements of transcendence) between Chagall and Malamud.

Other Works by Bernard Malamud

1. Write an essay in which you discuss *The Natural* as an allegory of natural man.

2. Compare and contrast the role of suffering in *The Assistant* and *The Fixer*.

3. Examine the function of satire and irony in *A New Life*.

4. Philip Roth has described the Jewish characters in Malamud's fiction as "a kind of invention, a metaphor to stand for certain human possibilities and certain human promises. . . . Malamud, as a writer of fiction, has not shown specific interest in the anxieties and dilemmas and corruptions of the modern American Jew. . . ." Explore this premise by examining the Jewish characters in *Rembrandt's Hat*.

5. Fidelman, who is an artist, can also be considered "a metaphor to stand for certain human possibilities and certain human promises." Discuss this contention by analyzing Fidelman's role in *Pictures of Fidelman: An Exhibition*. Be sure to explain the meaning of the happy ending in this work.

6. The introduction to *Bernard Malamud and the Critics* observes that Malamud, in common with many great writers, is concerned with man "evolving *his* world within a world he never made. And how man chooses *his own* world and what happens to man in the process of that choice constitute the significant world of Barnard Malamud's fiction." Examine the nature and consequences of Harry Lesser's choices in *The Tenants*.

7. *Pictures of Fidelman: An Exhibition* and Mary McCarthy's *Birds of America* both depict Americans in Europe. Compare and contrast the presentation of Americans and Europeans in these two works.

BIBLIOGRAPHY

Primary

The Natural. New York: Harcourt, Brace & World, 1952. A novel.
The Assistant. New York: Farrar, Straus & Giroux, 1957. A novel.
The Magic Barrel. New York: Farrar, Straus & Giroux, 1958. Short stories.
A New Life. New York: Farrar, Straus & Giroux, 1961. A novel.
Idiots First. New York: Farrar, Straus & Giroux, 1963. Short stories.
The Fixer. New York: Farrar, Straus & Giroux, 1966. A novel.
"Theme, Content and the 'New Novel,'" an essay adapted froom Malamud's acceptance speech at the National Book Awards presentation for 1966, printed in *The New York Times Book Review,* March 26, 1967, pp. 2, 29. Literary criticism.
Pictures of Fidelman: An Exhibition. New York: Farrar, Straus & Giroux, 1969. Short stories.
The Tenants. New York: Farrar, Straus & Giroux, 1971. A novel.
Rembrandt's Hat. New York: Farrar, Straus & Giroux, 1973. Short stories.

Secondary

Baumbach, Jonathan. "All Men Are Jews" in *The Landscape of Nightmare.* New York: New York Univ. Press, 1965. Brief comments about *A New Life* and *The Natural* and an extended examination of *The Assistant,* in which the author discusses Malamud as "a moral fabler and fantasist," who "writes of the conflicting demands of the inner and outer worlds of his heroes, of the tremulous private life confronted by a mythic public scene."
Field, Leslie A. and Joyce W., eds. *Bernard Malamud and the Critics.* New York: New York Univ. Press, 1970. An outstanding collection of essays by Rovit, Hoyt, Hassan, Klein, and others; divided into four sections: 1) the Jewish tradition; 2) myth, ritual, folklore; 3) varied approaches; and 4) specific novels and short stories (essay "The Stories" excerpted from *Bernard Malamud* by Sidney Richman).
Hassan, Ihab. *Radical Innocence: Studies in the Contemporary American Novel.* Princeton, N.J.: Princeton Univ. Press, 1961. Contains a per-

ceptive discussion of the "ironic, awkward, and inconclusive" purgation and rebirth of Frank Alpine in *The Assistant*.

Hoyt, Charles Alva. "Bernard Malamud and the New Romanticism" in *Contemporary American Novelists*, ed. by Harry T. Moore. Carbondale, Ill.: Southern Illinois Univ. Press, 1964. A provocative interpretation structured around the premise that Malamud's fiction embodies the "romantic rejection of objectivity."

Kazin, Alfred. "Bernard Malamud: The Magic and the Dread" in *Contemporaries*. Boston: Little, Brown, 1962. A review of *The Magic Barrel*, interesting for its comments on Malamud's "almost uncanny transformation of the old Jewish mysticism."

Klein, Marcus. "The Sadness of Goodness" in *After Alienation: American Novels in Mid-Century*. Cleveland: World, 1964. An insightful analysis that examines the continuity of Malamud's stories and novels.

Malin, Irving. *Jews and Americans*. Carbondale, Ill.: Southern Illinois Univ. Press, 1965. An examination of the writing of Karl Shapiro, Delmore Schwartz, Isaac Rosenfeld, Leslie Fiedler, Saul Bellow, Philip Roth, and Bernard Malamud—all of whom "deal with the Jew in America."

Mandel, Ruth B. "Bernard Malamud's *The Assistant* and *A New Life*: Ironic Affirmation." *Critique*, 7 (Winter 1964–65), 110–22. A treatment of "the process of redemption" in these two novels and of the problems of interpretation raised by the "shadowy and inscrutable" S. Levin.

Meeter, Glenn. *Philip Roth and Bernard Malamud: A Critical Essay.* Grand Rapids, Mich.: William B. Eerdmans Publishing Co., 1968. Explores Malamud and Roth as Jewish romantics.

Richman, Sidney. *Bernard Malamud.* New York: Twayne, 1966. An informative full-length critical study of Malamud's fiction.

Siegel, Ben. "Victims in Motion: Bernard Malamud's Sad and Bitter Clowns." *Northwest Review*, 5 (Spring 1962), 69–80. Reprinted in *Recent American Fiction*, ed. by Joseph J. Waldmeir. Boston: Houghton Mifflin, 1963. An examination of the "uncertain, unlucky, and unloved" protagonists of *The Natural, The Assistant,* and *The Magic Barrel*.

Tanner, Tony. "A New Life" in *City of Words: American Fiction 1950–1970*. London: Jonathan Cape Ltd., 1971. Reviews *A New Life* in the context of Malamud's other fiction.

. . . the very first thing a writer has to face is that he cannot be told what to write. You know, nobody asked me to be a writer; I chose it. Well, since I'm a man I have to assume I chose it; perhaps, in fact, I didn't choose it. But in any case, the one thing you have to do is try to tell the truth. And what everyone overlooks is that in order to do it—when the book comes out it may hurt you—but in order for me to do it, it had to hurt me first. I can only tell you about yourself as much as I can face about myself. And this has happened to everybody who's tried to live. You go through life for a long time thinking, No one has ever suffered the way I've suffered, my God, my God. And then you realize—You read something or you hear something, and you realize that your suffering does not isolate you; your suffering is your bridge. Many people have suffered before you, many people are suffering around you and always will, and all you can do is bring, hopefully, a little light into that suffering. Enough light so that the person who is suffering can begin to comprehend his suffering and begin to live with it and begin to change it, change the situation. We don't change anything; all we can do is invest people with the morale to change it for themselves.

FROM *James Baldwin, Nikki Giovanni: A Dialogue*

JAMES BALDWIN

The oldest of nine children, James Baldwin was born in New York City in 1924. As a child, Baldwin was an avid reader, journeying to the 135th Street branch of the New York Public Library three or four times a week and reading "everything there." He was also deeply religious, and, at fourteen, began to preach in the fundamentalist churches of Harlem.

After graduating from high school, he worked at a variety of jobs (in shipyards, in a factory, as a waiter) and started a highly autobiographical novel called *Crying Holy*. Ten years later it was published, to great acclaim, as *Go Tell It on the Mountain* (1953). About that novel, Baldwin's brother David has said, "That book cost him a great deal. . . . Jimmy had to understand a lot before he could write *Go Tell It on the Mountain*. Everything that happened to him, in and out of the family. Ten years. It's a life." By this time, Baldwin, who had been living in Europe since 1948, had established himself also as a brilliant and controversial essayist, with the appearance of such essays as "The Harlem Ghetto" and "Everybody's Protest Novel."

Returning to America in 1957, Baldwin became active in the civil rights movement. From his involvement came *The Fire Next Time* (1963) and *Blues for Mister Charlie* (1964). Disillusioned by the course of the civil rights movement in America and emotionally distraught over the murders of Martin Luther King and Malcolm X, Baldwin left the United States once again. After spending a year in Turkey, he returned to France, where he lives in a farmhouse in the village of St. Paul de Vence. Baldwin has chosen to live in France because that country provides a setting in which he can work without daily skirmishing on black-white racial issues.

Although undeniably a spokesman on such issues, Baldwin has universal concerns that are also reflected in his stories. For, as he has written, "One cannot deny the humanity of another without diminishing one's own: in the face of one's victim, one sees oneself."

THIS MORNING,
THIS EVENING,
SO SOON

"You are full of nightmares," Harriet tells me. She is in her dressing gown and has cream all over her face. She and my older sister, Louisa, are going out to be girls together. I suppose they have many things to talk about—they have *me* to talk about, certainly—and they do not want my presence. I have been given a bachelor's evening. The director of the film which has brought us such incredible and troubling riches will be along later to take me out to dinner.

I watch her face. I know that it is quite impossible for her to be as untroubled as she seems. Her self-control is mainly for my benefit—my benefit, and Paul's. Harriet comes from orderly and progressive Sweden and has reacted against all the advanced doctrines to which she has been exposed by becoming steadily and beautifully old-fashioned. We never fought in front of Paul, not even when he was a baby. Harriet does not so much believe in protecting children as she does in helping them to build a foundation on

327

which they can build and build again, each time life's high-flying steel ball knocks down everything they have built.

Whenever I become upset, Harriet becomes very cheerful and composed. I think she began to learn how to do this over eight years ago, when I returned from my only visit to America. Now, perhaps, it has become something she could not control if she wished to. This morning, at breakfast, when I yelled at Paul, she averted Paul's tears and my own guilt by looking up and saying, "My God, your father is cranky this morning, isn't he?"

Paul's attention was immediately distracted from his wounds, and the unjust inflicter of those wounds, to his mother's laughter. He watched her.

"It is because he is afraid they will not like his songs in New York. Your father is an *artiste, mon chou,* and they are very mysterious people, *les artistes.* Millions of people are waiting for him in New York, they are begging him to come, and they will give him a *lot* of money, but he is afraid they will not like him. Tell him he is wrong."

She succeeded in rekindling Paul's excitement about places he has never seen. I was also, at once, reinvested with all my glamour. I think it is sometimes extremely difficult for Paul to realize that the face he sees on record sleeves and in the newspapers and on the screen is nothing more or less than the face of his father—who sometimes yells at him. Of course, since he is only seven—going on eight, he will be eight years old this winter—he cannot know that I am baffled, too.

"Of course, you are wrong, you are silly," he said with passion—and caused me to smile. His English is strongly accented and is not, in fact, as good as his French, for he speaks French all day at school. French is really his first language, the first he ever heard. "You are the greatest singer in France"—sounding exactly as he must sound when he makes this pronouncement to his schoolmates—"the greatest *American* singer"—this concession was so gracefully made that it was not a concession at all, it added inches to my stature, America being only a glamorous word for Paul. It is the place from which his father came, and to which he now is going, a place which very few people have ever seen. But his aunt is one of them and he looked over at her. "Mme. Dumont says so, and she says he is a *great actor, too.*" Louisa nodded, smiling. "And she has seen *Les Fauves Nous Attendent*—five times!" This clinched it, of course. Mme. Dumont is our concierge and she has known Paul all his life. I suppose he will not begin to doubt anything she says until he begins to doubt everything.

He looked over at me again. "So you are wrong to be afraid."

"I was wrong to yell at you, too. I won't yell at you any more today."

"All right." He was very grave.

Louisa poured more coffee. "He's going to knock them dead in New York. You'll see."

"Mais bien sur," said Paul, doubtfully. He does not quite know what "knock them dead" means, though he was sure, from her tone, that she must have been agreeing with him. He does not quite understand this aunt, whom he met for the first time two months ago, when she arrived to spend the summer with us. Her accent is entirely different from anything he has ever heard. He does not really understand why, since she is my sister and his aunt, she should be unable to speak French.

Harriet, Louisa, and I looked at each other and smiled. "Knock them dead," said Harriet, "means *d'avoir un succès fou.* But you will soon pick up all the American expressions." She looked at me and laughed. "So will I."

"That's what he's afraid of." Louisa grinned. "We have *got* some expressions, believe me. Don't let anybody ever tell you America hasn't got a culture. Our culture is as thick as clabber milk."

"Ah," Harriet answered, "I know. I know."

"I'm going to be practicing later," I told Paul.

His face lit up. *"Bon."* This meant that, later, he would come into my study and lie on the floor with his papers and crayons while I worked out with the piano and the tape recorder. He knew that I was offering this as an olive branch. All things considered, we get on pretty well, my son and I.

He looked over at Louisa again. She held a coffee cup in one hand and a cigarette in the other; and something about her baffled him. It was early, so she had not yet put on her face. Her short, thick, graying hair was rougher than usual, almost as rough as my own—later, she would be going to the hairdresser's; she is fairer than I, and better-looking; Louisa, in fact, caught all the looks in the family. Paul knows that she is my older sister and that she helped to raise me, though he does not, of course, know what this means. He knows that she is a schoolteacher in the *American* South, which is not, for some reason, the same place as South America. I could see him trying to fit all these exotic details together into a pattern which would explain her strangeness—strangeness of accent, strangeness of manner. In comparison with the people he has always known, Louisa must seem, for all her generosity and laughter and affection, peculiarly uncertain of herself, peculiarly hostile and embattled.

I wondered what he would think of his Uncle Norman, older and much blacker than I, who lives near the Alabama town in which we were born. Norman will meet us at the boat.

*

Now Harriet repeats, "Nightmares, nightmares. Nothing ever turns out as badly as you think it will—in fact," she adds laughing, "I am happy to say that that would scarcely be possible."

Her eyes seek mine in the mirror—dark-blue eyes, pale skin, black hair. I had always thought of Sweden as being populated entirely by blondes, and I thought that Harriet was abnormally dark for a Swedish girl. But when we visited Sweden, I found out differently. "It is all a great racial salad, Europe, that is why I am sure that I will never understand your country," Harriet said. That was in the days when we never imagined that we would be going to it.

I wonder what she is really thinking. Still, she is right, in two days we will be on a boat, and there is simply no point in carrying around my load of apprehension. I sit down on the bed, watching her fix her face. I realize that I am going to miss this old-fashioned bedroom. For years, we've talked about throwing out the old junk which came with the apartment and re-placing it with less massive, modern furniture. But we never have.

"Oh, everything will probably work out," I say. "I've been in a bad mood all day long. I just can't sing any more." We both laugh. She reaches for a wad of tissues and begins wiping off the cream. "I wonder how Paul will like it, if he'll make friends—that's all."

"Paul will like any place where you are, where we are. Don't you worry about Paul."

Paul has never been called any names, so far. Only, once he asked us what the word *métis* meant and Harriet explained to him that it meant mixed blood, adding that the blood of just about everybody in the world was mixed by now. Mme. Dumont contributed bawdy and detailed cor-roboration from her own family tree, the roots of which were somewhere in Corsica; the moral of the story, as she told it, was that women were weak, men incorrigible, and *le bon Dieu* appallingly clever. Mme. Dumont's version is the version I prefer, but it may not be, for Paul, the most utili-tarian.

Harriet rises from the dressing table and comes over to sit in my lap. I fall back with her on the bed, and she smiles down into my face.

"Now, don't worry," she tells me, "please try not to worry. Whatever is coming, we will manage it all very well, you will see. We have each other and we have our son and we know what we want. So, we are luckier than most people."

I kiss her on the chin. "I'm luckier than most men."

"I'm a very lucky woman, too."

And for a moment we are silent, alone in our room, which we have shared so long. The slight rise and fall of Harriet's breathing creates an intermittent pressure against my chest, and I think how, if I had never left America, I would never have met her and would never have established a life of my own, would never have entered my own life. For everyone's life begins on a level where races, armies, and churches stop. And yet everyone's life is always shaped by races, churches, and armies; races, churches, armies menace, and have taken, many lives. If Harriet had been born in America, it would have taken her a long time, perhaps forever, to look on me as a man like other men; if I had met her in America, I would never have been able to look on her as a woman like all other women. The habits of public rage and power would also have been our private compulsions, and would have blinded our eyes. We would never have been able to love each other. And Paul would never have been born.

Perhaps, if I had stayed in America, I would have found another woman and had another son. But that other woman, that other son are in the limbo of vanished possibilities. I might also have become something else, instead of an actor-singer, perhaps a lawyer, like my brother, or a teacher, like my sister. But no, I am what I have become and this woman beside me is my wife, and I love her. All the sons I might have had mean nothing, since I *have* a son, I named him, Paul, for my father, and I love him.

I think of all the things I have seen destroyed in America, all the things that I have lost there, all the threats it holds for me and mine.

I grin up at Harriet. "Do you love me?"

"Of course not. I simply have been madly plotting to get to America all these years."

"What a patient wench you are."

"The Swedes are very patient."

She kisses me again and stands up. Louisa comes in, also in a dressing gown.

"I hope you two aren't sitting in here yakking about the *subject*." She looks at me. "My, you are the sorriest-looking celebrity I've ever seen. I've always wondered why people like you hired press agents. Now I know." She goes to Harriet's dressing table. "Honey, do you mind if I borrow some of that *mad* nail polish?"

Harriet goes over to the dressing table. "I'm not sure I know *which* mad nail polish you mean."

Harriet and Louisa, somewhat to my surprise, get on very well. Each seems to find the other full of the weirdest and most delightful surprises. Harriet has been teaching Louisa French and Swedish expressions, and

Louisa has been teaching Harriet some of the saltier expressions of the black South. Whenever one of them is not playing straight man to the other's accent, they become involved in long speculations as to how a language reveals the history and the attitudes of a people. They discovered that all the European languages contain a phrase equivalent to "to work like a nigger." ("Of course," says Louisa, "they've had black men working for them for a long time.") "Language is experience and language is power," says Louisa, after regretting that she does not know any of the African dialects. "That's what I keep trying to tell those dicty bastards down South. They get their own experience into the language, we'll have a great language. But, no, they all want to talk like white folks." Then she leans forward, grasping Harriet by the knee. "I tell them, honey, white folks ain't saying *nothing*. Not a thing are they saying—and *some* of them know it, they *need* what you got, the whole world needs it." Then she leans back, in disgust. "You think they listen to me? Indeed they do not. They just go right on, trying to talk like white folks." She leans forward again, in tremendous indignation. "You know some of them folks are *ashamed* of Mahalia Jackson? *Ashamed* of her, one of the greatest singers alive! They think she's common." Then she looks about the room as though she held a bottle in her hand and were looking for a skull to crack.

I think it is because Louisa has never been able to talk like this to any white person before. All the white people she has ever met needed, in one way or another, to be reassured, consoled, to have their consciences pricked but not blasted; could not, could not afford to hear a truth which would shatter, irrevocably, their image of themselves. It is astonishing the lengths to which a person, or a people, will go in order to avoid a truthful mirror. But Harriet's necessity is precisely the opposite: it is of the utmost importance that she learn everything that Louisa can tell her, and then learn more, much more. Harriet is really trying to learn from Louisa how best to protect her husband and her son. This is why they are going out alone tonight. They will have, tonight, as it were, a final council of war. I may be moody, but they, thank God, are practical.

Now Louisa turns to me while Harriet rummages about on the dressing table. "What time is Vidal coming for you?"

"Oh, around seven-thirty, eight o'clock. He says he's reserved tables for us in some very chic place, but he won't say where." Louisa wriggles her shoulders, raises her eyebrows, and does a tiny bump and grind. I laugh. "That's right. And then I guess we'll go out and get drunk."

"I hope to God you do. You've been about as cheerful as a cemetery these last few days. And, that way, your hangover will keep you from bugging us tomorrow."

"What about *your* hangovers? I know the way you girls drink."

"Well, we'll be paying for our own drinks," says Harriet, "so I don't think we'll have that problem. But *you're* going to be feted, like an international movie star."

"You sure you don't want to change your mind and come out with Vidal and me?"

"We're sure," Louisa says. She looks down at me and gives a small, amused grunt. "An international movie star. And I used to change your diapers. I'll be damned." She is grave for a moment. "Mama'd be proud of you, you know that?" We look at each other and the air between us is charged with secrets which not even Harriet will ever know. "Now, get the hell out of here, so we can get dressed."

"I'll take Paul on down to Mme. Dumont's."

Paul is to have supper with her children and spend the night there.

"For the last time," says Mme. Dumont and she rubs her hand over Paul's violently curly black hair. *"Tu vas nous manquer, tu sais?"* Then she looks up at me and laughs. "He doesn't care. He is only interested in seeing the big ship and all the wonders of New York. Children are never sad to make journeys."

"I would be very sad to go," says Paul, "but my father must go to New York to work and he wants me to come with him."

Over his head, Mme. Dumont and I smile at each other. *"Il est malin, ton gosse!"* She looks down at him again. "And do you think, my little diplomat, that you will like New York?"

"We aren't only going to New York," Paul answers, "we are going to California, too."

"Well, do you think you will like California?"

Paul looks at me. "I don't know. If we don't like it, we'll come back."

"So simple. Just like that," says Mme. Dumont. She looks at me. "It is the best way to look at life. Do come back. You know, we feel that you belong to us, too, here in France."

"I hope you do," I say. "I hope you do. I have always felt—always felt at home here." I bend down and Paul and I kiss each other on the cheek. We have always done so—but will we be able to do so in America? American fathers never kiss American sons. I straighten, my hand on Paul's shoulder. "You be good. I'll pick you up for breakfast, or, if you get up first you come and pick me up and we can hang out together tomorrow, while your *Maman* and your Aunt Louisa finish packing. They won't want two men hanging around the house."

"*D'accord.* Where shall we hang out?" On the last two words he stumbles a little and imitates me.

"Maybe we can go to the zoo, I don't know. And I'll take you to lunch at the Eiffel Tower, would you like that?"

"Oh, yes," he says, "I'd love that." When he is pleased, he seems to glow. All the energy of his small, tough, concentrated being charges an unseen battery and adds an incredible luster to his eyes, which are large and dark brown—like mine—and to his skin, which always reminds me of the colors of honey and the fires of the sun.

"OK, then." I shake hands with Mme. Dumont. "*Bonsoir, Madame,*" I ring for the elevator, staring at Paul. "*Ciao, Pauli.*"

"*Bonsoir, Papa.*"

And Mme. Dumont takes him inside.

Upstairs, Harriet and Louisa are finally powdered, perfumed, and jeweled, and ready to go: dry martinis at the Ritz, supper, "in some *very* expensive little place," says Harriet, and perhaps the Folies Bergère afterwards. "A real cornball, tourist evening," says Louisa. "I'm working on the theory that if I can get Harriet to act like an American now, she won't have so much trouble later."

"I very much doubt," Harriet says, "that I will be able to endure the Folies Bergère for three solid hours."

"Oh, then we'll duck across town to Harry's New York bar and drink mint juleps," says Louisa.

I realize that, quite apart from everything else, Louisa is having as much fun as she has ever had in her life. Perhaps she, too, will be sad to leave Paris, even though she has only known it for such a short time.

"Do people drink those in New York?" Harriet asks. I think she is making a list of the things people do or do not do in New York.

"*Some* people do." Louisa winks at me. "Do you realize that this Swedish chick's picked up an Alabama drawl?"

We laugh together. The elevator chugs to a landing.

"We'll stop and say goodnight to Paul," Harriet says. She kisses me. "Give our best to Vidal."

"Right. Have a good time. Don't let any Frenchmen run off with Louisa."

"I did not come to Paris to be protected, and if I had, this wild chick *you* married couldn't do it. I just *might* upset everybody and come home with a French count." She presses the elevator button and the cage goes down.

*

I walk back into our dismantled apartment. It stinks of departure. There are bags and crates in the hall which will be taken away tomorrow, there are no books in the bookcases, the kitchen looks as though we never cooked a meal there, never dawdled there, in the early morning or late at night, over coffee. Presently, I must shower and shave but now I pour myself a drink and light a cigarette and step out on our balcony. It is dusk, the brilliant light of Paris is beginning to fade, and the green of the trees is darkening.

I have lived in this city for twelve years. This apartment is on the top floor of a corner building. We look out over the trees and the roof tops to the Champ de Mars, where the Eiffel Tower stands. Beyond this field is the river, which I have crossed so often, in so many states of mind. I have crossed every bridge in Paris, I have walked along every *quai*. I know the river as one finally knows a friend, know it when it is black, guarding all the lights of Paris in its depths, and seeming, in its vast silence, to be communing with the dead who lie beneath it; when it is yellow, evil, and roaring, giving a rough time to tugboats and barges, and causing people to remember that it has been known to rise, it has been known to kill; when it is peaceful, a slick dark, dirty green, playing host to rowboats and *les bateaux mouches* and throwing up from time to time an extremely unhealthy fish. The men who stand along the *quais* all summer with their fishing lines gratefully accept the slimy object and throw it in a rusty can. I have always wondered who eats those fish.

And I walk up and down, up and down, glad to be alone.

It is August, the month when all Parisians desert Paris and one has to walk miles to find a barbershop or a laundry open in some tree-shadowed, silent side street. There is a single person on the avenue, a paratrooper walking toward École Militaire. He is also walking, almost certainly, and rather sooner than later, toward Algeria. I have a friend, a good-natured boy who was always hanging around the clubs in which I worked in the old days, who has just returned from Algeria, with a recurring, debilitating fever, and minus one eye. The government has set his pension at the sum, arbitrary if not occult, of fifty-three thousand francs every three months. Of course, it is quite impossible to live on this amount of money without working—but who will hire a half-blind invalid? This boy has been spoiled forever, long before his thirtieth birthday, and there are thousands like him all over France.

And there are fewer Algerians to be found on the streets of Paris now. The rug sellers, the peanut vendors, the postcard peddlers and moneychangers have vanished. The boys I used to know during my first years in Paris are scattered—or corralled—the Lord knows where.

Most of them had no money. They lived three and four together in rooms with a single skylight, a single hard cot, or in buildings that seemed abandoned, with cardboard in the windows, with erratic plumbing in a wet, cobblestoned yard, in dark, dead-end alleys, or on the outer, chilling heights of Paris.

The Arab cafés are closed—those dark, acrid cafés in which I used to meet with them to drink tea, to get high on hashish, to listen to the obsessive, stringed music which has no relation to any beat, any time, that I have ever known. I once thought of the North Africans as my brothers and that is why I went to their cafés. They were very friendly to me, perhaps one or two of them remained really fond of me even after I could no longer afford to smoke Lucky Strikes and after my collection of American sport shirts had vanished—mostly into their wardrobes. They seemed to feel that they had every right to them, since I could only have wrested these things from the world by cunning—it meant nothing to say that I had had no choice in the matter; perhaps I had wrested these things from the world by treason, by refusing to be identified with the misery of my people. Perhaps, indeed, I identified myself with those who were responsible for this misery.

And this was true. Their rage, the only note in all their music which I could not fail to recognize, to which I responded, yet had the effect of setting us more than ever at a division. They were perfectly prepared to drive all Frenchmen into the sea, and to level the city of Paris. But I could not hate the French, because they left me alone. And I love Paris, I will always love it, it is the city which saved my life. It saved my life by allowing me to find out who I am.

It was on a bridge, one tremendous, April morning, that I knew I had fallen in love. Harriet and I were walking hand in hand. The bridge was the Pont Royal, just before us was the great *horloge,* high and lifted up, saying ten to ten; beyond this, the golden statue of Joan of Arc, with her sword uplifted. Harriet and I were silent, for we had been quarreling about something. Now, when I look back, I think we had reached that state when an affair must either end or become something more than an affair.

I looked sideways at Harriet's face, which was still. Her dark-blue eyes were narrowed against the sun, and her full, pink lips were still slightly sulky, like a child's. In those days, she hardly ever wore make-up. I was in my shirt sleeves. Her face made me want to laugh and run my hand over her short dark hair. I wanted to pull her to me and say, *Baby, don't be mad at me,* and at that moment something tugged at my heart and made me catch my breath. There were millions of people all around us, but I was alone with Harriet. She was alone with me. Never, in all my life, until that moment, had I been alone with anyone. The world had always been with us, between us, defeating the quarrel we could not achieve, and making love impossible. During all the years of my life, until that moment, I had carried the menacing, the hostile, killing world with me everywhere. No matter what I was doing or saying or feeling, one eye had always been on the world—that world which I had learned to distrust almost as soon as I learned my name, that world on which I knew one could never turn one's back, the white man's world. And for the first time in my life I was free of it; it had not existed for me; I had been quarreling with my girl. It was our quarrel, it was entirely between us, it had nothing to do with anyone else in the world. For the first time in my life I had not been afraid of the patriotism of the mindless, in uniform or out, who would beat me up and treat the woman who was with me as though she were the lowest of untouchables. For the first time in my life I felt that no force jeopardized my right, my power, to possess and to protect a woman; for the first time, the first time, felt that the woman was not, in her own eyes or in the eyes of the world, degraded by my presence.

The sun fell over everything, like a blessing, people were moving all about us, I will never forget the feeling of Harriet's small hand in mine, dry and trusting, and I turned to her, slowing our pace. She looked up at me with her enormous, blue eyes, and she seemed to wait. I said, "Harriet. Harriet. *Tu sais, il y a quelque chose de très grave qui m'est arrivé. Je t'aime. Je t'aime. Tu me comprends,* or shall I say it in English?"

This was eight years ago, shortly before my first and only visit home.

That was when my mother died. I stayed in America for three months. When I came back, Harriet thought that the change in me was due to my grief—I was very silent, very thin. But it had not been my mother's death which accounted for the change. I had known that my mother was going to die. I had not known what America would be like for me after nearly four years away.

I remember standing at the rail and watching the distance between myself and Le Havre increase. Hands fell, ceasing to wave, handkerchiefs ceased to flutter, people turned away, they mounted their bicycles or got into their cars and rode off. Soon, Le Havre was nothing but a blur. I thought of Harriet, already miles from me in Paris, and I pressed my lips tightly together in order not to cry.

Then, as Europe dropped below the water, as the days passed and

337

passed, as we left behind us the skies of Europe and the eyes of everyone on the ship began, so to speak, to refocus, waiting for the first glimpse of America, my apprehension began to give way to a secret joy, a checked anticipation. I thought of such details as showers, which are rare in Paris, and I thought of such things as rich, cold, American milk and heavy, chocolate cake. I wondered about my friends, wondered if I had any left, and wondered if they would be glad to see me.

The Americans on the boat did not seem to be so bad, but I was fascinated, after such a long absence from it, by the nature of their friendliness. It was a friendliness which did not suggest, and was not intended to suggest, any possibility of friendship. Unlike Europeans, they dropped titles and used first names almost at once, leaving themselves, unlike the Europeans, with nowhere thereafter to go. Once one had become "Pete" or "Jane" or "Bill" all that could decently be known was known and any suggestion that there might be further depths, a person, so to speak, behind the name, was taken as a violation of that privacy which did not, paradoxically, since they trusted it so little, seem to exist among Americans. They apparently equated privacy with the unspeakable things they did in the bathroom or the bedroom, which they related only to the analyst, and then read about in the pages of best sellers. There was an eerie and unnerving irreality about everything they said and did, as though they were all members of the same team and were acting on orders from some invincibly cheerful and tirelessly inventive coach. I was fascinated by it. I found it oddly moving, but I cannot say that I was displeased. It had not occurred to me before that Americans, who had never treated me with any respect, had no respect for each other.

On the last night but one, there was a gala in the big ballroom and I sang. It had been a long time since I had sung before so many Americans. My audience had mainly been penniless French students, in the weird, Left Bank bistros I worked in those days. Still, I was a great hit with them and by this time I had become enough of a drawing card, in the Latin quarter and in St. Germain des Prés, to have attracted a couple of critics, to have had my picture in *France-soir,* and to have acquired a legal work permit which allowed me to make a little more money. Just the same, no matter how industrious and brilliant some of the musicians had been, or how devoted my audience, they did not know, they could not know, what my songs came out of. They did not know what was funny about it. It was impossible to translate: It damn well better be funny, or Laughing to keep from crying, or What did *I* do to be so black and blue?

The moment I stepped out on the floor, they began to smile, something opened in them, they were ready to be pleased. I found in their faces, as they watched me, smiling, waiting, an artless relief, a profound reassurance. Nothing was more familiar to them than the sight of a dark boy, singing, and there were few things on earth more necessary. It was under cover of darkness, my own darkness, that I could sing for them of the joys, passions, and terrors they smuggled about with them like steadily depreciating contraband. Under cover of the midnight fiction that I was unlike them because I was black, they could stealthily gaze at those treasures which they had been mysteriously forbidden to possess and were never permitted to declare.

I sang *I'm Coming, Virginia,* and *Take This Hammer,* and *Precious Lord.* They wouldn't let me go and I came back and sang a couple of the oldest blues I knew. Then someone asked me to sing *Swanee River,* and I did, astonished that I could, astonished that this song, which I had put down long ago, should have the power to move me. Then, if only, perhaps, to make the record complete, I wanted to sing *Strange Fruit,* but, on this number, no one can surpass the great, tormented Billie Holiday. So I finished with *Great Getting-Up Morning* and I guess I can say that if I didn't stop the show I certainly ended it. I got a big hand and I drank at a few tables and I danced with a few girls.

After one more day and one more night, the boat landed in New York. I woke up, I was bright awake at once, and I thought, *We're here.* I turned on all the lights in my small cabin and I stared into the mirror as though I were committing my face to memory. I took a shower and I took a long time shaving and I dressed myself very carefully. I walked the long ship corridors to the dining room, looking at the luggage piled high before the elevators and beside the steps. The dining room was nearly half empty and full of a quick and joyous excitement which depressed me even more. People ate quickly, chattering to each other, anxious to get upstairs and go on deck. Was it my imagination or was it true that they seemed to avoid my eyes? A few people waved and smiled, but let me pass; perhaps it would have made them uncomfortable, this morning, to try to share their excitement with me; perhaps they did not want to know whether or not it was possible for me to share it. I walked to my table and sat down. I munched toast as dry as paper and drank a pot of coffee. Then I tipped my waiter, who bowed and smiled and called me "sir" and said that he hoped to see me on the boat again. "I hope so, too," I said.

And was it true, or was it my imagination, that a flash of wondering comprehension, a flicker of wry sympathy, then appeared in the waiter's eyes? I walked upstairs to the deck.

There was a breeze from the water but the sun was hot and made me re-member how ugly New York summers could be. All of the deck chairs had been taken away and people milled about in the space where the deck chairs had been, moved from one side of the ship to the other, clambered up and down the steps, crowded the rails, and they were busy taking photo-graphs—of the harbor, of each other, of the sea, of the gulls. I walked slowly along the deck, and an impulse stronger than myself drove me to the rail. There it was, the great, unfinished city, with all its towers blazing in the sun. It came toward us slowly and patiently, like some enormous, cun-ning, and murderous beast, ready to devour, impossible to escape. I watched it come closer and I listened to the people around me, to their ex-citement and their pleasure. There was no doubt that it was real. I watched their shining faces and wondered if I were mad. For a moment I longed, with all my heart, to be able to feel whatever they were feeling, if only to know what such a feeling was like. As the boat moved slowly into the har-bor, they were being moved into safety. It was only I who was being floated into danger. I turned my head, looking for Europe, but all that stretched behind me was the sky, thick with gulls. I moved away from the rail. A big, sandy-haired man held his daughter on his shoulders, showing her the Statue of Liberty. I would never know what this statue meant to others, she had always been an ugly joke for me. And the American flag was flying from the top of the ship, above my head. I had seen the French flag drive the French into the most unspeakable frenzies, I had seen the flag which was nominally mine used to dignify the vilest purposes: now I would never, as long as I lived, know what others saw when they saw a flag. "There's no place like home," said a voice close by, and I thought, *There damn sure isn't.* I decided to go back to my cabin and have a drink.

There was a cablegram from Harriet in my cabin. It said: Be good. Be quick. I'm waiting. I folded it carefully and put it in my breast pocket. Then I wondered if I would ever get back to her. How long would it take me to earn the money to get out of this land? Sweat broke out on my fore-head and I poured myself some whiskey from my nearly empty bottle. I paced the tiny cabin. It was silent. There was no one down in the cabins now.

I was not sober when I faced the uniforms in the first-class lounge. There were two of them; they were not unfriendly. They looked at my passport, they looked at me. "You've been away a long time," said one of them.

"Yes," I said, "it's been a while."

"What did you do over there all that time?"—with a grin meant to hide more than it revealed, which hideously revealed more than it could hide.

I said, "I'm a singer," and the room seemed to rock around me. I held on to what I hoped was a calm, open smile. I had not had to deal with these faces in so long that I had forgotten how to do it. I had once known how to pitch my voice precisely between curtness and servility, and known what razor's edge of a pickaninny's smile would turn away wrath. But I had forgotten all the tricks on which my life had once depended. Once I had been an expert at baffling these people, at setting their teeth on edge, and dancing just outside the trap laid for me. But I was not an expert now. These faces were no longer merely the faces of two white men, who were my enemies. They were the faces of two white people whom I did not understand, and I could no longer plan my moves in accordance with what I knew of their cowardice and their needs and their strategy. That moment on the bridge had undone me forever.

"That's right," said one of them, "that's what it says, right here on the passport. Never heard of you, though." They looked up at me. "Did you do a lot of singing over there?"

"Some."

"What kind—concerts?"

"No." I wondered what I looked like, sounded like. I could tell nothing from their eyes. "I worked a few nightclubs."

"Nightclubs, eh? I guess they liked you over there."

"Yes," I said, "they seemed to like me all right."

"Well"—and my passport was stamped and handed back to me—"let's hope they like you over here."

"Thanks." They laughed—was it at me, or was it my imagination? and I picked up the one bag I was carrying and threw my trench coat over one shoulder and walked out of the first-class lounge. I stood in the slow-moving, murmuring line which led to the gangplank. I looked straight ahead and watched heads, smiling faces, step up to the shadow of the gangplank awning and then swiftly descend out of sight. I put my passport back in my breast pocket—*Be quick. I'm waiting*—and I held my landing card in my hand. Then, suddenly, there I was, standing on the edge of the boat, staring down the long ramp to the ground. At the end of the plank, on the ground, stood a heavy man in a uniform. His cap was pushed back from his gray hair and his face was red and wet. He looked up at me. This was the face I remembered, the face of my nightmares; perhaps hatred had caused me to know this face better than I would ever know the face of any lover. "Come on, boy," he cried, "come on, come on!"

And I almost smiled. I was home. I touched my breast pocket. I thought of a song I sometimes sang, *When will I ever get to be a man?* I came down the gangplank, stumbling a little, and gave the man my landing card.

Much later in the day, a customs inspector checked my baggage and waved me away. I picked up my bags and started walking down the long stretch which led to the gate, to the city.

And I heard someone call my name.

I looked up and saw Louisa running toward me. I dropped my bags and grabbed her in my arms and tears came to my eyes and rolled down my face. I did not know whether the tears were for joy at seeing her, or from rage, or both.

"How are you? How are you? You look wonderful, but, oh, haven't you lost weight? It's wonderful to see you again."

I wiped my eyes. "It's wonderful to see you, too, I bet you thought I was never coming back."

Louisa laughed. "I wouldn't have blamed you if you hadn't. These people are just as corny as ever, I swear I don't believe there's any hope for them. How's your French? Lord, when I think that it was I who studied French and now I can't speak a word. And you never went near it and you probably speak it like a native."

I grinned. *"Pas mal. Te me défends pas mal."* We started down the wide steps into the street. "My God," I said. "New York." I was not aware of its towers now. We were in the shadow of the elevated highway but the thing which most struck me was neither light nor shade, but noise. It came from a million things at once, from trucks and tires and clutches and brakes and doors; from machines shuttling and stamping and rolling and cutting and pressing; from the building of tunnels, the checking of gas mains, the laying of wires, the digging of foundations; from the chattering of rivets, the scream of the pile driver, the clanging of great shovels; from the battering down and the raising up of walls; from millions of radios and television sets and juke boxes. The human voices distinguished themselves from the roar only by their note of strain and hostility. Another fleshy man, uniformed and red faced, hailed a cab for us and touched his cap politely but could only manage a peremptory growl: "Right this way, miss. Step up, sir." He slammed the cab door behind us. Louisa directed the driver to the New Yorker Hotel.

"Do they take us there?"

She looked at me. "They got laws in New York, honey, it'd be the easiest thing in the world to spend all your time in court. But over at the New Yorker, I believe they've already got the message." She took my arm. "You see? In spite of all this chopping and booming, this place hasn't really changed very much. You still can't hear yourself talk."

And I thought to myself, Maybe that's the point.

Early the next morning we checked out of the hotel and took the plane for Alabama.

I am just stepping out of the shower when I hear the bell ring. I dry myself hurriedly and put on a bathrobe. It is Vidal, of course, and very elegant he is, too, with his bushy gray hair quite lustrous, his swarthy, cynical, gypsylike face shaved and lotioned. Usually he looks just any old way. But tonight his brief bulk is contained in a dark-blue suit and he has an ironical pearl stickpin in his blue tie.

"Come in, make yourself a drink. I'll be with you in a second."

"I am, *hélas!*, on time. I trust you will forgive me for my thoughtlessness."

But I am already back in the bathroom. Vidal puts on a record: Mahalia Jackson, singing *I'm Going to Live the Life I Sing About in My Song.*

When I am dressed, I find him sitting in a chair before the open window. The daylight is gone, but it is not exactly dark. The trees are black now against the darkening sky. The lights in windows and the lights of motorcars are yellow and ringed. The street lights have not yet been turned on. It is as though, out of deference to the departed day, Paris waited a decent interval before assigning her role to a more theatrical but inferior performer.

Vidal is drinking a whiskey and soda. I pour myself a drink. He watches me.

"Well. How are you, my friend? You are nearly gone. Are you happy to be leaving us?"

"No." I say this with more force than I had intended. Vidal raises his eyebrows, looking amused and distant. "I never really intended to go back there. I certainly never intended to raise my kid there—"

"*Mais, mon cher,*" Vidal says, calmly, "you are an intelligent man, you must have known that you would probably be returning one day." He pauses. "And, as for Pauli—did it never occur to you that he might wish one day to see the country in which his father and his father's fathers were born?"

"To do that, really, he'd have to go to Africa."

"America will always mean more to him than Africa, you know that."

"I don't know." I throw my drink down and pour myself another. "Why should he want to cross all that water just to be called a nigger? America never gave him anything."

"It gave him his father."

I look at him. "You mean, his father escaped."

Vidal throws back his head and laughs. If Vidal likes you, he is certain to laugh at you and his laughter can be very unnerving. But the look, the silence which follows this laughter can be very unnerving, too. And, now, in the silence, he asks me, "Do you really think that you have escaped anything? Come. I know you for a better man than that." He walks to the table which holds the liquor. "In that movie of ours which has made you so famous, and, as I now see, so troubled, what are you playing, after all? What is the tragedy of this half-breed troubadour if not, precisely, that he has taken all the possible roads to escape and that all these roads have failed him?" He pauses, with the bottle in one hand, and looks at me. "Do you remember the trouble I had to get a performance out of you? How you hated me, you sometimes looked as though you wanted to shoot me! And do you remember when the role of Chico began to come alive?" He pours his drink. "Think back, remember. I am a very great director, *mais pardon!* I could not have got such a performance out of anyone but you. And what were you thinking of, what was in your mind, what nightmare were you living with when you began, at last, to play the role—truthfully?" He walks back to his seat.

Chico, in the film, is the son of a Martinique woman and a French *colon* who hates both his mother and his father. He flees from the island to the capital, carrying his hatred with him. This hatred has now grown, naturally, to include all dark women and all white men, in a word, everyone. He descends into the underworld of Paris, where he dies. *Les fauves*—the wild beasts—refers to the life he has fled and to the life which engulfs him. When I agreed to do the role, I felt that I could probably achieve it by bearing in mind the North Africans I had watched in Paris for so long. But this did not please Vidal. The blowup came while we were rehearsing a fairly simple, straightforward scene. Chico goes into a sleazy Pigalle dance hall to beg the French owner for a particularly humiliating job. And this Frenchman reminds him of his father.

"You are playing this boy as though you thought of him as the noble savage," Vidal said, icily. *"Ça vient d'où*—all these ghastly mannerisms you are using all the time?"

Everyone fell silent, for Vidal rarely spoke this way. This silence told me that everyone, the actor with whom I was playing the scene and all the people in the "dance hall," shared Vidal's opinion of my performance and were relieved that he was going to do something about it. I was humiliated and too angry to speak; but perhaps I also felt, at the very bottom of my heart, a certain relief, an unwilling respect.

"You are doing it all wrong," he said, more gently. Then, "Come, let us have a drink together."

We walked into his office. He took a bottle and two glasses out of his desk. "Forgive me, but you put me in mind of some of those English *lady* actresses who love to play *putain* as long as it is always absolutely clear to the audience that they are really ladies. So perhaps they read a book, not usually, *hélas!, Fanny Hill,* and they have their chauffeurs drive them through Soho once or twice—and they come to the stage with a performance so absolutely loaded with detail, every bit of it meaningless, that there can be no doubt that they are acting. It is what the British call a triumph." He poured two cognacs. "That is what you are doing. Why? Who do you think this boy is, what do you think he is feeling, when he asks for this job?" He watched me carefully and I bitterly resented his look. "You come from America. The situation is not so pretty there for boys like you. I know you may not have been as poor as—as some—but is it really impossible for you to understand what a boy like Chico feels? Have you never, yourself, been in a similar position?"

I hated him for asking the question because I knew he knew the answer to it. "I would have had to be a very lucky black man not to have been in such a position."

"You would have had to be a very lucky *man.*"

"Oh, God," I said, "please don't give me any of this equality-in-anguish business."

"It is perfectly possible," he said, sharply, "that there is not another kind."

Then he was silent. He sat down behind his desk. He cut a cigar and lit it, puffing up clouds of smoke, as though to prevent us from seeing each other too clearly. "Consider this," he said. "I am a French director who has never seen your country. I have never done you any harm, except, perhaps, historically—I mean, because I am white—but I cannot be blamed for that—"

"But *I* can be," I said, "and I am! I've never understood why, if *I* have to pay for the history written in the color of my skin, *you* should get off scot-free!" But I was surprised at my vehemence, I had not known I was going to say these things, and by the fact that I was trembling and from the way he looked at me I knew that, from a professional point of view anyway, I was playing into his hands.

"What makes you think I *do?*" His face looked weary and stern. "I am a Frenchman. Look at France. You think that I—we—are not paying for our history?" He walked to the window, staring out at the rather grim little town in which the studio was located. "If it is revenge that you want, well, then, let me tell you, you will have it. You will probably have it, whether you want it or not, our stupidity will make it inevitable." He turned back into the room. "But I beg you not to confuse me with the happy people of your country, who scarcely know that there is such a thing as history and so, naturally, imagine that they can escape, as you put it, scot-free. That is what you are doing, that is what I was about to say. I was about to say that I am a French director and I have never been in your country and I have never done you any harm—but you are not talking to that man, in this room, now. You are not talking to Jean Luc Vidal, but to some other white man, whom you remember, who has nothing to do with me." He paused and went back to his desk. "Oh, most of the time you are not like this, I know. But it is there all the time, it must be, because when you are upset, this is what comes out. So you are not playing Chico truthfully, you are lying about him, and I will not let you do it. When you go back, now, and play this scene again, I want you to remember what has just happened in this room. You brought your past into this room. That is what Chico does when he walks into the dance hall. The Frenchman whom he begs for a job is not merely a Frenchman—he is the father who disowned and betrayed him and all the Frenchmen whom he hates." He smiled and poured me another cognac. "Ah! If it were not for *my* history, I would not have so much trouble to get the truth out of you." He looked into my face, half smiling. "And you, you are angry—are you not?—that I *ask* you for the truth. You think I have no right to ask." Then he said something which he knew would enrage me. "Who are you then, and what good has it done you to come to France, and how will you raise your son? Will you teach him never to tell the truth to anyone?" And he moved behind his desk and looked at me, as though from behind a barricade.

"You have no right to talk to me this way."

"Oh, yes, I do," he said. "I have a film to make and a reputation to maintain and I am going to get a performance out of you." He looked at his watch. "Let us go back to work."

I watch him now, sitting quietly in my living room, tough, cynical, crafty old Frenchman, and I wonder if he knows that the nightmare at the bottom of my mind, as I played the role of Chico, was all the possible fates of Paul. This is but another way of saying that I relived the disasters which had nearly undone me; but, because I was thinking of Paul, I discovered that I did not want my son ever to feel toward me as I had felt toward my own father. He had died when I was eleven, but I had watched the humiliations he had to bear, and I had pitied him. But was there not, in that pity, however painfully and unwillingly, also some contempt? For how could I *know* what he had borne? I knew only that I was his son. However he had loved me, whatever he had borne, I, his son, was despised. Even had he lived, he could have done nothing to prevent it, nothing to protect me. The best that he could hope to do was to prepare me for it; and even at that he had failed. How can one be prepared for the spittle in the face, all the tireless ingenuity which goes into the spite and fear of small, unutterably miserable people, whose greatest terror is the singular identity, whose joy, whose safety, is entirely dependent on the humiliation and anguish of others?

But for Paul, I swore it, such a day would never come. I would throw my life and my work between Paul and the nightmare of the world. I would make it impossible for the world to treat Paul as it had treated my father and me.

Mahalia's record ends. Vidal rises to turn it over. "Well?" He looks at me very affectionately. "Your nightmares, please!"

"Oh, I was thinking of that summer I spent in Alabama, when my mother died." I stop. "You know, but when we finally filmed that bar scene, I was thinking of New York. I was scared in Alabama, but I almost went crazy in New York. I was sure I'd never make it back here—back here to Harriet. And I knew if I didn't, it was going to be the end of me." Now Mahalia is singing *When the Saints Go Marching In*. "I got a job in the town as an elevator boy, in the town's big department store. It was a special favor, one of my father's white friends got it for me. For a long time, in the South, we all—depended—on the—*kindness*—of white friends." I take out a handkerchief and wipe my face. "But this man didn't like me. I guess I didn't seem grateful enough, wasn't enough like my father, what he thought my father was. And I couldn't get used to the town again, I'd been away too long, I hated it. It's a terrible town, anyway, the whole thing looks as though it's been built around a jailhouse. There's a room in the courthouse, a room where they beat you up. Maybe you're walking along the street one night, it's usually at night, but it happens in the daytime, too. And the police car comes up behind you and the cop says, 'Hey, boy. Come on over here.' So you go on over. He says, 'Boy, I believe you're drunk.' And, you see, if you say, 'No, no sir,' he'll beat you because you're calling him a liar. And if you say anything else, unless it's something to make him laugh, he'll take you in and beat you, just for fun. The trick is to think of some way for them to have their fun without beating you up."

The street lights of Paris click on and turn all the green leaves silver. "Or to go along with the ways *they* dream up. And they'll do anything, anything at all, to prove that you're no better than a dog and to make you feel like one. And they hated me because I'd been North and I'd been to Europe. People kept saying, I hope you didn't bring no foreign notions back here with you, boy. And I'd say, 'No sir,' or 'No ma'am,' but I never said it right. And there was a time, all of them remembered it, when I *had* said it right. But now they could tell that I despised them—I guess, no matter what, I wanted them to know that I despised them. But I didn't despise them any more than everyone else did, only the others never let it show. They knew how to keep the white folks happy, and it was easy—you just had to keep them feeling like they were God's favor to the universe. They'd walk around with great, big, foolish grins on their faces and the colored folks loved to see this, because they hated them so much. "Just look at So-and-So," somebody'd say. "His white is *on* him today." And when we didn't hate them, we pitied them. In America, that's usually what it means to have a white friend. You pity the poor bastard because he was born believing the world's a great place to be, and you know it's not, and you can see that he's going to have a terrible time getting used to this idea, if he ever gets used to it."

Then I think of Paul again, those eyes which still imagine that I can do anything, that skin, the color of honey and fire, his jet-black, curly hair. I look out at Paris again, and I listen to Mahalia. "Maybe it's better to have the terrible times first. I don't know. Maybe, then, you can have, *if* you live, a better life, a real life, because you had to fight so hard to get it away —you know?—from the mad dog who held it in his teeth. But then your life has all those tooth marks, too, all those tatters, and all that blood." I walk to the bottle and raise it. "One for the road?"

"Thank you," says Vidal.

I pour us a drink, and he watches me. I have never talked so much before, not about those things anyway. I know that Vidal has nightmares, because he knows so much about them, but he has never told me what his are. I think that he probably does not talk about his nightmares any more. I know that the war cost him his wife and his son, and that he was in prison in Germany. He very rarely refers to it. He has a married daughter who lives in England, and he rarely speaks of her. He is like a man who has learned to live on what is left of an enormous fortune.

We are silent for a moment.

"Please go on," he says, with a smile. "I am curious about the reality behind the reality of your performance."

"My sister, Louisa, never married," I say, abruptly, "because, once, years ago, she and the boy she was going with and two friends of theirs were out driving in a car and the police stopped them. The girl who was with them was very fair and the police pretended not to believe her when she said she was colored. They made her get out and stand in front of the headlights of the car and pull down her pants and raise her dress—they said that was the only way they could be sure. And you can imagine what they said, and what they did—and they were lucky, at that, that it didn't go any further. But none of the men could do anything about it. Louisa couldn't face the boy again, and I guess he couldn't face her." Now it is really growing dark in the room and I cross to the light switch. "You know, I know what that boy felt, I've felt it. They want you to feel that you're not a man, maybe that's the only way they can feel like men, I don't know. I walked around New York with Harriet's cablegram in my pocket as though it were some atomic secret, in *code*, and they'd kill me if they ever found out what it meant. You know, there's something wrong with people like that. And thank God Harriet was here, she *proved* that the world was bigger than the world they wanted me to live in, I *had* to get back here, get to a place where people were too busy with their own lives, *their private lives*, to make fantasies about mine, to set up walls around mine." I look at him. The light in the room has made the night outside blue-black and golden and the great searchlight of the Eiffel Tower is turning in the sky. "That's what it's like in America, for me, anyway. I always feel that I don't exist there, except in someone else's—usually dirty—mind. I don't know if you know what that means, but I do, and I don't want to put Harriet through that and I don't want to raise Paul there."

"Well," he says at last, "you are not required to remain in America forever, are you? You will sing in that elegant club which apparently feels that it cannot, much longer, so much as open its doors without you, and you will probably accept the movie offer, you would be very foolish not to. You will make a lot of money. Then, one day, you will remember that airlines and steamship companies are still in business and that France still exists. *That* will certainly be cause for astonishment."

Vidal was a Gaullist before de Gaulle came to power. But he regrets the manner of de Gaulle's rise and he is worried about de Gaulle's regime. "It is not the fault of *mon général*," he sometimes says, sadly. "Perhaps it is history's fault. I *suppose* it must be history which always arranges to bill a civilization at the very instant it is least prepared to pay."

Now he rises and walks out on the balcony, as though to reassure himself of the reality of Paris. Mahalia is singing *Didn't It Rain?* I walk out and stand beside him.

"You are a good boy—Chico," he says. I laugh. "You believe in love. You do not know all the things love cannot do, but"—he smiles—"love will teach you that."

We go, after dinner, to a Left Bank discothèque which can charge outrageous prices because Marlon Brando wandered in there one night. By accident, according to Vidal. "Do you know how many people in Paris are becoming rich—to say nothing of those, *hélas!*, who are going broke—on the off chance that Marlon Brando will lose his way again?"

He has not, presumably, lost his way tonight, but the discothèque is crowded with those strangely faceless people who are part of the night life of all great cities, and who always arrive, moments, hours, or decades late, on the spot made notorious by an event or a movement or a handful of personalities. So here are American boys, anything but beardless, scratching around for Hemingway; American girls, titillating themselves with Frenchmen and existentialism, while waiting for the American boys to shave off their beards; French painters, busily pursuing the revolution which ended thirty years ago; and the young, bored, perverted, American *arrivistes* who are buying their way into the art world via flattery and liquor, and the production of canvases as arid as their greedy little faces. Here are boys, of all nations, one step above the pimp, who are occasionally walked across a stage or trotted before a camera. And the girls, their enemies, whose faces are sometimes seen in ads, one of whom will surely have a tantrum before the evening is out.

In a corner, as usual, surrounded, as usual, by smiling young men, sits the drunken blonde woman who was once the mistress of a famous, dead painter. She is a figure of some importance in the art world, and so rarely has to pay for either her drinks or her lovers. An older Frenchman, who was once a famous director, is playing *quatre cent vingt-et-un* with the woman behind the cash register. He nods pleasantly to Vidal and me as we enter, but makes no move to join us, and I respect him for this. Vidal and I are obviously cast tonight in the role vacated by Brando: our entrance justifies the prices and sends a kind of shiver through the room. It is mar-

velous to watch the face of the waiter as he approaches, all smiles and deference and grace, not so much honored by our presence as achieving his
reality from it; excellence, he seems to be saying, gravitates naturally toward excellence. We order two whiskey and sodas. I know why Vidal sometimes comes here. He is lonely. I do not think that he expects ever to love
one woman again, and so he distracts himself with many.

Since this is a discothèque, jazz is blaring from the walls and record
sleeves are scattered about with a devastating carelessness. Two of them are
mine and no doubt, presently, someone will play the recording of the songs
I sang in the film.

"I thought," says Vidal, with a malicious little smile, "that your farewell to Paris would not be complete without a brief exposure to the perils of
fame. Perhaps it will help prepare you for America, where, I am told, the
populace is yet more carnivorous than it is here."

I can see that one of the vacant models is preparing herself to come to
our table and ask for an autograph, hoping, since she is pretty—she has,
that is, the usual female equipment, dramatized in the usual, modern way
—to be invited for a drink. Should the maneuver succeed, one of her boy
friends or girl friends will contrive to come by the table, asking for a light
or a pencil or a lipstick, and it will be extremely difficult not to invite this
person to join us, too. Before the evening ends, we will be surrounded. I
don't, now, know what I expected of fame, but I suppose it never occurred
to me that the light could be just as dangerous, just as killing, as the dark.

"Well, let's make it brief," I tell him. "Sometimes I wish that you weren't
quite so fond of me."

He laughs. "There are some very interesting people here tonight. Look."

Across the room from us, and now staring at our table, are a group of
American Negro students, who are probably visiting Paris for the first time.
There are four of them, two boys and two girls, and I suppose that they
must be in their late teens or early twenties. One of the boys, a gleaming,
curly-haired, golden-brown type—the color of his mother's fried chicken—
is carrying a guitar. When they realize we have noticed them, they smile
and wave—wave as though I were one of their possessions, as, indeed, I
am. Golden-brown is a mime. He raises his guitar, drops his shoulders,
and his face falls into the lugubrious lines of Chico's face as he approaches
death. He strums a little of the film's theme music, and I laugh and the table laughs. It is as though we were all back home and had met for a moment, on a Sunday morning, say, before a church or a poolroom or a barbershop.

And they have created a sensation in the discothèque, naturally, having managed, with no effort whatever, to outwit all the gleaming boys and girls. Their table, which had been of no interest only a moment before, has now become the focus of a rather pathetic attention; their smiles have made it possible for the others to smile, and to nod in our direction.

"Oh," says Vidal, "he does that far better than you ever did, perhaps I will make him a star."

"Feel free, *m'sieu, le bon Dieu,* I got mine." But I can see that his attention has really been caught by one of the girls, slim, tense, and dark, who seems, though it is hard to know how one senses such things, to be treated by the others with a special respect. And, in fact, the table now seems to be having a council of war, to be demanding her opinion or her cooperation. She listens, frowning, laughing; the quality, the force of her intelligence causes her face to keep changing all the time, as though a light played on it. And, presently, with a gesture she might once have used to scatter feed to chickens, she scoops up from the floor one of those dangling rag bags women love to carry. She holds it loosely by the drawstrings, so that it is banging somewhere around her ankle, and walks over to our table. She has an honest, forthright walk, entirely unlike the calculated, pelvic workout by means of which most women get about. She is small, but sturdily, economically, put together.

As she reaches our table, Vidal and I rise, and this throws her for a second. (It has been a long time since I have seen such an attractive girl.)

Also, everyone, of course, is watching us. It is really a quite curious moment. They have put on the record of Chico singing a sad, angry Martinique ballad; my own voice is coming at us from the walls as the girl looks from Vidal to me, and smiles.

"I guess you know," she says, "we weren't *about* to let you get out of here without bugging you just a little bit. We've only been in Paris just a couple of days and we thought for sure that we wouldn't have a chance of running into you anywhere, because it's in all the papers that you're coming home."

"Yes," I say, "yes. I'm leaving the day after tomorrow."

"Oh!" She grins. "Then we really *are* lucky." I find that I have almost forgotten the urchin-like grin of a colored girl. "I guess, before I keep babbling on, I'd better introduce myself. My name is Ada Holmes."

We shake hands. "This is Monsieur Vidal, the director of the film."

"I'm very honored to meet you, sir."

"Will you join us for a moment? Won't you sit down?" And Vidal pulls a chair out for her.

But she frowns contritely. "I really ought to get back to my friends." She looks at me. "I really just came over to say, for myself and all the kids, that we've got your records and we've seen your movie, and it means so much to us"—and she laughs, breathlessly, nervously, it is somehow more moving than tears—"more than I can say. Much more. And we wanted to know if you and your friend"—she looks at Vidal—"your *director*, Monsieur Vidal, would allow us to buy you a drink? We'd be very honored if you would."

"It is we who are honored," says Vidal, promptly, "*and* grateful. We were getting terribly bored with one another, thank God you came along."

The three of us laugh, and we cross the room.

The three at the table rise, and Ada makes the introductions. The other girl, taller and paler than Ada, is named Ruth. One of the boys is named Talley—"short for Talliafero"—and Golden-brown's name is Pete. "Man," he tells me, "I dig you the most. You tore me up, baby, tore me *up*."

"You tore up a lot of people," Talley says, cryptically, and he and Ruth laugh. Vidal does not know, but I do, that Talley is probably referring to white people.

They are from New Orleans and Tallahassee and North Carolina; are college students, and met on the boat. They have been in Europe all summer, in Italy and Spain, but are only just getting to Paris.

"We meant to come sooner," says Ada, "but we could never make up our minds to leave a place. I thought we'd never pry Ruth loose from Venice."

"I resigned myself," says Pete, "and just sat in the Piazza San Marco, drinking gin fizz and being photographed with the pigeons, while Ruth had herself driven *all* up and down the Grand Canal." He looks at Ruth. "Finally, thank heaven, it rained."

"She was working off her hostilities," says Ada, with a grin. "We thought we might as well let her do it in Venice, the opportunities in North Carolina are really terribly limited."

"There are some very upset people walking around down there," Ruth says, "and a couple of tours around the Grand Canal might do them a world of good."

Pete laughs. "Can't you just see Ruth escorting them to the edge of the water?"

"I haven't lifted my hand in anger yet," Ruth says, "but, oh Lord," and she laughs, clenching and unclenching her fists.

"You haven't been back for a long time, have you?" Talley asks me.

"Eight years. I haven't really lived there for twelve years."

Pete whistles. "I fear you are in for some surprises, my friend. There have been some changes made." Then, "Are you afraid?"

"A little."

"We all are," says Ada, "that's why I was so glad to get away for a little while."

"Then you haven't been back since Black Monday," Talley says. He laughs. "That's how it's gone down in Confederate history." He turns to Vidal. "What do people think about it here?"

Vidal smiles, delighted. "It seems extraordinarily infantile behavior, even for Americans, from whom, I must say, I have never expected very much in the way of maturity." Everyone at the table laughs. Vidal goes on. "But I cannot really talk about it, I do not understand it. I have never really understood Americans; I am an old man now, and I suppose I never will. There is something very nice about them, something very winning, but they seem so ignorant—so ignorant of life. Perhaps it is strange, but the only people from your country with whom I have ever made contact are black people—like my good friend, my discovery, here," and he slaps me on the shoulder. "Perhaps it is because we, in Europe, whatever else we do not know, or have forgotten, know about suffering. We have suffered here. You have suffered, too. But most Americans do not yet know what anguish is. It is too bad, because the life of the West is in their hands." He turns to Ada. "I cannot help saying that I think it is a scandal—and we may all pay very dearly for it—that a civilized nation should elect to represent it a man who is so simple that he thinks the world is simple." And silence falls at the table and the four young faces stare at him.

"Well," says Pete, at last, turning to me, "you won't be bored, man, when you get back there."

"It's much too nice a night," I say, "to stay cooped up in this place, where all I can hear is my own records." We laugh. "Why don't we get out of here and find a sidewalk café?" I tap Pete's guitar. "Maybe we can find out if you've got any talent."

"Oh, talent I've got," says Pete, "but character, man, I'm lacking."

So, after some confusion about the bill, for which Vidal has already made himself responsible. we walk out into the Paris night. It is very strange to feel that, very soon now, these boulevards will not exist for me. People will be walking up and down, as they are tonight, and lovers will be murmuring in the black shadows of the plane trees, and there will be these same still figures on the benches or in the parks—but they will not exist for me, I will not be here. For a long while Paris will no longer exist for me, except in my mind; and only in the minds of some people will I exist any longer for Paris. After departure, only invisible things are left, perhaps the life of the world is held together by invisible chains of memory and loss and love. So many things, so many people, depart! And we can only repossess them in our minds. Perhaps this is what the old folks meant, what my mother and my father meant, when they counseled us to keep the faith.

We have taken a table at the Deux Magots and Pete strums on his guitar and begins to play this song:

> Preach the word, preach the word, preach the word!
> If I never, never see you any more.
> Preach the word, preach the word.
> And I'll meet you on Canaan's shore.

He has a strong, clear, boyish voice, like a young preacher's, and he is smiling as he sings his song. Ada and I look at each other and grin, and Vidal is smiling. The waiter looks a little worried, for we are already beginning to attract a crowd, but it is a summer night, the gendarmes on the corner do not seem to mind, and there will be time, anyway, to stop us.

Pete was not there, none of us were, the first time this song was needed; and no one now alive can imagine what that time was like. But the song has come down the bloodstained ages. I suppose this to mean that the song is still needed, still has its work to do.

The others are all, visibly, very proud of Pete; and we all join him, and people stop to listen:

> Testify! Testify!
> If I never, never see you any more!
> Testify! Testify!
> I'll meet you on Canaan's shore!

In the crowd that has gathered to listen to us, I see a face I know, the face of a North African prize fighter, who is no longer in the ring. I used to know him well in the old days, but have not seen him for a long time. He looks quite well, his face is shining, he is quite decently dressed. And something about the way he holds himself, not quite looking at our table, tells me that he has seen me, but does not want to risk a rebuff. So I call him. "Boona!"

And he turns, smiling, and comes loping over to our table, his hands in his pockets. Pete is still singing and Ada and Vidal have taken off on a conversation of their own. Ruth and Talley look curiously, expectantly, at Boona. Now that I have called him over, I feel somewhat uneasy. I realize that I do not know what he is doing now, or how he will get along with any of these people, and I can see in his eyes that he is delighted to be in the presence of two young girls. There are virtually no North African women in Paris, and not even the dirty, rat-faced girls who live, apparently, in cafés

355

are willing to go with an Arab. So Boona is always looking for a girl, and because he is so deprived and because he is not Western, his techniques can be very unsettling. I know he is relieved that the girls are not French and not white. He looks briefly at Vidal and Ada. Vidal, also, though for different reasons, is always looking for a girl.

But Boona has always been very nice to me. Perhaps I am sorry that I called him over, but I did not want to snub him.

He claps one hand to the side of my head, as is his habit. "*Comment vas-tu, mon frère?* I have not see you, oh, for long time." And he asks me, as in the old days, "You all right? Nobody bother you?" And he laughs. "Ah! *Tu as fait le chemin, toi!* Now you are *vedette,* big star—wonderful!" He looks around the table, made a little uncomfortable by the silence that has fallen, now that Pete has stopped singing. "I have seen you in the movies—you know?—and I tell everybody, I know *him!*" He points to me, and laughs, and Ruth and Talley laugh with him. "That's right, man, you make me real proud, you make me cry!"

"Boona, I want you to meet some friends of mine." And I go round the table: "Ruth, Talley, Ada, Pete"—and he bows and shakes hands, his dark eyes gleaming with pleasure—"*et Monsieur Vidal, le metteur en scène du film qui t'a arraché des larmes.*"

"*Enchanté.*" But his attitude toward Vidal is colder, more distrustful. "Of course I have heard of Monsieur Vidal. He is the director of many films, many of them made me cry." This last statement is utterly, even insolently, insincere.

But Vidal, I think, is relieved that I will now be forced to speak to Boona and will leave him alone with Ada.

"Sit down," I say, "have a drink with us, let me have your news. What's been happening with you, what are you doing with yourself these days?"

"Ah," he sits down, "nothing very brilliant, my brother." He looks at me quickly, with a little smile. "You know, we have been having hard times here."

"Where are you from?" Ada asks him.

His brilliant eyes take her in entirely, but she does not flinch. "I am from Tunis." He says it proudly, with a little smile.

"From Tunis. I have never been to Africa, I would love to go one day."

He laughs. "Africa is a big place. Very big. There are many countries in Africa, many"—he looks briefly at Vidal—"different kinds of people, many colonies."

"But Tunis," she continues, in her innocence, "is free? Freedom is happening all over Africa. That's why I would like to go there."

356

"I have not been back for a long time," says Boona, "but all the news I get from Tunis, from my people, is not good."

"Wouldn't you like to go back?" Ruth asks.

Again he looks at Vidal. "That is not so easy."

Vidal smiles. "You know what I would like to do? There's a wonderful Spanish place not far from here, where we can listen to live music and dance a little." He turns to Ada. "Would you like that?"

He is leaving it up to me to get rid of Boona, and it is, of course, precisely for this reason that I cannot do it. Besides, it is no longer so simple.

"Oh, I'd love that," says Ada, and she turns to Boona. "Won't you come, too?"

"Thank you, mam'selle," he says, softly, and his tongue flicks briefly over his lower lip, and he smiles. He is very moved, people are not often nice to him.

In the Spanish place there are indeed a couple of Spanish guitars, drums, castanets, and a piano, but the uses to which these are being put carry one back, as Pete puts it, to the levee. "These are the wailingest Spanish cats I ever heard," says Ruth. "They didn't learn how to do this in Spain, no, they didn't, they been rambling. You ever hear anything like this going on in Spain?" Talley takes her out on the dance floor, which is already crowded. A very handsome Frenchwoman is dancing with an enormous, handsome black man, who seems to be her lover, who seems to have taught her how to dance. Apparently, they are known to the musicians, who egg them on with small cries of *"Olé!"* It is a very good-natured crowd, mostly foreigners, Spaniards, Swedes, Greeks. Boona takes Ada out on the dance floor while Vidal is answering some questions put to him by Pete on the entertainment situation in France. Vidal looks a little put out, and I am amused.

We are there for perhaps an hour, dancing, talking, and I am, at last, a little drunk. In spite of Boona, who is a very good and tireless dancer, Vidal continues his pursuit of Ada, and I begin to wonder if he will make it and I begin to wonder if I want him to.

I am still puzzling out my reaction when Pete, who has disappeared, comes in through the front door, catches my eye, and signals to me. I leave the table and follow him into the streets.

He looks very upset. "I don't want to bug you, man," he says, "but I fear your boy has goofed."

I know he is not joking. I think he is probably angry at Vidal because of Ada, and I wonder what I can do about it and why he should be telling me.

I stare at him, gravely, and he says, "It looks like he stole some money."

"Stole *money?* Who, Vidal?"

And then, of course, I get it, in the split second before he says, impatiently, "No, are you kidding? Your friend, the Tunisian."

I do not know what to say or what to do, and so I temporize with questions. All the time I am wondering if this can be true and what I can do about it if it is. The trouble is, I know that Boona steals, he would probably not be alive if he didn't, but I cannot say so to these children, who probably still imagine that everyone who steals is a thief. But he has never, to my knowledge, stolen from a friend. It seems unlike him. I have always thought of him as being better than that, and smarter than that. And so I cannot believe it, but neither can I doubt it. I do not know anything about Boona's life, these days. This causes me to realize that I do not really know much about Boona.

"Who did he steal it from?"

"From Ada. Out of her bag."

"How much?"

"Ten dollars. It's not an awful lot of money, but"—he grimaces—"none of us *have* an awful lot of money."

"I know." The dark side street on which we stand is nearly empty. The only sound on the street is the muffled music of the Spanish club. "How do you know it was Boona?"

He anticipates my own unspoken rejoinder. "Who else could it be? Besides—somebody *saw* him do it."

"Somebody saw him?"

"Yes."

I do not ask him who this person is, for fear that he will say it is Vidal.

"Well," I say, "I'll try to get it back." I think that I will take Boona aside and then replace the money myself. "Was it in dollars or in francs?"

"In francs."

I have no dollars and this makes it easier. I do not know how I can possibly face Boona and accuse him of stealing money from my friends. I would rather give him the benefit of even the faintest doubt. But, "Who saw him?" I ask.

"Talley. But we didn't want to make a thing about it—"

"Does Ada know it's gone?"

"Yes." He looks at me helplessly. "I know this makes you feel pretty bad, but we thought we'd better tell you, rather than"—lamely—"anybody else."

Now, Ada comes out of the club, carrying her ridiculous handbag, and with her face all knotted and sad. "Oh," she says, "I hate to cause all this trouble, it's not worth it, not for ten lousy dollars." I am astonished to see that she has been weeping, and tears come to her eyes now.

I put my arm around her shoulder. "Come on, now. You're not causing anybody any trouble and, anyway, it's nothing to cry about."

"It isn't your fault, Ada," Pete says, miserably.

"Oh, I ought to get a sensible handbag," she says, "like you're always telling me to do," and she laughs a little, then looks at me. "Please don't try to do anything about it. Let's just forget it."

"What's happening inside?" I ask her.

"Nothing. They're just talking. I think Mr. Vidal is dancing with Ruth. He's a great dancer, that little Frenchman."

"He's a great talker, too," Pete says.

"Oh, he doesn't mean anything," says Ada, "he's just having fun. He probably doesn't get a chance to talk to many American girls."

"He certainly made up for lost time tonight."

"Look," I say, "if Talley and Boona are alone, maybe you better go back in. We'll be in in a minute. Let's try to keep this as quiet as we can."

"Yeah," he says, "okay. We're going soon anyway, okay?"

"Yes," she tells him, "right away."

But as he turns away, Boona and Talley step out into the street, and it is clear that Talley feels that he has Boona under arrest. I almost laugh, the whole thing is beginning to resemble one of those mad French farces with people flying in and out of doors; but Boona comes straight to me.

"They say I stole money, my friend. You know me, you are the only one here who knows me, you know I would not do such a thing."

I look at him and I do not know what to say. Ada looks at him with her eyes full of tears and looks away. I take Boona's arm.

"We'll be back in a minute," I say. We walk a few paces up the dark, silent street.

"She say I take her money," he says. He, too, looks as though he is about to weep—but I do not know for which reason. "You know me, you know me almost twelve years, you think I do such a thing?"

Talley saw you, I want to say, but I cannot say it. Perhaps Talley only thought he saw him. Perhaps it is easy to see a boy who looks like Boona with his hand in an American girl's purse.

"If you not believe me," he says, "search me. Search me!" And he opens his arms wide, theatrically, and now there are tears standing in his eyes.

I do not know what his tears mean, but I certainly cannot search him. I want to say, I know you steal, I know you have to steal. Perhaps you took the money out of this girl's purse in order to eat tomorrow, in order not to be thrown into the streets tonight, in order to stay out of jail. This girl means nothing to you, after all, she is only an American, an American like me. Perhaps, I suddenly think, no girl means anything to you, or ever will again, they have beaten you too hard and kept you out in the gutter too long. And I also think, if you would steal from her, then of course you would lie to me, neither of us means anything to you; perhaps, in your eyes, we are simply luckier gangsters in a world which is run by gangsters. But I cannot say any of these things to Boona. I cannot say, Tell me the truth, nobody cares about the money any more.

So I say, "Of course I will not search you." And I realize that he knew I would not.

"I think it is that Frenchman who say I am a thief. They think we all are thieves." His eyes are bright and bitter. He loooks over my shoulder. "They have all come out of the club now."

I look around and they are all there, in a little dark knot on the sidewalk.

"Don't worry," I say. "It doesn't matter."

"You believe me? My brother?" And his eyes look into mine with a terrible intensity.

"Yes," I force myself to say, "yes, of course, I believe you. Someone made a mistake, that's all."

"You know, the way American girls run around, they have their sack open all the time, she could have lost the money anywhere. Why she blame me? Because I come from Africa?" Tears are glittering on his face. "Here she come now."

And Ada comes up the street with her straight, determined walk. She walks straight to Boona and takes his hand. "I am sorry," she says, "for everything that happened. Please believe me. It isn't worth all this fuss. I'm sure you're a very nice person, and"—she falters—"I must have lost the money, I'm sure I lost it." She looks at him. "It isn't worth hurting your feelings, and I'm terribly sorry about it."

"I no take your money," he says. "Really, truly, I no take it. Ask him"— pointing to me, grabbing me by the arm, shaking me—"he know me for years, he will tell you that I never, never steal!"

"I'm sure," she says. "I'm sure."

I take Boona by the arm again. "Let's forget it. Let's forget it all. We're all going home now, and one of these days we'll have a drink again and we'll forget all about it, all right?"

"Yes," says Ada, "let us forget it." And she holds out her hand.

Boona takes it, wonderingly. His eyes take her in again. "You are a very nice girl. Really. A very nice girl."

"I'm sure you're a nice person, too." She pauses. "Goodnight."

"Goodnight," he says, after a long silence.

Then he kisses me on both cheeks. *"Au revoir, mon frère."*

"Au revoir, Boona."

After a moment we turn and walk away, leaving him standing there.

"Did he take it?" asks Vidal.

"I tell you, I *saw* him," says Talley.

"Well," I say, "it doesn't matter now." I look back and see Boona's stocky figure disappearing down the street.

"No," says Ada, "it doesn't matter." She looks up. "It's almost morning."

"I would gladly," says Vidal, stammering, "gladly—"

But she is herself again. "I wouldn't think of it. We had a wonderful time tonight, a wonderful time, and I wouldn't think of it." She turns to me with that urchin-like grin. "It was wonderful meeting you. I hope you won't have too much trouble getting used to the States again."

"Oh, I don't think I will," I say. And then, "I hope you won't."

"No," she says, "I don't think anything they can do will surprise me any more."

"Which way are we all going?" asks Vidal. "I hope someone will share my taxi with me."

But he lives in the sixteenth arrondissement, which is not in anyone's direction. We walk him to the line of cabs standing under the clock at Odéon.

And we look each other in the face, in the growing morning light. His face looks weary and lined and lonely. He puts both hands on my shoulders and then puts one hand on the nape of my neck. "Do not forget me, Chico," he says. "You must come back and see us, one of these days. Many of us depend on you for many things."

"I'll be back," I say. "I'll never forget you."

He raises his eyebrows and smiles. *"Alors, Adieu."*

"Adieu, Vidal."

"I was happy to meet all of you," he says. He looks at Ada. "Perhaps we will meet again before you leave."

"Perhaps," she says. "Goodby, Monsieur Vidal."

"Goodby."

Vidal's cab drives away. "I also leave you now," I say. "I must go home and wake up my son and prepare for our journey."

I leave them standing on the corner, under the clock, which points to six. They look very strange and lost and determined, the four of them. Just before my cab turns off the boulevard, I wave to them and they wave back.

Mme. Dumont is in the hall, mopping the floor.

"Did all my family get home?" I ask. I feel very cheerful, I do not know why.

"Yes," she says, "they are all here. Paul is still sleeping."

"May I go in and get him?"

She looks at me in surprise. "Of course."

So I walk into her apartment and walk into the room where Paul lies sleeping. I stand over his bed for a long time.

Perhaps my thoughts traveled—travel through to him. He opens his eyes and smiles up at me. He puts a fist to his eyes and raises his arms. *"Bonjour, Papa."*

I lift him up. *"Bonjour.* How do you feel today?"

"Oh, I don't know yet," he says.

I laugh. I put him on my shoulder and walk out into the hall. Mme. Dumont looks up at him with her radiant, aging face.

"Ah," she says, "you are going on a journey! How does it feel?"

"He doesn't know yet," I tell her. I walk to the elevator door and open it, dropping Paul down to the crook of my arm.

She laughs again. "He will know later. What a journey! *Jusqu'au nouveau monde!"*

I open the cage and we step inside. "Yes," I say, "all the way to the new world." I press the button and the cage, holding my son and me, goes up.

JAMES BALDWIN: THE BLACK AND THE RED-WHITE-AND-BLUE

John V. Hagopian

James Baldwin's "This Morning, This Evening, So Soon," first published in 1960, appears to be a relatively simple story, but it is full of subtle and surprising complexities. A young American Negro, who has for 12 years been living in exile in Paris, where he has established a family (a Swedish wife and a 7-year-old son) and has found fame as a singer and actor, has decided to return to America. He is full of fear and anxiety, especially for his son who may suffer the spiritually crippling effects of American anti-Negro prejudice. But the experiences and reminiscences of his last 24 hours in Paris change his mood—they make him feel "very cheerful, I do not know why"—and he finds himself smiling at the prospect of taking his son "all the way to the new world." This story is an honest, articulate, even eloquent exploration of the inner thoughts and feelings of a sensitive Negro American about his own country—probably the finest piece of literature yet written on this powerfully charged subject.

The story is divided into three sections which might have been sub-titled (I) Family, (II) Friend, (III) Strangers; hence, it moves from the intimate center of the unnamed narrator's experiences outward into public life and society. Simultaneously, the narrator—and the reader—gains more and more understanding and insight into the complexities and changes in the current of his emotions, even though much happens that he does not fully understand. The "I" narrator tells us (in the present tense) about the events as they happen and (in the past tense) about his reminiscences, together with his own interpretations which are often much too explicit and preachy: "Everyone's life begins on a level where races, armies, and churches stop. And yet everyone's life is always shaped by races, churches, and armies; races, churches, and armies menace, and have taken, many lives."

Such comments give the reader the false notion that he is getting the meaning as well as the action from the narrator. As the narrator is intelligent and trained to be wary and critical, his observations are always appropriate to his character and are often apt and to the point. But he has had prejudices of his own ("I had always thought of Sweden as being populated entirely by blondes"), is super-sensitive to every act and gesture by a white man that might conceivably be interpreted as anti-Negro ("Was it my imagination or was it true that they seemed to avoid my eyes?"), and often speaks ("she is only an American like me") and feels ("I feel very cheerful, I do not know why") in ways that he does not fully understand. Hence the narrator does not, however much he may seem to, do all the reader's interpretive work for him. In fact, the fundamental meaning of the story remains implicit.

In the opening lines of the story, the narrator introduces the members of the intimate family circle: his wife Harriet; his sister Louisa, who has come to Paris for a brief holiday before accompanying him and his family back to America; his son Paul, to whom America is "only a glamorous word"; and "the director of the film," who remains unnamed at this point because he is not important until we reach the second section of the story. The strangers of the third section are, of course, not mentioned because the narrator is speculating on events *as they occur* and does not know who is going to appear or what is going to happen. Many of the undercurrents of the opening section will not have much impact on first reading because Baldwin holds back the vital information that the narrator and his sister are Negroes until after he has established his characters as a family unit. Only on second reading can we realize the immense tactfulness of Harriet when she explains to their son that his father's crankiness at breakfast "is because he is afraid they will not like his songs in New York. Your father is an *artiste, mon chou,* and they are very mysterious people, *les artistes.*" The Negro question is avoided because "Harriet does not so much believe in protecting children as she does in helping them to build a foundation [of love]on which they can build and build again, each time life's high-flying steel ball knocks down everything they have built." And only on second reading can we understand why Louisa must seem to Paul "peculiarly uncertain of herself, peculiarly hostile and embattled," or the sinister significance of her insistence to Harriet that "We have *got* some expressions, believe me. Don't let anybody ever tell you America hasn't got a culture. Our culture is as thick as clabber milk."

It is in an atmosphere of family love that the narrator's fears emerge: "Paul has never been called any names before." Well aware of the fact that in America he and Harriet would never have been able to love each other, he broods over "all the threats it holds for me and mine." And he shrewdly observes that "Harriet is really trying to learn from Louisa how best to protect her husband and her son." The largest image of this first section is that of a family group full of love and good will facing a threatening experience in which each is eager to help and protect the other.

After Harriet and Louisa leave to spend an evening in Paris and after Paul has been delivered to the safe-keeping of the concierge, the narrator returns to his apartment to await the visit of Vidal, the director of the film which has made him famous. On the balcony he smokes, looks at Paris where he has "always felt at home" (but see *Notes of a Native Son*, where Baldwin describes the horrible experience of incarceration in a Paris jail), meditates and reminisces: "I love Paris, I will always love it, it is the city which has saved my life . . . by allowing me to find out who I am." It was in Paris eight years before that he fell in love with Harriet just before returning to America for the funeral of his mother—"I felt . . . for the first time that the woman was not, in her own eyes or in the eyes of the world, degraded by my presence." He was afraid of America and eager to return to Harriet. New York seemed like "some enormous, cunning and murderous beast, ready to devour, impossible to escape," and he was especially vulnerable because he "had forgotten all the tricks [of appearing subservient to the whites] on which my life had once depended." There are few subtleties in this transitional part of the story. The narrator is ambivalent about America, fears it but is attracted to it. There is a fine little sketch of the noise and power of New York, capped with the observation that "the human voices distinguished themselves from the roar by their note of strain and hostility." When his sister Louisa, who had met him at the ship, directed the cab driver to the New Yorker Hotel, the narrator was surprised, for Negroes had formerly been discriminated against there. Obviously the country was changing, but Louisa's optimism is tempered with humorous caution: "this place really hasn't changed very much. You still can't hear yourself talk."

The second section of the story begins with the arrival of Jean Luc Vidal, a "tough, cynical, crafty old Frenchman," a former Gaullist whose wife and son were lost in the war and who had spent time in a Nazi prison. This man is very fond of the young Negro whom he has made into an international star in a film significantly entitled *Les Fauves Nous Attendent*. But Vidal has done more for him than that; he had taught him to express in his art, and thus to relieve, his deep-felt hatred, and he had exposed the narrator's self-pitying anti-white prejudice. Such reverse prejudice had prevented him from responding to any individual white man just as effectively as anti-Negro prejudice blinds white people to the individuality of Negroes: "I am a French director and I have never been in your country and I have never done you any harm—but . . . you are not talking to Jean Luc

Vidal, but to some other white man, whom you remember, who has nothing to do with me." To Vidal the narrator can speak openly of his fears at returning to a country where "I always feel that I don't exist, except in someone else's—usually dirty—mind . . . I don't want to put Harriet through that and I don't want to raise Paul there." Vidal reassures him that his return needn't be permanent, that his new status and the prospects of great wealth are worth the risk.

Section three opens at a discothèque where the narrator and Vidal encounter a group of touring American Negro students, two girls and two young men. The more beautiful of the girls approaches them, astonished at her luck "because it's in all the papers that you're coming home." These Negroes, like the narrator, obviously regard America as "home" despite the conditions of their life there. Their dialogue reveals their fear and hatred of the whites, but also their belligerent determination to fight back. One says, "I fear you are in for some surprises, my friend. There have been some changes made." Then, "Are you afraid?"

"A little."

"We all are," says another, "that's why I was so glad to get away *for a little while.*"

As the group goes bar-hopping, they are joined by an Arab named Boona, an erstwhile prize-fighter from Tunis and an acquaintance of the narrator. Though Boona is a disreputable fellow and obviously does not fit with the group, the narrator is trapped by his fear of expressing anti-Arab prejudice and cannot send him away. During the course of the night, Boona steals money from the purse of one of the girls; he is confronted and denies it—"Why she blame me? Because I come from Africa?" In this section of the story the narrator makes no commentaries on the action, and when the girl decides not to press the point ("I'm sure I lost it . . . It isn't worth hurting your feelings") we can only assume that she has observed the Arab's desperation and is therefore willing to endure the loss of the money. The party breaks up at dawn, and the narrator goes home, stopping at the concierge's apartment to pick up his son: "I feel very cheerful, I do not know why." The concierge, referring to their trip to America, says, "What a journey! *Jusqu'au nouveau monde!*"

> I open the cage [of the elevator] and we step inside. "Yes," I say, "all the way to the new world." I press the button and the cage, holding my son and me, goes up.

The symbolism of the ending is clear. Although this Negro and his son are in the cage of their Negro skins, they are rising in the world. But what, exactly, has happened to explain or justify this optimism? The answer is that as the story moves in wider and wider orbits around the private individuality of this Negro, we see that his original feeling that everything was divided into his oppressed self and the hostile world was false, that he is part of a history and a humanity that is far more complex than that. The narrator cannot identify himself simply as an oppressed person, for much of the world does *not* oppress him. He finds love not only from his Negro sister, but from a Swedish woman who marries him and gives him a son and from a French film director who teaches him some hard truths about life. In the film he had been obliged to portray a mulatto boy who hated "all dark women and all white men" and he had not been throwing himself fully and honestly into the role. Vidal had goaded him:

> "Have you never, yourself, been in a similar position?"
> I hated him for asking the question because I knew he had the answer to it. "I would have had to be a very lucky black man not to have been in such a position."
> "You would have had to be a very lucky *man*."
> "Oh, God," I said, "please don't give me any of this equality-in-anguish business."
> "It is perfectly possible," he said sharply, "that there is not another kind."

Vidal then gave him a stern lecture on history, pointing out that the white men—especially the French—are paying for their history of abuse of the colored peoples and that if revenge is what the Negro wants he will certainly have it. He then strikes home with a telling blow: "How will you raise your son? Will you teach him never to tell the truth to anyone?" The narrator then recalls how he had held his own father in pity and contempt for not being able to prevent or even to prepare for the humiliation and the anguish of Negro life in Alabama. "But for Paul . . . I swore I would make it impossible for the world to treat Paul as it had treated my father and me." But since the story does not end at that point, this must be taken as a temporary and transient stage in the narrator's development. And Vidal's wisdom, too, is by no means the last word.

The last word apparently has to do with Boona, i.e., with the contrast between the Arab from Tunis and the Negro from America, neither of whom wishes to go home. One of the Negro girls asks Boona, "Wouldn't you like to go back [to Tunis]?" and he replies, "That is not so easy." But their situations are not quite the same, as the narrator comes to realize; there is a profound difference in their racial histories. The Arabs do not identify themselves as Frenchmen, but the Negroes feel that they are Americans.

In his balcony meditation the narrator had mused on the plight of the Arabs in Paris and how their treatment had caused such a degeneration among them. "I once thought of the North Africans as my brothers" and responded to "their rage, the only note in all their music which I could not fail to recognize." Yet because "they were perfectly prepared to drive all Frenchmen into the sea and to level the city of Paris" he could not identify with them—partly because he owed his spiritual life to France and partly because his own rage against America is the anger one feels against the wrongs of a country one loves ("waiting for the first glimpse of America, my apprehension began to give way to a secret joy, a checked anticipation"). Furthermore, he had discovered aboard ship during his first voyage home that the white Americans "who had never treated me with any respect, had no respect for each other." True, they quickly came to call each other by their first names, but their friendliness "did not suggest and was not intended to suggest any possibility of friendship." And earlier in the story he had observed that the whites "could not afford to hear a truth which would shatter, irrevocably, their image of themselves." This is a condition which the Negro can and must help to correct. He shares with his sister Louisa the conviction that if the whites could be brought to confront the Negro honestly and to accept him for what he was—not only a fellow human being but a permanent and unshakable part of American culture— the entire culture could be made whole and healthy. Louisa had said that even Negroes must be brought to realize this truth:

> That's what I keep trying to tell those dicty bastards down South. They get their own experience into the language, we'll have a great language. But, no, they all want to talk like white folks . . . I tell them, honey, white folks ain't saying *nothing*. Not a thing are they saying—and *some* of them know it, they *need* what you got, the whole world needs it.

It is this kind of racial pride that the Arabs in France do not share with the Negroes in America, that has been buttressed by the narrator's observation of the understanding and kindness displayed by the Negro tourists toward Boona. That is what makes him cheerful at the end. It is an achievement that he can face with pride the prospect of being a Negro in America.

QUESTIONS

This Morning, This Evening, So Soon

POINT OF VIEW 1. Examine Baldwin's use of a first-person narrator in "This Morning, This Evening, So Soon." Indicate the relationship between point of view and mood, between point of view and sympathy. The essayist warns that "the narrator does not, however much he may seem to, do all the reader's interpretive work for him." Explain the meaning of this statement.

CHARACTERS 2. Why is Louisa integral to the structure and theme of the story? Why has Louisa chosen not to marry? 3. What does the narrator's judgment of his father reveal about his own attitudes toward Paul? 4. Is the narrator a developing or a static character? Explain. 5. With the exception of Boona, the characters in the narrator's family and those who figure in his public life—including all the Negroes, Harriet, Mme. Dumont, and Jean Luc Vidal—seem to have virtually no faults. How does this "goodness" support the contrast Baldwin presents between the narrator's life in Paris and the life of the Negro in the United States? 6. Each character seems to have been created to illuminate aspects of the narrator's situation, in particular, of his sense of and relation to life in the United States. Choose a character and show how he or she functions this way.

PLOT 7. The narrative moves "from the intimate center of the unnamed narrator's experiences outward into public life and society," but it also moves back and forth in time. One significant return to the past involves the narrator's experiences in America eight years prior to the narrative present. What specific insights into the narrator are gained by the recounting of these experiences? 8. Another major return to the past concerns the making of a film that has brought the narrator "incredible and troubling riches." What specific insights into the character of the narrator does this episode afford? What is the significance of the title of the film? 9. In what way does the title of the story hold the key to its narrative structure?

SETTING 10. In what ways does Baldwin effectively dramatize the contrasts between New York City and Paris?

STYLE 11. At times, the narrator as narrator and the narrator as protagonist seem to split into separate entities. That is, the narrator as character is a singer and actor who, in his encounters with the Arabs, the film director, and the white Americans, shows himself to be fallible, uncertain of his motives, and even ineloquent (" 'You have no right to talk to me this way' "). Yet the narrator as narrator is always capable of eloquent descriptions and intellectual judgments reminiscent of James Baldwin the essayist. Compare and contrast the character and styles of the narrator as narrator and the narrator as protagonist. 12. Point out passages in the story that could fit into an essay as easily as into a story. What seems to be the writer's purpose in such passages?

TONE 13. In this story, which explores "the inner thoughts and feelings of a sensitive Negro American about his own country," does Baldwin have control of esthetic distance? What devices has he used to "objectify" his subject matter?

James Baldwin: The Black and the Red-White-and-Blue

FOCUS 1. What are some of the "subtle and surprising complexities" that the essayist has discovered in "This Morning, This Evening, So Soon"? In your judgment, does the first sentence of the essay indicate its focus? Explain.

ORGANIZATION 2. How does the organization of the essay parallel what the essayist asserts is the organization of the story?

USING THE EVIDENCE 3. What evidence is cited in the essay to illustrate the contention that "the fundamental meaning of the story remains implicit"? 4. What evidence supports the assertion that "the largest image of this first section is that of a family group full of love and good will"? 5. The essay states that "Vidal's wisdom, too, is by no means the last word." How is this observation documented? 6. Can you find evidence in the essay to support the contention that the narrator *shares* Louisa's conviction that "if the whites could be brought to confront the Negro honestly and to accept him for what he was . . . the entire culture could be made whole and healthy"?

STYLE 7. How would you describe the diction in this essay? Can you find any examples of jargon?

MAKING LITERARY JUDGMENTS 8. What evidence, if any, can you find that the essayist views "This Morning, This Evening, So Soon" favorably because he finds it true to life? 9. The essayist describes the narrator's interpretations as being "often much too explicit and preachy." What criticism of Baldwin as a writer of fiction is implied in this statement? And what does the statement reveal about the essayist's view of what characterizes good fiction? 10. The essay states, "Many of the undercurrents of the opening section will not have much impact on first reading because Baldwin holds back the vital information that the narrator and his sister are Negroes until after he has established his characters as a family unit." Discuss your own experience and reactions when you read the opening section. For example, did you assume or suspect from the beginning that the narrator is a Negro because you know something about Baldwin's background and his other writing? How does Baldwin's withholding "the vital information that the narrator and his sister are Negroes" affect your understanding of the theme of this story?

SONNY'S BLUES

I read about it in the paper, in the subway, on my way to work. I read it, and I couldn't believe it, and I read it again. Then perhaps I just stared at it, at the newsprint spelling out his name, spelling out the story. I stared at it in the swinging lights of the subway car, and in the faces and bodies of the people, and in my own face, trapped in the darkness which roared outside.

It was not to be believed and I kept telling myself that, as I walked from the subway station to the high school. And at the same time I couldn't doubt it. I was scared, scared for Sonny. He became real to me again. A great block of ice got settled in my belly and kept melting there slowly all day long, while I taught my classes algebra. It was a special kind of ice. It kept melting, sending trickles of ice water all up and down my veins, but it never got less. Sometimes it hardened and seemed to expand until I felt my guts were going to come spilling out or that I was going to choke or scream.

This would always be at a moment when I was remembering some specific thing Sonny had once said or done.

When he was about as old as the boys in my classes his face had been bright and open, there was a lot of copper in it; and he'd had wonderfully direct brown eyes, and great gentleness and privacy. I wondered what he looked like now. He had been picked up, the evening before, in a raid on an apartment downtown, for peddling and using heroin.

I couldn't believe it: but what I mean by that is that I couldn't find any room for it anywhere inside me. I had kept it outside me for a long time. I hadn't wanted to know. I had had suspicions, but I didn't name them, I kept putting them away. I told myself that Sonny was wild, but he wasn't crazy. And he'd always been a good boy, he hadn't ever turned hard or evil or disrespectful, the way kids can, so quick, so quick, especially in Harlem. I didn't want to believe that I'd ever see my brother going down, coming to nothing, all that light in his face gone out, in the condition I'd already seen so many others. Yet it had happened and here I was, talking about algebra to a lot of boys who might, every one of them for all I knew, be popping off needles every time they went to the head. Maybe it did more for them than algebra could.

I was sure that the first time Sonny had ever had horse, he couldn't have been much older than these boys were now. These boys, now, were living as we'd been living then, they were growing up with a rush and their heads bumped abruptly against the low ceiling of their actual possibilities. They were filled with rage. All they really knew were two darknesses, the darkness of their lives, which was now closing in on them, and the darkness of the movies, which had blinded them to that other darkness, and in which they now, vindictively, dreamed, at once more together than they were at any other time, and more alone.

When the last bell rang, the last class ended, I let out my breath. It seemed I'd been holding it for all that time. My clothes were wet—I may have looked as though I'd been sitting in a steam bath, all dressed up, all afternoon. I sat alone in the classroom a long time. I listened to the boys outside, downstairs, shouting and cursing and laughing. Their laughter struck me for perhaps the first time. It was not the joyous laughter which— God knows why—one associates with children. It was mocking and insular, its intent was to denigrate. It was disenchanted, and in this, also, lay the authority of their curses. Perhaps I was listening to them because I was thinking about my brother and in them I heard my brother. And myself.

One boy was whistling a tune, at once very complicated and very simple, it seemed to be pouring out of him as though he were a bird, and it sounded very cool and moving through all that harsh, bright air, only just holding its own through all those other sounds.

I stood up and walked over to the window and looked down into the courtyard. It was the beginning of the spring and the sap was rising in the boys. A teacher passed through them every now and again, quickly, as though he or she couldn't wait to get out of that courtyard, to get those boys out of their sight and off their minds. I started collecting my stuff. I thought I'd better get home and talk to Isabel.

The courtyard was almost deserted by the time I got downstairs. I saw this boy standing in the shadow of a doorway, looking just like Sonny. I almost called his name. Then I saw that it wasn't Sonny, but somebody we used to know, a boy from around our block. He'd been Sonny's friend. He'd never been mine, having been too young for me, and, anyway, I'd never liked him. And now, even though he was a grown-up man, he still hung around that block, still spent hours on the street corners, was always high and raggy. I used to run into him from time to time and he'd often work around to asking me for a quarter or fifty cents. He always had some real good excuse, too, and I always gave it to him, I don't know why.

But now, abruptly, I hated him. I couldn't stand the way he looked at me, partly like a dog, partly like a cunning child. I wanted to ask him what the hell he was doing in the school courtyard.

He sort of shuffled over to me, and he said, "I see you got the papers. So you already know about it."

"You mean about Sonny? Yes, I already know about it. How come they didn't get you?"

He grinned. It made him repulsive and it also brought to mind what he'd looked like as a kid. "I wasn't there. I stay away from them people."

"Good for you." I offered him a cigarette and I watched him through the smoke. "You come all the way down here just to tell me about Sonny?"

"That's right." He was sort of shaking his head and his eyes looked strange, as though they were about to cross. The bright sun deadened his damp dark brown skin and it made his eyes look yellow and showed up the dirt in his kinked hair. He smelled funky. I moved a little away from him and I said, "Well, thanks. But I already know about it and I got to get home."

"I'll walk you a little ways," he said. We started walking. There were a couple of kids still loitering in the courtyard and one of them said goodnight to me and looked strangely at the boy beside me.

"What're you going to do?" he asked me. "I mean, about Sonny."

374

"Look. I haven't seen Sonny for over a year, I'm not sure I'm going to do anything. Anyway, what the hell *can* I do?"

"That's right," he said quickly, "ain't nothing you can do. Can't much help old Sonny no more, I guess."

It was what I was thinking and so it seemed to me he had no right to say it.

"I'm surprised at Sonny, though," he went on—he had a funny way of talking, he looked straight ahead as though he were talking to himself—"I thought Sonny was a smart boy, I thought he was too smart to get hung."

"I guess he thought so too," I said sharply, "and that's how he got hung. And how about you? You're pretty goddamn smart, I bet."

Then he looked directly at me, just for a minute. "I ain't smart," he said. "If I was smart, I'd have reached for a pistol a long time ago."

"Look. Don't tell *me* your sad story, if it was up to me, I'd give you one." Then I felt guilty—guilty, probably, for never having supposed that the poor bastard *had* a story of his own, much less a sad one, and I asked, quickly, "What's going to happen to him now?"

He didn't answer this. He was off by himself some place. "Funny thing," he said, and from his tone we might have been discussing the quickest way to get to Brooklyn, "when I saw the papers this morning, the first thing I asked myself was if I had anything to do with it. I felt sort of responsible."

I began to listen more carefully. The subway station was on the corner, just before us, and I stopped. He stopped, too. We were in front of a bar and he ducked slightly, peering in, but whoever he was looking for didn't seem to be there. The juke box was blasting away with something black and bouncy and I half watched the barmaid as she danced her way from the juke box to her place behind the bar. And I watched her face as she laughingly responded to something someone said to her, still keeping time to the music. When she smiled one saw the little girl, one sensed the doomed, still-struggling woman beneath the battered face of the semi-whore.

"I never *give* Sonny nothing," the boy said finally, "but a long time ago I come to school high and Sonny asked me how it felt." He paused, I couldn't bear to watch him, I watched the barmaid, and I listened to the music which seemed to be causing the pavement to shake. "I told him it felt great." The music stopped, the barmaid paused and watched the juke box until the music began again. "It did."

All this was carrying me some place I didn't want to go. I certainly didn't want to know how it felt. It filled everything, the people, the houses, the music, the dark, quicksilver barmaid, with menace; and this menace was their reality.

"What's going to happen to him now?" I asked again.

"They'll send him away some place and they'll try to cure him." He shook his head. "Maybe he'll even think he's kicked the habit. Then they'll let him loose"—he gestured, throwing his cigarette into the gutter. "That's all."

"What do you mean, that's *all?*"

But I knew what he meant.

"I *mean,* that's *all.*" He turned his head and looked at me, pulling down the corners of his mouth. "Don't you know what I mean?" he asked, softly.

"How the hell *would* I know what you mean?" I almost whispered it, I don't know why.

"That's right," he said to the air, "how would he know what I mean?" He turned toward me again, patient and calm, and yet I somehow felt him shaking, shaking as though he were going to fall apart. I felt that ice in my guts again, the dread I'd felt all afternoon; and again I watched the barmaid, moving about the bar, washing glasses, and singing. "Listen. They'll let him out and then it'll just start all over again. That's what I mean."

"You mean—they'll let him out. And then he'll just start working his way back in again. You mean he'll never kick the habit. Is that what you mean?"

"That's right," he said, cheerfully. "*You* see what I mean."

"Tell me," I said at last, "why does he want to die? He must want to die, he's killing himself, why does he want to die?"

He looked at me in surprise. He licked his lips. "He don't want to die. He wants to live. Don't nobody want to die, ever."

Then I wanted to ask him—too many things. He could not have answered, or if he had, I could not have borne the answers. I started walking. "Well, I guess it's none of my business."

"It's going to be rough on old Sonny," he said. We reached the subway station. "This is your station?" he asked. I nodded. I took one step down. "Damn!" he said, suddenly. I looked up at him. He grinned again. "Damn it if I didn't leave all my money home. You ain't got a dollar on you, have you? Just for a couple of days, is all."

All at once something inside gave and threatened to come pouring out of me. I didn't hate him any more. I felt that in another moment I'd start crying like a child.

"Sure," I said. "Don't sweat." I looked in my wallet and didn't have a dollar, I only had a five. "Here," I said. "That hold you?"

He didn't look at it—he didn't want to look at it. A terrible, closed look came over his face, as though he were keeping the number on the bill a secret from him and me. "Thanks," he said, and now he was dying to see me go. "Don't worry about Sonny. Maybe I'll write him or something."

"Sure," I said. "You do that. So long."

"Be seeing you," he said. I went on down the steps.

And I didn't write Sonny or send him anything for a long time. When I finally did, it was just after my little girl died, he wrote me back a letter which made me feel like a bastard.

Here's what he said:

> Dear brother,
>
> You don't know how much I needed to hear from you. I wanted to write you many a time but I dug how much I must have hurt you and so I didn't write. But now I feel like a man who's been trying to climb up out of some deep, real deep and funky hole and just saw the sun up there, outside. I got to get outside.
>
> I can't tell you much about how I got here. I mean I don't know how to tell you. I guess I was afraid of something or I was trying to escape from something and you know I have never been very strong in the head (smile). I'm glad Mama and Daddy are dead and can't see what's happened to their son and I swear if I'd known what I was doing I would never have hurt you so, you and a lot of other fine people who were nice to me and who believed in me.
>
> I don't want you to think it had anything to do with me being a musician. It's more than that. Or maybe less than that. I can't get anything straight in my head down here and I try not to think about what's going to happen to me when I get outside again. Sometime I think I'm going to flip and *never* get outside and sometime I think I'll come straight back. I tell you one thing, though, I'd rather blow my brains out than go through this again. But that's what they all say, so they tell me. If I tell you when I'm coming to New York and if you could meet me, I sure would appreciate it. Give my love to Isabel and the kids and I was sure sorry to hear about little Gracie. I wish I could be like Mama and say the Lord's will be done, but I don't know it seems to me that trouble is the one thing that never does get stopped and I don't know what good it does to blame it on the Lord. But maybe it does some good if you believe it.
>
> Your brother,
> Sonny

Then I kept in constant touch with him and I sent him whatever I could and I went to meet him when he came back to New York. When I saw him many things I thought I had forgotten came flooding back to me. This was because I had begun, finally, to wonder about Sonny, about the life that Sonny lived inside. This life, whatever it was, had made him older and thinner and it had deepened the distant stillness in which he had always moved. He looked very unlike my baby brother. Yet, when he smiled, when we shook hands, the baby brother I'd never known looked out from the depths of his private life, like an animal waiting to be coaxed into the light.

"How you been keeping?" he asked me.

"All right. And you?"

"Just fine." He was smiling all over his face. "It's good to see you again."

"It's good to see you."

The seven years difference in our ages lay between us like a chasm: I wondered if these years would ever operate between us as a bridge. I was remembering, and it made it hard to catch my breath, that I had been there when he was born; and I had heard the first words he had ever spoken. When he started to walk, he walked from our mother straight to me. I caught him just before he fell when he took the first steps he ever took in this world.

"How's Isabel?"

"Just fine. She's dying to see you."

"And the boys?"

"They're fine, too. They're anxious to see their uncle."

"Oh, come on. You know they don't remember me."

"Are you kidding? Of course they remember you."

He grinned again. We got into a taxi. We had a lot to say to each other, far too much to know how to begin.

As the taxi began to move, I asked, "You still want to go to India?"

He laughed. "You still remember that. Hell, no. This place is Indian enough for me."

"It used to belong to them," I said.

And he laughed again. "They damn sure knew what they were doing when they got rid of it."

Years ago, when he was around fourteen, he'd been all hipped on the idea of going to India. He read books about people sitting on rocks, naked, in all kinds of weather, but mostly bad, naturally, and walking barefoot through hot coals and arriving at wisdom. I used to say that it sounded to

378

me as though they were getting away from wisdom as fast as they could. I
think he sort of looked down on me for that.

"Do you mind," he asked, "if we have the driver drive alongside the
park? On the west side—I haven't seen the city in so long."

"Of course not," I said. I was afraid that I might sound as though I were
humoring him, but I hoped he wouldn't take it that way.

So we drove along, between the green of the park and the stony, lifeless
elegance of hotels and apartment buildings, toward the vivid, killing streets
of our childhood. These streets hadn't changed, though housing projects
jutted up out of them now like rocks in the middle of a boiling sea. Most
of the houses in which we had grown up had vanished, as had the stores
from which we had stolen, the basements in which we had first tried sex,
the rooftops from which we had hurled tin cans and bricks. But houses
exactly like the houses of our past yet dominated the landscape, boys exactly
like the boys we once had been found themselves smothering in these
houses, came down into the streets for light and air and found themselves
encircled by disaster. Some escaped the trap, most didn't. Those who got
out always left something of themselves behind, as some animals ampu-
tate a leg and leave it in the trap. It might be said, perhaps, that I had
escaped, after all, I was a school teacher; or that Sonny had, he hadn't lived
in Harlem for years. Yet, as the cab moved uptown through streets which
seemed, with a rush, to darken with dark people, and as I covertly studied
Sonny's face, it came to me that what we both were seeking through our
separate cab windows was that part of ourselves which had been left behind. It's always at the hour of trouble and confrontation that the missing
member aches.

We hit 110th Street and started rolling up Lenox Avenue. And I'd
known this avenue all my life, but it seemed to me again, as it had seemed
on the day I'd first heard about Sonny's trouble, filled with a hidden menace which was its very breath of life.

"We almost there," said Sonny.

"Almost." We were both too nervous to say anything more.

We live in a housing project. It hasn't been up long. A few days after it
was up it seemed uninhabitably new, now, of course, it's already rundown.
It looks like a parody of the good, clean, faceless life—God knows the people who live in it do their best to make it a parody. The beat-looking grass
lying around isn't enough to make their lives green, the hedges will never
hold out the streets, and they know it. The big windows fool no one, they
aren't big enough to make space out of no space. They don't bother with

379

the windows, they watch the TV screen instead. The playground is most popular with the children who don't play at jacks, or skip rope, or roller skate, or swing, and they can be found in it after dark. We moved in partly because it's not too far from where I teach, and partly for the kids; but it's really just like the houses in which Sonny and I grew up. The same things happen, they'll have the same things to remember. The moment Sonny and I started into the house I had the feeling that I was simply bringing him back into the danger he had almost died trying to escape.

Sonny has never been talkative. So I don't know why I was sure he'd be dying to talk to me when supper was over the first night. Everything went fine, the oldest boy remembered him, and the youngest boy liked him, and Sonny had remembered to bring something for each of them; and Isabel, who is really much nicer than I am, more open and giving, had gone to a lot of trouble about dinner and was genuinely glad to see him. And she's always been able to tease Sonny in a way that I haven't. It was nice to see her face so vivid again and to hear her laugh and watch her make Sonny laugh. She wasn't, or, anyway, she didn't seem to be, at all uneasy or embarrassed. She chatted as though there were no subject which had to be avoided and she got Sonny past his first, faint stiffness. And thank God she was there, for I was filled with that icy dread again. Everything I did seemed awkward to me, and everything I said sounded freighted with hidden meaning. I was trying to remember everything I'd heard about dope addiction and I couldn't help watching Sonny for signs. I wasn't doing it out of malice. I was trying to find out something about my brother. I was dying to hear him tell me he was safe.

"Safe!" my father grunted, whenever Mama suggested trying to move to a neighborhood which might be safer for children. "Safe, hell! Ain't no place safe for kids, nor nobody."

He always went on like this, but he wasn't, ever, really as bad as he sounded, not even on weekends, when he got drunk. As a matter of fact, he was always on the lookout for "something a little better," but he died before he found it. He died suddenly, during a drunken weekend in the middle of the war, when Sonny was fifteen. He and Sonny hadn't ever got on too well. And this was partly because Sonny was the apple of his father's eye. It was because he loved Sonny so much and was frightened for him, that he was always fighting with him. It doesn't do any good to fight with Sonny. Sonny just moves back, inside himself, where he can't be reached. But the principal reason that they never hit it off is that they were so much alike. Daddy was big and rough and loud-talking, just the opposite of Sonny, but they both had—that same privacy.

Mama tried to tell me something about this, just after Daddy died. I was home on leave from the army.

This was the last time I ever saw my mother alive. Just the same, this picture gets all mixed up in my mind with pictures I had of her when she was younger. The way I always see her is the way she used to be on a Sunday afternoon, say, when the old folks were talking after the big Sunday dinner. I always see her wearing pale blue. She'd be sitting on the sofa. And my father would be sitting in the easy chair, not far from her. And the living room would be full of church folks and relatives. There they sit, in chairs all around the living room, and the night is creeping up outside, but nobody knows it yet. You can see the darkness growing against the windowpanes and you hear the street noises every now and again, or maybe the jangling beat of a tambourine from one of the churches close by, but it's real quiet in the room. For a moment nobody's talking, but every face looks darkening, like the sky outside. And my mother rocks a little from the waist, and my father's eyes are closed. Everyone is looking at something a child can't see. For a minute they've forgotten the children. Maybe a kid is lying on the rug, half asleep. Maybe somebody's got a kid in his lap and is absent-mindedly stroking the kid's head. Maybe there's a kid, quiet and big-eyed, curled up in a big chair in the corner. The silence, the darkness coming, and the darkness in the faces frightens the child obscurely. He hopes that the hand which strokes his forehead will never stop—will never die. He hopes that there will never come a time when the old folks won't be sitting around the living room, talking about where they've come from, and what they've seen, and what's happened to them and their kinfolk.

But something deep and watchful in the child knows that this is bound to end, is already ending. In a moment someone will get up and turn on the light. Then the old folks will remember the children and they won't talk any more that day. And when light fills the room, the child is filled with darkness. He knows that every time this happens he's moved just a little closer to that darkness outside. The darkness outside is what the old folks have been talking about. It's what they've come from. It's what they endure. The child knows that they won't talk any more because if he knows too much about what's happened to *them*, he'll know too much too soon, about what's going to happen to *him*.

The last time I talked to my mother, I remember I was restless. I wanted to get out and see Isabel. We weren't married then and we had a lot to straighten out between us.

There Mama sat, in black, by the window. She was humming an old church song, *Lord, you brought me from a long ways off.* Sonny was out somewhere. Mama kept watching the streets.

"I don't know," she said, "if I'll ever see you again, after you go off from here. But I hope you'll remember the things I tried to teach you."

"Don't talk like that," I said, and smiled. "You'll be here a long time yet."

She smiled, too, but she said nothing. She was quiet for a long time. And I said, "Mama, don't you worry about nothing. I'll be writing all the time, and you be getting the checks. . . ."

"I want to talk to you about your brother," she said, suddenly. "If anything happens to me he ain't going to have nobody to look out for him."

"Mama," I said, "ain't nothing going to happen to you *or* Sonny. Sonny's all right. He's a good boy and he's got good sense."

"It ain't a question of his being a good boy," Mama said, "nor of his having good sense. It ain't only the bad ones, nor yet the dumb ones that gets sucked under." She stopped, looking at me. "Your Daddy once had a brother," she said, and she smiled in a way that made me feel she was in pain. "You didn't never know that, did you?"

"No," I said, "I never knew that," and I watched her face.

"Oh, yes," she said, "your Daddy had a brother." She looked out of the window again. "I know you never saw your Daddy cry. But I did—many a time, through all these years."

I asked her, "What happened to his brother? How come nobody's ever talked about him?"

This was the first time I ever saw my mother look old.

"His brother got killed," she said, "when he was just a little younger than you are now. I knew him. He was a fine boy. He was maybe a little full of the devil, but he didn't mean nobody no harm."

Then she stopped and the room was silent, exactly as it had sometimes been on those Sunday afternoons. Mama kept looking out into the streets.

"He used to have a job in the mill," she said, "and, like all young folks, he just liked to perform on Saturday nights. Saturday nights, him and your father would drift around to different places, go to dances and things like that, or just sit around with people they knew, and your father's brother would sing, he had a fine voice, and play along with himself on his guitar. Well, this particular Saturday night, him and your father was coming home from some place, and they were both a little drunk and there was a moon that night, it was bright like day. Your father's brother was feeling kind of good, and he was whistling to himself, and he had his guitar slung over his shoulder. They was coming down a hill and beneath them was a road that turned off from the highway. Well, your father's brother, being always kind of frisky, decided to run down this hill, and he did, with that guitar banging and clanging behind him, and he ran across the road, and he was making water behind a tree. And your father was sort of amused at him and he was still coming down the hill, kind of slow. Then he heard a car motor and that same minute his brother stepped from behind the tree, into the road, in the moonlight. And he started to cross the road. And your father started to run down the hill, he says he don't know why. This car was full of white men. They was all drunk, and when they seen your father's brother they let out a great whoop and holler and they aimed the car straight at him. They was having fun, they just wanted to scare him, the way they do sometimes, you know. But they was drunk. And I guess the boy, being drunk, too, and scared, kind of lost his head. By the time he jumped it was too late. Your father says he heard his brother scream when the car rolled over him, and he heard the wood of that guitar when it give, and he heard them strings go flying, and he heard them white men shouting, and the car kept on a-going and it ain't stopped till this day. And, time your father got down the hill, his brother weren't nothing but blood and pulp."

Tears were gleaming on my mother's face. There wasn't anything I could say.

"He never mentioned it," she said, "because I never let him mention it before you children. Your Daddy was like a crazy man that night and for many a night thereafter. He says he never in his life seen anything as dark as that road after the lights of that car had gone away. Weren't nothing, weren't nobody on that road, just your Daddy and his brother and that busted guitar. Oh, yes. Your Daddy never did really get right again. Till the day he died he weren't sure but that every white man he saw was the man that killed his brother."

She stopped and took out her handkerchief and dried her eyes and looked at me.

"I ain't telling you all this," she said, "to make you scared or bitter or to make you hate nobody. I'm telling you this because you got a brother. And the world ain't changed."

I guess I didn't want to believe this. I guess she saw this in my face. She turned away from me, toward the window again, searching those streets.

"But I praise my Redeemer," she said at last, "that He called your Daddy home before me. I ain't saying it to throw no flowers at myself, but, I declare, it keeps me from feeling too cast down to know I helped your father get safely through this world. Your father always acted like he was the roughest, strongest man on earth. And everybody took him to be like that. But if he hadn't had *me* there—to see his tears!"

She was crying again. Still, I couldn't move. I said, "Lord, Lord, Mama, I didn't know it was like that."

"Oh, honey," she said, "there's a lot that you don't know. But you are going to find it out." She stood up from the window and came over to me. "You got to hold on to your brother," she said, "and don't let him fall, no matter what it looks like is happening to him and no matter how evil you gets with him. You going to be evil with him many a time. But don't you forget what I told you, you hear?"

"I won't forget," I said. "Don't you worry, I won't forget. I won't let nothing happen to Sonny."

My mother smiled as though she were amused at something she saw in my face. Then, "You may not be able to stop nothing from happening. But you got to let him know you's *there*."

Two days later I was married, and then I was gone. And I had a lot of things on my mind and I pretty well forgot my promise to Mama until I got shipped home on a special furlough for her funeral.

And, after the funeral, with just Sonny and me alone in the empty kitchen, I tried to find out something about him.

"What do you want to do?" I asked him.

"I'm going to be a musician," he said.

For he had graduated, in the time I had been away, from dancing to the juke box to finding out who was playing what, and what they were doing with it, and he had bought himself a set of drums.

"You mean, you want to be a drummer?" I somehow had the feeling that being a drummer might be all right for other people but not for my brother Sonny.

"I don't think," he said, looking at me very gravely, "that I'll ever be a good drummer. But I think I can play a piano."

I frowned. I'd never played the role of the older brother quite so seriously before, had scarcely ever, in fact, *asked* Sonny a damn thing. I sensed myself in the presence of something I didn't really know how to handle, didn't understand. So I made my frown a little deeper as I asked: "What kind of musician do you want to be?"

He grinned. "How many kinds do you think there are?"

"Be *serious*," I said.

He laughed, throwing his head back, and then looked at me. "I *am* serious."

"Well, then, for Christ's sake, stop kidding around and answer a serious question. I mean, do you want to be a concert pianist, you want to play classical music and all that, or—or what?" Long before I finished he was laughing again. "For Christ's *sake*, Sonny!"

He sobered, but with difficulty. "I'm sorry. But you sound so—*scared!*" and he was off again.

"Well, you may think it's funny now, baby, but it's not going to be so funny when you have to make your living at it, let me tell you *that*." I was furious because I knew he was laughing at me and I didn't know why.

"No," he said, very sober now, and afraid, perhaps, that he'd hurt me, "I don't want to be a classical pianist. That isn't what interests me. I mean" —he paused, looking hard at me, as though his eyes would help me to understand, and then gestured helplessly, as though perhaps his hand would help—"I mean, I'll have a lot of studying to do, and I'll have to study *everything*, but, I mean, I want to play *with*—jazz musicians." He stopped. "I want to play jazz," he said.

Well, the word had never before sounded as heavy, as real, as it sounded that afternoon in Sonny's mouth. I just looked at him and I was probably frowning a real frown by this time. I simply couldn't see why on earth he'd want to spend his time hanging around nightclubs, clowning around on bandstands, while people pushed each other around a dance floor. It seemed —beneath him, somehow. I had never thought about it before, had never been forced to, but I suppose I had always put jazz musicians in a class with what Daddy called "good-time people."

"Are you *serious*?"

"Hell, yes, I'm serious."

He looked more helpless than ever, and annoyed, and deeply hurt.

I suggested, helpfully: "You mean—like Louis Armstrong?"

His face closed as though I'd struck him. "No. I'm not talking about none of that old-time, down home crap."

"Well, look, Sonny, I'm sorry, don't get mad. I just don't altogether get it, that's all. Name somebody—you know, a jazz musician you admire."

"Bird."

"Who?"

"Bird! Charlie Parker! Don't they teach you nothing in the goddamn army?"

I lit a cigarette. I was surprised and then a little amused to discover that

I was trembling. "I've been out of touch," I said. "You'll have to be patient with me. Now. Who's this Parker character?"

"He's just one of the greatest jazz musicians alive," said Sonny, sullenly, his hands in his pockets, his back to me. "Maybe *the* greatest," he added, bitterly, "that's probably why *you* never heard of him."

"All right," I said, "I'm ignorant. I'm sorry. I'll go out and buy all the cat's records right away, all right?"

"It don't," said Sonny, with dignity, "make any difference to me. I don't care what you listen to. Don't do me no favors."

I was beginning to realize that I'd never seen him so upset before. With another part of my mind I was thinking that this would probably turn out to be one of those things kids go through and that I shouldn't make it seem important by pushing it too hard. Still, I didn't think it would do any harm to ask: "Doesn't all this take a lot of time? Can you make a living at it?"

He turned back to me and half leaned, half sat, on the kitchen table. "Everything takes time," he said, "and—well, yes, sure, I can make a living at it. But what I don't seem to be able to make you understand is that it's the only thing I want to do."

"Well, Sonny," I said, gently, "you know people can't always do exactly what they *want* to do—"

"*No*, I don't know that," said Sonny, surprising me. "I think people *ought* to do what they want to do, what else are they alive for?"

"You getting to be a big boy," I said desperately, "it's time you started thinking about your future."

"I'm thinking about my future," said Sonny, grimly. "I think about it all the time."

I gave up. I decided, if he didn't change his mind, that we could always talk about it later. "In the meantime," I said, "you got to finish school." We had already decided that he'd have to move in with Isabel and her folks. I knew this wasn't the ideal arrangement because Isabel's folks are inclined to be dicty and they hadn't especially wanted Isabel to marry me. But I didn't know what else to do. "And we have to get you fixed up at Isabel's."

There was a long silence. He moved from the kitchen table to the window. "That's a terrible idea. You know it yourself."

"Do you have a *better* idea?"

He just walked up and down the kitchen for a minute. He was as tall as I was. He had started to shave. I suddenly had the feeling that I didn't know him at all.

He stopped at the kitchen table and picked up my cigarettes. Looking at me with a kind of mocking, amused defiance, he put one between his lips. "You mind?"

"You smoking already?"

He lit the cigarette and nodded, watching me through the smoke. "I just wanted to see if I'd have the courage to smoke in front of you." He grinned and blew a great cloud of smoke to the ceiling. "It was easy." He looked at my face. "Come on, now. I bet you was smoking at my age, tell the truth."

I didn't say anything but the truth was on my face, and he laughed. But now there was something very strained in his laugh. "Sure. And I bet that ain't all you was doing."

He was frightening me a little. "Cut the crap," I said. "We already decided that you was going to go and live at Isabel's. Now what's got into you all of a sudden?"

"*You* decided it," he pointed out. "*I* didn't decide nothing." He stopped in front of me, leaning against the stove, arms loosely folded. "Look, brother. I don't want to stay in Harlem no more, I really don't." He was very earnest. He looked at me, then over toward the kitchen window. There was something in his eyes I'd never seen before, some thoughtfulness, some worry all his own. He rubbed the muscle of one arm. "It's time I was getting out of here."

"Where do you want to *go*, Sonny?"

"I want to join the army. Or the navy, I don't care. If I say I'm old enough, they'll believe me."

Then I got mad. It was because I was so scared. "You must be crazy. You goddamn fool, what the hell do you want to go and join the *army* for?"

"I just told you. To get out of Harlem."

"Sonny, you haven't even finished *school*. And if you really want to be a musician, how do you expect to study if you're in the *army*?"

He looked at me, trapped, and in anguish. "There's ways. I might be able to work out some kind of deal. Anyway, I'll have the G.I. Bill when I come out."

"*If* you come out." We stared at each other. "Sonny, please. Be reasonable. I know the setup is far from perfect. But we got to do the best we can."

"I ain't learning nothing in school," he said. "Even when I go." He turned away from me and opened the window and threw his cigarette out into the narrow alley. I watched his back. "At least, I ain't learning nothing you'd want me to learn." He slammed the window so hard I thought the glass would fly out, and turned back to me. "And I'm sick of the stink of these garbage cans!"

"Sonny," I said, "I know how you feel. But if you don't finish school now, you're going to be sorry later that you didn't." I grabbed him by the shoulders. "And you only got another year. It ain't so bad. And I'll come back and I swear I'll help you do *whatever* you want to do. Just try to put up with it till I come back. Will you please do that? For me?"

He didn't answer and he wouldn't look at me.

"Sonny. You hear me?"

He pulled away. "I hear you. But you never hear anything *I* say."

I didn't know what to say to that. He looked out of the window and then back at me. "OK," he said, and sighed. "I'll try."

Then I said, trying to cheer him up a little, "They got a piano at Isabel's. You can practice on it."

And as a matter of fact, it did cheer him up for a minute. "That's right," he said to himself. "I forgot that." His face relaxed a little. But the worry, the thoughtfulness, played on it still, the way shadows play on a face which is staring into the fire.

But I thought I'd never hear the end of that piano. At first, Isabel would write me, saying how nice it was that Sonny was so serious about his music and how, as soon as he came in from school, or wherever he had been when he was supposed to be at school, he went straight to that piano and stayed there until suppertime. And, after supper, he went back to that piano and stayed there until everybody went to bed. He was at the piano all day Saturday and all day Sunday. Then he bought a record player and started playing records. He'd play one record over and over again, all day long sometimes, and he'd improvise along with it on the piano. Or he'd play one section of the record, one chord, one change, one progression, then he'd do it on the piano. Then back to the record. Then back to the piano.

Well, I really don't know how they stood it. Isabel finally confessed that it wasn't like living with a person at all, it was like living with sound. And the sound didn't make any sense to her, didn't make any sense to any of them—naturally. They began, in a way, to be afflicted by this presence that was living in their home. It was as though Sonny were some sort of god, or monster. He moved in an atmosphere which wasn't like theirs at all. They fed him and he ate, he washed himself, he walked in and out of their door; he certainly wasn't nasty or unpleasant or rude, Sonny isn't any of those things; but it was as though he were all wrapped up in some cloud, some fire, some vision all his own; and there wasn't any way to reach him.

At the same time, he wasn't really a man yet, he was still a child, and they had to watch out for him in all kinds of ways. They certainly couldn't throw him out. Neither did they dare to make a great scene about that piano because even they dimly sensed, as I sensed, from so many thousands of miles away, that Sonny was at that piano playing for his life.

But he hadn't been going to school. One day a letter came from the school board and Isabel's mother got it—there had, apparently, been other letters but Sonny had torn them up. This day, when Sonny came in, Isabel's mother showed him the letter and asked where he'd been spending his time. And she finally got it out of him that he'd been down in Greenwich Village, with musicians and other characters, in a white girl's apartment. And this scared her and she started to scream at him and what came up, once she began—though she denies it to this day—was what sacrifices they were making to give Sonny a decent home and how little he appreciated it.

Sonny didn't play the piano that day. By evening, Isabel's mother had calmed down but then there was the old man to deal with, and Isabel herself. Isabel says she did her best to be calm but she broke down and started crying. She says she just watched Sonny's face. She could tell, by watching him, what was happening with him. And what was happening was that they penetrated his cloud, they had reached him. Even if their fingers had been a thousand times more gentle than human fingers ever are, he could hardly help feeling that they had stripped him naked and were spitting on that nakedness. For he also had to see that his presence, that music, which was life or death to him, had been torture for them and that they had endured it, not at all for his sake, but only for mine. And Sonny couldn't take that. He can take it a little better today than he could then but he's still not very good at it and, frankly, I don't know anybody who is.

The silence of the next few days must have been louder than the sound of all the music ever played since time began. One morning, before she went to work, Isabel was in his room for something and she suddenly realized that all of his records were gone. And she knew for certain that he was gone. And he was. He went as far as the navy would carry him. He finally sent me a postcard from some place in Greece and that was the first I knew that Sonny was still alive. I didn't see him any more until we were both back in New York and the war had long been over.

He was a man by then, of course, but I wasn't willing to see it. He came by the house from time to time, but we fought almost every time we met.

I didn't like the way he carried himself, loose and dreamlike all the time, and I didn't like his friends, and his music seemed to be merely an excuse for the life he led. It sounded just that weird and disordered.

Then we had a fight, a pretty awful fight, and I didn't see him for months. By and by I looked him up, where he was living, in a furnished room in the Village, and I tried to make it up. But there were lots of other people in the room and Sonny just lay on his bed, and he wouldn't come downstairs with me, and he treated these other people as though they were his family and I weren't. So I got mad and then he got mad, and then I told him that he might just as well be dead as live the way he was living. Then he stood up and he told me not to worry about him any more in life, that he *was* dead as far as I was concerned. Then he pushed me to the door and the other people looked on as though nothing were happening, and he slammed the door behind me. I stood in the hallway, staring at the door. I heard somebody laugh in the room and then the tears came to my eyes. I started down the steps, whistling to keep from crying, I kept whistling to myself, *You going to need me, baby, one of these cold, rainy days.*

I read about Sonny's trouble in the spring. Little Grace died in the fall. She was a beautiful little girl. But she only lived a little over two years. She died of polio and she suffered. She had a slight fever for a couple of days, but it didn't seem like anything and we just kept her in bed. And we would certainly have called the doctor, but the fever dropped, she seemed to be all right. So we thought it had just been a cold. Then, one day, she was up, playing, Isabel was in the kitchen fixing lunch for the two boys when they'd come in from school, and she heard Grace fall down in the living room. When you have a lot of children you don't always start running when one of them falls, unless they start screaming or something. And, this time, Grace was quiet. Yet, Isabel says that when she heard that *thump* and then that silence, something happened in her to make her afraid. And she ran to the living room and there was little Grace on the floor, all twisted up, and the reason she hadn't screamed was that she couldn't get her breath. And when she did scream, it was the worst sound, Isabel says, that she'd ever heard in all her life, and she still hears it sometimes in her dreams. Isabel will sometimes wake me up with a low, moaning, strangled sound and I have to be quick to awaken her and hold her to me and where Isabel is weeping against me seems a mortal wound.

I think I may have written Sonny the very day that little Grace was buried. I was sitting in the living room in the dark, by myself, and I suddenly thought of Sonny. My trouble made his real.

One Saturday afternoon, when Sonny had been living with us, or, anyway, been in our house, for nearly two weeks, I found myself wandering aimlessly about the living room, drinking from a can of beer, and trying to work up the courage to search Sonny's room. He was out, he was usually out whenever I was home, and Isabel had taken the children to see their grandparents. Suddenly I was standing still in front of the living room window, watching Seventh Avenue. The idea of searching Sonny's room made me still. I scarcely dared to admit to myself what I'd be searching for. I didn't know what I'd do if I found it. Or if I didn't.

On the sidewalk across from me, near the entrance to a barbecue joint, some people were holding an old-fashioned revival meeting. The barbecue cook, wearing a dirty white apron, his conked hair reddish and metallic in the pale sun, and a cigarette between his lips, stood in the doorway, watching them. Kids and older people paused in their errands and stood there, along with some older men and a couple of very tough-looking women who watched everything that happened on the avenue, as though they owned it, or were maybe owned by it. Well, they were watching this, too. The revival was being carried on by three sisters in black, and a brother. All they had were their voices and their Bibles and a tambourine. The brother was testifying and while he testified two of the sisters stood together, seeming to say, amen, and the third sister walked around with the tambourine outstretched and a couple of people dropped coins into it. Then the brother's testimony ended and the sister who had been taking up the collection dumped the coins into her palm and transferred them to the pocket of her long black robe. Then she raised both hands, striking the tambourine against the air, and then against one hand, and she started to sing. And the two other sisters and the brother joined in.

It was strange, suddenly, to watch, though I had been seeing these street meetings all my life. So, of course, had everybody else down there. Yet, they paused and watched and listened and I stood still at the window. *"Tis the old ship of Zion,"* they sang, and the sister with the tambourine kept a steady, jangling beat, *"it has rescued many a thousand!"* Not a soul under the sound of their voices was hearing this song for the first time, not one of them had been rescued. Nor had they seen much in the way of rescue work being done around them. Neither did they especially believe in the holiness of the three sisters and the brother, they knew too much about them, knew where they lived, and how. The woman with the tambourine, whose voice dominated the air, whose face was bright with joy, was divided by very little from the woman who stood watching her, a cigarette between her heavy, chapped lips, her hair a cuckoo's nest, her face scarred and swollen from many beatings, and her black eyes glittering like coal. Perhaps they both knew this, which was why, when, as rarely, they addressed each other, they addressed each other as Sister. As the singing filled the air the watching, listening faces underwent a change, the eyes focusing on something within; the music seemed to soothe a poison out of them; and time seemed, nearly, to fall away from the sullen, belligerent, battered faces, as though they were fleeing back to their first condition, while dreaming of their last. The barbecue cook half shook his head and smiled, and dropped his cigarette and disappeared into his joint. A man fumbled in his pockets for change and stood holding it in his hand impatiently, as though he had just remembered a pressing appointment further up the avenue. He looked furious. Then I saw Sonny, standing on the edge of the crowd. He was carrying a wide, flat notebook with a green cover, and it made him look, from where I was standing, almost like a schoolboy. The coppery sun brought out the copper in his skin, he was very faintly smiling, standing very still. Then the singing stopped, the tambourine turned into a collection plate again. The furious man dropped in his coins and vanished, so did a couple of the women, and Sonny dropped some change in the plate, looking directly at the woman with a little smile. He started across the avenue, toward the house. He has a slow, loping walk, something like the way Harlem hipsters walk, only he's imposed on this his own half-beat. I had never really noticed it before.

I stayed at the window, both relieved and apprehensive. As Sonny disappeared from my sight, they began singing again. And they were still singing when his key turned in the lock.

"Hey," he said.

"Hey, yourself. You want some beer?"

"No. Well, maybe." But he came up to the window and stood beside me, looking out. "What a warm voice," he said.

They were singing *If I could only hear my mother pray again!*

"Yes," I said, "and she can sure beat that tambourine."

"But what a terrible song," he said, and laughed. He dropped his notebook on the sofa and disappeared into the kitchen. "Where's Isabel and the kids?"

"I think they went to see their grandparents. You hungry?"

"No." He came back into the living room with his can of beer. "You want to come some place with me tonight?"

I sensed, I don't know how, that I couldn't possibly say no. "Sure. Where?"

He sat down on the sofa and picked up his notebook and started leafing through it. "I'm going to sit in with some fellows in a joint in the Village."

"You mean, you're going to play, tonight?"

"That's right." He took a swallow of his beer and moved back to the window. He gave me a sidelong look. "If you can stand it."

"I'll try," I said.

He smiled to himself and we both watched as the meeting across the way broke up. The three sisters and the brother, heads bowed, were singing *God be with you till we meet again*. The faces around them were very quiet. Then the song ended. The small crowd dispersed. We watched the three women and the lone man walk slowly up the avenue.

"When she was singing before," said Sonny, abruptly, "her voice reminded me for a minute of what heroin feels like sometimes—when it's in your veins. It makes you feel sort of warm and cool at the same time. And distant. And—and sure." He sipped his beer, very deliberately not looking at me. I watched his face. "It makes you feel—in control. Sometimes you've got to have that feeling."

"Do you?" I sat down slowly in the easy chair.

"Sometimes." He went to the sofa and picked up his notebook again. "Some people do."

"In order," I asked, "to play?" And my voice was very ugly, full of contempt and anger.

"Well"—he looked at me with great, troubled eyes, as though, in fact, he hoped his eyes would tell me things he could never otherwise say—"they *think* so. And *if* they think so—!"

"And what do *you* think?" I asked.

He sat on the sofa and put his can of beer on the floor. "I don't know," he said, and I couldn't be sure if he were answering my question or pursuing his thoughts. His face didn't tell me. "It's not so much to *play*. It's to *stand* it, to be able to make it at all. On any level." He frowned and smiled: "In order to keep from shaking to pieces."

"But these friends of yours," I said, "they seem to shake themselves to pieces pretty goddamn fast."

"Maybe." He played with the notebook. And something told me that I should curb my tongue, that Sonny was doing his best to talk, that I should listen. "But of course you only know the ones that've gone to pieces. Some don't—or at least they haven't *yet* and that's just about all *any* of us can say." He paused. "And then there are some who just live, really, in hell, and they know it and they see what's happening and they go right on. I don't know." He sighed, dropped the notebook, folded his arms. "Some guys, you can tell from the way they play, they on something *all* the time. And you can see that, well, it makes something real for them. But of course," he picked up his beer from the floor and sipped it and put the can down again, "they *want* to, too, you've got to see that. Even some of them that say they don't—*some,* not all."

"And what about you?" I asked—I couldn't help it. "What about you? *Do you* want to?"

He stood up and walked to the window and remained silent for a long time. Then he sighed. "Me," he said. Then: "While I was downstairs before, on my way here, listening to that woman sing, it struck me all of a sudden how much suffering she must have had to go through—to sing like that. It's *repulsive* to think you have to suffer that much."

I said: "But there's no way not to suffer—is there, Sonny?"

"I believe not," he said and smiled, "but that's never stopped anyone from trying." He looked at me. "Has it?" I realized, with this mocking look, that there stood between us, forever, beyond the power of time or forgiveness, the fact that I had held silence—so long!—when he had needed human speech to help him. He turned back to the window. "No, there's no way not to suffer. But you try all kinds of ways to keep from drowning in it, to keep on top of it, and to make it seem—well, like *you*. Like you did something, all right, and now you're suffering for it. You know?" I said nothing. "Well you know," he said, impatiently, "why *do* people suffer? Maybe it's better to do something to give it a reason, *any* reason."

"But we just agreed," I said, "that there's no way not to suffer. Isn't it better, then, just to—take it?"

"But nobody just takes it," Sonny cried, "that's what I'm telling you! *Everybody* tries not to. You're just hung up on the *way* some people try—it's not *your* way!"

The hair on my face began to itch, my face felt wet. "That's not true," I said, "that's not true. I don't give a damn what other people do, I don't even care how they suffer. I just care how *you* suffer." And he looked at me. "Please believe me," I said, "I don't want to see you—die—trying not to suffer."

"I won't," he said, flatly, "die trying not to suffer. At least, not any faster than anybody else."

"But there's no need," I said, trying to laugh, "is there? in killing yourself."

I wanted to say more, but I couldn't. I wanted to talk about will power and how life could be—well, beautiful. I wanted to say that it was all within; but was it? or, rather, wasn't that exactly the trouble? And I wanted

to promise that I would never fail him again. But it would all have sounded
—empty words and lies.

So I made the promise to myself and prayed that I would keep it.

"It's terrible sometimes, inside," he said, "that's what's the trouble. You
walk these streets, black and funky and cold, and there's not really a living
ass to talk to, and there's nothing shaking, and there's no way of getting it
out—that storm inside. You can't talk it and you can't make love with it,
and when you finally try to get with it and play it, you realize *nobody's* listening. So *you've* got to listen. You got to find a way to listen."

And then he walked away from the window and sat on the sofa again,
as though all the wind had suddenly been knocked out of him. "Sometimes
you'll do *anything* to play, even cut your mother's throat." He laughed
and looked at me. "Or your brother's." Then he sobered. "Or your own."
Then: "Don't worry. I'm all right now and I think I'll *be* all right. But I
can't forget—where I've been. I don't mean just the physical place I've
been, I mean where I've *been*. And *what* I've been."

"What have you been, Sonny?" I asked.

He smiled—but sat sideways on the sofa, his elbow resting on the back,
his fingers playing with his mouth and chin, not looking at me. "I've been
something I didn't recognize, didn't know I could be. Didn't know anybody
could be." He stopped, looking inward, looking helplessly young, looking
old. "I'm not talking about it now because I feel *guilty* or anything like
that—maybe it would be better if I did, I don't know. Anyway, I can't really
talk about it. Not to you, not to anybody," and now he turned and faced
me. "Sometimes, you know, and it was actually when I was most *out* of the
world, I felt that I was in it, that I was *with* it, really, and I could play or I
didn't really have to *play*, it just came out of me, it was there. And I don't
know how I played, thinking about it now, but I know I did awful things,
those times sometimes, to people. Or it wasn't that I *did* anything to them
—it was that they weren't real." He picked up the beer can; it was empty;
he rolled it between his palms: "And other times—well, I needed a fix, I
needed to find a place to lean, I needed to clear a space to *listen*—and I
couldn't find it, and I—went crazy, I did terrible things to *me*, I was terrible *for* me." He began pressing the beer can between his hands, I
watched the metal begin to give. It glittered, as he played with it, like a
knife, and I was afraid he would cut himself, but I said nothing. "Oh well.
I can never tell you. I was all by myself at the bottom of something, stinking and sweating and crying and shaking, and I smelled it, you know? *my*
stink, and I thought I'd die if I couldn't get away from it and yet, all the

same, I knew that everything I was doing was just locking me in with it. And I didn't know," he paused, still flattening the beer can, "I didn't know, I still *don't* know, something kept telling me that maybe it was good to smell your own stink, but I didn't think that *that* was what I'd been trying to do—and—who can stand it?" and he abruptly dropped the ruined beer can, looking at me with a small, still smile, and then rose, walking to the window as though it were the lodestone rock. I watched his face, he watched the avenue. "I couldn't tell you when Mama died—but the reason I wanted to leave Harlem so bad was to get away from drugs. And then, when I ran away, that's what I was running from—really. When I came back, nothing had changed, I hadn't changed, I was just—older." And he stopped, drumming with his fingers on the windowpane. The sun had vanished, soon darkness would fall. I watched his face. "It can come again," he said, almost as though speaking to himself. Then he turned to me. "It can come again," he repeated. "I just want you to know that."

"All right," I said, at last. "So it can come again. All right."

He smiled, but the smile was sorrowful. "I had to try to tell you," he said.

"Yes," I said. "I understand that."

"You're my brother," he said, looking straight at me, and not smiling at all.

"Yes," I repeated, "yes. I understand that."

He turned back to the window, looking out. "All that hatred down there," he said, "all that hatred and misery and love. It's a wonder it doesn't blow the avenue apart."

We went to the only nightclub on a short, dark street, downtown. We squeezed through the narrow, chattering, jam-packed bar to the entrance of the big room, where the bandstand was. And we stood there for a moment, for the lights were very dim in this room and we couldn't see. Then, "Hello, boy," said a voice and an enormous black man, much older than Sonny or myself, erupted out of all that atmospheric lighting and put an arm around Sonny's shoulder. "I been sitting right here," he said, "waiting for you."

He had a big voice, too, and heads in the darkness turned toward us.

Sonny grinned and pulled a little away, and said, "Creole, this is my brother. I told you about him."

Creole shook my hand. "I'm glad to meet you, son," he said, and it was clear that he was glad to meet me *there*, for Sonny's sake. And he smiled, "You got a real musician in *your* family," and he took his arm from Sonny's shoulder and slapped him, lightly, affectionately, with the back of his hand.

"Well. Now I've heard it all," said a voice behind us. This was another musician, and a friend of Sonny's, a coal-black, cheerful-looking man, built close to the ground. He immediately began confiding to me, at the top of his lungs, the most terrible things about Sonny, his teeth gleaming like a lighthouse and his laugh coming up out of him like the beginning of an earthquake. And it turned out that everyone at the bar knew Sonny, or almost everyone; some were musicians, working there, or nearby, or not working, some were simply hangers-on, and some were there to hear Sonny play. I was introduced to all of them and they were all very polite to me. Yet, it was clear that, for them, I was only Sonny's brother. Here, I was in Sonny's world. Or, rather: his kingdom. Here, it was not even a question that his veins bore royal blood.

They were going to play soon and Creole installed me, by myself, at a table in a dark corner. Then I watched them, Creole, and the little black man, and Sonny, and the others, while they horsed around, standing just below the bandstand. The light from the bandstand spilled just a little short of them and, watching them laughing and gesturing and moving about, I had the feeling that they, nevertheless, were being most careful not to step into that circle of light too suddenly: that if they moved into the light too suddenly, without thinking, they would perish in flame. Then, while I watched, one of them, the small, black man, moved into the light and crossed the bandstand and started fooling around with his drums. Then— being funny and being, also, extremely ceremonious—Creole took Sonny by the arm and led him to the piano. A woman's voice called Sonny's name and a few hands started clapping. And Sonny, also being funny and being ceremonious, and so touched, I think, that he could have cried, but neither hiding it nor showing it, riding it like a man, grinned, and put both hands to his heart and bowed from the waist.

Creole then went to the bass fiddle and a lean, very bright-skinned brown man jumped up on the bandstand and picked up his horn. So there they were, and the atmosphere on the bandstand and in the room began to change and tighten. Someone stepped up to the microphone and announced them. Then there were all kinds of murmurs. Some people at the bar shushed others. The waitress ran around, frantically getting in the last orders, guys and chicks got closer to each other, and the lights on the bandstand, on the quartet, turned to a kind of indigo. Then they all looked different there. Creole looked about him for the last time, as though he were making certain that all his chickens were in the coop, and then he— jumped and struck the fiddle. And there they were.

All I know about music is that not many people ever really hear it. And even then, on the rare occasions when something opens within, and the music enters, what we mainly hear, or hear corroborated, are personal, private, vanishing evocations. But the man who creates the music is hearing something else, is dealing with the roar rising from the void and imposing order on it as it hits the air. What is evoked in him, then, is of another order, more terrible because it has no words, and triumphant, too, for that same reason. And his triumph, when he triumphs, is ours. I just watched Sonny's face. His face was troubled, he was working hard, but he wasn't with it. And I had the feeling that, in a way, everyone on the bandstand was waiting for him, both waiting for him and pushing him along. But as I began to watch Creole, I realized that it was Creole who held them all back. He had them on a short rein. Up there, keeping the beat with his whole body, wailing on the fiddle, with his eyes half closed, he was listening to everything, but he was listening to Sonny. He was having a dialogue with Sonny. He wanted Sonny to leave the shoreline and strike out for the deep water. He was Sonny's witness that deep water and drowning were not the same thing—he had been there, and he knew. And he wanted Sonny to know. He was waiting for Sonny to do the things on the keys which would let Creole know that Sonny was in the water.

And, while Creole listened, Sonny moved, deep within, exactly like someone in torment. I had never before thought of how awful the relationship must be between the musician and his instrument. He has to fill it, this instrument, with the breath of life, his own. He has to make it do what he wants it to do. And a piano is just a piano. It's made out of so much wood and wires and little hammers and big ones, and ivory. While there's only so much you can do with it, the only way to find this out is to try; to try and make it do everything.

And Sonny hadn't been near a piano for over a year. And he wasn't on much better terms with his life, not the life that stretched before him now. He and the piano stammered, started one way, got scared, stopped; started another way, panicked, marked time, started again; then seemed to have found a direction, panicked again, got stuck. And the face I saw on Sonny I'd never seen before. Everything had been burned out of it, and, at the same time, things usually hidden were being burned in, by the fire and fury of the battle which was occurring in him up there.

Yet, watching Creole's face as they neared the end of the first set, I had the feeling that something had happened, something I hadn't heard. Then they finished, there was scattered applause, and then, without an instant's warning, Creole started into something else, it was almost sardonic, it was *Am I Blue*. And, as though he commanded, Sonny began to play. Something began to happen. And Creole let out the reins. The dry, low, black man said something awful on the drums, Creole answered, and the drums talked back. Then the horn insisted, sweet and high, slightly detached perhaps, and Creole listened, commenting now and then, dry, and driving, beautiful and calm and old. Then they all came together again, and Sonny was part of the family again. I could tell this from his face. He seemed to have found, right there beneath his fingers, a damn brand-new piano. It seemed that he couldn't get over it. Then, for awhile, just being happy with Sonny, they seemed to be agreeing with him that brand-new pianos certainly were a gas.

Then Creole stepped forward to remind them that what they were playing was the blues. He hit something in all of them, he hit something in me, myself, and the music tightened and deepened, apprehension began to beat the air. Creole began to tell us what the blues were all about. They were not about anything very new. He and his boys up there were keeping it new, at the risk of ruin, destruction, madness, and death, in order to find new ways to make us listen. For, while the tale of how we suffer, and how we are delighted, and how we may triumph is never new, it always must be heard. There isn't any other tale to tell, it's the only light we've got in all this darkness.

And this tale, according to that face, that body, those strong hands on those strings, has another aspect in every country, and a new depth in every generation. Listen, Creole seemed to be saying, listen. Now these are Sonny's blues. He made the little black man on the drums know it, and the bright, brown man on the horn. Creole wasn't trying any longer to get Sonny in the water. He was wishing him Godspeed. Then he stepped back, very slowly, filling the air with the immense suggestion that Sonny speak for himself.

Then they all gathered around Sonny and Sonny played. Every now and again one of them seemed to say, amen. Sonny's fingers filled the air with life, his life. But that life contained so many others. And Sonny went all the way back, he really began with the spare, flat statement of the opening phrase of the song. Then he began to make it his. It was very beautiful because it wasn't hurried and it was no longer a lament. I seemed to hear with what burning he had made it his, with what burning we had yet to make it ours, how we could cease lamenting. Freedom lurked around us and I understood, at last, that he could help us to be free if we would listen, that he would never be free until we did. Yet, there was no battle in his face now. I heard what he had gone through, and would continue to go through until he came to rest in earth. He had made it his: that long line, of which we knew only Mama and Daddy. And he was giving it back, as everything must be given back, so that, passing through death, it can live forever. I saw my mother's face again, and felt, for the first time, how the stones of the road she had walked on must have bruised her feet. I saw the moonlit road where my father's brother died. And it brought something else back to me, and carried me past it, I saw my little girl again and felt Isabel's tears again, and I felt my own tears begin to rise. And I was yet aware that this was only a moment, that the world waited outside, as hungry as a tiger, and that trouble stretched above us, longer than the sky.

Then it was over. Creole and Sonny let out their breath, both soaking wet, and grinning. There was a lot of applause and some of it was real. In the dark, the girl came by and I asked her to take drinks to the bandstand. There was a long pause, while they talked up there in the indigo light and after awhile I saw the girl put a Scotch and milk on top of the piano for Sonny. He didn't seem to notice it, but just before they started playing again, he sipped from it and looked toward me, and nodded. Then he put it back on top of the piano. For me, then, as they began to play again, it glowed and shook above my brother's head like the very cup of trembling.

SUGGESTIONS FOR WRITING

The Stories

1. Compare and contrast the esthetic and thematic function of Baldwin's first-person narrator in "This Morning, This Evening, So Soon" with Malamud's Nat Lime in "Black Is My Favorite Color."

2. The essay on "This Morning, This Evening, So Soon" states that "the narrator does not, however much he may seem to, do all the reader's interpretive work for him." In similar fashion, the narrator of "Sonny's Blues" fails to do "the reader's interpretive work," although he too is intelligent, wary, and critical (qualities attributed by the essayist to the narrator of "This Morning, This Evening, So Soon"). Write an essay in which you show why the reader of "Sonny's Blues" must guard against "the false notion that he is getting the meaning as well as the action from the narrator."

3. Write an essay in which you examine the nature and function of images of light and dark in "Sonny's Blues."

4. Write an essay in which you treat *music* as holding the key to the theme or meaning of "Sonny's Blues."

5. Assuming the point of view of the narrator's brother Sonny, write a character sketch of the narrator.

Other Works by James Baldwin

1. The church plays an important role in *Go Tell It on the Mountain,* as it did in Baldwin's early life in Harlem. Discuss Baldwin's portrayal of religion in this novel.

2. In "Many Thousands Gone," Baldwin writes, "It is only in his music, which Americans are able to admire because a protective sentimentality limits their understanding of it, that the Negro in America has been able to tell his story." In *After Alienation,* Marcus Klein adds, "as an aid to the telling of his version of it, Baldwin has used Negro musical motifs. . . . The music contributes a tone, and that tone at the very least reinforces the yearning that anyway is in much of the work." Discuss music as a rhetorical device and a theme in selected stories from *Going to Meet the Man* and in either *Go Tell It on the Mountain* or *Another Country.*

3. In "The World of James Baldwin," Theodore Gross finds fault with the structure of *Another Country:* "When Baldwin transfers Rufus's vision of the white world to his sister Ida and has her develop a relationship with Rufus's closest white friend, Vivaldo, he loses firm control of his material." Write an essay in which you either support or refute Gross's statement by examining the relation between structure and theme in *Another Country.*

4. Concerning *The Amen Corner* (which was written in the 1950's shortly after *Go Tell It on the Mountain*), Baldwin observes that Sister Margaret's dilemma stemmed from trying to treat her husband and son as men and at the same time protecting them "from the bloody consequences of trying to be a man in this society." Compare the characters, the role of the church, and the themes of *The Amen Corner* and *Go Tell It on the Mountain.*

BIBLIOGRAPHY

Primary

Go Tell It on the Mountain. New York: Alfred A. Knopf, 1953. A novel.
Notes of a Native Son. Boston: Beacon Press, 1955. Essays.
Giovanni's Room. New York: Dial Press, 1956. A novel.
Nobody Knows My Name. New York: Dial Press, 1961. Essays.
Another Country. New York: Dial Press, 1962. A novel.
The Fire Next Time. New York: Dial Press, 1963. Essay.
Blues for Mister Charlie. New York: Dial Press, 1964. Drama.
Going to Meet the Man. New York: Dial Press, 1965. Short stories.
Tell Me How Long the Train's Been Gone. New York: Dial Press, 1968. A novel.
Amen Corner. New York: Dial Press, 1968. A play.
A Rap on Race [with Margaret Mead]. Philadelphia: Lippincott, 1971. A discussion.
James Baldwin, Nikki Giovanni: A Dialogue. Philadelphia: Lippincott, 1972. A discussion.
No Name in the Street. New York: Dial Press, 1972. Essays.

Secondary

Breit, Harvey. "James Baldwin and Two Footnotes" in *The Creative Present*, ed. by Nona Balakian and Charles Simmons. Garden City, N.Y.: Doubleday, 1963. An analysis of the relationship of Baldwin's role as a Negro leader to his achievement as an essayist and novelist.
Charney, Maurice. "James Baldwin's Quarrel with Richard Wright." *American Quarterly*, 15 (Spring 1963), 65–75. Affords insight into Baldwin's esthetic theory by exploring the differences between Baldwin and Wright.
Eckman, Fern Marja. *The Furious Passage of James Baldwin*. New York: M. Evans, 1966. A detailed, full-length biographical study.
Foster, David E. " 'Cause My House Fell Down: The Theme of the Fall in Baldwin's Novels." *Critique*, 13:2 (1971), 50–62. Discusses the theme of the fall in *Go Tell It on the Mountain, Giovanni's Room*, and *Another Country* and the meaning of its absence in *Tell Me How Long the Train's Been Gone*.

Gross, Theodore. "The World of James Baldwin." *Critique,* 7 (Winter 1964–65), 139–49. A general review of Baldwin's career and a thematic discussion of *Another Country.*

Harper, Howard M., Jr. *Desperate Faith: A Study of Bellow, Salinger, Mailer, Baldwin, and Updike.* Chapel Hill: Univ. of North Carolina Press, 1967. Analyzes the incompatibility of Baldwin's roles as "a fiery prophet of the racial apocalypse and a sensitive explorer of man's inmost nature."

Klein, Marcus. "James Baldwin: A Question of Identity" in *After Alienation: American Novels in Mid-Century.* Cleveland: World, 1964. A perceptive analysis of Baldwin's essays and fiction.

Newman, Charles. "The Lesson of the Master: Henry James and James Baldwin." *Yale Review,* 56 (Autumn 1966), 45–59. Uses *Another Country* to illustrate the "dialectical art" integral to Baldwin's fiction.

Podhoretz, Norman. "In Defense of James Baldwin" in *Doings and Undoings.* New York: Farrar, Straus & Giroux, 1964. A defense of *Another Country* for its "remorseless insistence on a truth which, however partial we may finally judge it to be, is nevertheless compelling as a perspective on the way we live now."

Sayre, Robert. "James Baldwin's Other Country" in *Contemporary American Novelists,* ed. by Harry T. Moore. Carbondale, Ill.: Southern Illinois Univ. Press, 1964. Examines the relationship between Baldwin's essays and novels. (A brief introduction to Baldwin given by Kay Boyle on the occasion of Baldwin's speaking at Wesleyan College precedes Sayre's essay.)

In the greatest fiction, the writer's moral sense coincides with his dramatic sense, and I see no way for it to do this unless his moral judgment is part of the very act of seeing, and he is free to use it. I have heard it said that belief in Christian dogma is a hindrance to the writer, but I myself have found nothing further from the truth. Actually, it frees the storyteller to observe. It is not a set of rules which fixes what he sees in the world. It affects his writing primarily by guaranteeing his respect for mystery.

· · ·

The novelist with Christian concerns will find in modern life distortions which are repugnant to him, and his problem will be to make these appear as distortions to an audience which is used to seeing them as natural; and he may well be forced to take ever more violent means to get his vision across to this hostile audience. When you can assume that your audience holds the same beliefs you do, you can relax a little and use more normal ways of talking to it; when you have to assume that it does not, then you have to make your vision apparent by shock—to the hard of hearing you shout, and for the almost blind you draw large and startling figures.

FROM *The Fiction Writer and His Country*

FLANNERY O'CONNOR

Mary Flannery O'Connor was born in Savannah, Georgia, in 1925. She majored in English literature and social science at the Georgia State College for Women and received a master's degree in creative writing from the University of Iowa. Serious illness—the tubercular skin disease lupus—brought her back to Georgia after two years in New York and Connecticut, and she spent the last fourteen years of her short life with her mother on a farm near Milledgeville. When the disease was in a remissive stage, she worked on her stories and novels; she also painted, raised peafowl and swans, engaged in lengthy and lively correspondence with friends, and traveled occasionally to give lectures. She died of lupus in 1964, at the age of 39.

During her lifetime O'Connor won two *Kenyon Review* fellowships in fiction, a National Institute of Arts and Letters grant, a Ford Foundation grant, and three O. Henry first prizes. In 1972, she was posthumously awarded the National Book Award in fiction for *The Complete Stories*.

A devout Roman Catholic, O'Connor drew sustenance not only from her own deep spirtuality and Catholic doctrine, but also from her keen interest in the life around her. "The Displaced Person" and "Everything That Rises Must Converge" show her ability to render dialect, her unfailing sense of humor, and her seemingly compulsive urge to tear apart the facades of polite, spiritually empty existence.

THE DISPLACED
PERSON

The peacock was following Mrs. Shortley up the road to the hill where she meant to stand. Moving one behind the other, they looked like a complete procession. Her arms were folded and as she mounted the prominence, she might have been the giant wife of the countryside, come out at some sign of danger to see what the trouble was. She stood on two tremendous legs, with the grand self-confidence of a mountain, and rose, up narrowing bulges of granite, to two icy blue points of light that pierced forward, surveying everything. She ignored the white afternoon sun which was creeping behind a ragged wall of cloud as if it pretended to be an intruder and cast her gaze down the red clay road that turned off from the highway.

The peacock stopped just behind her, his tail—glittering green-gold and blue in the sunlight—lifted just enough so that it would not touch the ground. It flowed out on either side like a floating train and his head on the long blue reed-like neck was drawn back as if his attention were fixed in the distance on something no one else could see.

Mrs. Shortley was watching a black car turn through the gate from the highway. Over by the toolshed, about fifteen feet away, the two Negroes, Astor and Sulk, had stopped work to watch. They were hidden by a mulberry tree but Mrs. Shortley knew they were there.

Mrs. McIntyre was coming down the steps of her house to meet the car. She had on her largest smile but Mrs. Shortley, even from her distance, could detect a nervous slide in it. These people who were coming were only hired help, like the Shortleys themselves or the Negroes. Yet here was the owner of the place out to welcome them. Here she was, wearing her best clothes and a string of beads, and now bounding forward with her mouth stretched.

The car stopped at the walk just as she did and the priest was the first to get out. He was a long-legged black-suited old man with a white hat on and a collar that he wore backwards, which, Mrs. Shortley knew, was what priests did who wanted to be known as priests. It was this priest who had arranged for these people to come here. He opened the back door of the car and out jumped two children, a boy and a girl, and then, stepping more slowly, a woman in brown, shaped like a peanut. Then the front door opened and out stepped the man, the Displaced Person. He was short and a little sway-backed and wore gold-rimmed spectacles.

Mrs. Shortley's vision narrowed on him and then widened to include the woman and the two children in a group picture. The first thing that struck her as very peculiar was that they looked like other people. Every time she had seen them in her imagination, the image she had got was of the three bears, walking single file, with wooden shoes on like Dutchmen and sailor hats and bright coats with a lot of buttons. But the woman had on a dress she might have worn herself and the children were dressed like anybody from around. The man had on khaki pants and a blue shirt. Suddenly, as Mrs. McIntyre held out her hand to him, he bobbed down from the waist and kissed it.

Mrs. Shortley jerked her own hand up toward her mouth and then after a second brought it down and rubbed it vigorously on her seat. If Mr. Shortley had tried to kiss her hand, Mrs. McIntyre would have knocked him into the middle of next week, but then Mr. Shortley wouldn't have kissed her hand anyway. He didn't have time to mess around.

She looked closer, squinting. The boy was in the center of the group, talking. He was supposed to speak the most English because he had learned some in Poland and so he was to listen to his father's Polish and say it in English and then listen to Mrs. McIntyre's English and say that in Polish. The priest had told Mrs. McIntyre his name was Rudolph and he was twelve and the girl's name was Sledgewig and she was nine. Sledgewig sounded to Mrs. Shortley like something you would name a bug, or vice versa, as if you named a boy Bollweevil. All of them's last name was something that only they themselves and the priest could pronounce. All she could make out of it was Gobblehook. She and Mrs. McIntyre had been calling them the Gobblehooks all week while they got ready for them.

There had been a great deal to do to get ready for them because they didn't have anything of their own, not a stick of furniture or a sheet or a dish, and everything had had to be scraped together out of things that Mrs. McIntyre couldn't use any more herself. They had collected a piece of odd furniture here and a piece there and they had taken some flowered chicken feed sacks and made curtains for the windows, two red and one green, because they had not had enough of the red sacks to go around. Mrs. McIntyre said she was not made of money and she could not afford to buy curtains. "They can't talk," Mrs. Shortley said. "You reckon they'll know what colors even is?" and Mrs. McIntyre had said that after what those people had been through, they should be grateful for anything they could get. She said to think how lucky they were to escape from over there and come to a place like this.

Mrs. Shortley recalled a newsreel she had seen once of a small room piled high with bodies of dead naked people all in a heap, their arms and legs tangled together, a head thrust in here, a head there, a foot, a knee, a part that should have been covered up sticking out, a hand raised clutching nothing. Before you could realize that it was real and take it into your head, the picture changed and a hollow-sounding voice was saying, "Time marches on!" This was the kind of thing that was happening every day in Europe where they had not advanced as in this country, and watching from her vantage point, Mrs. Shortley had the sudden intuition that the Gobblehooks, like rats with typhoid fleas, could have carried all those murderous ways over the water with them directly to this place. If they had come from where that kind of thing was done to them, who was to say they were not the kind that would also do it to others? The width and breadth of this question nearly shook her. Her stomach trembled as if there had been a slight quake in the heart of the mountain and automatically she moved down from her elevation and went forward to be introduced to them, as if she meant to find out at once what they were capable of.

She approached, stomach foremost, head back, arms folded, boots flopping gently against her large legs. About fifteen feet from the gesticulating group, she stopped and made her presence felt by training her gaze on the back of Mrs. McIntyre's neck. Mrs. McIntyre was a small woman of sixty with a round wrinkled face and red bangs that came almost down to two high orange-colored penciled eyebrows. She had a little doll's mouth and eyes that were a soft blue when she opened them wide but more like steel or granite when she narrowed them to inspect a milk can. She had buried one husband and divorced two and Mrs. Shortley respected her as a person nobody had put anything over on yet—except, ha, ha, perhaps the Shortleys. She held out her arm in Mrs. Shortley's direction and said to the Rudolph boy, "And this is Mrs. Shortley. Mr. Shortley is my dairyman. Where's Mr. Shortley?" she asked as his wife began to approach again, her arms still folded. "I want him to meet the Guizacs."

Now it was Guizac. She wasn't calling them Gobblehook to their face. "Chancey's at the barn," Mrs. Shortley said. "He don't have time to rest himself in the bushes like them niggers over there."

Her look first grazed the tops of the displaced people's heads and then revolved downwards slowly, the way a buzzard glides and drops in the air until it alights on the carcass. She stood far enough away so that the man would not be able to kiss her hand. He looked directly at her with little green eyes and gave her a broad grin that was toothless on one side. Mrs. Shortley, without smiling, turned her attention to the little girl who stood by the mother, swinging her shoulders from side to side. She had long braided hair in two looped pigtails and there was no denying she was a pretty child even if she did have a bug's name. She was better looking than either Annie Maude or Sarah Mae, Mrs. Shortley's two girls going on fifteen and seventeen but Annie Maude had never got her growth and Sarah Mae had a cast in her eye. She compared the foreign boy to her son, H. C., and H. C. came out far ahead. H. C. was twenty years old with her build and eyeglasses. He was going to Bible school now and when he finished he was going to start him a church. He had a strong sweet voice for hymns and could sell anything. Mrs. Shortley looked at the priest and was reminded that these people did not have an advanced religion. There was no telling what all they believed since none of the foolishness had been re-formed out of it. Again she saw the room piled high with bodies.

The priest spoke in a foreign way himself, English but as if he had a throatful of hay. He had a big nose and a bald rectangular face and head. While she was observing him, his large mouth dropped open and with a stare behind her, he said, "Arrrrrrr!" and pointed.

Mrs. Shortley spun around. The peacock was standing a few feet behind her, with his head slightly cocked.

"What a beauti-ful birdrrrd!" the priest murmured.

"Another mouth to feed," Mrs. McIntyre said, glancing in the peafowl's direction.

"And when does he raise his splendid tail?" asked the priest.

"Just when it suits him," she said. "There used to be twenty or thirty of those things on the place but I've let them die off. I don't like to hear them scream in the middle of the night."

"So beauti-ful," the priest said. "A tail full of suns," and he crept forward on tiptoe and looked down on the bird's back where the polished gold and green design began. The peacock stood still as if he had just come down from some sun-drenched height to be a vision for them all. The priest's homely red face hung over him, glowing with pleasure.

Mrs. Shortley's mouth had drawn acidly to one side. "Nothing but a pea-chicken," she muttered.

Mrs. McIntyre raised her orange eyebrows and exchanged a look with her to indicate that the old man was in his second childhood. "Well, we must show the Guizacs their new home," she said impatiently and she herded them into the car again. The peacock stepped off toward the mulberry tree where the two Negroes were hiding and the priest turned his absorbed face away and got in the car and drove the displaced people down to the shack they were to occupy.

Mrs. Shortley waited until the car was out of sight and then she made her way circuitously to the mulberry tree and stood about ten feet behind the two Negroes, one an old man holding a bucket half full of calf feed and the other a yellowish boy with a short woodchuck-like head pushed into a rounded felt hat. "Well," she said slowly, "yawl have looked long enough. What you think about them?"

The old man, Astor, raised himself. "We been watching," he said as if this would be news to her. "Who they now?"

"They come from over the water," Mrs. Shortley said with a wave of her arm. "They're what is called Displaced Persons."

"Displaced Persons," he said. "Well now. I declare. What do that mean?"

"It means they ain't where they were born at and there's nowhere for them to go—like if you was run out of here and wouldn't nobody have you."

"It seem like they here, though," the old man said in a reflective voice. "If they here, they somewhere."

"Sho is," the other agreed. "They here."

The illogic of Negro-thinking always irked Mrs. Shortley. "They ain't where they belong to be at," she said. "They belong to be back over yonder where everything is still like they been used to. Over here it's more advanced than where they come from. But yawl better look out now," she said and nodded her head. "There's about ten million billion more just like them and I know what Mrs. McIntyre said."

"Say what?" the young one asked.

"Places are not easy to get nowadays, for white or black, but I reckon I heard what she stated to me," she said in a sing-song voice.

"You liable to hear most anything," the old man remarked, leaning forward as if he were about to walk off but holding himself suspended.

"I heard her say, 'This is going to put the Fear of the Lord into those shiftless niggers!' " Mrs. Shortley said in a ringing voice.

The old man started off. "She say something like that every now and then," he said. "Ha. Ha. Yes indeed."

"You better get on in that barn and help Mr. Shortley," she said to the other one. "What you reckon she pays you for?"

"He the one sont me out," the Negro muttered. "He the one gimme something else to do."

"Well you better get to doing it then," she said and stood there until he moved off. Then she stood a while longer, reflecting, her unseeing eyes directly in front of the peacock's tail. He had jumped into the tree and his tail hung in front of her, full of fierce planets with eyes that were each ringed in green and set against a sun that was gold in one second's light and salmon-colored in the next. She might have been looking at a map of the universe but she didn't notice it any more than she did the spots of sky that cracked the dull green of the tree. She was having an inner vision instead. She was seeing the ten million billion of them pushing their way into new places over here and herself, a giant angel with wings as wide as a house, telling the Negroes that they would have to find another place. She turned herself in the direction of the barn, musing on this, her expression lofty and satisfied.

She approached the barn from an oblique angle that allowed her a look in the door before she could be seen herself. Mr. Chancey Shortley was adjusting the last milking machine on a large black and white spotted cow near the entrance, squatting at her heels. There was about a half-inch of cigarette adhering to the center of his lower lip. Mrs. Shortley observed it minutely for half a second. "If she seen or heard of you smoking in this barn, she would blow a fuse," she said.

Mr. Shortley raised a sharply rutted face containing a washout under each cheek and two long crevices eaten down both sides of his blistered mouth. "You gonter be the one to tell her?" he asked.

"She's got a nose of her own," Mrs. Shortley said.

Mr. Shortley, without appearing to give the feat any consideration, lifted the cigarette stub with the sharp end of his tongue, drew it into his mouth, closed his lips tightly, rose, stepped out, gave his wife a good round appreciative stare, and spit the smoldering butt into the grass.

"Aw Chancey," she said, "haw haw," and she dug a little hole for it with her toe and covered it up. This trick of Mr. Shortley's was actually his way of making love to her. When he had done his courting, he had not brought a guitar to strum or anything pretty for her to keep, but had sat on her porch steps, not saying a word, imitating a paralyzed man propped up to enjoy a cigarette. When the cigarette got the proper size, he would turn his eyes to her and open his mouth and draw in the butt and then sit there as if he had swallowed it, looking at her with the most loving look anybody could imagine. It nearly drove her wild and every time he did it, she wanted to pull his hat down over his eyes and hug him to death.

"Well," she said, going into the barn after him, "the Gobblehooks have come and she wants you to meet them, says, 'Where's Mr. Shortley?' and I says, 'He don't have time . . .'"

"Tote up them weights," Mr. Shortley said, squatting to the cow again.

"You reckon he can drive a tractor when he don't know English?" she asked. "I don't think she's going to get her money's worth out of them. That boy can talk but he looks delicate. The one can work can't talk and the one can talk can't work. She ain't any better off than if she had more niggers."

"I rather have a nigger if it was me," Mr. Shortley said.

"She says it's ten million more like them, Displaced Persons, she says that there priest can get her all she wants."

"She better quit messin with that there priest," Mr. Shortley said.

"He don't look smart," Mrs. Shortley said, "—kind of foolish."

"I ain't going to have the Pope of Rome tell me how to run no dairy," Mr. Shortley said.

"They ain't Eye-talians, they're Poles," she said. "From Poland where all them bodies were stacked up at. You remember all them bodies?"

"I give them three weeks here," Mr. Shortley said.

Three weeks later Mrs. McIntyre and Mrs. Shortley drove to the cane bottom to see Mr. Guizac start to operate the silage cutter, a new machine that Mrs. McIntyre had just bought because she said, for the first time, she had somebody who could operate it. Mr. Guizac could drive a tractor, use the rotary hay-baler, the silage cutter, the combine, the letz mill, or any other machine she had on the place. He was an expert mechanic, a carpenter, and a mason. He was thrifty and energetic. Mrs. McIntyre said she figured he would save her twenty dollars a month on repair bills alone. She said getting him was the best day's work she had ever done in her life. He could work milking machines and he was scrupulously clean. He did not smoke.

She parked her car on the edge of the cane field and they got out. Sulk, the young Negro, was attaching the wagon to the cutter and Mr. Guizac was attaching the cutter to the tractor. He finished first and pushed the colored boy out of the way and attached the wagon to the cutter himself, gesticulating with a bright angry face when he wanted the hammer or the screwdriver. Nothing was done quick enough to suit him. The Negroes made him nervous.

The week before, he had come upon Sulk at the dinner hour, sneaking with a croker sack into the pen where the young turkeys were. He had watched him take a frying-size turkey from the lot and thrust it in the sack and put the sack under his coat. Then he had followed him around the barn, jumped on him, dragged him to Mrs. McIntyre's back door and had acted out the entire scene for her, while the Negro muttered and grumbled and said God might strike him dead if he had been stealing any turkey, he had only been taking it to put some black shoe polish on its head because it had the sorehead. God might strike him dead if that was not the truth before Jesus. Mrs. McIntyre told him to go put the turkey back and then she was a long time explaining to the Pole that all Negroes would steal. She finally had to call Rudolph and tell him in English and have him tell his father in Polish, and Mr. Guizac had gone off with a startled disappointed face.

Mrs. Shortley stood by hoping there would be trouble with the silage machine but there was none. All of Mr. Guizac's motions were quick and accurate. He jumped on the tractor like a monkey and maneuvered the big orange cutter into the cane; in a second the silage was spurting in a green jet out of the pipe into the wagon. He went jolting down the row until he disappeared from sight and the noise became remote.

Mrs. McIntyre sighed with pleasure. "At last," she said, "I've got somebody I can depend on. For years I've been fooling with sorry people. Sorry people. Poor white trash and niggers," she muttered. "They've drained me dry. Before you all came I had Ringfields and Collins and Jarrells and Perkins and Pinkins and Herrins and God knows what all else and not a one of them left without taking something off this place that didn't belong to them. Not a one!"

Mrs. Shortley could listen to this with composure because she knew that if Mrs. McIntyre had considered her trash, they couldn't have talked about trashy people together. Neither of them approved of trash. Mrs. McIntyre continued with the monologue that Mrs. Shortley had heard oftentimes before. "I've been running this place for thirty years," she said, looking with a deep frown out over the field, "and always just barely making it. People think you're made of money. I have the taxes to pay. I have the insurance to keep up. I have the repair bills. I have the feed bills." It all gathered up and she stood with her chest lifted and her small hands gripped around her elbows. "Ever since the Judge died," she said, "I've barely been making ends meet and they all take something when they leave. The niggers don't leave —they stay and steal. A nigger thinks anybody is rich he can steal from and that white trash thinks anybody is rich who can afford to hire people as sorry as they are. And all I've got is the dirt under my feet!"

You hire and fire, Mrs. Shortley thought, but she didn't always say what she thought. She stood by and let Mrs. McIntyre say it all out to the end but this time it didn't end as usual. "But at last I'm saved!" Mrs. McIntyre said. "One fellow's misery is the other fellow's gain. That man there," and she pointed where the Displaced Person had disappeared, "—he has to work! He wants to work!" She turned to Mrs. Shortley with her bright wrinkled face. "That man is my salvation!" she said.

Mrs. Shortley looked straight ahead as if her vision penetrated the cane and the hill and pierced through to the other side. "I would suspicion salvation got from the devil," she said in a slow detached way.

"Now what do you mean by that?" Mrs. McIntyre asked, looking at her sharply.

Mrs. Shortley wagged her head but would not say anything else. The fact was she had nothing else to say for this intuition had only at that instant come to her. She had never given much thought to the devil for she felt that religion was essentially for those people who didn't have the brains to avoid evil without it. For people like herself, for people of gumption, it was a social occasion providing the opportunity to sing; but if she had ever given it much thought, she would have considered the devil the head of it and God the hanger-on. With the coming of these displaced people, she was obliged to give new thought to a good many things.

"I know what Sledgewig told Annie Maude," she said, and when Mrs. McIntyre carefully did not ask her what but reached down and broke off a sprig of sassafras to chew, she continued in a way to indicate she was not telling all, "that they wouldn't be able to live long, the four of them, on seventy dollars a month."

"He's worth raising," Mrs. McIntyre said. "He saves me money."

415

This was as much as to say that Chancey had never saved her money. Chancey got up at four in the morning to milk her cows, in winter wind and summer heat, and he had been doing it for the last two years. They had been with her the longest she had ever had anybody. The gratitude they got was these hints that she hadn't been saved any money.

"Is Mr. Shortley feeling better today?" Mrs. McIntyre asked.

Mrs. Shortley thought it was about time she was asking that question. Mr. Shortley had been in bed two days with an attack. Mr. Guizac had taken his place in the dairy in addition to doing his own work. "No he ain't," she said. "That doctor said he was suffering from over-exhaustion."

"If Mr. Shortley is over-exhausted," Mrs. McIntyre said, "then he must have a second job on the side," and she looked at Mrs. Shortley with almost closed eyes as if she were examining the bottom of a milk can.

Mrs. Shortley did not say a word but her dark suspicion grew like a black thunder cloud. The fact was that Mr. Shortley did have a second job on the side and that, in a free country, this was none of Mrs. McIntyre's business. Mr. Shortley made whisky. He had a small still back in the farthest reaches of the place, on Mrs. McIntyre's land to be sure, but on land that she only owned and did not cultivate, on idle land that was not doing anybody any good. Mr. Shortley was not afraid of work. He got up at four in the morning and milked her cows and in the middle of the day when he was supposed to be resting, he was off attending to his still. Not every man would work like that. The Negroes knew about his still but he knew about theirs so there had never been any disagreeableness between them. But with foreigners on the place, with people who were all eyes and no understanding, who had come from a place continually fighting, where the religion had not been reformed—with this kind of people, you had to be on the lookout every minute. She thought there ought to be a law against them. There was no reason they couldn't stay over there and take the places of some of the people who had been killed in their wars and butcherings.

"What's furthermore," she said suddenly, "Sledgewig said as soon as her papa saved the money, he was going to buy him a used car. Once they get them a used car, they'll leave you."

"I can't pay him enough for him to save money," Mrs. McIntyre said. "I'm not worrying about that. Of course," she said then, "if Mr. Shortley got incapacitated, I would have to use Mr. Guizac in the dairy all the time and I would have to pay him more. He doesn't smoke," she said, and it was the fifth time within the week that she had pointed this out.

"It is no man," Mrs. Shortley said emphatically, "that works as hard as Chancey, or is as easy with a cow, or is more of a Christian," and she folded her arms and her gaze pierced the distance. The noise of the tractor and cutter increased and Mr. Guizac appeared coming around the other side of the cane row. "Which can not be said about everybody," she muttered. She wondered whether, if the Pole found Chancey's still, he would know what it was. The trouble with these people was, you couldn't tell what they knew. Every time Mr. Guizac smiled, Europe stretched out in Mrs. Shortley's imagination, mysterious and evil, the devil's experiment station.

The tractor, the cutter, the wagon passed, rattling and rumbling and grinding before them. "Think how long that would have taken with men and mules to do it," Mrs. McIntyre shouted. "We'll get this whole bottom cut within two days at this rate."

"Maybe," Mrs. Shortley muttered, "if don't no terrible accident occur." She thought how the tractor had made mules worthless. Nowadays you couldn't give away a mule. The next thing to go, she reminded herself, will be niggers.

In the afternoon she explained what was going to happen to them to Astor and Sulk who were in the cow lot, filling the manure spreader. She sat down next to the block of salt under a small shed, her stomach in her lap, her arms on top of it. "All you colored people better look out," she said. "You know how much you can get for a mule."

"Nothing, no indeed," the old man said, "not one thing."

"Before it was a tractor," she said, "it could be a mule. And before it was a Displaced Person, it could be a nigger. The time is going to come," she prophesied, "when it won't be no more occasion to speak of a nigger."

The old man laughed politely. "Yes indeed," he said. "Ha ha."

The young one didn't say anything. He only looked sullen but when she had gone in the house, he said, "Big Belly act like she know everything."

"Never mind," the old man said, "your place too low for anybody to dispute with you for it."

She didn't tell her fears about the still to Mr. Shortley until he was back on the job in the dairy. Then one night after they were in bed, she said, "That man prowls."

Mr. Shortley folded his hands on his bony chest and pretended he was a corpse.

"Prowls," she continued and gave him a sharp kick in the side with her knee. "Who's to say what they know and don't know? Who's to say if he found it he wouldn't go right to her and tell? How you know they don't make liquor in Europe? They drive tractors. They got them all kinds of machinery. Answer me."

"Don't worry me now," Mr. Shortley said. "I'm a dead man."

"It's them little eyes of his that's foreign," she muttered. "And that way he's got a shrugging." She drew her shoulders up and shrugged several times. "Howcome he's got anything to shrug about?" she asked.

"If everybody was as dead as I am, nobody would have no trouble," Mr. Shortley said.

"That priest," she muttered and was silent for a minute. Then she said, "In Europe they probably got some different way to make liquor but I reckon they know all the ways. They're full of crooked ways. They never have advanced or reformed. They got the same religion as a thousand years ago. It could only be the devil responsible for that. Always fighting amongst each other. Disputing. And then get us into it. Ain't they got us into it twict already and we ain't got no more sense than to go over there and settle it for them and then they come on back over here and snoop around and find your still and go straight to her. And liable to kiss her hand any minute. Do you hear me?"

"No," Mr. Shortley said.

"And I'll tell you another thing," she said. "I wouldn't be a tall surprised if he don't know everything you say, whether it be in English or not."

"I don't speak no other language," Mr. Shortley murmured.

"I suspect," she said, "that before long there won't be no more niggers on this place. And I tell you what. I'd rather have niggers than them Poles. And what's furthermore, I aim to take up for the niggers when the time comes. When Gobblehook first come here, you recollect how he shook their hands, like he didn't know the difference, like he might have been as black as them, but when it come to finding out Sulk was taking turkeys, he gone on and told her. I known he was taking turkeys. I could have told her myself."

Mr. Shortley was breathing softly as if he were asleep.

"A nigger don't know when he has a friend," she said. "And I'll tell you another thing. I get a heap out of Sledgewig. Sledgewig said that in Poland they lived in a brick house and one night a man come and told them to get out of it before daylight. Do you believe they ever lived in a brick house?

"Airs," she said. "That's just airs. A wooden house is good enough for me. Chancey," she said, "turn thisaway. I hate to see niggers mistreated and run out. I have a heap of pity for niggers and poor folks. Ain't I always had?" she asked. "I say ain't I always been a friend to niggers and poor folks?

418

"When the time comes," she said, "I'll stand up for the niggers and that's that. I ain't going to see that priest drive out all the niggers."

Mrs. McIntyre bought a new drag harrow and a tractor with a power lift because she said, for the first time, she had someone who could handle machinery. She and Mrs. Shortley had driven to the back field to inspect what he had harrowed the day before. "That's been done beautifully!" Mrs. McIntyre said, looking out over the red undulating ground.

Mrs. McIntyre had changed since the Displaced Person had been working for her and Mrs. Shortley had observed the change very closely: she had begun to act like somebody who was getting rich secretly and she didn't confide in Mrs. Shortley the way she used to. Mrs. Shortley suspected that the priest was at the bottom of the change. They were very slick. First he would get her into his Church and then he would get his hand in her pocketbook. Well, Mrs. Shortley thought, the more fool she! Mrs. Shortley had a secret herself. She knew something the Displaced Person was doing that would floor Mrs. McIntyre. "I still say he ain't going to work forever for seventy dollars a month," she murmured. She intended to keep her secret to herself and Mr. Shortley.

"Well," Mrs. McIntyre said, "I may have to get rid of some of this other help so I can pay him more."

Mrs. Shortley nodded to indicate she had known this for some time. "I'm not saying those niggers ain't had it coming," she said. "But they do the best they know how. You can always tell a nigger what to do and stand by until he does it."

"That's what the Judge said," Mrs. McIntyre said and looked at her with approval. The Judge was her first husband, the one who had left her the place. Mrs. Shortley had heard that she had married him when she was thirty and he was seventy-five, thinking she would be rich as soon as he died, but the old man was a scoundrel and when his estate was settled, they found he didn't have a nickel. All he left her were the fifty acres and the house. But she always spoke of him in a reverent way and quoted his sayings, such as, "One fellow's misery is the other fellow's gain," and "The devil you know is better than the devil you don't."

"However," Mrs. Shortley remarked, "the devil you know is better than the devil you don't," and she had to turn away so that Mrs. McIntyre would not see her smile. She had found out what the Displaced Person was up to through the old man, Astor, and she had not told anybody but Mr. Shortley. Mr. Shortley had risen straight up in bed like Lazarus from the tomb.

"Shut your mouth!" he had said.

"Yes," she had said.

"Naw!" Mr. Shortley had said.

"Yes," she had said.

Mr. Shortley had fallen back flat.

"The Pole don't know any better," Mrs. Shortley had said. "I reckon that priest is putting him up to it is all. I blame the priest."

The priest came frequently to see the Guizacs and he would always stop in and visit Mrs. McIntyre too and they would walk around the place and she would point out her improvements and listen to his rattling talk. It suddenly came to Mrs. Shortley that he was trying to persuade her to bring another Polish family onto the place. With two of them here, there would be almost nothing spoken but Polish! The Negroes would be gone and there would be the two families against Mr. Shortley and herself! She began to imagine a war of words, to see the Polish words and the English words coming at each other, stalking forward, not sentences, just words, gabble gabble gabble, flung out high and shrill and stalking forward and then grappling with each other. She saw the Polish words, dirty and all-knowing and unreformed, flinging mud on the clean English words until everything was equally dirty. She saw them all piled up in a room, all the dead dirty words, theirs and hers too, piled up like the naked bodies in the newsreel. God save me! she cried silently, from the stinking power of Satan! And she started from that day to read her Bible with a new attention. She pored over the Apocalypse and began to quote from the Prophets and before long she had come to a deeper understanding of her existence. She saw plainly that the meaning of the world was a mystery that had been planned and she was not surprised to suspect that she had a special part in the plan because she was strong. She saw that the Lord God Almighty had created the strong people to do what had to be done and she felt that she would be ready when she was called. Right now she felt that her business was to watch the priest.

His visits irked her more and more. On the last one, he went about picking up feathers off the ground. He found two peacock feathers and four or five turkey feathers and an old brown hen feather and took them off with him like a bouquet. This foolish-acting did not deceive Mrs. Shortley any. Here he was: leading foreigners over in hoards to places that were not theirs, to cause disputes, to uproot niggers, to plant the Whore of Babylon in the midst of the righteous! Whenever he came on the place, she hid herself behind something and watched until he left.

It was on a Sunday afternoon that she had her vision. She had gone to drive in the cows for Mr. Shortley who had a pain in his knee and she was walking slowly through the pasture, her arms folded, her eyes on the distant low-lying clouds that looked like rows and rows of white fish washed up on a great blue beach. She paused after an incline to heave a sigh of exhaustion for she had an immense weight to carry around and she was not as young as she used to be. At times she could feel her heart, like a child's fist, clenching and unclenching inside her chest, and when the feeling came, it stopped her thought altogether and she would go about like a large hull of herself, moving for no reason; but she gained this incline without a tremor and stood at the top of it, pleased with herself. Suddenly while she watched, the sky folded back in two pieces like the curtain to a stage and a gigantic figure stood facing her. It was the color of the sun in the early afternoon, white-gold. It was of no definite shape but there were fiery wheels with fierce dark eyes in them, spinning rapidly all around it. She was not able to tell if the figure was going forward or backward because its magnificence was so great. She shut her eyes in order to look at it and it turned blood-red and the wheels turned white. A voice, very resonant, said the one word, "Prophesy!"

She stood there, tottering slightly but still upright, her eyes shut tight and her fists clenched and her straw sun hat low on her forehead. "The children of wicked nations will be butchered," she said in a loud voice. "Legs where arms should be, foot to face, ear in the palm of hand. Who will remain whole? Who will remain whole? Who?"

Presently she opened her eyes. The sky was full of white fish carried lazily on their sides by some invisible current and pieces of the sun, submerged some distance beyond them, appeared from time to time as if they were being washed in the opposite direction. Woodenly she planted one foot in front of the other until she had crossed the pasture and reached the lot. She walked through the barn like one in a daze and did not speak to Mr. Shortley. She continued up the road until she saw the priest's car parked in front of Mrs. McIntyre's house. "Here again," she muttered. "Come to destroy."

Mrs. McIntyre and the priest were walking in the yard. In order not to meet them face to face, she turned to the left and entered the feed house, a single-room shack piled on one side with flowered sacks of scratch feed. There were spilled oyster shells in one corner and a few old dirty calendars on the wall, advertising calf feed and various patent medicine remedies. One showed a bearded gentleman in a frock coat, holding up a bottle, and beneath his feet was the inscription, "I have been made regular by this marvelous discovery!" Mrs. Shortley had always felt close to this man as if he were some distinguished person she was acquainted with but now her mind was on nothing but the dangerous presence of the priest. She stationed herself at a crack between two boards where she could look out and see him and Mrs. McIntyre strolling toward the turkey brooder, which was placed just outside the feed house.

"Arrrr!" he said as they approached the brooder. "Look at the little biddies!" and he stooped and squinted through the wire.

Mrs. Shortley's mouth twisted.

"Do you think the Guizacs will want to leave me?" Mrs. McIntyre asked. "Do you think they'll go to Chicago or some place like that?"

"And why should they do that now?" asked the priest, wiggling his finger at a turkey, his big nose close to the wire.

"Money," Mrs. McIntyre said.

"Arrrr, give them some morrre then," he said indifferently. "They have to get along."

"So do I," Mrs. McIntyre muttered. "It means I'm going to have to get rid of some of these others."

"And arrre the Shortleys satisfactory?" he inquired, paying more attention to the turkeys than to her.

"Five times in the last month I've found Mr. Shortley smoking in the barn," Mrs. McIntyre said. "Five times."

"And arrre the Negroes any better?"

"They lie and steal and have to be watched all the time," she said.

"Tsk, tsk," he said. "Which will you discharge?"

"I've decided to give Mr. Shortley his month's notice tomorrow," Mrs. McIntyre said.

The priest scarcely seemed to hear her he was so busy wiggling his finger inside the wire. Mrs. Shortley sat down on an open sack of laying mash with a dead thump that sent feed dust clouding up around her. She found herself looking straight ahead at the opposite wall where the gentleman on the calendar was holding up his marvelous discovery but she didn't see him. She looked ahead as if she saw nothing whatsoever. Then she rose and ran to her house. Her face was an almost volcanic red.

She opened all the drawers and dragged out boxes and old battered suitcases from under the bed. She began to unload the drawers into the boxes, all the time without pause, without taking off the sunhat she had on her head. She set the two girls to doing the same. When Mr. Shortley came in, she did not even look at him but merely pointed one arm at him while she packed with the other. "Bring the car around to the back door," she said. "You ain't waiting to be fired!"

Mr. Shortley had never in his life doubted her omniscience. He perceived the entire situation in half a second and, with only a sour scowl, retreated out the door and went to drive the automobile around to the back.

They tied the two iron beds to the top of the car and the two rocking chairs inside the beds and rolled the two mattresses up between the rocking chairs. On top of this they tied a crate of chickens. They loaded the inside of the car with the old suitcases and boxes, leaving a small space for Annie Maude and Sarah Mae. It took them the rest of the afternoon and half the night to do this but Mrs. Shortley was determined that they would leave before four o'clock in the morning, that Mr. Shortley should not adjust another milking machine on this place. All the time she had been working, her face was changing rapidly from red to white and back again.

Just before dawn, as it began to drizzle rain, they were ready to leave. They all got in the car and sat there cramped up between boxes and bundles and rolls of bedding. The square black automobile moved off with more than its customary grinding noises as if it were protesting the load. In the back, the two long bony yellow-haired girls were sitting on a pile of boxes and there was a beagle hound puppy and a cat with two kittens somewhere under the blankets. The car moved slowly, like some overfreighted leaking ark, away from their shack and past the white house where Mrs. McIntyre was sleeping soundly—hardly guessing that her cows would not be milked by Mr. Shortley that morning—and past the Pole's shack on top of the hill and on down the road to the gate where the two Negroes were walking, one behind the other, on their way to help with the milking. They looked straight at the car and its occupants but even as the dim yellow headlights lit up their faces, they politely did not seem to see anything, or anyhow, to attach significance to what was there. The loaded car might have been passing mist in the early morning half-light. They continued up the road at the same even pace without looking back.

A dark yellow sun was beginning to rise in a sky that was the same slick dark gray as the highway. The fields stretched away, stiff and weedy, on either side. "Where we goin?" Mr. Shortley asked for the first time.

Mrs. Shortley sat with one foot on a packing box so that her knee was pushed into her stomach. Mr. Shortley's elbow was almost under her nose and Sarah Mae's bare left foot was sticking over the front seat, touching her ear.

"Where we goin?" Mr. Shortley repeated and when she didn't answer again, he turned and looked at her.

Fierce heat seemed to be swelling slowly and fully into her face as if it were welling up now for a final assault. She was sitting in an erect way in spite of the fact that one leg was twisted under her and one knee was almost into her neck, but there was a peculiar lack of light in her icy blue eyes. All the vision in them might have been turned around, looking inside her. She suddenly grabbed Mr. Shortley's elbow and Sarah Mae's foot at the same time and began to tug and pull on them as if she were trying to fit the two extra limbs onto herself.

Mr. Shortley began to curse and quickly stopped the car and Sarah Mae yelled to quit but Mrs. Shortley apparently intended to rearrange the whole car at once. She thrashed forward and backward, clutching at everything she could get her hands on and hugging it to herself, Mr. Shortley's head, Sarah Mae's leg, the cat, a wad of white bedding, her own big moonlike knee; then all at once her fierce expression faded into a look of astonishment and her grip on what she had loosened. One of her eyes drew near to the other and seemed to collapse quietly and she was still.

The two girls, who didn't know what had happened to her, began to say, "Where we goin, Ma? Where we goin'?" They thought she was playing a joke and that their father, staring straight ahead at her, was imitating a dead man. They didn't know that she had had a great experience or ever been displaced in the world from all that belonged to her. They were frightened by the gray slick road before them and they kept repeating in higher and higher voices, "Where we goin, Ma? Where we goin?" while their mother, her huge body rolled back still against the seat and her eyes like blue-painted glass, seemed to contemplate for the first time the tremendous frontiers of her true country.

2

"Well," Mrs. McIntyre said to the old Negro, "we can get along without them. We've seen them come and seen them go—black and white." She was standing in the calf barn while he cleaned it and she held a rake in her hand and now and then pulled a corn cob from a corner or pointed to a soggy spot that he had missed. When she discovered the Shortleys were gone, she was delighted as it meant she wouldn't have to fire them. The people she hired always left her—because they were that kind of people. Of all the families she had had, the Shortleys were the best if she didn't count the Displaced Person. They had been not quite trash; Mrs. Shortley was a good woman, and she would miss her but as the Judge used to say, you couldn't have your pie and eat it too, and she was satisfied with the D.P. "We've seen them come and seen them go," she repeated with satisfaction.

"And me and you," the old man said, stooping to drag his hoe under a feed rack, "is still here."

She caught exactly what he meant her to catch in his tone. Bars of sunlight fell from the cracked ceiling across his back and cut him in three distinct parts. She watched his long hands clenched around the hoe and his crooked old profile pushed close to them. You might have been here *before* I was, she said to herself, but it's mighty likely I'll be here when you're gone. "I've spent half my life fooling with worthless people," she said in a severe voice, "but now I'm through."

"Black and white," he said, "is the same."

"I am through," she repeated and gave her dark smock that she had thrown over her shoulders like a cape a quick snatch at the neck. She had on a broad-brimmed black straw hat that had cost her twenty dollars twenty years ago and that she used now for a sunhat. "Money is the root of all evil," she said. "The Judge said so every day. He said he deplored money. He said the reason you niggers were so uppity was because there was so much money in circulation."

The old Negro had known the Judge. "Judge say he long for the day when he be too poor to pay a nigger to work," he said. "Say when that day come, the world be back on its feet."

She leaned forward, her hands on her hips and her neck stretched and said, "Well that day has almost come around here and I'm telling each and every one of you: you better look sharp. I don't have to put up with foolishness any more. I have somebody now who *has* to work!"

The old man knew when to answer and when not. At length he said, "We seen them come and we seen them go."

"However, the Shortleys were not the worst by far," she said. "I well remember those Garrits."

"They was before them Collinses," he said.

"No, before the Ringfields."

"Sweet Lord, them Ringfields!" he murmured.

"None of that kind *want* to work," she said.

"We seen them come and we seen them go," he said as if this were a refrain. "But we ain't never had one before," he said, bending himself up until he faced her, "like what we got now." He was cinnamon-colored with eyes that were so blurred with age that they seemed to be hung behind cobwebs.

She gave him an intense stare and held it until, lowering his hands on the hoe, he bent down again and dragged a pile of shavings alongside the wheelbarrow. She said stiffly, "He can wash out that barn in the time it took Mr. Shortley to make up his mind he had to do it."

"He from Pole," the old man muttered.

"From Poland."

"In Pole it ain't like it is here," he said. "They got different ways of doing," and he began to mumble unintelligibly.

"What are you saying?" she said. "If you have anything to say about him, say it and say it aloud."

He was silent, bending his knees precariously and edging the rake along the underside of the trough.

"If you know anything he's done that he shouldn't, I expect you to report it to me," she said.

"It warn't like it was what he should ought or oughtn't," he muttered. "It was like what nobody else don't do."

"'You don't have anything against him," she said shortly, "and he's here to stay."

"We ain't never had one like him before is all," he murmured and gave his polite laugh.

"Times are changing," she said. "Do you know what's happening to this world? It's swelling up. It's getting so full of people that only the smart thrifty energetic ones are going to survive," and she tapped the words, smart, thrifty, and energetic out on the palm of her hand. Through the far end of the stall she could see down the road to where the Displaced Person was standing in the open barn door with the green hose in his hand. There was a certain stiffness about his figure that seemed to make it necessary for her to approach him slowly, even in her thoughts. She had decided this was because she couldn't hold an easy conversation with him. Whenever she said anything to him, she found herself shouting and nodding extravagantly and she would be conscious that one of the Negroes was leaning behind the nearest shed, watching.

"No indeed!" she said, sitting down on one of the feed racks and folding her arms, "I've made up my mind that I've had enough trashy people on this place to last me a lifetime and I'm not going to spend my last years fooling with Shortleys and Ringfields and Collins when the world is full of people who *have* to work."

"Howcome they so many extra?" he asked.

"People are selfish," she said. "They have too many children. There's no sense in it any more."

He had picked up the wheelbarrow handles and was backing out the door and he paused, half in the sunlight and half out, and stood there chewing his gums as if he had forgotten which direction he wanted to move in.

"What you colored people don't realize," she said, "is that I'm the one around here who holds all the strings together. If you don't work, I don't make any money and I can't pay you. You're all dependent on me but you each and every one act like the shoe is on the other foot."

It was not possible to tell from his face if he heard her. Finally he backed out with the wheelbarrow. "Judge say the devil he know is better than the devil he don't," he said in a clear mutter and turned and trundled off.

She got up and followed him, a deep vertical pit appearing suddenly in the center of her forehead, just under the red bangs. "The Judge has long since ceased to pay the bills around here," she called in a piercing voice.

He was the only one of her Negroes who had known the Judge and he thought this gave him title. He had had a low opinion of Mr. Crooms and Mr. McIntyre, her other husbands, and in his veiled polite way, he had congratulated her after each of her divorces. When he thought it necessary, he would work under a window where he knew she was sitting and talk to himself, a careful roundabout discussion, question and answer and then refrain. Once she had got up silently and slammed the window down so hard that he had fallen backwards off his feet. Or occasionally he spoke with the peacock. The cock would follow him around the place, his steady eye on the ear of corn that stuck up from the old man's back pocket or he would sit near him and pick himself. Once from the open kitchen door, she had heard him say to the bird, "I remember when it was twenty of you walking about this place and now it's only you and two hens. Crooms it was twelve. McIntyre it was five. You and two hens now."

And that time she had stepped out of the door onto the porch and said, "MISTER Crooms and MISTER McIntyre! And I don't want to hear you call either of them anything else again. And you can understand this: when that peachicken dies there won't be any replacements."

She kept the peacock only out of a superstitious fear of annoying the Judge in his grave. He had liked to see them walking around the place for he said they made him feel rich. Of her three husbands, the Judge was the one most present to her although he was the only one she had buried. He was in the family graveyard, a little space fenced in the middle of the back cornfield, with his mother and father and grandfather and three great aunts and two infant cousins. Mr. Crooms, her second, was forty miles away in the state asylum and Mr. McIntyre, her last, was intoxicated, she supposed, in some hotel room in Florida. But the Judge, sunk in the cornfield with his family, was always at home.

She had married him when he was an old man and because of his money but there had been another reason that she would not admit then, even to herself: she had liked him. He was a dirty snuff-dipping Court House figure, famous all over the country for being rich, who wore high-top shoes, a string tie, a gray suit with a black stripe in it, and a yellowed panama hat, winter and summer. His teeth and hair were tobacco-colored and his face a clay pink pitted and tracked with mysterious prehistoric-looking marks as if he had been unearthed among fossils. There had been a peculiar odor about him of sweaty fondled bills but he never carried money on him or had a nickel to show. She was his secretary for a few months and the old man with his sharp eye had seen at once that here was a woman who admired him for himself. The three years that he lived after they married were the happiest and most prosperous of Mrs. McIntyre's life, but when he died his estate proved to be bankrupt. He left her a mortgaged house and fifty acres that he had managed to cut the timber off before he died. It was as if, as the final triumph of a successful life, he had been able to take everything with him.

But she had survived. She had survived a succession of tenant farmers and dairymen that the old man himself would have found hard to outdo, and she had been able to meet the constant drain of a tribe of moody unpredictable Negroes, and she had even managed to hold her own against the incidental bloodsuckers, the cattle dealers and lumber men and the buyers and sellers of anything who drove up in pieced-together trucks and honked in the yard.

She stood slightly reared back with her arms folded under her smock and a satisfied expression on her face as she watched the Displaced Person turn off the hose and disappear inside the barn. She was sorry that the poor man had been chased out of Poland and run across Europe and had had to take up in a tenant shack in a strange country, but she had not been responsible for any of this. She had had a hard time herself. She knew what it was to struggle. People ought to have to struggle. Mr. Guizac had probably had everything given to him all the way across Europe and over here. He had probably not had to struggle enough. She had given him a job. She didn't know if he was grateful or not. She didn't know anything about him except that he did the work. The truth was that he was not very real to her yet. He was a kind of miracle that she had seen happen and that she talked about but that she still didn't believe.

She watched as he came out of the barn and motioned to Sulk, who was coming around the back of the lot. He gesticulated and then took something out of his pocket and the two of them stood looking at it. She started down the lane toward them. The Negro's figure was slack and tall and he was craning his round head forward in his usual idiotic way. He was a little better than half-witted but when they were like that they were always good workers. The Judge had said always hire you a half-witted nigger because they don't have sense enough to stop working. The Pole was gesticulating rapidly. He left something with the colored boy and then walked off and before she rounded the turn in the lane, she heard the tractor crank up. He was on his way to the field. The Negro was still hanging there, gaping at whatever he had in his hand.

She entered the lot and walked through the barn, looking with approval at the wet spotless concrete floor. It was only nine-thirty and Mr. Shortley had never got anything washed until eleven. As she came out at the other end, she saw the Negro moving very slowly in a diagonal path across the road in front of her, his eyes still on what Mr. Guizac had given him. He didn't see her and he paused and dipped his knees and leaned over his hand, his tongue describing little circles. He had a photograph. He lifted one finger and traced it lightly over the surface of the picture. Then he looked up and saw her and seemed to freeze, his mouth in a half-grin, his finger lifted.

"Why haven't you gone to the field?" she asked.

He raised one foot and opened his mouth wider while the hand with the photograph edged toward his back pocket.

"What's that?" she said.

"It ain't nothin," he muttered and handed it to her automatically.

It was a photograph of a girl of about twelve in a white dress. She had blond hair with a wreath in it and she looked forward out of light eyes that were bland and composed. "Who is this child?" Mrs. McIntyre asked.

"She his cousin," the boy said in a high voice.

"Well what are you doing with it?" she asked.

"She going to mah me," he said in an even higher voice.

"Marry you!" she shrieked.

"I pays half to get her over here," he said. "I pays him three dollar a week. She bigger now. She his cousin. She don't care who she mah she so glad to get away from there." The high voice seemed to shoot up like a nervous jet of sound and then fall flat as he watched her face. Her eyes were the color of blue granite when the glare falls on it, but she was not looking at him. She was looking down the road where the distant sound of the tractor could be heard.

"I don't reckon she goin to come nohow," the boy murmured.

"I'll see that you get every cent of your money back," she said in a toneless voice and turned and walked off, holding the photograph bent in two. There was nothing about her small stiff figure to indicate that she was shaken.

As soon as she got in the house, she lay down on her bed and shut her eyes and pressed her hand over her heart as if she were trying to keep it in place. Her mouth opened and she made two or three dry little sounds. Then after a minute she sat up and said aloud, "They're all the same. It's always been like this," and she fell back flat again.

"Twenty years of being beaten and done in and they even robbed his grave!" and remembering that, she began to cry quietly, wiping her eyes every now and then with the hem of her smock.

What she had thought of was the angel over the Judge's grave. This had been a naked granite cherub that the old man had seen in the city one day in a tombstone store window. He had been taken with it at once, partly because its face reminded him of his wife and partly because he wanted a genuine work of art over his grave. He had come home with it sitting on the green plush train seat beside him. Mrs. McIntyre had never noticed the resemblance to herself. She had always thought it hideous but when the Herrins left the angel left with them, all but its toes, for the ax old man Herrin had used to break it off with had struck slightly too high. Mrs. McIntyre had never been able to afford to have it replaced.

When she had cried all she could, she got up and went into the back hall, a closet-like space that was dark and quiet as a chapel and sat down on the edge of the Judge's black mechanical chair with her elbow on his desk. This was a giant roll-top piece of furniture pocked with pigeon holes full of dusty papers. Old bankbooks and ledgers were stacked in the half-open drawers and there was a small safe, empty but locked, set like a tabernacle in the center of it. She had left this part of the house unchanged since the old man's time. It was a kind of memorial to him, sacred because he had conducted his business here. With the slightest tilt one way or the other, the chair gave a rusty skeletal groan that sounded something like him when he had complained of his poverty. It had been his first principle to talk as if he were the poorest man in the world and she followed it, not only because he had but because it was true. When she sat with her intense constricted face turned toward the empty safe, she knew there was nobody poorer in the world than she was.

She sat motionless at the desk for ten or fifteen minutes and then as if she had gained some strength, she got up and got in her car and drove to the cornfield.

The road ran through a shadowy pine thicket and ended on top of a hill that rolled fan-wise down and up again in a broad expanse of tasseled green. Mr. Guizac was cutting from the outside of the field in a circular path to the center where the graveyard was all but hidden by the corn, and she could see him on the high far side of the slope, mounted on the tractor with the cutter and wagon behind him. From time to time, he had to get off the tractor and climb in the wagon to spread the silage because the Negro had not arrived. She watched impatiently, standing in front of her black coupe with her arms folded under her smock, while he progressed slowly around the rim of the field, gradually getting close enough for her to wave to him to get down. He stopped the machine and jumped off and came running forward, wiping his red jaw with a piece of grease rag.

"I want to talk to you," she said and beckoned him to the edge of the thicket where it was shady. He took off the cap and followed her, smiling, but his smile faded when she turned and faced him. Her eyebrows, thin and fierce as a spider's leg, had drawn together ominously and the deep vertical pit had plunged down from under the red bangs into the bridge of her nose. She removed the bent picture from her pocket and handed it to him silently. Then she stepped back and said, "Mr. Guizac! You would bring this poor innocent child over here and try to marry her to a half-witted thieving black stinking nigger! What kind of a monster are you!"

He took the photograph with a slowly returning smile. "My cousin," he said. "She twelve here. First Communion. Six-ten now."

Monster! she said to herself and looked at him as if she were seeing him for the first time. His forehead and skull were white where they had been protected by his cap but the rest of his face was red and bristled with short yellow hairs. His eyes were like two bright nails behind his gold-rimmed spectacles that had been mended over the nose with haywire. His whole face looked as if it might have been patched together out of several others. "Mr. Guizac," she said, beginning slowly and then speaking faster until she ended breathless in the middle of a word, "that nigger cannot have a white wife from Europe. You can't talk to a nigger that way. You'll excite him and besides it can't be done. Maybe it can be done in Poland but it can't be done here and you'll have to stop. It's all foolishness. That nigger don't have a grain of sense and you'll excite . . ."

"She in camp three year," he said.

431

"Your cousin," she said in a positive voice, "cannot come over here and marry one of my Negroes."

"She six-ten year," he said. "From Poland. Mamma die, pappa die. She wait in camp. Three camp." He pulled a wallet from his pocket and fingered through it and took out another picture of the same girl, a few years older, dressed in something dark and shapeless. She was standing against a wall with a short woman who apparently had no teeth. "She mamma," he said, pointing to the woman. "She die in two camp."

"Mr. Guizac," Mrs. McIntyre said, pushing the picture back at him, I will not have my niggers upset. I cannot run this place without my niggers. I can run it without you but not without them and if you mention this girl to Sulk again, you won't have a job with me. Do you understand?"

His face showed no comprehension. He seemed to be piecing all these words together in his mind to make a thought.

Mrs. McIntyre remembered Mrs. Shortley's words: "He understands everything, he only pretends he don't so as to do exactly as he pleases," and her face regained the look of shocked wrath she had begun with. "I cannot understand how a man who calls himself a Christian," she said, "could bring a poor innocent girl over here and marry her to something like that. I cannot understand it. I cannot!" and she shook her head and looked into the distance with a pained blue gaze.

After a second he shrugged and let his arms drop as if he were tired. "She no care black," he said. "She in camp three year."

Mrs. McIntyre felt a peculiar weakness behind her knees. "Mr. Guizac," she said, "I don't want to have to speak to you about this again. If I do, you'll have to find another place yourself. Do you understand?"

The patched face did not say. She had the impression that he didn't see her there. "This is my place," she said. "I say who will come here and who won't."

"Ya," he said and put back on his cap.

"I am not responsible for the world's misery," she said as an afterthought.

"Ya," he said.

"You have a good job. You should be grateful to be here," she added, "but I'm not sure you are."

"Ya," he said and gave his little shrug and turned back to the tractor.

She watched him get on and maneuver the machine into the corn again. When he had passed her and rounded the turn, she climbed to the top of the slope and stood with her arms folded and looked out grimly over the field. "They're all the same," she muttered, "whether they come from Poland or Tennessee. I've handled Herrins and Ringfields and Shortleys and

I can handle a Guizac," and she narrowed her gaze until it closed entirely around the diminishing figure on the tractor as if she were watching him through a gunsight. All her life she had been fighting the world's overflow and now she had it in the form of a Pole. "You're just like all the rest of them," she said, "—only smart and thrifty and energetic but so am I. And this is my place," and she stood there, a small black-hatted, black-smocked figure with an aging cherubic face, and folded her arms as if she were equal to anything. But her heart was beating as if some interior violence had already been done to her. She opened her eyes to include the whole field so that the figure on the tractor was no larger than a grasshopper in her widened view.

She stood there for some time. There was a slight breeze and the corn trembled in great waves on both sides of the slope. The big cutter, with its monotonous roar, continued to shoot it pulverized into the wagon in a steady spurt of fodder. By nightfall, the Displaced Person would have worked his way around and around until there would be nothing on either side of the two hills but the stubble, and down in the center, risen like a little island, the graveyard where the Judge lay grinning under his desecrated monument.

3

The priest, with his long bland face supported on one finger, had been talking for ten minutes about Purgatory while Mrs. McIntyre squinted furiously at him from an opposite chair. They were drinking ginger ale on her front porch and she had kept rattling the ice in her glass, rattling her beads, rattling her bracelet like an impatient pony jingling its harness. There is no moral obligation to keep him, she was saying under her breath, there is absolutely no moral obligation. Suddenly she lurched up and her voice fell across his brogue like a drill into a mechanical saw. "Listen!" she said, "I'm not theological. I'm practical! I want to talk to you about something practical!"

"Arrrrrrr," he groaned, grating to a halt.

She had put at least a finger of whisky in her own ginger ale so that she would be able to endure his full-length visit and she sat down awkwardly, finding the chair closer to her than she had expected. "Mr. Guizac is not satisfactory," she said.

The old man raised his eyebrows in mock wonder.

"He's extra," she said. "He doesn't fit in. I have to have somebody who fits in."

The priest carefully turned his hat on his knees. He had a little trick of waiting a second silently and then swinging the conversation back into his own paths. He was about eighty. She had never known a priest until she had gone to see this one on the business of getting her the Displaced Person. After he had got her the Pole, he had used the business introduction to try to convert her—just as she had supposed he would.

"Give him time," the old man said. "He'll learn to fit in. Where is that beautiful birrrrd of yours?" he asked and then said, "Arrrrr, I see him!" and stood up and looked out over the lawn where the peacock and the two hens were stepping at a strained attention, their long necks ruffled, the cock's violent blue and the hens' silver-green, glinting in the late afternoon sun.

"Mr. Guizac," Mrs. McIntyre continued, bearing down with a flat steady voice, "is very efficient. I'll admit that. But he doesn't understand how to get on with my niggers and they don't like him. I can't have my niggers run off. And I don't like his attitude. He's not in the least grateful for being here."

The priest had his hand on the screen door and he opened it, ready to make his escape. "Arrrr, I must be off," he murmured.

"I tell you if I had a white man who understood the Negroes, I'd have to let Mr. Guizac go," she said and stood up again.

He turned then and looked her in the face. "He has nowhere to go," he said. Then he said, "Dear lady, I know you well enough to know you wouldn't turn him out for a trifle!" and without waiting for an answer, he raised his hand and gave her his blessing in a rumbling voice.

She smiled angrily and said, "I didn't create his situation, of course."

The priest let his eyes wander toward the birds. They had reached the middle of the lawn. The cock stopped suddenly and curving his neck backwards, he raised his tail and spread it with a shimmering timbrous noise. Tiers of small pregnant suns floated in a green-gold haze over his head. The priest stood transfixed, his jaw slack. Mrs. McIntyre wondered where she had ever seen such an idiotic old man. "Christ will come like that!" he said in a loud gay voice and wiped his hand over his mouth and stood there, gaping.

Mrs. McIntyre's face assumed a set puritanical expression and she reddened. Christ in the conversation embarrassed her the way sex had her mother. "It is not my responsibility that Mr. Guizac has nowhere to go," she said. "I don't find myself responsible for all the extra people in the world."

The old man didn't seem to hear her. His attention was fixed on the cock who was taking minute steps backward, his head against the spread tail. "The Transfiguration," he murmured.

She had no idea what he was talking about. "Mr. Guizac didn't have to come here in the first place," she said, giving him a hard look.

The cock lowered his tail and began to pick grass.

"He didn't have to come in the first place," she repeated, emphasizing each word.

The old man smiled absently. "He came to redeem us," he said and blandly reached for her hand and shook it and said he must go.

If Mr. Shortley had not returned a few weeks later, she would have gone out looking for a new man to hire. She had not wanted him back but when she saw the familiar black automobile drive up the road and stop by the side of the house, she had the feeling that she was the one returning, after a long miserable trip, to her own place. She realized all at once that it was Mrs. Shortley she had been missing. She had had no one to talk to since Mrs. Shortley left, and she ran to the door, expecting to see her heaving herself up the steps.

Mr. Shortley stood there alone. He had on a black felt hat and a shirt with red and blue palm trees designed in it but the hollows in his long bitten blistered face were deeper than they had been a month ago.

"Well!" she said. "Where is Mrs. Shortley?"

Mr. Shortley didn't say anything. The change in his face seemed to have come from the inside; he looked like a man who had gone for a long time without water. "She was God's own angel," he said in a loud voice. "She was the sweetest woman in the world."

"Where is she?" Mrs. McIntyre murmured.

"Daid," he said. "She had herself a stroke on the day she left out of here." There was a corpse-like composure about his face. "I figure that Pole killed her," he said. "She seen through him from the first. She known he come from the devil. She told me so."

It took Mrs. McIntyre three days to get over Mrs. Shortley's death. She told herself that anyone would have thought they were kin. She rehired Mr. Shortley to do farm work though actually she didn't want him without his wife. She told him she was going to give thirty days' notice to the Displaced Person at the end of the month and that then he could have his job back in the dairy. Mr. Shortley preferred the dairy job but he was willing to wait. He said it would give him some satisfaction to see the Pole leave the place, and Mrs. McIntyre said it would give her a great deal of satisfaction. She confessed that she should have been content with the help she had in the first place and not have been reaching into other parts of the world for it. Mr. Shortley said he never had cared for foreigners since he had been in the first world's war and seen what they were like. He said he had seen all kinds then but that none of them were like us. He said he recalled the face of one man who had thrown a hand-grenade at him and that the man had had little round eye-glasses exactly like Mr. Guizac's.

"But Mr. Guizac is a Pole, he's not a German," Mrs. McIntyre said.

"It ain't a great deal of difference in them two kinds," Mr. Shortley had explained.

The Negroes were pleased to see Mr. Shortley back. The Displaced Person had expected them to work as hard as he worked himself, whereas Mr. Shortley recognized their limitations. He had never been a very good worker himself with Mrs. Shortley to keep him in line, but without her, he was even more forgetful and slow. The Pole worked as fiercely as ever and seemed to have no inkling that he was about to be fired. Mrs. McIntyre saw jobs done in a short time that she had thought would never get done at all. Still she was resolved to get rid of him. The sight of his small stiff figure moving quickly here and there had come to be the most irritating sight on the place for her, and she felt she had been tricked by the old priest. He had said there was no legal obligation for her to keep the Displaced Person if he was not satisfactory, but then he had brought up the moral one.

She meant to tell him that *her* moral obligation was to her own people, to Mr. Shortley, who had fought in the world war for his country and not to Mr. Guizac who had merely arrived here to take advantage of whatever he could. She felt she must have this out with the priest before she fired the Displaced Person. When the first of the month came and the priest hadn't called, she put off giving the Pole notice for a little longer.

Mr. Shortley told himself that he should have known all along that no woman was going to do what she said she was when she said she was. He didn't know how long he could afford to put up with her shilly-shallying. He thought himself that she was going soft and was afraid to turn the Pole out for fear he would have a hard time getting another place. He could tell her the truth about this: that if she let him go, in three years he would own his own house and have a television aerial sitting on top of it. As a matter of policy, Mr. Shortley began to come to her back door every evening to put certain facts before her. "A white man sometimes don't get the consideration a nigger gets," he said, "but that don't matter because he's still white, but sometimes," and here he would pause and look off into the distance, "a man that's fought and bled and died in the service of his native land don't get the consideration of one of them like them he was fighting. I ast you: is that right?" When he asked her such questions he could watch her face and tell he was making an impression. She didn't look too well these days. He noticed lines around her eyes that hadn't been there when he and Mrs. Shortley had been the only white help on the place. Whenever he thought of Mrs. Shortley, he felt his heart go down like an old bucket into a dry well.

The old priest kept away as if he had been frightened by his last visit but finally, seeing that the Displaced Person had not been fired, he ventured to call again to take up giving Mrs. McIntyre instructions where he remembered leaving them off. She had not asked to be instructed but he instructed anyway, forcing a little definition of one of the sacraments or of some dogma into each conversation he had, no matter with whom. He sat on her porch, taking no notice of her partly mocking, partly outraged expression as she sat shaking her foot, waiting for an opportunity to drive a wedge into his talk. "For," he was saying, as if he spoke of something that had happened yesterday in town, "when God sent his Only Begotten Son, Jesus Christ Our Lord"—he slightly bowed his head—"as a Redeemer to mankind, He . . ."

"Father Flynn!" she said in a voice that made him jump. "I want to talk to you about something serious!"

The skin under the old man's right eye flinched.

"As far as I'm concerned," she said and glared at him fiercely, "Christ was just another D. P."

He raised his hands slightly and let them drop on his knees. "Arrrrr," he murmured as if he were considering this.

"I'm going to let that man go," she said. "I don't have any obligation to him. My obligation is to the people who've done something for their country, not to the ones who've just come over to take advantage of what they can get," and she began to talk rapidly, remembering all her arguments. The priest's attention seemed to retire to some private oratory to wait until she got through. Once or twice his gaze roved out onto the lawn as if he were hunting some means of escape but she didn't stop. She told him how she had been hanging onto this place for thirty years, always just barely making it against people who came from nowhere and were going nowhere, who didn't want anything but an automobile. She said she had found out they were the same whether they came from Poland or Tennessee. When the Guizacs got ready, she said, they would not hesitate to leave her. She told him how the people who looked rich were the poorest of all because they had the most to keep up. She asked him how he thought she paid her feed bills. She told him she would like to have her house done over but she couldn't afford it. She couldn't even afford to have the monument restored over her husband's grave. She asked him if he would like to guess what her insurance amounted to for the year. Finally she asked him if he thought she was made of money and the old man suddenly let out a great ugly bellow as if this were a comical question.

When the visit was over, she felt let down, though she had clearly triumphed over him. She made up her mind now that on the first of the month, she would give the Displaced Person his thirty days' notice and she told Mr. Shortley so.

Mr. Shortley didn't say anything. His wife had been the only woman he was ever acquainted with who was never scared off from doing what she said. She said the Pole had been sent by the devil and the priest. Mr. Shortley had no doubt that the priest had got some peculiar control over Mrs. McIntyre and that before long she would start attending his Masses. She looked as if something was wearing her down from the inside. She was thinner and more fidgety and not as sharp as she used to be. She would look at a milk can now and not see how dirty it was and he had seen her lips move when she was not talking. The Pole never did anything the wrong way but all the same he was very irritating to her. Mr. Shortley himself did things as he pleased—not always her way—but she didn't seem to notice. She had noticed though that the Pole and all his family were getting fat; she pointed out to Mr. Shortley that the hollows had come out of their cheeks and that they saved every cent they made. "Yes'm, and one of these days he'll be able to buy and sell you out," Mr. Shortley had ventured to say, and he could tell that the statement had shaken her.

"I'm just waiting for the first," she had said.

Mr. Shortley waited too and the first came and went and she didn't fire him. He could have told anybody how it would be. He was not a violent man but he hated to see a woman done in by a foreigner. He felt that that was one thing a man couldn't stand by and see happen.

There was no reason Mrs. McIntyre should not fire Mr. Guizac at once but she put it off from day to day. She was worried about her bills and about her health. She didn't sleep at night or when she did she dreamed about the Displaced Person. She had never discharged any one before; they had all left her. One night she dreamed that Mr. Guizac and his family were moving into her house and that she was moving in with Mr. Shortley. This was too much for her and she woke up and didn't sleep again for several nights; and one night she dreamed that the priest came to call and droned on and on, saying, "Dear lady, I know your tender heart won't suffer you to turn the porrrrr man out. Think of the thousands of them, think of the ovens and the boxcars and the camps and the sick children and Christ Our Lord."

"He's extra and he's upset the balance around here," she said, "and I'm a logical practical woman and there are no ovens here and no camps and no Christ Our Lord and when he leaves, he'll make more money. He'll work at the mill and buy a car and don't talk to me—all they want is a car."

"The ovens and the boxcars and the sick children," droned the priest, "and our dear Lord."

"Just one too many," she said.

The next morning, she made up her mind while she was eating her breakfast that she would give him his notice at once, and she stood up and walked out of the kitchen and down the road with her table napkin still in her hand. Mr. Guizac was spraying the barn, standing in his swaybacked way with one hand on his hip. He turned off the hose and gave her an impatient kind of attention as if she were interfering with his work. She had not thought of what she would say to him, she had merely come. She stood in the barn door, looking severely at the wet spotless floor and the dripping stanchions. "Ya goot?" he said.

"Mr. Guizac," she said, "I can barely meet my obligations now." Then she said in a louder, stronger voice, emphasizing each word, "I have bills to pay."

"I too," Mr. Guizac said. "Much bills, little money," and he shrugged.

At the other end of the barn, she saw a long beak-nosed shadow glide like a snake halfway up the sunlit open door and stop; and somewhere behind her, she was aware of a silence where the sound of the Negroes shoveling had come a minute before. "This is my place," she said angrily. "All of you are extra. Each and every one of you are extra!"

"Ya," Mr. Guizac said and turned on the hose again.

She wiped her mouth with the napkin she had in her hand and walked off, as if she had accomplished what she came for.

Mr. Shortley's shadow withdrew from the door and he leaned against the side of the barn and lit half of a cigarette that he took out of his pocket. There was nothing for him to do now but wait on the hand of God to strike but he knew one thing: he was not going to wait with his mouth shut.

Starting that morning, he began to complain and to state his side of the case to every person he saw, black or white. He complained in the grocery store and at the courthouse and on the street corner and directly to Mrs. McIntyre herself, for there was nothing underhanded about him. If the

Pole could have understood what he had to say, he would have said it to him too. "All men was created free and equal," he said to Mrs. McIntyre, "and I risked my life and limb to prove it. Gone over there and fought and bled and died and come back on over here and find out who's got my job— just exactly who I been fighting. It was a hand-grenade come that near to killing me and I seen who threwed it—little man with eye-glasses just like his. Might have bought them at the same store. Small world," and he gave a bitter little laugh. Since he didn't have Mrs. Shortley to do the talking any more, he had started doing it himself and had found that he had a gift for it. He had the power of making other people see his logic. He talked a good deal to the Negroes.

"Whyn't you go back to Africa?" he asked Sulk one morning as they were cleaning out the silo. "That's your country, ain't it?"

"I ain't goin there," the boy said. "They might eat me up."

"Well, if you behave yourself it isn't any reason you can't stay here," Mr. Shortley said kindly. "Because you didn't run away from nowhere. Your granddaddy was brought. He didn't have a thing to do with coming. It's the people that run away from where they come from that I ain't got any use for."

"I never felt no need to travel," the Negro said.

"Well," Mr. Shortley said, "if I was going to travel again, it would be to either China or Africa. You go to either of them two places and you can tell right away what the difference is between you and them. You go to these other places and the only way you can tell is if they say something. And then you can't always tell because about half of them know the English language. That's where we make our mistake," he said, "—letting all them people onto English. There'd be a heap less trouble if everybody only knew his own language. My wife said knowing two languages was like having eyes in the back of your head. You couldn't put nothing over on her."

"You sho couldn't," the boy muttered, and then he added, "She was fine. She was sho fine. I never known a finer white woman than her."

Mr. Shortley turned in the opposite direction and worked silently for a while. After a few minutes he leaned up and tapped the colored boy on the shoulder with the handle of his shovel. For a second he only looked at him while a great deal of meaning gathered in his wet eyes. Then he said softly, "Revenge is mine, saith the Lord."

Mrs. McIntyre found that everybody in town knew Mr. Shortley's version of her business and that everyone was critical of her conduct. She began to understand that she had a moral obligation to fire the Pole and that she was shirking it because she found it hard to do. She could not stand the increasing guilt any longer and on a cold Saturday morning, she started off after breakfast to fire him. She walked down to the machine shed where she heard him cranking up the tractor.

There was a heavy frost on the ground that made the fields look like the rough backs of sheep; the sun was almost silver and the woods stuck up like dry bristles on the sky line. The countryside seemed to be receding from the little circle of noise around the shed. Mr. Guizac was squatting on the ground beside the small tractor, putting in a part. Mrs. McIntyre hoped to get the fields turned over while he still had thirty days to work for her. The colored boy was standing by with some tools in his hand and Mr. Shortley was under the shed about to get up on the large tractor and back it out. She meant to wait until he and the Negro got out of the way before she began her unpleasant duty.

She stood watching Mr. Guizac, stamping her feet on the hard ground, for the cold was climbing like a paralysis up her feet and legs. She had on a heavy black coat and a red head-kerchief with her black hat pulled down on top of it to keep the glare out of her eyes. Under the black brim her face had an abstracted look and once or twice her lips moved silently. Mr. Guizac shouted over the noise of the tractor for the Negro to hand him a screwdriver and when he got it, he turned over on his back on the icy ground and reached up under the machine. She could not see his face, only his feet and legs and trunk sticking impudently out from the side of the tractor. He had on rubber boots that were cracked and splashed with mud. He raised one knee and then lowered it and turned himself slightly. Of all the things she resented about him, she resented most that he hadn't left of his own accord.

Mr. Shortley had got on the large tractor and was backing it out from under the shed. He seemed to be warmed by it as if its heat and strength sent impulses up through him that he obeyed instantly. He had headed it toward the small tractor but he braked it on a slight incline and jumped off and turned back toward the shed. Mrs. McIntyre was looking fixedly at Mr. Guizac's legs lying flat on the ground now. She heard the brake on the large tractor slip and, looking up, she saw it move forward, calculating its own path. Later she remembered that she had seen the Negro jump silently out of the way as if a spring in the earth had released him and that she had seen Mr. Shortley turn his head with incredible slowness and stare silently over his shoulder and that she had started to shout to the Displaced Person but that she had not. She had felt her eyes and Mr. Shortley's eyes and the

Negro's eyes come together in one look that froze them in collusion forever, and she had heard the little noise the Pole made as the tractor wheel broke his backbone. The two men ran forward to help and she fainted.

She remembered, when she came to, running somewhere, perhaps into the house and out again but she could not remember what for or if she had fainted again when she got there. When she finally came back to where the tractors were, the ambulance had arrived. Mr. Guizac's body was covered with the bent bodies of his wife and two children and by a black one which hung over him, murmuring words she didn't understand. At first she thought this must be the doctor but then with a feeling of annoyance she recognized the priest, who had come with the ambulance and was slipping something into the crushed man's mouth. After a minute he stood up and she looked first at his bloody pants legs and then at his face which was not averted from her but was as withdrawn and expressionless as the rest of the countryside. She only stared at him for she was too shocked by her experience to be quite herself. Her mind was not taking hold of all that was happening. She felt she was in some foreign country where the people bent over the body were natives, and she watched like a stranger while the dead man was carried away in the ambulance.

That evening Mr. Shortley left without notice to look for a new position and the Negro, Sulk, was taken with a sudden desire to see more of the world and set off for the southern part of the state. The old man Astor could not work without company. Mrs. McIntyre hardly noticed that she had no help left for she came down with a nervous affliction and had to go to the hospital. When she came back, she saw that the place would be too much for her to run now and she turned her cows over to a professional auctioneer (who sold them at a loss) and retired to live on what she had, while she tried to save her declining health. A numbness developed in one of her legs and her hands and head began to jiggle and eventually she had to stay in bed all the time with only a colored woman to wait on her. Her eyesight grew steadily worse and she lost her voice altogether. Not many people remembered to come out to the country to see her except the old priest. He came regularly once a week with a bag of breadcrumbs and, after he had fed these to the peacock, he would come in and sit by the side of her bed and explain the doctrines of the Church.

THEMATIC CENTERS
IN "THE DISPLACED PERSON'

Eileen Baldeshwiler

In an essay on Greek tragedy, Gerard Manley Hopkins spoke of "two strains of thought running together," the "overthought" (which can be paraphrased) and the "underthought." The "overthought" of Flannery O'Connor's "The Displaced Person" is sensitively—and for the first time—explored in Robert Fitzgerald's *Sewanee Review* article "The Countryside and the True Country" (LXX, No. 3, July-September, 1962); but Fitzgerald's study leaves much of the tale's "underthought" unexamined, partly by intention and partly by a failure to discern the full significance of the peacock symbol and of the "displaced person" theme. Neither does Fitzgerald explore the connections between the two. Yet a fuller reading of the tale will show that "The Displaced Person" provides an admirable example of how symbolization, as Susanne Langer has pointed out, can be "both an end and an instrument."

In one of her conversations with the priest, Mrs. McIntyre impatiently remarks, "I'm not theological. I'm practical! I want to talk to you about something practical!" Whether or not she is a practical writer, Flannery O'Connor is most certainly a theological one, and "The Displaced Person" is essentially a probing of two deeply theological themes, the nature of Christian love or divine, supernatural charity, which in turn reflects its source in a theological event, the Incarnation. The remote springs of the story are Scriptural:

> "Master, which is the great commandment in the Law?" Jesus said to him, "Thou shalt love the Lord thy God with thy whole heart, and with thy whole soul, and with thy whole mind." This is the greatest and the first commandment. And the second is like it, "Thou shalt love thy neighbor as thyself." On these two commandments depend the whole Law and the Prophets. (Matt. 2:36-40)

and,

> Then the just will answer him, saying, "Lord, when did we see thee hungry, and feed thee; or thirsty, and give thee drink? And when did we see

443

thee a stranger and take thee in; or naked, and clothe thee? Or when did
we see thee sick, or in prison, and come to thee?" And answering the king
will say to them, "Amen I say to you, as long as you did it for one of these,
the least of my brethren, you did it for me." (Matt. 25:37-40)

. . .

Then they [on his left hand] will also answer and say, "Lord, when did
we see thee hungry, or thirsty, or a stranger, or naked, or sick, or in prison,
and did not minister to thee?" And he will answer them, saying, "Amen I
say to you, as long as you did not do it for one of these least ones, you
did not do it for me." (Matt. 25:44-46)

Interestingly enough, "The Displaced Person" is one of the few O'Connor
stories without a demoniac; but it is in fact more metaphysically subtle, for
in it evil is not defined in a person nor in an action but in an absence, the
absence of love, the "displacement" in the "displacer."

For the moment, let us be over-schematic and say that the peacock, as a
Christ figure, forms a thematic center for the story, with the major characters ranged around it. Thus the priest, literally in theological teaching an
alter Christus, is drawn most deeply to the peacock, admires and reverences
its beauty most, and connects it with the most supereminent Being of his
own experience, Christ. Mrs. McIntyre's feelings toward the bird and its
predecessors are grudging and hardfisted. At the most she tolerates the peacocks, retaining them on the farm because of some connection they seem
to have with her late husband, the Judge, who is, incidentally, the only
creature for whom Mrs. McIntyre has been able to experience anything
approaching love. She has decided that " 'when that peachicken dies there
won't be any replacements,' " for "she kept the peacock only out of a superstitious fear of annoying the Judge in his grave. He had liked to see them
walking around the place for he said they made him feel rich. Of her three
husbands, the Judge was the one most present to her although he was the
only one she had buried." Mrs. Shortley, on the contrary, sees the peacocks with her physical eyes but scarcely acknowledges their presence and
certainly grants them no significance.

But there is another and more obvious thematic center of the story: Mr.
Guizac, the "displaced person." Miss O'Connor so manipulates the story's
"overthought" and "underthought" that the major characters also range
themselves around Mr. Guizac on a descending scale from love to hate.
Thus the priest's charity toward the Guizacs is most active and Christ-like,
the Negroes are almost tolerant of him, while Mrs. McIntyre's and the
Shortleys' feelings regress from neutrality to suspicion to hatred. Moreover,

444

and here the symbolization begins to be an end as well as an instrument, a character's feelings toward the peacock may coincide with his feelings toward Mr. Guizac. The priest is attached to both, while Mrs. McIntyre's deepening indifference to the birds parallels her growing alienation from Guizac, and indeed from everyone. Mrs. Shortley calls the cock "nothing but a peachicken," her callousness in this regard exactly paralleling her lack of feeling for the Guizacs.

From a more "horizontal" viewpoint, the first half of the story is Mrs. Shortley's, and the action imitates her life and death as defined and controlled by the Guizacs. The second half of the story, Mrs. McIntyre's, is the playing out of her destiny as defined, also, by Mr. Guizac. As Fitzgerald puts it, "After Mrs. Shortley's death, her role as the giant wife of the countryside devolves upon Mrs. McIntyre, who being still more formidable will engage in a harder struggle." Uniting both halves of the story's "overthought" are the physical peacock and the Displaced Person; they unite the halves as "underthought" through their analogue, Christ, and the reality of supernatural love. As each major character defines himself in relationship to Mr. Guizac, so that character defines himself in relation to Christ. "As long as you did not do it for one of these least ones. . . ."

Henry LeClerq provides a full account of the peacock symbol and its use, tracing its provenance from pagan times to early Christian, and noting its very ancient use as a symbol of Christ:

> Le paon, qui est sans contestation, le plus somptueux des oiseaux domestiques de nos climats, offrait un type accompli au symbolisme. Sa chair incorruptible, sa parure reparaissant au printemps, permettaient d'en faire une image du Saveur qui avait échappé à la corruption du tombeau et qui renaissait chaque année au printemps dant un éblouissement de splendeur.[1] (*Dictionnaire D'Archeologie Chretienne et de Liturgie*, 1937, *Tome trezieme*, "Paon")

More recently, Van Treeck and Croft have noted that "The peacock was the ancient symbol of eternity and divinity. It was adopted by the Christians and is used in connection with symbols of the Savior to show His divine character." It is this ancient and accessible symbology which Miss O'Connor exploits in "The Displaced Person."

---

[1] [The quotation may be translated as follows:
The peacock, which is indisputably the most sumptuous of the domestic birds in our clime, offered a "ready-made" symbol. Its incorruptible flesh, its plumage reappearing in the spring, permitted making it an image of the Savior, who had escaped the corruption of the tomb and who was reborn each year in the spring in a dazzling burst of splendor. (*Dictionary of Christian Archeology and Liturgy*, 1937, Volume 13, "Peacock")]

The most explicit use of the peacock as symbol for Christ comes in a scene where the two are directly identified by the priest. Mrs. McIntyre has just explained her reasons why the Guizacs must leave the farm; the priest answers obliquely, expressing the hope that she will not send them away; then

> without waiting for an answer, he raised his hand and gave her his blessing in a rumbling voice.
>
> She smiled angrily and said, "I didn't create his situation, of course."
>
> The priest let his eyes wander toward the birds. They had reached the middle of the lawn. The cock stopped suddenly and curving his neck backwards, he raised his tail and spread it with a shimmering timbrous noise. Tiers of small pregnant suns floated in a green-gold haze over his head. The priest stood transfixed, his jaw slack. Mrs. McIntyre wondered where she had ever seen such an idiotic old man. "Christ will come like that!" he said in a loud gay voice and wiped his hand over his mouth and stood there, gaping.

But Miss O'Connor introduced the peacock with these same symbolic overtones at the very beginning of the story. In the opening line she depicts a strange procession-in-reverse in which "The peacock was following Mrs. Shortley up the road to the hill where she meant to stand," a line in which in fact Mrs. Shortley's entire story is forecast. A few lines later the bird is described more fully:

> The peacock stopped just behind her, his tail—glittering green-gold and blue in the sunlight—lifted just enough so that it would not touch the ground. It flowed out on either side like a floating train and his head on the long blue reed-like neck was drawn back as if his attention were fixed in the distance on something no one else could see.

The final detail underlines once more the spiritual blindness of Mrs. Shortley, who not only cannot see what the peacock sees but cannot even see the peacock.

After the Guizacs' arrival, there are a few moments of conversation during which Father Flynn first sees the peacock, a scene stressing Mrs. Shortley's blindness and Mrs. McIntyre's hardness and introducing for the first time the thematic associations of the peacock with the Displaced Person:

> Mrs. Shortley spun around. The peacock was standing a few feet behind her, with his head slightly cocked.
>
> "What a beauti-ful birdrrrd!" the priest murmured.

446

"Another mouth to feed," Mrs. McIntyre said, glancing in the peafowl's direction.

"And when does he raise his splendid tail?" asked the priest.

"Just when it suits him," she said. "There used to be twenty or thirty of those things on the place but I've let them die off. I don't like to hear them scream in the middle of the night."

"So beauti-ful," the priest said. "A tail full of suns," and he crept forward on tiptoe and looked down on the bird's back where the polished gold and green design began. The peacock stood still as if he had just come down from some sun-drenched height to be a vision for them all. The priest's homely red face hung over him, glowing with pleasure.

Mrs. Shortley's mouth had drawn acidly to one side. "Nothing but a peachicken," she muttered.

Mrs. McIntyre's annoyance at the nocturnal crying of the peacock provides an ironic commentary on her spiritual state, for according to the bestiaries, the night cry of the peacock resembles the call of the Christian in fear of losing grace in the darkness of life (as does the peacocks' cry in Wallace Stevens's "Domination of Black").

The parallel between Mrs. Shortley's relation to the Guizacs and to the peacock is further emphasized in a conversation Mrs. Shortley holds with the two Negroes not long after the arrival of the Poles. Displaced Persons, she explains, are those who "ain't where they belong to be at." Then,

. . . she stood a little while longer, reflecting, her unseeing eyes directly in front of the peacock's tail. He had jumped into the tree and his tail hung in front of her, full of fierce planets with eyes that were each ringed in green and set against a sun that was gold in one second's light and salmon-colored in the next. She might have been looking at a map of the universe but she didn't notice it any more than she did the spots of sky that cracked the dull green of the tree. She was having an inner vision instead.

Conscienceless incomprehension and self-seeking callousness have so blinded Mrs. Shortley, the essence of "good country people," that she can "see" neither the peacock nor the Displaced Person but only the inner side of her own capacious ego, a consciousness later inflated to the dimensions of a pseudo-apocalyptic vision. At death, though, "her eyes like blue-painted glass, seemed to contemplate for the first time the tremendous frontiers of her true country."

The last appearance of the peacock coincides with the last sentence of the story, in which the bird is again juxtaposed with the priest. Mrs. Mc-

Intyre, abandoned and invalid, almost sightless and voiceless, now lives alone, and

> Not many people remembered to come out to the country to see her except the old priest. He came regularly once a week with a bag of breadcrumbs and, after he had fed these to the peacock, he would come in and sit by the side of her bed and explain the doctrines of the Church.

The peacock is deliberately associated here with the bread of the Holy Eucharist, for, at the literal level, the peacock was and is a common decoration for repositories and other vessels containing the Blessed Sacrament. Ironically, though, Father Flynn can feed breadcrumbs only to a bird, unable to nourish Mrs. McIntyre with the true body and blood of Christ. Eucharistic imagery has played a significant part previously also in a detail characterizing Mrs. McIntyre—she loves money above all things—as she goes "into the back hall, a closet-like space that was dark and quiet as a chapel." Miss O'Connor depicts Mrs. McIntyre sitting down at the Judge's old roll-top desk containing bankbooks and ledgers stacked in the half open drawers and "a small safe, empty but locked, set like a tabernacle in the center of it." When Mrs. McIntyre sat "with her intense constricted face turned toward the empty safe, she knew there was nobody poorer in the world than she was."

Obviously, detaching the peacock symbol from the total weave of the story for purposes of a separate analysis is almost as impossible as it is to dissociate the peacock from the story's other thematic center, the "displaced person" motif. However true it is that the centers eventually coalesce in their analogue, Christ, the "displaced person" motif is developed more explicitly and has a more important part to play in the unfolding of the action. The depth and power of the motif ultimately derives, though, from Miss O'Connor's deliberate identification of the Displaced Person and Christ, sometimes directly by means of the prior identification of the peacock with Christ, as in a scene quoted above in which the priest has exclaimed of the peacock, "Christ will come like that!" The section continues:

> Mrs. McIntyre's face assumed a set puritanical expression and she reddened. Christ in the conversation embarrassed her the way sex had her mother. "It is not my responsibility that Mr. Guizac had nowhere to go," she said. "I don't find myself responsible for all the extra people in the world."
> The old man didn't seem to hear her. His attention was fixed on the cock who was taking minute steps backward, his head against the spread tail. "The Transfiguration," he murmured.

448

She had no idea what he was talking about. "Mr. Guizac didn't have to come here in the first place," she said, giving him a hard look.

The cock lowered his tail and began to pick grass.

"He didn't have to come in the first place," she repeated, emphasizing each word.

The old man smiled absently. "He came to redeem us," he said and blandly reached for her hand and shook it and said he must go.

Some time later, Mrs. McIntyre makes the connection between Christ and the Displaced Person brutally explicit. "For," the priest was saying

as if he spoke of something that had happened yesterday in town, "when God sent his Only Begotten Son, Jesus Christ Our Lord"—he slightly bowed his head—"as a Redeemer to mankind, He . . ."

"Father Flynn!" she said in a voice that made him jump. "I want to talk to you about something serious!"

The skin under the old man's right eye flinched.

"As far as I'm concerned," she said and glared at him fiercely, "Christ was just another D. P."

Ironically, in an earlier fit of enthusiasm over Mr. Guizac's success as a money-saver for her, Mrs. McIntyre had declared, "That man is my salvation!"

The culmination of the "underthought" of the Mrs. McIntyre plot thus occurs in the revelation of the woman's moral and spiritual condition as it is refracted through her view of Mr. Guizac, and beyond that, of Christ. Mrs. McIntyre's equation is, of course, perfectly logical and perfectly knowing, but it is also perfectly inverted; instead of seeing Christ in the Displaced Person, as Christian love demands, she sees Christ only as a Displaced Person. But on another level, it is precisely her spiritual blindness and hardness that have caused Christ to be for her a Displaced Person.

The revelation of Mrs. McIntyre's spiritual state through her view of the Guizacs is carefully prepared for and paralleled in other details that show she is totally self-centered and thus completely incapable of love. In a tirade against the old Negro she says, ". . . I'm the one around here who holds all the strings together. . . . You're all dependent on me. . . ." and she tells Mr. Guizac, "This is my place . . . . I say who will come here and who won't. . . . I am not responsible for the world's misery." From this standpoint, of course, everyone else is—or can become—"extra."

"Howcome they so many extra?" he asked.

"People are selfish," she said. "They have too many children. There's no sense in it any more."

Of Mr. Guizac, she says to the priest, "He's extra. . . . He doesn't fit in," and "I don't find myself responsible for all the extra people in the world." In the period while she delays dismissing Mr. Guizac, she dreams that Father Flynn comes to her and says,

> "Think of the thousands of them, think of the ovens and the boxcars and the camps and the sick children and Christ Our Lord."
> "He's extra and he's upset the balance around here," she said, "and I'm a logical practical woman and there are no ovens here and no camps and no Christ Our Lord. . . ."

Since she is capable only of self-interest and lacks any capacity for a true response to persons, Mrs. McIntyre, typically enough, has placed money at the center of her interest and endeavor. (The patent ironies of the process by which she is cheated first by the Judge and then by herself in her search for money need not be recapitulated here.) Mrs. McIntyre repeatedly refers to herself as not "made of money," but these demurs only underline her greed and acquisitiveness, and culminate in a scene in which she asked the priest "if he thought she was made of money and the old man suddenly let out a great ugly bellow as if this were a comical question."

By a variation of the "displaced person" motif, then, Flannery O'Connor shows that it is the displacer who is truly displaced. (Robert Fitzgerald is a little vague here: "It is a tale of the displacement of persons, of the human Person displaced.") Abandoning every altruistic and generous impulse, every vestige of natural compassion, the egoist abandons at once his capacity to love and to be loved supernaturally. He loses his self. But even in the process of hardening his heart toward others-in-Christ and Christ-in-others, he experiences with Mrs. McIntyre that "some interior violence" has already been done. The abandoner experiences most deeply of all his own abandonment; as Mr. Guizac died, Mrs. McIntyre "felt she was in some foreign country where the people bent over the body were natives, and she watched like a stranger. . . ."

Thus the fullest exploitation of the two thematic centers, the peacock and the Displaced Person, and their analogue, Christ, is reached in this final revelation that the displacer is the displaced. The denouement in the story's "overthought" coincides exactly with maximum revelation of the "underthought." Without the peacock symbol and the ironies playing about the "displaced person" motif, the story might not have been more than the *Time* (June 6, 1955) reviewer called it, "a powerful and moving tale of an innocent Pole who stumbles against the South's color bar." Flannery O'Connor's ability to create and control a strong story line and her use of realistic and naturalistic detail enables us to accept without question the physical reality and "inevitability" of both the Poles and the peacock, and they can thus serve perfectly as instruments. But the symbolization is also an end, for in these figures is already contained in germ the story's entire *raison d'etre*.

QUESTIONS

The Displaced Person

POINT OF VIEW 1. The central theme in this story concerns being displaced—being forced from one's "rightful" place. By presenting the story through the inside views of Mrs. Shortley and Mrs. McIntyre and by excluding us from the consciousness of the Negroes and the Guizacs, O'Connor heightens our awareness of her theme. Discuss the relationship between theme and point of view.

CHARACTERS 2. In many of her stories—including the two reprinted in this book—Flannery O'Connor portrays narrow-minded, self-righteous women whose status is threatened (by history, by Negroes, and so forth) but who affirm their "superiority" by virtue of the Negroes' lower position in society. The inability of these women to understand or even acknowledge their own motives, rationalizations, and fears gives O'Connor an opportunity to let them "hang themselves" with their own words, thoughts, and acts. In the following passage, Mrs. Shortley is beginning to formulate her strategy for dealing with the threat the Guizacs represent, a threat her pride and self-righteousness will not allow her to acknowledge. Show how each of her statements has more implications than she understands. From what you know of her character and situation, describe the assumptions and prejudices behind each sentence.

> "I suspect," she said, "that before long there won't be no more niggers on this place. And I tell you what. I'd rather have niggers than them Poles. And what's furthermore, I aim to take up for the niggers when the time comes. When Gobblehook first come here, you recollect how he shook their hands, like he didn't know the difference, like he might have been as black as them, but when it come to finding out Sulk was taking turkeys, he gone on and told her. I known he was taking turkeys. I could have told her myself." (p. 418)

451

3. The Guizacs and the Negroes are both aliens to Mrs. Shortley: She grants neither of them full human status. But the Guizacs represent an unfamiliar threat that she has to find ways of coping with in her own mind as well as practically. List her criticisms of the Guizacs and point out how her attitude toward them changes through the course of the story. 4. List at least three images that describe Mrs. Shortley and at least three that describe Mrs. McIntyre. What are the attitudes of the two women toward religion? In what other ways do they resemble each other? What sort of artistic and thematic concerns led O'Connor to treat them as "doubles"?

PLOT 5. Analyze the plot of this story by using the arrivals and departures of the characters as a pattern of organization. 6. What information does Mrs. Shortley possess that she tells only to her husband? When Mrs. McIntyre discovers this "secret," does she react as Mrs. Shortley predicted she would? 7. In what ways does the death of Mrs. Shortley foreshadow the decline of Mrs. McIntyre? What is the thematic significance of this foreshadowing? 8. Early in the story, in response to Mrs. McIntyre's admiration of how efficiently Mr. Guizac operated the new silage cutter and her appreciation of how quickly the cane bottom could be cut, Mrs. Shortley muttered, "Maybe, . . . if don't no terrible accident occur." Describe the events surrounding Mr. Guizac's death. Defend, or attack the statement that the displaced person's death was premeditated by Mr. Shortley. Is there any proof that Mr. Shortley was seeking revenge for the death of Mrs. Shortley?

SETTING 9. In what way does the setting make plausible the ignorant, distorted views the Shortleys have about Europe, the events of World Wars I and II, and the Catholic church? 10. Much of the story's action centers around the practical business of running a farm. How do Mrs. McIntyre's difficulties in coping with her employees make her a believable and even somewhat sympathetic character?

STYLE 11. Flannery O'Connor has said that the writer's ability to hear speech is one of his major assets. What idioms and speech patterns mark the Shortleys' speech as Southern and rural? Examine the patterns of Mrs. McIntyre's speech. On the basis of this evidence, can you ascertain that O'Connor is trying to establish a class distinction between Mrs. McIntyre and Mrs. Shortley? 12. From the time Mr. Shortley returns to the farm, the prose takes on a dry, matter-of-fact, summary-like quality. There is less dialogue and more descriptive statement. Discuss how this shift in style relates to the theme of the story. 13. In what ways does the Judge function as a symbol in this story? Consider his legacy to Mrs. McIntyre, his grave, and his office.

TONE   14. Irony has something in common with hypocrisy—that is, they both imply a certain "doubleness." The ironist says one thing but means another; the hypocrite proclaims virtues that he does not have. Flannery O'Connor, the ironist, makes good use of her hypocritical characters. For example, in defending her husband against Mrs. McIntyre's suspicion that he is secretly holding a second job, Mrs. Shortley thinks, ". . . in the middle of the day when he [Mr. Shortley] was supposed to be resting, he was off attending to his still. Not every man would work like that." Mrs. Shortley is announcing her husband's virtue, but the reader sees in the statement that Mr. Shortley is cheating Mrs. McIntyre. And "Not every man would work like that" has a double edge of irony— indeed, not every man would so deceive his employer. Analyze another incident or passage in the story where irony is produced by hypocrisy. 15. Although the action is horrifying and disturbing, there are flashes of humor in the narrative. Describe the nature of the comedy in this story. What is its effect on the story as a whole?

Thematic Centers in "The Displaced Person"

FOCUS   1. According to the essayist, the action in "The Displaced Person" revolves around two thematic centers. What are these separate but related thematic centers? As described in the essay, how are they related to each other?   2. How are they related to the "two deeply theological themes" that are probed in the story?

ORGANIZATION   3. Explain how the first paragraph serves to introduce the essay as a whole.   4. Obvious problems in organization occur when a writer analyzes two separate concepts—in this case, the two thematic centers. Where in the essay is each theme treated separately? Where are they discussed together? Is the organization satisfactory? Explain.   5. Would you describe the essayist's concern as being with the story's "overthought" or "underthought"? How has this emphasis influenced the organization of the essay?

USING THE EVIDENCE   6. How does the essayist support the contention that the peacock is a Christ symbol?   7. How does she justify her statement that the opening line of the narrative foreshadows Mrs. Shortley's entire story?   8. Can you find evidence in the story that allows the essayist to describe Mrs. Shortley's vision as "pseudo-apocalyptic"?   9. What evidence does the essayist offer to show that it is the displacer (Mrs. McIntyre) who is truly displaced?   10. A cynic might say that every critical essay is a false report since it necessarily shuts its eyes to ninety percent of what the story contains. For example, from the evidence in the story, it is possible to argue that the priest is not only old but also *senile.* If the priest is truly senile, would this "fact" alter the essayist's interpretation? Can you find any other major aspects of the story that the essay has not taken into consideration?

STYLE 11. Define the following terms: *alter Christus,* analogue, bestiaries, capacious, eucharistic imagery, provenance, and devolves.

MAKING LITERARY JUDGMENTS 12. In saying that "The Displaced Person" is "one of the few O'Connor stories without a demoniac" and is, therefore, "more metaphysically subtle," the essay is praising the story by saying that it is complex. That is, the essayist finds admirable a certain complexity of tone. This critical assumption posits that serious literature takes into account the intricacy and subtlety of all human life. Examine complexity as a criterion for making literary judgments. 13. Flannery O'Connor once stated that "It is the nature of fiction not to be good for much else unless it is good in itself." In what way is this critical assumption also the basis for the essayist's statement that the Poles and the peacock illustrate how symbols can be both an instrument and an end? 14. An implicit assumption in this essay is that Flannery O'Connor is a consciously theological writer. Consequently, the assumption follows that the story's effectiveness is related to its dramatic illumination of Catholic dogma. Clearly this is judging the story not on literary but on extrinsic considerations. In your opinion, is such an assumption justifiable as a basis for critical judgment? In what way are O'Connor's theological concerns the "extra dimension" in her fiction?

EVERYTHING THAT RISES
MUST CONVERGE

Her doctor had told Julian's mother that she must lose twenty pounds on account of her blood pressure, so on Wednesday nights Julian had to take her downtown on the bus for a reducing class at the Y. The reducing class was designed for working girls over fifty, who weighed from 165 to 200 pounds. His mother was one of the slimmer ones, but she said ladies did not tell their age or weight. She would not ride the buses by herself at night since they had been integrated, and because the reducing class was one of her few pleasures, necessary for her health, and *free*, she said Julian could at least put himself out to take her, considering all she did for him. Julian did not like to consider all she did for him, but every Wednesday night he braced himself and took her.

She was almost ready to go, standing before the hall mirror, putting on her hat, while he, his hands behind him, appeared pinned to the door frame, waiting like Saint Sebastian for the arrows to begin piercing him. The hat was new and had cost her seven dollars and a half. She kept saying, "Maybe I shouldn't have paid that for it. No, I shouldn't have. I'll take it off and return it tomorrow. I shouldn't have bought it."

Julian raised his eyes to heaven. "Yes, you should have bought it," he said. "Put it on and let's go." It was a hideous hat. A purple velvet flap came down on one side of it and stood up on the other; the rest of it was green and looked like a cushion with the stuffing out. He decided it was less comical than jaunty and pathetic. Everything that gave her pleasure was small and depressed him.

She lifted the hat one more time and set it down slowly on top of her head. Two wings of gray hair protruded on either side of her florid face, but her eyes, sky-blue, were as innocent and untouched by experience as they must have been when she was ten. Were it not that she was a widow who had struggled fiercely to feed and clothe and put him through school and who was supporting him still, "until he got on his feet," she might have been a little girl that he had to take to town.

"It's all right, it's all right," he said. "Let's go." He opened the door himself and started down the walk to get her going. The sky was a dying violet and the houses stood out darkly against it, bulbous liver-colored monstrosities of a uniform ugliness though no two were alike. Since this had been a fashionable neighborhood forty years ago, his mother persisted in thinking they did well to have an apartment in it. Each house had a narrow collar of dirt around it in which sat, usually, a grubby child. Julian walked with his hands in his pockets, his head down and thrust forward and his eyes glazed with the determination to make himself completely numb during the time he would be sacrificed to her pleasure.

The door closed and he turned to find the dumpy figure, surmounted by the atrocious hat, coming toward him. "Well," she said, "you only live once and paying a little more for it, I at least won't meet myself coming and going."

"Some day I'll start making money," Julian said gloomily—he knew he never would—"and you can have one of those jokes whenever you take the fit." But first they would move. He visualized a place where the nearest neighbors would be three miles away on either side.

"I think you're doing fine," she said, drawing on her gloves. "You've only been out of school a year. Rome wasn't built in a day."

She was one of the few members of the Y reducing class who arrived in hat and gloves and who had a son who had been to college. "It takes time," she said "and the world is in such a mess. This hat looked better on me than any of the others, though when she brought it out I said, 'Take that thing back. I wouldn't have it on my head,' and she said, 'Now wait till you

456

see it on,' and when she put it on me, I said, 'We-ull,' and she said, 'If you ask me, that hat does something for you and you do something for the hat, and besides,' she said, 'with that hat, you won't meet yourself coming and going.'"

Julian thought he could have stood his lot better if she had been selfish, if she had been an old hag who drank and screamed at him. He walked along, saturated in depression, as if in the midst of his martyrdom he had lost his faith. Catching sight of his long, hopeless, irritated face, she stopped suddenly with a grief-stricken look, and pulled back on his arm. "Wait on me," she said. "I'm going back to the house and take this thing off and to-morrow I'm going to return it. I was out of my head. I can pay the gas bill with that seven-fifty."

He caught her arm in a vicious grip. "You are not going to take it back," he said. "I like it."

"Well," she said, "I don't think I ought . . ."

"Shut up and enjoy it," he muttered, more depressed than ever.

"With the world in the mess it's in," she said, "it's a wonder we can enjoy anything. I tell you, the bottom rail is on the top."

Julian sighed.

"Of course," she said, "if you know who you are, you can go anywhere." She said this every time he took her to the reducing class. "Most of them in it are not our kind of people," she said, "but I can be gracious to anybody. I know who I am."

"They don't give a damn for your graciousness," Julian said savagely. "Knowing who you are is good for one generation only. You haven't the foggiest idea where you stand now or who you are."

She stopped and allowed her eyes to flash at him. "I most certainly do know who I am," she said, "and if you don't know who you are, I'm ashamed of you."

"Oh hell," Julian said.

"Your great-grandfather was a former governor of this state," she said. "Your grandfather was a prosperous landowner. Your grandmother was a Godhigh."

"Will you look around you," he said tensely, "and see where you are now?" and he swept his arm jerkily out to indicate the neighborhood, which the growing darkness at least made less dingy.

"You remain what you are," she said. "Your great-grandfather had a plantation and two hundred slaves."

"There are no more slaves," he said irritably.

"They were better off when they were," she said. He groaned to see that she was off on that topic. She rolled onto it every few days like a train on an open track. He knew every stop, every junction, every swamp along the way, and knew the exact point at which her conclusion would roll majestically into the station: "It's ridiculous. It's simply not realistic. They should rise, yes, but on their own side of the fence."

"Let's skip it," Julian said.

"The ones I feel sorry for," she said, "are the ones that are half white. They're tragic."

"Will you skip it?"

"Suppose we were half white. We would certainly have mixed feelings."

"I have mixed feelings now," he groaned.

"Well let's talk about something pleasant," she said. "I remember going to Grandpa's when I was a little girl. Then the house had double stairways that went up to what was really the second floor—all the cooking was done on the first. I used to like to stay down in the kitchen on account of the way the walls smelled. I would sit with my nose pressed against the plaster and take deep breaths. Actually the place belonged to the Godhighs but your grandfather Chestny paid the mortgage and saved it for them. They were in reduced circumstances," she said, "but reduced or not, they never forgot who they were."

"Doubtless that decayed mansion reminded them," Julian muttered. He never spoke of it without contempt or thought of it without longing. He had seen it once when he was a child before it had been sold. The double stairways had rotted and been torn down. Negroes were living in it. But it remained in his mind as his mother had known it. It appeared in his dreams regularly. He would stand on the wide porch, listening to the rustle of oak leaves, then wander through the high-ceilinged hall into the parlor that opened onto it and gaze at the worn rugs and faded draperies. It occurred to him that it was he, not she, who could have appreciated it. He preferred its threadbare elegance to anything he could name and it was because of it that all the neighborhoods they had lived in had been a torment to him—whereas she had hardly known the difference. She called her insensitivity "being adjustable."

"And I remember the old darky who was my nurse, Caroline. There was no better person in the world. I've always had a great respect for my colored friends," she said. "I'd do anything in the world for them and they'd . . ."

"Will you for God's sake get off that subject?" Julian said. When he got on a bus by himself, he made it a point to sit down beside a Negro, in reparation as it were for his mother's sins.

"You're mighty touchy tonight," she said. "Do you feel all right?"

"Yes I feel all right," he said. "Now lay off."

She pursed her lips. "Well, you certainly are in a vile humor," she observed. "I just won't speak to you at all."

They had reached the bus stop. There was no bus in sight and Julian, his hands still jammed in his pockets and his head thrust forward, scowled down the empty street. The frustration of having to wait on the bus as well as ride on it began to creep up his neck like a hot hand. The presence of his mother was borne in upon him as she gave a pained sigh. He looked at her bleakly. She was holding herself very erect under the preposterous hat, wearing it like a banner of her imaginary dignity. There was in him an evil urge to break her spirit. He suddenly unloosened his tie and pulled it off and put it in his pocket.

She stiffened. "Why must you look like *that* when you take me to town?" she said. "Why must you deliberately embarrass me?"

"If you'll never learn where you are," he said, "you can at least learn where I am."

"You look like a—thug," she said.

"Then I must be one," he murmured.

"I'll just go home," she said. "I will not bother you. If you can't do a little thing like that for me . . ."

Rolling his eyes upward, he put his tie back on. "Restored to my class," he muttered. He thrust his face toward her and hissed, "True culture is in the mind, the *mind*," he said, and tapped his head, "the mind."

"It's in the heart," she said, "and in how you do things and how you do things is because of who you *are*."

"Nobody in the damn bus cares who you are."

"I care who I am," she said icily.

The lighted bus appeared on top of the next hill and as it approached, they moved out into the street to meet it. He put his hand under her elbow and hoisted her up on the creaking step. She entered with a little smile, as if she were going into a drawing room where everyone had been waiting for her. While he put in the tokens, she sat down on one of the broad front seats for three which faced the aisle. A thin woman with protruding teeth and long yellow hair was sitting on the end of it. His mother moved up beside her and left room for Julian beside herself. He sat down and looked at the floor across the aisle where a pair of thin feet in red and white canvas sandals were planted.

His mother immediately began a general conversation meant to attract anyone who felt like talking. "Can it get any hotter?" she said and removed from her purse a folding fan, black with a Japanese scene on it, which she began to flutter before her.

"I reckon it might could," the woman with the protruding teeth said, "but I know for a fact my apartment couldn't get no hotter."

"It must get the afternoon sun," his mother said. She sat forward and looked up and down the bus. It was half filled. Everybody was white. "I see we have the bus to ourselves," she said. Julian cringed.

"For a change," said the woman across the aisle, the owner of the red and white canvas sandals. "I come on one the other day and they were thick as fleas—up front and all through."

"The world is in a mess everywhere," his mother said. "I don't know how we've let it get in this fix."

"What gets my goat is all those boys from good families stealing automobile tires," the woman with the protruding teeth said. "I told my boy, I said you may not be rich but you been raised right and if I ever catch you in any such mess, they can send you on to the reformatory. Be exactly where you belong."

"Training tells," his mother said. "Is your boy in high school?"

"Ninth grade," the woman said.

"My son just finished college last year. He wants to write but he's selling typewriters until he gets started," his mother said.

The woman leaned forward and peered at Julian. He threw her such a malevolent look that she subsided against the seat. On the floor across the aisle there was an abandoned newspaper. He got up and got it and opened it out in front of him. His mother discreetly continued the conversation in a lower tone but the woman across the aisle said in a loud voice, "Well that's nice. Selling typewriters is close to writing. He can go right from one to the other."

"I tell him," his mother said, "that Rome wasn't built in a day."

Behind the newspaper Julian was withdrawing into the inner compartment of his mind where he spent most of his time. This was a kind of mental bubble in which he established himself when he could not bear to be a part of what was going on around him. From it he could see out and judge but in it he was safe from any kind of penetration from without. It was the only place where he felt free of the general idiocy of his fellows. His mother had never entered it but from it he could see her with absolute clarity.

The old lady was clever enough and he thought that if she had started from any of the right premises, more might have been expected of her. She lived according to the laws of her own fantasy world, outside of which he had never seen her set foot. The law of it was to sacrifice herself for him after she had first created the necessity to do so by making a mess of things. If he had permitted her sacrifices, it was only because her lack of foresight had made them necessary. All of her life had been a struggle to act like a Chestny without the Chestny goods, and to give him everything she thought a Chestny ought to have; but since, said she, it was fun to struggle, why complain? And when you had won, as she had won, what fun to look back on the hard times! He could not forgive her that she had enjoyed the struggle and that she thought *she* had won.

What she meant when she said she had won was that she had brought him up successfully and had sent him to college and that he had turned out so well—good looking (her teeth had gone unfilled so that his could be straightened), intelligent (he realized he was too intelligent to be a success), and with a future ahead of him (there was of course no future ahead of him). She excused his gloominess on the grounds that he was still growing up and his radical ideas on his lack of practical experience. She said he didn't yet know a thing about "life," that he hadn't even entered the real world—when already he was as disenchanted with it as a man of fifty.

The further irony of all this was that in spite of her, he had turned out so well. In spite of going to only a third-rate college, he had, on his own initiative, come out with a first-rate education; in spite of growing up dominated by a small mind, he had ended up with a large one; in spite of all her foolish views, he was free of prejudice and unafraid to face facts. Most miraculous of all, instead of being blinded by love for her as she was for him, he had cut himself emotionally free of her and could see her with complete objectivity. He was not dominated by his mother.

The bus stopped with a sudden jerk and shook him from his meditation. A woman from the back lurched forward with little steps and barely escaped falling in his newspaper as she righted herself. She got off and a large Negro got on. Julian kept his paper lowered to watch. It gave him a certain satisfaction to see injustice in daily operation. It confirmed his view that with a few exceptions there was no one worth knowing within a radius of three hundred miles. The Negro was well dressed and carried a briefcase. He looked around and then sat down on the other end of the seat where the woman with the red and white canvas sandals was sitting. He immediately unfolded a newspaper and obscured himself behind it. Julian's mother's elbow at once prodded insistently into his ribs. "Now you see why I won't ride on these buses by myself," she whispered.

The woman with the red and white canvas sandals had risen at the same time the Negro sat down and had gone further back in the bus and taken the seat of the woman who had got off. His mother leaned forward and cast her an approving look.

Julian rose, crossed the aisle, and sat down in the place of the woman with the canvas sandals. From this position, he looked serenely across at his mother. Her face had turned an angry red. He stared at her, making his eyes the eyes of a stranger. He felt his tension suddenly lift as if he had openly declared war on her.

He would have liked to get in conversation with the Negro and to talk with him about art or politics or any subject that would be above the comprehension of those around them, but the man remained entrenched behind his paper. He was either ignoring the change of seating or had never noticed it. There was no way for Julian to convey his sympathy.

His mother kept her eyes fixed reproachfully on his face. The woman with the protruding teeth was looking at him avidly as if he were a type of monster new to her.

"Do you have a light?" he asked the Negro.

Without looking away from his paper, the man reached in his pocket and handed him a packet of matches.

"Thanks," Julian said. For a moment he held the matches foolishly. A NO SMOKING sign looked down upon him from over the door. This alone would not have deterred him; he had no cigarettes. He had quit smoking some months before because he could not afford it. "Sorry," he muttered and handed back the matches. The Negro lowered the paper and gave him an annoyed look. He took the matches and raised the paper again.

His mother continued to gaze at him but she did not take advantage of his momentary discomfort. Her eyes retained their battered look. Her face seemed to be unnaturally red, as if her blood pressure had risen. Julian allowed no glimmer of sympathy to show on his face. Having got the advantage, he wanted desperately to keep it and carry it through. He would have liked to teach her a lesson that would last her a while, but there seemed no way to continue the point. The Negro refused to come out from behind his paper.

Julian folded his arms and looked stolidly before him, facing her but as if he did not see her, as if he had ceased to recognize her existence. He visualized a scene in which, the bus having reached their stop, he would remain in his seat and when she said, "Aren't you going to get off?" he would look at her as at a stranger who had rashly addressed him. The corner they got off on was usually deserted, but it was well lighted and it would not hurt her to walk by herself the four blocks to the Y. He decided to wait until the time came and then decide whether or not he would let her get off by herself. He would have to be at the Y at ten to bring her back, but he could leave her wondering if he was going to show up. There was no reason for her to think she could always depend on him.

He retired again into the high-ceilinged room sparsely settled with large pieces of antique furniture. His soul expanded momentarily but then he became aware of his mother across from him and the vision shriveled. He studied her coldly. Her feet in little pumps dangled like a child's and did not quite reach the floor. She was training on him an exaggerated look of reproach. He felt completely detached from her. At that moment he could with pleasure have slapped her as he would have slapped a particularly obnoxious child in his charge.

He began to imagine various unlikely ways by which he could teach her a lesson. He might make friends with some distinguished Negro professor or lawyer and bring him home to spend the evening. He would be entirely justified but her blood pressure would rise to 300. He could not push her to the extent of making her have a stroke, and moreover, he had never been successful at making any Negro friends. He had tried to strike up an acquaintance on the bus with some of the better types, with ones that looked like professors or ministers or lawyers. One morning he had sat down next to a distinguished-looking dark brown man who had answered his questions with a sonorous solemnity but who had turned out to be an undertaker. Another day he had sat down beside a cigar-smoking Negro with a diamond ring on his finger, but after a few stilted pleasantries, the Negro had rung the buzzer and risen, slipping two lottery tickets into Julian's hand as he climbed over him to leave.

He imagined his mother lying desperately ill and his being able to secure only a Negro doctor for her. He toyed with that idea for a few minutes and then dropped it for a momentary vision of himself participating as a sympathizer in a sit-in demonstration. This was possible but he did not linger with it. Instead, he approached the ultimate horror. He brought home a beautiful suspiciously Negroid woman. Prepare yourself, he said. There is nothing you can do about it. This is the woman I've chosen. She's intelligent, dignified, even good, and she's suffered and she hasn't thought it *fun*. Now persecute us, go ahead and persecute us. Drive her out of here, but remember, you're driving me too. His eyes were narrowed and through the indignation he had generated, he saw his mother across the aisle, purple-faced, shrunken to the dwarf-like proportions of her moral nature, sitting like a mummy beneath the ridiculous banner of her hat.

He was tilted out of his fantasy again as the bus stopped. The door opened with a sucking hiss and out of the dark a large, gaily dressed, sullen-looking colored woman got on with a little boy. The child, who might have been four, had on a short plaid suit and a Tyrolean hat with a blue feather in it. Julian hoped that he would sit down beside him and that the woman would push in beside his mother. He could think of no better arrangement.

As she waited for her tokens, the woman was surveying the seating possibilities—he hoped with the idea of sitting where she was least wanted. There was something familiar-looking about her but Julian could not place what it was. She was a giant of a woman. Her face was set not only to meet opposition but to seek it out. The downward tilt of her large lower lip was like a warning sign: DON'T TAMPER WITH ME. Her bulging figure was encased in a green crepe dress and her feet overflowed in red shoes. She had on a hideous hat. A purple velvet flap came down on one side of it and stood up on the other; the rest of it was green and looked like a cushion with the stuffing out. She carried a mammoth red pocketbook that bulged throughout as if it were stuffed with rocks.

To Julian's disappointment, the little boy climbed up on the empty seat beside his mother. His mother lumped all children, black and white, into the common category, "cute," and she thought little Negroes were on the whole cuter than little white children. She smiled at the little boy as he climbed on the seat.

Meanwhile the woman was bearing down upon the empty seat beside Julian. To his annoyance, she squeezed herself into it. He saw his mother's face change as the woman settled herself next to him and he realized with satisfaction that this was more objectionable to her than it was to him. Her face seemed almost gray and there was a look of dull recognition in her eyes, as if suddenly she had sickened at some awful confrontation. Julian saw that it was because she and the woman had, in a sense, swapped sons. Though his mother would not realize the symbolic significance of this, she would feel it. His amusement showed plainly on his face.

The woman next to him muttered something unintelligible to herself. He was conscious of a kind of bristling next to him, a muted growling like that of an angry cat. He could not see anything but the red pocketbook upright on the bulging green thighs. He visualized the woman as she had stood waiting for her tokens—the ponderous figure, rising from the red shoes upward over the solid hips, the mammoth bosom, the haughty face, to the green and purple hat.

His eyes widened.

The vision of the two hats, identical, broke upon him with the radiance of a brilliant sunrise. His face was suddenly lit with joy. He could not believe that Fate had thrust upon his mother such a lesson. He gave a loud chuckle so that she would look at him and see that he saw. She turned her eyes on him slowly. The blue in them seemed to have turned a bruised purple. For a moment he had an uncomfortable sense of her innocence, but it lasted only a second before principle rescued him. Justice entitled him to laugh. His grin hardened until it said to her as plainly as if he were saying aloud: Your punishment exactly fits your pettiness. This should teach you a permanent lesson.

Her eyes shifted to the woman. She seemed unable to bear looking at him and to find the woman preferable. He became conscious again of the bristling presence at his side. The woman was rumbling like a volcano about to become active. His mother's mouth began to twitch slightly at one corner. With a sinking heart, he saw incipient signs of recovery on her face and realized that this was going to strike her suddenly as funny and was going to be no lesson at all. She kept her eyes on the woman and an amused smile came over her face as if the woman were a monkey that had stolen her hat. The little Negro was looking up at her with large fascinated eyes. He had been trying to attract her attention for some time.

"Carver!" the woman said suddenly. "Come heah!"

When he saw that the spotlight was on him at last, Carver drew his feet up and turned himself toward Julian's mother and giggled.

"Carver!" the woman said. "You heah me? Come heah!"

Carver slid down from the seat but remained squatting with his back against the base of it, his head turned slyly around toward Julian's mother, who was smiling at him. The woman reached a hand across the aisle and snatched him to her. He righted himself and hung backwards on her knees, grinning at Julian's mother. "Isn't he cute?" Julian's mother said to the woman with the protruding teeth.

"I reckon he is," the woman said without conviction.

The Negress yanked him upright but he eased out of her grip and shot across the aisle and scrambled, giggling wildly, onto the seat beside his love.

"I think he likes me," Julian's mother said, and smiled at the woman. I was the smile she used when she was being particularly gracious to an inferior. Julian saw everything lost. The lesson had rolled off her like rain on a roof.

The woman stood up and yanked the little boy off the seat as if she were snatching him from contagion. Julian could feel the rage in her at having no weapon like his mother's smile. She gave the child a sharp slap across his leg. He howled once and then thrust his head into her stomach and kicked his feet against her shins. "Be-have," she said vehemently.

465

The bus stopped and the Negro who had been reading the newspaper got off. The woman moved over and set the little boy down with a thump between herself and Julian. She held him firmly by the knee. In a moment he put his hands in front of his face and peeped at Julian's mother through his fingers.

"I see yoooooooo!" she said and put her hand in front of her face and peeped at him.

The woman slapped his hand down. "Quit yo' foolishness," she said, "before I knock the living Jesus out of you!"

Julian was thankful that the next stop was theirs. He reached up and pulled the cord. The woman reached up and pulled it at the same time. Oh my God, he thought. He had the terrible intuition that when they got off the bus together, his mother would open her purse and give the little boy a nickel. The gesture would be as natural to her as breathing. The bus stopped and the woman got up and lunged to the front, dragging the child, who wished to stay on, after her. Julian and his mother got up and followed. As they neared the door, Julian tried to relieve her of her pocketbook.

"No," she murmured, "I want to give the little boy a nickel."

"No!" Julian hissed. "No!"

She smiled down at the child and opened her bag. The bus door opened and the woman picked him up by the arm and descended with him, hanging at her hip. Once in the street she set him down and shook him.

Julian's mother had to close her purse while she got down the bus step but as soon as her feet were on the ground, she opened it again and began to rummage inside. "I can't find but a penny," she whispered, "but it looks like a new one."

"Don't do it!" Julian said fiercely between his teeth. There was a streetlight on the corner and she hurried to get under it so that she could better see into her pocketbook. The woman was heading off rapidly down the street with the child still hanging backward on her hand.

"Oh little boy!" Julian's mother called and took a few quick steps and caught up with them just beyond the lamppost. "Here's a bright new penny for you," and she held out the coin, which shone bronze in the dim light.

The huge woman turned and for a moment stood, her shoulders lifted and her face frozen with frustrated rage, and stared at Julian's mother. Then all at once she seemed to explode like a piece of machinery that had been given one ounce of pressure too much. Julian saw the black fist swing out with the red pocketbook. He shut his eyes and cringed as he heard the woman shout, "He don't take nobody's pennies!" When he opened his eyes, the woman was disappearing down the street with the little boy staring wide-eyed over her shoulder. Julian's mother was sitting on the sidewalk.

"I told you not to do that," Julian said angrily. "I told you not to do that!"

He stood over her for a minute, gritting his teeth. Her legs were stretched out in front of her and her hat was on her lap. He squatted down and looked her in the face. It was totally expressionless. "You got exactly what you deserved," he said. "Now get up."

He picked up her pocketbook and put what had fallen out back in it. He picked the hat up off her lap. The penny caught his eye on the sidewalk and he picked that up and let it drop before her eyes into the purse. Then he stood up and leaned over and held his hands out to pull her up. She remained immobile. He sighed. Rising above them on either side were black apartment buildings, marked with irregular rectangles of light. At the end of the block a man came out of a door and walked off in the opposite direction. "All right," he said, "suppose somebody happens by and wants to know why you're sitting on the sidewalk?"

She took the hand and, breathing hard, pulled heavily up on it and then stood for a moment, swaying slightly as if the spots of light in the darkness were circling around her. Her eyes, shadowed and confused, finally settled on his face. He did not try to conceal his irritation. "I hope this teaches you a lesson," he said. She leaned forward and her eyes raked his face. She seemed trying to determine his identity. Then, as if she found nothing familiar about him, she started off with a headlong movement in the wrong direction.

"Aren't you going on to the Y?" he asked.

"Home," she muttered.

"Well, are we walking?"

For answer she kept going. Julian followed along, his hands behind him. He saw no reason to let the lesson she had had go without backing it up with an explanation of its meaning. She might as well be made to understand what had happened to her. "Don't think that was just an uppity Negro woman," he said. "That was the whole colored race which will no longer take your condescending pennies. That was your black double. She can wear the same hat as you, and to be sure," he added gratuitously (because he thought it was funny), "it looked better on her than it did on you. What all this means," he said, "is that the old world is gone. The old manners are obsolete and your graciousness is not worth a damn." He thought bitterly of the house that had been lost for him. "You aren't who you think you are," he said.

She continued to plow ahead, paying no attention to him. Her hair had come undone on one side. She dropped her pocketbook and took no notice. He stooped and picked it up and handed it to her but she did not take it.

"You needn't act as if the world had come to an end," he said, "because it hasn't. From now on you've got to live in a new world and face a few realities for a change. Buck up," he said, "it won't kill you."

She was breathing fast.

"Let's wait on the bus," he said.

"Home," she said thickly.

"I hate to see you behave like this," he said. "Just like a child. I should be able to expect more of you." He decided to stop where he was and make her stop and wait for a bus. "I'm not going any farther," he said, stopping. "We're going on the bus."

She continued to go on as if she had not heard him. He took a few steps and caught her arm and stopped her. He looked into her face and caught his breath. He was looking into a face he had never seen before. "Tell Grandpa to come get me," she said.

He stared, stricken.

"Tell Caroline to come get me," she said.

Stunned, he let her go and she lurched forward again, walking as if one leg were shorter than the other. A tide of darkness seemed to be sweeping her from him. "Mother!" he cried. "Darling, sweetheart, wait!" Crumpling, she fell to the pavement. He dashed forward and fell at her side, crying, "Mamma, Mamma!" He turned her over. Her face was fiercely distorted. One eye, large and staring, moved slightly to the left as if it had become unmoored. The other remained fixed on him, raked his face again, found nothing and closed.

"Wait here, wait here!" he cried and jumped up and began to run for help toward a cluster of lights he saw in the distance ahead of him. "Help, help!" he shouted, but his voice was thin, scarcely a thread of sound. The lights drifted farther away the faster he ran and his feet moved numbly as if they carried him nowhere. The tide of darkness seemed to sweep him back to her, postponing from moment to moment his entry into the world of guilt and sorrow.

S U G G E S T I O N S   F O R   W R I T I N G

The Stories

1. The conflict in both "The Displaced Person" and "Eli, the Fanatic" is occasioned by the arrival of a group of "displaced persons." Write an essay in which you discuss the nature of the conflict and the theme of "displacement" in both stories.

2. Discover as many parallel objects, events, and characters as you can in "Everything That Rises Must Converge." Then write an essay in which you discuss the esthetic and thematic effects of this "twinning" or parallelism.

3. Find several passages in "Everything That Rises Must Converge" in which Julian's mother makes a statement that has more to it than she understands. Then, from what you know of her character and situation, write an essay in which you describe what is behind each statement.

4. Find several passages in "Everything That Rises Must Converge" in which Julian—through dialogue, thought, or deed—reveals his true or essential nature to the reader. Then write an essay in which you portray Julian as he appears to his mother, as he appears to the Negro man whom he sits beside on the bus, as he appears to himself, and as he appears to you.

5. Ostensibly, Flannery O'Connor could have ended "Everything That Rises Must Converge" with the clash between Julian's mother and the Negro woman. But the story continues, centering first around the convergence between Julian and his mother, and then finally on Julian himself. Write an essay in which you interpret the conclusion of this story—explaining why O'Connor did not end her story with the convergence of the two women.

6. Compare and contrast the nature and implication of charity as revealed in "Everything That Rises Must Converge" and in "A Gift from the City."

7. Compare and contrast the nature and implication of charity as revealed in "Everything That Rises Must Converge" and in "Black Is My Favorite Color."

Other Works by Flannery O'Connor

1. Write an essay in which you explore the esthetic and thematic effects of the parallelism or "twinning" of objects, events, and characters in the novel *Wise Blood*.

2. In *Violence in Recent Southern Fiction*, Louise Y. Gossett observes that in O'Connor's short stories "the secular expression of man's separation from God often takes the form of corrosive tension between parents and children, from which violence as an act or an attitude results." Examine the literal and symbolic implications of the conflict between generations as dramatized in stories from *A Good Man Is Hard to Find* and *Everything That Rises Must Converge*.

3. Discuss the nature and function of the grotesque in "The Lame Shall Enter First" and *The Violent Bear It Away*.

4. *The Complete Stories* contains stories written early in O'Connor's career as well as stories written shortly before her death. Find two stories with similar themes (and, if possible, similar subject matter—characters, plot, setting), from each period. Compare and contrast an "early" and "late" story to show the author's differing technical treatment of a common theme.

B I B L I O G R A P H Y

Primary

Wise Blood. New York: Harcourt, Brace & World, 1952. A novel.

A Good Man Is Hard to Find. New York: Harcourt, Brace & World, 1955. Short stories.

"The Fiction Writer and His Country" in *The Living Novel*, ed. by Granville Hicks. New York: Macmillan, 1957. An essay.

"The Church and the Fiction Writer." *America*, 96 (March 30, 1957), 733–35. An essay.

"Replies to Two Questions." *Esprit*, 3 (Winter 1959), 10.

The Violent Bear It Away. New York: Farrar, Straus & Giroux, 1960. Short stories.

Introduction to *A Memoir of Mary Ann*. By the Dominican Nuns of Our

Lady of Perpetual Help Home, Atlanta, Ga. New York: Farrar, Straus & Giroux, 1961.

"The Regional Writer." *Esprit,* 7 (Winter 1963), 31–35. An essay.

"Some Aspects of the Grotesque in Southern Literature." *Cluster Review,* seventh issue (March 1965), 5–6, 22. Included also in *The Added Dimension.* A lecture.

Everything That Rises Must Converge. Introduction by Robert Fitzgerald. New York: Farrar, Straus & Giroux, 1965. Short stories.

Mystery and Manners. Ed. by Sally and Robert Fitzgerald. New York: Farrar, Straus & Giroux, 1969. Essays.

The Complete Stories of Flannery O'Connor. New York: Farrar, Straus & Giroux, 1971. Short stories.

Secondary

Baumbach, Jonathan. "The Acid of God's Grace: The Fiction of Flannery O'Connor." *Georgia Review,* 17 (Fall 1963), 334–46. Reprinted, with alterations, as "The Acid of God's Grace," in *The Landscape of Nightmare: Studies in the Contemporary American Novel.* New York: New York Univ. Press, 1965. An examination of *Wise Blood.*

Critique, 2 (Fall 1958). Contains articles by Caroline Gordon on *Wise Blood;* Louis D. Rubin, Jr., on "literary fashions"; and Sister M. Bernetta Quinn, O.S.F., on Flannery O'Connor and J. F. Powers.

Feeley, Kathleen. *Flannery O'Connor: Voice of the Peacock.* New Brunswick, N.J.: Rutgers Univ. Press, 1972. Critical study that approaches the fiction of Flannery O'Connor through her interest in such subjects as theology, biblical commentary, meditative writing, and philosophy.

Ferris, Sumner J. "The Outside and the Inside: Flannery O'Connor's *The Violent Bear It Away.*" *Critique,* 3 (Winter–Spring 1960), 11–19. Develops the thesis that the major characters "are described in different ways by the title" of this "great religious novel."

Fitzgerald, Robert. "The Countryside and the True Country." *Sewanee Review,* 70 (Summer 1962), 380–94. An analysis of "The Displaced Person" that explores the concept that "estrangement from Christian plenitude" results in "estrangement from the true country of man."

The Flannery O'Connor Bulletin. Published annually by Georgia College, Milledgeville, Ga. Volume 1 (Autumn 1972). Contains four essays on O'Connor, "an affectionate recollection" of her (by Rose Lee Walston), and a description of the Flannery O'Connor collection of manuscripts and memorabilia now residing in the library of Georgia College.

Friedman, Melvin J. "Flannery O'Connor: Another Legend in Southern Fiction." *English Journal,* 51 (April 1962), 233–43. Reprinted in *Recent American Fiction: Some Critical Views,* ed. by Joseph J. Waldmeir. Boston: Houghton Mifflin, 1963. A revised and expanded version of this essay appears as the Introduction to *The Added Dimension*. A general discussion of Flannery O'Connor's fiction.

Friedman, Melvin J. and Lewis A. Lawson, eds. *The Added Dimension: The Art and Mind of Flannery O'Connor*. New York: Fordham Univ. Press, 1966. Contains ten essays by such critics as Frederick J. Hoffman, Louis D. Rubin, Jr., C. Hugh Holman, and F. Albert Duhamel; includes also an 80-page section entitled "Flannery O'Connor in Her Own Words."

Gossett, Louise Y. "The Test by Fire: Flannery O'Connor" in *Violence in Recent Southern Fiction*. Durham, N.C.: Duke Univ. Press, 1965. Discusses "the special function of violence" in O'Connor's fiction.

Hawkes, John. "Flannery O'Connor's Devil." *Sewanee Review*, 70 (Summer 1962), 395–407. Compares the writing of Flannery O'Connor and Nathanael West.

Hendin, Josephine. *The World of Flannery O'Connor*. Bloomington, Ind.: Indiana Univ. Press, 1970. A full-length critical biography.

Hyman, Stanley Edgar. *Flannery O'Connor*. Minneapolis: Univ. of Minnesota Press, 1966 (No. 54 of the University of Minnesota Pamphlets on American Writers). An examination of the principal metaphors, symbols, and themes in Flannery O'Connor's stories and novels.

Martin, Carter W. *The True Country: Themes in the Fiction of Flannery O'Connor*. Nashville, Tenn.: Vanderbilt Univ. Press, 1969. An intelligent, carefully documented interpretation; chapters include "The Gothic Impulse," "Comic and Grim Laughter," "The True Country: Flannery O'Connor's Sacramental View," and "The Countryside: Corruption of the Spirit."

Muller, Gilbert. *Nightmares and Visions*. Athens, Ga.: Univ. of Georgia Press, 1972. Pursues the "Catholic grotesque" in O'Connor's fiction.

All art is autobiographical. It is the record of an artist's psychic experience, his attempt to explain something to himself: and in the process of explaining it to himself, he explains it to others. When a work of art pleases us it is often because it recounts for us an experience close to our own, something we can recognize. And so we "like" the artist, because he is so human.

But there are works of art that explain nothing, that dispel order and sanity; works of art that contradict our experience and are therefore deeply offensive to us; works of art that refuse to make sense, that are perhaps dangerous because they are unforgettable. Picasso tells us that "Art is a lie that leads to the truth," and we understand by this paradox that a lie can make us see the truth, a lie can illuminate the truth for us, a lie—especially an extravagant, gorgeous lie —can make us sympathize with a part of the truth we had always successfully avoided. Instinctively, we want either lies that we can know as lies, or truth that we can know as truth. A newspaper in the mid-South declares bluntly: "We Print Only the Truth—No Fiction." But the two concepts are hopelessly mixed together, mysteriously confused. Nothing human is simple.

FROM a prefatory note to *Scenes from American Life*

JOYCE CAROL OATES

Joyce Carol Oates was born in 1938 in Lockport, New York, a small city near Buffalo. After graduating from Syracuse University, she studied at the University of Wisconsin where, in 1961, she received a master's degree in English.

Throughout her writing career, Oates has been the recipient of many literary awards, including a Guggenheim Fellowship and, for *A Garden of Earthly Delights*, a 1968 National Institute of Arts and Letters Award. In 1969, she won the National Book Award in fiction for the novel *Them*, and, since the early 1960's, her short stories have appeared almost yearly in *Prize Stories: The O. Henry Awards* and in *Best American Short Stories*.

Oates is one of the most prolific of the major contemporary writers and has sometimes published two or three volumes in a single year—evidence of an inherent ability to tell stories. Commenting on this propensity, Oates has said that she cannot remember an age when she was not creating fiction: "Before I could write, I drew pictures to tell my stories." Her literary works have not been limited to fiction, moreover, for they also include several plays and numerous poems, book reviews, and pieces of literary criticism. Married to Raymond Smith, she is presently a member of the English department at the University of Windsor, Ontario.

While the stories of Joyce Carol Oates exemplify, for the most part, the well-made story, some of the more recent ones experiment with unusual fictional forms and subjects. Thus, as will be evident, one of the stories here is fairly conventional, while the other is flagrantly unconventional. In both stories, however, Oates stays close to her obsessive thematic concerns: the anguish of love and its inevitable betrayal, and the neuroses that often twist and destroy the lives of her protagonists.

HOW I CONTEMPLATED THE WORLD FROM THE DETROIT HOUSE OF CORRECTION AND BEGAN MY LIFE OVER AGAIN

*NOTES FOR AN ESSAY FOR AN ENGLISH CLASS AT BALD-
WIN COUNTRY DAY SCHOOL; POKING AROUND IN DE-
BRIS; DISGUST AND CURIOSITY; A REVELATION OF THE
MEANING OF LIFE; A HAPPY ENDING . . .*

I   EVENTS

1. The girl (myself) is walking through Branden's, that excellent store. Suburb of a large famous city that is a symbol for large famous American cities. The event sneaks up on the girl, who believes she is herding it along with a small fixed smile, a girl of fifteen, innocently experienced. She dawdles in a certain style by a counter of costume jewelry. Rings, earrings, necklaces. Prices from $5 to $50, all within reach. All ugly. She eases over to the glove counter, where everything is ugly too. In her close-fitted coat with its black fur collar she contemplates the

luxury of Branden's, which she has known for many years: its many mild pale lights, easy on the eye and the soul, its elaborate tinkly decorations, its women shoppers with their excellent shoes and coats and hairdos, all dawdling gracefully, in no hurry.

Who was ever in a hurry here?

2. The girl seated at home. A small library, paneled walls of oak. Someone is talking to me. An earnest, husky, female voice drives itself against my ears, nervous, frightened, groping around my heart, saying, "If you wanted gloves, why didn't you say so? Why didn't you ask for them?" That store, Branden's, is owned by Raymond Forrest who lives on Du Maurier Drive. We live on Sioux Drive. Raymond Forrest. A handsome man? An ugly man? A man of fifty or sixty, with gray hair, or a man of forty with earnest, courteous eyes, a good golf game; who is Raymond Forrest, this man who is my salvation? Father has been talking to him. Father is not his physician; Dr. Berg is his physician. Father and Dr. Berg refer patients to each other. There is a connection. Mother plays bridge with . . . On Mondays and Wednesdays our maid Billie works at . . . The strings draw together in a cat's cradle, making a net to save you when you fall. . . .

3. *Harriet Arnold's.* A small shop, better than Branden's. Mother in her black coat, I in my close-fitted blue coat. Shopping. Now look at this, isn't this cute, do you want this, why don't you want this, try this on, take this with you to the fitting room, take this also, what's wrong with you, what can I do for you, why are you so strange . . . ? "I wanted to steal but not to buy," I don't tell her. The girl droops along in her coat and gloves and leather boots, her eyes scan the horizon, which is pastel pink and decorated like Branden's, tasteful walls and modern ceilings with graceful glimmering lights.

4. Weeks later, the girl at a bus stop. Two o'clock in the afternoon, a Tuesday; obviously she has walked out of school.

5. The girl stepping down from a bus. Afternoon, weather changing to colder. Detroit. Pavement and closed-up stores; grillwork over the windows of a pawnshop. What is a pawnshop, exactly?

II CHARACTERS

1. The girl stands five feet five inches tall. An ordinary height. Baldwin Country Day School draws them up to that height. She dreams along

the corridors and presses her face against the Thermoplex glass. No frost
or steam can ever form on that glass. A smudge of grease from her forehead . . . could she be boiled down to grease? She wears her hair loose
and long and straight in suburban teen-age style, 1968. Eyes smudged with
pencil, dark brown. Brown hair. Vague green eyes. A pretty girl? An ugly
girl? She sings to herself under her breath, idling in the corridor, thinking
of her many secrets (the thirty dollars she once took from the purse of a
friend's mother, just for fun, the basement window she smashed in her own
house just for fun) and thinking of her brother who is at Susquehanna
Boys' Academy, an excellent preparatory school in Maine, remembering
him unclearly . . . he has long manic hair and a squeaking voice and he
looks like one of the popular teen-age singers of 1968, one of those in a
group, *The Certain Forces, The Way Out, The Maniacs Responsible.* The
girl in her turn looks like one of those fieldsful of girls who listen to the
boys' singing, dreaming and mooning restlessly, breaking into high sullen
laughter, innocently experienced.

2. The mother. A Midwestern woman of Detroit and suburbs. Belongs
to the Detroit Athletic Club. Also the Detroit Golf Club. Also the Bloomfield Hills Country Club. The Village Women's Club at which lectures
are given each winter on Genet and Sartre and James Baldwin, by the
Director of the Adult Education Program at Wayne State University. . . .
The Bloomfield Art Association. Also the Founders Society of the Detroit
Institute of Arts. Also . . . Oh, she is in perpetual motion, this lady, hair
like blown-up gold and finer than gold, hair and fingers and body of in-
estimable grace. Heavy weighs the gold on the back of her hairbrush and
hand mirror. Heavy heavy the candlesticks in the dining room. Very heavy
is the big car, a Lincoln, long and black, that on one cool autumn day split
a squirrel's body in two unequal parts.

3. The father. Dr. ———. He belongs to the same clubs as #2. A
player of squash and golf; he has a golfer's umbrella of stripes. Candy
stripes. In his mouth nothing turns to sugar, however; saliva works no
miracles here. His doctoring is of the slightly sick. The sick are sent elsewhere (to Dr. Berg?), the deathly sick are sent back for more tests and
their bills are sent to their homes, the unsick are sent to Dr. Coronet (Isabel, a lady), an excellent psychiatrist for unsick people who angrily believe
they are sick and want to do something about it. If they demand a male
psychiatrist, the unsick are sent by Dr. ——— (my father) to Dr. Lowen-
stein, a male psychiatrist, excellent and expensive, with a limited practice.

4. Clarita. She is twenty, twenty-five, she is thirty or more? Pretty, ugly, what? She is a woman lounging by the side of a road, in jeans and a sweater, hitchhiking, or she is slouched on a stool at a counter in some roadside diner. A hard line of jaw. Curious eyes. Amused eyes. Behind her eyes processions move, funeral pageants, cartoons. She says, "I never can figure out why girls like you bum around down here. What are you looking for anyway?" An odor of tobacco about her. Unwashed underclothes, or no underclothes, unwashed skin, gritty toes, hair long and falling into strands, not recently washed.

5. Simon. In this city the weather changes abruptly, so Simon's weather changes abruptly. He sleeps through the afternoon. He sleeps through the morning. Rising, he gropes around for something to get him going, for a cigarette or a pill to drive him out to the street, where the temperature is hovering around 35°. Why doesn't it drop? Why, why doesn't the cold clean air come down from Canada; will he have to go up into Canada to get it? will he have to leave the Country of his Birth and sink into Canada's frosty fields . . . ? Will the F.B.I. (which he dreams about constantly) chase him over the Canadian border on foot, hounded out in a blizzard of broken glass and horns . . . ?

"Once I was Huckleberry Finn," Simon says, "but now I am Roderick Usher." Beset by frenzies and fears, this man who makes my spine go cold, he takes green pills, yellow pills, pills of white and capsules of dark blue and green . . . he takes other things I may not mention, for what if Simon seeks me out and climbs into my girl's bedroom here in Bloomfield Hills and strangles me, what then . . . ? (As I write this I begin to shiver. Why do I shiver? I am now sixteen and sixteen is not an age for shivering.) It comes from Simon, who is always cold.

III WORLD EVENTS

Nothing.

IV PEOPLE & CIRCUMSTANCES
   CONTRIBUTING TO THIS DELINQUENCY

Nothing.

V SIOUX DRIVE

George, Clyde G. 240 Sioux. A manufacturer's representative; children, a dog, a wife. Georgian with the usual columns. You think of the White

House, then of Thomas Jefferson, then your mind goes blank on the white pillars and you think of nothing. Norris, Ralph W. 246 Sioux. Public relations. Colonial. Bay window, brick, stone, concrete, wood, green shutters, sidewalk, lantern, grass, trees, blacktop drive, two children, one of them my classmate Esther (Esther Norris) at Baldwin. Wife, cars. Ramsey, Michael D. 250 Sioux. Colonial. Big living room, thirty by twenty-five, fireplaces in living room, library, recreation room, paneled walls wet bar five bathrooms five bedrooms two lavatories central air conditioning automatic sprinkler automatic garage door three children one wife two cars a breakfast room a patio a large fenced lot fourteen trees a front door with a brass knocker never knocked. Next is our house. Classic contemporary. Traditional modern. Attached garage, attached Florida room, attached patio, attached pool and cabana, attached roof. A front door mail slot through which pour *Time Magazine, Fortune, Life, Business Week,* the *Wall Street Journal,* the *New York Times,* the *New Yorker,* the *Saturday Review, M.D., Modern Medicine, Disease of the Month* . . . and also. . . . And in addition to all this, a quiet sealed letter from Baldwin saying: *Your daughter is not doing work compatible with her performance on the Stanford-Binet.* . . . And your son is not doing well, not well at all, very sad. Where is your son anyway? Once he stole trick-and-treat candy from some six-year-old kids, he himself being a robust ten. The beginning. Now your daughter steals. In the Village Pharmacy she made off with, yes she did, don't deny it, she made off with a copy of *Pageant Magazine* for no reason, she swiped a roll of Life Savers in a green wrapper and was in no need of saving her life or even in need of sucking candy; when she was no more than eight years old she stole, don't blush, she stole a package of Tums only because it was out on the counter and available, and the nice lady behind the counter (now dead) said nothing. . . . Sioux Drive. Maples, oaks, elms. Diseased elms cut down. Sioux Drive runs into Roosevelt Drive. Slow, turning lanes, not streets, all drives and lanes and ways and passes. A private police force. Quiet private police, in unmarked cars. Cruising on Saturday evenings with paternal smiles for the residents who are streaming in and out of houses, going to and from parties, a thousand parties, slightly staggering, the women in their furs alighting from automobiles bought of Ford and General Motors and Chrysler, very heavy automobiles. No foreign cars. Detroit. In 275 Sioux, down the block in that magnificent French-Normandy mansion, lives —————— himself, who has the C———— account itself, imagine that! Look at where he lives and look at the enormous trees and chimneys, imagine his many fireplaces, imagine his wife and children, imagine his wife's hair, imagine her fingernails, imagine her bathtub of smooth clean glowing pink, imagine their embraces, his trouser pockets filled with odd coins and keys and dust and peanuts, imagine their ecstasy on Sioux Drive, imagine their income tax returns, imagine their little boy's pride in his experimental car, a scaled-down C————, as he roars round the neighborhood on the sidewalks frightening dogs and Negro maids, oh imagine all these things, imagine everything, let your mind roar out all over Sioux Drive and Du Maurier Drive and Roosevelt Drive and Ticonderoga Pass and Burning Bush Way and Lincolnshire Pass and Lois Lane.

When spring comes, its winds blow nothing to Sioux Drive, no odors of hollyhocks or forsythia, nothing Sioux Drive doesn't already possess, everything is planted and performing. The weather vanes, had they weather vanes, don't have to turn with the wind, don't have to contend with the weather. There is no weather.

VI   DETROIT

There is always weather in Detroit. Detroit's temperature is always 32°. Fast-falling temperatures. Slow-rising temperatures. Wind from the north-northeast four to forty miles an hour, small-craft warnings, partly cloudy today and Wednesday changing to partly sunny through Thursday . . . small warnings of frost, soot warnings, traffic warnings, hazardous lake conditions for small craft and swimmers, restless Negro gangs, restless cloud formations, restless temperatures aching to fall out the very bottom of the thermometer or shoot up over the top and boil everything over in red mercury.

Detroit's temperature is 32°. Fast-falling temperatures. Slow-rising temperatures. Wind from the north-northeast four to forty miles an hour. . . .

VII   EVENTS

1. The girl's heart is pounding. In her pocket is a pair of gloves! In a plastic bag! Airproof breathproof plastic bag, gloves selling for twenty-five dollars on Branden's counter! In her pocket! Shoplifted! . . . In her purse is a blue comb, not very clean. In her purse is a leather billfold (a birthday present from her grandmother in Philadelphia) with snapshots of the family in clean plastic windows, in the billfold are bills, she doesn't know how many bills. . . . In her purse is an ominous note from her friend Tykie *What's this about Joe H. and the kids hanging around at Louise's Sat. night? You heard anything?* . . . passed in French class. In her purse is a lot of dirty yellow Kleenex, her mother's heart would break to see such very

dirty Kleenex, and at the bottom of her purse are brown hairpins and safety pins and a broken pencil and a ballpoint pen (blue) stolen from somewhere forgotten and a purse-size compact of Cover Girl Make-Up, Ivory Rose. . . . Her lipstick is Broken Heart, a corrupt pink; her fingers are trembling like crazy; her teeth are beginning to chatter; her insides are alive; her eyes glow in her head; she is saying to her mother's astonished face *I want to steal but not to buy.*

2. At Clarita's. Day or night? What room is this? A bed, a regular bed, and a mattress on the floor nearby. Wallpaper hanging in strips. Clarita says she tore it like that with her teeth. She was fighting a barbaric tribe that night, high from some pills; she was battling for her life with men wearing helmets of heavy iron and their faces no more than Christian crosses to breathe through, every one of those bastards looking like her lover Simon, who seems to breathe with great difficulty through the slits of mouth and nostrils in his face. Clarita has never heard of Sioux Drive. Raymond Forrest cuts no ice with her, nor does the C——— account and its millions; Harvard Business School could be at the corner of Vernor and 12th Street for all she cares, and Vietnam might have sunk by now into the Dead Sea under its tons of debris, for all the amazement she could show . . . her face is overworked, overwrought, at the age of twenty (thirty?) it is already exhausted but fanciful and ready for a laugh. Clarita says mournfully to me *Honey somebody is going to turn you out let me give you warning.* In a movie shown on late television Clarita is not a mess like this but a nurse, with short neat hair and a dedicated look, in love with her doctor and her doctor's patients and their diseases, enamored of needles and sponges and rubbing alcohol. . . . Or no: she is a private secretary. Robert Cummings is her boss. She helps him with fantastic plots, the canned audience laughs, no, the audience doesn't laugh because nothing is funny, instead her boss is Robert Taylor and they are not boss and secretary but husband and wife, she is threatened by a young starlet, she is grim, handsome, wifely, a good companion for a good man. . . . She is Claudette Colbert. Her sister too is Claudette Colbert. They are twins, identical. Her husband Charles Boyer is a very rich handsome man and her sister, Claudette Colbert, is plotting her death in order to take her place as the rich man's wife, no one will know because they are *twins.* . . . All these marvelous lives Clarita might have lived, but she fell out the bottom at the age of thirteen. At the age when I was packing my overnight case for a slumber party at Toni Deshield's she was tearing filthy sheets off a bed and scratching up a rash on her arms. . . . Thirteen is uncommonly young for a white girl

in Detroit, Miss Brock of the Detroit House of Correction said in a sad newspaper interview for the *Detroit News*; fifteen and sixteen are more likely. Eleven, twelve, thirteen are not surprising in colored . . . they are more precocious. What can we do? Taxes are rising and the tax base is falling. The temperature rises slowly but falls rapidly. Everything is falling out the bottom, Woodward Avenue is filthy, Livernois Avenue is filthy! Scraps of paper flutter in the air like pigeons, dirt flies up and hits you right in the eye, oh Detroit is breaking up into dangerous bits of newspaper and dirt, watch out. . . .

Clarita's apartment is over a restaurant. Simon her lover emerges from the cracks at dark. Mrs. Olesko, a neighbor of Clarita's, an aged white wisp of a woman, doesn't complain but sniffs with contentment at Clarita's noisy life and doesn't tell the cops, hating cops, when the cops arrive. I should give more fake names, more blanks, instead of telling all these secrets. I myself am a secret; I am a minor.

3. My father reads a paper at a medical convention in Los Angeles. There he is, on the edge of the North American continent, when the unmarked detective put his hand so gently on my arm in the aisle of Branden's and said, "Miss, would you like to step over here for a minute?"

And where was he when Clarita put her hand on my arm, that wintry dark sulphurous aching day in Detroit, in the company of closed-down barber shops, closed-down diners, closed-down movie houses, homes, windows, basements, faces . . . she put her hand on my arm and said, "Honey, are you looking for somebody down here?"

And was he home worrying about me, gone for two weeks solid, when they carried me off . . . ? It took three of them to get me in the police cruiser, so they said, and they put more than their hands on my arm.

4. I work on this lesson. My English teacher is Mr. Forest, who is from Michigan State. Not handsome, Mr. Forest, and his name is plain, unlike Raymond Forrest's, but he is sweet and rodentlike, he has conferred with the principal and my parents, and everything is fixed . . . treat her as if nothing has happened, a new start, begin again, only sixteen years old, what a shame, how did it happen?—nothing happened, nothing could have happened, a slight physiological modification known only to a gynecologist or to Dr. Coronet. I work on my lesson. I sit in my pink room. I look around the room with my sad pink eyes. I sigh, I dawdle, I pause, I eat up time, I am limp and happy to be home, I am sixteen years old suddenly, my head

hangs heavy as a pumpkin on my shoulders, and my hair has just been cut by Mr. Faye at the Crystal Salon and is said to be very becoming.

(Simon too put his hand on my arm and said, "Honey, you have got to come with me," and in his six-by-six room we got to know each other. Would I go back to Simon again? Would I lie down with him in all that filth and craziness? Over and over again.

a Clarita is being betrayed as in front of a Cunningham Drug Store she is nervously eying a colored man who may or may not have money, or a nervous white boy of twenty with sideburns and an Appalachian look, who may or may not have a knife hidden in his jacket pocket, or a husky red-faced man of friendly countenance who may or may not be a member of the Vice Squad out for an early twilight walk.)

I work on my lesson for Mr. Forest. I have filled up eleven pages. Words pour out of me and won't stop. I want to tell everything . . . what was the song Simon was always humming, and who was Simon's friend in a very new trench coat with an old high school graduation ring on his finger . . . ? Simon's bearded friend? When I was down too low for him, Simon kicked me out and gave me to him for three days, I think, on Fourteenth Street in Detroit, an airy room of cold cruel drafts with newspapers on the floor. . . . Do I really remember that or am I piecing it together from what they told me? Did they tell the truth? Did they know much of the truth?

VIII   CHARACTERS

1. Wednesdays after school, at four; Saturday mornings at ten. Mother drives me to Dr. Coronet. Ferns in the office, plastic or real, they look the same. Dr. Coronet is queenly, an elegant nicotine-stained lady who would have studied with Freud had circumstances not prevented it, a bit of a Catholic, ready to offer you some mystery if your teeth will ache too much without it. Highly recommended by Father! Forty dollars an hour, Father's forty dollars! Progress! Looking up! Looking better! That new haircut is so becoming, says Dr. Coronet herself, showing how normal she is for a woman with an I.Q. of 180 and many advanced degrees.

2. Mother. A lady in a brown suede coat. Boots of shiny black material, black gloves, a black fur hat. She would be humiliated could she know

that of all the people in the world it is my ex-lover Simon who walks most like her . . . self-conscious and unreal, listening to distant music, a little bowlegged with craftiness. . . .

3. Father. Tying a necktie. In a hurry. On my first evening home he put his hand on my arm and said, "Honey, we're going to forget all about this."

4. Simon. Outside, a plane is crossing the sky, in here we're in a hurry. Morning. It must be morning. The girl is half out of her mind, whimpering and vague; Simon her dear friend is wretched this morning . . . he is wretched with morning itself . . . he forces her to give him an injection with that needle she knows is filthy, she had a dread of needles and surgical instruments and the odor of things that are to be sent into the blood, thinking somehow of her father. . . . This is a bad morning, Simon says that his mind is being twisted out of shape, and so he submits to the needle that he usually scorns and bites his lip with his yellowish teeth, his face going very pale. *Ah baby!* he says in his soft mocking voice, which with all women is a mockery of love, *do it like this—Slowly—*And the girl, terrified, almost drops the precious needle but manages to turn it up to the light from the window . . . is it an extension of herself then? She can give him this gift then? *I wish you wouldn't do this to me,* she says, wise in her terror, because it seems to her that Simon's danger—in a few minutes he may be dead—is a way of pressing her against him that is more powerful than any other embrace. She has to work over his arm, the knotted corded veins of his arm, her forehead wet with perspiration as she pushes and releases the needle, staring at that mixture of liquid now stained with Simon's bright blood. . . . When the drug hits him she can feel it herself, she feels that magic that is more than any woman can give him, striking the back of his head and making his face stretch as if with the impact of a terrible sun. . . . She tries to embrace him but he pushes her aside and stumbles to his feet. *Jesus Christ,* he says. . . .

5. Princess, a Negro girl of eighteen. What is her charge? She is closed-mouthed about it, shrewd and silent, you know that no one had to wrestle her to the sidewalk to get her in here; she came with dignity. In the recreation room she sits reading *Nancy Drew and the Jewel Box Mystery,* which inspires in her face tiny wrinkles of alarm and interest: what a face! Light brown skin, heavy shaded eyes, heavy eyelashes, a serious sinister dark brow, graceful fingers, graceful wristbones, graceful legs, lips, tongue, a

sugar-sweet voice, a leggy stride more masculine than Simon's and my mother's, decked out in a dirty white blouse and dirty white slacks; vaguely nautical is Princess' style. . . . At breakfast she is in charge of clearing the table and leans over me, saying, *Honey you sure you ate enough?*

6. The girl lies sleepless, wondering. Why here, why not there? Why Bloomfield Hills and not jail? Why jail and not her pink room? Why downtown Detroit and not Sioux Drive? What is the difference? Is Simon all the difference? The girl's head is a parade of wonders. She is nearly sixteen, her breath is marvelous with wonders, not long ago she was coloring with crayons and now she is smearing the landscape with paints that won't come off and won't come off her fingers either. She says to the matron *I am not talking about anything,* not because everyone has warned her not to talk but because, because she will not talk; because she won't say anything about Simon, who is her secret. And she says to the matron, *I won't go home,* up until that night in the lavatory when everything was changed. . . . "No, I won't go home I want to stay here," she says, listening to her own words with amazement, thinking that weeds might climb everywhere over that marvelous $180,000 house and dinosaurs might return to muddy the beige carpeting, but never never will she reconcile four o'clock in the morning in Detroit with eight o'clock breakfasts in Bloomfield Hills. . . . oh, she aches still for Simon's hands and his caressing breath, though he gave her little pleasure, he took everything from her (five-dollar bills, ten-dollar bills, passed into her numb hands by men and taken out of her hands by Simon) until she herself was passed into the hands of other men, police, when Simon evidently got tired of her and her hysteria. . . . *No, I won't go home, I don't want to be bailed out.* The girl thinks as a *Stubborn and Wayward Child* (one of several charges lodged against her), and the matron understands her crazy white-rimmed eyes that are seeking out some new violence that will keep her in jail, should someone threaten to let her out. Such children try to strangle the matrons, the attendants, or one another . . . they want the locks locked forever, the doors nailed shut . . . and this girl is no different up until that night her mind is changed for her. . . .

IX   THAT NIGHT

Princess and Dolly, a little white girl of maybe fifteen, hardy however as a sergeant and in the House of Correction for armed robbery, corner her in the lavatory at the farthest sink and the other girls look away and file out to bed, leaving her. God, how she is beaten up! Why is she beaten up? Why do they pound her, why such hatred? Princess vents all the hatred of a thousand silent Detroit winters on her body, this girl whose body belongs to me, fiercely she rides across the Midwestern plains on this girl's tender bruised body . . . revenge on the oppressed minorities of America! revenge on the slaughtered Indians! revenge on the female sex, on the male sex, revenge on Bloomfield Hills, revenge revenge. . . .

X DETROIT

In Detroit, weather weighs heavily upon everyone. The sky looms large. The horizon shimmers in smoke. Downtown the buildings are imprecise in the haze. Perpetual haze. Perpetual motion inside the haze. Across the choppy river is the city of Windsor, in Canada. Part of the continent has bunched up here and is bulging outward, at the tip of Detroit; a cold hard rain is forever falling on the expressways. . . . Shoppers shop grimly, their cars are not parked in safe places, their windshields may be smashed and graceful ebony hands may drag them out through their shatterproof smashed windshields, crying, *Revenge for the Indians!* Ah, they all fear leaving Hudson's and being dragged to the very tip of the city and thrown off the parking roof of Cobo Hall, that expensive tomb, into the river. . . .

XI CHARACTERS WE ARE
FOREVER ENTWINED WITH

1. Simon drew me into his tender rotting arms and breathed gravity into me. Then I came to earth, weighed down. He said, *You are such a little girl,* and he weighed me down with his delight. In the palms of his hands were teeth marks from his previous life experiences. He was thirty-five, they said. Imagine Simon in this room, in my pink room: he is about six feet tall and stoops slightly, in a feline cautious way, always thinking, always on guard, with his scuffed light suede shoes and his clothes that are anyone's clothes, slightly rumpled ordinary clothes that ordinary men might wear to not-bad jobs. Simon has fair long hair, curly hair, spent languid curls that are like . . . exactly like the curls of wood shavings to the touch, I am trying to be exact . . . and he smells of unheated mornings and coffee and too many pills coating his tongue with a faint green-white scum. . . . Dear Simon, who would be panicked in this room and in this house (right now Billie ·is vacuuming next door in my parents' room; a vacuum cleaner's roar is a sign of all good things), Simon who is

said to have come from a home not much different from this, years ago, fleeing all the carpeting and the polished banisters . . . Simon has a deathly face, only desperate people fall in love with it. His face is bony and cautious, the bones of his cheeks prominent as if with the rigidity of his ceaseless thinking, plotting, for he has to make money out of girls to whom money means nothing, they're so far gone they can hardly count it, and in a sense money means nothing to him either except as a way of keeping on with his life. *Each Day's Proud Struggle,* the title of a novel we could read at jail. . . . Each day he needs a certain amount of money. He devours it. It wasn't love he uncoiled in me with his hollowed-out eyes and his courteous smile, that remnant of a prosperous past, but a dark terror that needed to press itself flat against him, or against another man . . . but he was the first, he came over to me and took my arm, a claim. We struggled on the stairs and I said, *Let me loose, you're hurting my neck, my face,* it was such a surprise that my skin hurt where he rubbed it, and afterward we lay face to face and he breathed everything into me. In the end I think he turned me in.

2. Raymond Forrest. I just read this morning that Raymond Forrest's father, the chairman of the board at ———, died of a heart attack on a plane bound for London. I would like to write Raymond Forrest a note of sympathy. I would like to thank him for not pressing charges against me one hundred years ago, saving me, being so generous . . . well, men like Raymond Forrest are generous men, not like Simon. I would like to write him a letter telling of my love, or of some other emotion that is positive and healthy. Not like Simon and his poetry, which he scrawled down when he was high and never changed a word . . . but when I try to think of something to say, it is Simon's language that comes back to me, caught in my head like a bad song, it is always Simon's language:

> *There is no reality only dreams*
> *Your neck may get snapped when you wake*
> *My love is drawn to some violent end*
> *She keeps wanting to get away*
> *My love is heading downward*
> *And I am heading upward*
> *She is going to crash on the sidewalk*
> *And I am going to dissolve into the clouds*

XII EVENTS

1. Out of the hospital, bruised and saddened and converted, with Princess' grunts still tangled in my hair . . . and Father in his overcoat, looking like a prince himself, come to carry me off. Up the expressway and out north to home. Jesus Christ, but the air is thinner and cleaner here. Monumental houses. Heartbreaking sidewalks, so clean.

2. Weeping in the living room. The ceiling is two stories high and two chandeliers hang from it. Weeping, weeping, though Billie the maid is *probably listening*. I will never leave home again. Never. Never leave home. Never leave this home again, never.

3. Sugar doughnuts for breakfast. The toaster is very shiny and my face is distorted in it. Is that my face?

4. The car is turning in the driveway. Father brings me home. Mother embraces me. Sunlight breaks in movieland patches on the roof of our traditional-contemporary home, which was designed for the famous automotive stylist whose identity, if I told you the name of the famous car he designed, you would all know, so I can't tell you because my teeth chatter at the thought of being sued . . . or having someone climb into my bedroom window with a rope to strangle me. . . . The car turns up the blacktop drive. The house opens to me like a doll's house, so lovely in the sunlight, the big living room beckons to me with its walls falling away in a delirium of joy at my return, Billie the maid is *no doubt* listening from the kitchen as I burst into tears and the hysteria Simon got so sick of. Convulsed in Father's arms, I say I will never leave again, never, why did I leave, where did I go, what happened, my mind is gone wrong, my body is one big bruise, my backbone was sucked dry, it wasn't the men who hurt me and Simon never hurt me but only those girls . . . my God, how they hurt me . . . I will never leave home again. . . . The car is perpetually turning up the drive and I am perpetually breaking down in the living room and we are perpetually taking the right exit from the expressway (Lahser Road) and the wall of the rest room is perpetually banging against my head and perpetually are Simon's hands moving across my body and adding everything up and so too are Father's hands on my shaking bruised back, far from the surface of my skin on the surface of my good blue cashmere coat (dry-cleaned for my release). . . . I weep for all the money here, for God in gold and beige carpeting, for the beauty of chandeliers

488

and the miracle of a clean polished gleaming toaster and faucets that run both hot and cold water, and I tell them, *I will never leave home, this is my home, I love everything here, I am in love with everything here.* . . .

I am home.

REMEMBERING, KNOWING, AND TELLING IN JOYCE CAROL OATES

Philip Stevick

The controlling figure of speech in most of our thought about realistic fiction is the visual metaphor. In contrast, for example, to fiction that seems vague and suggestive, we speak of *photographic* realism; vague and suggestive fiction we easily describe as *sketchy,* as if it were a pencil drawing, or *impressionistic,* as if it were a painting by Monet. Highly particular, highly social passages in fiction we call *scenes;* figures of speech we call *images;* the angle from which a fiction is narrated we call its *point of view;* and for the placing of the materials of fiction in relation to each other we use such words as *foregrounding, foreshadowing, foreshortening,* words suggesting perspective painting. A novelist's philosophical assumptions, as those assumptions are realized in his fiction, we call his *view* of the world or his *vision.* And in a famous passage from the preface to *The Nigger of the Narcissus* Conrad writes, "My task which I am trying to achieve is, by the power of the written word to make you hear, to make you feel—it is, before all, to make you *see.*"

It is understandable that our discussions of fiction should so often seem to equate telling a story, or reading a story, with seeing: fiction ordinarily puts us in touch with the shape and texture of visual experience with a sustained intensity that distinguishes fiction from the poetic and discursive forms. Still, it is at best a partial truth, at worst a considerable distortion, to say that fiction is seeing. Susanne Langer, in *Feeling and Form,* writes that fiction, far from being a direct report of sensory experience, projects the "virtual memory." Fiction, that is, is not a straight recollection of experience but rather a sequence of events presented *as if* remembered. And so it is that Robinson Crusoe does not *see* Friday's footprint, as if he were an on-the-scene reporter of a news event; he *remembers* what it was to have seen it many years before. Even fiction that is told from an author's point of view, rather than from the recollection of a first-person narrator, customarily uses the past tense, along with all of the techniques of shaping and dramatizing, so as to give the illusion not of experience being seen but of experience being remembered and recreated in the mind.

We read fiction differently when we allow ourselves to understand fiction writing as an act of virtual memory. We are likely to think of our own problems in bringing the past together into any kind of coherent shape, of the odd and inaccessible corners of the mind out of which the memory must work, of the ways in which time in the memory differs from time by the clock and space in the memory from space by the yardstick. We may think of the Freudian defense mechanisms of repression and sublimation by means of which experience is transmuted in the memory, of the way in which values are altered in the mind, so that matters of great importance become gradually neutral in the memory while other matters, neutral of value when they happened, become charged with significance by the memory. In short, we are likely to think less of the observing eye rendering for us a direct impression of the world than we are of the processes of consciousness through which the world is filtered.

A writer who understands his fiction as an act of virtual memory and who wishes to make this aspect of his fiction prominent and self-conscious, such a writer has a number of different courses open to him. The most obvious and familiar of these is to show the narrator in the act of remembering: David Copperfield, in Charles Dickens's *David Copperfield,* works quite explicitly at times at trying to call up the past, sort it out, get it right, put it together. Then again, fiction can show us the act of recollection only very intermittently or only at the end: Stephen Daedalus, in James Joyce's *Portrait of the Artist as a Young Man,* has, at the end of the book, become a writer, the writer who has just recalled and set down the book we are finishing. Still another possibility is to move the locus of the fiction back into the very process by which the fiction is made: instead of writing a story in which the teller seems to have remembered well enough to get his story put together, what we have in this case is a presentation of some chunks of raw recollection, some gaps, some data, some dead ends, all of which might be titled "Notes Toward the Story of My Life If I Can Ever Get It All Pulled Together."

This particular kind of experiment is unusual before the twentieth century; the most brilliant and extended example from an earlier time is Laurence Sterne's *Tristram Shandy,* written about 1760. Although *Tristram Shandy* is an endlessly complicated and problematic book, one thing about it is clear: that part of its quite irresistible comedy comes from the narrator's inability to make the fragments of his memory come together. That part of the awful pathos of the book comes from the same source is equally clear.

Tristram Shandy suggests the intricate effects that may come from allowing the process of a fiction to stand in some way unformed, drawing us into the very making of the book as we read it. Not only are we drawn into the composition of the work, its acts of selection and arrangement, but we also experience a kind of intimate emotionality that is quite different from what we experience in a "finished" story. If a story is finished or achieved, the speaker or writer has given away as much of his privacy as he wishes to give away, defended himself against embarrassments, found the formulas for presenting himself to the world as he wishes to be seen. A work that is still in process leaves the speaker or writer open and vulnerable, and we are likely to feel the stress and pathos of his inner life with the same kind of mixed tenderness and discomfort we might find in reading another person's private diary. Sterne's book also suggests the difficulty of the enterprise: it is easy to put together fragments, but it is not easy to find the right tone, not easy to make the fragments seem authentic yet intelligible, not easy to sustain a work that, by its very nature, must lack conventional plot. Yet Sterne shows, in a rather pure and original form, esthetic motives that have become, despite the difficulty of executing them, highly characteristic of twentieth-century art: the juxtapositions and montages of film, the cutting and pasting of collage, the open and unresolved effect of much twentieth-century fiction and poetry. Joyce's *Portrait of the Artist as a Young Man* ends with scraps from a diary, and Eliot's *Waste Land* ends with cryptic fragments written in exotic languages.

Judged against the general possibilities of fiction, Joyce Carol Oates's "How I Contemplated the World . . ." is, in some respects, surprising; in other respects it is not surprising at all. Despite the interest of twentieth-century artists in fragmentary forms and the processes of the mind, it is surprising, all the same, to find a short fiction, of the length of a conventional short story, in which the process of working up fragments out of the memory is made so prominent that it affects the very shape of the work upon the page. The short story in the twentieth century has tended to be among the most conservative of arts. There is, however, nothing very obscure or problematic about the language of the story. The shape of the sentences, the pattern of the prose, is familiar and conventional. The style, moreover, is ordinary enough (although less ordinary as the fiction nears its end); the word choices and the figures of speech fall well within the range that we might easily expect of a mind not much different from our own—literate and fluent, curious and observant, occasionally fond of a certain rhetorical flashiness but never poised and rarely very elegant. It is odd and surprising, however, to find a short fiction that is so aggressively non-linear: the story is so discontinuous that some important connections we understand only gradually and some we never learn at all. (Still, for all of its oddity of arrangement, the world of the fiction is familiar—for many of us it is our own world, of decaying city and comfortable suburb.) It is also peculiar to find so thin and unrealized a sense of social intercourse as one finds in the story. Other people have a flat and shadowy existence. They do not really converse or participate in dialogue but, sometimes coming alive for only a brief scene, say ritual phrases and tend to move about rather like puppets. Yet the narrator herself is remarkably realized, a stable ego at the center of the fiction, with continuity, coherence, and substance—in short, a character.

The story, finally, is unusual in the special kind of intensity it contains. Classic short fiction cultivates a number of devices that allow a story, short though it be, to figure forth the larger world—such devices as metaphor and symbol, irony and verbal indirection, allusion, and rhythmic patterning of various kinds. There is not much in Oates's story that can be called symbolic, not much that seems to insist upon thematic significance, not much of any of the classic techniques by which short fiction gains the intensity that forces us to consider it a compressed representation of large patterns of meaning. Thus the story has an unusual kind of starkness and literalness for short fiction that aspires to a degree of artistic seriousness. Yet for all its stark avoidance of the usual techniques of compression, the story is remarkably intense all the same. How it manages to represent discontinuous scraps from the memory, while avoiding many of the classic techniques of fictional art, yet manages also to be as intense and powerful as it is, is perhaps the most interesting question one can ask of the story.

II

When we begin poking around in our memories, what we find depends largely upon what we are looking for. If a psychiatrist asks us about our first day at school, if a prosecuting attorney asks us our whereabouts on a certain day, if a parent asks if we remember a childhood trip to Niagara Falls, then these are what we remember. To a remarkable extent, moreover, the very form of our recollection depends upon the formal expectations we carry in our minds as we begin exploring our memories. If we are telling an episode from our past in a social situation and would like the remembered episode to be highly dramatic, we remember it as being highly dramatic, though it may not have been so when it happened. If we are relating an episode from the past to an audience skeptical about whether the episode happened, we call up details and intricacies to persuade our audience that our recollection is accurate. If we begin to recollect in a mood of self-pity, then we heighten those elements from our past in which we were most buffeted by life. Above all, if we plan to write our recollections, the form our prose is going to take governs the very shape of the materials we bring up out of our memories. If we know that what we are going to write is a diary entry, then we set about remembering things that are different from those we remember if we know the work is to be a detailed, self-justifying autobiography for the largest possible audience.

"How I Contemplated . . ." consists of notes for an English-class essay (although as it proceeds it grows and changes into something more than this), an occasion that is both one of the most strained and artificial of writing situations as well as one of the most open and confidential. It is an artificial situation because in it one must attend to matters of form and structure, spelling and punctuation, word choice and rhetorical effect, all with a kind of nervous concentration that exists in few other kinds of communication. On the other hand, in such an essay one is encouraged ordinarily to write about one's self, to give shape and coherence to one's own experience, in a sense to "confess," and the relation between one's revealed self and the teacher, who is ordinarily one's only reader, is often as sacred and confidential as that of lawyer and client, psychiatrist and patient, priest and confessor. So it is that "How I Contemplated . . ." seems to vary from a tough defensiveness ("In this city the weather changes abruptly. . . . He sleeps through the afternoon. He sleeps through the morning.") to a pathetic vulnerability at the end. So it is that the story seems at times an exercise, with its carefully recalled descriptions laid out in a spirit of breezy self-confidence, and at times an authentic confession, recollected with difficulty and written in a crabbed, elliptical prose.

What is most obvious about the writing, of course, is that it is divided into sections and numbered, indicating in some general way a quest for order and shape and suggesting more specifically the form of the outline, that dreary form in which English compositions are supposed to be cast if they are to make sense when finished. The headings, numbers, and fragmentary effects look, at first glance, as if they were devices used to give an experimental gloss to the story. On the contrary, what they do is provide a necessary form for what has to get said. And the key to the necessity for form lies in the qualitative differences between the sections.

The sense of self, for example, shifts quite markedly from one section to another. In one section, the narrator will speak of "the girl," as if she were writing a fiction about someone else; in another section, she will write about "my mother," making explicit what we know all along—that the subject of the story is not "the girl" but "I"—and varying the distance of the narration from intense self-involvement to self-detachment. The style, as well, changes from section to section. At times the diction has a schoolgirl quality about it: elements of experience are "excellent" or "marvelous" or "magnificent." Often this wide-eyed quality seems to be ironic, the narrator's way of telling us that she is *not* impressed. Just as often, it seems not ironic at all, and the schoolgirl prose suggests that she is impressed, with a perfectly authentic naiveté. Yet there is nothing of that schoolgirl ingenuousness, for example, about the section that begins "5. Princess, a Negro girl of eighteen." The qualitative difference between the sections is most noticeable in the plain bulk of the paragraphs. "World Events," the narrator writes. And it is a peculiar, ambiguous heading: does she really expect to be able to provide a kind of global setting for her own personal drama? does she think her teacher would wish her to, if she could? In any case, nothing comes to her mind. And the effect upon the reader is potentially quite haunting, for he sees the narrator invent a heading under which nothing can be arranged, a box into which nothing can fit, a class of which there are no members. Yet a few lines later, the narrator recalls the details of Sioux Drive with a concreteness and plenitude that become obsessive as the description goes on, a vehicle for her contempt for the sheer abundance of her suburban culture.

In several of the sections the texture of the writing suggests the outer limits of the natural world, an area of magical metamorphoses. Can a person be boiled into grease, she wonders, noticing a smudge of grease from her forehead? Can a squirrel be split in two by a Lincoln? Simon imagines himself to be Huckleberry Finn and Roderick Usher; Clarita is transformed, at the movies, into Robert Cummings' secretary or Claudette Colbert. The blowing dirt of Detroit is imagined evidence that Detroit is breaking up into little pieces. All of these incidental images relate, of course, to the central metamorphosis of the story, the understandable but unexplainable transformation of suburban daughter into shoplifter, runaway, institutional delinquent, whore, and suburban daughter once again. Yet the prevailing reality of the story, in most of the sections, is finally not magical but all too natural. And the human limitations are figured forth by the plain descriptive details out of which so much of the story is made.

"Words pour out of me and won't stop. I want to tell everything," writes the narrator, and a few lines later, "Do I really remember that or am I piecing it together from what they told me?" So it is that the story is less about a group of events than about remembering those events, finding words for them, fitting them together. We are always entitled to ask of a work that comes to us as unconnected fragments why we should be forced to expend the extra effort to read something that does not give the appearance of being fully achieved. In the case of "How I Contemplated . . ." the answer is obvious. In its fragments lies its truth. By joining together, without really joining together, what is understood and what is not, what is remembered and what is almost forgotten, what can be contemplated only with scorn and what can be recalled with joy, what can be formed and shaped by the mind and what can only remain formless, the story succeeds both in reporting with great power the process of trying to know the self and in drawing the reader into that process.

A fiction made with bits and scraps of the memory need not end; most likely it will merely stop. For how can the process of consciousness and the effort of recollection ever really come to an end, short of death? If we imagine ourselves lying on the psychiatrist's couch, trying to dredge up our significant past, we know that the hour ends not when we succeed in finding a suitable conclusion but when the analyst says, "I'm sorry but I'm afraid our time is up for today." "How I Contemplated . . . ," however, does end, and that ending is likely to be moving for some readers, troublesome for others.

Most American fiction moves toward an ending that is alienated and self-assertive, not integrative but individualistic. Characters in American fiction tend to rebel, break loose, go it alone—like Huck Finn, to "light out for the territory." They tend not to come home, get married, settle down, make their peace with the domestic virtues and the prevailing cultural assumptions. But the narrator of "How I Contemplated . . ." does come home, and, however contradictory her emotions, it is clear that in some quite powerful sense she is sorry she left and glad to be back. When a serious fiction, especially one that strikes us as being audacious and unusual, ends with a homecoming heavily charged with such emotions as these, it invites us to respond to that ending, as if it were asking us to take a dare. Having been encouraged to feel the narrator's scorn for the shallow opulence of her suburban world, shall we now understand the ending as a symbolic statement of reconciliation to the cashmere and chrome of Bloomfield Hills?

It is, in fact, the power of the story that it can make us assent to a resolution that is neither very fashionable nor very traditional. Recall that the story purports to tell us a very limited range of truth, all located within the virtual memory of the narrator. Nothing in the ending need be construed as meaning that all is well in Bloomfield Hills. What the story, finally, can be seen to contain is the experience of some days, not many, and some pages, a dozen or so, in which the narrator has learned, with difficulty, that comfort is better than pain, civility is better than rudeness, health is better than illness, warmth is better than cold, soft is better than hard, clean is better than dirty. Father strokes her back by stroking her cashmere coat while Simon strokes her body. The first is remote, the second direct. But who is to say that the first, with its decency, its comfort, and its quite real love is inferior to the second, with its pain, its exploitation, and its brutishness?

Q U E S T I O N S

How I Contemplated the World from the Detroit House of Correction and Began My Life Over Again

POINT OF VIEW 1. Comment on the effect of the dramatized narrator's referring to herself alternately in the first person and the third person. When in the story do the switches in person occur? Can you find any logic behind this "illogical" use of pronouns? 2. Were Joyce Carol Oates to violate narrative perspective and offer the reader other points of view (such as the father's or Simon's), how would the reader's relationship to the narrator be changed by this widening of perspective?

CHARACTERS 3. Although flat and imperfectly realized, the minor characters are each, in his own way, important to understanding the narrator's state of mind. Explain this view by citing qualities of the narrator that are represented by one or more of the minor characters. 4. Raymond Forrest is never a direct participant in the action of the story but is, nonetheless, very important to the story's meaning. Explain. 5. Describe the relationships between: Clarita and Simon; Clarita and the narrator; Dr. Isabel Coronet and the narrator; and Princess and the narrator.

PLOT 6. Although events, as described by the narrator, move back and forth in time and place, these same events—unscrambled and put into

497

chronological order—can be construed as encompassing the five stages of a conventional plot: exposition, rising action, turning point, falling action, and resolution. Explain. 7. Would you describe this story as having a happy ending? Why or why not?

SETTING 8. The narrator's description of Bloomfield Hills is very particularized; we are given specific information about her room, parents' house, neighborhood, and so on. The descriptions of Detroit, on the other hand, are largely unspecific. Find examples to support this observation, and explain the effect of these different modes of description on the story's meaning.

STYLE 9. As the essay contends, "the process of working up fragments out of the memory is made so prominent that it affects the very shape of the work upon the page." Explain this statement in view of the contention that technique is meaning. 10. Examine the narrator's diction. Is her word choice appropriate to her age, social class, and education? Is her language consistent? 11. Joyce Carol Oates makes us aware that some headings in the narrator's outline are meaningless to the protagonist— that they are a formality she acknowledges as part of a well-rounded essay. What are these headings? What is the effect of including them in the story? 12. Discuss the function of irony in this story.

TONE 13. Do you find yourself sympathetic to the protagonist? Why or why not? 14. Even though the outline form makes clear that the essay is unfinished, the reader knows that Oates has finished her story; that it is the narrator, and not the author, who lacks control. Examine the implications of this discrepancy between narrator and author. In your opinion, what is the author's attitude toward her subject? What is your concept of the implied author as a result of the "core of norms and choices" in the narrative?

Remembering, Knowing, and Telling in Joyce Carol Oates

FOCUS 1. In what ways does the title of the essay suggest the author's thesis? 2. Discuss the paragraph in Part II that, in your opinion, best expresses the essay's controlling idea.

ORGANIZATION 3. Do you feel that the introductory material in Part I provides background information essential to your understanding of the essay as a whole? Explain. If you think that some of this information could be deleted, what would you omit? 4. How does the first paragraph of Part II relate to the remainder of the section? to the essay as a whole?

USING THE EVIDENCE   5. The essay contends that there is "nothing very obscure or problematic about the language of the story. The shape of the sentences, the pattern of the prose, is familiar and conventional." What evidence can you find in the story to support this contention?   6. What portions of the story support the observation that "the story is so discontinuous that some important connections we understand only gradually and some we never learn at all"?

STYLE   7. The essay alludes to various novels: *The Nigger of the Narcissus, Robinson Crusoe, David Copperfield, A Portrait of the Artist as a Young Man, Tristram Shandy,* and *Huckleberry Finn.* Do you find these references helpful or unhelpful? Explain.   8. The essay contains many examples of parallel structure (for instance, "Still, it is at best a partial truth, at worst a considerable distortion, to say that fiction is seeing"). Find other examples of parallelism. What is the effect of this stylistic device on the reader?

MAKING LITERARY JUDGMENTS   9. By stating that it is unusual "to find so thin and unrealized a sense of social intercourse as one finds in this story," the essay implies that most fiction concerns itself with a fully realized sense of social intercourse. Do you agree? Support your answer with references to other stories you have read in this collection.   10. The essayist remarks on the scarcity of "classic techniques by which short fiction gains the intensity that forces us to consider it a compressed representation of large patterns of meaning." He finds the story's "starkness and literalness" unusual for "short fiction that aspires to a degree of artistic seriousness." Do you agree that metaphor, symbol, irony, allusion, and rhythmic patterning give short fiction its special intensity? Do you find these devices absent in this story?   11. Do you agree with the essayist's assertion that, unlike "How I Contemplated . . . ," most American works of fiction have endings that are "alienated and self-assertive, not integrative but individualistic"? Support your answer with references to stories in this collection.

ACCOMPLISHED DESIRES

There was a man she loved with a violent love, and she spent much of her time thinking about his wife.

No shame to it, she actually followed the wife. She followed her to Peabody's Market, which was a small, dark, crowded store, and she stood in silence on the pavement as the woman appeared again and got into her station wagon and drove off. The girl, Dorie, would stand as if paralyzed, and even her long fine blond hair seemed paralyzed with thought—her heart pounded as if it too was thinking, planning—and then she would turn abruptly as if executing one of the steps in her modern dance class and cross through Peabody's alley and out to the Elks' Club parking lot and so up toward the campus, where the station wagon was bound.

Hardly had the station wagon pulled into the driveway when Dorie, out of breath, appeared a few houses down and watched. How that woman got out of her car!—you could see the flabby expanse of her upper leg, white flesh that should never be exposed, and then she turned and leaned in, probably with a grunt, to get shopping bags out of the back seat. Two of her children ran out to meet her, without coats or jackets. They had nervous, darting bodies—Dorie felt sorry for them—and their mother rose, straightening, a stout woman in a colorless coat, either scolding them or teasing them, one bag in either muscular arm—and so—so the mother and children went into the house and Dorie stood with nothing to stare at except the battered station wagon, and the small snowy wilderness that was the Arbers' front yard, and the house itself. It was a large, ugly, peeling Victorian home in a block of similar homes, most of which had been fixed up by the faculty members who rented them. Dorie, who had something of her own mother's shrewd eye for hopeless, cast-off things, believed that the house could be remodeled and made presentable—but as long as he remained married to *that woman* it would be slovenly and peeling and ugly.

She loved that woman's husband with a fierce love that was itself a little ugly. Always a rather stealthy girl, thought to be simply quiet, she had entered his life by no accident—had not appeared in his class by accident—but every step of her career, like every outfit she wore and every expression on her face, was planned and shrewd and desperate. Before her twenties she had not thought much about herself; now she thought about herself continuously. She was leggy, long-armed, slender, and had a startled look—but the look was stylized now, and attractive. Her face was denuded of make-up and across her soft skin a galaxy of freckles glowed with health. She looked like a girl about to bound onto the tennis courts—and she did play tennis, though awkwardly. She played tennis with *him*. But so confused with love was she that the game of tennis, the relentless slamming of the ball back and forth, had seemed to her a disguise for something else, the way everything in poetry or literature was a disguise for something else—for love?—and surely he must know, or didn't he know? Didn't he guess? There were many other girls he played tennis with, so that was nothing special, and her mind worked and worked while she should have slept, planning with the desperation of youth that has never actually been young—planning how to get him, how to get him, for it seemed to her that she would never be able to overcome her desire for this man.

The wife was as formidable as the husband. She wrote narrow volumes of poetry Dorie could not understand and he, the famous husband, wrote novels and critical pieces. The wife was a big, energetic, high-colored woman; the husband, Mark Arber, was about her size though not so high-colored—his complexion was rather putty-colored, rather melancholy. Dorie thought about the two of them all the time, awake or asleep, and she could feel the terrible sensation of blood flowing through her body, a flowing of desire that was not just for the man but somehow for the woman as well, a desire for her accomplishments, her fame, her children, her ugly house, her ugly body, her very life. She had light, frank blue eyes and people whispered that she drank; Dorie never spoke of her.

The college was a girls' college, exclusive and expensive, and every girl who remained there for more than a year understood a peculiar, even freakish kinship with the place—as if she had always been there and the other girls, so like herself with their sleepy unmade-up faces, the skis in winter and the bicycles in good weather, the excellent expensive professors, and the excellent air—everything, everything had always been there, had existed for centuries. They were stylish and liberal in their cashmere sweaters with soiled necks; their fingers were stained with ballpoint ink; and like them, Dorie understood that most of the world was wretched and would never come to this college, never, would be kept back from it by armies of helmeted men. She, Dorie Weinheimer, was not wretched but supremely fortunate, and she must be grateful always for her good luck, for there was no justification for her existence any more than there was any justification for the wretched lots of the world's poor. And there would flash to her mind's eye a confused picture of dark-faced starving mobs, or emaciated faces out of an old-fashioned Auschwitz photograph, or something—some dreary horror from the *New York Times'* one hundred neediest cases in the Christmas issue— She had, in the girls' soft, persistent manner, an idealism-turned-pragmatism under the influence of the college faculty, who had all been idealists at Harvard and Yale as undergraduates but who were now in their forties, and as impatient with normative values as they were with their students' occasional lockets-shaped-into-crosses; Mark Arber was the most disillusioned and the most eloquent of the Harvard men.

In class he sat at the head of the seminar table, leaning back in his leather-covered chair. He was a rather stout man. He had played football once in a past Dorie could not quite imagine, though she wanted to imagine it, and he had been in the war—one of the wars—she believed it had been World War II. He had an ugly, arrogant face and discolored teeth. He read poetry in a raspy, hissing, angry voice. "Like Marx, I believe that poetry has had enough of love; the hell with it. Poetry should now cultivate the whip," he would say grimly, and Dorie would stare at him to see if he was serious. There were four senior girls in this class and they sometimes asked him questions or made observations of their own, but there was no consistency in his reaction. Sometimes he seemed not to hear, sometimes he nodded enthusiastically and indifferently, sometimes he opened his eyes and looked at them, not distinguishing among them, and said: "A remark like that is quite characteristic." So she sat and stared at him and her heart seemed to turn to stone, wanting him, hating his wife and envying her violently, and the being that had been Dorie Weinheimer for twenty-one years changed gradually through the winter into another being, obsessed with jealousy. She did not know what she wanted most, this man or the victory over his wife.

She was always bringing poems to him in his office. She borrowed books from him and puzzled over every annotation of his. As he talked to her he picked at his fingernails, settled back in his chair, and he talked on in his rushed, veering, sloppy manner, as if Dorie did not exist or were a crowd, or a few intimate friends, it hardly mattered, as he raved about frauds in contemporary poetry, naming names, "that bastard with his sonnets," "that cow with her daughter-poems," and getting so angry that Dorie wanted to protest, no, no, why are you angry? Be gentle. Love me and be gentle.

When he failed to come to class six or seven times that winter the girls were all understanding. "Do you think he really is a genius?" they asked. His look of disintegrating, decomposing recklessness, his shiny suit and bizarre loafer shoes, his flights of language made him so different from their own fathers that it was probable he was a genius; these were girls who believed seriously in the existence of geniuses. They had been trained by their highly paid, verbose professors to be vaguely ashamed of themselves, to be silent about any I.Q. rated under 160, to be uncertain about their talents within the school and quite confident of them outside it— and Dorie, who had no talent and only adequate intelligence, was always silent about herself. Her talent perhaps lay in her faithfulness to an obsession, her cunning patience, her smile, her bared teeth that were a child's teeth and yet quite sharp. . . .

One day Dorie had been waiting in Dr. Arber's office for an hour, with some new poems for him. He was late but he strode into the office as if he had been hurrying all along, sitting heavily in the creaking swivel chair, panting; he looked a little mad. He was the author of many reviews in New York magazines and papers and in particular the author of three short, frightening novels, and now he had a burned-out, bleached-out look. Like any of the girls at this college, Dorie would have sat politely if one of her professors set fire to himself, and so she ignored his peculiar stare and began her rehearsed speech about—but what did it matter what it was about? The poems of Emily Dickinson or the terrible yearning of Shelley or her own terrible lust, what did it matter?

He let his hand fall onto hers by accident. She stared at the hand, which was like a piece of meat—and she stared at him and was quite still. She was pert and long-haired, in the chair facing him, an anonymous student and a minor famous man, and every wrinkle of his sagging, impatient face was bared to her in the winter sunlight from the window—and every thread of blood in his eyes—and quite calmly and politely she said, "I guess I should tell you, Dr. Arber, that I'm in love with you. I've felt that way for some time."

"You what, you're what?" he said. He gripped her feeble hand as if clasping it in a handshake. "What did you say?" He spoke with an amazed, slightly irritated urgency, and so it began.

II

His wife wrote her poetry under an earlier name, Barbara Scott. Many years before she had had a third name, a maiden name—Barbara Cameron —but it belonged to another era about which she never thought except under examination from her analyst. She had a place cleared in the dirty attic of her house and she liked to sit up there, away from the children, and look out the small octagon of a window, and think. People she saw from her attic window looked bizarre and helpless to her. She herself was a hefty, perspiring woman, and all her dresses—especially her expensive ones—were stained under the arms with great lemon-colored half-moons no dry cleaner could remove. Because she was so large a woman, she was quick to see imperfections in others, as if she used a magnifying glass. Walking by her window on an ordinary morning were an aged tottering woman, an enormous Negro woman—probably someone's cleaning lady— and a girl from the college on aluminum crutches, poor brave thing, and the white-blond child from up the street who was precocious and demonic. Her own children were precocious and only slightly troublesome. Now two of them were safe in school and the youngest, the three-year-old, was asleep somewhere.

Barbara Scott had won the Pulitzer Prize not long before with an intricate sonnet series that dealt with the "voices" of many people; her energetic, coy line was much imitated. This morning she began a poem that her agent was to sell, after Barbara's death, to the *New Yorker*:

> *What awful wrath*
> *what terrible betrayal*
> *and these aluminum crutches, rubber-tipped. . . .*

She had such a natural talent that she let words take her anywhere. Her decade of psychoanalysis had trained her to hold nothing back; even when she had nothing to say, the very authority of her technique carried her on. So she sat that morning at her big, nicked desk—over the years the children had marred it with sharp toys—and stared out the window and waited for more inspiration. She felt the most intense kind of sympathy when she saw someone deformed—she was anxious, in a way, to see deformed people because it released such charity in her. But apart from the girl on the crutches she saw nothing much. Hours passed and she realized that her husband had not come home; already school was out and her two boys were running across the lawn.

When she descended the two flights of stairs to the kitchen, she saw that the three-year-old, Geoffrey, had opened a white plastic bottle of ammonia and had spilled it on the floor and on himself; the stench was sickening. The two older boys bounded in the back door as if spurred on by the argument that raged between them, and Barbara whirled upon them and began screaming. The ammonia had spilled onto her slacks. The boys ran into the front room and she remained in the kitchen, screaming. She sat down heavily on one of the kitchen chairs. After half an hour she came to herself and tried to analyze the situation. Did she hate these children, or did she hate herself? Did she hate Mark? Or was her hysteria a form of love, or was it both love and hate together . . . ? She put the ammonia away and made herself a drink.

When she went into the front room she saw that the boys were playing with their mechanical inventors' toys and had forgotten about her. Good. They were self-reliant. Slight, cunning children, all of them dark like Mark and prematurely aged, as if by the burden of their prodigious intelligences, they were not always predictable: they forgot things, lost things, lied about things, broke things, tripped over themselves and each other, mimicked classmates, teachers, and their parents, and often broke down into pointless tears. And yet sometimes they did not break down into tears when Barbara punished them, as if to challenge her. She did not always know what she had given birth to: they were so remote, even in their struggles and assaults, they were so fictional, as if she had imagined them herself. It had been she who'd imagined them, not Mark. Their father had no time. He was always in a hurry, he had three aged typewriters in his study and paper in each one, an article or a review or even a novel in progress in each of the machines, and he had no time for the children except to nod grimly at them or tell them to be quiet. He had been so precocious himself, Mark Arber, that after his first, successful novel at the age of

twenty-four he had had to whip from place to place, from typewriter to
typewriter, in a frantic attempt to keep up with—he called it keeping up
with his "other self," his "real self," evidently a kind of alter ego who was
always typing and creating, unlike the real Mark Arber. The real Mark
Arber was now forty-five and he had made the transition from "promis-
ing" to "established" without anything in between, like most middle-aged
critics of prominence.

Strachey, the five-year-old, had built a small machine that was both a
man and an automobile, operated by the motor that came with the set of
toys. "This is a modern centaur," he said wisely, and Barbara filed that
away, thinking perhaps it would do well in a poem for a popular, slick
magazine. . . . She sat, unbidden, and watched her boys' intense work with
the girders and screws and bolts, and sluggishly she thought of making
supper, or calling Mark at school to see what had happened . . . that morning he had left the house in a rage and when she went into his study, prim
and frowning, she had discovered four or five crumpled papers in his wastebasket. It was all he had accomplished that week.

Mark had never won the Pulitzer Prize for anything. People who knew
him spoke of his slump, familiarly and sadly; if they disliked Mark they
praised Barbara, and if they disliked Barbara they praised Mark. They
were "established" but it did not mean much, younger writers were being
discovered all the time who had been born in the mid- or late-forties,
strangely young, terrifyingly young, and people the Arbers' age were being crowded out, hustled toward the exits. . . . Being "established" should
have pleased them, but instead it led them to long spiteful bouts of eating
and drinking in the perpetual New England winter.

She made another drink and fell asleep in the chair. Sometime later her
children's fighting woke her and she said, "Shut up," and they obeyed at
once. They were playing in the darkened living room, down at the other
end by the big brick fireplace that was never used. Her head ached. She
got to her feet and went out to make another drink.

Around one o'clock Mark came in the back door. He stumbled and put
the light on. Barbara, in her plaid bathrobe, was sitting at the kitchen
table. She had a smooth, shiny, bovine face, heavy with fatigue. Mark said,
"What the hell are you doing here?"

She attempted a shrug of her shoulders. Mark stared at her. "I'm getting
you a housekeeper," he said. "You need more time for yourself, for your
work. For your work," he said, twisting his mouth at the word to show what
he thought of it. "You shouldn't neglect your poetry so we're getting in a
housekeeper, not to do any heavy work, just to sort of watch things—in

other words—a kind of external consciousness. You should be freed from ordinary considerations."

He was not drunk but he had the appearance of having been drunk, hours before, and now his words were muddled and dignified with the air of words spoken too early in the morning. He wore a dirty tweed overcoat, the same coat he'd had when they were married, and his necktie had been pulled off and stuffed somewhere, and his puffy, red face looked mean. Barbara thought of how reality was too violent for poetry and how poetry, and the language itself, shimmered helplessly before the confrontation with living people and their demands. "The housekeeper is here. She's outside," Mark said. "I'll go get her."

He returned with a college girl who looked like a hundred other college girls. "This is Dorie, this is my wife Barbara, you've met no doubt at some school event, here you are," Mark said. He was carrying a suitcase that must have belonged to the girl. "Dorie has requested room and board with a faculty family. The Dean of Women arranged it. Dorie will babysit or something—we can put her in the spare room. Let's take her up."

Barbara had not yet moved. The girl was pale and distraught; she looked about sixteen. Her hair was disheveled. She stared at Barbara and seemed about to speak.

"Let's take her up, you want to sit there all night?" Mark snarled.

Barbara indicated with a motion of her hand that they should go up without her. Mark, breathing heavily, stomped up the back steps and the girl followed at once. There was no indication of her presence because her footsteps were far too light on the stairs. She said nothing, and only a slight change in the odor of the kitchen indicated something new—a scent of cologne, hair scrubbed clean, a scent of panic. Barbara sat listening to her heart thud heavily inside her and she recalled how, several years before, Mark had left her and had turned up at a friend's apartment in Chicago— he'd been beaten up by someone on the street, an accidental event—and how he had blackened her eye once in an argument over the worth of Samuel Richardson, and how—there were many other bitter memories—and of course there had been other women, some secret and some known—and now this—

So she sat thinking with a small smile of how she would have to dismiss this when she reported it to their friends: *Mark has had this terrible block for a year now, with his novel, and so . . .*

She sat for a while running through phrases and explanations, and when she climbed up the stairs to bed she was grimly surprised to see him in their bedroom, asleep, his mouth open and his breath raspy and exhausted. At the back of the house, in a small oddly shaped maid's room, slept the girl; in their big dormer room slept the three boys, or perhaps they only pretended to sleep; and only she, Barbara, stood in the dark and contemplated the bulk of her own body, wondering what to do and knowing that there was nothing she would do, no way for her to change the process of events any more than she could change the heavy fact of her body itself. There was no way to escape what the years had made her.

III

From that time on they lived together like a family. Or it was as Mark put it: "Think of a babysitter here permanently. Like the Lunt girl, staying on here permanently to help, only we won't need that one any more." Barbara made breakfast for them all, and then Mark and Dorie drove off to school and returned late, between six and six-thirty, and in the evenings Mark worked hard at his typewriters, going to sit at one and then the next and then the next, and the girl, Dorie, helped Barbara with the dishes and odd chores and went up to her room, where she studied . . . or did something, she must have done something.

Of the long afternoons he and the girl were away Mark said nothing. He was evasive and jaunty; he looked younger. He explained carefully to Dorie that when he and Mrs. Arber were invited somewhere she must stay home and watch the children, that she was not included in these invitations; and the girl agreed eagerly. She did so want to help around the house! She had inherited from her background a dislike for confusion—so the mess of the Arber house upset her and she worked for hours picking things up, polishing tarnished objects Barbara herself had forgotten were silver, cleaning, arranging, fixing. As soon as the snow melted she was to be seen outside, raking shyly through the flower beds. How to explain her to the neighbors? Barbara said nothing.

"But I didn't think we lived in such a mess. I didn't think it was so bad," Barbara would say to Mark in a quiet, hurt voice, and he would pat her hand and say, "It isn't a mess, she just likes to fool around. I don't think it's a mess."

It was fascinating to live so close to a young person. Barbara had never been young in quite the way Dorie was young. At breakfast—they ate crowded around the table—everyone could peer into everyone else's face, there were no secrets, stale mouths and bad moods were inexcusable, all the wrinkles of age or distress that showed on Barbara could never be hidden, and not to be hidden was Mark's guilty enthusiasm, his habit of saying,

"*We* should go to . . . ," "*We* are invited . . ." and the "we" meant either him and Barbara, or him and Dorie, but never all three; he had developed a new personality. But Dorie was fascinating. She awoke to the slow gray days of spring with a panting, wondrous expectation, her blond hair shining, her freckles clear as dabs of clever paint on her heartbreaking skin, her teeth very, very white and straight, her pert little lips innocent of lipstick and strangely sensual . . . yes, it was heartbreaking. She changed her clothes at least twice a day while Barbara wore the same outfit—baggy black slacks and a black sweater—for weeks straight. Dorie appeared downstairs in cashmere sweater sets that were the color of birds' eggs, or of birds' fragile legs, and white trim blouses that belonged on a genteel hockey field, and bulky pink sweaters big as jackets, and when she was dressed casually she wore stretch slacks that were neatly secured by stirrups around her long, narrow, white feet. Her eyes were frankly and emptily brown, as if giving themselves up to every observer. She was so anxious to help that it was oppressive; "No, I can manage, I've been making breakfast for eight years by myself," Barbara would say angrily, and Dorie, a chastised child, would glance around the table not only at Mark but at the children for sympathy. Mark had a blackboard set up in the kitchen so that he could test the children's progress in languages, and he barked out commands for them—French or Latin or Greek words—and they responded with nervous glee, clacking out letters on the board, showing off for the rapt, admiring girl who seemed not to know if they were right or wrong.

"Oh, how smart they are—how wonderful everything is," Dorie breathed.

Mark had to drive to Boston often because he needed his prescription for tranquillizers refilled constantly, and his doctor would not give him an automatic refill. But though Barbara had always looked forward to these quick trips, he rarely took her now. He went off with Dorie, now his "secretary," who took along a notebook decorated with the college's insignia to record his impressions in, and since he never gave his wife warning she could not get ready in time, and it was such an obvious trick, so crudely cruel, that Barbara stood in the kitchen and wept as they drove out. . . . She called up friends in New York but never exactly told them what was going on. It was so ludicrous, it made her seem such a fool. Instead she chatted and barked with laughter; her conversations with these people were always so witty that nothing, nothing seemed very real until she hung up the receiver again; and then she became herself, in a drafty college-owned house in New England, locked in this particular body.

She stared out the attic window for hours, not thinking. She became a

state of being, a creature. Downstairs the children fought, or played peacefully, or rifled through their father's study, which was forbidden, and after a
certain amount of time something would nudge Barbara to her feet and she
would descend slowly, laboriously, as if returning to the real world where
any ugliness was possible. When she slapped the boys for being bad, they
stood in meek defiance and did not cry. "Mother, you're out of your mind,"
they said. "Mother, you're losing control of yourself."

"It's your father who's out of his mind!" she shouted.

She had the idea that everyone was talking about them, everyone.
Anonymous, worthless people who had never published a line gloated over
her predicament; high-school baton twirlers were better off than Barbara
Scott, who had no dignity. Dorie, riding with Mark Arber on the expressway to Boston, was at least young and stupid, anonymous though she was,
and probably she too had a slim collection of poems that Mark would
manage to get published . . . and who knew what would follow, who
could tell? Dorie Weinheimer was like any one of five hundred or five
thousand college girls and was no one, had no personality, and yet Mark
Arber had somehow fallen in love with her, so perhaps everyone would
eventually fall in love with her . . . ? Barbara imagined with panic the
parties she knew nothing about to which Mark and his new girl went:
Mark in his slovenly tweed suits, looking like his own father in the thirties,
and Dorie chic as a Vogue model in her weightless bones and vacuous face.

"Is Dorie going to stay here long?" the boys kept asking.

"Why, don't you like her?"

"She's nice. She smells nice. Is she going to stay long?"

"Go ask your father that," Barbara said angrily.

The girl was officially boarding with them; it was no lie. Every year
certain faculty families took in a student or two, out of generosity or
charity, or because they themselves needed the money, and the Arbers
themselves had always looked down upon such hearty liberalism. But now
they had Dorie, and in Peabody's Market Barbara had to rush up and
down the aisles with her shopping cart, trying to avoid the wives of other
professors who were sure to ask her about the new boarder; and she had to
buy special things for the girl, spinach and beets and artichokes, while
Barbara and Mark liked starches and sweets and fat, foods that clogged up
the blood vessels and strained the heart and puffed out the stomach. While
Barbara ate and drank hungrily, Dorie sat chaste with her tiny forkfuls of
food, and Barbara could eat three platefuls to Dorie's one; her appetite
increased savagely just in the presence of the girl. (The girl was always
asking politely, "Is it the boys who get the bathroom all dirty?" or "Could

I take the vacuum cleaner down and have it fixed?" and these questions, polite as they were, made Barbara's appetite increase savagely.)

In April, after Dorie had been boarding with them three and a half months, Barbara was up at her desk when there was a rap on the plywood door. Unused to visitors, Barbara turned clumsily and looked at Mark over the top of her glasses. "Can I come in?" he said. "What are you working on?"

There was no paper in her typewriter. "Nothing," she said.

"You haven't shown me any poems lately. What's wrong?"

He sat on the window ledge and lit a cigarette. Barbara felt a spiteful satisfaction to see how old he looked—he hadn't her fine, fleshed-out skin, the smooth complexion of an overweight woman; he had instead the bunched, baggy complexion of an overweight man whose weight keeps shifting up and down. Good. Even his fingers shook as he lit the cigarette.

"This is the best place in the house," he said.

"Do you want me to give it up to Dorie?"

He stared at her. "Give it up—why? Of course not."

"I thought you might be testing my generosity."

He shook his head, puzzled. Barbara wondered if she hated this man or if she felt a writer's interest in him. Perhaps he was insane. Or perhaps he had been drinking again; he had not gone out to his classes this morning and she'd heard him arguing with Dorie. "Barbara, how old are you?" he said.

"Forty-three. You know that."

He looked around at the boxes and other clutter as if coming to an important decision. "Well, we have a little problem here."

Barbara stared at her blunt fingernails and waited.

"She got herself pregnant. It seems on purpose."

"She what?"

"Well," Mark said uncomfortably, "she did it on purpose."

They remained silent. After a while, in a different voice he said, "She claims she loves children. She loves our children and wants some of her own. It's a valid point, I can't deny her her rights . . . but . . . I thought you should know about it in case you agree to help."

"What do you mean?"

"Well, I have something arranged in Boston," he said, not looking at her, "and Dorie has agreed to it . . . though reluctantly . . . and unfortunately I don't think I can drive her myself . . . you know I have to go to Chicago. . . ."

Barbara did not look at him.

"I'm on this panel at the University of Chicago, with John Ciardi. You know, it's been set up for a year, it's on the state of contemporary poetry —you know—I can't possibly withdraw from it now—"

"And so?"

"If you could drive Dorie in—"

"If I could drive her in?"

"I don't see what alternative we have," he said slowly.

"Would you like a divorce so you can marry her?"

"I have never mentioned that," he said.

"Well, would you?"

"I don't know."

"Look at me. Do you want to marry her?"

A nerve began to twitch in his eye. It was a familiar twitch—it had been with him for two decades. "No, I don't think so. I don't know—you know how I feel about disruption."

"Don't you have any courage?"

"Courage?"

"If you want to marry her, go ahead. I won't stop you."

"Do you want a divorce yourself?"

"I'm asking you. It's up to you. Then Dorie can have her baby and fulfill herself," Barbara said with a deathly smile. "She can assert her rights as a woman twenty years younger than I. She can become the third Mrs. Arber and become automatically envied. Don't you have the courage for it?"

"I had thought," Mark said with dignity, "that you and I had an admirable marriage. It was different from the marriages of other people we know—part of it is that we don't work in the same area, yes, but the most important part lay in our understanding of each other. It has taken a tremendous generosity on your part, Barbara, over the last three months and I appreciate it," he said, nodding slowly, "I appreciate it and I can't help asking myself whether . . . whether I would have had the strength to do what you did, in your place. I mean, if you had brought in—"

"I know what you mean."

"It's been an extraordinary marriage. I don't want it to end on an impulse, anything reckless or emotional," he said vaguely. She thought that he did look a little mad, but quietly mad; his ears were very red. For the first time she began to feel pity for the girl who was, after all, nobody, and who had no personality, and who was waiting in the ugly maid's room for her fate to be decided.

"All right, I'll drive her to Boston," Barbara said.

IV

Mark had to leave the next morning for Chicago. He would be gone, he explained, about a week—there was not only the speaking appearance but other things as well. The three of them had a kind of farewell party the night before. Dorie sat with her frail hand on her flat, child's stomach and drank listlessly, while Barbara and Mark argued about the comparative merits of two English novelists—their literary arguments were always witty, superficial, rapid, and very enjoyable. At two o'clock Mark woke Dorie to say good-by and Barbara, thinking herself admirably discreet, went upstairs alone.

She drove Dorie to Boston the next day. Dorie was a mother's child, the kind of girl mothers admire—clean, bright, passive—and it was a shame for her to be so frightened. Barbara said roughly, "I've known lots of women who've had abortions. They lived."

"Did you ever have one?"

"No."

Dorie turned away as if in reproach.

"I've had children and that's harder, maybe. It's thought to be harder," Barbara said, as if offering the girl something.

"I would like children, maybe three of them," Dorie said.

"Three is a good number, yes."

"But I'd be afraid . . . I wouldn't know what to do. . . . I don't know what to do now. . . ."

She was just a child herself, Barbara thought with a rush of sympathy; of all of them it was Dorie who was most trapped. The girl sat with a scarf around her careless hair, staring out the window. She wore a camel's hair coat like all the girls and her fingernails were colorless and uneven, as if she had been chewing them.

"Stop thinking about it. Sit still."

"Yes," the girl said listlessly.

They drove on. Something began to weigh at Barbara's heart, as if her flesh were aging moment by moment. She had never liked her body. Dorie's body was so much more prim and chaste and stylish, and her own body belonged to another age, a hearty nineteenth century where fat had been a kind of virtue. Barbara thought of her poetry, which was light and sometimes quite clever, the poetry of a girl, glimmering with half-seen visions and echoing with peculiar off-rhymes—and truly it ought to have been Dorie's poetry and not hers. She was not equal to her own writing. And, on the highway like this, speeding toward some tawdry destination, she had the sudden terrible conviction that language itself did not matter and that nothing mattered ultimately except the body, the human body and the bodies of other creatures and objects: what else existed?

Her own body was the only real fact about her. Dorie, huddled over in her corner, was another real fact and they were going to do something about it, defeat it. She thought of Mark already in Chicago, at a cocktail party, the words growing like weeds in his brain and his wit moving so rapidly through the brains of others that it was, itself, a kind of lie. It seemed strange to her that the two of them should move against Dorie, who suffered because she was totally real and helpless and gave up nothing of herself to words.

They arrived in Boston and began looking for the street. Barbara felt clumsy and guilty and did not dare to glance over at the girl. She muttered aloud as they drove for half an hour, without luck. Then she found the address. It was a small private hospital with a blank gray front. Barbara drove past it and circled the block and approached it again. "Come on, get hold of yourself," she said to Dorie's stiff profile, "this is no picnic for me either."

She stopped the car and she and Dorie stared out at the hospital, which looked deserted. The neighborhood itself seemed deserted. Finally Barbara said, with a heaviness she did not yet understand, "Let's find a place to stay tonight first. Let's get that settled." She took the silent girl to a motel on a boulevard and told her to wait in the room, she'd be back shortly. Dorie stared in a drugged silence at Barbara, who could have been her mother—there flashed between them the kind of camaraderie possible only between mother and daughter—and then Barbara left the room. Dorie remained sitting in a very light chair of imitation wood and leather. She sat so that she was staring at the edge of the bureau; occasionally her eye was attracted by the framed picture over the bed, of a woman in a red evening gown and a man in a tuxedo observing a waterfall by moonlight. She sat like this for quite a while, in her coat. A nerve kept twitching in her thigh but it did not bother her; it was a most energetic, thumping twitch, as if her very flesh were doing a dance. But it did not bother her. She remained there for a while, waking to the morning light, and it took her several panicked moments to remember where she was and who had brought her here. She had the immediate thought that she must be safe—if it was morning she must be safe—and someone had taken care of her, had seen what was best for her and had carried it out.

V

And so she became the third Mrs. Arber, a month after the second one's death. Barbara had been found dead in an elegant motel across the city, the Paradise Inn, which Mark thought was a brave, cynical joke; he took Barbara's death with an alarming, rhetorical melodrama, an alcoholic melancholy Dorie did not like. Barbara's "infinite courage" made Dorie resentful. The second Mrs. Arber had taken a large dose of sleeping pills and had died easily, because of the strain her body had made upon her heart; so that was that. But somehow it wasn't—because Mark kept talking about it, speculating on it, wondering: "She did it for the baby, to preserve life. It's astonishing, it's exactly like something in a novel," he said. He spoke with a perpetual guilty astonishment.

She married him and became Mrs. Arber, which surprised everyone. It surprised even Mark. Dorie herself was not very surprised, because a daydreamer is prepared for most things and in a way she had planned even this, though she had not guessed how it would come about. Surely she had rehearsed the second Mrs. Arber's suicide and funeral already a year before, when she'd known nothing, could have guessed nothing, and it did not really surprise her. Events lost their jagged edges and became hard and opaque and routine, drawing her into them. She was still a daydreamer, though she was Mrs. Arber. She sat at the old desk up in the attic and leaned forward on her bony elbows to stare out the window, contemplating the hopeless front yard and the people who strolled by, some of them who —she thought—glanced toward the house with a kind of amused contempt, as if aware of her inside. She was almost always home.

The new baby was a girl, Carolyn. Dorie took care of her endlessly and she took care of the boys; she hadn't been able to finish school. In the evening when all the children were at last asleep Mark would come out of his study and read to her in his rapid, impatient voice snatches of his new novel, or occasionally poems of his late wife's, and Dorie would stare at him and try to understand. She was transfixed with love for him and yet —and yet she was unable to locate this love in this particular man, unable to comprehend it. Mark was invited everywhere that spring; he flew all the way out to California to take part in a highly publicized symposium with George Steiner and James Baldwin, and Dorie stayed home. Geoffrey was seeing a psychiatrist in Boston and she had to drive him in every other day, and there was her own baby, and Mark's frequent visitors who arrived often without notice and stayed a week—sleeping late, staying up late, drinking, eating, arguing—it was exactly the kind of life she had known would be hers, and yet she could not adjust to it. Her baby was somehow mixed up in her mind with the other wife, as if it had been that woman's and only left to her, Dorie, for safekeeping. She was grateful that her baby was a girl because wasn't there always a kind of pact or understanding between women?

In June two men arrived at the house to spend a week, and Dorie had to cook for them. They were long, lean, gray-haired young men who were undefinable, sometimes very fussy, sometimes reckless and hysterical with wit, always rather insulting in a light, veiled manner Dorie could not catch. They were both vegetarians and could not tolerate anyone eating meat in their presence. One evening at a late dinner Dorie began to cry and had to leave the room, and the two guests and Mark and even the children were displeased with her. She went up to the attic and sat mechanically at the desk. It did no good to read Barbara Scott's poetry because she did not understand it. Her understanding had dropped to tending the baby and the boys, fixing meals, cleaning up and shopping, and taking the station wagon to the garage perpetually . . . and she had no time to go with the others to the tennis courts, or to accompany Mark to New York . . . and around her were human beings whose lives consisted of language, the grace of language, and she could no longer understand them. She felt strangely cheated, a part of her murdered, as if the abortion had taken place that day after all and something had been cut permanently out of her.

In a while Mark climbed the stairs to her. She heard him coming, she heard his labored breathing. "Here you are," he said, and slid his big beefy arms around her and breathed his liquory love into her face, calling her his darling, his beauty. After all, he did love her, it was real and his arms were real, and she still loved him although she had lost the meaning of that word. "Now will you come downstairs and apologize, please?" he said gently. "You've disturbed them and it can't be left like this. You know how I hate disruption."

She began weeping again, helplessly, to think that she had disturbed anyone, that she was this girl sitting at a battered desk in someone's attic, and no one else, no other person who might confidently take upon herself the meaning of this man's words—she was herself and that was a fact, a final fact she would never overcome.

SUGGESTIONS FOR WRITING

The Stories

1. Does the fragmentary form used in "How I Contemplated . . ." draw you into the story—that is, force your participation in its events— more than the conventional structure used in "Accomplished Desires"? Explain by referring to your thought processes and emotional responses as you read the two stories.

2. Despite the experimental form in which 'How I Contemplated . . ." is cast, both this story and "Accomplished Desires" are essentially melodramatic in subject matter. Examine these stories as melodrama and compare and contrast their events, characters, and themes.

3. Discuss the function of setting in both "How I Contemplated . . ." and "Accomplished Desires."

4. Try rewriting "Accomplished Desires" from the point of view of Mark, Barbara, or Dorie, casting your story in the form of an outline similar to that of "How I Contemplated. . . ."

5. Discuss the use of irony in "Accomplished Desires."

Other Works by Joyce Carol Oates

1. *Expensive People* has been described by its author as the second of her three novels dealing "with social and economic facts of life in America, combined with unusually sensitive—but hopefully representative—young men and women, who confront the puzzle of American life in different ways and come to different ends." Explore the thematic ramifications of the "social and economic facts of life" presented in this novel or one of the two others, *A Garden of Earthly Delights* and *Them*. Be sure to describe the relationship between the social fabric and the sensibility of the protagonist.

2. "I am really a romantic writer in the tradition of Stendhal and Flaubert," Oates said in 1969. Basing your views on *A Garden of Earthly Delights*, support or contest this declaration of literary antecedents.

3. In *Expensive People*, Oates makes her first-person narrator rather unreliable; he also plays games with his hypothetical reader, commenting on books and articles that offer advice to the aspiring writer and quoting from his mother's notebooks. Explore the experimental tech-

niques used in this novel; be sure to include your analysis of the use of *the process of fiction* as subject matter.

4. The short stories of Joyce Carol Oates often end in violence. Discuss the nature and function of violence in three or more of the stories collected in *Upon the Sweeping Flood*. Do you find the violence literary and unconvincing, as one critic contends? Is violence too facile a solution for the social and personal reality depicted in the stories? Is it at odds with the author's stylistically graceful prose?

BIBLIOGRAPHY

Primary

By the North Gate. New York: Vanguard Press, 1963. Short stories.

With Shuddering Fall. New York: Vanguard Press, 1964. A novel.

The Sweet Enemy. Unpublished. A play (performed at the Actors Studio Workshop, New York City, 1965).

Upon the Sweeping Flood and Other Stories. New York: Vanguard Press, 1966. Short stories.

A Garden of Earthly Delights. New York: Vanguard Press, 1967. A novel.

Expensive People. New York: Vanguard Press, 1968. A novel.

Women in Love and Other Poems. New York: Albondacani Press, 1968. Poems.

Them. New York: Vanguard Press, 1969. A novel.

Anonymous Sins and Other Poems. Baton Rouge, La.: Louisiana State Univ. Press, 1969. Poems.

The Edge of Impossibility. New York: Vanguard Press, 1970. Literary criticism.

Love and Its Derangements. Baton Rogue, La.: Louisiana State Univ. Press, 1970. Poems.

Sunday Dinner. Unpublished. A play (performed at the American Place Theatre, New York City, 1970).

The Wheel of Love. New York: Vanguard Press, 1970. Short stories.

Wonderland. New York: Vanguard Press, 1971. A novel.

Marriages and Infidelities. New York: Vanguard Press, 1972. Short stories.

Ontological Proof of My Existence. Unpublished. A play (performed at the Cubiculo, New York City, 1972).

Scenes from American Life: Contemporary Short Fiction. New York: Random House, 1972. Anthology (edited).
Do With Me What You Will. New York: Vanguard Press, 1973. A novel.

Secondary

Bower, Warren. "Bliss in the First Person." *Saturday Review,* 51 (October 26, 1968), 34–35. An interview with Joyce Carol Oates that focuses on *Expensive People.*

Dalton, Elizabeth. "Joyce Carol Oates: Violence in the Head." *Commentary,* 49 (June 1970), 75–77. Examines the mixture of two styles in Oates' fiction: a naturalism that depicts rural and urban desolation, and a tendency to push beyond naturalism toward "transcendent meaning"; finds the literary correctness of the fiction antithetical to the violence that pervades it.

Hicks, Granville. "What Is Reality?" *Saturday Review,* 51 (October 26, 1968), 33–34. A review of *Expensive People* that explores the novel's concern with the "impact of suburban life on the sensibility of the narrator."

Kuehl, Linda. "An Interview with Joyce Carol Oates." *Commonweal,* 91 (December 5, 1969), 307–10. Oates discusses her literary antecedents, fictional theories, and her fiction (in particular *Them*).

McCormick, Lucienne P. "A Bibliography of Works By and About Joyce Carol Oates." *American Literature,* 43 (March 1971), 124–32. Helpful for its listing of short stories and their original place of publication and for its lengthy list of reviews about the fiction of Oates.

Quirino, Leonard. Review of *A Garden of Earthly Delights. Novel: A Forum on Fiction,* 2 (Winter 1969), 188–90. Finds fault with the clichéd treatment of important themes in this novel.

Sullivan, Walter. "The Artificial Demon: Joyce Carol Oates and the Dimensions of the Real." *The Hollins Critic,* 9 (December 1972), 1–12. An overview of the fiction that criticizes Oates for her "tendency to let her people go insane"; theorizes that the writer's forte lies in the short story rather than the novel.

. . . we have specified that everyone who comes to us from this day forward must take twelve hours of you a week, for which they will receive three points credit per semester, and, as well, a silver spoon in the "Heritage" pattern. Don't hang back. We are sure you are up to it. Many famous teachers teach courses in themselves; why should you be different, just because you are a wimp and a lame, objectively speaking? Courage. The anthology of yourself which will be used as a text is even now being assembled by underpaid researchers in our textbook division, drawing upon the remembrances of those who hated you and those (a much smaller number) who loved you. You will be adequate in your new role. See? Your life is saved. The instructions do not make distinctions between those lives which are worth saving and those which are not. Your life is saved. Congratulations. I'm sorry.

FROM "What to do Next"

DONALD BARTHELME

Born in Philadelphia, Pennsylvania, in 1931, Donald Barthelme grew up in Houston, Texas. He served in the Army in Korea and Japan and has worked as a newspaper reporter, museum director, and managing editor of *Location,* an art and literature review. At present, he lives in New York City.

In recent years, Barthelme's fiction has appeared regularly in the *New Yorker,* and his short stories have also been published in such magazines as *Paris Review, Contact, New World Writing,* and *Harper's Bazaar.* In 1972, Barthelme earned a National Institute of Arts and Letters grant in fiction, and, in the same year, he received a National Book Award in children's literature for *The Slightly Irregular Fire Engine or the Hithering Thithering Djinn.*

"Fragments are the only forms I trust," writes Barthelme in one of his stories, and several critics have used this statement to explain his stylistic practices and intentions. Literary fragments are, by definition, open-ended, unanchored in time and place, tentative, suggestive of process rather than of finished product, and unconventional in that they often violate established syntactical patterns of language. In Barthelme's fiction the fragments most often consist of newspaper clichés, advertising slogans, academic jargon, verbal puns, and tag lines from stale jokes: waste products of our word-stuffed lives. But, according to one of his former editors, although Barthelme seems to spend a lot of time in despair, "he's not alienated; he knows what's going on; he makes experimental writing important; and he writes just as *he* sees things." About himself Barthelme has said, "I try to avoid saying anything directly and just hope that something emerges from what has been [written]."

THE INDIAN UPRISING

We defended the city as best we could. The arrows of the Comanches came in clouds. The war clubs of the Comanches clattered on the soft, yellow pavements. There were earthworks along the Boulevard Mark Clark and the hedges had been laced with sparkling wire. People were trying to understand. I spoke to Sylvia. "Do you think this is a good life?" The table held apples, books, long-playing records. She looked up. "No."

Patrols of paras and volunteers with armbands guarded the tall, flat buildings. We interrogated the captured Comanche. Two of us forced his head back while another poured water into his nostrils. His body jerked, he choked and wept. Not believing a hurried, careless, and exaggerated report of the number of casualties in the outer districts where trees, lamps, swans had been reduced to clear fields of fire we issued entrenching tools to those who seemed trustworthy and turned the heavy-weapons companies so that we could not be surprised from that direction. And I sat there getting drunker and drunker and more in love and more in love. We talked.

"Do you know Fauré's 'Dolly'?"

"Would that be Gabriel Fauré?"

"It would."

"Then I know it," she said. "May I say that I play it at certain times, when I am sad, or happy, although it requires four hands."

"How is that managed?"

"I accelerate," she said, "ignoring the time signature."

And when they shot the scene in the bed I wondered how you felt under the eyes of the camermen, grips, juicers, men in the mixing booth: excited? stimulated? And when they shot the scene in the shower I sanded a hollow-core door working carefully against the illustrations in texts and whispered instructions from one who had already solved the problem. I had made after all other tables, one while living with Nancy, one while living with Alice, one while living with Eunice, one while living with Marianne.

Red men in waves like people scattering in a square startled by something tragic or a sudden, loud noise accumulated against the barricades we had made of window dummies, silk, thoughtfully planned job descriptions (including scales for the orderly progress of other colors), wine in demijohns, and robes. I analyzed the composition of the barricade nearest me and found two ashtrays, ceramic, one dark brown and one dark brown with an orange blur at the lip; a tin frying pan; two-litre bottles of red wine; three-quarter-litre bottles of Black & White, aquavit, cognac, vodka, gin, Fad #6 sherry; a hollow-core door in birch veneer on black wrought-iron legs; a blanket, red-orange with faint blue stripes; a red pillow and a blue pillow; a woven straw wastebasket; two glass jars for flowers; corkscrews and can openers; two plates and two cups, ceramic, dark brown; a yellow-and-purple poster; a Yugoslavian carved flute, wood, dark brown; and other items. I decided I knew nothing.

The hospitals dusted wounds with powders the worth of which was not quite established, other supplies having been exhausted early in the first day. I decided I knew nothing. Friends put me in touch with a Miss R., a teacher, unorthodox they said, excellent they said, successful with difficult cases, steel shutters on the windows made the house safe. I had just learned via an International Distress Coupon that Jane had been beaten up by a dwarf in a bar on Tenerife but Miss R. did not allow me to speak of it. "You know nothing," she said, "you feel nothing, you are locked in a most savage and terrible ignorance, I despise you, my boy, *mon cher,* my heart. You may attend but you must not attend now, you must attend later, a day or a week or an hour, you are making me ill. . . ." I nonevaluated these remarks as Korzybski instructed. But it was difficult. Then they pulled back in a feint near the river and we rushed into that sector with a reinforced battalion hastily formed among the Zouaves and cabdrivers. This unit was crushed in the afternoon of a day that began with spoons and letters in hallways and under windows where men tasted the history of the heart, cone-shaped muscular organ that maintains *circulation of the blood.*

But it is you I want now, here in the middle of this Uprising, with the streets yellow and threatening, short, ugly lances with fur at the throat and ✓ inexplicable shell money lying in the grass. It is when I am with you that I am happiest, and it is for you that I am making this hollow-core door table with black wrought-iron legs. I held Sylvia by her bear-claw necklace. "Call off your braves," I said. "We have many years left to live." There was a sort of muck running in the gutters, yellowish, filthy stream suggesting excrement, or nervousness, a city that does not know what it has done to deserve baldness, errors, infidelity. "With luck you will survive until matins," Sylvia said. She ran off down the Rue Chester Nimitz, uttering shrill cries. *Non serious*

Then it was learned that they had infiltrated our ghetto and that the people of the ghetto instead of resisting had joined the smooth, well-coördinated attack with zipguns, telegrams, lockets, causing that portion of the line held by the I.R.A. to swell and collapse. We sent more heroin into the ghetto, and hyacinths, ordering another hundred thousand of the pale, delicate flowers. On the map we considered the situation with its strung-out inhabitants and merely personal emotions. Our parts were blue and their parts were green. I showed the blue-and-green map to Sylvia. "Your parts are green," I said. "You gave me heroin first a year ago," Sylvia said. She ran off down George C. Marshall Allée, uttering shrill cries. Miss R. pushed me into a large room painted white (jolting and dancing in the soft light, and I was excited! and there were people watching!) in which there were two chairs. I sat in one chair and Miss R. sat in the other. She wore a blue dress containing a red figure. There was nothing exceptional about her. I was disappointed by her plainness, by the bareness of the room, by the absence of books.

The girls of my quarter wore long blue mufflers that reached to their knees. Sometimes the girls hid Comanches in their rooms, the blue mufflers together in a room creating a great blue fog. Block opened the door. He was carrying weapons, flowers, loaves of bread. And he was friendly, kind, enthusiastic, so I related a little of the history of torture, reviewing the technical literature quoting the best modern sources, French, German, and

American, and pointing out the flies which had gathered in anticipation of some new, cool color.

"What is the situation?" I asked.

"The situation is liquid," he said. "We hold the south quarter and they hold the north quarter. The rest is silence."

"And Kenneth?"

"That girl is not in love with Kenneth," Block said frankly. "She is in love with his coat. When she is not wearing it she is huddling under it. Once I caught it going down the stairs by itself. I looked inside. Sylvia."

Once I caught Kenneth's coat going down the stairs by itself but the coat was a trap and inside a Comanche who made a thrust with his short, ugly knife at my leg which buckled and tossed me over the balustrade through a window and into another situation. Not believing that your body brilliant as it was and your fat, liquid spirit distinguished and angry as it was were stable quantities to which one could return on wires more than once, twice, or another number of times I said: "See the table?"

In Skinny Wainwright Square the forces of green and blue swayed and struggled. The referees ran out on the field trailing chains. And then the blue part would be enlarged, the green diminished. Miss R. began to speak. "A former king of Spain, a Bonaparte, lived for a time in Bordentown, New Jersey. But that's no good." She paused. "The ardor aroused in men by the beauty of women can only be satisfied by God. That is *very* good (it is Valéry) but it is not what I have to teach you, goat, muck, filth, heart of my heart." I showed the table to Nancy. "See the table?" She stuck out her tongue red as a cardinal's hat. "I made such a table once," Block said frankly. "People all over America have made such tables. I doubt very much whether one can enter an American home without finding at least one such table, or traces of its having been there, such as faded places in the carpet." And afterward in the garden the men of the 7th Cavalry played Gabrieli, Albinoni, Marcello, Vivaldi, Boccherini. I saw Sylvia. She wore a yellow ribbon, under a long blue muffler. "Which side are you on," I cried, "after all?"

"The only form of discourse of which I approve," Miss R. said in her dry, tense voice, "is the litany. I believe our masters and teachers as well as plain citizens should confine themselves to what can safely be said. Thus when I hear the words *pewter, snake, tea, Fad #6 sherry, serviette, fenestration, crown, blue* coming from the mouth of some public official, or some raw youth, I am not disappointed. Vertical organization is also possible," Miss R. said, "as in

pewter
snake
tea
Fad #6 sherry
serviette
fenestration
crown
blue.

I run to liquids and colors," she said, "but you, you may run to something else, my virgin, my darling, my thistle, my poppet, my own. Young people," Miss R. said, "run to more and more unpleasant combinations as they sense the nature of our society. Some people," Miss R. said, "run to conceits or wisdom but I hold to the hard, brown, nutlike word. I might point out that there is enough aesthetic excitement here to satisfy anyone but a damned fool." I sat in solemn silence.

Fire arrows lit my way to the post office in Patton Place where members of the Abraham Lincoln Brigade offered their last, exhausted letters, postcards, calendars. I opened a letter but inside was a Comanche flint arrowhead played by Frank Wedekind in an elegant gold chain and congratulations. Your earring rattled against my spectacles when I leaned forward to touch the soft, ruined place where the hearing aid had been. "Pack it in! Pack it in!" I urged, but the men in charge of the Uprising refused to listen to reason or to understand that it was real and that our water supply had evaporated and that our credit was no longer what it had been, once.

We attached wires to the testicles of the captured Comanche. And I sat there getting drunker and drunker and more in love and more in love. When we threw the switch he spoke. His name, he said, was Gustave Aschenbach. He was born at L———, a country town in the province of Silesia. He was the son of an upper official in the judicature, and his forebears had all been officers, judges, departmental functionaries. . . . And you can never touch a girl in the same way more than once, twice, or another number of times however much you may wish to hold, wrap, or otherwise fix her hand, or look, or some other quality, or incident, known to you previously. In Sweden the little Swedish children cheered when we managed nothing more remarkable than getting off a bus burdened with packages, bread and liver-paste and beer. We went to an old church and sat in the royal box. The organist was practicing. And then into the graveyard next to the church. *Here lies Anna Pedersen, a good woman.* I threw a mushroom on the grave. The officer commanding the garbage dump reported by radio that the garbage had begun to move.

Jane! I heard via an International Distress Coupon that you were beaten up by a dwarf in a bar on Tenerife. That doesn't sound like you, Jane. Mostly you kick the dwarf in his little dwarf groin before he can get his teeth into your tasty and nice-looking leg, don't you, Jane? Your affair with Harold is reprehensible, you know that, don't you, Jane? Harold is married to Nancy. And there is Paula to think about (Harold's kid), and Billy (Harold's other kid). I think your values are peculiar, Jane! Strings of language extend in every direction to bind the world into a rushing, ribald whole.

And you can never return to felicities in the same way, the brilliant body, the distinguished spirit recapitulating moments that occur once, twice, or another number of times in rebellions, or water. The rolling consensus of the Comanche nation smashed our inner defenses on three sides. Block was firing a greasegun from the upper floor of a building designed by Emery Roth & Sons. "See the table?" "Oh, pack it in with your bloody table!" The city officials were tied to trees. Dusky warriors padded with their forest tread into the mouth of the mayor. "Who do you want to be?" I asked Kenneth and he said he wanted to be Jean-Luc Godard but later when time permitted conversations in large, lighted rooms, whispering galleries with black-and-white Spanish rugs and problematic sculpture on calm, red catafalques. The sickness of the quarrel lay thick in the bed. I touched your back, the white, raised scars.

We killed a great many in the south suddenly with helicopters and rockets but we found that those we had killed were children and more came from the north and from the east and from other places where there are children preparing to live. "Skin," Miss R. said softly in the white, yellow room. "This is the Clemency Committee. And would you remove your belt and shoelaces." I removed my belt and shoelaces and looked (rain shattering from a great height the prospects of silence and clear, neat rows of houses in the subdivisions) into their savage black eyes, paint, feathers, beads.

MOVING THROUGH
"THE INDIAN UPRISING"

Charles Thomas Samuels

Readers who come to "The Indian Uprising" with expectations inspired by most other short fiction may soon feel frustrated. As the introduction to this volume rightly asserts, the first purpose of narrative is the relating of an event or series of events. Although events occur in Donald Barthelme's story, they are so briefly presented and so puzzlingly mixed that we seem to be viewing them through the window of a fast moving train. No less fleeting are the story's characters, since, though names are mentioned and dialogue is spoken, the people who speak and act are never fixed for us by description. To make matters more unsettling, we are never told quite where or when the action is taking place. Even when ingredients common to other short stories pop up in this one, what we are most aware of is the bubbling of the stew.

Since the story works, in part, by resisting our habitual expectations about narrative, we must first see how far it yields to them; that is, to what extent it offers us the genre's fundamentals: plot, characters, setting, and theme. Advanced or experimental art, of which this is an example, normally makes some contact with its antecedents while moving beyond them— otherwise means of dealing with it would be denied the audience. Barthelme helps us to deal with "The Indian Uprising" by simulating conventional narrative practice. Only after we have taken his aid and read the story as we have always read stories can we see how and why he parts company with the standard model. Hence the following discussion initially posits more narrative coherence than the story will ultimately be seen to possess; it puts things together too neatly at first so that it can eventually show why they remain apart.

"The Indian Uprising" seems to be a first-person account of a city besieged by Comanches. Immediately after introducing us to this situation, however, the narrator shifts, without warning, to a conversation he has had with a girl named Sylvia. The repetition of this shift in the following paragraph warns us that close attention must be paid if we are to have any idea of what is going on.

Next the narrator begins to think about the girl's experience as an actress in a seemingly erotic film, thereby adding an interior plot element to the two exterior ones (the uprising and the conversation). While she made the film, as he recalls, he busied himself by building her a table from the wood of a door. He also recalls having constructed similar tables while living with other women. At this point his recollection is broken off by a new development in the uprising, and, as he will do throughout the tale, the narrator moves from presenting his private life or thoughts to describing the battle.

Subsequently a fourth plot element is introduced. For some reason, the narrator decides that he knows nothing and needs enlightenment. Friends put him in touch with a reputedly effective teacher, but when he goes to her she will not let him discuss a disturbing message he has just received from a girl named Jane. As before, the account of the uprising resumes. Sylvia, whom we now discover is a participant in the rebellion, appears and warns the narrator that he will be lucky if he lasts until morning.

Indeed, the battle has heated up. The Comanches have invaded and won over the ghetto despite the shipments of drugs and flowers with which the narrator's side had thought to command its loyalty. Sylvia reappears to demonstrate that the pacification program has failed.

Forced by the teacher, Miss R., into a nearly empty room, the narrator now alternates between thoughts of war and other thoughts so rapidly that we lose our sense of an ongoing plot. Instead of hearing the anticipated conversation with Miss R., we are told of his talk with a man named Block about Sylvia's affair with a man named Kenneth. Then we are brought back into Miss R.'s room, where the interview takes place.

When it is over, the narrator goes to a post office, where he picks up a letter containing an arrowhead. Afterward, he urges his comrades to surrender, but they refuse, engaging instead in a torture more severe than one described in an earlier interrogation scene. The narrator participates in this act, whereupon events become more frantic and more unclear. He breaks into his most puzzling reverie, only to be brought out of it by the news that a garbage dump has begun to move and because he receives a second message from Jane. This, in turn, sets off a series of thoughts about Jane's affair with a married man, the uprising, Kenneth, and so forth. As the warfare gets more brutal, the narrator suddenly finds himself in another room with Miss R., but this time she is accompanied by savages, and the story ends with a captured narrator contemplating their "black eyes, paint, feathers, beads."

Our triumph over the story's elusiveness demands not only that we fathom the plot but that we identify the characters. Some of them come from other fiction (Gustave Aschenbach from Thomas Mann's *Death in Venice*) or from real life (Frank Wedekind, the German playwright). Similarly identifiable through the reader's independent knowledge are the story's temporal and spatial settings. We need to know that the Comanches flourished in nineteenth-century Wyoming but are now settled mainly in Oklahoma, that the I.R.A. operates in Ireland, that the Abraham Lincoln Brigade fought in the Spanish Civil War, and that most of the streets in the city are named after World War II generals in order to understand that the action isn't occurring in a fixed time and place. Because "The Indian Uprising" merges fact and fiction, here and there, now and then, reading it forces a process of sorting things out. This forced participation causes us to experience an anxiety analogous to the stress felt by the narrator.

However complex and subtle in meaning, most stories at least allow us to contemplate a self-contained and fully delineated action. Instead, "The Indian Uprising" doesn't so much dramatize an action as provide a series of notations from which it is possible to infer a dramatic shape. This notational quality not only forces us to complete the plot, characters, and setting but also requires that we put together an idea of the theme.

At the outset "The Indian Uprising" posits two thematic bonds: between movies and real life and between love and war. The Comanche uprising is a cliché of Western films, but it takes place here in a landscape crammed with references to actual battles. In this respect, Barthelme's technique resembles cinematic montage and recalls most particularly the last scene of the Marx Brothers' comedy *Duck Soup,* wherein a war in the mythical kingdom of Fredonia manages to include warriors, wild animals, athletes, and others—from both newsreels and fiction.

Barthelme alludes to movies, books, and music because they are parts of the cultural experience of the people whose condition the story treats. When, in the first paragraph, the narrator asks Sylvia whether "this is a good life," "this" refers not only to the uprising already indicated but also to the serial monogamy and cultural confusion that subsequent clues will show him to be confronting on a personal level. For now, however, the narrator doesn't oppose the girl who plays Fauré's saccharine piano pieces regardless of her mood and the composition's technical requirements; he rather uses liquor to help him fall in love. Although a devotee of books and classical music, the girl appears in skin-flicks; just as the narrator, a devotee of falling in love, signals the state with an oddly inappropriate gesture (table-making) which, moreover, he has performed promiscuously. Though apparently now living with Sylvia, he longs for Jane, but Jane is having an affair with a married man—when she is not battling lascivious dwarfs on Tenerife. "Strings of language," as the narrator says, "extend in every direction to bind the world into a rushing, ribald whole." Everyone seems to copulate with everyone as easily as words may be formed into sentences. The characters in the story aren't any more than names to us because that's what they are to each other.

Hence, in her long-delayed lesson, Miss R. offers an alternative not only to accepted linguistic practice but, by inference, to accepted erotic behavior. "Young people," she avers, "run to more and more unpleasant combinations as they sense the nature of our society." Equally misguided to her are those who, in a search for art ("conceits") or wisdom, attempt to put words together in meaningful orders. She counsels even so "difficult [a] case" as the narrator to a kind of resignation by recommending that he learn how to savor the individual word (and woman?) without straining after assertion or meaning.

But the narrator responds to her advice in "solemn silence." He would like the warfare to cease; he finds adultery "reprehensible" and regrets that "you can never return to felicities in the same way, the brilliant body, the distinguished spirit recapitulating moments that occur once, twice, or another number of times in rebellions, or water." In a world of impermanence, where love is always turning into hatred, war characterizes the emotional climate. This the narrator finds upsetting.

Yet his condition itself seems abetted by an inability or unwillingness to act on this feeling. Only in fragments does the narrator acknowledge that he feels disturbed, and he is no more able to connect observations to produce a coherent resolve than he is to connect permanently with a woman.

Thus, in the first paragraph, although the subject is warfare, the language is pacific. Arrows come in "clouds," and the defenders have "laced" the hedges with "sparkling" barbed wire. Paradoxically, the falling arrows "clatter" on pavements that are "soft." As the story progresses, both the war and the narrator's attitude become more turbulent, but he never strikes a decisively negative posture. This is left to the reader who, by picking his way among the shards of insight, must come to understand that something has been wrecked.

Like the plot and characters, meaning is scattered through the tale, cohering through juxtaposition and analogy. In moving through "The Indian Uprising" we must be as alert to verbal echoes as if we were reading a poem and to patterns of tone color as if we were studying a collage.

Initially, as has been said, we supply the tone. When the narrator describes the torture of a Comanche, he does so neutrally, just as he neutrally conjoins getting drunk and falling in love. Both the larger juxtapositions (torture and love/drunkenness) and the smaller ones (love and liquor) suggest that the narrator isn't making distinctions, and this is supported by his failure to mock, as the reader must, the ludicrous dialogue of the lady who plays "Dolly." That such neutrality may not be limited to him is an inference we can draw from the next paragraph, which wonders whether his girlfriend was stimulated and excited by becoming an object of voyeurism.

Because the barricade he soon turns to inspect was formed from domestic items, the uprising begins to seem metaphoric. And because the narrator decides at this moment that he needs enlightenment, we infer that the teacher to whom he goes might be expected to help him understand why men and women throw up defenses against each other. To him the barricade is just a list of its contents; perhaps Miss R. will tell him what the list means.

But, as we later learn, Miss R. herself regards lists as the supreme form of utterance. Nor will she help him to deal with the message he carries from Jane (itself another example of sexual warfare) or with the longing that, as we later learn, Jane inspires. He attempts to respond to her dismissal with sophisticated indifference—according to the dictates of a popular semanticist (Alfred Korzybski)—"but it was difficult." Then he notes that one of the units fighting on his side has been defeated. In describing the defeat, he recalls that the day had begun with spoons (recalling the domestic components of the barricade) and letters (cf. the International Distress Coupon from Jane) and thereby places himself among the men described in the rest of the sentence as having "tasted the history of the heart." Yet he immediately plays against the romantic tone of that phrase by emphatically asserting that the heart is only a physiological organ.

Despite this unillusioned factuality, the narrator seems something of a romantic. He wishes he might have a permanent love affair, insists that he is making a table this time for the girl with whom he is happiest, and tells Sylvia to call off the uprising. He regards his surroundings, with apparent regret, as "a city that does not know what it has done to deserve baldness, errors, infidelity."

Henceforth the erotic significance of the uprising becomes unmistakable.

We hear that the weapons include not only zipguns but "telegrams" and "lockets" and that Sylvia's braves have won over the ghetto despite the fact that men had sought to pacify its inhabitants with drugs, both literal (heroin) and figurative (the flowers given as signs of affection). Barthelme includes an allusion here to reenforce his meaning. Echoing the "Hyacinth girl" in T. S. Eliot's *Waste Land,* who tells her impotent lover, "You gave me hyacinths first a year ago," Sylvia mocks the narrator by asserting that he gave her heroin instead. Eliot's line itself alludes to a myth about love so as to point out a comparative decline in love's significance in the modern world; Barthelme, by parodying Eliot, indicates an even deeper decline. At this moment, Miss R. pushes the narrator into a room where, by recalling language he used to describe his girlfriend making an erotic film ("I was excited! and there were people watching!"), he associates the impending lesson with sex. But he is disappointed to find that his mentor seems "[un]exceptional" and, as we later see, she counsels him to the very indifference that might cause a skin-flick performer to simulate sex before a crowd of "cameramen, grips, juicers. . . ."

Before the lesson takes place, the narrator recalls that the girls of his neighborhood conceal Comanches; he associates their behavior with torture when he concludes his discussion with Block by saying that flies "had gathered in anticipation of some new, cool color" other than the blue of the girls' mufflers. Again an allusion is employed in an ironic way. When Block responds to the narrator's inquiry about the progress of the uprising, he concludes with Hamlet's dying words, "The rest is silence." But whereas Hamlet spoke these words after completing his moral rebellion against, among other things, easy adultery, *amoral* rebellion and easy adultery are never-ending in the narrator's world.

Block's explanation of the affair between Sylvia and Kenneth maintains this tone of irony through the comic description of a coat marching downstairs. The image is funny, but not its implication that women love only the superficial aspects of men and, because the coat conceals a Comanche, that sexual relations are antagonistic. Moreover, because the narrator first uses "situation" to refer to the uprising and then says that discovering a Comanche in Kenneth's coat threw him "into another situation" with a woman, we realize that affairs equal war. Further verbal echoes suggest that the continual succession of liaisons (the serial offering of tables) is caused by the impossibility of being certain that a woman's body and spirit offer the basis for permanent loyalty.

Why this is so Miss R. eventually explains when she quotes Valéry.

She wishes to teach the narrator resignation to incoherence rather than to explain its causes. But before Miss R. can praise meaningless litanies, "the hard, brown, nutlike word" that can be recited in either vertical or horizontal lists, Barthelme cuts into the narrator's thoughts a confirmation of Valéry's aphorism ("The ardor aroused in men by the beauty of women can only be satisfied by God"). And then the narrator recalls that, when he made his characteristic love offering to a girl named Nancy, the stuckout tongue with which she rebuffed him was "red as a cardinal's hat"; this suggests another limited intermediary between man and God: the church. Block also suggests that proofs of the attempt at love exist all over America. But when Sylvia presently flashes by wearing a movie symbol of feminine beauty and fidelity (an allusion to the John Ford Western about women and an Indian uprising, *She Wore a Yellow Ribbon*), the narrator notices that it is covered by the long blue muffler under which "the girls of [his] quarter" hide Comanches. "Which side are you on," he cries out; a man can never tell whether a woman promises permanent love or hostility.

In the narrator's case, the latter seems more likely because when he leaves Miss R. he picks up a letter containing an arrowhead "played by" a playwright famous for his portrayal of women as man's destruction (see Wedekind's *Erdgeist*). And now the cutting becomes more rapid, the action more hallucinatory, and the tone exacerbated.

Torture is explicitly connected with sex; the defending troops attach "wires to the testicles of the captured Comanche," who turns out to be Gustave Aschenbach, the hero of Mann's *Death in Venice* and the epitome of man immolating himself through the pursuit of beauty and love. Aschenbach now begins to tell his story, but so casually that the narrator, suffering a kind of breakdown, offers his own more enervated babble: about the impossibility of permanence but also about examples of permanent value (the innocent excitement of children, the music in a church listened to from "the royal box," a woman who lies buried under commemoration of her fulfillment of others). Because he immediately thinks of Jane and only now mentions or reprehends her promiscuity and sexual combativeness, we infer that the previous images of value underlie these judgments.

However, nothing fruitful comes of them. As the uprising continues, the narrator's side eventually resorts to the murder of children (despite his tender thoughts of them), which is appropriate in a world characterized by sexual enmity. By the end of the story, the narrator realizes that any "prospects" of peace and regular domesticity ("neat rows of houses in the subdivisions") have been "shattered." Captured by the enemy, he is told by

Miss R., who we now learn was in league with them, that he will be granted clemency; the story ends before we are told what that might be.

The foregoing account is an attempt at a tolerably comprehensive analysis of the plot, characters, and theme of "The Indian Uprising." It minimizes the strangeness of the story so as to make Barthelme's techniques available to analytical practices developed for the reading of conventional fiction. Having assimilated "The Indian Uprising" to the model from which it departs, we must now remind ourselves that the departure is considerable.

We must remember that the story doesn't so much have a plot as a series of references to acts, none of which is either fully described or plausibly represented. It isn't a fantasy, where the world is not our own but at least seems equally entire and coherent; nor, for the same reason, is it an allegory, though there are local symbols. Because the story keeps referring to a number of actions and because it contains a conclusion of sorts, enough narrative development is simulated to provide unity, but the obscure connections between one action and another preclude causality, on which plot depends.

What causality exists is really sequence, although we may sometimes want to take the sequence as reflecting psychological causes within the narrator. For example, after telling us that he joined in the torture of Aschenbach, the narrator asserts that "you can never touch a girl in the same way more than once," and so forth, and then recalls some unlocated prior experiences that seem to express permanence. Calling "Jane!" he now takes a negative attitude toward her behavior, although he had previously reported it neutrally. Because our reading experience has told us that a narrative event is a consequence of previous narrative events and that a first-person point of view reflects the speaker's character, we are tempted to view the judgment of Jane as somehow a consequence of the narrator's previous recollections. That is, our reading habits dispose us to fill in the unspecified links between his having tortured Aschenbach while "getting drunker and drunker and more in love and more in love" and his subsequent regret that love is finite. From this we infer that the subsequent images of permanence are evoked in response to that regret and that, in their turn, they authorize his final reprehension of Jane. Note, however, that no such causality is declared in the story. Nor is the narrator presented as a fully developed biographical entity. Apart from sparse details of his love life—and these nonliteral—we know virtually nothing about him. He is little more than the voice that records actions, statements, and allusions. More completely here than in other fiction, the narrator is words. As with the "plot," cross references among these words, together with a gradual explicitness of statement and the disturbing increase in tempo, make us feel that we have a coherent and developing character, but the absence of causality and characterization establish this as an illusion.

In truth, "The Indian Uprising" is a sequence of assertions or clues and the effects that both inspire. Whereas in an ordinary story an event is important partly because of its motivational effect on subsequent events, in Barthelme it is important only because of its effect on the reader; this arises not so much because of the event itself but because of its juxtaposition with other undescribed events. Incongruity and the reader's response to it are what the story is after. Similarly the "characters" are little more than items in the account of the narrator, who himself lacks the plausibility lent fictional characters by the actions we see them perform or by an authorial voice describing them.

Barthelme doesn't want us to study the narrator but rather the shifts in "his" prose. Accordingly, he doesn't endow the narrator with a unified consciousness aware of its own alterations. For example, the narrator doesn't come to recognize that serial table-giving is ludicrous; rather, Barthelme chooses to represent promiscuity through this inherently ludicrous symbol and the story comes more and more to state that promiscuity is not only bizarre but reprehensible.

Barthelme's story minimizes one of the classic problems of the fiction writer. Since conventionally plotted and peopled stories set up strong parallels to the real world, we often overlook their details because of our interest in the simulacra of action and character. With reflection, we realize that both are composed of words, but a conventional story is, paradoxically, successful in the degree that it makes us forget that fact. To be engrossed is to ignore the language that engrosses us, just as we ignore the means of an anecdotalist in real life because of our interest in his message. Barthelme gives us just enough of the appearance of plot or character to hold interest, but, by scrambling sequence, eliminating motivation, and so on, he forces us to pay closer attention to each word than we are accustomed to doing. Miss R. may be something of a villain in the tale, but she clearly speaks for her creator when she asserts that there is enough "aesthetic excitement [in a word] to satisfy anyone but a damned fool."

Putting words together well is not only an expression of Barthelme's craftsmanship; it is his way of renewing the force of his subject. We have all read stories about the destabilizing effect of promiscuity and the beleaguerment of love in the modern world; the very metaphor underlying "The Indian Uprising" is a commonplace, but, since it gets at an essential truth, not thereby to be avoided. Barthelme's puzzling devices are attempts to shake this familiar theme and strategy out of their familiarity, to reactivate their power by making them recalcitrant and even hostile to a reader who wants to look at old things in an old way.

That there are antecedents for Barthelme's unusual style should bother us as little as it bothers him. In part, his characteristic allusions to Eliot occur not only for effect but as homage to the imagist and allusive verse that is clearly one of his models. Similarly, Barthelme doesn't hide his debt to popular culture or to absurdist theater. Just as his stories aren't as arbitrary as they may first seem, his style isn't as uniquely bizarre. To realize this is not to deny his originality but to acknowledge that innovative art either builds on its forebears or becomes marginal and obscure. People who have read and appreciated such stories as those by Updike, Roth, and Malamud will be able to appreciate what Barthelme accomplishes by following his models rather than theirs (and, of course, what he thereby forfeits). One doesn't admire "The Indian Uprising" for insight or imitation but for the feelings that the prose evokes about matters that might leave us cold were they not so represented and also for the sheer pleasure in seeing how these feelings are produced. What these feelings are (and that, for example, there are many moments of wild comedy amid the anguish) this essay has barely suggested. Rather, it has sought to clear up enough of the reader's probable bafflement so that he may begin to examine the story's texture and thereby to see the brilliance of Donald Barthelme's performance.

QUESTIONS

The Indian Uprising

POINT OF VIEW   1. The essay describes the dramatized narrator as being "little more than the voice that records actions, statements, and allusions. More completely here than in other fiction, the narrator is words." Do you agree with this statement? If so, explain why. If not, write a brief, coherent essay showing that the narrator is more than words.   2. Examine the function of the dramatized narrator in relation to the concerns and techniques of experimental fiction and to the story's meaning.

CHARACTERS   3. Discuss the role played by Miss R., a teacher. How do her actions relate to the story's meaning?   4. The captured Comanche tells his captors that his name is Gustave Aschenbach and that he was born in a country town in the province of Silesia. Is this reference to Thomas Mann's character absurd and meaningless, or does this juxtaposition contribute to the story's meaning? Can you find other contradictions in the description of the characters? 5. What is Sylvia's relationship to the narrator? to Kenneth? to Block? 6. The essay contends that "the characters in the story aren't any more than names to us because that's what they are to each other." Do you agree with this judgment? Explain.

PLOT 7. As the essay observes, the events that comprise the action of the story move on several levels. Considering only the overt level of the battle itself, describe the events of the "uprising." Is there a turning point? a resolution? 8. In what ways, if any, can the battle with the Comanches be considered an objective correlative for the other, less overt battles waged by the narrator?

SETTING 9. The imaginary city that is the setting provides important clues about the story's meaning. What descriptions of the city are offered and what insights do they give the reader?

STYLE 10. Miss R. acknowledges that while some individuals prefer conceits or wisdom, she holds to "the hard, brown, nutlike word. I might point out that there is enough aesthetic excitement here to satisfy anyone but a damned fool." Apply this statement to an examination of Barthelme's prose style in this story. 11. The first paragraph presages, in a remarkable shorthand, the story's meaning. Explain. 12. Show how Barthelme uses language to underscore the pervasiveness of violence and the apathy with which we view man's inhumanity to man. 13. In a critical review, William H. Gass says that "it is impossible to overpraise such a sentence" as: "This unit was crushed in the afternoon of a day that began with spoons and letters in hallways and under windows where men tasted the history of the heart, cone-shaped muscular organ that maintains *circulation of the blood*." Do you agree? Discuss your attitude toward such prose.

TONE 14. In the same review, Gass praises Barthelme for having "the art to make a treasure out of trash, to see *out* from inside it, the world as it's faceted by colored jewelglass." Do you agree that, in this story, Barthelme is able to *use* dreck, not simply write about it? Explain. 15. The essay contends that the neutrality of the narrator means that the reader must supply the tone. Yet Barthelme's decision to make his narrator neutral is a conscious choice that shapes our image of the implied author. Explain.

Moving Through "The Indian Uprising"

FOCUS 1. Explain why the essayist chose, in the first section of the essay, to discuss the story as though it had "more narrative coherence than the story will ultimately be seen to possess." 2. Do you agree that the thesis of the essay is that the theme of "The Indian Uprising" is created "by the story's language"? Why or why not? Can you find a better statement of the essay's thesis?

ORGANIZATION 3. Why does the essayist discuss the various levels of "plot" in much greater detail than he does the characters? 4. Show how the organization of the essay is appropriate to the story it discusses.

USING THE EVIDENCE 5. How does the essayist support his interpretation of the uprising as erotic? 6. What evidence does the essayist offer to show that the story posits a connection between "movies and real life"? How does the essayist relate this connection to Barthelme's prose style?

STYLE 7. Do you find that the essayist's explanation of allusions increases your understanding of the story? Explain. Does the essayist clarify all the allusions in the story?

MAKING LITERARY JUDGMENTS 8. The essay contends that most stories, regardless of their complexity and subtlety, "allow us to contemplate a self-contained and fully delineated action." Do you agree with this judgment? Support your answer with references to stories in this collection. 9. The essay states that "in an ordinary story an event is important partly because of its motivational effect on subsequent events, [whereas] in Barthelme it is important only because of its effect on the reader." Do you agree? Explain.

CITY LIFE

Elsa and Ramona entered the complicated city. They found an apartment without much trouble, several rooms on Porter Street. Curtains were hung. Bright paper things from a Japanese store were placed here and there.

—You'd better tell Charles that he can't come see us until everything is ready.

Ramona thought: I don't want him to come at all. He will go into a room with Elsa and close the door. I will be sitting outside reading the business news. Britain Weighs Economic Curbs. Bond Rate Surge Looms. Time will pass. Then, they will emerge. Acting as if nothing had happened. Elsa will make coffee. Charles will put brandy from his flat silver flask into the coffee. We will all drink the coffee with the brandy in it. Ugh!

—Where shall we put the telephone books?

—Put them over there, by the telephone.

Elsa and Ramona went to the $2 plant store. A man stood outside selling individual peacock feathers. Elsa and Ramona bought several hanging plants in white plastic pots. The proprietor put the plants in brown paper bags.

—Water them every day, girls. Keep them wet.

—We will.

Elsa uttered a melancholy reflection on life: It goes faster and faster! Ramona said: It's so difficult!

Charles accepted a position with greater responsibilities in another city.

—I'll be able to get in on weekends sometimes.

—Is this a real job?

—Of course, Elsa. You don't think I'd fool you, do you?

Clad in an extremely dark gray, if not completely black, suit, he had shaved his mustache.

—This outfit doesn't let you wear them.

Ramona heard Elsa sobbing in the back bedroom. I suppose I should sympathize with her. But I don't.

2.

Ramona received the following letter from Charles:

Dear Ramona—

Thank you, Ramona, for your interesting and curious letter. It is true that I have noticed you sitting there, in the living room, when I visit Elsa. I have many times made mental notes about your appearance, which I consider in no way inferior to that of Elsa herself. I get a pretty electric reaction to your taste in clothes, too. Those upper legs have not been lost on me. But the trouble is, when two girls are living together, one must make a choice. One can't have them both, in our society. This prohibition is enforced by you girls, chiefly, together with older ladies, who if the truth were known probably don't care, but nevertheless feel that standards must be upheld, somewhere. I have Elsa, therefore I can't have you. (I know that there is a philosophical problem about "being" and "having" but I can't discuss that now because I'm a little rushed due to the pressures of my new assignment.) So that's what obtains at the moment, most excellent Ramona. That's where we stand. Of course the future may be different. It not infrequently is.

Hastily,
Charles.

—What are you reading?
—Oh, it's just a letter.
—Who is it from?
—Oh, just somebody I know.
—Who?
—Oh, nobody.
—Oh.

Ramona's mother and father came to town from Montana. Ramona's thin father stood on the Porter Street sidewalk wearing a business suit and a white cowboy hat. He was watching his car. He watched from the steps of the house for a while, and then watched from the sidewalk a little, and then watched from the steps again. Ramona's mother looked in the suitcases for the present she had brought.

—Mother! You shouldn't have brought me such an expensive present!
—Oh, it wasn't all that expensive. We wanted you to have something for the new apartment.
—An original gravure by René Magritte!
—Well, it isn't very big. It's just a small one.

Whenever Ramona received a letter forwarded to her from her Montana home, the letter had been opened and the words "Oops! Opened by mistake!" written on the envelope. But she forgot that in gazing at the handsome new Magritte print, a picture of a tree with a crescent moon cut out of it.

—It's fantastically beautiful! Where shall we hang it?
—How about on the wall?

3.

At the University the two girls enrolled in the Law School.

—I hear the Law School's tough, Elsa stated, but that's what we want, a tough challenge.

—You are the only two girls ever to be admitted to our Law School, the Dean observed. Mostly, we have men. A few foreigners. Now I am going to tell you three things to keep an eye on: 1) Don't try to go too far too fast. 2) Wear plain clothes. And 3) Keep your notes clean. And if I hear the words "Yoo hoo" echoing across the quadrangle, you will be sent down instantly. We don't use those words in this school.

—I like what I already know, Ramona said under her breath.

Savoring their matriculation, the two girls wandered out to sample the joys of Pascin Street. They were closer together at this time than they had ever been. Of course, they didn't want to get too close together. They were afraid to get too close together.

Elsa met Jacques. He was deeply involved in the struggle.

—What is this struggle about, exactly, Jacques?

—My God, Elsa, your eyes! I have never seen that shade of umber in anyone's eyes before. Ever.

Jacques took Elsa to a Mexican restaurant. Elsa cut into her *cabrito con queso*.

—To think that this food was once a baby goat!

Elsa, Ramona, and Jacques looked at the dawn coming up over the hanging plants. Patterns of silver light and so forth.

—You're not afraid that Charles will bust in here unexpectedly and find us?

—Charles is in Cleveland. Besides, I'd say you were with Ramona. Elsa giggled.

Ramona burst into tears.

Elsa and Jacques tried to comfort Ramona.

—Why don't you take a 21-day excursion-fare trip to "preserves of nature"?

—If I went to a "preserve of nature," it would turn out to be nothing but a terrible fen!

Ramona thought: He will go into a room with Elsa and close the door. Time will pass. Then they will emerge, acting as if nothing had happened. Then the coffee. Ugh!

4.

Charles in Cleveland.

"Whiteness"

"Vital skepticism"

Charles advanced very rapidly in the Cleveland hierarchy. That sort of situation that develops sometimes wherein managers feel threatened by gifted subordinates and do not assign them really meaningful duties but instead shunt them aside into dead areas where their human potential is wasted did not develop in Charles' case. His devoted heart lifted him to the highest levels. It was Charles who pointed out that certain operations had been carried out more efficiently "when the cathedrals were white," and in time the entire Cleveland structure was organized around his notions: "whiteness," "vital skepticism."

Two men held Charles down on the floor and a third slipped a needle into his hip.

He awakened in a vaguely familiar room.

—Where am I? he asked the nurselike person who appeared to answer his ring.

—Porter Street, this creature said. Mlle. Ramona will see you shortly. In the meantime, drink some of this orange juice.

Well, Charles thought to himself, I cannot but admire the guts and address of this brave girl, who wanted me so much that she engineered this whole affair—my abduction from Cleveland and removal to these beloved rooms, where once I was entertained by the beautiful Elsa. And now I must see whether my key concepts can get me out of this "fix," for "fix" it is. I shouldn't have written that letter. Perhaps if I wrote another letter? A followup?

Charles formed the letter to Ramona in his mind.

Dear Ramona—

Now that I am back in your house, tied down to this bed with these steel bands around my ankles, I understand that perhaps my earlier letter to you was subject to misinterpretation etc. etc.

Elsa entered the room and saw Charles tied down on the bed.

—That's against the law!

—Sit down, Elsa. Just because you are a law student you want to proclaim the rule of law everywhere. But some things don't have to do with the law. Some things have to do with the heart. The heart, which was our great emblem and cockade, when the cathedrals were white.

—I'm worried about Ramona, Elsa said. She has been missing lectures. And she has been engaging in hilarity at the expense of the law.

—Jokes?

—Gibes. And now this extra-legality. Your sequestration.

Charles and Elsa looked out of the window at the good day.

—See that blue in the sky. How wonderful. After all the gray we've had.

5.

Elsa and Ramona watched the Motorola television set in their pajamas.

—What else is on? Elsa asked.

Ramona looked in the newspaper.

—On 7 there's "Johnny Allegro" with George Raft and Nina Foch. On 9 "Johnny Angel" with George Raft and Claire Trevor. On 11 there's "Johnny Apollo" with Tyrone Power and Dorothy Lamour. On 13 is "Johnny Concho" with Frank Sinatra and Phyllis Kirk. On 2 is "Johnny Dark" with Tony Curtis and Piper Laurie. On 4 is "Johnny Eager" with Robert Taylor and Lana Turner. On 5 is "Johnny O'Clock" with Dick Powell and Evelyn Keyes. On 31 is "Johnny Trouble" with Stuart Whitman and Ethel Barrymore.

—What's this one we're watching?

—What time is it?

—Eleven-thirty-five.

—"Johnny Guitar" with Joan Crawford and Sterling Hayden.

6.

Jacques, Elsa, Charles and Ramona sat in a row at the sun dance. Jacques was sitting next to Elsa and Charles was sitting next to Ramona. Of course Charles was also sitting next to Elsa but he was leaning toward Ramona mostly. It was hard to tell what his intentions were. He kept his hands in his pockets.

—How is the struggle coming, Jacques?

—Quite well, actually. Since the Declaration of Rye we have accumulated many hundreds of new members.

Elsa leaned across Charles to say something to Ramona.

—Did you water the plants?

The sun dancers were beating the ground with sheaves of wheat.

—Is that supposed to make the sun shine, or what? Ramona asked.

—Oh, I think it's just sort of to . . . honor the sun. I don't think it's supposed to make it do anything.

Elsa stood up.

—That's against the law!

—Sit down, Elsa.

Elsa became pregnant.

7.

"This young man, a man though only eighteen . . ."
A large wedding scene
Charles measures the church
Elsa and Jacques bombarded with flowers

Fathers and mothers riding on the city railway
The minister raises his hands
Evacuation of the sacristy: bomb threat
Black limousines with ribbons tied to their aerials
Several men on balconies who appear to be signalling, or applauding
Traffic lights
Pieces of blue cake
Champagne

8.

—Well, Ramona, I am glad we came to the city. In spite of everything.

—Yes, Elsa, it has turned out well for you. You are Mrs. Jacques Tope now. And soon there will be a little one.

—Not so soon. Not for eight months. I am sorry, though, about one thing. I hate to give up Law School.

—Don't be sorry. The Law needs knowledgeable civilians as well as practitioners. Your training will not be wasted.

—That's dear of you. Well, goodbye.

Elsa and Jacques and Charles went into the back bedroom. Ramona remained outside with the newspaper.

—Well, I suppose I might as well put the coffee on, she said to herself. Rats!

9.

Laughing aristocrats moved up and down the corridors of the city.

Elsa, Jacques, Ramona and Charles drove out to the combined race track and art gallery. Ramona had a Heineken and everyone else had one too. The tables were crowded with laughing aristocrats. More laughing aristocrats arrived in their carriages drawn by dancing matched pairs. Some drifted in from Flushing and São Paulo. Management of the funded indebtedness was discussed; the Queen's behavior was discussed. All of the horses ran very well, and the pictures ran well too. The laughing aristocrats sucked on the heads of their gold-headed canes some more.

Jacques held up his degrees from the New Yorker Theatre, where he had been buried in the classics, when he was twelve.

—I remember the glorious debris underneath the seats, he said, and I remember that I hated then, as I do now, laughing aristocrats.

The aristocrats heard Jacques talking. They all raised their canes in the

air, in rage. A hundred canes shattered in the sun, like a load of antihista-
mines falling out of an airplane. More laughing aristocrats arrived in phae-
tons and tumbrels.

As a result of absenting himself from Cleveland for eight months,
Charles had lost his position there.

—It is true that I am part of the laughing-aristocrat structure, Charles
said. I don't mean I am one of them. I mean I am their creature. They hold
me in thrall.

Laughing aristocrats who invented the cost-plus contract . . .

Laughing aristocrats who invented the real estate broker . . .

Laughing aristocrats who invented Formica . . .

Laughing aristocrats wiping their surfaces clean with a damp cloth . . .

Charles poured himself another brilliant green Heineken.

—To the struggle!

10.

The Puerto Rican painters have come, as they do every three years, to
paint the apartment!

The painters, Emmanuel and Curtis, heaved their buckets, rollers, lad-
ders and drop cloths up the stairs into the apartment.

—What shade of white do you want this apartment painted?

A consultation.

—How about plain white?

—Fine, Emmanuel said. That's a mighty good-looking Motorola television set you have there. Would you turn it to Channel 47, *por favor?*
There's a film we'd like to see. We can paint and watch at the same time.

—What's the film?

—"Victimas de Pecado," with Pedro Vargas and Ninon Sevilla.

Elsa spoke to her husband, Jacques.

—Ramona has frightened me.

—How?

—She said one couldn't sleep with someone more than four hundred
times without being bored.

—How does she know?

—She saw it in a book.

—Well, Jacques said, we only do what we really want to do about 11
per cent of the time. In our lives.

—11 per cent!

At the Ingres Gardens, the great singer Moonbelly sang a song of rage.

11.

Vercingetorix, leader of the firemen, reached for his red telephone.

—Hello, is this Ramona?

—No, this is Elsa. Ramona's not home.

—Will you tell her that the leader of all the firemen called?

Ramona went out of town for a weekend with Vercingetorix. They went to his farm, about eighty miles away. In the kitchen of the farm, bats attacked them. Vercingetorix could not find his broom.

—Put a paper bag over them. Where is a paper bag?

—The groceries, Vercingetorix said.

Ramona dumped the groceries on the floor. The bats were zooming around the room uttering audible squeaks. With the large paper bag in his hands Vercingetorix made weak capturing gestures toward the bats.

—God, if one gets in my hair, Ramona said.

—They don't want to fly into the bag, Vercingetorix said.

—Give me the bag, if one gets in my hair I'll croak right here in front of you.

Ramona put the paper bag over her head just as a bat banged into her.

—What was that?

—A bat, Vercingetorix said, but it didn't get into your hair.

—Damn you, Ramona said, inside the bag, why can't you stay in the city like other men?

Moonbelly emerged from the bushes and covered her arms with kisses.

12.

Jacques persuaded Moonbelly to appear at a benefit for the signers of the Declaration of Rye, who were having a little legal trouble. Three hundred younger people sat in the church. Paper plates were passed up and down the rows. A number of quarters were collected.

Moonbelly sang a new song called "The System Cannot Withstand Close Scrutiny."

> The system cannot withstand close scrutiny
> The system cannot withstand close scrutiny
> The system cannot withstand close scrutiny
> The system cannot withstand close scrutiny
> Etc.

Jacques spoke briefly and well. A few more quarters showered down on the stage.

At the party after the benefit Ramona spoke to Jacques, because he was handsome and flushed with triumph.

—Tell me something.

—All right Ramona what do you want to know?

—Do you promise to tell me the truth?

—Of course. Sure.

—Can one be impregnated by a song?

—I think not. I would say no.

—While one is asleep, possibly?

—It's not very likely.

—What sort of people have hysterical pregnancies?

—Well, you know. Sort of nervous girls.

—If a hysterical pregnancy results in a birth, is it still considered hysterical?

—No.

—Rats!

13.

Charles and Jacques were trying to move a parked Volkswagen. When a Volkswagen is parked with its parking brake set you need three people to move it, usually.

A third person was sighted moving down the street.

—Say, buddy, could you give us a hand for a minute?

—Sure, the third person said.

Charles, Jacques, and the third person grasped the VW firmly in their hands and heaved. It moved forward opening up a new parking space where only half a space had been before.

—Thanks, Jacques said. Now would you mind helping us unload this panel truck here? It contains printed materials pertaining to the worldwide struggle for liberation from outmoded ways of thought that hold us in thrall.

—I don't mind.

Charles, Jacques, and Hector carried the bundles of printed material up the stairs into the Porter Street apartment.

—What does this printed material say, Jacques?

—It says that the government has promised to give us some of our money back if it loses the war.

—Is that true?

—No. And now, how about a drink?

Drinking their drinks they regarded the black trombone case which rested under Hector's coat.

—Is that a trombone case?

Hector's eyes glazed.

Moonbelly sat on the couch, his great belly covered with plants and animals.

—It's good to be what one is, he said.

14.

Ramona's child was born on Wednesday. It was a boy.

—But Ramona! Who is responsible? Charles? Jacques? Moonbelly? Vercingetorix?

—It was a virgin birth, unfortunately, Ramona said.

—But what does this imply about the child?

—Nothing, Ramona said. It was just an ordinary virgin birth. Don't bother your pretty head about it, Elsa dear.

However much Ramona tried to soft-pedal the virgin birth, people persisted in getting excited about it. A few cardinals from the Sacred Rota dropped by.

—What is this you're claiming here, foolish girl?

—I claim nothing, Your Eminence. I merely report.

—Give us the name of the man who has compromised you!

—It was a virgin birth, sir.

Cardinal Maranto frowned in several directions.

—There can't be another Virgin Birth!

Ramona modestly lowered her eyes. The child, Sam, was wrapped in a blanket with his feet sticking out.

—Better cover those feet.

—Thank you, Cardinal. I will.

15.

Ramona went to class at the Law School carrying Sam on her hip in a sling.

—What's that?

—My child.

—I didn't know you were married.

—I'm not.

—That's against the law! I think.

—What law is it against?

The entire class regarded the teacher.

—Well there is a law against fornication on the books, but of course it's not enforced very often ha ha. It's sort of difficult to enforce ha ha.

—I have to tell you, Ramona said, that this child is not of human man conceived. It was a virgin birth. Unfortunately.

A few waves of smickers washed across the classroom.

A law student named Harold leaped to his feet.

—Stop this smickering! What are we thinking of? To make mock of this fine girl! Rot me if I will permit it! Are we gentlemen? Is this lady our colleague? Or are we rather beasts of the field? This Ramona, this trull . . . No, that's not what I mean. I mean that we should think not upon her peculations but on our own peculations. For, as Augustine tells us, if for some error or sin of our own, sadness seizes us, let us not only bear in mind that an afflicted spirit is a sacrifice to God but also the words: for as water quencheth a flaming fire, so almsgiving quencheth sin; and for I desire, He says, mercy rather than sacrifice. As, therefore, if we were in danger from fire, we should, of course, run for water with which to extinguish it, and should be thankful if someone showed us water nearby, so if some flame of sin has arisen from the hay of our passions, we should take delight in this, that the ground for a work of great mercy is given to us. Therefore—

Harold collapsed, from the heat of his imagination.

A student in a neighboring seat looked deeply into Sam's eyes.

—They're brown.

16.

Moonbelly was fingering his axe.

—A birth hymn? Do I really want to write a birth hymn?

—What do I really think about this damn birth?

—Of course it's within the tradition.

—Is this the real purpose of cities? Is this why all these units have been brought together, under the red, white and blue?

—Cities are erotic, in a depressing way. Should that be my line?

—Of course I usually do best with something in the rage line. However—

—C . . . F . . . C . . . F . . . C . . . F . . . G7 . . .

Moonbelly wrote "Cities Are Centers of Copulation."

The recording company official handed Moonbelly a gold record marking the sale of a million copies of "Cities Are Centers of Copulation."

17.

Charles and Jacques were still talking to Hector Guimard, the former trombone player.

—Yours is not a modern problem, Jacques said. The problem today is not angst but lack of angst.

—Wait a minute, Jacques. Although I myself believe that there is nothing wrong with being a trombone player, I can understand Hector's feeling. I know a painter who feels the same way about being a painter. Every morning he gets up, brushes his teeth, and stands before the empty canvas. A terrible feeling of being *de trop* comes over him. So he goes to the corner and buys the Times, at the corner newsstand. He comes back home and reads the Times. During the period in which he's coupled with the Times he is all right. But soon the Times is exhausted. The empty canvas remains. So (usually) he makes a mark on it, some kind of mark that is not what he means. That is, any old mark, just to have something on the canvas. Then he is profoundly depressed because what is there is not what he meant. And it's time for lunch. He goes out and buys a pastrami sandwich at the deli. He comes back and eats the sandwich meanwhile regarding the canvas with the wrong mark on it out of the corner of his eye. During the afternoon, he paints out the mark of the morning. This affords him a measure of satisfaction. The balance of the afternoon is spent in deciding whether or not to venture another mark. The new mark, if one is ventured, will also, inevitably, be misconceived. He ventures it. It is misconceived. It is, in fact, the worst kind of vulgarity. He paints out the second mark. Anxiety accumulates. However, the canvas is now, in and of itself, because of the wrong moves and the painting out, becoming rather interesting-looking. He goes to the A. & P. and buys a TV Mexican dinner and many bottles of Carta Blanca. He comes back to his loft and eats the Mexican dinner and drinks a couple of Carta Blancas, sitting in front of his canvas. The canvas is, for one thing, no longer empty. Friends drop in and congratulate him on having a not-empty canvas. He begins feeling better. A something has been wrested from the nothing. The quality of the something is still at issue—he is by no means home free. And of course all of painting—the whole art—has moved on somewhere else, it's not where his head is, and he knows that, but nevertheless he—

—How does this apply to trombone playing? Hector asked.

—I had the connection in my mind when I began, Charles said.

—As Goethe said, theory is gray, but the golden tree of life is green.

18.

Everybody in the city was watching a movie about an Indian village menaced by a tiger. Only Wendell Corey stood between the village and the tiger. Furthermore Wendell Corey had dropped his rifle—or rather the tiger had knocked it out of his hands—and was left with only his knife. In addition, the tiger had Wendell Corey's left arm in his mouth up to the shoulder.

Ramona thought about the city.

—I have to admit we are locked in the most exquisite mysterious muck. This muck heaves and palpitates. It is multi-directional and has a mayor. To describe it takes many hundreds of thousands of words. Our muck is only a part of a much greater muck—the nation-state—which is itself the creation of that muck of mucks, human consciousness. Of course all these things also have a touch of sublimity—as when Moonbelly sings, for example, or all the lights go out. What a happy time that was, when all the electricity went away! If only we could re-create that paradise! By, for instance, all forgetting to pay our electric bills at the same time. All nine million of us. Then we'd all get those little notices that say unless we remit within five days the lights will go out. We all stand up from our chairs with the notice in our hands. The same thought drifts across the furrowed surface of nine million minds. We wink at each other, through the walls.

At the Electric Company, a nervousness appeared as Ramona's thought launched itself into parapsychological space.

Ramona arranged names in various patterns.

> Vercingetorix
> Moonbelly
> Charles
>
> Moonbelly
> Charles
> Vercingetorix
>
> Charles
> Vercingetorix
> Moonbelly

—Upon me, their glance has fallen. The engendering force was, perhaps, the fused glance of all of them. From the millions of units crawling about on the surface of the city, their wavering desirous eye selected me. The pupil enlarged to admit more light: more me. They began dancing little dances of suggestion and fear. These dances constitute an invitation of unmistakable import—an invitation which, if accepted, leads one down many muddy roads. I accepted. What was the alternative?

SUGGESTIONS FOR WRITING

The Stories

1. Discuss the function and ramifications of Barthelme's use of the effaced narrator's point of view in "City Life."

2. In his essay on "The Indian Uprising," Charles Thomas Samuels declares, "Putting words together well is not only an expression of Barthelme's craftsmanship; it is his way of renewing the force of his subject." Examine "City Life" in view of this hypothesis.

3. Compare and contrast the use of fragments in "The Indian Uprising" and "How I Contemplated. . . ." Be sure to consider technique in relation to meaning.

4. Focusing on the city as setting, write an essay that compares and contrasts "A Gift from the City" and "City Life."

Other Works by Donald Barthelme

1. In *City of Words*, Tony Tanner writes: "To introduce *Snow White* into the contemporary world is obviously to gain the opportunity for ironies, incongruities, clashes of genre . . . and indirect sentimentality. . . ." Explore each of these "opportunities" in Barthelme's *Snow White*.

2. Barthelme's fiction has been compared to Pop Art. Drawing examples from the stories in either *Unspeakable Practices, Unnatural Acts* or *City Life*, support or contest this assertion.

3. Barthelme's dissatisfaction with language and his obsessive concern with the phenomenology of the creative process supply the content of many of his short stories and of the novella *Snow White*. Stanley

Trachtenberg comments, "Along with denying the possibility of providing fictional equivalents of reality, the form of *Snow White* questions the discursive ability of language even to express that denial." Apply these observations to stories in *Come Back, Dr. Caligari* and *Sadness*.

4. In many of Barthelme's stories, words usurp the place of characters in more conventional fiction (as Charles Thomas Samuels says of "The Indian Uprising"—the narrator is words). Discuss this metamorphosis and its stylistic and thematic implications in stories from *City Life* and *Sadness*.

5. Both John Updike and Donald Barthelme write for the *New Yorker*, and, although their styles are divergent, they share similar preoccupations, settings, fictional personages, and events. Using Updike's *Museums and Women and Other Stories* and Barthelme's *City Life*, discuss their shared "world."

BIBLIOGRAPHY

Primary

Come Back, Dr. Caligari. Boston: Little, Brown, 1964. Short stories.
Snow White. New York: Atheneum, 1967. (Originally published in the *New Yorker*, February 18, 1967.) A novella.
Unspeakable Practices, Unnatural Acts. New York: Farrar, Straus & Giroux, 1968. Short stories.
City Life. New York: Farrar, Straus & Giroux, 1970. Short stories.
The Slightly Irregular Fire Engine or the Hithering Thithering Djinn. New York: Farrar, Straus & Giroux, 1971. Children's book.
Sadness. New York: Farrar, Straus & Giroux, 1972. Short stories.

Secondary

Gass, William H. "The Leading Edge of the Trash Phenomenon" in *Fiction and the Figures of Life*. New York: Alfred A. Knopf, 1970. A review of *Unspeakable Practices, Unnatural Acts* that emphasizes "The Indian Uprising."
Gillen, F. "Donald Barthelme's City: A Guide." *Twentieth Century Literature*, 18 (January 1972), 37–44. A thematic exploration of Barthelme's short stories.

Krupnick, Mark L. "Notes from the Funhouse." *Modern Occasions,* 1 (Fall 1970), 108–12. Review of *City Life* that criticizes Barthelme for failing to supply "opposing images of passion or aesthetic bliss to redeem all this *dreck.* . . . What is exhausted for Barthelme are not merely certain formal possibilities of fiction but emotion itself."

Longleigh, Peter J. "Donald Barthelme's *Snow White.*" *Critique,* 11:3 (1969), 30–34. Either a mildly humorous tongue-in-cheek analysis of *Snow White* or a highly pretentious symbolic, mythical, psychological, and sociological interpretation that finds correspondences between Barthelme and Shakespeare, Melville, Wittgenstein, Hume, Kierkegaard, Aristotle, Beckett, Joyce, Eliot, Baldwin, and Sophocles—among others.

Mudrick, Marvin. "Sarraute, Duras, Burroughs, Barthelme, and a Postscript." *The Hudson Review,* 20 (Autumn 1967), 473–86. Discusses *Snow White* and *Come Back, Dr. Caligari* (on pp. 482–85), describing the former as "a remarkably slick pseudo–avant-garde novel."

Shadoian, Jack. "Notes on Donald Barthelme's *Snow White.*" *Western Humanities Review,* 24 (Winter 1970), 73–75. A sympathetic review that finds the tone of *Snow White* "a serious matter" despite its suggesting "that life isn't worth taking seriously."

Tanner, Tony. *City of Words: American Fiction 1950–1970.* London: Jonathan Cape Ltd., 1971. Discusses the meaning of fragmentation in Barthelme's fiction, pp. 400–406.

Trachtenberg, Stanley. "Modes of Imperception." *The Kenyon Review,* 29 (September 1967), 561–68. Discusses *Snow White* (on pp. 563–65) as an anti-novel that ridicules "not only what is seen but the conventional manner of perception."

You shouldn't pay very much attention to anything writ-
ers say. They don't know why they do what they do. They're
like good tennis players or good painters, who are just full
of nonsense, pompous and embarrassing, or merely mistaken,
when they open their mouths. All sports, for example, all
knacks and skills, become close to second nature with experts.
When writers speak of things like inspiration and characters
taking over and space-time grids, it's usually because they
don't know why they do the things they do. And, if you be-
gin to think about it too much, I guess you might tie yourself
in knots, like when you think consciously about tying your
necktie or tying your shoes. At least I have never heard much
that any writer has said about writing that didn't embarrass
me, including the things I say about it.

FROM "John Barth: An Interview"

JOHN BARTH

John Barth was born in Cambridge, Maryland, in 1930. After graduating from high school, where he was a drummer in the school band, Barth enrolled in New York's Juilliard School of Music to study orchestration. His interest in music continues into the present, and, as a writer, he often sees himself as an orchestrator of old literary devices.

Barth transferred after one term at Juilliard to Johns Hopkins University, where he studied journalism and literature and worked part-time in the classics library. Of this work experience he has said: "One was permitted to get lost for hours in that splendiferous labyrinth and intoxicate, engorge oneself with *story*. Especially I became enamoured of the great tale-cycles and collections. . . . Most of those spellbinding liars I have forgotten, but never Scheherazade." Barth received a bachelor's degree from Johns Hopkins in 1951 and, in 1952, a master's degree.

A teacher as well as a writer, Barth was a member of the English department at Pennsylvania State University from 1953 to 1965, and for the next seven years, was associated with the State University of New York at Buffalo. In 1972, he returned to Johns Hopkins to teach in the university's writing workshop. Barth's stories and essays have appeared in a wide range of periodicals, including *Esquire, Atlantic, Yale Review,* and *Kenyon Review.* He has been the recipient of a National Institute of Arts and Letters grant and, in 1972, was co-winner of a National Book Award in fiction, for *Chimera.*

Barth's intimate knowledge of the history, geography, and inhabitants of Dorchester County, Maryland—the region he knew as a boy—is apparent in much of his fiction, including such works as *The Floating Opera* (1967), *The Sot-Weed Factor* (1967), and the "Ambrose" stories of *Lost in the Funhouse* (1968). Barth has also found delight and instruction in "the old tales" and encourages young writers to do the same: ". . . it is refreshing, it seems to me, for writers to become interested in yarns—elaborate lies. The *Arabian Nights* may be a better mentor for many than, say, J. D. Salinger. There is a Hindu thing that I've always wanted to go clear through. I believe it's Hindu. It's called *The Ocean of Story,* and I keep seeing it on the shelf in the library. Four feet long. Wouldn't it be wonderful to have written that?"

L⊕ST IN

THE FUNH⊕USE

For whom is the funhouse fun? Perhaps for lovers. For
Ambrose it is *a place of fear and confusion*. He has come to the seashore
with his family for the holiday, *the occasion of their visit is Independence
Day, the most important secular holiday of the United States of America.*
A single straight underline is the manuscript mark for italic type, *which
in turn* is the printed equivalent to oral emphasis of words and phrases as
well as the customary type for titles of complete works, not to mention.
Italics are also employed, in fiction stories especially, for "outside," intrusive, or artificial voices, such as radio announcements, the texts of telegrams
and newspaper articles, et cetera. They should be used *sparingly*. If passages originally in roman type are italicized by someone repeating them,
it's customary to acknowledge the fact. *Italics mine.*

Ambrose was "at that awkward age." His voice came out high-pitched
as a child's if he let himself get carried away; to be on the safe side, therefore, he moved and spoke with *deliberate calm* and *adult gravity*. Talking

soberly of unimportant or irrelevant matters and listening consciously to the sound of your own voice are useful habits for maintaining control in this difficult interval. *En route* to Ocean City he sat in the back seat of the family car with his brother Peter, age fifteen, and Magda G———, age fourteen, a pretty girl and exquisite young lady, who lived not far from them on B——— Street in the town of D———, Maryland. Initials, blanks, or both were often substituted for proper names in nineteenth-century fiction to enhance the illusion of reality. It is as if the author felt it necessary to delete the names for reasons of tact or legal liability. Interestingly, as with other aspects of realism, it is an *illusion* that is being enhanced, by purely artificial means. Is it likely, does it violate the principle of verisimilitude, that a thirteen-year-old boy could make such a sophisticated observation? A girl of fourteen is *the psychological coeval* of a boy of fifteen or sixteen; a thirteen-year-old boy, therefore, even one precocious in some other respects, might be three years *her emotional junior.*

Thrice a year—on Memorial, Independence, and Labor Days—the family visits Ocean City for the afternoon and evening. When Ambrose and Peter's father was their age, the excursion was made by train, as mentioned in the novel *The 42nd Parallel* by John Dos Passos. Many families from the same neighborhood used to travel together, with dependent relatives and often with Negro servants; schoolfuls of children swarmed through the railway cars; everyone shared everyone else's Maryland fried chicken, Virginia ham, deviled eggs, potato salad, beaten biscuits, iced tea. Nowadays (that is, in 19—, the year of our story) the journey is made by automobile—more comfortably and quickly though without the extra fun though without the *camaraderie* of a general excursion. It's all part of the deterioration of American life, their father declares; Uncle Karl supposes that when the boys take *their* families to Ocean City for the holidays they'll fly in Autogiros. Their mother, sitting in the middle of the front seat like Magda in the second, only with her arms on the seat-back behind the men's shoulders, wouldn't want the good old days back again, the steaming trains and stuffy long dresses; on the other hand she can do without Autogiros, too, if she has to become a grandmother to fly in them.

Description of physical appearance and mannerisms is one of several standard methods of characterization used by writers of fiction. It is also important to "keep the senses operating"; when a detail from one of the five senses, say visual, is "crossed" with a detail from another, say auditory, the reader's imagination is oriented to the scene, perhaps unconsciously. This procedure may be compared to the way surveyors and navigators de-

termine their positions by two or more compass bearings, a process known
as triangulation. The brown hair on Ambrose's mother's forearms gleamed
in the sun like. Though right-handed, she took her left arm from the
seat-back to press the dashboard cigar lighter for Uncle Karl. When the
glass bead in its handle glowed red, the lighter was ready for use. The smell
of Uncle Karl's cigar smoke reminded one of. The fragrance of the ocean
came strong to the picnic ground where they always stopped for lunch,
two miles inland from Ocean City. Having to pause for a full hour almost
within sound of the breakers was difficult for Peter and Ambrose when
they were younger; even at their present age it was not easy to keep their
anticipation, *stimulated by the briny spume,* from turning into short temper. The Irish author James Joyce, in his unusual novel entitled *Ulysses,*
now available in this country, uses the adjectives *snot-green* and *scrotum-
tightening* to describe the sea. Visual, auditory, tactile, olfactory, gustatory.
Peter and Ambrose's father, while steering their black 1936 LaSalle sedan
with one hand, could with the other remove the first cigarette from a white
pack of Lucky Strikes and, more remarkably, light it with a match fore-
fingered from its book and thumbed against the flint paper without being
detached. The matchbook cover merely advertised U. S. War Bonds and
Stamps. A fine metaphor, simile, or other figure of speech, in addition to
its obvious "first-order" relevance to the thing it describes, will be seen
upon reflection to have a second order of significance: it may be drawn
from the *milieu* of the action, for example, or be particularly appropriate
to the sensibility of the narrator, even hinting to the reader things of which
the narrator is unaware; or it may cast further and subtler lights upon the
thing it describes, sometimes ironically qualifying the more evident sense
of the comparison.

To say that Ambrose's and Peter's mother was *pretty* is to accomplish
nothing; the reader may acknowledge the proposition, but his imagination
is not engaged. Besides, Magda was also pretty, yet in an altogether different way. Although she lived on B——— Street she had very good
manners and did better than average in school. Her figure was very well
developed for her age. Her right hand lay casually on the plush upholstery
of the seat, very near Ambrose's left leg, on which his own hand rested. The
space between their legs, between her right and his left leg, was out of the
line of sight of anyone sitting on the other side of Magda, as well as anyone glancing into the rear-view mirror. Uncle Karl's face resembled Peter's
—rather, vice versa. Both had dark hair and eyes, short husky statures, deep
voices. Magda's left hand was probably in a similar position on her left

side. The boy's father is difficult to describe; no particular feature of his appearance or manner stood out. He wore glasses and was principal of a T——— County grade school. Uncle Karl was a masonry contractor.

Although Peter must have known as well as Ambrose that the latter, because of his position in the car, would be the first to see the electrical towers of the power plant at V———, the halfway point of their trip, he leaned forward and slightly toward the center of the car and pretended to be looking for them through the flat pinewoods and tuckahoe creeks along the highway. For as long as the boys could remember, "looking for the Towers" had been a feature of the first half of their excursions to Ocean City, "looking for the standpipe" of the second. Though the game was childish, their mother preserved the tradition of rewarding the first to see the Towers with a candy-bar or piece of fruit. She insisted now that Magda play the game; the prize, she said, was "something hard to get nowadays." Ambrose decided not to join in; he sat far back in his seat. Magda, like Peter, leaned forward. Two sets of straps were discernible through the shoulders of her sun dress; the inside right one, a brassiere-strap, was fastened or shortened with a small safety pin. The right armpit of her dress, presumably the left as well, was damp with perspiration. The simple strategy for being first to espy the Towers, which Ambrose had understood by the age of four, was to sit on the right-hand side of the car. Whoever sat there, however, had also to put up with the worst of the sun, and so Ambrose, without mentioning the matter, chose sometimes the one and sometimes the other. Not impossibly Peter had never caught on to the trick, or thought his brother hadn't simply because Ambrose on occasion preferred shade to a Baby Ruth or tangerine.

The shade-sun situation didn't apply to the front seat, owing to the windshield; if anything the driver got more sun, since the person on the passenger side not only was shaded below by the door and dashboard but might swing down his sunvisor all the way too.

"Is that them?" Magda asked. Ambrose's mother teased the boys for letting Magda win, insinuating that "somebody [had] a girlfriend." Peter and Ambrose's father reached a long thin arm across their mother to butt his cigarette in the dashboard ashtray, under the lighter. The prize this time for seeing the Towers first was a banana. Their mother bestowed it after chiding their father for wasting a half-smoked cigarette when everything was so scarce. Magda, to take the prize, moved her hand from so near Ambrose's that he could have touched it as though accidentally. She offered to share the prize, things like that were so hard to find; but everyone insisted it was hers alone. Ambrose's mother sang an iambic trimeter couplet from a popular song, femininely rhymed:

> *"What's good is in the Army;*
> *What's left will never harm me."*

Uncle Karl tapped his cigar ash out the ventilator window; some particles were sucked by the slipstream back into the car through the rear window on the passenger side. Magda demonstrated her ability to hold a banana in one hand and peel it with her teeth. She still sat forward; Ambrose pushed his glasses back onto the bridge of his nose with his left hand, which he then negligently let fall to the seat cushion immediately behind her. He even permitted the single hair, gold, on the second joint of his thumb to brush the fabric of her skirt. Should she have sat back at that instant, his hand would have been caught under her.

Plush upholstery prickles uncomfortably through gabardine slacks in the July sun. The function of the *beginning* of a story is to introduce the principal characters, establish their initial relationships, set the scene for the main action, expose the background of the situation if necessary, plant motifs and foreshadowings where appropriate, and initiate the first complication or whatever of the "rising action." Actually, if one imagines a story called "The Funhouse," or "Lost in the Funhouse," the details of the drive to Ocean City don't seem especially relevant. The *beginning* should recount the events between Ambrose's first sight of the funhouse early in the afternoon and his entering it with Magda and Peter in the evening. The *middle* would narrate all relevant events from the time he goes in to the time he loses his way; middles have the double and contradictory function of delaying the climax while at the same time preparing the reader for it and fetching him to it. Then the *ending* would tell what Ambrose does while he's lost, how he finally finds his way out, and what everybody makes of the experience. So far there's been no real dialogue, very little sensory detail, and nothing in the way of a *theme*. And a long time has gone by already without anything happening; it makes a person wonder. We haven't even reached Ocean City yet: we will never get out of the funhouse.

The more closely an author identifies with the narrator, literally or metaphorically, the less advisable it is, as a rule, to use the first-person narrative viewpoint. Once three years previously the young people *aforementioned* played Niggers and Masters in the backyard; when it was Ambrose's turn to be the Master and theirs to be Niggers Peter had to go serve his evening papers; Ambrose was afraid to punish Magda alone, but she led him to the whitewashed Torture Chamber between the woodshed and the privy in the Slaves Quarters; there she knelt sweating among bamboo rakes and dusty Mason jars, pleadingly embraced his knees, and while bees droned in the lattice as if on an ordinary summer afternoon, purchased clemency at a surprising price set by herself. Doubtless she remembered nothing of this event; Ambrose on the other hand seemed unable to forget the least detail of his life. He even recalled how, standing beside himself with awed impersonality in the reeky heat, he'd stared the while at an empty cigar box in which Uncle Karl kept stone-cutting chisels: beneath the words *El Producto,* a laureled, loose-toga'd lady regarded the sea from a marble bench; beside her, forgotten or not yet turned to, was a five-stringed lyre. Her chin reposed on the back of her right hand; her left depended negligently from the bench-arm. The lower half of scene and lady was peeled away; the words EXAMINED BY ———— were inked there into the wood. Nowadays cigar boxes are made of pasteboard. Ambrose wondered what Magda would have done, Ambrose wondered what Magda would do when she sat back on his hand as he resolved she should. Be angry. Make a teasing joke of it. Give no sign at all. For a long time she leaned forward, playing cow-poker with Peter against Uncle Karl and Mother and watching for the first sign of Ocean City. At nearly the same instant, picnic ground and Ocean City standpipe hove into view; an Amoco filling station on their side of the road cost Mother and Uncle Karl fifty cows and the game; Magda bounced back, clapping her right hand on Mother's right arm; Ambrose moved clear "in the nick of time."

At this rate our hero, at this rate our protagonist will remain in the funhouse forever. Narrative ordinarily consists of alternating dramatization and summarization. One symptom of nervous tension, paradoxically, is repeated and violent yawning; neither Peter nor Magda nor Uncle Karl nor Mother reacted in this manner. Although they were no longer small children, Peter and Ambrose were each given a dollar to spend on boardwalk amusements in addition to what money of their own they'd brought along. Magda too, though she protested she had ample spending money. The boys' mother made a little scene out of distributing the bills; she pretended that her sons and Magda were small children and cautioned them not to spend the sum too quickly or in one place. Magda promised with a merry laugh and, having both hands free, took the bill with her left. Peter laughed also and pledged in a falsetto to be a good boy. His imitation of a child was not clever. The boys' father was tall and thin, balding, fair-complexioned. Assertions of that sort are not effective; the reader may acknowledge the proposition, but. We should be much farther along than we are; something has gone wrong; not much of this preliminary rambling seems relevant. Yet everyone begins in the same place; how is it that most go along without difficulty but a few lose their way?

"Stay out from under the boardwalk," Uncle Karl growled from the side of his mouth. The boys' mother pushed his shoulder *in mock annoyance*. They were all standing before Fat May the Laughing Lady who advertised the funhouse. Larger than life, Fat May mechanically shook, rocked on her heels, slapped her thighs while recorded laughter—uproarious, female—came amplified from a hidden loudspeaker. It chuckled, wheezed, wept; tried in vain to catch its breath; tittered, groaned, exploded raucous and anew. You couldn't hear it without laughing yourself, no matter how you felt. Father came back from talking to a Coast-Guardsman on duty and reported that the surf was spoiled with crude oil from tankers recently torpedoed offshore. Lumps of it, difficult to remove, made tarry tidelines on the beach and stuck on swimmers. Many bathed in the surf nevertheless and came out speckled; others paid to use a municipal pool and only sunbathed on the beach. We would do the latter. We would do the latter. We would do the latter.

Under the boardwalk, matchbook covers, grainy other things. What is the story's theme? Ambrose is ill. He perspires in the dark passages; candied apples-on-a-stick, delicious-looking, disappointing to eat. Funhouses need men's and ladies' room at intervals. Others perhaps have also vomited in corners and corridors; may even have had bowel movements liable to be stepped in in the dark. The word *fuck* suggests suction and/or and/or flatulence. Mother and Father; grandmothers and grandfathers on both sides; great-grandmothers and great-grandfathers on four sides, et cetera. Count a generation as thirty years: in approximately the year when Lord Baltimore was granted charter to the province of Maryland by Charles I, five hundred twelve women—English, Welsh, Bavarian, Swiss—of every class and character, received into themselves the penises the intromittent organs of five hundred twelve men, ditto, in every circumstance and posture, to conceive the five hundred twelve ancestors of the two hundred fifty-six ancestors of the et cetera et cetera et cetera et cetera et cetera et cetera et cetera et cetera of the author, of the narrator, of this story, *Lost in the Funhouse*. In alleyways, ditches, canopy beds, pinewoods, bridal suites, ship's cabins, coach-and-fours, coaches-and-four, sultry toolsheds; on the cold sand under boardwalks, littered with *El Producto* cigar butts, treasured with Lucky Strike cigarette stubs, Coca-Cola caps, gritty turds, cardboard lollipop sticks, matchbook covers warning that A Slip of the Lip Can

Sink a Ship. The shluppish whisper, continuous as seawash round the globe, tidelike falls and rises with the circuit of dawn and dusk.

Magda's teeth. She *was* left-handed. Perspiration. They've gone all the way, through, Magda and Peter, they've been waiting for hours with Mother and Uncle Karl while Father searches for his lost son; they draw french-fried potatoes from a paper cup and shake their heads. They've named the children they'll one day have and bring to Ocean City on holidays. Can spermatozoa properly be thought of as male animalcules when there are no female spermatozoa? They grope through hot, dark windings, past Love's Tunnel's fearsome obstacles. Some perhaps lose their way.

Peter suggested then and there that they do the funhouse; he had been through it before, so had Magda, Ambrose hadn't and suggested, his voice cracking on account of Fat May's laughter, that they swim first. All were chuckling, couldn't help it; Ambrose's father, Ambrose's and Peter's father came up grinning like a lunatic with two boxes of syrup-coated popcorn, one for Mother, one for Magda; the men were to help themselves. Ambrose walked on Magda's right; being by nature left-handed, she carried the box in her left hand. Up front the situation was reversed.

"What are you limping for?" Magda inquired of Ambrose. He supposed in a husky tone that his foot had gone to sleep in the car. Her teeth flashed. "Pins and needles?" It was the honeysuckle on the lattice of the former privy that drew the bees. Imagine being stung there. How long is this going to take?

The adults decided to forgo the pool; but Uncle Karl insisted they change into swimsuits and do the beach. "He wants to watch the pretty girls," Peter teased, and ducked behind Magda from Uncle Karl's pretended wrath. "You've got all the pretty girls you need right here," Magda declared, and Mother said: "Now that's the gospel truth." Magda scolded Peter, who reached over her shoulder to sneak some popcorn. "Your brother and father aren't getting any." Uncle Karl wondered if they were going to have fireworks that night, what with the shortages. It wasn't the shortages, Mr. M——— replied; Ocean City had fireworks from pre-war. But it was too risky on account of the enemy submarines, some people thought.

"Don't seem like Fourth of July without fireworks," said Uncle Karl. The inverted tag in dialogue writing is still considered permissible with proper names or epithets, but sounds old-fashioned with personal pronouns. "We'll have 'em again soon enough," predicted the boys' father. Their mother declared she could do without fireworks: they reminded her too much of the real thing. Their father said all the more reason to shoot off a few now and again. Uncle Karl asked *rhetorically* who needed reminding, just look at people's hair and skin.

"The oil, yes," said Mrs. M———.

Ambrose had a pain in his stomach and so didn't swim but enjoyed watching the others. He and his father burned red easily. Magda's figure was exceedingly well developed for her age. She too declined to swim, and got mad, and became angry when Peter attempted to drag her into the pool. She always swam, he insisted; what did she mean not swim? Why did a person come to Ocean City?

"Maybe I want to lay here with Ambrose," Magda teased.

Nobody likes a pedant.

"Aha," said Mother. Peter grabbed Magda by one ankle and ordered Ambrose to grab the other. She squealed and rolled over on the beach blanket. Ambrose pretended to help hold her back. Her tan was darker than even Mother's and Peter's. "Help out, Uncle Karl!" Peter cried. Uncle Karl went to seize the other ankle. Inside the top of her swimsuit, however, you could see the line where the sunburn ended and, when she hunched her shoulders and squealed again, one nipple's auburn edge. Mother made them behave themselves. "*You* should certainly know," she said to Uncle Karl. Archly. "That when a lady says she doesn't feel like swimming, a gentleman doesn't ask questions." Uncle Karl said excuse *him*; Mother winked at Magda; Ambrose blushed; stupid Peter kept saying "Phooey on *feel like!*" and tugging at Magda's ankle; then even he got the point, and cannonballed with a holler into the pool.

"I swear," Magda said, in mock *in feigned* exasperation.

The diving would make a suitable literary symbol. To go off the high board you had to wait in a line along the poolside and up the ladder. Fellows tickled girls and goosed one another and shouted to the ones at the top to hurry up, or razzed them for bellyfloppers. Once on the springboard some took a great while posing or clowning or deciding on a dive or getting up their nerve; others ran right off. Especially among the younger fellows the idea was to strike the funniest pose or do the craziest stunt as you fell, a thing that got harder to do as you kept on and kept on. But whether you hollered *Geronimo!* or *Sieg heil!*, held your nose or "rode a bicycle," pretended to be shot or did a perfect jacknife or changed your mind halfway down and ended up with nothing, it was over in two seconds, after all that wait. Spring, pose, splash. Spring, neat-o, splash. Spring, aw fooey, splash.

The grown-ups had gone on; Ambrose wanted to converse with Magda; she was remarkably well developed for her age; it was said that that came from rubbing with a turkish towel, and there were other theories. Ambrose could think of nothing to say except how good a diver Peter was, who was showing off for her benefit. You could pretty well tell by looking at their bathing suits and arm muscles how far along the different fellows were. Ambrose was glad he hadn't gone in swimming, the cold water shrank you up so. Magda pretended to be uninterested in the diving; she probably weighed as much as he did. If you knew your way around in the funhouse like your own bedroom, you could wait until a girl came along and then slip away without ever getting caught, even if her boyfriend was right with her. She'd think *he* did it! It would be better to be the boyfriend, and act outraged, and tear the funhouse apart.

Not act; *be*.

"He's a master diver," Ambrose said. In feigned admiration. "You really have to slave away at it to get that good." What would it matter anyhow if he asked her right out whether she remembered, even teased her with it as Peter would have?

There's no point in going farther; this isn't getting anybody anywhere; they haven't even come to the funhouse yet. Ambrose is off the track, in some new or old part of the place that's not supposed to be used; he strayed into it by some one-in-a-million chance, like the time the roller-coaster car left the tracks in the nineteen-teens against all the laws of physics and sailed over the boardwalk in the dark. And they can't locate him because they don't know where to look. Even the designer and operator have forgotten this other part, that winds around on itself like a whelk shell. That winds around the right part like the snakes on Mercury's caduceus. Some people, perhaps, don't "hit their stride" until their twenties, when the growing-up business is over and women appreciate other things besides wisecracks and teasing and strutting. Peter didn't have one-tenth the imagination *he* had, not one-tenth. Peter did this naming-their-children as a joke, making up names like Aloysius and Murgatroyd, but Ambrose knew *exactly* how it would feel to be married and have children of your own, and be a loving husband and father, and go comfortably to work in the mornings and to bed with your wife at night, and wake up with her there. With a breeze coming through the sash and birds and mockingbirds singing in the Chinese-cigar trees. His eyes watered, there aren't enough ways to say that. He would be quite famous in his line of work. Whether Magda was his wife or not, one evening when he was wise-lined and gray at the temples he'd smile gravely, at a fashionable dinner party, and remind her of his youthful passion. The time they went with his family to Ocean City; the *erotic fantasies* he used to have about her. How long ago it seemed, and childish! Yet tender, too, *n'est-ce pas?* Would she have imagined that the world-famous whatever remembered how many strings were on the lyre on the bench beside the girl on the label of the cigar box he'd stared at in the toolshed at age ten while she, age eleven. Even then he had felt *wise beyond his years;* he'd stroked her hair and said in his deepest voice and correctest English, as to a dear child: "I shall never forget this moment."

But though he had breathed heavily, groaned as if ecstatic, what he'd really felt throughout was an odd detachment, as though someone else were Master. Strive as he might to be transported, he heard his mind take notes upon the scene: *This is what they call* passion. *I am experiencing it.* Many of the digger machines were out of order in the penny arcades and could not be repaired or replaced for the duration. Moreover the prizes, made now in USA, were less interesting than formerly, pasteboard items for the most part, and some of the machines wouldn't work on white pennies. The gypsy fortuneteller machine might have provided a foreshadowing of the climax of this story if Ambrose had operated it. It was even dilapidateder than most: the silver coating was worn off the brown metal handles, the glass windows around the dummy were cracked and taped, her kerchiefs and silks long-faded. If a man lived by himself, he could take a department-store mannequin with flexible joints and modify her in certain ways. *However:* by the time he was that old he'd have a real woman. There was a machine that stamped your name around a white-metal coin with a star in the middle: A———. His son would be the second, and when the lad reached thirteen or so he would put a strong arm around his shoulder and tell him calmly: "It is perfectly normal. We have all been through it. It will not last forever." Nobody knew how to be what they were right. He'd smoke a pipe, teach his son how to fish and softcrab, assure him he needn't worry about himself. Magda would certainly give, Magda would certainly yield a great deal of milk, although guilty of occasional solecisms. It don't taste so bad. Suppose the lights came on now!

The day wore on. You think you're yourself, but there are other persons in you. Ambrose gets hard when Ambrose doesn't want to, *and obversely.* Ambrose watches them disagree; Ambrose watches him watch. In the funhouse mirror room you can't see yourself go on forever, because no matter how you stand, your head gets in the way. Even if you had a glass periscope, the image of your eye would cover up the thing you really wanted to see. The police will come; there'll be a story in the papers. That must be where it happened. Unless he can find a surprise exit, an unofficial back-door or escape hatch opening on an alley, say, and then stroll up to the family in front of the funhouse and ask where everybody's been; *he's* been out of the place for ages. That's just where it happened, in that last lighted room: Peter and Magda found the right exit; he found one that you weren't supposed to find and strayed off into the works somewhere. In a perfect funhouse you'd be able to go only one way, like the divers off the high board; getting lost would be impossible; the doors and halls would work like minnow traps or the valves in veins.

On account of German U-boats, Ocean City was "browned out": street-lights were shaded on the seaward side; shopwindows and boardwalk amusement places were kept dim, not to silhouette tankers and Liberty-ships for torpedoing. In a short story about Ocean City, Maryland, during World War II, the author could make use of the image of sailors on leave in the penny arcades and shooting galleries, sighting through the crosshairs of toy machine guns at swastika'd subs, while out in the black Atlantic a U-boat skipper squints through his periscope at real ships outlined by the glow of penny arcades. After dinner the family strolled back to the amusement end of the boardwalk. The boys' father had burnt red as always and was masked with Noxzema, a minstrel in reverse. The grown-ups stood at the end of the boardwalk where the Hurricane of '33 had cut an inlet from the ocean to Assawoman Bay.

"Pronounced with a long *o*," Uncle Karl reminded Magda with a wink. His shirt sleeves were rolled up; Mother punched his brown biceps with the arrowed heart on it and said his mind was naughty. Fat May's laugh came suddenly from the funhouse, as if she'd just got the joke; the family laughed too at the coincidence. Ambrose went under the boardwalk to search for out-of-town matchbook covers with the aid of his pocket flash-light; he looked out from the edge of the North American continent and wondered how far their laughter carried over the water. Spies in rubber rafts; survivors in lifeboats. If the joke had been beyond his understanding, he could have said: *"The laughter was over his head."* And let the reader see the serious wordplay on second reading.

He turned the flashlight on and then off at once even before the woman whooped. He sprang away, heart athud, dropping the light. What had the man grunted? Perspiration drenched and chilled him by the time he scram-bled up to the family. "See anything?" his father asked. His voice wouldn't come; he shrugged and violently brushed sand from his pants legs.

"Let's ride the old flying horses!" Magda cried. I'll never be an author. It's been forever already, everybody's gone home, Ocean City's deserted, the ghost-crabs are tickling across the beach and down the littered cold streets. And the empty halls of clapboard hotels and abandoned funhouses. A tidal wave; an enemy air raid; a monster-crab swelling like an island from the sea. *The inhabitants fled in terror.* Magda clung to his trouser leg; he alone knew the maze's secret. "He gave his life that we might live," said Uncle Karl with a scowl of pain, as he. The fellow's hands had been tattooed; the woman's legs, the woman's fat white legs had. *An astonishing coincidence.* He yearned to tell Peter. He wanted to throw up for excitement. They hadn't even chased him. He wished he were dead.

One possible ending would be to have Ambrose come across another lost person in the dark. They'd match their wits together against the funhouse, struggle like Ulysses past obstacle after obstacle, help and encourage each other. Or a girl. By the time they found the exit they'd be closest friends, sweethearts if it were a girl; they'd know each other's inmost souls, be bound together *by the cement of shared adventure;* then they'd emerge into the light and it would turn out that his friend was a Negro. A blind girl. President Roosevelt's son. Ambrose's former archenemy.

Shortly after the mirror room he'd groped along a musty corridor, his heart already misgiving him at the absence of phosphorescent arrows and other signs. He'd found a crack of light—not a door, it turned out, but a seam between the plyboard wall panels—and squinting up to it, espied a small old man, *in appearance not unlike* the photographs at home of Ambrose's late grandfather, nodding upon a stool beneath a bare, speckled bulb. A crude panel of toggle- and knife-switches hung beside the open fuse box near his head; elsewhere in the little room were wooden levers and ropes belayed to boat cleats. At the time, Ambrose wasn't lost enough to rap or call; later he couldn't find that crack. Now it seemed to him that he'd possibly dozed off for a few minutes somewhere along the way; certainly he was exhausted from the afternoon's sunshine and the evening's problems; he couldn't be sure he hadn't dreamed part or all of the sight. Had an old black wall fan droned like bees and shimmied two flypaper streamers? Had the funhouse operator—gentle, somewhat sad and tired-appearing, in expression not unlike the photographs at home of Ambrose's late Uncle Konrad—murmured in his sleep? Is there really such a person as Ambrose, or is he a figment of the author's imagination? Was it Assawoman Bay or Sinepuxent? Are there other errors of fact in this fiction? Was there another sound besides the little slap slap of thigh on ham, like water sucking at the chine-boards of a skiff?

When you're lost, the smartest thing to do is stay put till you're found, hollering if necessary. But to holler guarantees humiliation as well as rescue; keeping silent permits some saving of face—you can act surprised at the fuss when your rescuers find you and swear you weren't lost, if they do. What's more you might find your own way yet, *however belatedly.*

573

"Don't tell me your foot's still asleep!" Magda exclaimed as the three young people walked from the inlet to the area set aside for ferris wheels, carrousels, and other carnival rides, they having decided in favor of the vast and ancient merry-go-round instead of the funhouse. What a sentence, everything was wrong from the outset. People don't know what to make of him, he doesn't know what to make of himself, he's only thirteen, *athletically and socially inept,* not astonishingly bright, but there are antennae; he has . . . some sort of receivers in his head; things speak to him, he understands more than he should, the world winks at him through its objects, grabs grinning at his coat. Everybody else is in on some secret he doesn't know; they've forgotten to tell him. Through simple *procrastination* his mother put off his baptism until this year. Everyone else had it done as a baby; he'd assumed the same of himself, as had his mother, so she claimed, until it was time for him to join Grace Methodist-Protestant and the oversight came out. He was mortified, but pitched sleepless through his private catechizing, intimidated by the ancient mysteries, a thirteen year old would never say that, resolved to experience conversion like St. Augustine. When the water touched his brow and Adam's sin left him, he contrived by a strain like defecation to bring tears into his eyes—but felt nothing. There was some simple, radical difference about him; he hoped it was genius, feared it was madness, devoted himself to amiability and inconspicuousness. Alone on the seawall near his house he was seized by the terrifying transports he'd thought to find in toolshed, in Communion-cup. The grass was alive! The town, the river, himself, were not imaginary; time roared in his ears like wind; the world was *going on!* This part ought to be dramatized. The Irish author James Joyce once wrote. Ambrose M———— is going to scream.

There is no *texture of rendered sensory detail,* for one thing. The faded distorting mirrors beside Fat May; the impossibility of choosing a mount when one had but a single ride on the great carrousel; the *vertigo attendant on his recognition* that Ocean City was worn out, the place of fathers and grandfathers, straw-boatered men and parasoled ladies survived by their amusements. Money spent, the three paused at Peter's insistence beside Fat May to watch the girls get their skirts blown up. The object was to tease Magda, who said: "I swear, Peter M————, you've got a one-track mind! Amby and me aren't *interested* in such things." In the tumbling-barrel, too, just inside the Devil's-mouth entrance to the funhouse, the girls were up-ended and their boyfriends and others could see up their dresses if they cared to. Which was the whole point, Ambrose realized. Of the entire funhouse! If you looked around, you noticed that almost all the people on the boardwalk were paired off into couples except the small children; in a way, that was the whole point of Ocean City! If you had X-ray eyes and could see everything going on at that instant under the boardwalk and in all the hotel rooms and cars and alleyways, you'd realize that all that normally *showed,* like restaurants and dance halls and clothing and test-your-strength machines, was merely preparation and intermission. Fat May screamed.

Because he watched the goings-on from the corner of his eye, it was Ambrose who spied the half-dollar on the boardwalk near the tumbling-barrel. Losers weepers. The first time he'd heard some people moving through a corridor not far away, just after he'd lost sight of the crack of light, he'd decided not to call to them, for fear they'd guess he was scared and poke fun; it sounded like roughnecks; he'd hoped they'd come by and he could follow in the dark without their knowing. Another time he'd heard just one person, unless he imagined it, bumping along as if on the other side of the plywood; perhaps Peter coming back for him, or Father, or Magda lost too. Or the owner and operator of the funhouse. He'd called out once, as though merrily: "Anybody know where the heck we are?" But the query was too stiff, his voice cracked, when the sounds stopped he was terrified: maybe it was a queer who waited for fellows to get lost, or a longhaired filthy monster that lived in some cranny of the funhouse. He stood rigid for hours it seemed like, scarcely respiring. His future was shockingly clear, in outline. He tried holding his breath to the point of unconsciousness. There ought to be a button you could push to end your life absolutely without pain; disappear in a flick, like turning out a light. He would push it instantly! He despised Uncle Karl. But he despised his father too, for not being what he was supposed to be. Perhaps his father hated *his* father, and so on, and his son would hate him, and so on. Instantly!

Naturally he didn't have nerve enough to ask Magda to go through the funhouse with him. With incredible nerve and to everyone's surprise he invited Magda, quietly and politely, to go through the funhouse with him. "I warn you, I've never been through it before," he added, *laughing easily;* "but I reckon we can manage somehow. The important thing to remember, after all, is that it's meant to be a *fun*house; that is, a place of amusement. If people really got lost or injured or too badly frightened in it, the owner'd go out of business. There'd even be lawsuits. No character in a work of fiction can make a speech this long without interruption or acknowledgment from the other characters."

Mother teased Uncle Karl: "Three's a crowd, I always heard." But actually Ambrose was relieved that Peter now had a quarter too. Nothing was what it looked like. Every instant, under the surface of the Atlantic Ocean, millions of living animals devoured one another. Pilots were falling in flames over Europe; women were being forcibly raped in the South Pacific. His father should have taken him aside and said: "There is a simple secret to getting through the funhouse, as simple as being first to see the Towers. Here it is. Peter does not know it; neither does your Uncle Karl. You and I are different. Not surprisingly, you've often wished you weren't. Don't think I haven't noticed how unhappy your childhood has been! But you'll understand, when I tell you, why it had to be kept secret until now. And you won't regret not being like your brother and your uncle. *On the contrary!*" If you knew all the stories behind all the people on the boardwalk, you'd see that *nothing* was what it looked like. Husbands and wives often hated each other; parents didn't necessarily love their children; et cetera. A child took things for granted because he had nothing to compare his life to and everybody acted as if things were as they should be. Therefore each saw himself as the hero of the story, when the truth might turn out to be that he's the villain, or the coward. And there wasn't one thing you could do about it!

Hunchbacks, fat ladies, fools—that no one chose what he was was unbearable. In the movies he'd meet a beautiful young girl in the funhouse; they'd have hairs-breadth escapes from real dangers; he'd do and say the right things; she also; in the end they'd be lovers; their dialogue lines would match up; he'd be perfectly at ease; she'd not only like him well enough, she'd think he was *marvelous*; she'd lie awake thinking about *him,* instead of vice versa—the way *his* face looked in different lights and how he stood and exactly what he'd said—and yet that would be only one small episode in his wonderful life, among many many others. Not a *turning point* at all. What had happened in the toolshed was nothing. He hated, he loathed his parents! One reason for not writing a lost-in-the-funhouse story is that either everybody's felt what Ambrose feels, in which case it goes without saying, or else no normal person feels such things, in which case Ambrose is a freak. "Is anything more tiresome, in fiction, than the problems of sensitive adolescents?" And it's all too long and rambling, as if the author. For all a person knows the first time through, the end could be just around any corner; perhaps, *not impossibly* it's been within reach any number of times. On the other hand he may be scarcely past the start, with everything yet to get through, an intolerable idea.

Fill in: His father's raised eyebrows when he announced his decision to do the funhouse with Magda. Ambrose understands now, but didn't then, that his father was wondering whether he knew what the funhouse was *for*—especially since he didn't object, as he should have, when Peter decided to come along too. The ticket-woman, witchlike, mortifying him when inadvertently he gave her his name-coin instead of the half-dollar, then unkindly calling Magda's attention to the birthmark on his temple: "Watch out for him, girlie, he's a marked man!" She wasn't even cruel, he understood, only vulgar and insensitive. Somewhere in the world there was a young woman with such splendid understanding that she'd see him entire, like a poem or story, and find his words so valuable after all that when he confessed his apprehensions she would explain why they were in fact the very things that made him precious to her . . . and to Western Civilization! There was no such girl, the simple truth being. Violent yawns as they approached the mouth. Whispered advice from an old-timer on a bench near the barrel: "Go crabwise and ye'll get an eyeful without upsetting!" Composure vanished at the first pitch: Peter hollered joyously, Magda tumbled, shrieked, clutched her skirt; Ambrose scrambled crabwise, tight-lipped with terror, was soon out, watched his dropped name-coin slide among the couples. Shamefaced he saw that to get through expeditiously was not the point; Peter feigned assistance in order to trip Magda up, shouted "I see Christmas!" when her legs went flying. The old man, his latest betrayer, cackled approval. A dim hall then of black-thread cobwebs and recorded gibber: he took Magda's elbow to steady her against revolving discs set in the slanted floor to throw your feet out from under, and explained to her in a calm, deep voice his theory that each phase of the funhouse was triggered either automatically, by a series of photoelectric devices, or else manually by operators stationed at peepholes. But he lost his voice thrice as the discs unbalanced him; Magda was anyhow squealing; but at one point she clutched him about the waist to keep from falling, and her right cheek pressed for a moment against his belt-buckle. Heroically he drew her up, it was his chance to clutch her close as if for support and say: "I love you." He even put an arm lightly about the small of her back before a sailor-and-girl pitched into them from behind, sorely treading his left big toe and knocking Magda asprawl with them. The sailor's girl was a string-haired hussy with a loud laugh and light blue drawers; Ambrose realized that he wouldn't have said "I love you" anyhow, and was smitten with self-contempt. How much better it would be to be that common sailor! A wiry little Seaman 3rd, the fellow squeezed a girl to each side and stumbled hilarious into the mirror room, closer to Magda in thirty seconds than Ambrose had got in thirteen years. She giggled at something the fellow said to Peter; she drew her hair from her eyes with a movement so womanly it struck Ambrose's heart; Peter's smacking her backside then seemed particularly coarse. But Magda made a pleased indignant face and cried, "All right for *you*, mister!" and pursued Peter into the maze without a backward glance. The sailor followed after, leisurely, drawing his girl against his hip; Ambrose understood not only that they were all so relieved to be rid of his burdensome company that they didn't even notice his absence, but that he himself shared their relief. Stepping from the treacherous passage at last into the mirror-maze, he saw once again, more clearly than ever, how readily he deceived himself into supposing he was a person. He even foresaw, wincing at his dreadful self-knowledge, that he would repeat the deception, at ever-rarer intervals, all his wretched life, so fearful were the alternatives. Fame, madness, suicide; perhaps all three. It's not believable that so young a boy could articulate that reflection, and in fiction the merely true must always yield to the plausible. Moreover, the symbolism is in places heavy-footed. Yet Ambrose M——— understood, as few adults do, that the famous loneliness of the great was no popular myth but a general truth—furthermore, that it was as much cause as effect.

All the preceding except the last few sentences is exposition that should've been done earlier or interspersed with the present action instead of lumped together. No reader would put up with so much with such *prolixity*. It's interesting that Ambrose's father, though presumably an intelligent man (as indicated by his role as grade-school principal), neither encouraged nor discouraged his sons at all in any way—as if he either didn't care about them or cared all right but didn't know how to act. If this fact should contribute to one of them's becoming a celebrated but wretchedly unhappy scientist, was it a good thing or not? He too might someday face the question; it would be useful to know whether it had tortured his father for years, for example, or never once crossed his mind.

In the maze two important things happened. First, our hero found a name-coin someone else had lost or discarded: *AMBROSE,* suggestive of the famous lightship and of his late grandfather's favorite dessert, which his mother used to prepare on special occasions out of coconut, oranges, grapes, and what else. Second, as he wondered at the endless replication of his image in the mirrors, second, as he *lost himself in the reflection* that the necessity for an observer makes perfect observation impossible, better make him eighteen at least, yet that would render other things unlikely, he heard Peter and Magda chuckling somewhere together in the maze. "Here!" "No, here!" they shouted to each other; Peter said, "Where's Amby?" Magda murmured. "Amb?" Peter called. In a pleased, friendly voice. He didn't reply. The truth was, his brother was a *happy-go-lucky youngster* who'd've been better off with a regular brother of his own, but who seldom complained of his lot and was generally cordial. Ambrose's throat ached; there aren't enough different ways to say that. He stood quietly while the two young people giggled and thumped through the glittering maze, hurrah'd their discovery of its exit, cried out in joyful alarm at what next beset them. Then he set his mouth and followed after, as he supposed, took a wrong turn, strayed into the pass *wherein he lingers yet*.

The action of conventional dramatic narrative may be represented by a diagram called Freitag's Triangle:

or more accurately by a variant of that diagram:

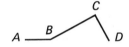

in which *AB* represents the exposition, *B* the introduction of conflict, *BC* the "rising action," complication, or development of the conflict, *C* the climax, or turn of the action, *CD* the dénouement, or resolution of the conflict. While there is no reason to regard this pattern as an absolute necessity, like many other conventions it became conventional because great numbers of people over many years learned by trial and error that it was effective; one ought not to forsake it, therefore, unless one wishes to forsake as well the effect of drama or has clear cause to feel that deliberate violation of the "normal" pattern can better can better effect that effect. This can't go on much longer; it can go on forever. He died telling stories to himself in the dark; years later, when that vast unsuspected area of the funhouse came to light, the first expedition found his skeleton in one of its labyrinthine corridors and mistook it for part of the entertainment. He died of starvation telling himself stories in the dark; but unbeknownst unbeknownst to him, an assistant operator of the funhouse, happening to overhear him, crouched just behind the plyboard partition and wrote down his every word. The operator's daughter, an exquisite young woman with a figure unusually well developed for her age, crouched just behind the partition and transcribed his every word. Though she had never laid eyes on him, she recognized that here was one of Western Culture's truly great imaginations, the eloquence of whose suffering would be an inspiration to unnumbered. And her heart was torn between her love for the misfortunate young man (yes, she loved him, though she had never laid though she knew him only—but how well!—through his words, and the deep, calm voice in which he spoke them) between her love et cetera and her womanly intuition that only in suffering and isolation could he give voice et cetera. Lone dark dying. Quietly she kissed the rough plyboard, and a tear fell upon the page. Where she had written in shorthand *Where she had written in shorthand* Where she had written in shorthand *Where she* et cetera. A long time ago we should have passed the apex of Freitag's Triangle and made brief work of the *dénouement;* the plot doesn't rise by meaningful steps but winds upon itself, digresses, retreats, hesitates, sighs, collapses, expires. The climax of the story must be its protagonist's discovery of a way to get through the funhouse. But he has found none, may have ceased to search.

What relevance does the war have to the story? Should there be fireworks outside or not?

Ambrose wondered, languished, dozed. Now and then he fell into his habit of rehearsing to himself the unadventurous story of his life, narrated from the third-person point of view, from his earliest memory parenthesis of maple leaves stirring in the summer breath of tidewater Maryland end of parenthesis to the present moment. Its principal events, on this telling, would appear to have been *A, B, C,* and *D.*

He imagined himself years hence, successful, married, at ease in the world, the trials of his adolescence far behind him. He has come to the seashore with his family for the holiday: how Ocean City has changed! But at one seldom at one ill-frequented end of the boardwalk a few derelict amusements survive from times gone by: the great carrousel from the turn of the century, with its monstrous griffins and mechanical concert band; the roller coaster rumored since 1916 to have been condemned; the mechanical shooting gallery in which only the image of our enemies changed. His own son laughs with Fat May and wants to know what a funhouse is; Ambrose hugs the sturdy lad close and smiles around his pipestem at his wife.

The family's going home. Mother sits between Father and Uncle Karl, who teases him good-naturedly who chuckles over the fact that the comrade with whom he'd fought his way shoulder to shoulder through the funhouse had turned out to be a blind Negro girl—to their mutual discomfort, as they'd opened their souls. But such are the walls of custom, which even. Whose arm is where? How must it feel. He dreams of a funhouse vaster by far than any yet constructed; but by then they may be out of fashion, like steamboats and excursion trains. Already quaint and seedy: the draperied ladies on the frieze of the carrousel are his father's father's mooncheeked dreams; if he thinks of it more he will vomit his apple-on-a-stick.

He wonders: will he become a regular person? Something has gone wrong; his vaccination didn't take; at the Boy-Scout initiation campfire he only pretended to be deeply moved, as he pretends to this hour that it is not so bad after all in the funhouse, and that he has a little limp. How long will it last? He envisions a truly astonishing funhouse, incredibly complex yet utterly controlled from a great central switchboard like the console of a pipe organ. Nobody had enough imagination. He could design such a place himself, wiring and all, and he's only thirteen years old. He would be its operator: panel lights would show what was up in every cranny of its cunning of its multifarious vastness; a switch-flick would ease this fellow's way, complicate that's, to balance things out; if anyone seemed lost or frightened, all the operator had to do was.

He wishes he had never entered the funhouse. But he has. Then he wishes he were dead. But he's not. Therefore he will construct funhouses for others and be their secret operator—though he would rather be among the lovers for whom funhouses are designed.

FOUND IN THE BARTHHOUSE: NOVELIST AS SAVIOR

Edgar H. Knapp

Nor is there singing school but studying
Monuments of its own magnificence

W. B. *Yeats*

After John Barth's "Lost in the Funhouse" appeared in *The Atlantic* of November, 1967, common men had a taste of terror, the mad felt a twinge of sympathy, and a faint and tweedy generation of English professors found themselves in the mirror-maze of a new fiction.

Warning. You cannot read "Lost in the Funhouse" simply for the fun of it. Read it three times: once, to get knocked off your feet; again to regain your balance; and then to be knocked down again. Perhaps a fourth time . . . for the fun of it.

The story adheres to the archetypal pattern of passage through difficult ways, and the hero seems to be a thirteen-year-old boy on a family outing to Ocean City, Maryland, during World War II. The story line is straight. It's the how of the tale that up-ends one. Its mixture of myth, masque, cinema, and symposium makes "Lost in the Funhoue" one of the oldest and freshest of stories.

MYTH

The setting of Barth's story is intensely true to the texture of life in tidewater Maryland, 1943. Lucky Strike's green has gone to war; V——— (Vienna) is the halfway point of the trip to the shore; at the end of the boardwalk is an inlet the Hurricane of '33 had cut to Sinepuxent Bay (which the author can't bear to leave as Assawoman). Nevertheless, the setting has another dimension: it is an ironic garden. At the Ocean City amusement park the roller coaster, rumored to be condemned in 1916, still runs; many machines are broken and the prizes are made of pasteboard (in the USA). Everyone except Ambrose M——— and his father exudes and ingests the carnival spirit—on Independence Day in a time of national crisis. Barth ruminates: "In a short story about Ocean City, Maryland, during World War II the author could make use of the image of sailors on leave in the penny arcades and shooting galleries, sighting through the cross-hairs of toy machine guns at swastika'd subs, while out in the black Atlantic a U-boat skipper squints through his periscope at real ships outlined by the glow of penny arcades." In a slight variation on the independence theme, Ambrose recalls that, five years before, the kids played "Niggers and Masters" in the backyard. And on the day of the story, even the sensitive hero is uncomfortable to think that a Negro boy might help him through the funhouse. The boardwalk is a begrimed paradise to which there is no return: "Already quaint and seedy: the draperied ladies on the frieze of the carrousel are his father's father's mooncheeked dreams; if he thinks of it more he will vomit his apple-on-a-stick."

Ambrose at thirteen suffers from undescended identity. He has experienced two initiation ceremonies which left him cold: one sexual, in a toolshed at the age of eight; another religious, at his own belated baptism during the year of the story. (Each involved kneeling and the forgiveness of a master.) Ideally, such acts as these betoken man's communion with his own kind and with his God, but to the aggravation of his sense of loss, Ambrose "felt nothing." He feigned passion, he feigned tears. From time to time he even pretends to be a real person. And so it is his identity he seeks in a funhouse world where nothing is as it seems.

The dark passageways of the funhouse increase his sense of isolation. Still he must find his way out himself. Peeping through a crack in a plywood wall, Ambrose sees the lonely, old funhouse operator (God?) asleep at the switch. An ironic epiphany. Especially as we interpret the funhouse as world (and the world as funhouse), the mythic structure becomes more visible. Ambrose's adventures are like heroic suffering, death, and resurrection (if indeed one sees him as out of the funhouse at the story's end). The witchlike ticket-seller calls him a marked man. And we recall the tumble of unconscious formulation which follows his brush with life in the raw (*"an astonishing coincidence"*) under the boardwalk: "Magda clung to his trouser leg: he alone knew the maze's secret. 'He gave his life that we might live,' said Uncle Karl with a scowl of pain, as he." These words relate to a subsequent dream scene in the funhouse when a Magda-like assistant operator transcribes the hero's inspirational message, the more beautiful for his "lone dark dying." Mention of the Ambrose Lightship, beacon to lost seafarers, and the meaning of *Ambrose* (divine) and echoes of *ambrosia* (that bee-belabored stuff of immortality) reenforce the mythic overtones of his characterization.

MASQUE

This Ambrose seems clearly to be the protagonist but in another sense he is not. The "quaint and seedy" sextet may be the hero—each aspects of generalized man. Ambrose and father, both thin, fair-skinned, and bespectacled, combine as soulful tenors; brother Peter and Uncle Karl, both squat and swarthy, thump out a basso counterpoint, with which the two women harmonize as one voice—a sexy alto, limited in range. (They complement each other, appearing to be an at-once-sinister-and-dexterous female unit, the reflections of one another.)

Perceived as aspects of the same personality, Ambrose and his father represent acute awareness of experience and artistic intuition. Unlike his lustful, mesomorphic brother and uncle, Ambrose is seized by "terrifying transports": "The grass was alive! The town, the river, himself, were not imaginary; time roared in his ears like wind; the world was *going on!*" Peter and Uncle Karl represent "the withness of the body," Whitehead's phrase, which Delmore Schwartz uses as an epigraph to his poem "The Heavy Bear":

> That heavy bear who sleeps with me,
> Howls in his sleep for a world of sugar,
>
> .   .   .   .
>
> Stretches to embrace the very dear
> With whom I would walk without him near,
> Touches her grossly, although a word
> Would bare my heart and make me clear.

Womankind is the honey that keeps the heavy bear "lumbering." (The women held the syrup-coated popcorn.) Also, the naming within the party of the flesh is symbolic: *Magda* for Mary Magdalene, sinful woman; *Peter*, meaning rock; *Karl*, man of the common people, who is coincidentally a stone mason and an inveterate cigar smoker. (He kept his stone-cutting chisels in an empty cigar box.)

The sextet enacts a masque-like drama symbolic of the inner transactions which result in human behavior. Members of the "heavy bear" quartet communicate by tactile and kinesthetic means—playful shoves, tugs, punches, and slaps. Prufrock-like, Ambrose recoils from physical contact: the brown hair on his mother's forearms gleams in the sun; he sees perspiration patches at Magda's armpits. (He even gets to play the crab scuttling across the turning funhouse floors.) In the car he removes his hand "in the nick of time," and later in the funhouse he fails to embrace Magda in keeping with his vision.

Additional support to the sextet theory: the two males of each generation, although their actions contrast, share the same woman without deceit or suspicion. Nor is there conflict between corresponding members of the different generations. Although communication is strained between the separate selves, still they gravitate toward one another in artificial ways. For instance, at poolside Ambrose feigns interest in the diving; Magda, disinterest. (" 'He's a *master* diver,' Ambrose said. . . . 'You really have to *slave* away at it to get that good.' " [Italics mine]). These oscillations toward and away from members of the same generation are true to the tensions of personality, or man divided within himself. But besides these synchronic vibrations, the diachronic, or generation-to-generation, echoes have special implications in this Barth story—particularly the reveries in which Ambrose sees himself, standing before Fat May, with Ambrose the Third. ("Magda would yield a great deal of milk although guilty of occasional solecisms.") The mirrored manners of father and son, Mrs. M———— and Magda, Uncle Karl and Peter—their adherence to the same old routines—speak to us of the shaping role of inheritance. The story brings to mind the Freudian quip that when two lovers take to bed they are accompanied by both sets of parents.

CINEMA

Whereas the action of the story is mythic and its characterization is related to archetypal masque, its scenic values—its choreography—derive from cinematic techniques. The scenic splicing is suggestive—and not only in a ribald sense. The interstitching of dream and action supports the basic theme of the merging of illusion and reality. Other splices create abrupt switches, with utter absence of transition, from narrative flow to textbook exposition, reminding us that not even the story is real. The action is suspended—reminiscent of the lights dimming and the actors freezing at intervals in Samuel Beckett's play *Waiting for Godot*—and then the motion picture resumes. Another and more conventional sort of juxtaposition is also used, as when Fat May's canned laughter sounds ironically over images of war and death.

Perhaps the most intriguing aspect of Barth's scenic art is his use of symbolic ballet. Reenforcing the masque-like characterization, the physical interrelationships in the "blocking" of particular scenes are allegorical. For instance, the story opens and closes with the thematically loaded formation of the older generation in the front seat—the woman between the competing interests of the spirit and the flesh—reflected by the younger generation behind. Barth avoids perfect symmetry by contrasting the arm position of the sexually mature mother with that of the sexually maturing Magda (from B————— Street), who has her arms down, but "at the ready."

The theme is only slightly varied as the *sextet* swings down the boardwalk to the swimming pool, the heavy bears next to the syrup-coated popcorn. The mirror motif is intensified at the pool: Peter grasps one ankle of the squirming Magda; Uncle Karl goes for the other ankle. Had either looked up he would have seen his reflection! The communion motif, as well, is reflected in the choreography, being subtly varied from the sexual to the religious: first by the child kneeling in sin in the toolshed and later by the fallen woman clutching her savior in supplication in the funhouse.

Not only scenic arrangement but also the varied sensory appeals of Barth's imagery support the illusion-reality theme. Paint peels from the hotels—themselves facades, within which lovers may pretend passion. Not only do the mirrors within the funhouse distort and confuse but also the sounds of fumbling bees and lapping wavelets re-echo in Amby's ears. He suffers from vertigo, if not labyrinthitis. And "candied apples-on-a-stick, delicious-looking, [were] disappointing to eat."

SYMPOSIUM

And so we have a significant human experience imaginatively presented in structure and textures organically related to the whole. But the story has one more funhouse dimension which is most puzzling—its point of view. Although Barth's story is spun from the consciousness of the protagonist, a precocious adolescent, in the telling at least six distinct bands of mental formulation seem to be randomly mixed: (1) report of the action proper, (2) recollection of past experience, (3) conscious contrivance of a reasonable future, (4) uncontrolled swings into a fantastic future, (5) consciousness of problems of composition, and (6) recollection of sections from a handbook for creative writers. (After a while the reader can visualize the author seated before a console, gleefully pushing buttons according to the sprung rhythm of his whim.) The first four bands on the list qualify as spritely narrative; the last two, as the conscience of an author not completely free from the shackles of conventional fiction. The relationship which is generated between these technical obtrusions and the rest of the story is that of a symposium. We have a running Platonic dialogue between the experimental Barth and the tradition out of which his work has grown. The dialectic is undeniable, but what is the artistic reason for it? It obtrudes upon the illusion of reality. And it has to be Barth's strategy—similar to Pirandello's and Wilder's experiments in the theatre—to remind the reader continually of the contrivance of literature, the fact that a story is the semblance of lived-experience, not experience. The frequent italicized phrases are likewise reminders of the artificiality of fiction. One purpose could be to wean us from the particular in time and place so that we will appreciate the universality of Amby's fate, that he is also ourselves, and that we have our opportunities for heroism.

But wait; we're not out of the funhouse yet. Could it be that Barth's story, and not Barth himself, is playing the bright, young heterosexual Phaedrus to a tired, old Socrates, who is in fact the nineteenth-century short story? (Peruse Barth's essay "The Literature of Exhaustion" in *The Atlantic* of August, 1967, and you have to believe it.) This doesn't vitiate other interpretations of the story-within-the-story; it is merely an additional crown to the apple-within-an-apple nest of "Lost in the Funhouse."

Granted this detachment and accepting the universality of the human experience represented by the M———— family's journey, an allegory of the flesh and the spirit, we are in position to appreciate one more tantalizing suggestion: that one generation of the M———— family is symbolic not only of essential M-a-n but also of essential M-y-t-h—the attempt in story form to help man find his way in the non-human world. The earliest of these fictions portrayed gods as the main strugglers. Hence, the divine characteristics of Ambrose, which set him apart from the common man; his wanderings in a strange dark underworld; his yearning to discover his identity.

When we see a generation of the M———— family as a story, the reappearance of the old structure and dynamics in later generations takes on fresh significance. The Fourth of July trip as family tradition, which Ambrose sees himself reenacting with his own son, is like a recurring plot in the history of the short story. As every man is like his father, every story bears a likeness to its archetype. The generation-to-generation resemblances suggest the relationships within literary genres. As Northrop Frye points out, individual works of literature reveal "family likenesses resembling the species, genera, and phyla of biology."

Fiction as we have known it, Barth implies, is at the water's edge. The myth-carrying vehicles have not changed radically (train, car, autogiro), and these recurring outings of the monomyth are distastefully decked with anachronistic trappings. Mention of "the draperied ladies on the frieze of the carrousel [who are seen as] his father's father's mooncheeked dreams" is a comment on "the literature of exhausted possibility," as critic John Barth has labeled it.

And so in a central room of the funhouse, the maze of mirrors, we have the eye. We trust it, as we have learned to, and its imperfect perception goes to a bleary brain: a flickering of self-knowledge (Ambrose did find his name coin there—symbolic of himself). But with it the *awful* chain of reflection cast backward and forward, in space and time. Outside is the funhouse of a lifetime. Beyond that, the history of humanity and the extension of its possibilities. And encompassing that, the marvelous funhouse of imaginative conception, which can project images, construct funhouses, *et cetera et cetera et cetera*. We are reminded of E. M. Forster's Mrs. Moore who, speaking God's name to the sky, finds that "outside the arch there seemed to be always another arch, beyond the remotest echo a silence." And we can come to the chimerical conclusion that the eye in the funhouse is that of a seeker for a sign: that of son searching for father; man, for God; author, for muse. (The hero is amb—"O brightening glance . . ." Could six characters be in search of an author?) And, of course, the eye in the funhouse is yours and mine. The quiet terror with which the story concludes is not fictional; it rouses the body's hair against our invocation of disbelief! Selfhood is not easy. Best be a common man and not think about it.

But I'm still worried about Ambrose. Did he make it out of the funhouse? If I can still be worried about him after peering down and up these other echoing funhouse corridors, then I consider the story to be a really good one. I tend to believe the dissembling narrator when he says, "The family's going home. Mother sits between Father and Uncle Karl who teases him [Ambrose] . . ." and I say he's out of the Ocean City funhouse, though still in his funhouse world, as much "a place of fear and confusion" as it was. The voice of convention, nevertheless, has reminded us that the climax will be reached when the protagonist is out. But Ambrose doesn't have climaxes and he will expire in his funhouse world. Lost as he is, he can find purpose in life—at least make "a stay against confusion" (and have a fighting chance for one sort of immortality)—through imaginative design. The Whiffenpoofs are lost too, but "the magic of their singing" makes it a joy to be lost with them. And from another angle, we know that when the operator of our funhouse sets the tumbling-barrel

turning, struggle for equilibrium does beget fresh intellectual and/or intuitive formulation. And so the funhouse for *man thinking* is a womb of possibility from which he may be reborn. I ruminate: if in one house of fiction we discover that we are lost and toppled and we regain our equilibrium, even to our knees, the author will have found us and so saved himself, according to the terrible and wonderful necessity which only he can know.

QUESTIONS

Lost in the Funhouse

POINT OF VIEW 1. When does the reader discover that Ambrose is a dramatized narrator? What is the impact of this discovery? 2. In the following passage, Ambrose fantasizes about his future and also discusses an aspect of fiction writing:

> Stepping from the treacherous passage at last into the mirror-maze, he saw once again, more clearly than ever, how readily he deceived himself into supposing he was a person. He even foresaw, wincing at his dreadful self-knowledge, that he would repeat the deception, at ever-rarer intervals, all his wretched life, so fearful were the alternatives. Fame, madness, suicide; perhaps all three. It's not believable that so young a boy could articulate that reflection, and in fiction the merely true must always yield to the plausible.

Comment on the effect of John Barth, a mature writer, using the point of view of Ambrose, his younger self, to talk about Barth in the present. In what other passages does Ambrose "imagine" himself in the future?

CHARACTERS 3. The essay describes Magda and Ambrose's mother as complementing each other, "appearing to be an at-once-sinister-and-dextrous female unit, the reflections of one another." Do you agree with this statement? Support your view with specific references to the story. 4. As in the passage quoted in question 2, Ambrose tries several times in the narrative to convince us that his remarks about fiction and human nature are within the intellectual and emotional grasp of a thirteen-year old boy. Do you agree, or do you find these statements and explanation out of character? Explain. 5. Ambrose compares the funhouse operato

JOHN BARTH

to a relative. Which one? Discuss the significance of the funhouse operator to Ambrose as a character; to the meaning of the story as a whole. 6. What advice is offered to Ambrose by an old man sitting near the tumbling-barrel inside the funhouse? Why does Ambrose initially accept and then reject this advice? 7. Why does Ambrose despise his father "for not being what he was supposed to be"?

PLOT 8. Find the many references to conventions of plot that occur in this story. Does the story itself adhere to any of these conventions? If so, which one(s)? Would we be interested in reading a story totally devoid of plot? 9. What statement about plot in conventional narrative is Barth trying to make in this story?

SETTING 10. Describe the effect of this story's being set during World War II. 11. Discuss the literal and symbolic functions of the amusement park as the generalized location for the story.

STYLE 12. Throughout the story, the prose shifts stylistically as Ambrose attempts to reconcile his emotional reactions to both his family and Magda, his insights into fiction writing, and his fantasies. Cite several examples to support this contention. Discuss your response to these stylistic shifts. Do you find them objectionable? 13. The story has, as one of its concerns, the process of fiction. Do you object to being reminded that you are reading a story—that fiction is an artifact? Explain.

TONE 14. Describe Barth's attitude toward his thirteen-year-old self. 15. Describe Barth's attitude toward himself as an author. 16. Describe Barth's attitude toward the writing of fiction.

Found in the Barthhouse: Novelist as Savior

FOCUS 1. Show how the funhouse (as literal place and as symbol) is used to unify the essay and give it focus.

ORGANIZATION 2. List the four parts into which the essay is divided. In your opinion, does the fourth part, *symposium*, state the essayist's thesis more clearly than the other three parts? Explain. 3. Is the essayist justified in beginning his four-part discussion with *myth* rather than with one of the other topics?

USING THE EVIDENCE 4. Does the essay offer sufficient evidence to prove that "Lost in the Funhouse" is "one of the oldest and freshest of stories"? 5. In the section labeled *symposium*, the essayist mentions "at least six

distinct bands of mental formulation." List these six bands. Does the essay offer sufficient examples of each? Supply as many other examples as you can.   6. How does the essayist support his view that the story derives its choreography from cinematic techniques?

STYLE   7. What is the meaning of the word *masque*? Is the interpretation of the story as masque sufficiently clear?   8. Explain the allusions in the following sentence: "Could it be that Barth's story, and not Barth himself, is playing the bright, young heterosexual Phaedrus to a tired, old Socrates, who is in fact the nineteenth-century short story?"

MAKING LITERARY JUDGMENTS   9. Concerning Ambrose, the essayist writes: "Lost as he is, he can find purpose in life—at least make 'a stay against confusion' (and have a fighting chance for one sort of immortality)—through imaginative design." Explain this statement in relation to the creating of literature.   10. Explain the meaning of the following passage as it applies to literature:

> The Fourth of July trip as family tradition, which Ambrose sees himself reenacting with his own son, is like a recurring plot in the history of the short story. As every man is like his father, every story bears a likeness to its archetype.

Enlarge upon this hypothesis through references to other stories in the collection.   11. In describing the reception accorded to "Lost in the Funhouse" when it appeared in 1967, the essayist writes that "common men had a taste of terror, the mad felt a twinge of sympathy, and a faint and tweedy generation of English professors found themselves in the mirror-maze of a new fiction." Each clause represents a judgment about literature. Explain.   12. What judgment about literature is implied in the following statement: "If I can still be worried about him [Ambrose] after peering down and up these other echoing funhouse corridors, then I consider the story to be a really good one"?

NIGHT-SEA JOURNEY

"One way or another, no matter which theory of our journey is correct, it's myself I address; to whom I rehearse as to a stranger our history and condition, and will disclose my secret hope though I sink for it.

"Is the journey my invention? Do the night, the sea, exist at all, I ask myself, apart from my experience of them? Do I myself exist, or is this a dream? Sometimes I wonder. And if I am, who am I? The Heritage I supposedly transport? But how can I be both vessel and contents? Such are the questions that beset my intervals of rest.

"My trouble is, I lack conviction. Many accounts of our situation seem plausible to me—where and what we are, why we swim and whither. But implausible ones as well, perhaps especially those, I must admit as possibly correct. Even likely. If at times, in certain humors—stroking in unison, say, with my neighbors and chanting with them 'Onward! Upward!'—I have supposed that we have after all a common Maker, Whose nature and motives we may not know, but Who engendered us in some mysterious wise and launched us forth toward some end known but to Him—if (for a moodslength only) I have been able to entertain such notions, very popular in certain quarters, it is because our night-sea journey partakes of their absurdity. One might even say: I can believe them *because* they are absurd.

"Has that been said before?

"Another paradox: it appears to be these recesses from swimming that sustain me in the swim. Two measures onward and upward, flailing with the rest, then I float exhausted and dispirited, brood upon the night, the sea, the journey, while the flood bears me a measure back and down: slow progress, but I live, I live, and make my way, aye, past many a drownèd comrade in the end, stronger, worthier than I, victims of their unremitting *joie de nager*. I have seen the best swimmers of my generation go under. [Ginsberg] Numberless the number of the dead! Thousands drown as I think this thought, millions as I rest before returning to the swim. And scores, hundreds of millions have expired since we surged forth, brave in our innocence, upon our dreadful way. 'Love! Love!' we sang then, a quarter-billion strong, and churned the warm sea white with joy of swimming! Now all are gone down—the buoyant, the sodden, leaders and followers, all gone under, while wretched I swim on. Yet these same reflective intervals that keep me afloat have led me into wonder, doubt, despair—strange emotions for a swimmer!—have led me, even, to suspect . . . that our night-sea journey is without meaning.

"Indeed, if I have yet to join the hosts of the suicides, it is because [Camus] (fatigue apart) I find it no meaningfuller to drown myself than to go on swimming.

"I know that there are those who seem actually to enjoy the night-sea; who claim to love swimming for its own sake, or sincerely believe that 'reaching the Shore,' 'transmitting the Heritage' (*Whose* Heritage, I'd like to know? And to whom?) is worth the staggering cost. I do not. Swimming itself I find at best not actively unpleasant, more often tiresome, not infrequently a torment. Arguments from function and design don't impress me: granted that we can and do swim, that in a manner of speaking our long tails and streamlined heads are 'meant for' swimming; it by no [design] means follows—for me, at least—that we *should* swim, or otherwise endeavor to 'fulfill our destiny.' Which is to say, Someone Else's destiny, since ours, so far as I can see, is merely to perish, one way or another, soon or late. The heartless zeal of our (departed) leaders, like the blind ambition and good cheer of my own youth, appalls me now; for the death of my comrades I am inconsolable. If the night-sea journey has justification, it is not for us swimmers ever to discover it.

"Oh, to be sure, 'Love!' one heard on every side: 'Love it is that drives and sustains us!' I translate: we don't know *what* drives and sustains us, only that we are most miserably driven and, imperfectly, sustained. *Love* is how we call our ignorance of what whips us. 'To reach the Shore,' then: but what if the Shore exists in the fancies of us swimmers merely, who dream it to account for the dreadful fact that we swim, have always and only swum, and continue swimming *living* without respite (myself excepted) until we die? Supposing even that there *were* a Shore—that, as a cynical companion of mine once imagined, we rise from the drowned to discover all those vulgar superstitions and exalted metaphors to be literal truth: the giant Maker of us all, the Shores of Light beyond our night-sea journey! —whatever would a swimmer do there? The fact is, when we imagine the Shore, what comes to mind is just the opposite of our condition: no more night, no more sea, no more journeying. In short, the blissful estate of the drowned.

" 'Ours not to stop and think; ours but to swim and sink. . . .' Because a moment's thought reveals the pointlessness of swimming. 'No matter,' I've heard some say, even as they gulped their last: 'The night-sea journey may be absurd, but here we swim, will-we nill-we, against the flood, onward and upward, toward a Shore that may not exist and couldn't be reached if it did.' The thoughtful swimmer's choices, then, they say, are two: give over thrashing and go under for good, or embrace the absurdity; affirm in and for itself the night-sea journey; swim on with neither motive nor destination, for the sake of swimming, and compassionate moreover with your fellow swimmer, we being all at sea and equally in the dark. I find neither course acceptable. If not even the hypothetical Shore can justify a sea-full of drownèd comrades, to speak of the swim-in-itself as somehow doing so strikes me as obscene. I continue to swim—but only because blind habit, blind instinct, blind fear of drowning are still more strong than the horror of our journey. And if on occasion I have assisted a fellow-thrasher, joined in the cheers and songs, even passed along to others strokes of genius from the drownèd great, it's that I shrink by temperament from making myself conspicuous. To paddle off in one's own direction, assert one's independent right-of-way, overrun one's fellows without compunction, or dedicate oneself entirely to pleasures and diversions without regard for conscience—I can't finally condemn those who journey in this wise; in half my moods I envy them and despise the weak vitality that keeps me from following their example. But in reasonabler moments I remind myself that it's their very freedom and self-responsibility I reject, as more dramatically absurd, in our senseless circumstances, than tailing along in conventional fashion.

Suicides, rebels, affirmers of the paradox—nay-sayers and yea-sayers alike to our fatal journey—I finally shake my head at them. And splash sighing past their corpses, one by one, as past a hundred sorts of others: friends, enemies, brothers; fools, sages, brutes—and nobodies, million upon million. I envy them all.

"A poor irony: that I, who find abhorrent and tautological the doctrine of survival of the fittest (*fitness* meaning, in my experience, nothing more than survival-ability, a talent whose only demonstration is the fact of survival, but whose chief ingredients seem to be strength, guile, callousness), may be the sole remaining swimmer! But the doctrine is false as well as repellent: Chance drowns the worthy with the unworthy, bears up the unfit with the fit by whatever definition, and makes the night-sea journey essentially *haphazard* as well as murderous and unjustified.

" 'You only swim once.' Why bother, then?

" 'Except ye drown, ye shall not reach the Shore of Life.' Poppycock.

"One of my late companions—that same cynic with the curious fancy, among the first to drown—entertained us with odd conjectures while we waited to begin our journey. A favorite theory of his was that the Father does exist, and did indeed make us and the sea we swim—but not a-purpose or even consciously; He made us, as it were, despite Himself, as we make waves with every tail-thrash, and may be unaware of our existence. Another was that He knows we're here but doesn't care what happens to us, inasmuch as He creates (voluntarily or not) other seas and swimmers at more or less regular intervals. In bitterer moments, such as just before he drowned, my friend even supposed that our Maker wished us unmade; there was indeed a Shore, he'd argue, which could save at least some of us from drowning and toward which it was our function to struggle—but for reasons unknowable to us He wanted desperately to prevent our reaching that happy place and fulfilling our destiny. Our 'Father,' in short, was our adversary and would-be killer! No less outrageous, and offensive to traditional opinion, were the fellow's speculations on the nature of our Maker: that He might well be no swimmer Himself at all, but some sort of monstrosity, perhaps even tailless; that He might be stupid, malicious, insensible, perverse, or asleep and dreaming; that the end for which He created and launched us forth, and which we flagellate ourselves to fathom, was perhaps immoral, even obscene. Et cetera, et cetera: there was no end to the chap's conjectures, or the impoliteness of his fancy; I have reason to suspect that his early demise, whether planned by 'our Maker' or not, was expedited by certain fellow-swimmers indignant at his blasphemies.

"In other moods, however (he was given to moods as I), his theorizing would become half-serious, so it seemed to me, especially upon the subjects of Fate and Immortality, to which our youthful conversations often turned. Then his harangues, if no less fantastical, grew solemn and obscure, and if he was still baiting us, his passion undid the joke. His objection to popular opinions of the hereafter, he would declare, was their claim to general validity. Why need believers hold that *all* the drownèd rise to be judged at journey's end, and non-believers that drowning is final without exception? In *his* opinion (so he'd vow at least), nearly everyone's fate was permanent death; indeed he took a sour pleasure in supposing that every 'Maker' made thousands of separate seas in His creative lifetime, each populated like ours with millions of swimmers, and that in almost every instance both sea and swimmers were utterly annihilated, whether accidentally or by malevolent design. (Nothing if not pluralistic, he imagined there might be millions and billions of 'Fathers,' perhaps in some 'night-sea' of their own!) However—and here he turned infidels against him with the faithful—he professed to believe that in possibly a single night-sea per thousand, say, one of its quarter-billion swimmers (that is, one swimmer in two hundred and fifty billions) achieved a qualified immortality. In some cases the rate might be slightly higher; in others it was vastly lower, for just as there are swimmers of every degree of proficiency, including some who drown before the journey starts, unable to swim at all, and others created drowned, as it were, so he imagined what can only be termed impotent Creators, Makers unable to Make, as well as uncommonly fertile ones and all grades between. And it pleased him to deny any necessary relation between a Maker's productivity and His other virtues— including, even, the quality of His creatures.

"I could go on (*he* surely did) with his elaboration of these mad notions —such as that swimmers in other night-seas needn't be of our kind; that Makers themselves might belong to different *species*, so to speak; that our particular Maker mightn't Himself be immortal, or that we might be not only His emissaries but His 'immortality,' continuing His life and our own, transmogrified, beyond our individual deaths. Even this modified immortality (meaningless to me) he conceived as relative and contingent, subject to accidental or deliberate termination: his pet hypothesis was that Makers and swimmers *each generate the other*—against all odds, their number being so great—and that any given 'immortality-chain' could terminate after any number of cycles, so that what was 'immortal' (still speaking relatively) was only the cyclic process of incarnation, which itself might have a beginning and an end. Alternatively he liked to imagine cycles within cycles, either finite or infinite: for example, the 'night-sea,' as it were, in which Makers 'swam' and created night-seas and swimmers like ourselves, might be the creation of a larger Maker, Himself one of many, Who in turn et cetera. Time itself he regarded as relative to our experience, like magnitude: who knew but what, with each thrash of our tails, minuscule seas and swimmers, whole eternities, came to pass—as ours, perhaps, and our Maker's Maker's, was elapsing between the strokes of some supertail, in a slower order of time?

"Naturally I hooted with the others at this nonsense. We were young then, and had only the dimmest notion of what lay ahead; in our ignorance we imagined night-sea journeying to be a positively heroic enterprise. Its meaning and value we never questioned; to be sure, some must go down by the way, a pity no doubt, but to win a race requires that others lose, and like all my fellows I took for granted that I would be the winner. We milled and swarmed, impatient to be off, never mind where or why, only to try our youth against the realities of night and sea; if we indulged the skeptic at all, it was as a droll, half-contemptible mascot. When he died in the initial slaughter, no one cared.

"And even now I don't subscribe to all his views—but I no longer scoff. The horror of our history has purged me of opinions, as of vanity, confidence, spirit, charity, hope, vitality, everything—except dull dread and a kind of melancholy, stunned persistence. What leads me to recall his fancies is my growing suspicion that I, of all swimmers, may be the sole survivor of this fell journey, tale-bearer of a generation. This suspicion, together with the recent sea-change, suggests to me now that nothing is impossible, not even my late companion's wildest visions, and brings me to a certain desperate resolve, the point of my chronicling.

"Very likely I have lost my senses. The carnage at our setting out; our decimation by whirlpool, poisoned cataract, sea-convulsion; the panic stampedes, mutinies, slaughters, mass suicides; the mounting evidence that none will survive the journey—add to these anguish and fatigue; it were a miracle if sanity stayed afloat. Thus I admit, with the other possibilities, that the present sweetening and calming of the sea, and what seems to be a kind of vasty presence, song, or summons from the near upstream, may be hallucinations of disordered sensibility. . . .

"Perhaps, even, I am drowned already. Surely I was never meant for the rough-and-tumble of the swim; not impossibly I perished at the outset and have only imagined the night-sea journey from some final deep. In any case, I'm no longer young, and it is we spent old swimmers, disabused of every illusion, who are most vulnerable to dreams.

"Sometimes I think I am my drownèd friend.

"Out with it: I've begun to believe, not only that *She* exists, but that She lies not far ahead, and stills the sea, and draws me Herward! Aghast, I recollect his maddest notion: that our destination (which existed, mind, in but one night-sea out of hundreds and thousands) was no Shore, as commonly conceived, but a mysterious being, indescribable except by paradox and vaguest figure: wholly different from us swimmers, yet our complement; the death of us, yet our salvation and resurrection; simultaneously our journey's end, mid-point, and commencement; not membered and thrashing like us, but a motionless or hugely gliding sphere of unimaginable dimension; self-contained, yet dependent absolutely, in some wise, upon the chance (always monstrously improbable) that one of us will survive the night-sea journey and reach . . . Her! *Her,* he called it, or *She,* which is to say, Other-than-a-he. I shake my head; the thing is too preposterous; it is myself I talk to, to keep my reason in this awful darkness. There is no She! There is no You! I rave to myself; it's Death alone that hears and summons. To the drowned, all seas are calm. . . .

"Listen: my friend maintained that in every order of creation there are two sorts of creators, contrary yet complementary, one of which gives rise to seas and swimmers, the other to the Night-which-contains-the-sea and to What-waits-at-the-journey's-end: the former, in short, to destiny, the latter to destination (and both profligately, involuntarily, perhaps indifferently or unwittingly). The 'purpose' of the night-sea journey—but not necessarily of the journeyer or of either Maker!—my friend could describe only in abstractions: *consummation, transfiguration, union of contraries, transcension of categories.* When we laughed, he would shrug and admit that he understood the business no better than we, and thought it ridiculous, dreary, possibly obscene. 'But one of you,' he'd add with his wry smile, 'may be the Hero destined to complete the night-sea journey and be one with Her. Chances are, of course, you won't make it.' He himself, he declared, was not even going to try; the whole idea repelled him; if we chose to dismiss it as an ugly fiction, so much the better for us; thrash, splash, and be merry, we were soon enough drowned. But there it was, he could not say how he knew or why he bothered to tell us, any more than he could say what would happen after She and Hero, Shore and Swimmer, 'merged identities' to become something both and neither. He quite agreed with me that if the issue of that magical union had no memory of the night-sea journey, for example, it enjoyed a poor sort of immortality; even poorer if, as he rather imagined, a swimmer-hero plus a She equaled or became merely another Maker of future night-seas and the rest, at such incredible expense of life. This being the case—he was persuaded it was

—the merciful thing to do was refuse to participate; the genuine heroes, in his opinion, were the suicides, and the hero of heroes would be the swimmer who, in the very presence of the Other, refused Her proffered 'immortality' and thus put an end to at least one cycle of catastrophes.

"How we mocked him! Our moment came, we hurtled forth, pretending to glory in the adventure, thrashing, singing, cursing, strangling, rationalizing, rescuing, killing, inventing rules and stories and relationships, giving up, struggling on, but dying all, and still in darkness, until only a battered remnant was left to croak 'Onward, upward,' like a bitter echo. Then they too fell silent—victims, I can only presume, of the last frightful wave —and the moment came when I also, utterly desolate and spent, thrashed my last and gave myself over to the current, to sink or float as might be, but swim no more. Whereupon, marvelous to tell, in an instant the sea grew still! Then warmly, gently, the great tide turned, began to bear me, as it does now, onward and upward will-I nill-I, like a flood of joy—and I recalled with dismay my dead friend's teaching.

"I am not deceived. This new emotion is Her doing; the desire that possesses me is Her bewitchment. Lucidity passes from me; in a moment I'll cry 'Love!' bury myself in Her side, and be 'transfigured.' Which is to say, I die already; this fellow transported by passion is not I; *I am he who abjures and rejects the night-sea journey!* I. . . .

"I am all love. 'Come!' She whispers, and I have no will.

"You who I may be about to become, whatever You are: with the last twitch of my real self I beg You to listen. It is *not* love that sustains me! No; though Her magic makes me burn to sing the contrary, and though I drown even now for the blasphemy, I will say truth. What has fetched me across this dreadful sea is a single hope, gift of my poor dead comrade: that You may be stronger-willed than I, and that by sheer force of concentration I may transmit to You, along with Your official Heritage, a private legacy of awful recollection and negative resolve. Mad as it may be, my dream is that some unimaginable embodiment of myself (or myself plus Her if that's how it must be) will come to find itself expressing, in however garbled or radical a translation, some reflection of these reflections. If against all odds this comes to pass, may You to whom, through whom I speak, do what I cannot: terminate this aimless, brutal business! Stop Your hearing against Her song! Hate love!

"Still alive, afloat, afire. Farewell then my penultimate hope: that one may be sunk for direst blasphemy on the very shore of the Shore. Can it be (my old friend would smile) that only utterest nay-sayers survive the night? But even that were Sense, and there is no sense, only senseless love, senseless death. Whoever echoes these reflections: be more courageous than their author! An end to night-sea journeys! Make no more! And forswear me when I shall forswear myself, deny myself, plunge into Her who summons, singing . . .

"'Love! Love! Love!'"

SUGGESTIONS FOR WRITING

The Stories

1. Charles Thomas Samuels suggests that "The Indian Uprising" makes use of a considerable number of cinematic elements; and in reviewing "Lost in the Funhouse," Edgar H. Knapp also discusses such elements. Compare and contrast the two stories in terms of their incorporation of "cinema" into their technique.

2. In Barth's "Dunyazadiad," Scheherazade declares:

   —whether it's a magic spell or a magic story with the answer in it or a magic anything—it comes down to particular words in the story we're reading, right? And those words are made from the letters of our alphabet: a couple-dozen squiggles we can draw with this pen. This is the key . . . ! And the treasure, too, if we can only get our hands on it! It's as if—as if the key to the treasure *is* the treasure!

   Explain this insight as it relates to "Lost in the Funhouse."

3. Write an essay in which you explain Edgar H. Knapp's statement, that "the funhouse for *man thinking* is a womb of possibility from which he may be reborn." You may want to apply this observation to situations other than those described in the story.

4. Both "Lost in the Funhouse" and "How I Contemplated . . ." can be considered anti-mimetic in that both "remind the reader continually of the contrivance of literature, the fact that a story is the semblance of lived-experience, not experience." Show how each of these stories is, in its own way, anti-mimetic.

5. Is "Night-Sea Journey" too philosophical and too satirical to be classified as a short story? Explain by offering a definition of short fiction and showing how "Night-Sea Journey" fulfills or negates that definition.

6. Charles Thomas Samuels describes the narrator of "The Indian Uprising" as being "little more than the voice that records actions,

statements, and allusions"—of being "words." Is this statement also true of the dramatized narrator of "Nights-Sea Journey"? Explain.

7. Discuss the many-faceted comedy of "Night-Sea Journey."

8. Discuss the limitations and possibilities of contemporary fiction as put forth in "Night-Sea Journey."

Other Works by John Barth

1. Barth has said that he wishes more of his students would read Robert Musil's *The Man Without Qualities*: "That book is one of the giants that doesn't get spoken of when people are speaking of Joyce, Kafka, and Mann. A real New American Novel." Write a comprehensive essay in which you compare *The Man Without Qualities* to *The End of the Road*.

2. Gerhard Joseph has observed that "the educational experience either as theme or all-encompassing metaphor" is basic to Barth's fiction. Explore "the educational experience" as structure and theme in *The End of the Road, Giles Goat-Boy*, or *Lost in the Funhouse*.

3. The characters in Barth's fiction are often "inverted doubles" of each other. Examine this doubling in *The End of the Road* and *Lost in the Funhouse*.

4. Barth often depicts triangular relationships. Discuss the structural and thematic implications of the "triangles" that occur in *The End of the Road* and *Lost in the Funhouse*.

5. Examine the varied narrators found in *Lost in the Funhouse*. Are the stories in this collection unified by a consistent tone?

6. *The Sot-Weed Factor* has been described as parodying "the grand costume novel, Elizabethan literature, Ph.D. theses, and mankind at large." Examine this novel as multi-faceted parody.

7. Using *Giles Goat-Boy*, explore Tony Tanner's thesis (in *City of Words*) that language, while part of a pervasive "entropic clutter," must be used both to convey this clutter and at the same time to rebel against it. You may find it helpful to consult "The Literature of Exhaustion," by John Barth (*Atlantic Monthly*, August 1967). In this article, Barth discusses Borges' description of the Baroque as "that style which deliberately exhausts (or tries to exhaust) its possibilities and borders upon its own caricature."

8. Barth has described Scheherazade as his favorite story-teller:

> The story of deflowered Scheherazade, yarning tirelessly through the dark hours to save her neck, corresponds to a number of things

at once and flashes meaning from all its facets. For me its rich dark circumstances, mixing the subtle and the coarse, the comic and the grim, the realistic and the fantastic, the apocalyptic and the hopeful, figure, among other things, both the estate of the fictioner in general and the particular endeavors and aspirations of this one, at least, who can wish nothing better than to spin like that vizier's excellent daughter, through what nights remain to him, tales within tales, fullstored with "description and discourse and rare traits and anecdotes and moral instances and reminiscences . . . proverbs and parables, chronicles and pleasantries, quips and jests, stories and . . . dialogues and histories and elegies and other verses."

Examine "Dunyazadiad" (from *Chimera*) to see how well Barth's story (modestly subtitled "The second greatest story ever told") matches those of his acknowledged mentor. In your analysis, be sure to consider Barth's use of the process of fiction as subject matter.

9. Examine Barth's use of the Bellerophon/Pegasus/Chimera myth in "Perseid" (from *Chimera*).

BIBLIOGRAPHY

Primary

Giles Goat-Boy. New York: Doubleday, 1966. A novel.
The End of the Road. rev. ed. New York: Doubleday, 1967. A novel.
The Floating Opera. rev. ed. New York: Doubleday, 1967. A novel.
The Sot-Weed Factor. rev. ed. New York: Doubleday, 1967. A novel.
Lost in the Funhouse. New York: Doubleday, 1968. Short stories.
Chimera. New York: Random House, 1972. A novel.

Secondary

Bienstock, Beverly Gray. "Lingering on the Autognostic Verge: John Barth's *Lost in the Funhouse*." *Modern Fiction Studies*, 19 (Spring 1973), 69–78. Interprets the stories in *Lost in the Funhouse* as centering on "the search for one's identity amidst the tangled skeins of past, present, and future"; emphasis on "Menelaiad" and "Lost in the Funhouse."

Critique. 13:3 (1972). An issue devoted to John Barth and John Fowles. Includes a bibliography as well as the following articles on Barth:

Kyle, Carol A. "The Unity of Anatomy: The Structure of Barth's *Lost in the Funhouse*," 31–43; McDonald, James L. "Barth's Syllabus: The Frame of *Giles Goat-Boy*," 5–10; Slethang, Gordon E. "Barth's Refutation of the Idea of Progress," 11–29; and Weixlmann, Joseph N. "John Barth: A Bibliography," 45–55.

Hauck, Richard Boyd. *A Cheerful Nihilism: Confidence and "The Absurd" in American Humorous Fiction*. Bloomington, Ind.: Indiana Univ. Press, 1971. Places Barth in the tradition of such writers as Melville, Twain, and Faulkner whose response to nihilism is not despair but humor—writers who create in spite of a clear recognition that creation may mean nothing.

Hinden, Michael. *"Lost in the Funhouse*: Barth's Use of the Recent Past." *Twentieth Century Literature*, 19 (April 1973), 107–18. Explores the premise that, for Barth, the past provides new materials for new art; offers extended analysis of "Night-Sea Journey."

Joseph, Gerhard. *John Barth*. Minneapolis: Univ. of Minnesota Press, 1970 (No. 91 of the University of Minnesota Pamphlets on American Writers). Traces "the irreversible quality of Barth's drift from time-bound realism to timeless fable"; includes a bibliography.

Majdiak, Daniel. "Barth and the Representation of Life." *Criticism*, 12 (Winter 1970), 51–67. Shows that *The End of the Road* is not as conventional a novel as critics have assumed—that in the character of Horner "we find Barth's first serious challenge to the epistemology of realism and the concept of character and identity assumed in traditional fiction."

Olderman, Raymond M. "The Grail Knight Goes to College" in *Beyond the Wasteland: A Study of the American Novel in the Nineteen-Sixties*. New Haven and London: Yale Univ. Press, 1972. Emphasis on *Giles Goat-Boy*; Barth's fiction is used to support premise that the dominant pattern in the novel of the sixties continues the movement away from the realistic novel and toward a contemporary version of romance.

Scholes, Robert. "Fabulation and Epic Vision" in *The Fabulators*. New York: Oxford Univ. Press, 1967. Examines *Giles Goat-Boy*: "a work of genuine epic vision, a fantastic mosaic constructed from the fragments of our own life and traditions, calculated to startle us into new perceptions of epic hero and saviour."

Tanner, Tony. "What is the Case?" in *City of Words: American Fiction 1950–1970*. London: Jonathan Cape Ltd., 1971. Discusses the fiction from *The Floating Opera* to *Lost in the Funhouse*. Shows Barth's drift away from "reality" and his "corrosive doubt about identity and its relation to language."

NOTES
ON THE ESSAYISTS

Barbara McKenzie is the author of *Mary McCarthy* (Twayne, 1966) and the recipient of a master's degree from the University of Miami and of a doctorate from Florida State University. A specialist in contemporary American fiction and in communications, she has taught at Drew University and is now on the faculty of the University of Georgia.

John M. Warner received his master's and doctoral degrees from Harvard University, where he was a Teaching Fellow. Now a teacher at Drew University, he is a specialist in eighteenth-century literature and in modern British prose and poetry.

James R. Hollis, who received a doctorate from Drew University, is the author of *Harold Pinter: The Poetics of Silence* (Southern Illinois University Press, 1970). He has taught at Upsala College, Drew University, and Kirkland College and is now on the faculty of Manchester College.

Ruth M. Vande Kieft is the author of *Eudora Welty* (Twayne, 1962) and articles on such literary figures as Sir Thomas Brown, Melville, Dickens, and Flannery O'Connor. She received a master's degree and a doctorate from the University of Michigan and has also studied at Oxford University. Formerly on the faculty at Wellesley College, she now teaches at Queens College of the City University of New York.

Merrill Maguire Skaggs is the author of *The Folk of Southern Fiction: A Study in Local Color Traditions* (University of Georgia Press, 1972). She received a master's degree and a doctorate from Duke University and has since been a college teacher and an editor of literature textbooks.

John V. Hagopian is the author of *J. F. Powers* (Twayne, 1968). A specialist in modern American and English literature and in literary theory and criticism, he has served as Fulbright Professor at Kiel and as Chairman of American Studies at the University of the Saar, Germany. He holds a master's degree from Wayne State University and a doctoral degree from Western Reserve University. The author of more than a hundred articles, he currently teaches at the State University of New York at Binghamton.

Eileen Baldeshwiler (formerly Sister M. Joselyn) received a master's degree from the University of Minnesota and a doctorate from Fordham University. She has published many articles in the field of literary criticism and has translated several books on theology. A specialist in literary theory, she teaches courses in prose fiction and in literary criticism at Loyola University in Chicago.

Philip Stevich received a master's degree from Kent State University and a doctorate from Ohio State University. He now teaches English at Temple University and is the author of *The Chapter in Fiction: Theories of Narrative Division* (Syracuse University Press, 1970) and editor of *Anti-Story: An Anthology of Experimental Fiction* (The Free Press, 1971). Among his notable articles on literature is "Scheherazade runs out of plots, goes on talking; the king, puzzled, listens: an essay on new fiction" (*TriQuarterly,* Winter 1973).

Charles Thomas Samuels, who teaches English at Williams College, received a master's degree from Ohio State University and a doctorate from the University of California at Berkeley. He is the film critic of *The American Scholar,* editor of *A Casebook on Film* (Van Nostrand, 1970), and author of *John Updike* (University of Minnesota Press, 1969), *The Ambiguity of Henry James* (University of Illinois, 1971), and *Encountering Directors* (Putnam, 1972). Formerly a Fulbright lecturer, he has also held fellowships from the American Council of Learned Societies and from the National Endowment for the Humanities.

Edgar H. Knapp received a master's degree from Boston University and a doctorate from Columbia University. He is now a teacher of English and secondary education at Pennsylvania State University. The author of many literary articles, he is also the editor of *Introduction to Poetry* (McCormick-Mathers, 1965) and a co-editor of *Ideas and Patterns in Literature* (Harcourt Brace Jovanovich, 1970).

INDEX

Italic numbers in an entry locate the story or essay that is the subject of the entry. In a story entry, the numbers following the italic numbers locate the critical essay about that story.

C
D   6
E   7
F   8
G   9
H   0
I   1
J